Dramatists Guild
RESOURCE DIRECTORY

2018

NEW COLOR EDGE TABS

FIND THE SECTION YOU WANT MORE EASILY

this book belongs to:

NAME

DG MEMBERSHIP #

DRAMATISTS GUILD RESOURCE DIRECTORY™

©2017 Dramatists Guild of America, Inc.
The Dramatists Guild Resource Directory is a trademark of Dramatists Guild of America, Inc.

PRINTED BY Acutrack, Inc.

EDITORS: Joey Stocks & Amelia French
DESIGN: Bekka Lindström
DATA ASSISTANTS: Abby Barr, Sarah Rebell, Tari Stratton, Zack Turner

SPECIAL THANKS: Aurin Squire

All Rights Reserved. Compiled and published by the Dramatists Guild of America, Inc. No part of this book may be reproduced without prior written permission from Dramatists Guild of America, Inc., 1501 Broadway, Suite 701, New York, NY 10036 or (212) 398-9366.

ADVERTISING OPPORTUNITIES:
Contact Joey Stocks, Director of Publications at jstocks@dramatistsguild.com or call (212) 398-9366, Ext. 16.

Dramatists Guild of America

OFFICERS

Doug Wright
President

Lisa Kron
Vice President

Lynn Nottage
Secretary

Julia Jordan
Treasurer

STAFF

Ralph Sevush
Advisor to Council, Executive Director of Business Affairs

Tina Fallon
Executive Director of Creative Affairs

Claudia Stuart
Director of Finance & Administration

David Faux
Associate Executive Director of Business Affairs

Tari Stratton
Director of Education, Events, & Outreach

Joey Stocks
Director of Publications

Deborah Murad
Director of Business Affairs

Amy VonVett
Manager of Business Affairs

Zack Turner
Director of Marketing & Online Media

Emmanuel Wilson
Director of Membership

Jenna Chrisphonteh
Director of Community Engagement

Bekka Lindström
Graphic Designer

Sarah Rebell
Office Administrator

Lily Dwoskin, Kristin Kapinos
Office Assistants

Gary Garrison
Director, DGI

Jordan Stovall
Executive Administrator, DGI & Regional Rep Program

Amelia French
Publications Assistant

COUNCIL

Lee Adams
Lynn Ahrens
Kristen Anderson-Lopez
David Auburn
Dan Berkowitz
Susan Birkenhead
Craig Carnelia
Kirsten Childs
Kia Corthron
Gretchen Cryer
Kristoffer Diaz
Christopher Durang
Jules Feiffer
William Finn
Stephen Flaherty
Maria Irene Fornes
Rebecca Gilman
Daniel Goldfarb
Micki Grant
Amanda Green
John Guare
Carol Hall
Sheldon Harnick
Donna Hoke
Mark Hollmann
Tina Howe
Timothy Huang
Branden Jacobs-Jenkins
Chirstine Toy Johnson
Julia Jordan
John Kander
Arthur Kopit
Michael Korie
Lisa Kron
Tony Kushner
James Lapine
Warren Leight
Mike Lew
David Lindsay-Abaire
Andrew Lippa
Robert Lopez
Emily Mann
Donald Margulies
Terrence McNally
Alan Menken
Lin-Manuel Miranda
Marsha Norman
Lynn Nottage
Austin Pendleton
Douglas Post
Theresa Rebeck
Jonathan Reynolds
Nikkole Salter
Stephen Schwartz
John Patrick Shanley
David Shire
Stephen Sondheim
Lloyd Suh
Gwydion Suilebhan
Jeffrey Sweet
Alfred Uhry
Teresa Coleman Wash
John Weidman
Michael Weller
George C. Wolfe
Charlayne Woodard
Doug Wright
Maury Yeston

DG REGIONAL REPRESENTATIVES

Suze Allen
Kathleen Cahill
Gab Cody
Cheryl Coons
Allyson Currin
Dewey Davis-Thompson
Charlene Donaghy
William R. Duell
Brent Englar
Liz Fentress
Rob Florence
Patrick Gabridge
Josh Gershick
Jacqueline Goldfinger
Anita Gonzalez
Josh Hartwell
Laurie Flanigan Hegge
Donna Hoke
Stephen Kaplan
Duane Kelly
Andy Landis
Michael McKeever
Francesca Piantadosi
Sheila Rinear
Kim Stinson
Aoise Stratford
David Todd
Pamela Turner
Teresa Coleman Wash
Hartley Wright

PUBLICATIONS COMMITTEE

Amanda Green
Chair
Lynn Ahrens
Kirsten Childs
Nathan Alan Davis
Daniel Goldfarb
Adam Gwon
Tina Howe
Chisa Hutchinson
Christine Toy Johnson
David Kirshenbaum
Michael Korie
Deborah Zoe Laufer
Michele Lowe
Lin-Manuel Miranda
Lynn Nottage
Jonathan Marc Sherman
Caridad Svich

TABLE OF CONTENTS

- DRAMATIST'S BILL OF RIGHTS 4
- DG POLICY ON SUBMISSION 5
- DG BEST PRACTICES FOR CONTESTS & FESTIVALS 6
- SUBMISSION CALENDAR 12

CAREER DEVELOPMENT PROFESSIONALS
- Accountants 38
- Agents 39
- Attorneys 48
- Publishers 55

CAREER DEVELOPMENT OPPORTUNITIES
- Colonies & Residencies 65
- Conferences & Festivals 82
- Contests 117
- Grants & Fellowships 145
- Theatres 169

EDUCATIONAL OPPORTUNITIES
- Colleges & Universities 292
- Developmental Workshops 299
- Other Educational Opportunities 316

WRITER RESOURCES
- Emergency Funds 319
- Membership & Service Organizations 324
- Products & Other Services 346
- Bookstores 350
- Playwrights Welcome 352

ADDITIONAL RESOURCES
- The Submission Letter and Production Resume 357
- Suggested Formats for Plays and Musicals 360
- Business Affairs FAQ 366
- Dramatists Guild Sample Contract Guide 370

INDEX 371

HOW TO USE THIS DIRECTORY

1. ALWAYS VERIFY THE INFORMATION LISTED. These listings have been updated and checked as of November 1, 2017. This Directory is only updated once a year. The information inside can and will change throughout the year. Where applicable, we have listed websites, addresses, and emails. Be diligent. Take the time to verify the deadlines, submission materials, etc. Internet access and research will be required for most submissions.

2. IF YOU SEE SOMETHING, SAY SOMETHING. We want this directory to be the best it can be. If you discover a missing date, a contact change, or even a better way to organize the material included here, let us know! Email the editor at jstocks@dramatistsguild.com.

3. LISTINGS & ADS DO NOT CONSTITUTE AN ENDORSEMENT FROM THE GUILD. Please be advised that the inclusion or omission of a listing or advertisement does not constitute approval or disapproval of that organization by the Guild, its council, officers, employees, agents, or affiliates. Guild members are individually responsible for their submissions and should fully evaluate an opportunity before submitting their work. As of November 1, 2017, contests with submission fees exceeding $50 have not been included.

4. JOIN THE GUILD. If you want access to our Business Affairs Department and free edition of this directory, apply for membership here: www.dramatistsguild.com/register

The Dramatist's Bill of Rights

Long before playwrights or musical theatre writers join the Dramatists Guild, they often struggle professionally in small-to-medium-sized theatres throughout the country. It is essential, therefore, that dramatists know their rights, which the Dramatists Guild has defended for nearly 100 years. In order to protect the dramatist's unique vision, which has always been the strength of the theatre, s/he needs to understand this fundamental principle: dramatists own and control their work.

The Guild recommends that any production involving a dramatist incorporate a written agreement in which both theatres/producers and writers acknowledge certain key rights with each other.

In Process and Production

ARTISTIC INTEGRITY.

No one (e.g., directors, actors, dramaturgs) can make changes, alterations, and/or omissions to your script – including the text, title, and stage directions – without your consent. This is called "script approval."

APPROVAL OF PRODUCTION ELEMENTS.

You have the right to approve the cast, director, and designers (and, for a musical, the choreographer, orchestrator, arranger, and musical director, as well), including their replacements. This is called "artistic approval."

RIGHT TO BE PRESENT.

You always have the right to attend casting, rehearsals, previews and performances.

Compensation

ROYALTIES.

You are generally entitled to receive a royalty. While it is possible that the amount an author receives may be minimal for a small to medium-sized production, some compensation should always be paid if any other artistic collaborator in the production is being paid, or if any admission is being charged. If you are a member of the Guild, you can always call our business office to discuss the standard industry royalties for various levels of production.

BILLING CREDIT.

You should receive billing (typographical credit) on all publicity, programs, and advertising distributed or authorized by the theatre. Billing is part of your compensation and the failure to provide it properly is a breach of your rights.

Ownership

OWNERSHIP OF INTELLECTUAL PROPERTY.

You own the copyright of your dramatic work. Authors in the theatre business do not assign (i.e., give away or sell in entirety) their copyrights, nor do they ever engage in "work-for-hire." When a university, producer or theatre wants to mount a production of your play, you actually license (or lease) the public performance rights to your dramatic property to that entity for a finite period of time.

OWNERSHIP OF INCIDENTAL CONTRIBUTIONS.

You own all approved revisions, suggestions, and contributions to the script made by other collaborators in the production, including actors, directors, and dramaturgs. You do not owe anyone any money for these contributions. If a theatre uses dramaturgs, you are not obligated to make use of any ideas the dramaturg might have. Even when the input of a dramaturg or director is helpful to the playwright, dramaturgs and directors are still employees of the theatre, not the author, and they are paid for their work by the theatre/producer. It has been well-established in case law, beginning with "the *Rent* Case" (Thompson v. Larson) that neither dramaturgs nor directors (nor any other contributors) may be considered a co-author of a play, unless (i) they've collaborated with you from the play's inception, (ii) they've made a copyrightable contribution to the play, and (iii) you have agreed in writing that they are a co-author.

SUBSIDIARY RIGHTS.

After the small or medium-sized production, you not only own your script, but also the rights to market and sell it to all different media (e.g., television, radio, film, internet) in any commercial market in the world. You are not obligated to sign over any portion of your project's future revenues to any third party (fellow artist, advisor, director, producer) as a result of a production, unless that production is a professional (i.e., Actor's Equity) premiere production (including sets, costumes and lighting), of no less than 21 consecutive paid public performances for which the author has received appropriate billing, compensation, and artistic approvals.

FUTURE OPTIONS.

Rather than granting the theatre the right to share in future proceeds, you may choose to grant a non-exclusive option to present another production of your work within six months or one year of the close of the initial production. No option should be assignable without your prior written consent.

AUTHOR'S CONTRACT.

The only way to ensure that you get the benefit of the rights listed above is through a written contract with the producer, no matter how large or small the entity. The Guild's Department of Business Affairs offers a model "production contract" and is available to review any contracts offered to you, and advise as to how those contracts compare to industry standards.

We realize that making demands of a small theatre is a difficult task. However, **you should feel confident in presenting this Bill of Rights to the Artistic Director, Producer, Literary Manager, or university administrator as a starting point for discussion**. At the very least, any professional in the dramatic arts should realize that it is important for writers to understand the nature of their work – not just the artistic aspects, but the business side, as well – and that they stand together as a community, for their mutual benefit and survival, and for the survival of theatre as a viable art form in the 21st century.

DG Policy on Submission

The Dramatists Guild of America denounces the practice by some theatres, festivals, contests and educational programs of charging excessive fees to dramatists who submit their work for consideration, as well as the unfair encumbrances they put on works they have not produced.

Members should understand that submission fees are not the norm and, when required, the festival should offer something significant in return for the writer's investment, such as a cash prize, a residency, or a production. Reading fees are in no case acceptable, as most festivals receive that money from other grant sources, and, in any event, writers should not have to pay to have their work read nor should they be required to fund a prize or production, either in whole or in part. So, any request for submission fees should be accompanied by a complete explanation of how those fees are to be spent. Contests and festivals should also announce the names of all finalists and winners to all of the participants.

In addition to the issue of submission fees, The Guild feels that any organization's future participation in the life of a play must be earned by their actual production of it. Therefore, the Guild disapproves of any encumbrances put on a play by a festival or contest when they are only acting as a presenting organization and are not actually the producer of the particular work. Such contests and festivals should provide full disclosure on what encumbrances, if any, will be placed on a participant's work (including any share of the play's subsidiary income or any future production options on it) and this information should be stated clearly in the organization's printed and electronic materials related to the event.

However, in order to further the Guild's goal of making our members as well informed as possible about legitimate submission opportunities, we post most of the listings we receive from sponsors, omitting only those listings that charge exorbitant fees (in our view) or about whom we have received multiple member complaints. So be advised that the inclusion or omission of a listing in the Guild's various publications does not constitute either approval or disapproval of that organization's practices by the Guild. Guild members are individually responsible for their submissions and should fully evaluate an opportunity before submitting their work.

Please contact Business Affairs (businessaffairs@dramatistsguild.com) with any questions or if you need assistance in evaluating a particular opportunity.

Submission Disclaimer

Please be advised that the inclusion or omission of a listing does not constitute approval or disapproval of that organization by the Guild, its council, officers, employees, agents, or affiliates. Guild members are individually responsible for their submissions and should fully evaluate an opportunity before submitting their work. Please contact Business Affairs (businessaffairs@dramatistsguild.com) with any questions or if you need assistance in evaluating a particular opportunity.

Dramatists Guild's Best Practices:

DG Festival Committee

Donna Hoke
Committee Chair

Julius Galacki

David Guaspari

Stephen Kaplan

Deborah Murad

Rich Orloff

Eric Sanders

Ralph Sevush

Jordan K. Stovall

Kathleen Warnock

If a theatre festival, conference, or contest were the most perfect, playwright-centered, ethical opportunity, what would it look like? That question drove the creation of this document, a template for theatre entities desiring to run programs with the Dramatists Guild Bill of Rights and #playwrightrespect informing its rules and policies, and a tool for playwrights* to make educated decisions about where to send their work.

Devising this list was the easy part; after all, we've all bristled at submission fees, no results notification, or directors who want to shut us out. So we had no problem agreeing, for example, that no submission fee is best practice, but, in declaring such, we had to acknowledge that some high-profile, career-building opportunities do charge them—and aren't likely to change. Of course playwrights want to be informed if they aren't selected, but, again, we know of top prizes that don't offer that courtesy. In fact, in seeking examples of totally compliant opportunities, we found that while a great number come close to checking all the boxes, few actually do.

Naturally, we wish they all did, but we're pragmatic. Even as we recognize good and great opportunities that aren't perfect, we present and encourage the Best Practices Guidelines as ideal industry standard. In publishing this, we hope theaters are motivated to amend their programs to hew as closely to this list as their own needs and practicalities allow.

For playwrights, the Best Practices Guidelines are a yardstick by which to compare opportunities, and a standard to point to when engaging with theatres employing questionable practices. While some Best Practices inherently carry more weight than others, nothing is a deal-breaker if a playwright doesn't want it to be. But with transparency about what is right, fair, and ethical—indeed, best—playwrights are empowered to make informed and individual submission choices.

The word "playwright" can also refer to writers of musical theatre, depending on the submission requirements of the festival, conference, or contest.

CONTESTS & FESTIVALS

EACH BEST PRACTICE IS NUMBERED AND CORRESPONDS TO THE ANNOTATIONS IN THE ADJACENT COLUMN.

Festival or Contest Information:

1 Best Practice: The organization outlines the nature of the contest/festival's award, whether a cash prize, a production, a reading, or some other form of artistic development, professional advancement opportunity (e.g., publicity, networking, residency), or benefit (e.g., free tickets).

2 Best Practice: The organization provides information on its history (including the organization's board and staff). It also provides a description of the venue.

Types of Plays and Authors:

3 Best Practice: The organization clearly states what subset, if any, of authors (e.g., age, sex) and plays (e.g., length, genre, theme, cast size, tech-

---

1 *The organization should detail the benefits of participating in its festival or contest. Doing so enables the author to evaluate each given opportunity.*

2 *Authors have many submission opportunities and face a constant and arduous task in sorting and assessing them. Providing a list of individuals involved in the organization, past winners, and notable attendees, as well as a description of the venue, helps the author see and assess the value the organization has added to past works and could add to the author's own work.*

3 *One of the main goals of an organization's submission guidelines is to inform the author about the types of works the organization is seeking. Unless an organization plans to consider any and all works, it should offer a clear and detailed description of the type of work it will consider. This has the mutual benefit of allowing authors to focus their time, money, and energy, while ensuring that the organization receives entries that are in line with its goals.*

Many previously produced plays make wonderful regional premieres! The Guild applauds organizations that consider previously produced plays.

4 *There is nothing wrong with an organization limiting its pool of applicants to those who meet specific criteria. However, when these criteria are based on vague terminology (e.g., "unproduced" or "premiere"), it often leads to confusion for the author, unnecessary inquiries, and an inefficient submission process. Far too often, authors are selected as "winners" or "finalists" only to be disqualified before opening night because they misunderstood the organization's definition of a specific term. This is unfortunate for both the author and the organization and can easily be avoided if terms are defined at the outset.*

For the sake of consistency and clarity, it is an "acceptable practice" for an organization to define its own terms, but it's a "best practice" to use the following standard definitions:

"Published Work" – A dramatic work (play, lyric, libretto, or musical composition) that has been (a) fixed in a tangible medium (including digital formats), (b) reasonably capable of being copied and/or distributed, and

(c) either (i) commercially distributed by a third-party publisher or (ii) self-published with at least 1000 copies sold via commercial distribution.

"Unproduced script" – A script that has not been "professionally" produced. Readings, staged readings, AEA workshops, developmental productions, amateur productions, concert versions, etc., are not professional productions.

"Professional production" – A fully-staged, royalty-paying, public production that utilizes at least one performer who belongs to a live performing arts union or guild (e.g., AEA, AGMA, AGVA), employed under such performer's union or guild contract.

"Premiere" – The first royalty-paying professional production in a territory, presented for no less than twelve performances, with an official press opening, and with tickets sold to the general public, including subscribers.

5 *An author often spends significant amounts of time and money before seeing a return on a script. Organizations should be sensitive to the financial situation of the people whose work allows the organizations to grow and profit. A simple gesture such as offering a digital submission option is invaluable to an author, who would otherwise need to pay for postage and photocopies. Hard copy requests should be limited to one copy. While it is an "acceptable practice" for organizations to request hard copy scripts, it is a "best practice" to offer a digital option.*

6 *The goal of any contest or festival is to identify the very best script. Offering blind submissions mitigates against personal bias in the selection process and promotes diversity in selected works. So, organizations should have a clearly stated process for assuring a blind submission and evaluation process.*

7 *Organizations should understand that not all authors have access to particular scriptwriting software. As such, they should allow submissions in any stage play format. At a minimum, they should accept DG standard formatting.*

8 *Transparency is paramount in hosting a contest or festival. Organizations should be honest when stating how many winners, finalists, slots, etc. are available for any*

nical limitations) it seeks for its contest/festival.

4 **Best Practice:** The organization uses standard DG definitions for any term used in connection with script submissions (e.g., "unpublished scripts," "unproduced scripts," "professional productions"). Any deviation from standard DG definitions is clearly noted.

The Submission:

5 **Best Practice:** The organization accepts a free or inexpensive form of submission (e.g., email).

6 **Best Practice:** The organization uses blind submissions throughout the selection process.

7 **Best Practice:** The organization accepts any stage play format or, at a minimum, DG standard format. Furthermore, the organization specifies the desired length of any synopsis.

8 **Best Practice:** The organization provides information on the number of submissions an individual applicant may submit and the actual number of works to be selected.

9 **Best Practice:** The organization provides a timeline that specifies a submission deadline and a date when the selected works will be announced.

CONTESTS & FESTIVALS

10 **Best Practice:** The organization acknowledges receipt of all submissions, alerts all applicants of the outcome, and states whether it returns hard copy scripts (subject to receipt of a SASE).

11 **Best Practice:** The organization does not require the author to sign a contract as part of the submission process.

12 **Best Practice:** The organization does not require a submission fee. Furthermore, the organization imposes no other obligation on the author or encumbrance on the work (e.g., ticket sales, participation fees, technical rentals, hiring fees, marketing, or other selling obligations), except for do-it-yourself ("DIY") productions.

Productions:

13 **Best Practice:** At the time it offers the winning author a production, the organization provides the author with a production contract that preserves authorial rights.

14 **Best Practice:** If the organization charges admission to the production, the author is compensated.

15 **Best Practice:** The organization provides copies of reviews, photos, marketing materials, and media mentions.

---

given opportunity. Too often, the Guild hears of organizations calling for "open submissions," when submissions have actually been pre-selected and there are fewer available slots than advertised. This is frustrating for the author and damages the organization's reputation. Toward this end, it is helpful if the organization discloses the number of applications it received in past years.

9 *Offering authors a detailed timeline allows them to set their expectations and track their submissions. This is mutually beneficial because it reduces the number of status inquiries the organization receives. When announcing winners, it is also helpful to include information on the number of applications the organization received.*

10 *Acknowledging receipt of a submission, alerting applicants to the outcome, and returning hard copy scripts (if author has provided a SASE) are all simple ways to show care and respect for the author. Such practices also reduce the number of inquiries and follow-up letters sent to the organization.*

11 *Forcing an applicant to sign a contract at the time of submission is a coercive act. First, such contracts often impose "non-negotiable" contract terms that erode an author's ability to negotiate a fair and reasonable deal. Second, even where contract terms are negotiable, because the producing entity has not yet committed to producing the script, the author is put in a position of negotiating at a time when their bargaining power is at its lowest. At all times, authors are encouraged to sign contracts that are consistent with the DG Bill of Rights.*

12 *The Guild has long disapproved of excessive submission fees, which not only undermine the benefit of any "award" or "royalty," but also impose financial hardship on the author.*

Any other authorial obligations should be clearly noted up front; this is particularly true for DIY and similar festivals that require authors to self-produce their works.

13 *Please see Best Practice #20 for a discussion on contract review, negotiation, and authorial rights.*

14 The Guild suggests that authors be paid industry-standard rates for any production, even in a festival or contest. Although the Guild is aware that a standard payment may not be feasible, the author should be compensated if tickets are being sold.

15 Photos, videos, press releases, articles, etc., are invaluable to an author and have the added benefit of promoting the festival and contest. If it is not possible to provide the author with these materials, the theatre should provide some follow-up (e.g., a few words about how the play was received and some photos).

16 As a general principle, non-profit organizations, which already benefit from sizable monetary transfers from the public through their tax-exempt status, should not request future royalties, future participation, or future options. Still, the Guild recognizes that some organizations do request these rights. In such instances, the organization should adhere to industry standard rates and practices. Specifically, the organization must earn subsidiary rights, future interests, and future performance rights by "vesting," which is typically defined as presenting a professional production of no less than 21 paid public performances (with no more than eight previews and an official press opening) and appropriately compensating the author.

Subsidiary rights should follow industry-standard rates. Future royalties for the organization should be limited to the next commercial production that takes place within one to two years after the initial production, so as to compensate the organization if significant elements of its production move to a new venue. (Typically, the same director and at least half of the same cast and creatives.) Finally, as a general rule, encumbrances (like future options) should be limited by time, nature, territory, and venue, and should not be assignable.

17 One of the most valuable assets an author can offer a producer is the right to present the "world premiere" of a script. The author should seek to reserve this term for the instance in which it will yield the greatest benefit. World premiere rights are only appropriate if the organization is presenting a professional production for an extended period of time (at

16 **Best Practice:** The organization never takes future production rights or future participation for ten-minute plays, one-act plays, or DIY productions. Rather, it seeks these rights **only** when it premieres a full-length work for an extended run (e.g., 21 paid, public performances), where the author is properly compensated pursuant to a written contract.

17 **Best Practice:** The organization only requests world premiere rights if it is presenting (a) a professional (e.g., Equity) production, (b) for at least twelve performances, (c) with an official press opening, and (d) with tickets sold to the general public, including subscribers.

Authorial Rights:

18 **Best Practice:** The organization recognizes standard authorial rights as defined in the DG's Bill of Rights, including script approval, creative approval, the right to be present, and billing.

19 **Best Practice:** If the organization requires the author to attend an event or performance, it pays for the author's related expenses.

Contract Negotiation:

20 **Best Practice:** The organization gives the author ample opportunity to evaluate, negotiate, and/or reject any production, publishing, or other contract. This includes the right to negotiate audio-visual rights and other uses of the play. Any proposed contract is presented well in advance of the contest/festival, and the producer acts in good faith to offer and complete all contracts in a timely manner.

DIY Festivals:

21 **Best Practice:** The organization makes its submission guidelines available to the public from the beginning of the application period;

• makes clear the specific obligations and expenses that are the responsibility of a self-producing author, including participation fees, technical rentals, tech hiring fees, or any other selling obligation (e.g., tickets);

• makes clear the specific obligations and expenses that are the responsibility of the festival;

• provides for an equitable allocation of rights and liabilities, indemnification from festival activities, and a clear understanding of the nature and quality of the advertising and promotional material to be used for the festival;

• requires no subsidiary rights or other encumbrances on the author or on the author's work;

consults with the self-producing author with regard to scheduling, venue, press/marketing, and selection of crew and staff; and

• shares ticket sales with a self-producing author in a manner that reflects his or her production and operating expenses.

least twelve performances) with tickets sold to the general public.

18 *An author's standard rights are described in the DG Bill of Rights on page 82.*

19 *Although standard industry practice grants authors the right to attend casting sessions, rehearsals, and performances, such attendance is not required. If an organization requires the author's presence, it should pay the author's expenses (travel, hotel, per-diem, etc.). Failing to do so not only imposes a financial burden on the author, but also undermines the value of a royalty or award offered by the organization.*

20 *A contract signed today may affect an author's work for many years. As such, an author should be given the opportunity to read and understand the terms of a proposed deal in advance of submission or acceptance. An author should not feel pressured or forced to agree to the terms of a contract and should be encouraged to negotiate a deal that is fair. Although allowing for negotiation is a "best practice," the theater is not obligated to negotiate if its contract is consistent with the DG Bill of Rights. In any event, the Guild recommends that contracts be signed well before the first rehearsal. Contract negotiations should never be delayed until after the production closes.*

21 *Self-production opportunities involve a different set of expectations than the typical contest or festival. For DIY festivals, the organization should seek to clarify the rights and responsibilities of the producing author and the nature of the support that the organization will offer. As the producing entity, the author should have a strong voice in matters relating to the production. Moreover, the organization should not seek subsidiary rights or any other encumbrance because the organization is not the "producer" and, therefore, has not earned these rights.*

12 SUBMISSION DEADLINES 2017

December 2017

1
- New Works Initiative...pg. 307
- Finger Lakes Musical Theatre Festival... pg. 93
- The Orchard Project...pg. 77
- New Hampshire Institute of Art...pg. 294
- Vanderbilt University Writer-in-Residence...pg. 166

2

3

4

5
- Kitchen Dog Theater New Works Festival... pg. 98

6

7
- McKnight National Playwriting Residency and Commission...pg. 75

8

9

10

11

12

13

14
- Many Voices Fellowships...pg. 157

15
- Jewish Women's Theatre...pg. 219
- Emerging Artist Theatre New Work Series...pg. 92
- RLTP Playwright In Residence...pg. 78
- CEC ArtsLink...pg. 150
- Tutterow Fellows Program...pg. 165

SUBMISSION DEADLINES 2017

December 2017

16	George R. Kernodle New Play Award... pg. 124
17	
18	
19	
20	
21	
22	
23	
24	
25	
26	
27	
28	
29	
30	
31	Jackie White Memorial Children's Playwriting Contest... pg. 127 Black Box New Play Festival...pg. 86

SUBMISSION DEADLINES 2018

January

1 — Summer Pride Festival...pg. 112

2

3

4 — Kumu Kahua Theatre/UHM Theatre Department Playwriting Contest...pg. 129

5 — Cincinnati Fringe Festival...pg. 88

6

7 — Discovery New Musical Theatre Festival...pg. 91

8 — Leah Ryan's FEWW Playwriting Prize...pg. 129

9

10

11 — Jerome Fellowships...pg. 155
NEA Translation Projects...pg. 159

12 — King's Shorts Festival of Ten Minute Plays...pg. 98

13

14 — The Robert Chesley/Victor Bumbalo Playwriting Grant...pg. 164

15 —
- Southern Playwrights Competition...pg. 139
- VCCA (Virginia Center for the Creative Arts)...pg. 80
- MacDowell Colony...pg. 75
- Bogliasco Foundation...pg. 68
- Arkansas New Play Festival...pg. 84
- Ross Alternative Works (RAW)...pg. 311
- Summerfield G. Roberts Award...pg. 140
- Playwrights Gallery...pg. 309
- Centre Stage [SC] New Play Festival...pg. 88
- Hambidge Center...pg. 71
- Cincinnati Fringe Next Festival...pg. 89

SUBMISSION DEADLINES 2018

	15
	16
	17
McKnight Fellowship in Playwriting...pg. 157 Helene Wurlitzer Foundation of New Mexico...pg. 73	18
Moss Hart and Kitty Carlisle New Play Initiative...pg. 132	19
	20
	21
	22
	23
	24
	25
	26
	27
	28
	29
	30
Idaho Commission on the Arts...pg. 154   Leighton Artists Studios...pg. 74
Virgin Islands Council on the Arts...pg. 167	31

January

SUBMISSION DEADLINES 2018

February

1
- W. Keith Hedrick Playwriting Contest…pg. 143
- Dionysia New Play Competition…pg. 122
- U.S. - Japan Creative Artists' Program…pg. 79
- SOUND BITES 10-Minute Musical Festival…pg. 112
- Brody Arts Fund…pg. 150
- Indiana Arts Commission (IAC)…pg. 155

2

3

4

5

6

7

8

9

10

11

12

13

14
- San Francisco Fringe Festival…pg. 111

15
- Woodstock Byrdcliffe Guild…pg. 80
- New Voices Project…pg. 307
- Shakespeare's New Contemporaries Project…pg. 139
- ATHE Award for Excellence In Playwriting…pg. 118
- McNerney Playwriting Contest…pg. 131
- Jane Chambers Playwriting Award…pg. 127
- Harold Morton Landon Translation Award…pg. 125

SUBMISSION DEADLINES 2018

February

	16
	17
Headwaters New Play Festival...pg. 95 ATHE Awards...pg. 118	18
	19
	20
	21
	22
	23
	24
	25
	26
	27
Helen McCloy Scholarship for Mystery Writing...pg. 154 10-Minute Play Festival...pg. 82 Play Competition for Youth Theatre...pg. 136	28
	29
	30
	31

SUBMISSION DEADLINES 2018

March

1
- Ucross Foundation Residency Program…pg. 79
- Millay Colony for the Arts…pg. 75
- Alabama State Council on the Arts…pg. 145
- National Ten Minute Play Contest…pg. 133
- Kimmel Harding Nelson (KHN) Center for the Arts…pg. 73
- New Voice Play Festival…pg. 104
- Smith and Kraus…pg. 62
- Young Writers Showcase…pg. 314
- Woodward/Newman Drama Award…pg. 144
- Clauder Competition for New England Playwrights…pg. 121

2

3

4

5
- Aurand Harris Children's Theatre Grants and Fellowship…pg. 149

6

7
- NEA Literature Fellowships: Creative Writing…pg. 159

8

9

10

11

12

13

14

15
- Princess Grace Foundation USA Playwriting Fellowship…pg. 162

SUBMISSION DEADLINES 2018

March

Laura Jane Musser Fund Rural Arts Program…pg. 156	16
	17
	18
	19
Sewanee Writers' Conference…pg. 111	20
	21
	22
Wisconsin Arts Board…pg. 168	23
	24
	25
	26
	27
	28
	29
	30
International MUT Author's Competition for Musical Entertainment Theatre…pg. 126	31

April

SUBMISSION DEADLINES 2018

1	New York Mills Arts Retreat...pg. 76 Julie Harris Playwright Awards...pg. 128 Fade To Black Play Festival...pg. 93 Chaim Schwartz Foundation...pg. 150
2	
3	
4	
5	
6	
7	
8	
9	
10	
11	
12	
13	The Dr. Floyd Gaffney Playwriting Competition...pg. 122
14	
15	Black & Latino Playwrights Conference...pg. 86

SUBMISSION DEADLINES 2018

April 21

	16
	17
	18
	19
	20
	21
	22
Essential Theatre Playwriting Award...pg. 123	23
	24
	25
	26
	27
	28
	29
Geva Theatre Center...pg. 208	30

SUBMISSION DEADLINES 2018

May

1	ReOrient Festival of Short Plays...pg. 110 New Voices One-Act Play Competition...pg. 133
2	
3	
4	8x10 TheatreFest...pg. 82
5	
6	
7	
8	
9	
10	
11	
12	
13	
14	
15	Kleban Prize in Musical Theatre...pg. 156

SUBMISSION DEADLINES 2018

	16
	17
	18
	19
	20
	21
	22
	23
	24
	25
	26
	27
	28
	29
Theatre Brut Short-Play Festival...pg. 113	30
Phoenix Theatre [IN]...pg. 245 Baltimore Playwrights Festival...pg. 85	31

MAY

June

SUBMISSION DEADLINES 2018

1	California Young Playwrights Contest…pg. 119
2	Headlands Center for the Arts…pg. 72
3	
4	
5	
6	
7	
8	
9	
10	
11	
12	
13	
14	
15	Towson University Prize for Literature…pg. 142

SUBMISSION DEADLINES 2018

June

	16
	17
	18
	19
	20
	21
	22
	23
	24
Artist Trust...pg. 148	25
	26
	27
	28
	29
IATI Theatre (Instituto Arte Teatral Internacional)...pg. 214	30

July

1
Mario Fratti & Fred Newman Political Play Contest...pg. 130

8 Tens @ 8 Festival...pg. 117

Script Tease of Short Plays Competition...pg. 139

Charles M. Getchell Award...pg. 120

Santa Cruz Actors' Theatre...pg. 257

2

3

4

5

6

7

8

9

10

11

12

13

14

15

SUBMISSION DEADLINES 2018

July

	16
	17
	18
	19
	20
	21
	22
	23
	24
	25
	26
	27
	28
	29
	30
	31

August

1	Marathon of One-Act Plays...pg. 100 Stoneham Theatre...pg. 265
2	
3	
4	
5	
6	
7	
8	
9	
10	
11	
12	
13	
14	
15	

SUBMISSION DEADLINES 2018

	16
	17
	18
	19
	20
	21
	22
	23
	24
	25
	26
	27
	28
	29
	30
	31

August

SUBMISSION DEADLINES 2018

September

1. Ohio Arts Council...pg. 161
2.
3.
4.
5.
6.
7.
8.
9.
10.
11.
12.
13.
14.
15. Playwrights First...pg. 137

SUBMISSION DEADLINES 2018

September

	16
	17
	18
	19
	20
	21
	22
	23
	24
	25
	26
	27
	28
	29
Siena Art Institute Summer Residency Program...pg. 78 AACT New Play Fest...pg. 82 City Theatre National Award for Short Playwriting Contest...pg. 120	30

SUBMISSION DEADLINES 2018

October

1	
2	
3	
4	
5	
6	
7	
8	
9	
10	
11	
12	
13	
14	
15	ShowOff! Ten-Minute Playwriting Festival…pg. 112 Great Plains Theatre Conference…pg. 94

SUBMISSION DEADLINES 2018

October

	16
	17
	18
	19
	20
	21
	22
	23
	24
	25
	26
	27
	28
	29
	30
Dayton Playhouse Futurefest...pg. 90	31

SUBMISSION DEADLINES 2018

November

1	North Carolina Arts Council...pg. 160 Will Geer Theatricum Botanicum...pg. 287
2	
3	
4	
5	
6	
7	
8	
9	
10	
11	
12	
13	
14	
15	

SUBMISSION DEADLINES 2018

November

	16
	17
	18
	19
	20
	21
	22
	23
	24
	25
	26
	27
	28
	29
	30

December

1	
2	
3	
4	
5	
6	
7	
8	
9	
10	
11	
12	
13	
14	
15	Premiere Stages Play Festival…pg. 109

SUBMISSION DEADLINES 2018

December

	16
	17
	18
	19
	20
	21
	22
	23
	24
	25
	26
	27
	28
	29
	30
Robert J. Pickering Award for Playwriting Excellence...pg. 138	31

ACCOUNTANTS

DR TAXGUY, LLC
WEBSITE: www.drtaxguy.com **EMAIL**: Don@Drtaxguy.com
PHONE: (866) 741-8294 **ADDRESS**: 222 Broadway, Ste 1917, New York NY 10038

GANER, GROSSBACH AND GANER
WEBSITE: www.gggcpa.com **EMAIL**: mganer@gggcpa.com
PHONE: (212) 873-1472 **ADDRESS**: 1995 Broadway, 16th Fl, New York NY 10023

GIORDANO, COHEN, FASTIGGI, LUCIANO, & CO., P.A.
EMAIL: michael@gcfl-cpa.com **PHONE**: (973) 377-2009
ADDRESS: PO Box 267, 147 Columbia Turnpike, Ste 100, Florham Park NJ 07923

KIMERLING AND WISDOM
WEBSITE: www.kwllc.us **EMAIL**: rwisdom@kwllc.us **PHONE**: (212) 986-0892
ADDRESS: 150 Broadway, Rm 1105, New York NY 10038
NOTES: Est. 1970. Kimerling & Wisdom's mission is to establish a strong mutual understanding of your financial issues in order to formulate creative and practical strategies to help you achieve your financial goals.

MARKS PANETH & SHRON LLP
WEBSITE: www.markspaneth.com **PHONE**: (212) 503-8800
ADDRESS: 685 3rd Ave, New York NY 10017
NOTES: Est. 1907. Nationally ranked, full-service public accounting firm for individuals and companies in the entertainment industry.

ROBERT M. PESCE, CPA
WEBSITE: www.marcumllp.com/PEOPLE/ROBERT-PESCE
EMAIL: robert.pesce@marcumllp.com
PHONE: (212) 485-5730 **ADDRESS**: Marcum LLP, 750 3rd Ave, New York NY 10017
NOTES: Mr. Pesce provides a variety of accounting, business management, consulting, and tax planning services that enable his clients to become more profitable and efficient.

SHEDLER AND COHEN
WEBSITE: www.shedcocpa.com **EMAIL**: mshedler@shedcoCPA.com
PHONE: (212) 564-6656 **ADDRESS**: 350 5th Ave, #3505, New York NY 10118

SPIELMAN, KOENIGSBERG AND PARKER (SKP)
WEBSITE: www.skpny.com **EMAIL**: rkoenigsberg@skpny.com
PHONE: (212) 453-2510 **ADDRESS**: 888 7th Ave, 35th Fl, New York NY 10106

RSO ADVISORS
WEBSITE: www.rsoadvisors.com **EMAIL:** info@rsoadvisors.com
ADDRESS: 16130 Ventura Blvd Ste 550, Encino CA 91436
NOTES: Tax, retirement, and wealth advisors.

AGENTS & MANAGERS

A.M. HEATH & COMPANY, LTD.
WEBSITE: www.amheath.com **EMAIL:** enquiries@amheath.com
PHONE: +44 (0) 207 242 2811
ADDRESS: 6 Warwick Ct, Holborn, London WC1R 5DJ United Kingdom
NOTES: Founded in 1919, A.M.Heath is one of the UK's leading literary agencies. We represent established contemporary authors, rising stars and some of the iconic writers of the 20th Century. Our focus is on working with authors to exploit the potential of their writing in as many arenas as possible. Our agents work closely together to ensure that we cover all areas of the business and each author benefits from the shared expertise of our tight-knit and supportive team. We no longer accept paper submissions.

AO INTERNATIONAL TALENT AGENCY
EMAIL: aoegel@aoiagency.com **PHONE:** (773) 754-7628
ADDRESS: A5240 N Sheridan Rd, Ste 814, Chicago IL 60640

UNITED AGENTS [A P WATT]
WEBSITE: www.unitedagents.co.uk **EMAIL:** info@unitedagents.co.uk
PHONE: +44 (0) 203 214 0800
ADDRESS: 12-26 Lexington St, London W1F 0LE United Kingdom
NOTES: Est. 1875.

ABOVE THE LINE AGENCY
WEBSITE: www.abovethelineagency.com **EMAIL:** abovethelineagency@gmail.com
PHONE: (310) 859-6115 **ADDRESS:** 468 N Camden Dr, Ste 400, Beverly Hills CA 90210
NOTES: Online submission only.

ABRAMS ARTISTS AGENCY
WEBSITE: www.abramsartists.com/literary.html
EMAIL: contactNY@abramsartists.com **PHONE:** (646) 486-4600
ADDRESS: 275 7th Ave, 26th Fl, New York NY 10001
NOTES: Abrams Artists Agency does not accept unsolicited material. Professional referral only.

AGENTS & MANAGERS

AGENCE ARTISTIQUE DUCHESNE
WEBSITE: www.agenceduchesne.com   **EMAIL:** info@agenceduchesne.com
PHONE: (514) 274-4607
ADDRESS: 6031 avenue du Parc, Montréal, QB, H2V 4H4, Canada
NOTES: Est. 1991. Our mission is to represent artists in different fields, (including playwrights, music composers, stage directors, stage designers, and translators), both in Quebec and abroad.

AGENCY FOR THE PERFORMING ARTS [LA]
WEBSITE: www.apa-agency.com   **EMAIL:** mailroom@apa-agency.com
PHONE: (310) 888-4200   **ADDRESS:** 405 S Beverly Dr, Beverly Hills CA 90210

AGENCY FOR THE PERFORMING ARTS [NY]
WEBSITE: www.apa-agency.com   **EMAIL:** nymailroom@apanewyork.com
PHONE: (212) 621-3098   **ADDRESS:** 250 W 57th St, Ste 1701, New York NY 10107
NOTES: Currently not accepting unsolicited submissions.

ALPERN GROUP
EMAIL: mail@alperngroup.com   **PHONE:** (818) 528-1111
ADDRESS: 15645 Royal Oak Rd, Encino CA 91436

ANN RITTENBERG LITERARY AGENCY
WEBSITE: www.rittlit.com   **EMAIL:** info@rittlit.com

ANN WRIGHT REPRESENTATIVES
EMAIL: AnnWrightReps@gmail.com   **PHONE:** (212) 764-6770
ADDRESS: 165 W 46th St, Ste 1105, New York NY 10036

ARTS MANAGEMENT SERVICES, LLC
EMAIL: joanneb@artsmanagementservices.com   **PHONE:** (415) 928-0380
ADDRESS: 2101 California St, Ste 2, San Francisco CA 94115

ASPLAND MANAGEMENT
EMAIL: dennisaspland@aol.com   **PHONE:** (212) 245-9111
ADDRESS: 245 W 55th St, Ste 1102, New York NY 10019

THE BARBARA HOGENSON AGENCY, INC.
EMAIL: Bhogenson@aol.com   **PHONE:** (212) 874-8084
ADDRESS: 165 West End Avenue, #19C, New York NY 10023
NOTES: Est. 1994. Response time: 2 months.

BEACON ARTISTS AGENCY
EMAIL: beaconagency@hotmail.com   **PHONE:** (212) 736-6630
ADDRESS: 120 E 56th St, Ste 540, New York NY 10002

AGENTS & MANAGERS

BOHEMIA GROUP
WEBSITE: www.bohemiaent.com **EMAIL:** info@bohemiaent.com
PHONE: (323) 462-5800
ADDRESS: 1680 N Vine St, Ste 518, Hollywood CA 90028

BRET ADAMS AGENCY
WEBSITE: www.bretadamsltd.net **PHONE:** (212) 765-5630
ADDRESS: 448 W 44th St, New York NY 10036
NOTES: Est. 1953. Staff: Bruce Ostler, Mark Orsini; Alexis Williams; Kate Herzlin (Literary); Margi Rountree, Ken Melamed (Acting). Query must include professional recommendation. We cannot accept unsolicited material, nor can we return any unsolicited material sent to us. Any person who is interested in becoming a client would do best to have someone we work with recommend them to us personally.

CHARLOTTE GUSAY LITERARY AGENCY
WEBSITE: www.gusay.com **EMAIL:** gusay1@ca.rr.com **PHONE:** (310) 559-0831
ADDRESS: 10532 Blythe Ave, Los Angeles CA 90064

CURTIS BROWN GROUP LTD. [UK]
WEBSITE: www.curtisbrown.co.uk **EMAIL:** cb@curtisbrown.com
PHONE: +44 (0) 207-393-4400 **ADDRESS:** Haymarket House, 28-29 Haymarket, London SW1Y 4SP United Kingdom

CURTIS BROWN LTD. [US]
WEBSITE: www.curtisbrown.com **EMAIL:** info@cbltd.com
PHONE: (212) 473-5400 **ADDRESS:** 10 Astor Pl, 3rd Fl, New York NY 10003

DARTMOUTH MANAGEMENT
EMAIL: dmanage@rcn.com **PHONE:** (212) 580-4747
ADDRESS: 208 W 71st St, New York NY 10023

ELEPHANT EYE THEATRICAL, LLC
EMAIL: contact@elephanteye.com
ADDRESS: The Tree Studios, 4 E Ohio St, Chicago IL 60611

ERIC GLASS LTD.
EMAIL: eglassltd@aol.com **PHONE:** +44 (0) 207-229-9500
ADDRESS: 25 Ladbroke Crescent, London W11 1PS United Kingdom

FIFI OSCARD AGENCY, INC.
WEBSITE: www.fifioscard.com **EMAIL:** agency@fifioscard.com
PHONE: (212) 764-1100 **ADDRESS:** 110 W 40 St, 16th Fl, New York NY 10018
NOTES: Est. 1956.

AGENTS & MANAGERS

GAGE GROUP, INC.
EMAIL: gagegroupla@gmail.com **PHONE:** (818) 905-3800
ADDRESS: 14724 Ventura Blvd, Sherman Oaks CA 91403
NOTES: Est. 1975. Submissions not returned. Response: 3 months.

GEORGES BORCHARDT AGENCY
EMAIL: anne@gbagency.com **PHONE:** (212) 753-5785
ADDRESS: 136 E 57th St, New York NY 10022

GERSH AGENCY [LA]
WEBSITE: www.gersh.com **EMAIL:** info@gershla.com **PHONE:** (310) 274-6611
ADDRESS: 232 N Canon Dr, Ste 201, Beverly Hills CA 90210

GERSH AGENCY [NY]
WEBSITE: www.gersh.com **PHONE:** (212) 634-8169
ADDRESS: 41 Madison Ave, 33rd Fl, New York NY 10010
NOTES: Must be submitted through professional recommendation.

GLORIA STERN LITERARY AGENCY
WEBSITE: www.geocities.com/athens/1980/writers.html
EMAIL: cywrite@juno.com **PHONE:** (818) 508-6296
ADDRESS: 12535 Chandler Blvd, #3, North Hollywood CA 91607

GREENSPAN ARTISTS MANAGEMENT
EMAIL: mail@greenspankohan.com
ADDRESS: 8748 Holloway Dr, 2nd Fl, West Hollywood CA 90069

GRUBMAN SHIRE & MEISELAS, P.C.
PHONE: (212) 554-0430
ADDRESS: 152 W 57th St, 31st Fl, New York NY 10019

GSK TALENT (GRANT, SAVIC, KOPALOFF)
WEBSITE: www.gsktalent.com **EMAIL:** contact@gsktalent.com
PHONE: (323) 782-1854
ADDRESS: 6399 Wilshire Blvd, #415, Los Angeles CA 90048

GURMAN AGENCY LLC
WEBSITE: www.gurmanagency.com **EMAIL:** assistant@gurmanagency.com
PHONE: (212) 749-4618
ADDRESS: 14 Penn Plz, Ste 1703, New York NY 10122
NOTES: Est. 1993. Professional referral only.

HARDEN CURTIS ASSOCIATES
WEBSITE: www.hardencurtis.com **EMAIL:** info@hardencurtis.com

AGENTS & MANAGERS

PHONE: (212) 977-8502
ADDRESS: 214 W 29th St, Ste 1203, New York NY 10001
NOTES: Est. 1995. Response time: 2 months.

HARRY FOX AGENCY, INC.
WEBSITE: www.harryfox.com
ADDRESS: 711 3rd Ave, New York NY 10017

HELEN MERRILL LTD.
EMAIL: info@hmlartists.com   **PHONE:** (212) 226-5015
ADDRESS: 295 Lafayette St, #915, New York NY 10012

INNOVATIVE ARTISTS [LA]
EMAIL: literary@iala.com
ADDRESS: 1505 10th St, Santa Monica CA 90401

INTERNATIONAL CREATIVE MANAGEMENT (ICM) [CA]
WEBSITE: www.icmtalent.com   **PHONE:** (310) 550-4000
ADDRESS: 10250 Constellation Blvd, Los Angeles CA 90067

INTERNATIONAL CREATIVE MANAGEMENT (ICM) [NY]
WEBSITE: www.icmtalent.com   **PHONE:** (212) 556-5600
ADDRESS: 65 E 55th St, New York NY 10022

INTERNATIONAL CREATIVE MANAGEMENT (ICM) [UK]
WEBSITE: www.icmtalent.com   **PHONE:** +44 (0) 208-004-5315
ADDRESS: Marlborough House, 10 Earlham St, 3rd Fl, London WC2H 9LN United Kingdom

JANA LUKER AGENCY
EMAIL: luker@castnet.com   **PHONE:** (310) 441-2822
ADDRESS: 1923½ Westwood Blvd, #3, Los Angeles CA 90025

JONATHAN CLOWES LTD.
WEBSITE: www.jonathanclowes.co.uk   **EMAIL:** admin@jonathanclowes.co.uk
PHONE: +44 (0) 207-722-7674   **ADDRESS:** 10 Iron Bridge Rd, Bridge Approach, London NW1 8BD United Kingdom

JUDI FARKAS MANAGEMENT
EMAIL: jgfarkas@mac.com   **PHONE:** (323) 939-9880

JUDY BOALS, INC.
WEBSITE: www.judyboals.com   **EMAIL:** info@judyboals.com
PHONE: (212) 500-1424   **ADDRESS:** 307 W 38th St, Ste 812, New York NY 10018
NOTES: Professional recommendation only.

AGENTS & MANAGERS

JUDY DAISH ASSOCIATES LTD.
EMAIL: judy@judydaish.com **PHONE:** +44 (0) 208-964-8811
ADDRESS: 2 St Charles Pl, London W10 6EG United Kingdom
NOTES: No unsolicited manuscripts accepted.

KNIGHT HALL AGENCY
WEBSITE: www.knighthallagency.com **EMAIL:** office@knighthallagency.com
PHONE: +44 (0) 203-397-2901 **ADDRESS:** 7 Mallow St, Lower Ground Floor, London EC1Y 8RQ United Kingdom

LEGACIES AGENCY
WEBSITE: www.legacytalentandentertainment.com
EMAIL: info@legacytalentllc.com **PHONE:** (704) 334-7727
ADDRESS: 501 Woodstock Cir, Bradenton FL 34209

LINN SAND AGENCY
EMAIL: lsandagency@sbcglobal.net **ADDRESS:** 10940 Wilshire Blvd, Ste 1400, Los Angeles CA 90024

LITERARY ARTISTS REPRESENTATIVES
EMAIL: LitArtists@aol.com **PHONE:** (212) 787-3808
ADDRESS: 575 West End Ave, New York NY 10024

MACNAUGHTON LORD REPRESENTATION
WEBSITE: www.mlrep.com **EMAIL:** info@mlrep.com
PHONE: +44 (0) 208-741-0606 **ADDRESS:** 16 Crucifix Ln, 2nd Fl, London SE1 3JW United Kingdom

MANATT, PHELPS & PHILIPS LLP
WEBSITE: www.manatt.com **EMAIL:** fbernstein@manatt.com
PHONE: (310) 312-4166 **ADDRESS:** 11355 W Olympic Blvd, Los Angeles CA 90064

MARGOT MILES & MATT HARVEY LITERARY TALENT AGENCY
EMAIL: agent6713@aol.com **PHONE:** (323) 871-5864
ADDRESS: 836 N La Cienega Blvd, #358, West Hollywood CA 90069

MCINTOSH & OTIS, INC.
EMAIL: info@mcintoshandotis.com **PHONE:** (212) 687-7400
ADDRESS: Attn: Elizabeth Winick, 353 Lexington Ave, Ste 202, New York NY 10016

MCLAUGHLIN & STERN
WEBSITE: www.mclaughlinstern.com **EMAIL:** info@mclaughlinstern.com

AGENTS & MANAGERS

PHONE: (212) 448-1100 **ADDRESS:** 260 Madison Ave, 18th Fl, New York NY 10016

MONTEIRO ROSE AGENCY INC.
WEBSITE: www.monteiro-rose.com **EMAIL:** monrose@monteiro-rose.com
PHONE: (818) 501-1177 **ADDRESS:** 17514 Ventura Blvd, #205, Encino CA 91316

NATIONAL ASSOCIATION OF TALENT REPRESENTATIVES
WEBSITE: www.natragents.com **EMAIL:** NATRmail@gmail.com
ADDRESS: 315 W 57th St, New York NY 10019

NIAD MANAGEMENT
WEBSITE: www.Niadmanagement.com **EMAIL:** info@niadmanagement.com
PHONE: (818) 774-0051 **ADDRESS:** 15021 Ventura Blvd, Ste 860, Sherman Oaks CA 91403

NICOLOSI & CO., INC.
WEBSITE: www.nicolosi-co.com **EMAIL:** jnicolosi@nicolosi-co.com
PHONE: (212) 633-1010 **ADDRESS:** 150 W 25th St, Ste 1200, New York NY 10001

OPUS 3 ARTISTS
WEBSITE: www.opus3artists.com **EMAIL:** info@opus3artists.com
PHONE: (212) 584-7500 **ADDRESS:** 470 Park Ave S, 9th Fl, New York NY 10016

PARADIGM [LA]
WEBSITE: www.paradigmagency.com **EMAIL:** books@paradigmagency.com
PHONE: (310) 288-8000 **ADDRESS:** 360 N Crescent Dr, North Bldg, Beverly Hills CA 90210

PARADIGM [NY]
WEBSITE: www.paradigmagency.com **EMAIL:** books@paradigmagency.com
PHONE: (212) 897-6400 **ADDRESS:** 140 Broadway, 26th Fl, New York NY 10005
NOTES: Est. 1992. Paradigm represents actors, playwrights, composers, lyricists, directors, choreographers, and designers of the top productions on Broadway and around the world.

PEREGRINE WHITTLESEY AGENCY
EMAIL: pwwagy@aol.com **PHONE:** (212) 787-1802
ADDRESS: 279 Central Park W, New York NY 10024

PETERS, FRASER & DUNLOP LTD.
EMAIL: info@pfd.co.uk **PHONE:** +44 (0) 207-344-1000
ADDRESS: Drury House, 34-43 Russell St, London WC2B 5HA United Kingdom

AGENTS & MANAGERS

PHILIP SPITZER LITERARY AGENCY
WEBSITE: www.spitzeragency.com **EMAIL:** kim.lombardini@spitzeragency.com
ADDRESS: 50 Talmage Farm Ln, East Hampton, NY 11937

ROBERT A. FREEDMAN DRAMATIC AGENCY, INC.
WEBSITE: www.robertfreedmanagency.com
EMAIL: info@robertfreedmanagency.com **PHONE:** (212) 840-5760
ADDRESS: 1501 Broadway, Ste 2310, New York NY 10036
NOTES: Est. 1928. We accept queries by email (fill out form on our website) and regular mail; however, we cannot guarantee a response to emailed queries. Query letters should be no more than two pages and should include a synopsis of the play and information about the author and his or her writing credits. Do not send a complete script.

ROSALIE CALABRESE MANAGEMENT
EMAIL: rcmgt@yahoo.com **PHONE:** (212) 663-6620
ADDRESS: PO Box 20580, Park West St, New York NY 10025

S. VERLAG FISCHER
EMAIL: barbara.perlmutter@bpbooks.net **PHONE:** (212) 222-6242
ADDRESS: 370 Central Park W, Ste 410, New York NY 10025

SCOTT MAURO ENTERTAINMNET
WEBSITE: www.scottmauroentertainment.com
EMAIL: scott@scottmauroentertainment.com **PHONE:** (323) 841-1751
ADDRESS: 1149 N Gower St, Ste 200, Los Angeles CA 90038

THE SHARLAND ORGANISATION
WEBSITE: www.sharlandorganisation.co.uk **EMAIL:** tso@btconnect.com
PHONE: +44 (0) 193-362-6600 **ADDRESS:** Manor House, Manor St, Raunds, Northamptonshire NN9 6AJ United Kingdom

SMC ARTISTS
WEBSITE: www.smcartists.com **PHONE:** (818) 505-9600
ADDRESS: 1525 Aviation Blvd, Ste 1000, Redondo Beach CA 90278

SOIREE FAIR, INC.
WEBSITE: www.soireefair.com **EMAIL:** Literary@soireefair.com
PHONE: (973) 783-9051 **ADDRESS:** 133 Midland Ave, Ste 10, Montclair NJ 7042
NOTES: Est. 1995. Scripts accepted through industry referral only.

STERLING LORD LITERISTIC
WEBSITE: www.sll.com **EMAIL:** info@sll.com **PHONE:** (212) 780-6050
ADDRESS: 115 Broadway, New York NY 10006

AGENTS & MANAGERS

SUSAN SCHULMAN LITERARY AGENCY
EMAIL: schulman@aol.com **PHONE:** (212) 713-1633
ADDRESS: 454 W 44th St, New York NY 10036
NOTES: Est. 1980. We specialize in representing foreign rights, motion picture, television, and allied rights, live stage including commercial theater, opera and dance adaptations, new media rights including e-book and digital applications, and other subsidiary rights on behalf of North American publishers and literary agents.

THE AGENCY [UK]
WEBSITE: www.theagency.co.uk **EMAIL:** info@theagency.co.uk
PHONE: +44 (0) 207-727-1346
ADDRESS: 24 Pottery Ln, Holland Park, London W11 4L2 United Kingdom
NOTES: We are unable to consider unsolicited material, unless it has been recommended by a producer, development executive or course tutor. If this is the case, please email a CV, covering letter and details of your referee to the relevant agent, or to info@theagency.co.uk. Please do not email more than one agent at a time.

THE BOHRMAN AGENCY
EMAIL: cb@thebohrmanagency.com **PHONE:** (310) 550-5444
ADDRESS: 8899 Beverly Blvd, #811, Los Angeles CA 90048

THE MARTON AGENCY, INC.
WEBSITE: www.martonagency.com **EMAIL:** info@martonagency.com
PHONE: (212) 255-1908 **ADDRESS:** Attn: Tonda Marton, 1 Union Sq W, Rm 815, New York NY 10003
NOTES: Specializes in brokering foreign-language rights to US theatre works. Promotes plays to associates abroad, generally after a production has been mounted in the US.

TSU TSU UNLIMITED
WEBSITE: www.tsutsuunlimited.com **EMAIL:** tsutsu007@gmail.com
PHONE: (212) 989 3424 **ADDRESS:** 145 W 12th St, #1-4, New York NY 10011

UNITED TALENT AGENCY [LA]
WEBSITE: www.unitedtalent.com **EMAIL:** sfoassistant@unitedtalent.com
PHONE: (310) 385-2800 **ADDRESS:** 9336 Civic Ctr Dr, Beverly Hills CA 90210
NOTES: UTA operates exclusively by referral and does not accept unsolicited materials or solicitations of any kind. Any such materials will be returned or destroyed at the agency's discretion.

UNITED TALENT AGENCY [NY]
EMAIL: mediarelations@unitedtalent.com **PHONE:** (212) 659-2600
ADDRESS: 888 7th Ave, 7th Fl, New York NY 10106

WILLIAM KERWIN AGENCY
WEBSITE: www.williamkerwinagency.com **EMAIL:** wka@williamkerwinagency.com **PHONE:** (323) 469-5155 **ADDRESS:** 1605 N Cahuenga Blvd, #202, Los Angeles CA 90028

WILLIAM MORRIS ENDEAVOR [NY]
WEBSITE: www.wmeentertainment.com   **PHONE:** (212) 586-5100 **ADDRESS:** 11 Madison Ave, 18th Fl, New York NY 10010
NOTES: Formed in 1898, William Morris Agency is the longest-running talent agency. In 2009, WMA merged with Endeavor to become one of the leading entertainment and media companies with an unparalleled list of artists and content creators. In 2014, WME acquired IMG, the global leader in sports, events, media and fashion, forming WME | IMG.

WYLIE AGENCY
EMAIL: mail@wylieagency.com **PHONE:** (212) 246-0069 **ADDRESS:** 250 W 57th St, Ste 2114, New York NY 10107

ATTORNEYS

CANE LAW LLP
WEBSITE: www.canelaw.com **EMAIL:** info@canelaw.com **PHONE:** (212) 627-7000 **ADDRESS:** 200 Park Ave, New York NY 10166

CASE ARTS LAW LLC
WEBSITE: www.caseartslaw.com **EMAIL:** contact@caseartslaw.com **PHONE:** (312) 234-9926 **ADDRESS:** 53 W Jackson Blvd, Ste 209, Chicago IL 60604
NOTES: Case Arts Law LLC provides sophisticated legal representation to fine arts clients in a wide range of legal matters, including contract, labor and employment, intellectual property, and litigation matters.

CLINTONS SOLICITORS
WEBSITE: www.clintons.co.uk **EMAIL:** jcohen@clintons.co.uk **PHONE:** +44 (0) 207-379-6080 **ADDRESS:** 55 Drury Ln, Attn: John Cohen, Sr Partner, London WC2B 5RZ United Kingdom

COWAN, DEBAETS, ABRAHAMS & SHEPPARD
WEBSITE: www.cdas.com **PHONE:** (212) 974-7474 **ADDRESS:** 40 W 57th St, 21st Fl, New York NY 10019
NOTES: For more than 25 years Cowan, DeBaets, Abrahams & Sheppard LLP has

provided legal counsel to leading media and entertainment clients, from individual creators, to corporations, associations, and non-profit organizations.

D. KRAUSZ AND ASSOCIATES, ATTORNEYS AT LAW
WEBSITE: www.dianefkrausz.com **EMAIL:** dkrausz@aol.com
PHONE: (212) 244-5292
ADDRESS: 33 W 19th St, 4th Fl, New York NY 10011

DANIEL AHARONI & PARTNERS LLP
WEBSITE: www.danielaharoni.com **EMAIL:** office@danielaharoni.com
PHONE: (212) 605-0035 Ext 2 **ADDRESS:** 575 Madison Ave, Ste 1006, New York NY 10022
NOTES: We help our clients achieve their dream to live and work in the United States by guiding them through the complex labyrinth of immigration laws, regulations, and procedures of multiple government agencies.

DAVID H. FRIEDLANDER, ESQ.
WEBSITE: www.dfriedlander.com **EMAIL:** david@dfriedlander.com
PHONE: (914) 241-1277 **ADDRESS:** 81 Park Dr., Mount Kisco, NY 10549
NOTES: David Friedlander practices entertainment and intellectual property law, and is admitted to practice in New York and California.

DAY & KOCH LLP
WEBSITE: www.dayandkoch.com **EMAIL:** info@dayandkoch.com
PHONE: (503) 224-4900 **ADDRESS:** 1435 NW 19th Ave, Portland OR 97209
NOTES: Day & Koch LLP represents creative companies, individuals, and entrepreneurs in business and corporate transactions, entertainment, and intellectual property law. Day & Koch is an "AV" rated law firm, the highest rating attainable in the Martindale-Hubbell Law Directory.

DIPERNA ASSOCIATES
WEBSITE: www.dipernaassociates.com **EMAIL:** leacpa@dipernaassociates.com
PHONE: (212) 675-3000 **ADDRESS:** 225 W 35th St, Ste 802, New York NY 10001

DONALDSON & CALLIF, LLP
WEBSITE: www.donaldsoncallif.com **EMAIL:** michael@donaldsoncallif.com
PHONE: (310) 277-8394 **ADDRESS:** 400 S Beverly Dr, Ste 400, Beverly Hills CA 90210

DRINKER BIDDLE & REATH LLP
WEBSITE: www.drinkerbiddle.com **PHONE:** (202) 354-1333
ADDRESS: 1 Logan Sq, Ste 2000, Philadelphia PA 19103
NOTES: Drinker Biddle is a national, full-service law firm providing litigation, regulatory and business solutions to public and private corporations, multinational Fortune 100 companies and start-ups.

ATTORNEYS

FRANKFURT, KURNIT, KLEIN AND SELZ
WEBSITE: www.fkks.com **EMAIL:** info@fkks.com **PHONE:** (212) 980-0120
ADDRESS: 488 Madison Ave, 10th Fl, New York NY 10022
NOTES: Long recognized as a leading media, entertainment, and advertising law firm, Frankfurt Kurnit Klein + Selz, PC, has grown to provide the highest quality legal services to clients in a wide range of industries and disciplines.

FRANKLIN, WEINRIB, RUDELL & VASSALLO PC
WEBSITE: www.fwrv.com **EMAIL:** info@fwrv.com **PHONE:** (212) 935-5500
ADDRESS: 488 Madison Ave, New York NY 10022

GELFAND, RENNERT, & FELDMAN
WEBSITE: www.grfllp.com **EMAIL:** info@grfllp.com **PHONE:** (310) 553-1707
ADDRESS: 1880 Century Park E, 16th Fl, Los Angeles CA 90067

HIRSCH WALLERSTEIN HAYUM MATLOF + FISHMAN
EMAIL: bhirsch@hwhmf.com **PHONE:** (310) 703-1700
ADDRESS: 10100 Santa Monica Blvd, Ste 1700, Los Angeles CA 90067

INNES SMOLANSKY, ATTORNEY AT LAW
EMAIL: innes@filmlegal.com **PHONE:** (718) 499-5633
ADDRESS: 761 Carroll St, Brooklyn NY 11215

JOHN J. TORMEY III, PLLC
WEBSITE: www.tormey.org **EMAIL:** jtormey@optonline.net
PHONE: (212) 410-4142 **ADDRESS:** 1324 Lexington Ave, PMB 188, New York NY 10128
NOTES: Entertainment Transactional Legal Work, Project Placement Work, and General Law Practice.

LAW OFFICE OF ANDREW B. PERETZ P.A
EMAIL: aperetz@comcast.net **PHONE:** (954) 558-8829
ADDRESS: 1 E Broward Blvd, Wachovia Tower, Ft Lauderdale FL 33301

LAW OFFICE OF GARY N. DASILVA
EMAIL: mail@garydasilva.com **PHONE:** (310) 318-5665
ADDRESS: 111 N Sepulveda Blvd, #250, Manhattan Beach CA 90266

LAW OFFICES OF BARTLEY F. DAY
EMAIL: allmedia@hevanet.com **PHONE:** (503) 291-9300
ADDRESS: 1001 SW 5th Ave, Ste 1100, Portland OR 97204

LAW OFFICE OF GHENYA B. GRANT
EMAIL: ggrant@gbg-law.com **PHONE:** (212) 835-1613
ADDRESS: 5 Penn Plz, 23rd Fl, New York NY 10001
NOTES: Entertainment attorney providing legal counsel and representation in corporate formation and governance, contracts, trademark, copyright, and licensing matters.

LAW OFFICE OF GORDON P. FIREMARK
WEBSITE: www.firemark.com **EMAIL:** gfiremark@firemark.com
PHONE: (310) 443-4185 **ADDRESS:** 10940 Wilshire Blvd, 16th Fl, Los Angeles CA 90024
NOTES: We are dedicated to the legal and business affairs requirements of clients in the entertainment and media industries.

LAW OFFICE OF J.J. SHERMAN, P.C.
WEBSITE: www.jjshermanlaw.com **PHONE:** (213) 984-1806
ADDRESS: 4470 W Sunset Blvd, #610, Los Angeles CA 90027
NOTES: Licensed in New York, California, and D.C.

LAW OFFICE OF JEFFREY L. GRAUBART, P.C.
WEBSITE: www.entertainmentlaw.la **EMAIL:** info@jlgraubart.com
PHONE: (626) 304-2800 **ADDRESS:** 800 E Colorado Blvd, #840, Pasadena CA 91101
NOTES: Est. 1971. We are a general, business and civil practice offering a wide range of legal services.

LAW OFFICES OF LLOYD J. JASSIN
WEBSITE: www.copylaw.com **EMAIL:** jassin@copylaw.com
PHONE: (212) 354-4442 **ADDRESS:** 1560 Broadway, #400, New York NY 10036

LAW OFFICES OF NOEL L. SILVERMAN
WEBSITE: www.nls-law.com **EMAIL:** nsilverman@nls-law.com
PHONE: (212) 758-2020 **ADDRESS:** 200 Park Ave S, #1614, New York NY 10003

LAW OFFICES OF PETER M. THALL
WEBSITE: www.thallentlaw.com **EMAIL:** nazava@thallentlaw.com
PHONE: (212) 245-6221 **ADDRESS:** Attn: Natasha Azava, Esq, 10 W End Ave, Ste 7K, New York NY 10023

LAW OFFICES OF RICHARD GARMISE, PLLC
PHONE: (212) 354-8474 **ADDRESS:** 1776 Broadway, Ste 1002, New York NY 10019

ATTORNEYS

LAW OFFICES OF ROBERT G PIMM
WEBSITE: www.rgpimm.com   **PHONE:** (925) 374-1442
ADDRESS: 2977 Ygnacio Valley Rd, #265, Walnut Creek CA 94598

LAZARUS & HARRIS LLP
WEBSITE: www.lazhar.com   **EMAIL:** info@lazhar.com   **PHONE:** (212) 302-5252
ADDRESS: 561 7th Ave, 11th Fl, New York NY 10018

LEAVENS, STRAND, GLOVER & ADLER, LLC
WEBSITE: www.lsglegal.com   **EMAIL:** tleavens@lsglegal.com
PHONE: (312) 488-4170   **ADDRESS:** 203 N LaSalle St, Ste 2550, Chicago IL 60601
NOTES: An entertainment, media, & intellectual property law firm concentrating our practice on matters involving creative industries and endeavors.

LEVINE, PLOTKIN & MENIN
WEBSITE: www.lpmny.com   **EMAIL:** info@lpmny.com   **PHONE:** (212) 245-6565
ADDRESS: 888 7th Ave, 10th Fl, New York NY 10106

LICHTER, GROSSMAN, NICHOLS, ADLER & FELDMAN, INC.
WEBSITE: www.lgna.com   **EMAIL:** info@lgna.com
ADDRESS: 9200 Sunset Blvd, Ste 1200, West Hollywood CA 90069

LOEB & LOEB
EMAIL: sgelblum@loeb.com   **PHONE:** (212) 407-4000
ADDRESS: 345 Park Ave, New York NY 10022

MEISTER SEELIG & FEIN LLP
WEBSITE: www.meisterseelig.com   **EMAIL:** emr@msf-law.com
PHONE: (617) 371-2979   **ADDRESS:** 60 State St, Ste 700, Boston MA 02109

MENAKER & HERRMANN LLP
WEBSITE: www.mhjur.com   **EMAIL:** info@mhjur.com   **PHONE:** (212) 545-1900
ADDRESS: 10 E 40th St, 43rd Fl, New York NY 10016

MICHAEL BLAHA, ESQ.
WEBSITE: www.blahalaw.com   **EMAIL:** mike@blahalaw.com
PHONE: (800) 419-3013   **ADDRESS:** 2530 Wilshire Blvd, 3rd Fl, Santa Monica CA 90403
NOTES: The Law Offices of Michael R. Blaha is an entertainment law firm that provides clients in Los Angeles, Hollywood and throughout Southern California with sound legal counsel and results-oriented advocacy focused on helping institutions and individuals resolve legal issues in an efficient and cost-effective manner so they can concentrate on their entertainment careers and businesses.

ATTORNEYS

PAUL, WEISS, RIFKIND, WHARTON & GARRISON
WEBSITE: www.paulweiss.com **PHONE:** (212) 373-3000
ADDRESS: 1285 Ave of the Americas, New York NY 10019
NOTES: Our highly regarded group represents individuals and companies involved in all aspects of the entertainment industry, including film, television, publishing, music, new media, live stage, and sports.

PEIKOFF MAHAN LAW OFFICE
EMAIL: michele@peikoffmahan.com **PHONE:** (212) 343-9600
ADDRESS: 173 E Broadway, Ste C-1, New York NY 10002

PETER D. SINGH, JR.
WEBSITE: www.wsmblaw.com **EMAIL:** psingh@wsmblaw.com
PHONE: (267) 218-1062
ADDRESS: 6 E 39th St, 6th Fl, New York, NY 10016

RABIN PANERO & HERRICK
WEBSITE: www.rabinpaneroherrick.com **EMAIL:** contact@rabinpaneroherrick.com
PHONE: (914) 948-2222 **ADDRESS:** 44 Church St, White Plains NY 10601
NOTES: Rabin, Panero & Herrick (RPH) is a law firm founded on two generations of experience in a wide range of real estate, business and estate matters. Our notable business experience and well-respected legal practice has been a recipe for success that drives unique insights into our clients' legal affairs. Our attorneys are passionate about what we do, and our commitment to personal service is what separates us from the crowd. We understand that important life events can be a stressful time and we strive to make your involvement with the legal system as painless as possible.

ROBERTA L. KORUS, ATTORNEY AT LAW
WEBSITE: www.robertakorus.com **EMAIL:** robertakorus@gmail.com
PHONE: (914) 269-8120 **ADDRESS:** 3 Emmalon Ave, N White Plains NY 10603
NOTES: Focusing on contracts and intellectual property rights for the entertainment industry.

ROBERTS RITHOLZ LEVY SANDERS CHIDEKEL & FIELDS LLP
EMAIL: mkim@robritlaw.com **PHONE:** (212) 448-1800
ADDRESS: 235 Park Ave S, 3rd Fl, New York, NY 10003

ROBINSON, BROG, LEINWAND, GREENE, GENOVESE & GLUCK
WEBSITE: www.robinsonbrog.com **EMAIL:** info@robinsonbrog.com
PHONE: (212) 603-6308 **ADDRESS:** 875 3rd Ave, 9th Fl, New York NY 10022

S. JEAN WARD
WEBSITE: www.fkks.com **EMAIL:** sjward@fkks.com **PHONE:** (212) 826-5584
ADDRESS: 488 Madison Ave, New York NY 10022

NOTES

SAPER LAW
WEBSITE: www.saperlaw.com **PHONE:** (312) 527-4100
ADDRESS: 505 N LaSalle, Ste 350, Chicago IL 60654
NOTES: Saper Law is an intellectual property, social media, and business law firm with headline grabbing clients and cases.

SCHRECK, ROSE, AND DAPELLO
EMAIL: schreckrose@srdlaw.com **PHONE:** (212) 832-1977
ADDRESS: 1790 Broadway, 20th Fl, New York NY 10019

SENDROFF & BARUCH, LLP
WEBSITE: www.sendroffbaruch.com **EMAIL:** msendroff@sendroffbaruch.com
PHONE: (212) 840-6400
ADDRESS: 1500 Broadway, #2201, New York NY 10036

SHUKAT ARROW HAFER WEBER & HERBSMAN, LLP
WEBSITE: www.musiclaw.com **EMAIL:** info@musiclaw.com
PHONE: (212) 582-7614
ADDRESS: 494 8th Ave, 6th Fl, New York NY 10001

WASHINGTON SQUARE ARTS AND FILM
EMAIL: bmiller@washingtonsquarearts.com **PHONE:** (212) 253-0333
ADDRESS: 310 Bowery, 2nd Fl, New York NY 10012

WINSLETT STUDNICKY MCCORMICK & BOMSER LLP
WEBSITE: www.wsmblaw.com **EMAIL:** abomser@wsmblaw.com
ADDRESS: 6 E 39th St, 6th Fl, New York NY 10016

PUBLISHERS

ALFRED MUSIC PUBLISHING
WEBSITE: www.alfred.com **EMAIL:** pr@alfred.com **PHONE:** (646) 449-0063
ADDRESS: 540 Broadway, #305, New York NY 10012

APPLAUSE THEATRE & CINEMA BOOKS
EMAIL: info@halleonard.com **PHONE:** (800) 637-2852
DESCRIPTION: Imprint of Hal Leonard.

ARTAGE PUBLICATIONS' SENIOR THEATRE RESOURCE CENTER
WEBSITE: www.seniortheatre.com **EMAIL:** bonniev@seniortheatre.com
PHONE: 800-858-4998 **ADDRESS:** 7845 SW Capitol Hwy Ste 12, Portland OR 97219
DESCRIPTION: For over 20 years, older performers and their directors have turned to the Senior Theatre Resource Center for plays, books, and materials that charm audiences. Whether amateur or skilled professional, we have something for everyone. With worldwide customers, ArtAge is proud of our personalized, prompt service. We always remember that our mission is to help older performers fulfill their theatrical dreams.
DEADLINE TYPE: Rolling **PREFERRED GENRE:** Plays or Musicals
PREFERRED LENGTH: Any Length **FEE:** No **AGENT ONLY:** No

ARTE PUBLICO PRESS
WEBSITE: artepublicopress.com **EMAIL:** mtristan@Central.uh.edu
PHONE: (713) 743-2845 **FAX:** (713) 743-3080
ADDRESS: 452 Cullen Performance Hall, Houston TX 77204

ASIAN AMERICAN WRITERS WORKSHOP
WEBSITE: www.aaww.org **EMAIL:** desk@aaww.org **PHONE:** (212) 494-0061
FAX: (212) 494-0062 **ADDRESS:** 16 W 32nd St, #10A, New York NY 10001

BAKER'S PLAYS
WEBSITE: www.bakersplays.com **EMAIL:** publications@bakersplays.com
PHONE: (212) 206-8990 **FAX:** (212) 627-7753
ADDRESS: 45 W 25th St, #9, New York NY 10010
FEE: No **AGENT ONLY:** No

BEAUFORT BOOKS
WEBSITE: www.beaufortbooks.com **EMAIL:** info@beaufortbooks.com
PHONE: (212) 727-0222 **ADDRESS:** 27 W 20th St, #1102, New York NY 10011

BIG DOG PUBLISHING
WEBSITE: www.bigdogplays.com **EMAIL:** info@bigdogplays.com
FAX: (605) 791-0186 **ADDRESS:** PO Box 1401, Rapid City SD 57709

PUBLISHERS

DESCRIPTION: Est. 2005. We welcome submissions from new and established playwrights. Plays for family and school audiences (K-12). Publishes 25-40 plays/year. Response time: 2-3 months. No email submissions please.
PREFERRED GENRE: Plays or Musicals **PREFERRED LENGTH:** Any Length
SPECIAL INTEREST: Theatre for Young Audiences **FEE:** No **AGENT ONLY:** No

BOOSEY AND HAWKES
WEBSITE: www.boosey.com **EMAIL:** composers.us@boosey.com
PHONE: (212) 358-5300 **ADDRESS:** 229 W 28th St, #11, New York NY 10001
DESCRIPTION: Composers and Repertoire Directorate

BROADWAY PLAY PUBLISHING, INC.
WEBSITE: www.broadwayplaypub.com **EMAIL:** info@broadwayplaypub.com
PHONE: (212) 772-8334 **FAX:** (212) 772-8358
ADDRESS: 224 E 62nd St, New York NY 10065
DESCRIPTION: Est. 1982. Broadway Play Publishing Inc generally acquires plays after a definitive production on or off-Broadway, in London's West End, or at a professional regional theater.
PREFERRED GENRE: Plays **PREFERRED LENGTH:** Full-length **FEE:** No **AGENT ONLY:** No

BROOKLYN PUBLISHERS
WEBSITE: www.brookpub.com **EMAIL:** editor@brookpub.com
PHONE: (432) 550-5532 **FAX:** (432) 368-0340
ADDRESS: 1841 Cord St, Odessa TX 79762

CAMBRIDGE UNIVERSITY PRESS
WEBSITE: www.cambridge.org **EMAIL:** customer_service@cambridge.org
PHONE: (212) 337-5000 **ADDRESS:** 1 Liberty Plz, 20th Fl, New York NY 10006

CONTEMPORARY DRAMA SERVICE
WEBSITE: www.contemporarydrama.com **EMAIL:** editor@meriwether.com
PHONE: (719) 594-4422 **FAX:** (719) 594-9916
ADDRESS: 885 Elkton Dr, Colorado Springs CO 80907
PREFERRED GENRE: Plays or Musicals **PREFERRED LENGTH:** Any Length
FEE: No **AGENT ONLY:** No

CURRENCY PRESS
WEBSITE: www.currency.com.au **EMAIL:** proposals@currency.com.au
ADDRESS: PO Box 2287, Strawberry Hills, NSW 2012 Australia
DESCRIPTION: Publisher/distributor of performing arts books on Australian drama, film, and music (including play and film scripts) in Australia & New Zealand.

If your play has been professionally produced in Australia, send the script along with details of its production history and any reviews you would like to include. Plays that have not been professionally produced will not be considered for publication except in our Current Theatre Series.

PREFERRED GENRE: Plays **PREFERRED LENGTH:** Full-length **FEE:** No **AGENT ONLY:** No

PUBLISHERS

DRAMATIC PUBLISHING COMPANY
WEBSITE: www.dramaticpublishing.com **EMAIL:** SubmissionsEditor@dpcplays.com
PHONE: (800) 448-7469 **ADDRESS:** 311 Washington St, Woodstock IL 60098
DESCRIPTION: Est. 1885. Response: 4-6 months.
PREFERRED GENRE: All genres **PREFERRED LENGTH:** Any Length
FEE: No **AGENT ONLY:** No

DRAMATISTS PLAY SERVICE, INC.
WEBSITE: www.dramatists.com **EMAIL:** publications@dramatists.com
PHONE: (212) 683-8960 **ADDRESS:** 440 Park Ave S, New York NY 10016
DESCRIPTION: Electronic submissions only. We generally acquire plays after successful productions in New York City, London, or at a major regional theatre. If your show has not yet been produced in a notable venue, you might be better served to put your time and energy into pursuing a production. Response time: 6 mos.
PREFERRED GENRE: Plays or Musicals **PREFERRED LENGTH:** Full-length **FEE:** No
AGENT ONLY: No

ELDRIDGE PUBLISHING COMPANY, INC.
WEBSITE: www.histage.com **EMAIL:** newworks@histage.com
PHONE: (850) 385-2463 **ADDRESS:** PO Box 4904, Lancaster PA 17604
DESCRIPTION: Please submit plays and musicals suitable for performance by community theatres and junior and senior high schools. We welcome shows on all subjects; however, shows with explicit adult content or graphically defined situations do not fit our market. For musicals, please include an audio sample of several songs and a few pages from the score. Response time: 2 mos.
PREFERRED GENRE: All genres **PREFERRED LENGTH:** Any Length **FEE:** No
AGENT ONLY: No

EMPIRE PUBLISHING SERVICE
EMAIL: empirepubsvc@att.net **PHONE:** (818) 784-8918
ADDRESS: PO Box 1344 Studio City CA 91614, Studio City CA 91614
PREFERRED GENRE: All Genres **PREFERRED LENGTH:** Any Length **FEE:** No
AGENT ONLY: No

FOCUS PUBLISHING
WEBSITE: www.focuspublishing.com **EMAIL:** info@focuspublishing.com
PHONE: 800-913-6287 **ADDRESS:** PO Box 665, Bemidji MN 56619-0665

FOX PLAYS
WEBSITE: www.foxplays.com **EMAIL:** sales@foxplays.com
PHONE: +61 (03) 9428 9064
DESCRIPTION: Based in Australia, Fox Plays publishes the plays, books, and musicals created by Cenarth Fox, for children, teens and adults.
PREFERRED GENRE: Plays or Musicals

NOTES

PUBLISHERS

G. SCHIRMER, INC. / ASSOCIATED MUSIC PUBLISHERS, INC.
WEBSITE: www.musicsalesclassical.com **EMAIL:** schirmer@schirmer.com
PHONE: (212) 254-2100 **ADDRESS:** 180 Madison Ave, Fl 24, New York NY 10016

GREEN INTEGER
WEBSITE: www.greeninteger.com **EMAIL:** info@greeninteger.com
PHONE: (323) 857-1115 **ADDRESS:** 6022 Wilshire Blvd, #202C, Los Angeles CA 90036
PREFERRED GENRE: Plays

GROVE ATLANTIC PRESS
WEBSITE: www.groveatlantic.com **EMAIL:** sales@groveatlantic.com
PHONE: (212) 614-7850 **ADDRESS:** 154 W 14th St, New York NY 10011

HAL LEONARD
WEBSITE: www.halleonard.com **EMAIL:** sales@halleonard.com
PHONE: (414) 774-3630 **ADDRESS:** PO Box 13819, Milwaukee WI 53213
DESCRIPTION: Est. 1947. The world's largest music print publisher.

HAVESCRIPTS.COM
WEBSITE: www.havescripts.com **EMAIL:** inbasket@havescripts.com
ADDRESS: 204 Oakengate Turn, Virginia Beach VA 23462
PREFERRED GENRE: Plays **PREFERRED LENGTH:** Any Length **FEE:** No

HEINEMANN
WEBSITE: www.heinemann.com **EMAIL:** doria.turner@heinemann.com
PHONE: (603) 431-7894 **FAX:** (603) 437-7840 **ADDRESS:** 361 Hanover St, Portsmouth NH 03801

JAC PUBLISHING & PROMOTIONS
WEBSITE: www.jacneed.com/JAC/JAC.htm **EMAIL:** submissions@jacneed.com
PHONE: (781) 272-2066 **FAX:** (781) 229-2676 **ADDRESS:** 4 Princeton Rd, PO Box 88, Burlington MA 01803

LAZY BEE SCRIPTS
WEBSITE: www.lazybeescripts.co.uk **EMAIL:** enquiries@lazybeescripts.co.uk
PHONE: +44 (0) 161-355-2374 **TWITTER:** @LazyBeeScripts
ADDRESS: 4 Marsham Dr, Marple, Stockport SK6 7DP United Kingdom
DESCRIPTION: Submission queries via a form on our web site. (There is no submissions fee, but we offer an optional Appraisal process for which there is a fee in return for thorough feedback.)
PREFERRED GENRE: Plays or Musicals **FEE:** No

LILLENAS PUBLISHING COMPANY
WEBSITE: www.lillenasdrama.com **EMAIL:** drama@lillenas.com

PUBLISHERS

PHONE: (816) 931-1900 **FAX:** (816) 412-8390
ADDRESS: Lillenas Drama Resources, PO Box 419527, Kansas City MO 64141

LIMELIGHT SCRIPTS
WEBSITE: www.limelightscripts.co.uk **EMAIL:** info@limelightscripts.co.uk
PHONE: +44 (0) 779-499-0307 **ADDRESS:** 152 Southey Hill, Sheffield S5 8BN United Kingdom

MIND'S EAR AUDIO PRODUCTIONS
WEBSITE: www.minds-ear.org **EMAIL:** mindsear@minds-ear.org
ADDRESS: 5661 W Bedrock Rd, Bloomington IN 47403

MOOSE HIDE BOOKS
WEBSITE: www.moosehidebooks.com **EMAIL:** mooseenterprises@on.aibn.com
PHONE: (705) 779-3331 **FAX:** (707) 779-3331 **ADDRESS:** 684 Walls Rd, Prince Twp ON P6A-6K4 Canada
DESCRIPTION: Response time is one month. We no longer publish new works, rather wish to assist authors through our story editing service, mentor editing, and script development.
PREFERRED GENRE: All genres **FEE:** No **AGENT ONLY:** No

MUSICAL THEATRE INTERNATIONAL
WEBSITE: www.mtishows.com **PHONE:** (212) 541-4684
ADDRESS: 423 W 55th St, 2nd Fl, New York NY 10019
DESCRIPTION: Est. 1952. Performances licensed, all venues. MTI is a secondary licensing agency and prefers musicals that have been produced.
PREFERRED GENRE: Musical Theatre

MYSTERIES BY MOUSHEY INC.
WEBSITE: www.mysteriesbymoushey.com **EMAIL:** info@mysteriesbymoushey.com
PHONE: (330) 678-3893 **FAX:** (330) 434-9376
ADDRESS: PO Box 3593, Kent OH 44240

NEWMUSICALS.COM
WEBSITE: www.newmusicals.com **EMAIL:** info@newmusicals.com
PHONE: (860) 236-0592 **ADDRESS:** 22 Grenhart St, West Hartford CT 06117
PREFERRED GENRE: Musical theatre **PREFERRED LENGTH:** Full-length **FEE:** No
AGENT ONLY: No

NEXT STAGE PRESS
WEBSITE: www.nextstagepress.net **EMAIL:** submissions@nextstagepress.net
ADDRESS: 11174 Josephine Way, Northglenn CO 80233
DESCRIPTION: We have suspended open submissions and are now taking submissions by referral from one of our playwrights.
PREFERRED GENRE: All genres **PREFERRED LENGTH:** Any Length
FEE: No **AGENT ONLY:** No

NORMAN MAINE PUBLISHING
WEBSITE: www.normanmaineplays.com **EMAIL:** info@normanmaineplays.com
FAX: (605) 791-0186 **ADDRESS:** PO Box 1401, Rapid City SD 57709
DESCRIPTION: Est. 2005. Plays for community, professional, and university theatre. Prefer produced/award-winning work. No email submissions please.
PREFERRED GENRE: Plays or Musicals **PREFERRED LENGTH:** Any Length **FEE:** No
AGENT ONLY: No

ORIGINAL WORKS PUBLISHING
WEBSITE: www.originalworksonline.com **EMAIL:** subdept@originalworksonline.com
ADDRESS: 7080 Hollywood Blvd, Ste 1100, Los Angeles CA 90028
DESCRIPTION: Est. 2000. Original Works is a publishing and licensing house for stage plays. Original Works is known as the home for bold, innovative, original new plays. Unsolicited submissions accepted year-round by e-mail only. Response time: 3-6 months.
PREFERRED GENRE: Plays **PREFERRED LENGTH:** Any Length **FEE:** No
AGENT ONLY: No

PERFORMER STUFF
WEBSITE: www.performerstuff.com **EMAIL:** info@performerstuff.com
PHONE: (407) 351-5900 **TWITTER:** @PerformerStuff
ADDRESS: 6626 Kingspointe Pkwy, Orlando FL 32819
DESCRIPTION: PerformerStuff.com is an online community, created for and powered by performers and entertainment industry professionals, offering monologues, audition cuts, full sheet music, performance coaching, a free resume builder, free user profiles, and educational resources. Published and unpublished playwrights and composers welcome. Please submit inquiries via the contact page (www.performerstuff.com/pwlandingpage). (Response: 1-2 weeks.) Questions? Visit the Playwright FAQ page (www.performerstuff.com/documents/PlaywrightFAQ.pdf).
PREFERRED GENRE: Plays or Musicals **PREFERRED LENGTH:** Any Length
FEE: No **AGENT ONLY:** No

PIONEER DRAMA SERVICE
WEBSITE: www.pioneerdrama.com **EMAIL:** submissions@pioneerdrama.com
PHONE: (303) 779-4035 **FAX:** (303) 779-4315
ADDRESS: PO Box 4267, Englewood CO 80155

PLAYERS PRESS, INC.
PHONE: (818) 789-4980 **ADDRESS:** PO Box 1132, Studio City CA 91614
PREFERRED GENRE: All Genres **PREFERRED LENGTH:** Full-lenngth **FEE:** No
AGENT ONLY: No

PLAYSCRIPTS, INC.
WEBSITE: www.playscripts.com/submit **EMAIL:** info@playscripts.com
PHONE: (866) 639-7529 **ADDRESS:** 450 Seventh Ave, Ste 809, New York NY 10123
DESCRIPTION: Est. 1998. Acting editions sold and performances licensed to amateur/professional venues worldwide. Playscripts does not currently accept unsolicited

PUBLISHERS

submissions but accepts submissions at any time through an agent, manager, or entertainment lawyer.

PREFERRED GENRE: Plays **PREFERRED LENGTH:** Any Length
FEE: No **AGENT ONLY:** Yes

PLAYSTAGE JUNIOR
WEBSITE: www.schoolplaysandpantos.com **EMAIL:** lynn@schoolplaysandpantos.com
PHONE: +44 (0) 776 965 3136
ADDRESS: 140 Buckingham Palace Rd, London SW1W 9SA United Kingdom

POND PLAYS (A DIVISION OF BEAVER'S POND PRESS)
WEBSITE: www.beaverspondpress.com **PHONE:** (952) 829-8818
TWITTER: @BPPress **ADDRESS:** 7108 Ohms Ln, Edina MN 55439
PREFERRED GENRE: Plays **PREFERRED LENGTH:** Any Length **FEE:** No
AGENT ONLY: No **DESCRIPTION:** A publishing resource for the independent playwright.

PRISM INTERNATIONAL
WEBSITE: www.prism.arts.ubc.ca **EMAIL:** prismpoetry@gmail.com
PHONE: (604) 822-2514 **FAX:** (604) 822-3616 **ADDRESS:** Buchanan E462, 1866 Main Mall, Vancouver BC V6T 1Z1 Canada

NOTES

THE MUSICAL COMPANY

| THEATRICAL LICENSING | MUSIC PUBLISHING | CAST RECORDING |

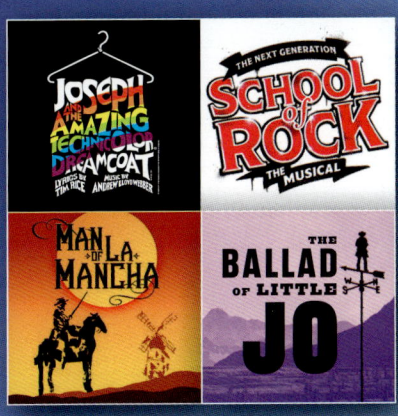

WWW.THEMUSICALCOMPANY.COM

RODGERS & HAMMERSTEIN ORGANIZATION THEATRICALS

WEBSITE: www.rnh.com **EMAIL:** Theater@rnh.com **PHONE:** (212) 541-6600 **FAX:** (212) 586-6155 **TWITTER:** @RnH_Org **ADDRESS:** 229 W 28th St, 11th Fl, New York NY 10001

DESCRIPTION: Theatrical Licensing Agent and Music Publisher. Quotes expire 3 months after being created. **FEE:** No **AGENT ONLY:** No

SAMUEL FRENCH, INC.

WEBSITE: www.samuelfrench.com **EMAIL:** info@samuelfrench.com **PHONE:** (866) 598-8449 **TWITTER:** @SamuelFrenchNYC **ADDRESS:** 235 Park Ave S, 5th Fl, New York NY 10003

DESCRIPTION: Est. 1830. Samuel French is the world's leading publisher and licensor of plays and musicals. The company's catalog features some of the most acclaimed work ever written for the stage and titles by writers at the forefront of contemporary drama. Samuel French is proud to have served as a leader in theatrical publishing and licensing for over 180 years and is committed to the future by championing for playwrights, innovating the industry, and celebrating all those who make theatre around the world.

PREFERRED GENRE: Plays or Musicals **PREFERRED LENGTH:** Any Length **FEE:** No **AGENT ONLY:** No

SHAWNEE PRESS

EMAIL: info@shawneepress.com

DESCRIPTION: Imprint of Hal Leonard.

SINISTER WISDOM

WEBSITE: www.sinisterwisdom.org **PHONE:** (813) 502-5549 **TWITTER:** @Sinister_Wisdom **ADDRESS:** 2333 McIntosh Rd, Dover FL 33527

DESCRIPTION: Sinister Wisdom is a multicultural lesbian literary & art journal that publishes four issues each year. Publishing since 1976, Sinister Wisdom works to create a multicultural, multi-class lesbian space.

PREFERRED GENRE: Plays **PREFERRED LENGTH:** 10-minute **FEE:** No **AGENT ONLY:** No

SMITH AND KRAUS

WEBSITE: www.smithandkraus.com **EMAIL:** editor@smithandkraus.com **PHONE:** (207) 523-2585 **ADDRESS:** 177 Lyme Rd, Hanover NH 03755

DESCRIPTION: Smith & Kraus, theatrical trade publisher, welcomes submissions of both full length and 10-minute plays for its annual ten-minute play anthology, and for its annual monologue anthologies, edited by Lawrence Harbison. 10-minute plays must be produced originally between 1 May 2017 and 30 April 2018. All submissions must include a title page with contact information for the author or agent. Send via e-mail to LRHarbison1@gmail.com.

SUBMISSION DEADLINE: 03/01/2018 **DEADLINE TYPE:** Annual **PREFERRED GENRE:** Plays **PREFERRED LENGTH:** Full-length & 10-minute **FEE:** No **AGENT ONLY:** No

PUBLISHERS

STEELE SPRING STAGE RIGHTS
WEBSITE: www.stagerights.com **EMAIL:** info@stagerights.com
PHONE: (323) 739-0413 **ADDRESS:** 3845 Cazador St, Los Angeles CA 90065
DESCRIPTION: Based in Los Angeles and founded in 2000, Stage Rights is one of the foremost independent theatrical publishers in the United States, providing stage performance rights for a wide range of plays and musicals to theater companies, schools, and other producing organizations across the country and internationally.
PREFERRED GENRE: Plays or Musicals **PREFERRED LENGTH:** Full-length **FEE:** No
AGENT ONLY: No

THEATREFOLK
WEBSITE: www.theatrefolk.com/submissions **EMAIL:** submissions@theatrefolk.com
PHONE: (866) 245-9138 **FAX:** (877) 245-9138 **ADDRESS:** 228 Park Ave S, #32457, New York NY 10003
DESCRIPTION: We publish plays specifically for student performers. Production should be simple. Response time: 6-8 weeks. Please review our submission policy before submitting.
PREFERRED GENRE: Plays **PREFERRED LENGTH:** Any Length **FEE:** No
AGENT ONLY: No

NOTES

MUSIC THEATRE INTERNATIONAL

We look forward to working with you.

mtishows.com

THEATREFORUM
WEBSITE: www.theatreforum.org **EMAIL:** TheatreForum@ucsd.edu
FAX: (858) 534-1080 **ADDRESS:** 9500 Gilman Dr, MCO344, La Jolla CA 92093
DESCRIPTION: Est. 1992. Plays must have been professionally produced. Submit via email.
PREFERRED GENRE: Plays **PREFERRED LENGTH:** Full-length
FEE: No **AGENT ONLY:** No

THEATRICAL RIGHTS WORLDWIDE
WEBSITE: www.theatricalrights.com **EMAIL:** licensing@theatricalrights.com
PHONE: (646) 736-3232 **ADDRESS:** 1180 Ave of the Americas, 8th Fl, New York NY 10036
DESCRIPTION: Est. 2006. If you feel your musical is ready for production, please send a hard copy of your script, samples of your music, and an audio CD, as well as any production history to the attention of Bay Wellington, Director of Submission.
PREFERRED GENRE: Musicals **PREFERRED LENGTH:** Any Length
FEE: No **AGENT ONLY:** No

UNIVERSITY OF HAWAI'I PRESS
WEBSITE: www.uhpress.hawaii.edu/journals.aspx **EMAIL:** uhpbooks@hawaii.edu
PHONE: (808) 956-8833 **ADDRESS:** 2840 Kolowalu St, Journals Dept, Honolulu HI 96822
DESCRIPTION: Dedicated to performing arts of Asia; traditional, modern, original, and translated plays.
PREFERRED GENRE: Plays **PREFERRED LENGTH:** Any length **SPECIAL INTEREST:** Asian; Native Hawaiian or Other Pacific Islander **FEE:** No

UNIVERSITY OF MISSOURI PRESS
EMAIL: upress@missouri.edu **PHONE:** (800) 621-2736 **FAX:** (800) 621-8476
ADDRESS: 113 Heinkel, Bldg 201, S 7th St, Columbia MO 65211

WW NORTON AND COMPANY
WEBSITE: wwnorton.com **PHONE:** (212) 354-5500 **ADDRESS:** 500 5th Ave, # 6, New York NY 10110

YOUTHPLAYS
WEBSITE: www.youthplays.com **EMAIL:** info@youthplays.com
PHONE: (424) 703-5315 **ADDRESS:** 7119 W Sunset Blvd, #390, Los Angeles CA 90046
DESCRIPTION: We publish plays for young actors and audiences. Particular needs include flexible to large cast One-Act (30-35 minutes) comedies for high school and middle school actors, adaptations, and plays and playwrights that reflect diversity (bilingual scripts welcome!). Deadline is ongoing for regular submissions.
PREFERRED GENRE: Plays **PREFERRED LENGTH:** 1-Act (under 1 hour)
SPECIAL INTEREST: Theatre for Young Audiences **FEE:** No **AGENT ONLY:** No

COLONIES & RESIDENCIES

ABRONS AIRSPACE PROGRAM
WEBSITE: www.abronsartscenter.org/artist-residencies **EMAIL:** AbronsAIRspace@henrystreet.org **PHONE:** (212) 598-0400 **FAX:** (212) 388-1418
TWITTER: @AbronsArtsCtr **ADDRESS:** 466 Grand St, New York NY 10002
DESCRIPTION: The AIRspace playwright residency program aims to support writing for the theater by offering playwrights space, time and institutional resources within a theater setting in which to create new work. The two year long residency includes a dedicated private office space for up to two separate resident artists annually. Additionally, playwrights are provided ongoing rehearsal space to develop new material and Abrons provides technical, marketing and administrative support in the presentation of work-in-progress showings in our blackbox theaters. See website or call for details.
SUBMISSION MATERIALS: Check website for updated information.

AFRICAN AMERICAN AND AFRICAN PLAYWRIGHTS CREATIVE RESIDENCY
PARENT ORGANIZATION: Camargo Foundation
WEBSITE: camargofoundation.org/programs/partnership-programs
EMAIL: apply@camargofoundation.org **PHONE:** + 33 (0)4 42 01 11 5
ADDRESS: 1 avenue Maurice Jermini, Cassis 13260 France
DESCRIPTION: The Camargo Foundation, with generous support from the National Endowment for the Arts and the Jerome Foundation, is excited to announce a four-week residency program for mid-career/established African-American and African playwrights. Four participants from the United States and four from the African continent, all of whom are interested in the intersection and interaction, whether historic or contemporary, between the United States and Africa, will be hosted at the Camargo Foundation in Cassis, France, from May 28 - June 25, 2018.
DEADLINE TYPE: Annual **GENRE:** All Genres **PREFERRED LENGTH:** Any Length
FEE: No **AGENT ONLY:** No

ALTOS DE CHAVON
WEBSITE: altosdechavon.edu.do/en/artists-residence-program
EMAIL: admisiones@altosdechavon.com **PHONE:** (809) 563-2802
ADDRESS: Altos de Chavón, La Romana, Dominican Republic
DESCRIPTION: Est. 1981. The Artists in Residence program aims to sponsor an educational and cultural interchange between Dominican and foreign artists. In this program, painters, sculptors, ceramicists, photographers, writers, musicians, and architects from different countries come together to live and work in Altos de Chavón for three months. They receive housing and a studio for their use, and during their stay they interact with their Dominican counterparts, sharing experiences and ideas in the different disciplines.
SUBMISSION MATERIALS: Check website for submission information. **FEE:** Yes

ANAM CARA WRITER'S AND ARTIST'S RETREAT

WEBSITE: www.anamcararetreat.com **EMAIL:** info@anamcararetreat.com
PHONE: +353 (0) 277 4441 **FAX:** (353) 277-4448
ADDRESS: Eyeries, Beara, Bantry Cork P75 DP66 Ireland
DESCRIPTION: Est. 1998. Anam Cara, an Irish retreat for writers and artists overlooking Coulagh Bay and the mountains and farmlands of the sub-tropical Beara Peninsula in West Cork. To check availability, rates, and deposit policy, please contact Sue at anamcararetreat@gmail.com or submit your request in the Contact Us section of the website.
SUBMISSION MATERIALS: Check website for additional information.
GENRE: All Genres **PREFERRED LENGTH:** Any Length **FEE:** Yes **AGENT ONLY:** No

ARTIST'S COTTAGE, THE

PARENT ORGANIZATION: Salamanca Arts Centre
WEBSITE: www.salarts.org.au/venue/the-artists-cottage
EMAIL: venues@salarts.org.au **TWITTER:** @salarts
ADDRESS: 77 Salamanca Pl, Hobart Tasmania 7000 Australia
DESCRIPTION: The Artist's Cottage is available to artist of all disciplines. Used by visiting artists and their families, the sunny cottage is ideal short-term accommodation for singles or groups. This completely self-contained 3 bedroom cottage can provide you with everything you need to work undisturbed.
SUBMISSION MATERIALS: Artists wishing to apply for the discounted rates must provide evidence of their Residency to be eligible. To request a booking for your Arts Residency please contact the Venues Coordinator on 03 6234 8414 or venues@salarts.org.au. Please see website for rates and details. **FEE:** No **AGENT ONLY:** No

ARTSCAPE GIBRALTAR POINT

WEBSITE: www.artscapegibraltarpoint.ca/artist-residences/
EMAIL: AGP@artscape.ca **PHONE:** (416) 392-1038 **FAX:** (416) 392-1059
TWITTER: @gibraltarpoint **ADDRESS:** 171 E Liberty St, #224, Toronto ON M6K 3P6 Canada
DESCRIPTION: Est. 1999. We host two types of artist residencies: self-directed, and programmed. Every Writing Studio in our dedicated quiet "Writers' Wing" includes a large desk and comfortable chair. Composer Studios are located in converted school portables and are separate from the rest of the residency centre. The 750 square-foot studios have an open-concept layout with a bedroom area, comfort zone and a large work table. The studios are not 100% soundproof, but are adequate for composing. See website for rates and details. **FEE:** Yes **AGENT ONLY:** No

ATLANTIC CENTER FOR THE ARTS

WEBSITE: atlanticcenterforthearts.org/residencies/master-artist-residency-schedule **EMAIL:** iriascos@atlanticcenterforthearts.org
PHONE: (386) 427-6975 **TWITTER:** Atlantic_Center
ADDRESS: 1414 Art Center Ave, New Smyrna Beach FL 32168
DESCRIPTION: Est. 1982. Residencies of 3 weeks with master artists. Workspace includes black box theater, music studio, dance studio, painting and sculpture studio, writing studio, and resource library.

SUBMISSION MATERIALS: Check website for additional information.

GENRE: Plays   **FEE:** Yes

BALTIC CENTRE FOR WRITERS & TRANSLATORS (BCWT)

WEBSITE: www.bcwt.org/GetDoc?meta_id=1403
EMAIL: baltic.centre@gotlandica.se   **PHONE:** 46-498-218-385
ADDRESS: Uddens Grand 3, SE-621 56, Visby 62156 Sweden

BAU INSTITUTE

WEBSITE: www.bauinstitute.org   **EMAIL:** info@bauinstitute.org
PHONE: (646) 712-2475   **ADDRESS:** 133 Wooster Street, 7F, New York NY 10012
SUBMISSION MATERIALS: Check website for additional information.
GENRE: All genres   **PREFERRED LENGTH:** Any Length   **FEE:** Yes

BAU INSTITUTE ARTS RESIDENCY

PARENT ORGANIZATION: Camargo Foundation
WEBSITE: www.bauinstitute.org/index.php?page=cassis-france
DESCRIPTION: In 2014 BAU Institute launched a new arts residency hosted by the Camargo Foundation in Cassis, France. It provides BAU Institute funded Fellowships for the realization of projects in the arts; it provides artists with live-work apartments at The Camargo Foundation at no cost. Creative practioners demonstrating a serious commitment to their practice and a desire to work independently within an international community are welcome to apply.
2018 DATES: July 22- August 19, 2017. PLEASE CHECK OUR WEBSITE FOR THE OPEN CALL ANNOUNCEMENT UPDATED DEADLINE INFORMATION. Please apply during the open call period only.
GENRE: All Genres   **PREFERRED LENGTH:** Any Length   **FEE:** Yes   **AGENT ONLY:** No

BETC GENERATIONS RESIDENCY

PARENT ORGANIZATION: Boulder Ensemble Theatre Company
WEBSITE: betc.org/programs-events/generations   **EMAIL:** info@betc.org
PHONE: (303) 351-2382   **TWITTER:** @betctheatre
ADDRESS: 2590 Walnut St #1, Boulder CO 80302
DESCRIPTION: Each season, BETC selects one playwright through a national competition to join us in Boulder for a one-week residency. During the residency week, the playwright works with a professional director, dramaturg, and actors to develop the selected script. The week concludes with a public reading and post-reading conversation. BETC takes pleasure in supporting our parent playwright residents' writing careers post-residency, and advocating for production of their plays through connections within the National New Play Network. 2018 competition guidelines will be posted in June 2018 on our website and through the New Play Exchange, with a September 2018 deadline. See website for details.
GENRE: Plays   **PREFERRED LENGTH:** Full-length   **FEE:** No   **AGENT ONLY:** No

BLUE MOUNTAIN CENTER

WEBSITE: www.bluemountaincenter.org/dates-and-guidelines

EMAIL: bmc@bluemountaincenter.org **PHONE:** (518) 352-7391 **FAX:** (518) 352-7700 **ADDRESS:** Box 109, Blue Mt Lake NY 12812
DESCRIPTION: Blue Mountain Center values racial, economic and environmental justice and gender equality. We encourage applications from people of color, women and LGBTQ artists and activists. Contact us if you have concerns or barriers to participating in a BMC Residency.
SUBMISSION MATERIALS: Check website for additional information. **FEE:** Yes

BOGLIASCO FOUNDATION
WEBSITE: bfny.org/en/home **EMAIL:** info@bfny.org **PHONE:** (212) 486-0874 **TWITTER:** @BogliascoFdn **ADDRESS:** 1 E 53rd St, 8th Fl, New York NY 10022
DESCRIPTION: An American nonprofit with a program in Italy, the Bogliasco Foundation awards one-month residential Fellowships to individuals of all ages and nationalities who have made significant contributions in the arts and humanities. To be eligible for a Fellowship, applicants should demonstrate significant achievement in their disciplines, commensurate with their age and experience. Online application only. Application deadlines: January 15th for residencies during the subsequent fall semester, and April 15th for residences during the subsequent spring semester.
SUBMISSION MATERIALS: Check website for additional information.
GENRE: All Genres **PREFERRED LENGTH:** Any Length **FEE:** Yes

BRECKENRIDGE CREATIVE ARTS: TIN SHOP AND ROBERT WHYTE HOUSE RESIDENCY
WEBSITE: www.breckcreate.org/opportunities/tin-shop-call-to-artists
EMAIL: info@breckcreate.org **PHONE:** (970) 453-3187 **ADDRESS:** 150 W Adams Ave, PO Box 4269, Breckenridge CO 80424
DESCRIPTION: The Tin Shop Artists-in-Residence program provides time and space for artists to work on their medium of choice, while providing public interaction in the form of open studio hours and workshops to complement the growing Breckenridge Arts District. Artists also engage with the local school district. The Tin Shop has a working studio on the main level and a small fully furnished studio apartment on the upper level. Seeking artists in a variety of mediums to fill a one year time period, January 2018 – December 2018, with flexible residency terms. Residencies are approximately one month. There is no charge for artists to stay at the Tin Shop. Artists are responsible for all transportation costs, food and materials for personal work. There are opportunities for artists to earn income during their residency through workshops, educational programs, lectures, and demos.
DEADLINE: See website **DEADLINE TYPE:** Annual **GENRE:** All Genres **PREFERRED LENGTH:** Any Length **FEE:** No **AGENT ONLY:** No

BRICLAB RESIDENCY
WEBSITE: www.bricartsmedia.org/artist-opportunities/residencies/briclab-residency **EMAIL:** briclab@bricartsmedia.org **PHONE:** (718) 683-5600 **TWITTER:** @BRICartsmedia **ADDRESS:** 647 Fulton Street, Brooklyn NY 11217
DESCRIPTION: BRIClab is a commissioning and residency development program for Brooklyn and New York City-based artists to explore and expand the possibilities of their work in music, dance, theater and multi-disciplinary perfor-

mance. Free and open exploration and intentional commitment to process – with the support of the staff and resources that BRIC offers – are at the heart of the BRIClab program. Artists receive stipends and an intensive residency in BRIC's Artist Studio with development time, opportunities for artistic mentoring, and work-in-process performances.

PREFERRED LENGTH: Any Length **FEE:** Yes

BROWN FOUNDATION FELLOWS PROGRAM AT THE DORA MAAR HOUSE

WEBSITE: mfah.org/fellowships/doramaarhouse/fellowship **EMAIL:** doramaarhouse@mfah.org **PHONE:** (713) 639-7300 **ADDRESS:** 1001 Bissonnet, Houston TX 77005

DESCRIPTION: The Brown Foundation Fellows Program, based at the Dora Maar House in Ménerbes, France, provides residencies of one to three months for mid-career professionals in the arts and humanities to concentrate on their fields of expertise. The Brown Foundation Fellows Program at the Dora Maar House is made possible through a grant from the Brown Foundation, Inc., in Houston. The program has been directed by the Museum of Fine Arts Houston since 2006. **FEE:** Yes

BYRDCLIFFE ARTS COLONY ARTIST-IN-RESIDENCE (AIR)

WEBSITE: www.woodstockguild.org/artist-residencies
EMAIL: air@woodstockguild.org **PHONE:** (845) 679-2079 **FAX:** (845) 679-4529
ADDRESS: 34 Tinker St, Woodstock NY 12498

DESCRIPTION: Since its founding in 1902, Byrdcliffe has welcomed artists—Bob Dylan, Philip Guston, Eva Hesse, and hundreds more—to and live and work surrounded by 250 acres of the Catskill Mountains' serene natural beauty. Byrdcliffe offers several types of residency ranging from four weeks to five months for artists in multiple disciplines.

SUBMISSION MATERIALS: See website for information. **AGENT ONLY:** No

CAMARGO CORE PROGRAM

PARENT ORGANIZATION: Camargo Foundation
WEBSITE: camargofoundation.org **EMAIL:** apply@camargofoundation.org
ADDRESS: 1 avenue Maurice Jermini, Cassis 13260 France

DESCRIPTION: The historical and flagship program of the Foundation. Each year an international call is launched through which 18 fellows (9 artists and 9 scholars/thinkers) are selected. The program offers time and space in a contemplative environment to think, create, and connect. By encouraging groundbreaking research and experimentation, it supports the visionary work of artists, scholars and thinkers in the Arts and Humanities. By encouraging multidisciplinary and interdisciplinary approaches, it intends to foster connections between research and creation. Artists applicants should be the primary creators of a new work/project and have achieved a track record of publications/performances/exhibitions, credits, awards and/or grants. We are interested in artists who have a fully developed, mature artistic voice. Applicants may include those who have been commissioned for multiple projects. When applying, artists will have to choose among the following subcategories: Visual Artists / Chore-

ographers and Performance Artists / Writers and Playwrights / Film, Video and Digital Artists / Composers and Sound Artists / Multidisciplinary Artists.
DEADLINE: see website **GENRE:** All Genres **PREFERRED LENGTH:** Any Length
FEE: No **AGENT ONLY:** No

CENTRUM ARTISTIC RESIDENCIES PROGRAM
WEBSITE: www.centrum.org/residencies **EMAIL:** mworthley@centrum.org
PHONE: (360) 385-3102 **ADDRESS:** Box 1158, Port Townsend WA 98368
DESCRIPTION: Centrum's Artist Residency Program was established in 1980 as a resource for artists and creative thinkers of all genres. We are located on Washington's Olympic Peninsula, in the beautiful and inspiring setting of Fort Worden State Park, which is nestled in the Victorian seaport and arts community of Port Townsend.
SUBMISSION MATERIALS: Check website for additional information.
GENRE: All genres **FEE:** Yes

COLLEGE OF LITERARY TRANSLATORS OF SENEFFE (CTLS)
WEBSITE: www.users.skynet.be/sky80640/informat.htm **EMAIL:** ctls@skynet.be
PHONE: (322) 569-6812 **FAX:** (322) 569-6812
ADDRESS: 749 chaussee de Waterloo, Brussels 1180 Belgium
DESCRIPTION: The Seneffe European College hosts literary translators from all over the world for a period of 15 days to a month and a half. All language combinations are welcome, however, our primary purpose is to promote the translation of French-language literature in Belgium. Priority is given to translators of Belgian authors. We provide residents with almost all the works of Belgian writers old and contemporary, regularly invite Belgian authors to seminars, and organize shows or readings in the Orangery and the Little Baroque theatre located in the area. The Seneffe College tries as much as possible to bring together the translators of the same author and to allow the translators to meet the writer(s). Translators are supported for housing and food. Translators of Belgian writers also benefit from a per diem, provided that the follow-up of their work is ensured, among others with a publishing house. Every year, the Ministry of the French Community of Belgium awards a prize to a translator who has contributed by the quality of his translations to the influence of the French-language literature of Belgium.
SUBMISSION MATERIALS: Candidates will be selected on the basis of a registration file accompanied by a Curriculum vitae. The registration form should be requested from the Director of the College: Françoise Wuilmart.
DEADLINE TYPE: Rolling

DJERASSI RESIDENT ARTISTS PROGRAM
WEBSITE: www.djerassi.org/apply **EMAIL:** judy@djerassi.org
PHONE: (650) 747-1250 **ADDRESS:** 2325 Bear Gulch Rd, Woodside CA 94062

DORLAND MOUNTAIN ARTS COLONY
WEBSITE: www.dorlandartscolony.com/residency-information.html
EMAIL: info@dorlandartscolony.org **PHONE:** (951) 302-3837

ADDRESS: PO Box 6, Temecula CA 92593
GENRE: All genres **PREFERRED LENGTH:** Any Length **FEE:** Yes

EDWARD F. ALBEE FOUNDATION, THE
WEBSITE: www.albeefoundation.org/guidelines--submitting.html
EMAIL: info@albeefoundation.org **PHONE:** (212) 226-2020
FAX: (212) 226-5551 **ADDRESS:** 14 Harrison St., New York NY 10013
DESCRIPTION: The Edward F. Albee Foundation exists to serve writers and visual artists from all walks of life, by providing time and space in which to work without disturbance.
SUBMISSION MATERIALS: Online only. 2017 submission deadline has passed. Check website for updated information.
GENRE: Plays **PREFERRED LENGTH:** Full-length **FEE:** No **AGENT ONLY:** No

EUROPEAN TRANSLATORS' COLLEGE
WEBSITE: www.euk-straelen.de/deutsch/das-kollegium **EMAIL:** euk.straelen@t-online.de **PHONE:** 011 (492) 834-1069 **FAX:** 011 (492) 834-7544
ADDRESS: Postfach 1162, Straelen D-47628 Germany

GELL: A FINGER LAKES CREATIVE RETREAT
WEBSITE: www.wab.org/gell-center-residencies-2/ **EMAIL:** Kathyp@wab.org
PHONE: (585) 473-2590 **FAX:** (585) 442-9333 **ADDRESS:** 6581 W Hollow Rd, Naples NY 14512
SUBMISSION MATERIALS: Check website for updated information. **FEE:** No

GROUND FLOOR SUMMER RESIDENCY LAB
PARENT ORGANIZATION: Berkeley Repertory Theatre
WEBSITE: www.berkeleyrep.org/groundfloor **EMAIL:** groundfloorapps@berkeleyrep.org **PHONE:** (510) 647-2900 **FAX:** (510) 647-2976 **ADDRESS:** Berkeley Repertory Theatre, 999 Harrison St, Berkeley CA 94710
DESCRIPTION: We invite artists to apply with projects that would benefit from a residency in Berkeley for 1–4 weeks. Berkeley Rep will provide transportation, housing, rehearsal space, basic technical support, and a modest stipend. Applicants must be available for residency between June 5 and July 1, 2018. Previous applicants may reapply. There is no limit on the number of projects an artist may apply with. We do accept applications from international artists.
SUBMISSION MATERIALS: The Ground Floor application window for the 2018 Summer Residency Lab has closed. Applications for 2019 will be accepted starting in Fall 2018.
DEADLINE TYPE: Annual **GENRE:** Plays or Musicals **PREFERRED LENGTH:** Any Length
FEE: No **AGENT ONLY:** No

HAMBIDGE CENTER
WEBSITE: www.hambidge.org/program-overview.html **EMAIL:** center@hambidge.org **PHONE:** (706) 746-5718 **FAX:** (706) 746-9933
ADDRESS: PO Box 339, Rabun Gap GA 30568
DESCRIPTION: Hambidge provides a residency program that empowers talented individuals to explore, develop, and express their creative voices. Situated on 600

acres in the mountains of north Georgia, Hambidge is a sanctuary of time and space that inspires individuals working in a broad range of disciplines to create works of the highest caliber. Apply from December 1st through January 15th for the May through August residency period. Apply from March 1st through April 15th for the September through December residency period. Apply from August 1st through September 15th for the mid-February through April residency period.

SUBMISSION MATERIALS: Proposal, bio, resume, work sample

DEADLINE: 01/15/2018 **FEE:** Yes **AGENT ONLY:** No

HAROLD CLURMAN PLAYWRIGHTS DIVISION

WEBSITE: www.stellaadler.com/cultural-center/playwrights-division
EMAIL: stevewhite@stellaadler.com **PHONE:** (212) 689-0087
ADDRESS: 31 W 27th St, 3rd Fl, New York NY 10001

HAWTHORNDEN RETREAT FOR WRITERS

WEBSITE: www.transartists.org/air/hawthornden-castle **EMAIL:** transartists@dutchculture.nl **PHONE:** +44 (0)131-440-2180 **ADDRESS:** Hawthornden Castle, Lasswade, Midlothian EH18 1EG United Kingdom

DESCRIPTION: The international retreat for writers at Hawthornden Castle has been founded to provide a peaceful setting where creative writers can work without disturbance.

SUBMISSION MATERIALS: Any creative writer, from any part of the world, who has already published may apply for a Fellowship at Hawthornden. Please send a letter of interest via postal mail and they should get back to you with more information to apply. **DEADLINE TYPE:** Rolling **FEE:** No

HEADLANDS CENTER FOR THE ARTS

WEBSITE: www.headlands.org/program/air **EMAIL:** hblake@headlands.org
PHONE: (415) 331-2787 **ADDRESS:** 944 Fort Barry, Sausalito CA 94965

DESCRIPTION: The Artist in Residence (AIR) program awards fully sponsored residencies to approximately 45 local, national, and international artists each year. Residencies of four to ten weeks include studio space, chef-prepared meals, comfortable housing, and travel and living stipends.

SUBMISSION MATERIALS: Resume, letter of interest, work sample

DEADLINE: 06/02/2018 **FEE:** Yes **AGENT ONLY:** No

HEDGEBROOK WOMEN WRITERS IN RESIDENCE

WEBSITE: www.hedgebrook.org/writers-in-residence
EMAIL: vitoz@hedgebrook.org **PHONE:** (360) 321-4786
ADDRESS: PO Box 1231, Freeland WA 98249

DESCRIPTION: Hedgebrook is on Whidbey Island, about thirty-five miles northwest of Seattle. Situated on 48-acres of forest and meadow facing Puget Sound, with a view of Mount Rainier, the retreat hosts writers from all over the world for residencies of two to six weeks, at no cost to the writer.

SUBMISSION MATERIALS: The deadline for 2018 residency has passed. Check website for updated information. **FEE:** Yes **AGENT ONLY:** No

COLONIES & RESIDENCIES

HELENE WURLITZER FOUNDATION OF NEW MEXICO
WEBSITE: www.wurlitzerfoundation.org **EMAIL:** HWF@taosnet.com
PHONE: (575) 758-2413 **FAX:** (575) 758-2559
ADDRESS: PO Box 1891, Taos NM 87571
DESCRIPTION: Est. 1954. The Foundation's mission is to "Support the artist and the creative process" and serves as a haven for visual artists, literary artists and music composers. We are located on fifteen acres in the heart of Taos, New Mexico, a four-hundred-year-old multicultural community renowned for its popularity with artists. The Foundation offers three months of rent-free and utility-paid housing to grantees. Our eleven guest houses, or casitas, are fully furnished and provide residents with a peaceful setting in which to pursue their creative endeavors.
SUBMISSION MATERIALS: Online application
DEADLINE: 01/18/2018 **DEADLINE TYPE:** Annual **FEE:** Yes **AGENT ONLY:** No

INTERNATIONAL COLLEGE OF LITERARY TRANSLATORS (CITL)
WEBSITE: www.atlas-citl.org/conditions-de-sejour/ **PHONE:** +33 049 052 0550
TWITTER: ATLAStrad **ADDRESS:** Espace Van Gogh, Arles 13200 France
DESCRIPTION: Est. 1987. The CITL's mission is to host in residence literary translators from all over the world, as well as authors wishing to work for a while with their translator, researchers, and linguists.
SUBMISSION MATERIALS: See website for updates. **FEE:** No **AGENT ONLY:** No

IWP RESIDENCY
PARENT ORGANIZATION: IWP Residency
WEBSITE: iwp.uiowa.edu/residency **EMAIL:** christopher-merrill@uiowa.edu
PHONE: (319) 335-0128 **FAX:** (319) 335-3843 **TWITTER:** @UIIWP
ADDRESS: 430 N Clinton St, Iowa City IA 52242
DESCRIPTION: The International Writing Program (IWP) is a unique conduit for the world's literatures, connecting well-established writers from around the globe, bringing international literature into classrooms, introducing American writers to other cultures through reading tours, and serving as a clearinghouse for literary news and a wealth of archival and pedagogical materials. Since 1967, over fourteen hundred writers from more than 150 countries have been in residence at the University of Iowa.
SUBMISSION MATERIALS: See website for updates.
GENRE: Plays **PREFERRED LENGTH:** Full-length **FEE:** No **AGENT ONLY:** No

KIMMEL HARDING NELSON (KHN) CENTER FOR THE ARTS
WEBSITE: www.khncenterforthearts.org/residency.php **EMAIL:** info@khncenterforthearts.org **PHONE:** (402) 874-9600 **FAX:** (402) 874-9600
ADDRESS: 801 3rd Corso, Nebraska City NE 68410
DESCRIPTION: The Kimmel Harding Nelson Center for the Arts offers approximately 70 juried residencies per year to visual artists, writers, composers, and interdisciplinary artists from across the country and around the world. Application deadlines are March 1 for July - December residencies and September 1 for January - June residencies annually. **DEADLINE:** 03/01/2018 **FEE:** Yes **AGENT ONLY:** No

KLAUSTRID ARTIST-IN-RESIDENCE PROGRAM
WEBSITE: www.skriduklaustur.is/index.php/en/air-program **EMAIL:** klaustur@skriduklaustur.is **PHONE:** (354) 471-2990 **FAX:** (354) 471-2991
ADDRESS: Skriduklaustur, 701 Egilsstadir, Egilsstadir IS-707 Iceland
DESCRIPTION: Klaustrið (the Monastery) is a residence managed by The Institute of Gunnar Gunnarsson. It is situated at Skriðuklaustur Culture Center in East Iceland in the beautiful home of the Icelandic writer Gunnar Gunnarsson.
SUBMISSION MATERIALS: See website for updated information.

LA CENTRALE GALERIE POWERHOUSE
WEBSITE: www.lacentrale.org/en/prix-powerhouse
EMAIL: galerie@lacentrale.org **PHONE:** (514) 871-0268
ADDRESS: 4296 Blvd St-Laurent, Montreal QC H2W1Z3 Canada
DESCRIPTION: Annual performance residency. Est. 1973. The centre welcomes submissions by self-identified under-represented artists working in dialogue with issues of gender equality and social justice.
SUBMISSION MATERIALS: Check website for updated information.
FEE: No **AGENT ONLY:** No

LA MAMA PLAYWRIGHT RETREAT
WEBSITE: www.lamama.org/programs/la-mama-umbria/ **EMAIL:** web@lamama.org **PHONE:** (212) 475-7710 **ADDRESS:** 74-A E 4th St, New York NY 10003
DESCRIPTION: La Mama Umbria International is a non-profit cultural center and artist residence founded in 1990 by legendary theatre pioneer, Ellen Stewart. Dedicated to artistic experimentation, research, and learning, La MaMa Umbria is a place where artists from around the world meet to create, and to share work and ideas.
SUBMISSION MATERIALS: See website for info. **FEE:** Yes **AGENT ONLY:** No

LANESBORO RESIDENCY PROGRAM FELLOWSHIPS
WEBSITE: www.lanesboroarts.org/artist-residency-program
EMAIL: adam@lanesboroarts.org **PHONE:** (507) 467-2446
ADDRESS: PO Box 152, Lanesboro MN 55949
DESCRIPTION: Since 2001, the Lanesboro Artist Residency Program has welcomed emerging artists of all disciplines to live, work and create in the context of the greater Lanesboro community.
SUBMISSION MATERIALS: The application deadline for the 2018 Lanesboro Artist Residency Program has passed. The application deadline for residencies taking place in 2019 will be announced online. **FEE:** No **AGENT ONLY:** No

LEIGHTON ARTISTS STUDIOS
WEBSITE: www.banffcentre.ca/programs/independent-residencies-leighton-artists-studios/20180501 **EMAIL:** arts_info@banffcentre.ca
PHONE: (800) 565-9989 **FAX:** (403) 762-6345
ADDRESS: 107 Tunnel Mountain Dr, Box 1020, Banff AB T1L 1H5 Canada
DESCRIPTION: Independent residencies in the Leighton Artists Studios offer artists the ability to delve into their work as a solitary retreat, as well as the option to engage

within the larger Banff Centre community.
SUBMISSION MATERIALS: Online application, project proposal, resume, letters of recommendation, portfolio **DEADLINE**: 01/31/2018 **FEE**: Yes **AGENT ONLY**: No

MACDOWELL COLONY
WEBSITE: www.macdowellcolony.org/apply **EMAIL**: admissions@macdowellcolony.org **PHONE**: (603) 924-3886 **TWITTER**: @MacDowellColony
ADDRESS: 100 High St, Peterborough NH 03458
DESCRIPTION: The MacDowell Colony provides time, space, and an inspiring environment to artists of exceptional talent. A MacDowell Fellowship, or residency, consists of exclusive use of a studio, accommodations, and three prepared meals a day for up to eight weeks. There are no residency fees.
SUBMISSION MATERIALS: Fall 2018 deadline: April 15, 2018. Winter/Spring 2019 deadline: September 15, 2018.
DEADLINE: 01/15/2018 **DEADLINE TYPE**: Rolling **FEE**: Yes **AGENT ONLY**: No

MCKNIGHT NATIONAL PLAYWRITING RESIDENCY AND COMMISSION
PARENT ORGANIZATION: Playwrights' Center [MN]
WEBSITE: www.pwcenter.org/programs/mcknight-national-residency-and-commission **EMAIL**: juliab@pwcenter.org **PHONE**: (612) 332-7481
FAX: (612) 332-6037 **ADDRESS**: 2301 Franklin Ave E, Minneapolis MN 55406
DESCRIPTION: Supported by a grant from the McKnight Foundation, this program aids in the commissioning and development of new works from nationally recognized playwrights. Benefits include a $15,000 commission, at least two U.S. round-trip airline tickets, housing during the residency period, up to $5,750 in workshop funds to support the development of the play, and a public reading of the commissioned play.
SUBMISSION MATERIALS: Full script, resume, project proposal, letter of recommendation **DEADLINE**: 12/07/2017 **GENRE**: Plays **PREFERRED LENGTH**: Full-length
FEE: No **AGENT ONLY**: No

MILLAY COLONY FOR THE ARTS
WEBSITE: www.millaycolony.org/programs/residencies-artists-millay-colony-arts/
EMAIL: residency@millaycolony.org **PHONE**: (518) 392-3103
ADDRESS: 454 East Hill Rd, Box 3, Austerlitz NY 12017
DESCRIPTION: The Millay Colony is an artists residency program in Upstate New York offering one-month and two-week retreats to six visual artists, writers and composers each month between April and November. We also offer a select number of group residencies for collaborating artists and virtual residencies for those who can't spend prolonged time away from home. We welcome artists of all ages, from all cultures and communities, and in all stages of their career.
SUBMISSION MATERIALS: Deadline: October 1 or March 1. Statuses of all applications are emailed out either late January for the October 1st deadline, or mid-May for the March 1st deadline. **DEADLINE**: 03/01/2018 **FEE**: Yes

MISSOULA COLONY
PARENT ORGANIZATION: Montana Repertory Theater

WEBSITE: montanarep.org/missoula-colony-22-2017   **EMAIL:** salina.chatlain@umontana.edu   **PHONE:** (406) 243-6809   **ADDRESS:** Montana Repertory Theatre, School of Theatre & Dance, University of Montana, Missoula MT 59812
DESCRIPTION: Est. 1996. The Colony convenes at the University of Montana in Missoula annually. Contact Salina Chatlain, Assistant to the Artistic Director, for more information.   **FEE:** No   **AGENT ONLY:** No

NATIONAL WINTER PLAYWRIGHTS RETREAT
PARENT ORGANIZATION: HBMG Foundation
WEBSITE: www.hbmgfoundation.org/foundation/writers-retreats.aspx
EMAIL: annzarate@hbmgfoundation.org   **PHONE:** (512) 573-8114
ADDRESS: 2800 E Whitestone Blvd, Ste 120, #224, Cedar Park TX 78613
DESCRIPTION: A playwright based retreat, the National Winter Playwrights Retreat prioritizes the playwright, not the work being produced. Playwrights have an opportunity to have work read or sung, conversation over dinners and coffees, sightseeing in the San Juan Mountains, and an introduction to local theatres. See website for more information.   **SUBMISSION MATERIALS:** Apply by email.   **GENRE:** Plays   **PREFERRED LENGTH:** Full-length   **FEE:** No   **AGENT ONLY:** No

NEW ORLEANS WRITERS' RESIDENCY
WEBSITE: www.neworleanswritersresidency.org
EMAIL: mail@neworleanswritersresidency.org   **TWITTER:** @NolaResidency
DESCRIPTION: In every culture, writers have played an important role in both society and revolution by voicing unspoken truths. This July, the NOLA Writers' Residency will offer a small group of writers a four week writing retreat to focus on getting better at doing just that. The retreat will cover lodging, airfare up to $500, and a stipend of $200 per week to cover food and entertainment. During those four weeks, you will have complete freedom to plan your time in ways that best support your writing and build lifelong connections with other writers. You will also have the opportunity to receive in-depth personal mentoring in everything from writing routines to the details of your craft, by Kat, our resident mentor, career counselor, and editor extraordinaire. Published and unpublished writers are encouraged to apply. Selection is based on quality of writing.

NEW YORK MILLS ARTS RETREAT
WEBSITE: www.kulcher.org/programs/artist-retreat
EMAIL: nymills@kulcher.org   **PHONE:** (218) 385-3339   **FAX:** (218) 385-3366
ADDRESS: PO Box 246, New York Mills MN 56567
DESCRIPTION: The Arts Retreat artist residency program of the Cultural Center in New York Mills focuses on providing dedicated artists time for creative development and exploration. The program offers a unique taste of life in rural Minnesota while allowing the artists virtually uninterrupted time in which to immerse themselves in their artwork. Deadline: April 1 for residencies from July – December; October 1 for residencies from January – June.   **DEADLINE:** 04/01/2018

NORTON ISLAND RESIDENCY PROGRAM
WEBSITE: www.easternfrontier.com/program.html
EMAIL: webmaster@easternfrontier.com   **ADDRESS:** Stephen T. Dunn, Chairman

Eastern Frontier Education Foundation, 446 Long Ridge Rd, Bedford NY 10506
DESCRIPTION: In 2000, the Norton Island Residency Program, under the leadership of the Eastern Frontier Education Foundation, was founded as a nonprofit and developed to create an ideal place for artists to paint, write, sculpt and compose.
SUBMISSION MATERIALS: Online application. **FEE:** Yes **AGENT ONLY:** No

NYFA IN RESIDENCE
PARENT ORGANIZATION: New York Foundation for the Arts
WEBSITE: www.nyfa.org/Content/Show/NYFA%20in%20Residence
EMAIL: help@nyfa.org **PHONE:** (212) 366-6900 **FAX:** (212) 366-1778
TWITTER: @nyfacurrent **ADDRESS:** 20 Jay St, 7th Fl, Brooklyn NY 11201
DESCRIPTION: NYFA offers national and international residencies to artists working in all disciplines. See website for specific opportunities and submission information.

ONE COMPANY'S WRITER'S RESIDENCY RETREAT AT DOLITTLE FARM
WEBSITE: oneconyc.com/writers-residency **EMAIL:** nick@oneconyc.com
ADDRESS: 406 W 45th St, #5D New York NY 10036
DESCRIPTION: One Company's Writer's Residency Retreat at DoLittle Farm is a four day residency at DoLittle farm in Long Valley, NJ. Transportation to and from NYC is provided. The stay is in an 8 bedroom, 4 bath home on a private lake. Meals are NOT provided. However, there is a grocery store nearby and a full kitchen for the participants use. No more than five participants will be in residence at one time.

THE ORCHARD PROJECT
WEBSITE: www.exchangenyc.org/content/orchard-project
EMAIL: info@orchardproject.com **PHONE:** (646) 760-6767
TWITTER: @exchangenyc **ADDRESS:** 310 W 72nd St, 8A, New York NY 10023
DESCRIPTION: The Orchard Project is one of the preeminent theatre laboratories in the United States, designed to fuel innovation in performance and support bold voices and big new ideas. Companies join the Orchard Project for overlapping residencies, during which they are provided with free rehearsal space, room & board, and support from fellow artists. Throughout the residencies, open rehearsals invite industry members from around the country to play an active role in the development of new works. **DEADLINE:** 12/01/2017 **FEE:** Yes **AGENT ONLY:** No

RAGDALE FOUNDATION
WEBSITE: www.ragdale.org/residency/apply **EMAIL:** admissions@ragdale.org
PHONE: (847) 234-1063 **FAX:** (847) 234-1063
ADDRESS: 1260 N Green Bay Rd, Lake Forest IL 60045
DESCRIPTION: Nearly 200 residencies and fellowships are now offered annually to creative professionals of all types, making Ragdale one of the largest interdisciplinary artists' communities in the country. Each session, 13 artists-in-residence experience uninterrupted time for dedicated work on a 5-acre historic campus beside a beautiful 50-acre prairie, 30 miles north of Chicago. With live/work studios, all meals provided, and unmatched staff support, Ragdale lets artists focus on what's most important: creating new work.

SUBMISSION MATERIALS: Online only. Resume, work sample, letters of recommendation, artists statement. **DEADLINE TYPE:** Rolling **FEE:** Yes **AGENT ONLY:** No

RESIDENCY FLAT IN GRÖNDAL'S HOUSE
PARENT ORGANIZATION: Rithöfundasamband Íslands (Writers' Union of Iceland)
WEBSITE: rsi.is/english/grondals-house **EMAIL:** bokmenntaborgin@reykjavik.is
PHONE: +354 411 6020
DESCRIPTION: Gröndalshús is the charming former home of writer, illustrator and scholar Benedikt Gröndal (1826-1907). This writer's home in the heart of the old town in Reykjavík has been renovated and opened as a cultural house and residency in 2017, run by Reykjavík City. The house is in Grjótaþorp, on the corner of Fischersund and Mjóstræti. The ground floor houses a residency flat for visiting writers, artists, scholars and translators of Icelandic literature who want to work on their art in Reykjavik. It can be rented for a period of 2 – 8 weeks for this purpose. See website for rates and details.

RESIDENT PLAYWRIGHT PROGRAM
PARENT ORGANIZATION: Chicago Dramatists
WEBSITE: www.chicagodramatists.org **EMAIL:** mbeals@chicagodramatists.org
PHONE: (312) 633-0630 **TWITTER:** @ChiDrama
ADDRESS: 1105 W Chicago Ave, Chicago IL 60642
DESCRIPTION: This six-year residency provides Chicago-area playwrights with the resources to develop their plays and grow as artists.

RHINEBECK WRITERS RETREAT
WEBSITE: www.rhinebeckwriters.org **EMAIL:** rhinebeckwriters@gmail.com
PHONE: (845) 266-0192 **ADDRESS:** 7 Hummingbird Way, Staatsburg NY 12580
GENRE: Musicals **PREFERRED LENGTH:** Any Length **FEE:** Yes

RLTP PLAYWRIGHT IN RESIDENCE
WEBSITE: roadlesstraveledproductions.org **EMAIL:** jelston@roadlesstraveledproductions.org **ADDRESS:** Road Less Traveled Productions, P.O. Box 542, Buffalo NY 14205 **GENRE:** Plays **PREFERRED LENGTH:** Any Length **FEE:** Yes

ROCKY MOUNTAIN NATIONAL PARK ARTIST-IN-RESIDENCE PROGRAM
WEBSITE: www.nps.gov/romo **PHONE:** (970) 586-1206
ADDRESS: 1000 Hwy 36, Estes Park CO 80517

SHENANDOAH INTERNATIONAL PLAYWRIGHTS
WEBSITE: www.shenanarts.org **EMAIL:** theatre@shenanarts.org
PHONE: (540) 248-1868 **ADDRESS:** Box 1, Verona VA 24482
GENRE: All genres **PREFERRED LENGTH:** Full-length **FEE:** Yes

SIENA ART INSTITUTE SUMMER RESIDENCY PROGRAM
WEBSITE: www.sienaart.org/index.php?p=111&l=eng **EMAIL:** office@sienaart.org
TWITTER: @sienaart **ADDRESS:** Via Tommaso Pendola 37 - 53100, Siena Italy

DESCRIPTION: The Siena Art Institute's Summer Residency Program grants accomplished professional artists & writers a studio space at the Siena Art Institute & a private one-bedroom apartment in the historic city center of Siena, as well as flight compensation for getting to and from Italy. Summer Residents are granted uninterrupted time to pursue their own independent projects, as well as the opportunity to explore the area of Siena and interact with the local community.
SUBMISSION MATERIALS: Online only.
DEADLINE: 09/30/2018 **DEADLINE TYPE:** Annual **FEE:** Yes **AGENT ONLY:** No

SPACE ON RYDER FARM
WEBSITE: www.spaceonryderfarm.org **EMAIL:** residencies@spaceonryderfarm.org **PHONE:** (646) 833-8159 **ADDRESS:** PO Box 699, New York NY 10013
GENRE: All genres **PREFERRED LENGTH:** Any Length **FEE:** Yes **AGENT ONLY:** No

TYRONE GUTHRIE CENTRE
WEBSITE: www.tyroneguthrie.ie/apply/guidelines **EMAIL:** info@tyroneguthrie.ie **PHONE:** (353) 475-4003
DESCRIPTION: The Tyrone Guthrie Centre promotes excellence and innovation in the arts by providing residential opportunities and workspaces for artists with a proven record of achievement.
SUBMISSION MATERIALS: Online only. **DEADLINE TYPE:** Rolling
GENRE: Plays **FEE:** No **AGENT ONLY:** No

U.S. - JAPAN CREATIVE ARTISTS' PROGRAM
WEBSITE: www.jusfc.gov/creative-artists-programs/creative-artists-program-how-to-apply-2 **EMAIL:** jusfc@jusfc.gov **PHONE:** (202) 653-9800
ADDRESS: 1201 15th St NW, #330, Washington DC 20005
DESCRIPTION: Each year five leading US-based artists are selected and provided funds to spend three to five months in Japan. This residency program allows artists to research and experience both the traditional and contemporary artistic milieu of Japan. Artists are free to live anywhere in the country to pursue activities of greatest relevance to their creative process.
SUBMISSION MATERIALS: See website for submission information.
DEADLINE: 02/01/2018 **FEE:** Yes **AGENT ONLY:** No

UCROSS FOUNDATION RESIDENCY PROGRAM
WEBSITE: www.ucrossfoundation.org/residency-program/apply
EMAIL: rsalvatore@ucross.org **PHONE:** (307) 737-2291
ADDRESS: 30 Big Red Ln, Clearmont WY 82835
DESCRIPTION: There are two residency sessions annually. Application deadlines are March 1 for Fall Session, which runs from August through the first Friday in December, and October 1 for Spring Session, which runs from March through the first Friday in June. Residencies vary in length from two to six weeks.
SUBMISSION MATERIALS: Applications are only accepted by online submission.
DEADLINE: 03/01/2018 **DEADLINE TYPE:** Annual **GENRE:** Plays or Musicals
PREFERRED LENGTH: Full-length **FEE:** Yes **AGENT ONLY:** No

UMASS NEW PLAY LAB
WEBSITE: umass.edu/theater/umass-new-play-lab   **EMAIL:** gina@theater.umass.edu   **PHONE:** (413) 545-3490   **ADDRESS:** Fine Arts Ctr 112, Amherst MA 01003   **DEADLINE TYPE:** Annual   **GENRE:** Plays   **PREFERRED LENGTH:** Full-length   **FEE:** No   **AGENT ONLY:** No

VCCA (VIRGINIA CENTER FOR THE CREATIVE ARTS)
WEBSITE: www.vcca.com/main/apply   **EMAIL:** vcca@vcca.com   **PHONE:** (434) 946-7236   **ADDRESS:** 154 San Angelo Dr, Amherst VA 24521   **SUBMISSION MATERIALS:** Online applications are accepted through SlideRoom on VCCA's website.   **DEADLINE:** 01/15/2018   **GENRE:** Plays   **PREFERRED LENGTH:** Any Length   **FEE:** Yes   **AGENT ONLY:** No

VILLA MONTALVO ARTIST RESIDENCY PROGRAM
WEBSITE: www.montalvoarts.org/programs/residency   **EMAIL:** kfunk@villamontalvo.org   **PHONE:** (408) 961-5818   **FAX:** (408) 961-5850   **ADDRESS:** PO Box 158, Saratoga CA 95071   **DESCRIPTION:** Lucas Artists Fellows are selected through an international selection process, which is held for each discipline approximately every three years. The Lucas Artists Residency Program (LAP) relies on a group of over 200 nominators who are each requested to nominate three artists of exceptional merit. Nominated artists are then invited to submit a full dossier on their work, which is reviewed by a jury of experts in each discipline. Approximately 24 artists in each discipline are selected every three years. Artists are awarded three months in residency at LAP, which can be taken over three years.

WOMEN'S WORK LAB
PARENT ORGANIZATION: New Perspectives Theatre Company   **WEBSITE:** www.newperspectivestheatre.org/programs/womenswork/index.html   **EMAIL:** contact@nptnyc.org   **PHONE:** (212) 630-9945   **FAX:** (212) 730-2030   **ADDRESS:** New Perspectives Theatre, 456 W 37th St, New York NY 10018   **DESCRIPTION:** The WOMEN'S WORK LAB for short plays provides a supportive and nurturing environment to emerging and mid-career women playwrights. Four to six members are selected each year, along with a similar number of directors. The LAB meets monthly (Sundays) from February through June, allowing for time in between sessions for writers to continue to develop and revise their work in response to feedback.   **GENRE:** Plays   **PREFERRED LENGTH:** 1-Act (under 1 hour)

WOODSTOCK BYRDCLIFFE GUILD
WEBSITE: www.woodstockguild.org/air-program   **EMAIL:** air@woodstockguild.org   **PHONE:** (845) 679-2079   **ADDRESS:** 34 Tinker St, Woodstock NY 12498   **DESCRIPTION:** The Byrdcliffe short-term Artist in Residence program provides visual artists, writers, architects, and composers of exceptional talent with uninterrupted time and creative space within the serene natural setting of the Byrdcliffe Art Colony. Lasting four weeks, the residency offers artists private studio time within a community of peers. Artists are invited to participate in open studios, work-shares, field trips to

cultural institutions and artists' studios, and communal dinners, or they can choose to work in solitude during their entire stay.

SUBMISSION MATERIALS: Resume, work sample, letters of recommendation
DEADLINE: 02/15/2018   **GENRE**: Plays   **PREFERRED LENGTH**: Full-length   **FEE**: Yes
AGENT ONLY: No

WRITERS OMI AT LEDIG HOUSE

WEBSITE: www.artomi.org/program.php?Writers-Omi-4   **EMAIL**: writers@artomi.org
PHONE: (212) 206-6060   **ADDRESS**: Art Omni Ledig House, 55 5th Ave, 15th Fl, New York NY 10003
DESCRIPTION: We welcome published writers and translators of every type of literature. International, cultural and creative exchange is a foundation of our mission, and a wide distribution of national background is an important part of our selection process.
SUBMISSION MATERIALS: The 2018 application cycle is now closed. Please check website on August 20, 2018, for information regarding applying for a 2019 residency.
FEE: Yes   **AGENT ONLY**: No

WRITERS' RESIDENCE IN GUNNARSHÚS

PARENT ORGANIZATION: Rithöfundasamband Íslands (Writers' Union of Iceland)
WEBSITE: rsi.is/english/the-writers-residence-in-gunnarshus   **EMAIL**: rsi@rsi.is
PHONE: +354 568 3190
DESCRIPTION: An apartment for visiting writers has been available in Gunnarshús since 1999. Gunnarshús is centrally located in Reykjavík (10 min by bus to downtown). The 60 square meter apartment, which is in the basement, comprises a living-room / study, a kitchen, and a bathroom. It is available for periods of 1 to 8 weeks at a time. See website for rates and details.
DEADLINE TYPE: Rolling   **FEE**: No   **AGENT ONLY**: No

YADDO

WEBSITE: www.yaddo.org/apply/guidelines   **EMAIL**: cwilliams@yaddo.org
PHONE: (518) 584-0746   **ADDRESS**: PO Box 395 - Union Ave, Saratoga Springs NY 12866
DESCRIPTION: The January 1 deadline is for residencies starting May of the same year, through February of the following year. Application portal opens November 1st. Notification of results is sent via email by March 15th. The August 1 deadline is for residencies starting November of the same year through May of the following year. Application portal opens June 1st. Notification of results is sent via email by October 1s
SUBMISSION MATERIALS: Online only.   **DEADLINE**: 01/01/2018
GENRE: Plays or Musicals   **FEE**: Yes   **AGENT ONLY**: No

CONFERENCES & FESTIVALS

4TH STREET THEATRE - 6X10 PLAY FESTIVAL
PARENT ORGANIZATION: 4th Street Theater
WEBSITE: 4thstreetncca.com/6x10 **EMAIL:** Lpauli2006@comcast.net **PHONE:** (219) 926-7875 **ADDRESS:** PO Box 2281, Chesterton IN 46304
SUBMISSION MATERIALS: See website for details.
GENRE: Plays **PREFERRED LENGTH:** 10-minute **FEE:** No

8X10 THEATREFEST
WEBSITE: weathervaneplayhouse.com/8x10TheatreFest **EMAIL:** sdavis@weathervaneplayhouse.com **PHONE:** 330-836-2626 **TWITTER:** @WeathervanePlay **ADDRESS:** 1301 Weathervane Ln, Akron Ohio 44313
DESCRIPTION: Weathervane Playhouse celebrates the art of the short-format play with the eighth annual 8x10 TheatreFest. Eight plays, 10 minutes each!
SUBMISSION MATERIALS: See website for details. **DEADLINE:** 05/04/2018
GENRE: Plays **PREFERRED LENGTH:** 10-minute **FEE:** Yes **AGENT ONLY:** No

10-MINUTE PLAY FESTIVAL
PARENT ORGANIZATION: Arkansas Theatre Collective
WEBSITE: arkansastheatrecollective.org **EMAIL:** rachel@arkansastheatrecollective.org **PHONE:** 4792591370 **ADDRESS:** Arkansas Theatre Collective, PO Box 3068, Fayetteville AR 72701
DESCRIPTION: ATC produces four 10 Minute play festivals a year. See our website to discover each individual festival's theme and deadline.
DEADLINE: 02/28/2018 **DEADLINE TYPE:** Annual **GENRE:** All genres **PREFERRED LENGTH:** 10-minute

21ST CENTURY VOICES NEW PLAY FESTIVAL
PARENT ORGANIZATION: American Stage [FL]
WEBSITE: www.americanstage.org/play-submissions **EMAIL:** 21stCenturyVoices@americanstage.org **PHONE:** (727) 823-7529 **TWITTER:** @AmericanStage **ADDRESS:** 163 3rd St N, St. Petersburg FL 33701
DESCRIPTION: Dedicated to developing and presenting new works for the stage that speak to a contemporary audience in a fresh and compelling way. Includes an annual staged reading festival and fully produced plays receiving one of their first three professional productions at American Stage. Submission requests and instructions will be posted on our website Spring 2018. Please visit website for updates & info.
DEADLINE TYPE: Annual **GENRE:** Plays **PREFERRED LENGTH:** Full-length **FEE:** No **AGENT ONLY:** No

AACT NEW PLAY FEST
PARENT ORGANIZATION: American Association of Community Theatre
WEBSITE: www.aact.org/newplayfest **EMAIL:** newplayfest@aact.org
PHONE: 817-732-3177 **FAX:** (817) 732-3178 **ADDRESS:** 1300 Gendy St, Fort

Worth TX 76107

DESCRIPTION: Play submissions are in even years; submit 8/01/2018 – 9/30/2018 for the 2020 cycle. One of the largest new works festivals in the country. Six community theatres around the country produce the top six plays of the festival. Royalty paid to playwright and some travel expenses for playwright to attend world premiere opening included. Winning plays cannot have been presented as fully staged productions; the NewPlayFest production will be a world premiere. Dramatic Publishing Company publishes winning plays in an anthology.
DEADLINE: 09/30/2018 **DEADLINE TYPE:** Biennial **GENRE:** Plays
PREFERRED LENGTH: Full-length **FEE:** Yes **AGENT ONLY:** No

ABOUT LOVE FESTIVAL

WEBSITE: www.tomosuruplayers.com/about-love-for-writers **EMAIL:** tomosuru@gmail.com **PHONE:** (604) 417-0714 **ADDRESS:** 303-828 Gilford St, Vancouver BC V6G 2N6 Canada
DESCRIPTION: The goal of the festival is to provide encouragement for emerging playwrights, the opportunity to emerging directors to work with exciting new works, and to showcase dedicated talented actors.
SUBMISSION MATERIALS: See website for details.
DEADLINE TYPE: Annual **GENRE:** Plays **PREFERRED LENGTH:** 15 Min **FEE:** Yes

ACTIVATE: MIDWEST NEW PLAY FESTIVAL

WEBSITE: www.wmich.edu/theatre/activate-midwest **EMAIL:** activatemidwest@gmail.com **PHONE:** (269) 387-3220 **ADDRESS:** 1329 Bretton Dr, Kalamazoo MI 49006
DESCRIPTION: A strong preference will be given to scripts with the majority of the characters in the 18-35 age range (appropriate for college age actors). Submit only one (1) play per year. Play must be unproduced and unpublished.
GENRE: Plays **PREFERRED LENGTH:** Full-length **FEE:** No **AGENT ONLY:** No

ALABAMA SHAKESPEARE FESTIVAL - SOUTHERN WRITERS' PROJECT

WEBSITE: southernwritersproject.net/?page_id=6 **EMAIL:** swp@asf.net
PHONE: (334) 271-5300 **FAX:** (334) 271-5348 **ADDRESS:** 1 Festival Dr, Montgomery AL 36117
DESCRIPTION: Accepts original scripts and adaptations, not professionally produced, that meet one or more of the following criteria: You are a Southern Writer. Your script is set in the South, or deals specifically with Southern issues, characters, or themes. Submissions are accepted year-round.
DEADLINE TYPE: Rolling **GENRE:** All genres **PREFERRED LENGTH:** Full-length
FEE: No **AGENT ONLY:** No

ALAP NEW WORKS LAB

WEBSITE: www.laplaywrights.org **EMAIL:** JMunozProulx@LAPlaywrights.org
PHONE: (323) 696-ALAP (2527) **ADDRESS:** 7190 Sunset Boulevard, #1050, Los Angeles CA 90046
DESCRIPTION: The Lab is intended to help playwrights by providing initial readings of

new plays which have reached that stage of development where hearing them out loud, with professional actors reading the roles, is the most logical, helpful next step. Only current members of ALAP are eligible to submit to the New Works Lab.

AMY'S HORSE

WEBSITE: www.amyshorse.com   **EMAIL:** submissions@amyshorse.com

DESCRIPTION: Amy's Horse is accepting submissions for its podcast series that plays around the world and releases new episodes twice monthly each featuring a couple new works. The podcast brings together writers and actors to read new works and chat and maybe have a drink. The twist is that all the participants are working remotely from the comfort of their own homes.

GENRE: Plays or Musicals   **PREFERRED LENGTH:** 10-minute   **FEE:** No

APPALACHIAN FESTIVAL OF PLAYS & PLAYWRIGHTS

PARENT ORGANIZATION: Barter Theatre

WEBSITE: www.bartertheatre.com/shows/afpp   **EMAIL:** apfestival@bartertheatre.com

PHONE: (276) 619-3316   **FAX:** (276) 619-3335   **ADDRESS:** PO Box 867, C/O Barter Theatre, Abingdon VA 24212

DESCRIPTION: This annual festival celebrates the richness of the Appalachian tradition by showcasing the stories of the region, both past and present, and the inspiration it provides the writers who live here.

SUBMISSION MATERIALS: Plays must be written by an Appalachian playwright (currently living in the Appalachian Mountains which, for our purposes, run from New York to Alabama) OR the plays must be set in the Appalachian region. Plays must be unpublished and must not have had a full professional production. See website for details.

DEADLINE TYPE: Annual   **GENRE:** Plays   **PREFERRED LENGTH:** Full-length   **FEE:** No

AGENT ONLY: No

ARKANSAS NEW PLAY FESTIVAL

PARENT ORGANIZATION: TheatreSquared

WEBSITE: www.arkansasnewplayfest.com   **EMAIL:** anpf@theatre2.org

PHONE: (479) 445-6333   ADDRESS: Theatre Squared, PO Box 4188, Fayetteville AR 72701

DESCRIPTION: Est. 2009. Two-week workshop and public staged readings of four new plays, plus an off-book workshop production of one new play, each June at TheatreSquared. For writers outside Arkansas, agent submissions or professional referrals only. Submissions accepted September 1 through January 15.

DEADLINE: 01/15/2018   **DEADLINE TYPE:** Annual   **GENRE:** Plays

PREFERRED LENGTH: Full-length   **FEE:** No

ARKANSAS WRITERS CONFERENCE

WEBSITE: www.arkansaswritersconference.org   **EMAIL:** jdaviscpa@aol.com

PHONE: (501) 915-0708   **ADDRESS:** 1115 Gillette Dr, Little Rock AR 72227

DESCRIPTION: Seeking work featuring older characters and concerns of seniors.

SUBMISSION MATERIALS: Full script.

GENRE: All genres   **PREFERRED LENGTH:** Any Length   **FEE:** No

CONFERENCES & FESTIVALS

ASHLAND NEW PLAYS FESTIVAL
WEBSITE: www.ashlandnewplays.org **EMAIL:** submissions@ashlandnewplays.org
PHONE: (541) 488-7995 **ADDRESS:** PO Box 3314, Ashland Oregon 97520
DESCRIPTION: An international playwright competition that culminates in the reading of four new plays chosen from hundreds of submissions by a cadre of volunteer readers. The event includes rehearsals and two staged readings of each winning play. The winning playwrights receive a $1,500 stipend and local accommodations. ANPF's Fall Festival submissions deadline is December 31 or until we reach 400 submissions, whichever comes first.
DEADLINE: 12/31/17 **DEADLINE TYPE:** Annual **GENRE:** Plays
PREFERRED LENGTH: Full-length **FEE:** No **AGENT ONLY:** No

AUSTIN LATINO NEW PLAY FESTIVAL
PARENT ORGANIZATION: Teatro Vivo
WEBSITE: teatrovivo.org/productions/alnpf2018 **EMAIL:** austinlnpf@gmail.com
TWITTER: @teatrovivotx **PHONE:** (915) 252-1712
ADDRESS: PO Box 42374, Austin TX 78704
DESCRIPTION: The Austin Latino New Play Festival, produced annually by Teatro Vivo in collaboration with ScriptWorks, brings together playwrights and audiences for staged readings and rich conversations about new works of Latino theatre. Each reading presents a different full-length work. The festival includes a student piece and a theatre-for-youth piece.
SUBMISSION MATERIALS: See website for submission information.
DEADLINE: 12/15/17 **DEADLINE TYPE:** Annual **GENRE:** Plays
PREFERRED LENGTH: Full-length **SPECIAL INTEREST:** Hispanic or Latinx **FEE:** No

BALTIMORE PLAYWRIGHTS FESTIVAL
WEBSITE: www.baltplayfest.org/submit-a-play **EMAIL:** librarian@baltplayfest.org
PHONE: (410) 218-9123 **ADDRESS:** PO Box 38122, Baltimore MD 21231
DESCRIPTION: Est 1981. Playwrights must currently reside or work in Maryland or the District of Columbia or have previously maintained their primary domicile, or place of employment, within Maryland or DC.
SUBMISSION MATERIALS: See website for updates and details.
DEADLINE: 05/31/2018 **DEADLINE TYPE:** Annual **GENRE:** Plays **PREFERRED LENGTH:** Any Length **FEE:** Yes **AGENT ONLY:** No

BAY AREA PLAYWRIGHTS FESTIVAL
PARENT ORGANIZATION: Playwrights Foundation
WEBSITE: bayareaplaywrightsfestival.org/submissions-2018 **EMAIL:** literary@playwrightsfoundation.org **PHONE:** (415) 626-2176 **TWITTER:** @pwfoundation
ADDRESS: 1616 16th St, Ste 350, San Francisco CA 94103
DESCRIPTION: Est. 1976. The oldest and most successful new play festival in the US. The festival has continuously discovered original and distinctive new voices in the theater, and invested in the development of their work. Playwrights Foundation accepts scripts via a blind submission process. Submissions are open to all playwrights living in North America and writing primarily in English. Special attention is given to Bay Area writers, emerging writers, and writers of color.

SUBMISSION MATERIALS: See website for details. **DEADLINE TYPE:** Annual
GENRE: Plays **PREFERRED LENGTH:** Full-length **FEE:** Yes **AGENT ONLY:** No

BILINGUAL FOUNDATION OF THE ARTS (BFA)
WEBSITE: www.bfatheatre.org **EMAIL:** bfamanagement@sbcglobal.net **PHONE:** (213) 437-0500 **FAX:** (323) 225-1250 **TWITTER:** @BFAtheatre **ADDRESS:** 421 N Ave 19, Los Angeles CA 90031
DESCRIPTION: Est. 1973. Summer reading fest of new works. The festival's purpose is to offer a clean entertainment alternative, accessible to all families of Los Angeles. The fest features a mix of themes as well as grass-root theatre groups and award-winning companies. Call (213) 437-0500 for more info.
DEADLINE TYPE: Annual **GENRE:** All genres

BILL & PEGGY HUNT PLAYWRIGHT FESTIVAL
WEBSITE: burienactorstheatre.org/get-involved/playrights-festival **EMAIL:** info@burienactorstheatre.org **PHONE:** (206) 242-5180 **TWITTER:** @BAT_tweeting **ADDRESS:** Box 48121, Burien WA 98148
DESCRIPTION: The mission of the Bill and Peggy Hunt Playwrights Festival is to encourage, promote and showcase previously unproduced theater works written by Washington state residents.
SUBMISSION MATERIALS: See website for updates and details.

BLACK & LATINO PLAYWRIGHTS CONFERENCE
WEBSITE: www.theatreanddance.txstate.edu/Productions/BLPC.html **EMAIL:** el18@txstate.edu **PHONE:** (512) 245-2147 **ADDRESS:** Texas State University, 601 University Dr, San Marcos TX 78666
DESCRIPTION: The special interests for submissions are both African American and Latino/a. The deadline for submission is April 15 every year to be considered for the following September's conference.
SUBMISSION MATERIALS: Email submissions only. See website for details.
DEADLINE: 04/15/2018 **GENRE:** Plays **PREFERRED LENGTH:** Full-length
SPECIAL INTEREST: All **FEE:** No **AGENT ONLY:** No

BLACK BOX NEW PLAY FESTIVAL
WEBSITE: galleryplayers.com **EMAIL:** info@galleryplayers.com **PHONE:** (718) 832-0617 **TWITTER:** @tgpbrooklyn **ADDRESS:** 199 14th St, Brooklyn NY 11215
DESCRIPTION: Each play selected will be given a black box production at Gallery Players and will be performed in a festival format with non-equity actors. Playwrights must be available for rehearsals and use this as an opportunity to continue work on their play.
SUBMISSION MATERIALS: Plays must be unproduced; must be the play's world premiere. Length may be from 10 minutes to 45 minutes. No monologues. No period costume pieces. We do not accept email submissions. See website for full details.
DEADLINE: 12/31/2017 **DEADLINE TYPE:** Annual **GENRE:** Plays
PREFERRED LENGTH: 1-Act (under 1 hour) **FEE:** No **AGENT ONLY:** No

BLACK PLAYWRIGHTS FESTIVAL

PARENT ORGANIZATION: Black Ensemble Theater
WEBSITE: blackensembletheater.org/outreach/black-playwrights-intiative
EMAIL: blackensemble@aol.com **PHONE:** (773) 769-4451 **FAX:** (773) 769-4533 **TWITTER:** @blackensemble **ADDRESS:** 4520 N Beacon, Chicago IL 60640
DESCRIPTION: Year-round open submissions. Clearly note script is for festival.
SUBMISSION MATERIALS: See website for updates.
DEADLINE TYPE: Rolling **PREFERRED LENGTH:** Full-length

BLANK THEATRE COMPANY YOUNG PLAYWRIGHTS FESTIVAL

WEBSITE: www.theblank.com/young-playwrights-festival
EMAIL: info@TheBlank.com **PHONE:** (323) 871-8018 **FAX:** (323) 661-3903
TWITTER: @TheBlankTheatre **ADDRESS:** PO Box 38756, Hollywood CA 90038
DESCRIPTION: Est. 1990. Every June, The Blank Theatre produces the 12 best plays by playwrights ages 9 to 19, chosen from a nationwide competition. Submissions open January 2018. **SUBMISSION MATERIALS:** Check website for updates.

BOSTON THEATER MARATHON

WEBSITE: www.bu.edu/bpt/our-programs/boston-theatre-marathon
EMAIL: newplays@bu.edu **PHONE:** (617) 353-5899 **FAX:** (617) 353-6196
ADDRESS: 949 Commonwealth Ave, Boston MA 2215
DESCRIPTION: Est. 1999. Fifty 10-minute plays by 50 New England playwrights by 50 New England theaters over the course of a single day. Production: small orchestra, minimal set. **SUBMISSION MATERIALS:** Online only. Check website for details.
DEADLINE: 11/15/2017 **DEADLINE TYPE:** Annual **GENRE:** All genres
PREFERRED LENGTH: 10-minute **FEE:** No **AGENT ONLY:** No

BOULDER INTERNATIONAL FRINGE FESTIVAL

WEBSITE: www.boulderfringe.com **EMAIL:** info@boulderfringe.com
PHONE: (720) 563-9950 **TWITTER:** @BoulderFringe **ADDRESS:** 1020 Portland St, Boulder CO 80302
DESCRIPTION: The Boulder Fringe provides a platform for artists to showcase their artwork, often in non-traditional spaces. We educate about independent art that is accessible and affordable with an annual 12-day performance art festival that brings together local, national, and international shows and other events in Boulder.
SUBMISSION MATERIALS: Email for more information.

BREAKING GROUND FESTIVAL

WEBSITE: www.huntingtontheatre.org/season/new-work/breaking-ground
EMAIL: chaugland@huntingtontheatre.org **PHONE:** (617) 273-1502
ADDRESS: 281 Huntington Ave, Boston MA 2115
DESCRIPTION: Est. 2004. Breaking Ground is the Huntington Theatre Company's festival of new work. The festival highlights the work of local playwrights and presents

national writers in partnership with the Huntington.

SUBMISSION MATERIALS: Check website for updates.

DEADLINE TYPE: Annual   **GENRE:** Plays   **PREFERRED LENGTH:** Full-length

CAPITAL STAGE - PLAYWRIGHTS REVOLUTION

PARENT ORGANIZATION: Capital Stage
WEBSITE: capstage.org/play-a-part/script-submissions-for-playwrights-revolution
EMAIL: literarymanager@capstage.org   **PHONE:** (916) 476-3116
ADDRESS: 2215 J St, Sacramento CA 95816
DESCRIPTION: This series of staged readings seeks to identify and develop exciting new plays and playwrights. These new works are brought to theatrical life through a series of staged readings performed by professional actors in Capital Stage's intimate theatre.
SUBMISSION MATERIALS: Email PDFs of submissions preferred. Check website for info and updates.   **GENRE:** All genres   **PREFERRED LENGTH:** Full-length   **FEE:** No

CATALYST SERIES

WEBSITE: www.intermediaarts.org/catalyst-series-present-your-work11
EMAIL: info@IntermediaArts.org   **ADDRESS:** 2822 Lyndale Ave S, Minneapolis MN 55408
DESCRIPTION: The Catalyst Series co-presents new work in the performing arts, dance, visual arts, and film in partnership with you: artists, groups and organizations in our community focused on art, equity, dialogue, and social change. The Catalyst Series places a particular emphasis on increasing the visibility of and providing a platform for artists whose voices have historically been underrepresented in the arts.
SUBMISSION MATERIALS: See website for details.

CENTRE STAGE [SC] NEW PLAY FESTIVAL

PARENT ORGANIZATION: Centre Stage [SC]
WEBSITE: centrestage.org/new-play-festival-submissions/
EMAIL: npfsubmissions@centrestage.org   **PHONE:** (864) 233-6733
TWITTER: @centrestagesc   **ADDRESS:** 501 River St, Greenville SC 29601
DESCRIPTION: Est. 2002. Three finalists must be in attendance at the Festival where they will receive staged readings. Centre Stage will assist the playwright finalists with travel expenses and will provide accommodations during their stay. Prize: $500 and possible future production.
SUBMISSION MATERIALS: Synopsis, full script. Scripts will not be returned.
DEADLINE: 01/15/2018   **DEADLINE TYPE:** Annual   **GENRE:** Plays   **PREFERRED LENGTH:** Full-length   **FEE:** Yes   **AGENT ONLY:** No

CINCINNATI FRINGE FESTIVAL

WEBSITE: www.cincyfringe.com   **EMAIL:** cincyfringe@knowtheatre.com
PHONE: (513) 300-5669   **ADDRESS:** 1120 Jackson St, Cincinnati OH 45202
DESCRIPTION: Est. 2004. Annual Fringe Festival late May/early June. During the festival local, regional, national, and international artists invade downtown Cincinnati for 12 days of artistic celebration in both traditional and non-traditional spaces.

CONFERENCES & FESTIVALS

SUBMISSION MATERIALS: Application; materials will not be returned
DEADLINE: 01/05/2018 **GENRE:** Plays or Musicals
PREFERRED LENGTH: 1-Act (under 1 hour) **FEE:** Yes **AGENT ONLY:** No

CINCINNATI FRINGE NEXT FESTIVAL
WEBSITE: www.cincyfringe.com **EMAIL:** cincyfringe@knowtheatre.com
PHONE: (513) 300-5669 **ADDRESS:** 1120 Jackson St, Cincinnati OH 45202
DESCRIPTION: Est. 2011. Conceived, written, directed, performed, and produced entirely by local high school-aged artists, FringeNext represents the future of theatre by giving these younger artists a chance to flex their theatrical voices in an uninhibited and unique setting. **DEADLINE:** 01/15/2018 **GENRE:** All genres **PREFERRED LENGTH:** 1-Act (under 1 hour) **FEE:** Yes

CITY WRIGHTS PLAYWRIGHTS CONFERENCE
WEBSITE: www.citytheatre.com/citywrights **EMAIL:** susan@citytheatre.com
PHONE: (305) 755-9401 **TWITTER:** @CityTheatreFL **ADDRESS:** 444 Brickell Ave, #229, Miami FL 33131
DESCRIPTION: Be inspired by new ideas, playwriting techniques, attend readings of fresh new work, receive feedback in creative workshop of your new works, all led by Master Playwrights. Learn the latest in professional development sessions all from leading industry experts.
DEADLINE TYPE: Annual **GENRE:** Plays **PREFERRED LENGTH:** 10-minute

COE COLLEGE PLAYWRITING FESTIVAL
PARENT ORGANIZATION: Coe College
WEBSITE: www.coe.edu/academics/theatrearts/theatrearts_playwritingfestival
PHONE: 3193998624 **ADDRESS:** 1220 1st Ave NE, Cedar Rapids IA 52402
DESCRIPTION: Winning playwright receives a $500 award plus travel, room and board for a week-long residency at Coe. The winning play will receive a staged reading for the public. Playwright attends play writing class as a visiting guest artist.
SUBMISSION MATERIALS: Synopsis, full script, SASE **GENRE:** Plays **FEE:** No

COLORADO NEW PLAY SUMMIT
PARENT ORGANIZATION: Denver Center for the Performing Arts (DCPA)
WEBSITE: www.denvercenter.org/events/colorado-new-play-summit
EMAIL: playsubmissions@dcpa.org **PHONE:** (303) 893-4000 **FAX:** (303) 825-2117
ADDRESS: 1101 13th St, Denver CO 80204
DESCRIPTION: After workshopping their pieces for a week with professional actors, directors and dramaturgs, playwrights test the waters with the initial readings during the Launch Weekend. The following week is spent fine-tuning their pieces based on the feedback from theatre lovers and creatives alike before presenting revised versions on the Festival Weekend.
SUBMISSION MATERIALS: We accept unproduced, original, full-length plays and musicals, which must be submitted by a literary agent. Playwrights residing in Colorado, Wyoming, Montana, Idaho, Arizona, New Mexico or Utah may send plays directly without an agent. We have a special interest in plays written by and for African-Americans and Latinos, by women playwrights and we are also interested in plays written for

young audiences. Adaptations will be considered if you have secured underlying rights.
DEADLINE TYPE: Rolling **GENRE:** Plays or Musicals **PREFERRED LENGTH:** Full-length
SPECIAL INTEREST: Black or African American; Hispanic or Latinx; Theatre for Young Audiences **FEE:** No **AGENT ONLY:** Yes

CONTEMPORARY AMERICAN THEATER FESTIVAL
WEBSITE: www.catf.org **EMAIL:** eherendeen@catf.org **PHONE:** (304) 876-3473
TWITTER: @thinktheater **ADDRESS:** Box 429, Shepherdstown WV 25443
DESCRIPTION: Est. 1991. The ultimate theater experience hosted by Sheperd University. CATF accepts manuscripts submitted by an agent or an industry colleague only.
AGENT ONLY: Yes

DAYTON PLAYHOUSE FUTUREFEST
WEBSITE: www.daytonplayhouse.org **EMAIL:** futurefest@thedaytonplayhouse.com
PHONE: (937) 424-8477 **FAX:** (937) 333-2827 **ADDRESS:** PO Box 3017, Dayton OH 45401
DESCRIPTION: Est. 1991. Dayton Playhouse has sponsored FutureFest, a festival of new and unproduced plays for over 25 years, put on by a community theater run entirely by volunteers. Submissions are accepted between August 1 - October 31
SUBMISSION MATERIALS: See website for details. **DEADLINE:** 10/31/2018
DEADLINE TYPE: Annual **GENRE:** Plays **PREFERRED LENGTH:** Full-length **FEE:** Yes
AGENT ONLY: No

DEATHSCRIBE FESTIVAL
PARENT ORGANIZATION: WildClaw Theatre
WEBSITE: www.wildclawtheatre.com/project/deathscribe-x **EMAIL:** literary@wildclawtheatre.com **ADDRESS:** 3900 N Monticello, Chicago IL 60613
DESCRIPTION: The Annual Deathscribe Festival of Horror Radio Plays seeks submissions of 10-minute radio plays in the horror genre, formatted for radio with sound cues included. Limit 2 submissions per author, per year.
GENRE: Radio plays **PREFERRED LENGTH:** 10-minute **FEE:** No **AGENT ONLY:** No

DELAWARE YOUNG PLAYWRIGHTS FESTIVAL (DYPF)
PARENT ORGANIZATION: Delaware Theatre Company
WEBSITE: www.delawaretheatre.org/young-playwrights-festival
EMAIL: johannaschloss@delawaretheatre.org **PHONE:** (302) 594-1104
TWITTER: @DelawareTheatre **ADDRESS:** Delaware Theatre Company, 200 Water St, Wilmington DE 19801
DESCRIPTION: DYPF is a program designed to provide an outlet for DE students grades 8-12 to get the professional playwright treatment. From standards-based feedback on first-round drafts to thorough workshops with industry professionals, playwrights selected in DTC's festival bring their ideas from page to stage. If you or your school want to get involved, contact the Education Department at (302)-594-1104, ext. 249, 204, or 226.
DEADLINE TYPE: Annual **GENRE:** Plays **FEE:** No **AGENT ONLY:** No

CONFERENCES & FESTIVALS

DISCOVERY NEW MUSICAL THEATRE FESTIVAL
WEBSITE: www.bsudiscoveryfestival.com/new-musical **EMAIL:** bsudiscoveryfestival@gmail.com **PHONE:** (765) 285-5557 **TWITTER:** @BSUTheatreFest
ADDRESS: Ball State University, 2000 W University Ave, Muncie IN 47306
DESCRIPTION: Students review selections choose three finalists for concert performances in May 2018. All three shows will be considered for development and production opportunities in future Ball State Department of Theatre and Dance seasons.
DEADLINE: 01/07/2018 **DEADLINE TYPE:** Biennial **GENRE:** Musicals
PREFERRED LENGTH: Any Length **FEE:** No **AGENT ONLY:** No

DOWNTOWN URBAN ARTS FESTIVAL
PARENT ORGANIZATION: Creative Ammo Inc.
WEBSITE: www.duafnyc.com **EMAIL:** info@duafnyc.com **PHONE:** (212) 807-1337
TWITTER: @DUAFNYC **ADDRESS:** 18 E 41st St, New York NY 10017
DESCRIPTION: Est. 2001. DUTF is a movement to bring about social change through the arts. Our objectives are to foster growth in the creation of new works and in the careers of a multicultural, cross section of artists; to create an artists' community and support the play development process; and to cultivate new urban audiences by making theater more affordable and accessible.
GENRE: Plays or Musicals **PREFERRED LENGTH:** Any Length **SPECIAL INTEREST:** Asian; Black or African American; Hispanic or Latinx; LGBT+ **FEE:** No

EAST END FRINGE FESTIVAL
WEBSITE: www.eastendfringefest.com **EMAIL:** eastendfringefestival@gmail.com
ADDRESS: 34 Red Creek Cir, Hampton Bays NY 11946
DESCRIPTION: This diverse and intimate theatrical event debuted Summer 2017 at the historic Vail-Leavitt Music Hall. As a catalyst for cultural and community development, The East End Fringe Festival is dedicated to connecting adventurous emerging and established artists, appreciative audiences and supportive businesses and organizations to foster the growth of creative arts on Long Island.
SUBMISSION MATERIALS: No fee for early bird submissions. Check website for updates and information.
DEADLINE TYPE: Annual **GENRE:** Plays **PREFERRED LENGTH:** Any Length **FEE:** No

ECODRAMA PLAYWRIGHT FESTIVAL
WEBSITE: www.earthmattersonstage.com/new-play-competition
EMAIL: uaa_emosfestival@alaska.edu **FAX:** (775) 521-9206
ADDRESS: University of Alaska Anchorage, Dept of Theatre and Dance, 3211 Providence Dr, Anchorage AK 99508
DESCRIPTION: Est. 2004, Earth Matters on Stage (EMOS) Ecodrama Playwrights Festival was founded in order to call forth and foster new dramatic works that respond to the ecological crisis, and, as part of that response, to explore new possibilities of being in relationship with the more-than-human world. EMOS calls for new plays that not only focus on current and historic environmental issues, but also enliven and transform our experience of the world around us, inspire us to listen better, and instill a deeper or more complex sense of our ecological communities.
SUBMISSION MATERIALS: Electronic submissions only. Scripts must be original works

which have not been published and have not had an Equity or full professional premiere production. See website for updates and details.

DEADLINE TYPE: Biennial **GENRE:** Plays **PREFERRED LENGTH:** Full-length

EDINBURGH FESTIVAL FRINGE

WEBSITE: www.edfringe.com **EMAIL:** participants@edfringe.com **PHONE:** +44 (0) 131-226-0026 **TWITTER:** @EdFringe **ADDRESS:** 180 High St, Edinburgh EH1 1QS United Kingdom

DESCRIPTION: Every year thousands of performers take to hundreds of stages all over Edinburgh to present shows for every taste. From big names in the world of entertainment to unknown artists looking to build their careers, the festival caters for everyone and includes theatre, comedy, dance, physical theatre, circus, cabaret, children's shows, musicals, opera, music, spoken word, exhibitions and events.

GENRE: All Genres **PREFERRED LENGTH:** Any Length **FEE:** Yes **AGENT ONLY:** No

EDMONTON INTERNATIONAL FRINGE FESTIVAL

WEBSITE: www.fringetheatre.ca/festival/artists **EMAIL:** murray.utas@fringetheatre.ca **PHONE:** (780) 448-9000 **FAX:** (780) 431-1893 **TWITTER:** @edmontonfringe **ADDRESS:** 10330 84 Ave, Edmonton AB T6E 2G9 Canada

DESCRIPTION: Our Festival hosts approximately 1,500 artists each year. 100% of the ticket price goes directly to artists, allowing you to collectively earn more than $1.2M through the box office each year. We adhere to the CAFF guidelines – producing a non-juried, uncensored Festival.

SUBMISSION MATERIALS: Online application. See website for updates and fees.

DEADLINE: 11/20/2017 **DEADLINE TYPE:** Annual **FEE:** Yes **AGENT ONLY:** No

EMERGING ARTIST THEATRE NEW WORK SERIES

PARENT ORGANIZATION: Emerging Artists Theatre **WEBSITE:** www.newworkseries.com/terms-and-conditions.php **EMAIL:** eattheatre@gmail.com **PHONE:** (212) 247-2429 **TWITTER:** @EATisTweeting **ADDRESS:** 15 W 28th St, 3rd Fl, New York NY 10001

DESCRIPTION: As there is no fee for submissions or participation, we ask all artists involved in the series to try to fill the 99-seat house. Artists do not receive a percentage of box office, but again, there is no charge to you and we use the box office income to cover the expenses of the series—theatre rental, staffing, programs, etc. Each show will receive ONE performance during the festival.

SUBMISSION MATERIALS: Online submissions. See website for details and application. **DEADLINE:** 12/15/2017 **GENRE:** All genres **PREFERRED LENGTH:** 1-Act (under 1 hour) **SPECIAL INTEREST:** LGBT+ **FEE:** No **AGENT ONLY:** No

EU

WEBSITE: 2entertaintheidea.wixsite.com/entertainus **EMAIL:** 2entertaintheidea@gmail.com **ADDRESS:** 144 Hester St, Apt 1, New York NY 10013

DESCRIPTION: An evening of Monologues & Shorts. A medium-brow charity event to benefit the NY Foundling. The 90 minute show will be made up of original and contemporary monologues and shorts followed by a reception. The show will be filmed and each performer/writer will receive the movie file of their individual performance as well as any social media and press exposure that may occur around the event.

SUBMISSION MATERIALS: Email submissions in PDF or Word. See website for updates and details. **DEADLINE TYPE:** Annual **GENRE:** Plays **PREFERRED LENGTH:** 10-minute

EVENING OF NEW PLAYS
WEBSITE: naplesplayers.org **EMAIL:** info@naplesplayers.org
PHONE: (239) 434-1141 **ADDRESS:** 701 5th Ave South, Naples FL 34102
DESCRIPTION: Opportunities incl. ETC play readings (for writers in Lee and surrounding counties.

FADE TO BLACK PLAY FESTIVAL
WEBSITE: www.fadetoblackfest.com/script-submission **EMAIL:** submissions@wmgellc.com **PHONE:** (832) 877-7609 **ADDRESS:** 16370 Angel Island Ln, Houston TX 77053
DESCRIPTION: Fade To Black is Houston's first national play festival to showcase the new works of African American playwrights.
SUBMISSION MATERIALS: Your play must be an original, not previously produced, unpublished work written by an African American playwright. Online submission form on website. After submission form is completed, email pdf of original work to submissions@wmgellc.com.
DEADLINE: 04/01/2018 **DEADLINE TYPE:** Annual **GENRE:** Plays
PREFERRED LENGTH: 10-minute **SPECIAL INTEREST:** Black or African American
FEE: No **AGENT ONLY:** No

FINGER LAKES MUSICAL THEATRE FESTIVAL
WEBSITE: fingerlakesmtf.com/the-pitch/writers **EMAIL:** PiTCHSubmissions@FingerLakesMTF.com **PHONE:** (315) 255-1305 **TWITTER:** @FingerLakesMTF
ADDRESS: 17 William St, 2nd Fl, Auburn NY 13021
DESCRIPTION: The Finger Lakes Musical Theatre Festival presents classic and contemporary works, new musicals, and in-school arts education for a diverse audience, to spur social awareness and cultural development in the Finger Lakes region. Home to the PiTCH–For Writers.
SUBMISSION MATERIALS: For the PiTCH, download submission cover sheet from website. Include 100-250-word summary, working draft of script, Demo recordings of at least 50% of songs in the show, etc. See website for complete info.
DEADLINE: 12/01/2017 **DEADLINE TYPE:** Annual **GENRE:** Musicals
PREFERRED LENGTH: 1-Act (under 1 hour) **FEE:** Yes **AGENT ONLY:** No

FIRST FLIGHT NEW PLAY FESTIVAL
PARENT ORGANIZATION: Boomerang Theatre Company
WEBSITE: www.boomerangtheatre.org **EMAIL:** literary@boomerangtheatre.org
TWITTER: @boomerangtheatr **ADDRESS:** Boomerang Theatre Company, PO Box 237166, New York NY 10023
DESCRIPTION: One of the premiere new play development festivals in Indie Theatre. Each play selected to participate in the festival received 6 hours of rehearsal time over the course of one week, culminating in a public reading of the play for a supportive audience.
SUBMISSION MATERIALS: Resume, synopsis, 10 pg sample. See website for up-

dates and info.
DEADLINE TYPE: Annual   **GENRE:** Plays   **PREFERRED LENGTH:** Full-length   **FEE:** No

FRESH FRUIT FESTIVAL
WEBSITE: www.freshfruitfestival.com   **EMAIL:** Exec@FreshFruitFestival.com
ADDRESS: All Out Arts, 131 W 35th St, 8th Fl, New York NY 10001
DEADLINE: See website   **GENRE:** Plays or Musicals   **PREFERRED LENGTH:** Any Length   **SPECIAL INTEREST:** LGBT+   **FEE:** No   **AGENT ONLY:** No

GEORGIA THEATRE CONFERENCE
WEBSITE: georgiatheatreweb.wix.com/gtc-website   **EMAIL:** gtc.newplaycomp@gmail.com   **PHONE:** (912) 478-0503   **ADDRESS:** PO Box 8091, Statesboro GA 30458
DESCRIPTION: Est. 1965, GTC seeks to encourage and coordinate a close relationship among the community, educational and professional theatres in Georgia; maintain quality in both live theatre and theatre education.
SUBMISSION MATERIALS: Website indicates there is a new play festival, but there is no submission information currently posted.
GENRE: Plays   **PREFERRED LENGTH:** 1-Act (under 1 hour)   **FEE:** No   **AGENT ONLY:** No

GOING TO THE RIVER
WEBSITE: www.goingtotheriver.com   **EMAIL:** director@goingtotheriver.com
ADDRESS: 790 Riverside Dr, New York NY 10032
DESCRIPTION: Founded by the late Curt Dempster and Elizabeth Van Dyke in 1999 at the Ensemble Studio Theatre, for the purpose of developing, producing and providing a New York City 'home base' for a community of female playwrights of color. GTTR consists of a River Writers Unit at The Lark, an annual Reading Series of New Work, a Festival of Short Plays, a festival of solo pieces known as Going to the River All By Yo'Self, Workshops, special events that include panels, classes, and conversations with Distinguished Guests at various venues in New York City.
SUBMISSION MATERIALS: Email for more information.   **GENRE:** Plays   **PREFERRED LENGTH:** Any Length   **SPECIAL INTEREST:** Feminism/Women's Rights   **FEE:** No

GREAT PLAINS THEATRE CONFERENCE
WEBSITE: www.gptcplays.com/submit-your-play-to-gptc
EMAIL: theatreconference@mccneb.edu   **PHONE:** (531) 622-2618
TWITTER: @GPTCNebraska   **ADDRESS:** PO Box 3777, Omaha NE 68103
DESCRIPTION: Founded in 2006 under the vision and leadership of Dr. Jo Ann C. McDowell, President Emeriti of Metropolitan Community College. At the time, the concept of a national playwriting conference was uncharted territory for both the College and the community.
SUBMISSION MATERIALS: Plays that have received an Equity production, plays for young audiences, and musicals will not be considered. Equity showcase productions are acceptable, as well as adaptations. See website for more details.
DEADLINE: 10/15/2018   **DEADLINE TYPE:** Annual   **GENRE:** Plays
PREFERRED LENGTH: Any Length   **FEE:** Yes   **AGENT ONLY:** No

CONFERENCES & FESTIVALS

GREENSBORO FRINGE FESTIVAL
WEBSITE: www.greensborofringefestival.org **EMAIL:** gsofringefest@gmail.com
PHONE: 336-549-7431 **TWITTER:** @GSOFringeFest **ADDRESS:** 200 N Davie St Ste 101, Greensboro NC 27401
DESCRIPTION: The Greensboro Fringe Festival, which began in 2003 as a way for independent theatre producers to combine resources and reach broader audiences, has grown and become more diverse.
SUBMISSION MATERIALS: Online application. **GENRE:** All Genres **PREFERRED LENGTH:** Any Length **FEE:** No

HEADWATERS NEW PLAY FESTIVAL
PARENT ORGANIZATION: Creede Repertory Theatre
WEBSITE: creederep.org/headwaters **EMAIL:** headwaters@creederep.com
PHONE: (719) 658-2540 **FAX:** (719) 658-2343 **TWITTER:** @CreedeTheatre
ADDRESS: PO Box 269, Creede CO 81130
DESCRIPTION: Mission: To foster the development of new plays for CRT's stages and beyond. Unleash vibrant new work into the world of theatre, because new voices and stories reflect back to us the shared anxieties and aspirations of our age.
SUBMISSION MATERIALS: To be considered for the Headwaters New Play Festival, a play must never have had a professional production and the playwright must be available to attend the workshop week. Since 2015's festival, our goal has been to more accurately reflect the diversity of human experience by reserving one of our two slots for a female playwright. Plays must be submitted digitally in PDF format. Hard copies will not be considered. See website for full guidelines.
DEADLINE: 02/18/2018 **DEADLINE TYPE:** Annual **GENRE:** Plays
PREFERRED LENGTH: Full-length **FEE:** No **AGENT ONLY:** No

HUBBARD HALL WINTER CARNIVAL OF NEW WORK
WEBSITE: www.hubbardhall.org/get-involved/winter-carnival-submissions
EMAIL: info@hubbardhall.org **PHONE:** (518) 677-2495 **ADDRESS:** Hubbard Hall, 25 E Main St, Cambridge NY 12816
DESCRIPTION: Check website for updates, or email for information.
GENRE: Plays **PREFERRED LENGTH:** 1-Act (under 1 hour) **FEE:** No **AGENT ONLY:** No

HUMANA FESTIVAL
PARENT ORGANIZATION: Actors Theatre of Louisville
WEBSITE: www.actorstheatre.org/humana-festival-of-new-american-plays
EMAIL: awegener@actorstheatre.org **PHONE:** (502) 584-1265
TWITTER: @ATLouisville **ADDRESS:** Actors Theatre of Louisville, 316 W Main St, Louisville KY 40202
DESCRIPTION: Est. 1976. Festival of 10-12 fully produced new plays (world premieres) running February-April. Unagented writers may submit a synopsis and 10-page sample from script for consideration. Check website for festival dates.
GENRE: Plays **PREFERRED LENGTH:** Full-length **FEE:** No **AGENT ONLY:** Yes

INTERNATIONAL PLAYWRIGHTS FESTIVAL

PARENT ORGANIZATION: Warner Theatre
WEBSITE: www.warnertheatre.org/6th-annual-international-playwright-festival.html
EMAIL: warnersubmissions@gmail.com **TWITTER:** @WarnerCT
ADDRESS: 68 Main St, Torrington CT 06790

DESCRIPTION: The Warner International Playwrights Festival recognizes the work of emerging and established playwrights from across the country and around the globe. The Festival gives playwrights a forum for production of their one-act plays that engage and entertain audiences through exploration of the human experience and the human spirit.

SUBMISSION MATERIALS: Submit plays in standard Samuel French playwriting format - 12 point font, character name centered or 3.5 inches from left margin, 1" margin all around. Plays should be emailed to: warnersubmissions@gmail.com. See website for more info. **DEADLINE TYPE:** Annual **GENRE:** Plays **PREFERRED LENGTH:** 1-Act (under 1 hour) **FEE:** No **AGENT ONLY:** No

IRVINGTON TOWN HALL THEATER: STAGE DOOR PLAYWRIGHTS FESTIVAL

WEBSITE: www.irvingtontheater.com/theatre-festival
EMAIL: ithtstagedoorplaywrights@gmail.com **PHONE:** (914) 591-6602
TWITTER: @ITH_Theater **ADDRESS:** 85 Main St, Irvington NY 10533

DESCRIPTION: The ITHT Stage Door Playwrights Festival celebrates original plays developed by local and NY metro area playwrights. It is dedicated to providing an arena for theatrical exploration of significant historical and modern issues that are relevant to our times.

SUBMISSION MATERIALS: Seeking submissions of One Acts 45-60 minutes long or portion of play that are self-contained and can be performed for an audience with their clear understanding of content.

DEADLINE TYPE: Annual **GENRE:** Plays **PREFERRED LENGTH:** 1-Act (under 1 hour) **FEE:** No **AGENT ONLY:** No

ITHACA FRINGE FESTIVAL

WEBSITE: www.ithacafringe.com **EMAIL:** george@ithacafringe.com
PHONE: (607) 351-3765 **TWITTER:** @IthacaFringe
ADDRESS: PO Box 403, Spencer NY 14851

DESCRIPTION: The Ithaca Fringe Festival develops new audiences, stimulates economic growth and supports the creative community. Five participating groups will be invited, all drawn by random lottery. Alternates will be drawn at the same time. Each selected group will get four performances, one each day of the festival. You bring your whole show, actors, tech, and whatever you need. Each performing group will receive 100% of its box office after small ticket processing fees assessed by Brownpapertickets. Each performing group will get at least two reviews. See the website for specific submission guidelines.

SUBMISSION MATERIALS: Begins accepting applications Nov 1, 2017. Check website for info and updates.

GENRE: All genres **PREFERRED LENGTH:** Full-length **FEE:** Yes **AGENT ONLY:** No

CONFERENCES & FESTIVALS

JAW: A PLAYWRIGHTS FESTIVAL
PARENT ORGANIZATION: Portland Center Stage at the Armory [OR]
WEBSITE: www.pcs.org/jaw **EMAIL:** jaw@pcs.org **PHONE:** (503) 445-3700
FAX: (503) 445-3721 **ADDRESS:** 128 NW 11th Ave, Portland OR 97209
DESCRIPTION: See website for eligibility and submission instructions.
DEADLINE: 11/20/2017 **DEADLINE TYPE:** Annual **GENRE:** Plays or Musicals
PREFERRED LENGTH: Full-length **FEE:** No **AGENT ONLY:** No

JET FEST
WEBSITE: www.jettheatre.org/copy-of-get-involved **EMAIL:** c.bremer@jettheatre.org
PHONE: (248) 788-2900 **ADDRESS:** Jewish Ensemble Theater, 6600 W Maple Rd, West Bloomfield MI 48322
DESCRIPTION: JET encourages all playwrights over 18 to submit their work. JET's programming generally reflects issues of social conscience and human rights both in drama and comedy. Use our past productions as a guide and if you have questions, contact us by phone.
SUBMISSION MATERIALS: Submit a blind copy of your script, securely bound, typed in standard play format, with pages numbered. Include a list of characters/descriptions, scene breakdown, and a brief synopsis of your play. Your script(s) should be accompanied by a cover letter, including playwright contact information (name, address, phone number, e-mail address) and resume. Musicals must include a demo CD. If applicable, also submit a photocopy of your Dramatists Guild membership card.
DEADLINE TYPE: Annual **GENRE:** Plays or Musicals **PREFERRED LENGTH:** Full-length
SPECIAL INTEREST: Jewish **FEE:** Waived for DG Members **AGENT ONLY:** No

KENNEDY CENTER AMERICAN COLLEGE THEATER FESTIVAL (KC/ACTF)
WEBSITE: www.KCACTF.org **EMAIL:** ghenry@kennedy-center.org
PHONE: (202) 416-8857 **TWITTER:** @kencen
ADDRESS: Kennedy Center, Washington DC 20566
DESCRIPTION: Est. 1969. KCACTF is a national theater program involving 20,000 students from colleges and universities nationwide which has served as a catalyst in improving the quality of college theater in the US.
GENRE: All genres **PREFERRED LENGTH:** Any Length **FEE:** No **AGENT ONLY:** No

KENTUCKY WOMEN WRITERS CONFERENCE
WEBSITE: womenwriters.as.uky.edu **EMAIL:** kentuckywomenwriters@gmail.com
PHONE: (859) 257-2874 **TWITTER:** @KYWomenWriters
ADDRESS: 232 E. Maxwell St., Lexington KY 40503
DESCRIPTION: Est. 1979. Kentucky Women Writers is the longest running literary festival of women in the nation, launched to showcase the talents and issues unique to female writers.
SPECIAL INTEREST: Feminism/Women's Rights **FEE:** No **AGENT ONLY:** No

KENYON PLAYWRIGHTS' CONFERENCE
WEBSITE: www.kenyoninstitute.org/programs/playwrights-conference

EMAIL: kenyoninstitute@kenyon.edu **PHONE:** (740) 427-5250 **FAX:** (740) 427-7041 **TWITTER:** @KenyonInstitute **ADDRESS:** 209 Chase Ave, Gambier OH 43022
DESCRIPTION: Write every day, surrounded by some of the most exciting early-stage play development in the U.S. and U.K. Seminars led by literary managers and faculty, the space to write in the afternoon and hear your work read in the evenings.
SUBMISSION MATERIALS: Online application. Please submit a paragraph (no more than 250 words) about why you are applying to this workshop and what you hope to take away from it. Additionally, please submit a sample scene of no more than five pages. If you are planning to work on a particular play at the conference, your sample must be from that play. Please also submit a biography (no more than 250 words).
GENRE: Plays **PREFERRED LENGTH:** Any Length **FEE:** Yes **AGENT ONLY:** No

KIDS RULE THE 8X10 FESTIVAL
WEBSITE: luckypennynapa.com/index.php?option=com_content&view=article&id=171:q8-x10-festival-of-10-minute-playsq&catid=35:upcoming-productions&Itemid=178 **EMAIL:** info@luckypennynapa.com **PHONE:** (707) 738-2920 **ADDRESS:** Lucky Penny Productions, 1357 Foster Rd, Napa CA 94558
DESCRIPTION: At the beginning of each new year we ask writers from all over the country to send us scripts for ten-minute plays. We receive 100-200 each year, and our reading committee pours over them all and chooses eight plays that they feel are the best of the bunch. We then bring in a team of about 20 directors and actors to bring these stories to life.
DEADLINE TYPE: Annual **GENRE:** Plays **PREFERRED LENGTH:** 10-minute **FEE:** Yes

KING'S SHORTS FESTIVAL OF TEN MINUTE PLAYS
PARENT ORGANIZATION: Kings Theatre
WEBSITE: kingstheatre.ca/events/kings-shorts **EMAIL:** verilea@yahoo.ca
PHONE: 902-245-2309 **ADDRESS:** 209 St. George St, PO Box 161, Annapolis Royal, Nova Scotia B0S 1A0 Canada
DESCRIPTION: Submissions should have a limited amount of characters (1-6) and should not have been previously produced in any form. Playwrights should avoid wording that might offend. Playwrights may submit a maximum of two plays, using a different pseudonym per script. The organizing committee will choose eight plays, by eight different playwrights, to be staged by the Annapolis Royal Drama Group utilizing local directors. Of those eight, one will be chosen by Theatre Nova Scotia as the winning entry and receive a prize of $300. A second place winner will receive a prize of $150.
DEADLINE: 01/12/2018 **DEADLINE TYPE:** Annual **GENRE:** Plays
PREFERRED LENGTH: 10-minute **FEE:** Yes **AGENT ONLY:** No

KITCHEN DOG THEATER NEW WORKS FESTIVAL
PARENT ORGANIZATION: Kitchen Dog Theater
WEBSITE: www.kitchendogtheater.org/script-submissions **EMAIL:** haley@kitchendogtheater.org **PHONE:** (214) 953-2258 **TWITTER:** @Kitchen_Dog
ADDRESS: Trinity River Arts Center, 2600 N Stemmons Freeway, Ste 180, Dallas TX 75207
DESCRIPTION: Est. 1990. Selected scripts receive 15-20 hours of rehearsal, one pub-

CONFERENCES & FESTIVALS

lic reading in June, and a $100 honorarium for the playwright. We are using the New Play Exchange exclusively for submissions for our New Works Festival. Playwrights may submit only one script. An eligible script aligns with the mission of our theater and has never received a full professional production.

SUBMISSION MATERIALS: We are only accepting submissions through the New Play Exchange (NPX) – no hard copies or emailed submissions accepted.
DEADLINE: 12/05/2017 **GENRE:** Plays **PREFERRED LENGTH:** Full-length **FEE:** No
AGENT ONLY: No

LAGUARDIA PERFORMING ARTS CENTER ROUGH DRAFT FESTIVAL
WEBSITE: www.siteline.vendini.com/site/lpac.nyc/rough-draft-festival-application-2018
EMAIL: scddy25@gmail.com **PHONE:** (718) 482-5151 **ADDRESS:** 31-10 Thomson Ave, Long Island City NY 11101
DESCRIPTION: The Rough Draft Festival (RDF) is a two-week spring arts festival that celebrates artists/organizations and their work under development.
SUBMISSION MATERIALS: Check websites for updated information.
DEADLINE TYPE: Annual **GENRE:** Plays **PREFERRED LENGTH:** Any Length **FEE:** No
AGENT ONLY: No

LAKESHORE PLAYERS 10-MINUTE PLAY FESTIVAL
PARENT ORGANIZATION: Lakeshore Players Theatre
WEBSITE: lakeshoreplayers.org/play-contest-details **EMAIL:** office@lakeshore-players.org **PHONE:** (651) 426-3275 **TWITTER:** @LPT_Arts **ADDRESS:** 4820 Stewart Ave, White Bear Lake MN 55110
DESCRIPTION: Lakeshore Players Theatre is accepting submissions for 10-minute plays. Finalist plays will be produced at our Annual Festival. See website for details.
SUBMISSION MATERIALS: Email two PDFs or mail two copies.
DEADLINE TYPE: Annual **GENRE:** Plays **PREFERRED LENGTH:** 10-minute

LAST FRONTIER THEATRE CONFERENCE
WEBSITE: www.theatreconference.org **EMAIL:** dlmoore@alaska.edu
PHONE: (907) 834-1614 **ADDRESS:** PO Box 97, Valdez AK 99686
DESCRIPTION: The Last Frontier Theatre Conference strives to create an educational experience for playwrights, actors, directors, and theatre enthusiasts that enriches participants' minds and inspires their souls. Participants are completely immersed in the theatre arts for eight days, with a blend of performances, developmental readings, classes, and social events. The Conference does not cover transportation to Alaska.
GENRE: All Genres **PREFERRED LENGTH:** Any Length **FEE:** No **AGENT ONLY:** No

LIFT-OFF NEW PLAY SERIES
PARENT ORGANIZATION: The Navigators Theatre Company
WEBSITE: www.navigatorstheater.com/submissions **PHONE:** (716) 491-4744
TWITTER: @_TheNavigators
DESCRIPTION: See website for submission dates. **DEADLINE TYPE:** Annual **GENRE:** Plays **PREFERRED LENGTH:** Any Length **SPECIAL INTEREST:** Feminism/Women's Rights **FEE:** Waived for DG Members **AGENT ONLY:** No

LITTLE FESTIVAL OF THE UNEXPECTED

PARENT ORGANIZATION: Portland Stage Company [ME]
WEBSITE: www.portlandstage.org/work-with-us/for-playwrights/little-festival-submissions **EMAIL:** literary@portlandstage.org **PHONE:** (207) 774-1043
TWITTER: @PortlandStageCo **ADDRESS:** Portland Stage, Box 1458, Portland ME 04104
DESCRIPTION: Est. 1989. An annual event dedicated to public readings of new works. Three playwrights are in residence each year at the festival as they continue to develop their scripts with input from actors, directors, dramaturgs, and audience members.
SUBMISSION MATERIALS: Playwrights who do not have agents may submit 10-page dialogue samples for consideration. Dialogue samples must be accompanied by a synopsis, production history and character breakdown. Submissions of 10-page samples (from playwrights) must be sent by U.S. Mail only – no e-mails, faxes, etc. Mail to Attn: Literary Manager.
GENRE: Plays **PREFERRED LENGTH:** Full-length **FEE:** No **AGENT ONLY:** Yes

LOS ANGELES WOMEN'S THEATRE FESTIVAL

WEBSITE: www.lawtf.org/application_2018.html **EMAIL:** submissions@lawtf.org
PHONE: (818) 760-0408 **TWITTER:** @LAWTF **ADDRESS:** 11411 Cumpston St, #204, Los Angeles CA 91601
DESCRIPTION: The Los Angeles Women's Theatre Festival (LAWTF) empowers women artists to engage and inspire communities through the production of multidisciplinary solo performers and educational outreach. The Annual Festival honors the achievement of extraordinary women in theatre.
SUBMISSION MATERIALS: LAWTF is currently seeking female solo artists of all ethnicities and ages with original performance pieces: actors, performance artists, dancers, comedians, storytellers, singers, and performance poems from throughout the world. See website for details.
SPECIAL INTEREST: Feminism/Women's Rights **FEE:** Yes **AGENT ONLY:** No

MACH 33 FESTIVAL

WEBSITE: tacit.caltech.edu/mach33/submissions **EMAIL:** arden.e.thomas@gmail.com **PHONE:** (626) 395-3696 **ADDRESS:** Theatre Arts at Cal Tech, 275 S Hill Ave, Pasadena CA 91125
DESCRIPTION: Mach 33 features plays by Los Angeles-area playwrights that center on scientific, mathematical, and technological questions. Please see our website for more details, including Festival information and submission requirements.
SUBMISSION MATERIALS: All plays must be submitted electronically in PDF format. All submissions should include a cover page with play title, author name, date of most recent revision, contact Information, and synopsis. See website for details and updates.
DEADLINE TYPE: Annual **GENRE:** Plays **PREFERRED LENGTH:** Full-length **FEE:** No

MARATHON OF ONE-ACT PLAYS

PARENT ORGANIZATION: Ensemble Studio Theater (EST)
WEBSITE: www.ensemblestudiotheatre.org/marathon-of-one-act-plays
EMAIL: literary@ensemblestudiotheatre.org **PHONE:** (212) 247-4982

TWITTER: @ESTnyc **ADDRESS:** 549 W 52nd St, New York NY 10019
DESCRIPTION: Inspired by the format in which Tennessee Williams and Eugene O'Neill honed their craft, EST held its first Marathon in 1977. Praised by critics and beloved by audiences, it launched an industry-wide revival of the short play form and broke new ground by putting new and established writers together on one stage.
SUBMISSION MATERIALS: Non-member playwrights may submit a single script, no longer than 30 minutes, which has not been reviewed in New York. We prefer email submissions, which can be sent to literary@estnyc.org. Please include your name and contact information in the body of your email but send the script without identifying information.
DEADLINE: 08/01/2018 **DEADLINE TYPE:** Bi-annual **GENRE:** All genres
PREFERRED LENGTH: 1-Act (under 1 hour)

MIDTOWN INTERNATIONAL THEATRE FESTIVAL
WEBSITE: www.midtownfestival.org/mitf-scripts.html
EMAIL: midtownfestival@gmail.com
ADDRESS: 347 W 36th St, #1204, New York NY 10018
DESCRIPTION: Est. 2000. MITF celebrates the diversity of theatre in NYC and beyond. We emphasize imaginative, low-tech staging. We now produce 3 festivals a year.
GENRE: All genres **PREFERRED LENGTH:** Any Length **FEE:** Yes **AGENT ONLY:** No

MIDWEST REGIONAL BLACK THEATRE FESTIVAL
PARENT ORGANIZATION: Cincinnati Black Theatre Company
WEBSITE: www.cincyblacktheatre.com **EMAIL:** cbtctickets@gmail.com
PHONE: (513) 241-6060 **FAX:** (513) 241-6671 **ADDRESS:** 5919 Hamilton Ave, Cincinnati OH 45224
DESCRIPTION: The Midwest Regional Black Theatre Festival is a biennial two-week event produced by CBTC showcasing and presenting the outstanding talent of local, regional and national theatre arts professionals and non-professionals, adults and children. See website for details and updates.

MIND THE GAP BRITBITS SHORT PLAY FESTIVAL
PARENT ORGANIZATION: Mind The Gap Theatre
WEBSITE: www.mindthegaptheatre.net/get-involved.html **EMAIL:** allaboard@mindthegaptheatre.com **PHONE:** (212) 252-3137 **TWITTER:** @mindthegapny
ADDRESS: 535 W 23rd St, S11G, New York NY 10011
DESCRIPTION: Writer must be native UK playwright.
GENRE: Plays **PREFERRED LENGTH:** 10-minute **FEE:** Yes **AGENT ONLY:** Yes

MINNESOTA FRINGE FESTIVAL
WEBSITE: www.fringefestival.org/artists **EMAIL:** info@fringefestival.org
PHONE: (612) 872-1212 **FAX:** (612) 872-3460 **TWITTER:** @mnfringe
ADDRESS: 528 Hennepin Ave, #503, Minneapolis MN 55403
DESCRIPTION: Each year Minnesota Fringe Festival works with more than 1000 artists to organize a performing arts extravaganza that features an array of genres. In the interest of fairness, Fringe artists are selected by random luck of the draw through an un-juried and un-curated process. Participants self-produce.

SUBMISSION MATERIALS: Artist applications are available on our website in mid-November with a mid-February deadline.
DEADLINE TYPE: Annual **GENRE:** All genres **PREFERRED LENGTH:** Any Length
FEE: Yes **AGENT ONLY:** No

MINNESOTA SHORTS FESTIVAL OF PLAYS
WEBSITE: www.mnshorts.com **EMAIL:** mnshorts@yahoo.com
PHONE: (507) 420-1881
ADDRESS: 805 Garfield Ave, North Mankato MN 56003
DESCRIPTION: In 2018, we will be doing a 10th anniversary show with the Best plays over the first nine years, so the festival will NOT be taking submissions in 2018. In 2019, we'll go back to our regular submissions from Jan 1, 2019 to Feb 1, 2019.
DEADLINE: 02/01/2019 **GENRE:** Plays **PREFERRED LENGTH:** 10-minute
FEE: No **AGENT ONLY:** No

NATIONAL ALLIANCE FOR MUSICAL THEATRE (NAMT)
WEBSITE: namt.org/festivalsconcerts/festival-submissions **EMAIL:** ciera@namt.org
PHONE: (212) 714-6668 **TWITTER:** @NAMT
ADDRESS: 520 8th Ave, #301, New York NY 10018
DESCRIPTION: Est. 1985. NAMT is an Equity Showcase of eight musicals in 45-minute presentations over two days. Participants will receive a stipend from NAMT.
SUBMISSION MATERIALS: You will be asked to upload a PDF of the script and a PDF of a 20-pg excerpt when you fill out the online application. See website for details.
GENRE: Musicals **PREFERRED LENGTH:** Full-length **FEE:** Yes **AGENT ONLY:** No

NATIONAL BLACK THEATRE FESTIVAL
PARENT ORGANIZATION: North Carolina Black Repertory Company
WEBSITE: ncblackrep.org/2019-submissions **EMAIL:** info@ncblackrep.org
PHONE: (336) 723-2266 **TWITTER:** @NCBlackRep
ADDRESS: 610 Coliseum Dr, Winston-Salem NC 27106
DESCRIPTION: Est. 1989. The festival is produced by the North Carolina Black Repertory Company. There are several submission opportunities, each with different deadlines.
SUBMISSION MATERIALS: See website for updates and information.
DEADLINE TYPE: Biennial **GENRE:** All genres **PREFERRED LENGTH:** Full-length
SPECIAL INTEREST: Black or African American **FEE:** No **AGENT ONLY:** No

NATIONAL MUSIC THEATER CONFERENCE – THE EUGENE O'NEILL THEATER CENTER
PARENT ORGANIZATION: The Eugene O'Neill Theater Center
WEBSITE: www.theoneill.org/summer-conferences/nmtc
EMAIL: litoffice@theoneill.org **PHONE:** (860) 443-5378
FAX: (860) 443-9653 **TWITTER:** @ONeill_Center
ADDRESS: The O'Neill, 305 Great Neck Rd, Waterford CT 6385
DESCRIPTION: Mission: To provide a supportive and challenging environment in which

emerging and established creative artists can take huge risks in order to refine and illuminate their work's vision during its formative stages. Each summer, the National Music Theater Conference includes several playwrights, lyricists, and composers endeavoring to create fresh and bold work from an array of music theater genres.

SUBMISSION MATERIALS: Application details and deadline change annually. Please consult website for additional information.

DEADLINE TYPE: Annual **GENRE:** Musicals **PREFERRED LENGTH:** Full-length **FEE:** Yes **AGENT ONLY:** No

NATIONAL PLAYWRIGHTS CONFERENCE – THE EUGENE O'NEILL THEATER CENTER

PARENT ORGANIZATION: The Eugene O'Neill Theater Center
WEBSITE: www.theoneill.org/summer-conferences/npc
EMAIL: litoffice@theoneill.org **PHONE:** (860) 443-5378 **FAX:** (860) 443-9653
TWITTER: @ONeill_Center **ADDRESS:** 305 Great Neck Rd, Waterford CT 06385
DESCRIPTION: Est. 1964. Month residency (June-July), includes 4-day workshop and two in-hand readings with professional actors and directors. Assistance: stipend, room/board, travel. Application details and deadline change annually. Please consult website for additional information.
SUBMISSION MATERIALS: Application details and deadline change annually. Please consult website for additional information.
DEADLINE TYPE: Annual **GENRE:** Plays **PREFERRED LENGTH:** Full-length **FEE:** Yes
AGENT ONLY: No

NATIVE VOICES ANNUAL SHORT PLAY FESTIVAL

WEBSITE: theautry.org/events/signature-programs/native-voices/annual-call-scripts
EMAIL: nvliteraryassociate@gmail.com **PHONE:** (619) 421-2182
FAX: (619) 421-2182 **TWITTER:** @nativevoices
ADDRESS: 4700 Western Heritage Way, Los Angeles CA 90027
DESCRIPTION: Please note that we only accept submissions written for the stage or theatre by Native American, Alaska Native, Hawaiian, and First Nations artists.
SUBMISSION MATERIALS: See website for updates and information.
DEADLINE TYPE: Annual **GENRE:** All Genres **PREFERRED LENGTH:** 10-minute
SPECIAL INTEREST: American Indian or Alaskan Native **FEE:** No **AGENT ONLY:** No

NEW GROUND THEATRE FESTIVAL

PARENT ORGANIZATION: Cleveland Play House
WEBSITE: www.clevelandplayhouse.com/shows/new-ground-theatre-festival
EMAIL: submissions@clevelandplayhouse.com **PHONE:** (216) 795-7000
TWITTER: @ClevePlayHouse
ADDRESS: 1901 E 13th St, Ste 200, Cleveland OH 44114
DESCRIPTION: Est. 1995. Reading series of unoptioned/unproduced new plays. Author must be resident of Ohio.
SUBMISSION MATERIALS: Check website in March for updates.
FEE: No **AGENT ONLY:** Yes

NEW SOUTH PLAY FESTIVAL

PARENT ORGANIZATION: Horizon Theatre Company [GA]
WEBSITE: www.horizontheatre.com/get-involved/play-submissions
EMAIL: submissions@horizontheatre.com   **PHONE:** (404) 523-1477
FAX: (404) 584-8815   **TWITTER:** @horizontheatre
ADDRESS: Box 5376, Atlanta GA 31107
DESCRIPTION: The New South Play Festival has been dedicated to producing new plays from, for, and about the contemporary South since 1999. The Festival focuses on new plays by writers who live or have roots in the South, creating stories that our relevant to our community today. The Festival is particularly interested in plays by women and African Americans. See website for details.
SUBMISSION MATERIALS: We accept the following types of submissions:
- Agent submissions that meet our mission
- Previously professionally produced plays that meet our mission
- For plays with no previous professional productions, the play must meet the mission of the New South Play Festival
- We do not accept submissions of unproduced plays by individual writers that do not meet our New South Play Festival mission

DEADLINE TYPE: Annual   **GENRE:** Plays   **PREFERRED LENGTH:** Full-length   **FEE:** No
AGENT ONLY: No

NEW VOICE PLAY FESTIVAL

PARENT ORGANIZATION: Old Opera House Theatre Co.
WEBSITE: www.oldoperahouse.org/new_voice_submit.html
EMAIL: ooh@oldoperahouse.org   **PHONE:** (304) 752-4420
TWITTER: @OldOperaHouse   **ADDRESS:** Old Opera House Theatre Company, 204 N George St, Charles Town WV 25414
SUBMISSION MATERIALS: Online submissions only. Only unpublished, non-musical works are acceptable. Plays enjoying a previous public "reading" or that have not been staged in more than one other theatre are acceptable. See website for more information.
DEADLINE: 03/01/2018   **DEADLINE TYPE:** Annual   **GENRE:** Plays
PREFERRED LENGTH: One Act   **FEE:** Yes   **AGENT ONLY:** No

NEW WORKS FESTIVAL

PARENT ORGANIZATION: TheatreWorks Silicon Valley
WEBSITE: www.theatreworks.org/new-works-initiative/new-works-festival
EMAIL: boxoffice@theatreworks.org   **PHONE:** (650) 463-1960
TWITTER: @TheatreWorksSV   **ADDRESS:** PO Box 50458, Palo Alto CA 94303-0458
DESCRIPTION: TheatreWorks' New Works Festival is an opportunity to experience new plays and musicals in their early stages of development. The Festival has launched many new works onto TheatreWorks' mainstage and on to productions nationally.
SUBMISSION MATERIALS: TheatreWorks accepts full-length scripts year-round from literary agents and theatre professionals with whom we have an existing professional relationship. We welcome script submissions to our mainstage season as well as our New Works Initiative. We look for well-written, well-constructed plays that celebrate the human spirit, speak to our diverse community, and advance the art of the Ameri-

can theatre.

DEADLINE TYPE: Rolling **GENRE:** Plays or Musicals **FEE:** No **AGENT ONLY:** Yes

NEW WORKS FESTIVAL AT LONG BEACH PLAYHOUSE
WEBSITE: www.lbplayhouse.org/show/new-works-festival
EMAIL: newworks@lbplayhouse.org **PHONE:** (562) 494-1014
ADDRESS: 5021 East Anaheim St, Long Beach CA 90804
GENRE: Plays **PREFERRED LENGTH:** Full-length **FEE:** Yes **AGENT ONLY:** No

NEW YORK INTERNATIONAL FRINGE FESTIVAL (FRINGENYC)
WEBSITE: www.fringenyc.org **EMAIL:** info@FringeNYC.org **PHONE:** (212) 279-4488 **FAX:** (212) 279-4466 **ADDRESS:** 518 E 6th St #BW, New York NY 10009
DESCRIPTION: In October of 2018, we'll present: FringeNYC – A smaller adjudicated festival, all within one block, area, or complex; Convening – of indie theatre, featuring panels, workshops, speakers; FringeBYOV – a twist on Bring Your Own Venue, where venues in other boroughs bring their own artists. See website for updates and details.

NEWTACTICS (NEW PLAY FESTIVAL)
PARENT ORGANIZATION: The Actors Company Theatre (TACT)
WEBSITE: tactnyc.org/category/newtactics-new-play-festival **EMAIL:** newTACTics@tactnyc.org **PHONE:** (212) 645-8228 **FAX:** (212) 462-2678 **TWITTER:** @TACTnyc **ADDRESS:** 900 Broadway #905, New York NY 10003
DESCRIPTION: newTACTics seeks new original full length plays that have not yet been published or received a full production in New York City. Submissions from playwrights of all levels of experience are accepted on an open basis year round.
SUBMISSION MATERIALS: Please submit a PDF, along with a bio and synopsis, of the most recent draft via email. **PREFERRED LENGTH:** Full-length **FEE:** No

NEXT ACT!
PARENT ORGANIZATION: Capital Repertory Theatre
WEBSITE: www.capitalrep.org **EMAIL:** mhall@capitalrep.org **PHONE:** (518) 462-4531 **TWITTER:** @theREPny **ADDRESS:** 111 N Pearl St, Albany NY 12207
DESCRIPTION: Next Act! is an expansion of Capital Repertory Theatre's continued commitment to the development of new work.
SUBMISSION MATERIALS: Check website for updates.
GENRE: All genres **PREFERRED LENGTH:** Any Length

NEXT STAGE THEATRE FESTIVAL (NSTF)
PARENT ORGANIZATION: Toronto Fringe Festival
WEBSITE: fringetoronto.com/year-round/artist-opportunities
EMAIL: general@fringetoronto.com **PHONE:** (416) 966-1062
TWITTER: @Toronto_Fringe **ADDRESS:** Fringe of Toronto Theatre Festival, 204-688 Richmond St W, Toronto Ontario M6J 1C5 Canada

DESCRIPTION: The Next Stage Theatre Festival (NSTF) is a 12-day celebration of indie theatre that takes place every January at Factory Theatre. While our summer Fringe shows are selected by lottery, our 10 NSTF shows are programmed by a jury of industry professionals.

SUBMISSION MATERIALS: Anyone who has participated as a primary artist in a CAFF festival is eligible to apply. Examples of primary artists are: producer, playwright, director. Check website for updates and details.

DEADLINE TYPE: Annual **GENRE:** Plays or Musicals **PREFERRED LENGTH:** Any Length **FEE:** Yes **AGENT ONLY:** No

NORTH PARK PLAYWRIGHT FESTIVAL

WEBSITE: www.northparkvaudeville.com/PlaywrightFestivalWebpage.html
EMAIL: jfbushnell@cox.net **PHONE:** (619) 220-8663 **ADDRESS:** 2031 El Cajon Blvd, San Diego CA 92104

DESCRIPTION: Provides a platform for brand new, 10 minute plays written by playwrights from around the world. Over the past twelve years more than 440 new plays have been produced. We seek short new plays that are easily staged and have casts with no more than four people. Our theater is very small and we normally use a minimal set concept in this festival.

SUBMISSION MATERIALS: Check website for updates.

GENRE: Plays **PREFERRED LENGTH:** 10-minute **FEE:** No **AGENT ONLY:** No

ORLANDO INTERNATIONAL FRINGE THEATRE FESTIVAL

WEBSITE: www.orlandofringe.org/2018-application-info **EMAIL:** producer@orlandofringe.org **PHONE:** (407) 648-0077 **FAX:** (407) 540-9878 **ADDRESS:** 812 E Rollins St, Ste 300, Orlando FL 32803

DESCRIPTION: Check website for updated submission information.

DEADLINE: 11/15/2017 **DEADLINE TYPE:** Annual **FEE:** Yes **AGENT ONLY:** No

PAN THEATER TEN MINUTE PLAY FEST

WEBSITE: www.pantheater.com **EMAIL:** david@pantheater.com **PHONE:** (415) 261-1641 **ADDRESS:** 287 17th St, #220, Oakland CA 94612

DESCRIPTION: Est. 2004. Check website for details.

PARK PLAYS FESTIVAL

PARENT ORGANIZATION: Queens Theatre

WEBSITE: www.queenstheatre.org/content/park-plays-festival **EMAIL:** parkplays@queenstheatre.org **ADDRESS:** Queens Theatre, 14 United Nations Ave S, Flushing NY 11352

DESCRIPTION: Park Plays is a festival of ten short plays exploring and celebrating the events, environs, and denizens of Flushing Meadows Corona Park. Five plays will be commissioned from internationally known playwrights, and half will be selected from an open submissions process.

SUBMISSION MATERIALS: Check website for updated information.

DEADLINE TYPE: Annual **GENRE:** Plays **PREFERRED LENGTH:** 10-minute **FEE:** No **AGENT ONLY:** No

PENN STATE NU MUSICAL THEATRE FESTIVAL

WEBSITE: www.psunewmusicals.psu.edu **EMAIL:** psunumusicals@psu.edu **PHONE:** (814) 865-7305 **ADDRESS:** c/o PSU School of Theatre, 210 Theatre Building, University Park PA 16801

DESCRIPTION: Est. 2006. The festival explores, encourages, and fosters new works of musical theatre by today's progressive playwrights and composers in an educational setting, giving students at Penn State access to the collaborative process between the artist, the art form, and the professional world of musical theatre.

SUBMISSION MATERIALS: Hard copy submissions only. Check website for updated information. **DEADLINE TYPE:** Annual **GENRE:** Musicals **PREFERRED LENGTH:** Full-length **FEE:** No

PHILADELPHIA CHILDREN'S FESTIVAL

WEBSITE: www.annenbergcenter.org **PHONE:** (215) 898-9080 **ADDRESS:** 3680 Walnut St, Philadelphia PA 19104

PHILADELPHIA YOUNG PLAYWRIGHTS' FESTIVAL

WEBSITE: www.phillyyoungplaywrights.org **EMAIL:** info@phillyyoungplaywrights.org **PHONE:** (215) 665-9226 **ADDRESS:** 1219 Vine St, Fl 3, Philadelphia PA 19107

DESCRIPTION: Check website for updated information.

DEADLINE TYPE: Annual **GENRE:** Plays

PHILLLY FRINGE

WEBSITE: www.fringearts.com/all-presentations/phillyfringe17 **EMAIL:** fringeinfo@livearts-fringe.org **PHONE:** (215) 413-9006 **FAX:** (215) 413-9007 **TWITTER:** @FringeArts **ADDRESS:** 140 N Columbus Blvd, Philadelphia PA 19106

SUBMISSION MATERIALS: Check website for information **GENRE:** All genres

PHOENIX THEATRE FESTIVAL OF NEW AMERICAN THEATRE

PARENT ORGANIZATION: Phoenix Theatre [AZ]

WEBSITE: www.phoenixtheatre.com/festival **EMAIL:** info@phoenixtheatre.com **PHONE:** (602) 889-6321 **ADDRESS:** 100 E McDowell Rd, C/O Robert Harper, Phoenix AZ 85004

DESCRIPTION: Submissions for the 2018 Festival of New American Theatre are closed, Please check website in April 2018 for guidelines for the 2019 Festival.

GENRE: Plays or Musicals **PREFERRED LENGTH:** Full-length **FEE:** Waived for DG Members **AGENT ONLY:** No

PICK OF THE VINE SHORT PLAY FESTIVAL

PARENT ORGANIZATION: Little Fish Theatre (LFT)

WEBSITE: www.littlefishtheatre.org/wp/participate/submit-a-script/ **EMAIL:** LFTpickofthevine@gmail.com **TWITTER:** @lilfishtheatre **ADDRESS:** 777 Centre St, San Pedro CA 90731

DESCRIPTION: There will be a $50 flat fee royalty payment to playwrights per play produced. Plays will have no more than 10 actors and run no more than 15 minutes.
SUBMISSION MATERIALS: Check website for updated information.
DEADLINE TYPE: Annual   **GENRE:** Plays   **PREFERRED LENGTH:** 10-minute   **FEE:** No
AGENT ONLY: No

PITTSBURGH NEW WORKS FESTIVAL (PNWF)
WEBSITE: www.pittsburghnewworks.org   **EMAIL:** info@pittsburghnewworks.org   **PHONE:** (412) 881-6888   **FAX:** (412) 490-8313   **ADDRESS:** PO Box 42419, Pittsburgh PA 15203
DESCRIPTION: Est. 1991. See website for updated information.

PLANET CONNECTIONS THEATRE FESTIVITY
WEBSITE: planetconnections.org   **EMAIL:** planetbrockh@gmail.com
PHONE: (917) 338-9541   **ADDRESS:** 85 Delancey St, Ste 33, Brooklyn NY 10002
DESCRIPTION: New York's premiere socially conscious and eco-friendly, not-for-profit theatre festival. The festival is designed to invoke the power of art in motivating philanthropy, community outreach, and social change.
SUBMISSION MATERIALS: See website for updated information.
GENRE: Plays   **PREFERRED LENGTH:** Full-length   **FEE:** Yes   **AGENT ONLY:** No

PLAYFEST
PARENT ORGANIZATION: Orlando Shakespeare Theater
WEBSITE: www.orlandoshakes.org/playfest/playfest-2017/
EMAIL: cynthiaw@orlandoshakes.org   **PHONE:** (407) 447-1700
ADDRESS: Orlando Shakespeare Theatre, 812 E Rollins St, Orlando FL 32803
DESCRIPTION: Annual festival presenting up to seven new plays in staged readings.
SUBMISSION MATERIALS: Check website for updated information.
DEADLINE TYPE: Annual   **GENRE:** Plays   **PREFERRED LENGTH:** Full-length   **FEE:** No
AGENT ONLY: No

PLAYPENN CONFERENCE
PARENT ORGANIZATION: PlayPenn
WEBSITE: www.playpenn.org/application/?mc_cid=beaca65b9e&mc_eid=455804896b   **EMAIL:** info@playpenn.org   **PHONE:** 215-242-2813
TWITTER: @PlayPennLIVE
ADDRESS: 100 S Broad St, Ste 1318, Philadelphia PA 19110
DESCRIPTION: PlayPenn's annual conference includes workshops and readings of new plays, forums for artists, seminars, and classes, all centered around fostering artists by providing as many resources possible.
SUBMISSION MATERIALS: See website for updates.   **DEADLINE TYPE:** Annual   **GENRE:** Plays   **PREFERRED LENGTH:** Full-length

PLAYS IN PROGRESS SERIES
WEBSITE: www.athenaprojectarts.org/get-involved/submit/

EMAIL: literarymanager@athenaprojectfestival.org
ADDRESS: Athena Project, 2344 E Iliff Ave, Denver CO 80210
DESCRIPTION: Submissions are now closed for our 2018 series. For our 2019 Festival, the deadline for submission will be during Spring 2018 – please check website for more details. **GENRE:** Plays **PREFERRED LENGTH:** Full-length **FEE:** No

PLAYWRIGHTS VOICED
PARENT ORGANIZATION: Relative Theatrics
WEBSITE: www.relativetheatrics.com/playwrights-voiced.html
EMAIL: relativetheatrics@gmail.com **TWITTER:** @rtheatrics
ADDRESS: 710 E Garfield St, #278, Laramie WY 82070
DESCRIPTION: Check website for information about future dates and submission guidelines.
GENRE: Plays **PREFERRED LENGTH:** Full-length **FEE:** No **AGENT ONLY:** No

PLAYWRIGHTS' WEEK
WEBSITE: www.larktheatre.org/what-we-do/our-initiatives/playwrights-week
EMAIL: andreah@larktheatre.org **PHONE:** (212) 246-2676] **ADDRESS:** 311 W 43rd St, Ste 406, New York NY 10036
DESCRIPTION: Playwrights' Week serves as the central entry point for play submissions at The Lark and encourages the development of new voices.
SUBMISSION MATERIALS: See website for updated information.
GENRE: Plays **PREFERRED LENGTH:** Full-length **FEE:** No **AGENT ONLY:** No

PREMIERE STAGES PLAY FESTIVAL
PARENT ORGANIZATION: Premiere Stages at Kean University
WEBSITE: www.premierestagesatkean.com/play-festival **EMAIL:** pfsubmit@kean.edu
PHONE: (908) 737-4092 **FAX:** (908) 737-4636 **TWITTER:** @PremiereStages
ADDRESS: 1000 Morris Ave, |235, Union N| 7083
DESCRIPTION: From September 15th to December 15th, Premiere Stages will accept submissions of unproduced plays (previous readings, workshops, and showcases are acceptable) written by playwrights affiliated with the greater metropolitan area (New York, New Jersey, Connecticut, Pennsylvania, and Delaware). Four plays are selected for development and one receives an Equity production.
SUBMISSION MATERIALS: Synopsis, character breakdown, play history, bio/resume, 10 pg. sample **DEADLINE:** 12/15/2018 **GENRE:** Plays **PREFERRED LENGTH:** Full-length
FEE: No **AGENT ONLY:** No

RAUCOUS CAUCUS
PARENT ORGANIZATION: Box Wine Theatre
WEBSITE: boxwinetheatre.com/get-involved **EMAIL:** info@boxwinetheatre.com
ADDRESS: 4721 41st St, #A1, New York NY 11104
DESCRIPTION: Submissions are now closed for Raucous Caucus 2017. Check website for updated information.
GENRE: Plays **PREFERRED LENGTH:** 1-Act (under 1 hour) **FEE:** No **AGENT ONLY:** No

REORIENT FESTIVAL OF SHORT PLAYS

PARENT ORGANIZATION: Golden Thread Productions
WEBSITE: www.goldenthread.org/programs/reorient **EMAIL:** gtpsubmissions@gmail.com **PHONE:** (415) 626-4061 **TWITTER:** @goldenthread
ADDRESS: 1695 18th St, #C101, San Francisco CA 94107
DESCRIPTION: Est. 1999. Presenting alternative perspectives of the Middle East and showcasing the multiplicity of stories, voices and styles from the region. This ambitious festival, now presented biennially, turns San Francisco into a mecca for innovative, spirited, and thought-provoking theatre from and about the Middle East. ReOrient welcomes artists who challenge the dominant depictions of the Middle East and audiences who seek unconventional and provocative programming.
SUBMISSION MATERIALS: Check website for updated information.
DEADLINE: 05/01/2018 **DEADLINE TYPE:** Biennial **GENRE:** Plays
PREFERRED LENGTH: 1-Act (under 1 hour) **FEE:** No **AGENT ONLY:** No

REP LAB SHORT PLAY FESTIVAL

PARENT ORGANIZATION: Milwaukee Repertory Theater
WEBSITE: www.milwaukeerep.com/Tickets--Events/201617-Season/Rep-Lab
EMAIL: DSladky@MilwaukeeRep.com **PHONE:** (414) 224-1761 **FAX:** (414) 224-9097 **ADDRESS:** 108 E Wells St, Milwaukee WI 53202
DESCRIPTION: Check website for updated information.
DEADLINE TYPE: Annual **GENRE:** Plays **PREFERRED LENGTH:** 1-Act (under 1 hour)
FEE: No **AGENT ONLY:** No

REVERB PLAY FESTIVAL

PARENT ORGANIZATION: Echo Theatre Company [OK]
WEBSITE: www.echotheatreco.org **EMAIL:** echotheatreco@gmail.com **PHONE:** (870) 918-4371 **ADDRESS:** 1908 W Cameron St, Tulsa OK 74127
DESCRIPTION: At press, the website has not been updated. Email Echo Theatre Company for more information. **GENRE:** Plays **FEE:** No **AGENT ONLY:** No

RISK IS THIS...NEW EXPERIMENTAL PLAYS FESTIVAL

PARENT ORGANIZATION: Cutting Ball Theater
WEBSITE: www.cuttingball.com/script-submissions **EMAIL:** ariel@cuttingball.com **PHONE:** (415) 419-3584 **ADDRESS:** 141 Taylor St, San Francisco CA 94102
DESCRIPTION: Check website for updated information.
GENRE: Plays **PREFERRED LENGTH:** Full-length **FEE:** Yes **AGENT ONLY:** No

SAMUEL FRENCH OFF-OFF BROADWAY SHORT-PLAY FESTIVAL, THE

PARENT ORGANIZATION: Samuel French, Inc.
WEBSITE: www.oobfestival.com **EMAIL:** oobfestival@samuelfrench.com **PHONE:** (212) 206-8990 **FAX:** (212) 206-1429 **TWITTER:** @OOBFestival **ADDRESS:** Samuel French, Inc, 235 Park Ave S, New York NY 10003
DESCRIPTION: Est. 1976. The Samuel French Off Off Broadway Short Play Festival offers a prize of publication and licensing for six short plays in the notable

OFF OFF BROADWAY FESTIVAL PLAYS series. In addition, the 24 semi-finalists each receive a full production in one of New York City's leading Off Broadway theatres.
SUBMISSION MATERIALS: Submissions for the 43rd annual Off Off Broadway Short Play Festival will open in late 2017. **GENRE:** Plays or Musicals **PREFERRED LENGTH:** 15-minute **FEE:** No **AGENT ONLY:** No

SAN FRANCISCO FRINGE FESTIVAL
WEBSITE: www.sffringe.org **EMAIL:** mail@sffringe.org **ADDRESS:** 156 Eddy St, San Francisco CA 94102
DESCRIPTION: Est 1991. The Fringe is open to all artists, with performers selected through a public lottery. This creates diversity with performers emerging and re-emerging across a range of disciplines and ethnicities.
DEADLINE: 02/14/2018 **FEE:** No **AGENT ONLY:** No

SEVEN DEVILS PLAYWRIGHTS CONFERENCE
WEBSITE: www.idtheater.org/submit-a-play.html **EMAIL:** ap@idtheater.org **ADDRESS:** Id Theater, 143 E 8th St, Brooklyn NY 11218
DESCRIPTION: The Seven Devils Playwrights Conference supports the development of plays that embrace, explore and challenge the diverse geographical, philosophical, cultural, aesthetic and political landscape of the American experience - rural and urban, east and west, coastal and inland. We're interested in addressing the needs, hopes, concerns and ambitions of American audiences.
SUBMISSION MATERIALS: Full script, resume. Online submission only.
DEADLINE TYPE: Annual **GENRE:** Plays **PREFERRED LENGTH:** Full-length **FEE:** Yes **AGENT ONLY:** No

SEWANEE WRITERS' CONFERENCE
WEBSITE: www.sewaneewriters.org/applications **EMAIL:** swc@sewanee.edu **PHONE:** (931) 598-1654 **TWITTER:** @sewaneewriters **ADDRESS:** 119 Gailor Hall, Stamler Center, 735 University Ave, Sewanee TN 37383-1000
DESCRIPTION: Est. 1990. Conference in late July. Limited number of scholarships and fellowships available on a competitive basis. See website for details and deadlines. **DEADLINE:** 03/20/2018 **DEADLINE TYPE:** Annual **GENRE:** Plays **PREFERRED LENGTH:** Any Length **FEE:** No **AGENT ONLY:** No

SHE NYC ARTS AND SHE LA ARTS
WEBSITE: www.shenycarts.org/faq **TWITTER:** @shenyc_arts
DESCRIPTION: Established in 2015, SheNYC Arts became NYC's first festival devoted to producing full-length plays, musicals, and adaptations by women writers. In 2018, She NYC will become bi-coastal! The first annual She LA Arts festival will run in tandem with the She NYC Arts festival in summer 2018. For more information please visit www.shenycarts.org.
SUBMISSION MATERIALS: Online submission. See website for updated details.
GENRE: Plays or Musicals **PREFERRED LENGTH:** Full-length **SPECIAL INTEREST:** Feminism/Women's Rights **FEE:** Yes **AGENT ONLY:** No

SHOVEL TOWN 10-MINUTE PLAY FESTIVAL, THE

WEBSITE: www.facebook.com/shoveltown10minuteplayfestival **EMAIL:** stedfastdrama@gmail.com **PHONE:** (508) 801-0936 **ADDRESS:** 50 Oliver St, N Easton MA 2356

DESCRIPTION: The Shovel Town 10-Minute Play Festival began in 2014. It is sponsored by The Stedfast School of Music and Arts in Conjunction with the Easton Shovel Town Cultural District. Its mission is to provide an opportunity for a wide range of actors to perform, while providing a high-quality evening of entertainment for the entire family. The Third Annual Shovel Town 10-Minute Play Festival will be held September 15th and 16th, 2017.

GENRE: Plays **PREFERRED LENGTH:** 10-minute **FEE:** No **AGENT ONLY:** No

SHOWOFF! TEN-MINUTE PLAYWRITING FESTIVAL

PARENT ORGANIZATION: Camino Real Playhouse
WEBSITE: www.caminorealplayhouse.org/showoff-submit.html
EMAIL: box_office@sbcglobal.net **PHONE:** (949) 248-0808
ADDRESS: Camino Real Playhouse, 31776 El Camino Real, San Juan Capistrano CA 92675
SUBMISSION MATERIALS: Please submit your plays unbound (stapled is OK) with your full contact info on the title page. Submit by mail only.
DEADLINE: 10/15/2018 **DEADLINE TYPE:** Annual **GENRE:** Plays
PREFERRED LENGTH: 10-minute **FEE:** Yes **AGENT ONLY:** No

SOUND BITES 10-MINUTE MUSICAL FESTIVAL

PARENT ORGANIZATION: Theatre Now New York
WEBSITE: www.soundbites.tnny.org/index.php/submit **EMAIL:** soundbites@tnny.org **PHONE:** (212) 845-9824 **TWITTER:** @soundbitesny
ADDRESS: 520 8th Ave, Ste 311, New York NY 10018
DESCRIPTION: SOUND BITES is an annual musical theatre festival which showcases ten 10-minute musicals or musical excerpts in one evening.
DEADLINE: 02/01/2018 **GENRE:** Musicals **PREFERRED LENGTH:** 10-minute **FEE:** No
AGENT ONLY: No

STRATFORD SHAKESPEARE FESTIVAL [ON]

WEBSITE: www.stratfordfestival.ca/AboutUs/NewPlayDevelopment
PHONE: (519) 271-4040 **ADDRESS:** Box 520, Stratford ON N5A 4M9 Canada

SUMMER PRIDE FESTIVAL

PARENT ORGANIZATION: Vermont Pride Theater
WEBSITE: www.chandler-arts.org **EMAIL:** kenrives@gmail.com
PHONE: 802-728-6464 **ADDRESS:** 71-73 Main St, Randolph VT 05060
DESCRIPTION: Vermont Pride Theater at Chandler (VPT) requests submissions for its eighth annual Summer Pride Festival, July 20-22 and 27-29, 2018 in the historic Chandler Center for the Arts, Randolph (VT). We are seeking full-length scripts with strong LGBTQ content that present the issues and concerns of today's LGBTQ persons, especially those living in rural areas, in a positive way. Scripts should have

a mid-sized ensemble, preferably all adults. Staging in a community-theater setting should be feasible. Plays that have been previously produced or published are welcome and should be submitted with performance history. Scripts should be e-mailed to VPT producer Sharon Rives no later than January 1st. For more information about the festival or VPT, feel free to contact Ms. Rives.

DEADLINE: 01/01/2018 **DEADLINE TYPE:** Annual **GENRE:** Plays
PREFERRED LENGTH: Full-length **SPECIAL INTEREST:** LGBT+

SUMMER SHORTCUTS
PARENT ORGANIZATION: Open Eye Theater
WEBSITE: www.theopeneyetheater.org/summer-shortcuts.html
EMAIL: openeye@catskill.net **PHONE:** (845) 586-1660
ADDRESS: PO Box 959, 960 Main St, Margaretville NY 12455
DESCRIPTION: Est. 2010. Plays must be family friendly. We are especially interested in plays with good roles for young teens and/or senior adults. Please check back later for the 2018 submissions deadline.
GENRE: Plays **PREFERRED LENGTH:** 10-minute **SPECIAL INTEREST:** Senior; Theatre for Young Audiences **FEE:** No **AGENT ONLY:** No

SUMMER SHORTS
WEBSITE: www.citytheatre.com/summer-shorts **EMAIL:** susan@citytheatre.com
PHONE: (305) 755-9401 **FAX:** (305) 755-9404
ADDRESS: 444 Brickell Ave, #229, Miami FL 33131
GENRE: Plays **PREFERRED LENGTH:** 10-minute **FEE:** No **AGENT ONLY:** No

SUMMERFEST FESTIVAL
PARENT ORGANIZATION: New York Theater Festival
WEBSITE: www.newyorktheaterfestival.com/submissions-2018-summerfest-closed/ **EMAIL:** venustheaterfestival@gmail.com
ADDRESS: 441 West 26 Street, New York NY 10001
DESCRIPTION: Submission accepted from everywhere in the U.S. Shows from outside of NY and NJ can only run if the entire cast and crew are from New York City. Submissions must be between 10 and 90 minutes long. If your play is selected, you are give a 3 performance run. Cash prizes awarded.
GENRE: Plays **FEE:** Yes **AGENT ONLY:** No

THEATRE BRUT SHORT-PLAY FESTIVAL
PARENT ORGANIZATION: New Jersey Repertory Company
WEBSITE: www.njrep.org/plays/theatrebrut1.htm **EMAIL:** njrep@njrep.org
ADDRESS: 179 Broadway, Long Branch NJ 07740
DEADLINE: 05/30/2018 **DEADLINE TYPE:** Annual **GENRE:** Plays
PREFERRED LENGTH: 10-minute **FEE:** No **AGENT ONLY:** No

THEATRE THREE [NY] ONE-ACT PLAY FESTIVAL
PARENT ORGANIZATION: Theatre Three [NY]
WEBSITE: theatrethree.com/oaf.html **EMAIL:** Info@TheatreThree.com

PHONE: (631) 928-9202 **FAX:** (631) 928-9120 **ADDRESS:** Attn. Jeffrey Sanzel, Artistic Director, PO Box 512, Port Jefferson NY 11777

DESCRIPTION: Stipend: $125.00. Only UNPRODUCED works will be accepted. Plays that have had staged readings are eligible. No adaptations or children's plays.

Cast size maximum: 10. Length: 40-minutes maximum. No minimum. Settings should be simple or suggested. Playwrights may make multiple submissions. (These need not be made under separate cover.) Please do not submit works that have been previously submitted.

SUBMISSION MATERIALS: Full script, resume, cover letter, synopsis. If playwrights wish to have their works returned, an appropriate SASE must also be included.

DEADLINE TYPE: Annual **GENRE:** Plays **PREFERRED LENGTH:** 1-Act (under 1 hour) **FEE:** No **AGENT ONLY:** No

TINY STOREFRONT CONCERT SERIES

WEBSITE: www.underscoretheatre.org/underlings **EMAIL:** isaac.loomer@yahoo.com
ADDRESS: PO Box 408748, Chicago IL 60640

DESCRIPTION: Are you a brilliant musical theatre composer, writing the freshest new songs that the world needs to hear? Well you've come to the right place. We are the number one Chicago venue for promoting new composers of musical theatre.

SUBMISSION MATERIALS: Submit your sheet music and/or optional demo recordings to isaac.loomer@yahoo.com for consideration to be included in our quarterly concert series! Arrangements can be piano/vocal, lead sheets, or any combination of piano/drums/guitar.

DEADLINE TYPE: Rolling **GENRE:** Musicals **FEE:** No **AGENT ONLY:** No

TORONTO FRINGE FESTIVAL

WEBSITE: fringetoronto.com/year-round/artist-opportunities
EMAIL: general@fringetoronto.com **PHONE:** (416) 966-1062
FAX: (416) 966-5072 **ADDRESS:** 344 Bloor St, #208, Toronto ON M5S 3A7 Canada

DESCRIPTION: Toronto Fringe offers a variety of opportunities to connect your art with an audience including a New Play Contest and the Paul O'Sullivan Prize for Musical Theatre.

SUBMISSION MATERIALS: Fees, materials, and deadlines vary. Check website for updates & info.

DEADLINE TYPE: Annual **GENRE:** Plays or Musicals **PREFERRED LENGTH:** Full-length **FEE:** Yes **AGENT ONLY:** No

VANCOUVER FRINGE FESTIVAL

WEBSITE: www.vancouverfringe.com/for-artists **EMAIL:** info@vancouverfringe.com
PHONE: (604) 257-0350 **TWITTER:** @VancouverFringe
ADDRESS: #203 - 1398 Cartwright St, Vancouver BC V6H 3R9 Canada

SUBMISSION MATERIALS: Check website for updated submission information.

GENRE: Plays **PREFERRED LENGTH:** Any Length **FEE:** Yes **AGENT ONLY:** No

CONFERENCES & FESTIVALS 115

WARNER INTERNATIONAL PLAYWRIGHTS FESTIVAL
PARENT ORGANIZATION: Warner Theatre
WEBSITE: www.warnertheatre.org/6th-annual-international-playwright-festival.html
EMAIL: warnersubmissions@gmail.com **ADDRESS:** 68 Main St, Torrington CT 6790
DESCRIPTION: The Warner International Playwrights Festival recognizes the work of emerging and established playwrights from across the country and around the globe. The Festival gives playwrights a forum for production of their one-act plays that engage and entertain audiences through exploration of the human experience and the human spirit. **SUBMISSION MATERIALS:** Check website for updates.
GENRE: Plays **PREFERRED LENGTH:** 1-Act (under 1 hour) **FEE:** No **AGENT ONLY:** No

WILLIAMSTOWN THEATRE FESTIVAL
WEBSITE: www.wtfestival.org/work-learn/artistic **EMAIL:** submissions@wtfestival.org
PHONE: (212) 395-9090 **ADDRESS:** 229 W 42nd St, #801, New York NY 10036
GENRE: Plays **PREFERRED LENGTH:** Full-length **FEE:** No **AGENT ONLY:** Yes

WINTERFEST FESTIVAL
PARENT ORGANIZATION: New York Theater Festival
WEBSITE: www.newyorktheaterfestival.com/winterfest-festivals/how-to-submit-winterfest-theater-festival **EMAIL:** thespistheaterfestival@gmail.com

NOTES

CONFERENCES & FESTIVALS

ADDRESS: 441 W 26 St, New York NY 10001

DESCRIPTION: Submission accepted from everywhere in the U.S. Shows from outside of NY and NJ can only run if the entire cast and crew are from New York City. Submissions must be between 10 and 90 minutes long. If your play is selected, you are give a 3 performance run. Cash prizes awarded. **FEE:** Yes

WORDPLAY

PARENT ORGANIZATION: Bricolage Production Company
WEBSITE: www.bricolagepgh.org/programs/program-listings/wordplay-main
EMAIL: submissions@wordplayshow.com **PHONE:** (412) 471-0999
ADDRESS: Bricolage Production Company, 937 Liberty Ave., 1st Fl, Pittsburgh PA 15222
DESCRIPTION: WordPlay is a new spin on the age-old tradition of storytelling. WordPlay stories don't have a specific theme, but we love funny stories and poignant stories and all combinations thereof. However, we try to steer clear of the maudlin and overly sentimental. 1,500 to 2,000 words max.
GENRE: Plays **FEE:** No

WORDS CUBED

PARENT ORGANIZATION: Utah Shakespeare Festival
WEBSITE: www.bard.org/words-cubed-submission **EMAIL:** words3@bard.org
PHONE: (435) 586-7880 **TWITTER:** @UtahShakespeare
ADDRESS: 351 W Center St, Cedar City UT 84720
DESCRIPTION: As part of an ongoing commitment to create a diverse body of work, Words Cubed, a new play initiative at the Utah Shakespeare Festival, nurtures and develops openly-submitted and commissioned-based new plays by providing a professionally supported (i.e. funded) platform for readings, workshops, and fully realized productions.
SUBMISSION MATERIALS: Online submissions only. See website for details.
DEADLINE TYPE: Annual **GENRE:** Plays or Musicals
PREFERRED LENGTH: Full-length **FEE:** No **AGENT ONLY:** No

YOUNG PLAYWRIGHTS FESTIVAL

PARENT ORGANIZATION: Center Stage [MD]
WEBSITE: www.centerstage.org/education/young-playwrights-festival **EMAIL:** education@centerstage.org **PHONE:** (410) 986-4042 **ADDRESS:** Center Stage, 700 N. Calvert Street, Baltimore MD 21202
DESCRIPTION: Students in grades K-12 throughout the state of Maryland are eligible and may even get to see their play on stage. Numerous plays are honored each year with workshops, in-school performances, and even performances at Center Stage.
GENRE: Plays **PREFERRED LENGTH:** Any Length **FEE:** No **AGENT ONLY:** No

CONTESTS

8 TENS @ 8 FESTIVAL
WEBSITE: www.sccat.org **EMAIL:** sccactorstheatre@gmail.com
PHONE: (831) 335-4409
ADDRESS: Santa Cruz Actors' Theatre, PO Box 7084, Santa Cruz CA 95061
DESCRIPTION: Est. 1995. Submissions are accepted year-round, but must meet the summer deadline of July 1. Over the following six months, eight plays are anonymously selected by a panel of judges, then rehearsed for three months, before premiering in front of a sold-out audience. Please see website for updates.
DEADLINE: 07/01/2018 **GENRE:** Plays **LENGTH:** 10-minute **FEE:** Yes
AGENT ONLY: No

ALASKA NATIVE PLAYS COMPETITION
WEBSITE: theatre.uaa.alaska.edu **EMAIL:** afdpe@uaa.alaska.edu
PHONE: (907) 786-1792 **FAX:** (907) 786-1799
ADDRESS: Theatre & Dance Dept, 3211 Providence Dr, Anchorage AK 99508
DESCRIPTION: See website.

AMERICAN SCANDINAVIAN FOUNDATION TRANSLATION PRIZE
WEBSITE: www.amscan.org **EMAIL:** grants@amscan.org
PHONE: (212) 879-9779 **FAX:** (212) 686-2115
ADDRESS: 58 Park Ave, New York NY 10016
SUBMISSION MATERIALS: Please see website for updates.
LENGTH: Any Length **FEE:** No **AGENT ONLY:** No

AMERICAN TRANSLATORS ASSOCIATION (ATA) HONORS AND AWARDS
WEBSITE: www.atanet.org/aboutus/honorsandawards.php **EMAIL:** ata@atanet.org
PHONE: (703) 683-6100 **FAX:** (703) 683-6122
ADDRESS: American Translators, 225 Reinekers Ln, #590, Alexandria VA 22314
DESCRIPTION: ATA presents annual and biennial awards to encourage, reward, and publicize outstanding work done by both seasoned professionals and students of our craft. See website for different award opportunities.

ANNA ZORNIO MEMORIAL CHILDREN'S THEATRE PLAYWRITING AWARD
WEBSITE: cola.unh.edu/theatre-dance/program/anna-zornio-childrens-theatre-playwriting-award **EMAIL:** mike.wood@unh.edu
PHONE: (603) 862-3038 **FAX:** (603) 862-0298 **ADDRESS:** UNH Theatre/Dance Dept, PCAC, 30 Academic Way, Durham NH 3824
DESCRIPTION: Est. 1979. See website for details. **GENRE:** Plays or Musicals
LENGTH: Full-length **SPECIAL INTEREST:** TYA **FEE:** No **AGENT ONLY:** No

ANNUAL BLANK THEATRE COMPANY YOUNG PLAYWRIGHTS FESTIVAL

WEBSITE: www.youngplaywrights.com **EMAIL:** info@theblank.com
PHONE: (323) 662-7734 **ADDRESS:** 1301 Lusicle Ave, Los Angeles CA 90026
DESCRIPTION: See website. Submissions open January 2018.

ARTHUR W. STONE NEW PLAY AWARD

WEBSITE: performingarts.latech.edu **EMAIL:** stoneplaywritingaward@yahoo.com
PHONE: (318) 257-2711 **FAX:** (318) 257-4571
ADDRESS: Louisiana Tech University, Box 8608, Ruston LA 71272
SUBMISSION MATERIALS: Email (DOC, FDR, RTF formats) 9/11 themed work only. Submit author bio and production history.
GENRE: Plays or Musicals **LENGTH:** Full-length **FEE:** No

ARTS & LETTERS PRIZE IN DRAMA

WEBSITE: artsandletters.gcsu.edu **EMAIL:** al.journal@gcsu.edu
PHONE: (478) 445-1289
ADDRESS: Georgia College, GCSU Campus Box 89, Milledgeville GA 31061
SUBMISSION MATERIALS: Separate cover sheet with playwright information
GENRE: Plays **LENGTH:** 1-Act (under 1 hour) **FEE:** Yes **AGENT ONLY:** No

ATHE AWARD FOR EXCELLENCE IN PLAYWRITING

WEBSITE: www.athe.org/?page=Playwriting **EMAIL:** cdonaghy@unomaha.edu
ADDRESS: PO Box 1290, Boulder CO 80306 **DEADLINE:** 02/15/2018
GENRE: Plays **LENGTH:** Full-length **FEE:** No

ATHE AWARDS

WEBSITE: www.athe.org/?page=Awards **EMAIL:** vpawards@athe.org
PHONE: 1 (800) 918-9216 **FAX:** 1 (800) 809-6374
ADDRESS: 1000 Westgate Dr, Ste 252, St Paul MN 55114
DESCRIPTION: See website. **DEADLINE:** 02/18/2018

AUGUST WILSON NEW PLAY INITIATIVE

PARENT ORGANIZATION: Congo Square Theatre Company
WEBSITE: www.congosquaretheatre.org **EMAIL:** literary@congosquaretheatre.org
PHONE: (773) 296-1108
ADDRESS: Congo Square Theatre, 4434 S Lake Park Ave, Chicago IL 60653
DESCRIPTION: Congo Square is interested in full-length plays, translations, adaptations, musicals and performance art. We request plays with no previous production history. Congo Square will only consider independent submissions to The August Wilson New Play Initiative.
SUBMISSION MATERIALS: Synopsis, cast list, SASE, relevant production info/readings/history/playwright resume, full copy of script as a Word document or PDF. Electronic submissions preferred. See website for details.
DEADLINE: 11/15/2017 **DEADLINE TYPE:** Annual **GENRE:** Plays

LENGTH: Full-length **FEE:** Yes **AGENT ONLY:** No

AURAND HARRIS MEMORIAL PLAYWRITING AWARD
PARENT ORGANIZATION: New England Theatre Conference (NETC)
WEBSITE: www.netconline.org/aurand-harris-award.php
EMAIL: mail@netconline.org **PHONE:** (617) 851-8535 **FAX:** (203) 288-5938
ADDRESS: NETC, 167 Cherry St #331, Milford CT 06460
DESCRIPTION: Est. 1997. A panel of judges named by the NETC Executive Board will administer this award. Two cash prizes will be awarded: First Prize of $1000, and Second Prize of $500. The judges may withhold prizes if in their opinion no play merits the award. A staged reading of the prize-winning scripts may be given, followed by critique and discussion.
SUBMISSION MATERIALS: See website for details. **DEADLINE TYPE:** Annual
GENRE: Plays **LENGTH:** Full-length

BABES WITH BLADES - JOINING SWORD AND PEN
WEBSITE: babeswithblades.org/jsp-17-18-submission
EMAIL: swordandpen@babeswithblades.org **TWITTER:** @BabesWithBlades
ADDRESS: Babes With Blades, 7016 N Greenview #2, Chicago IL 60626
DESCRIPTION: The winner receives the Margaret W. Martin Award: the play undergoes development via BWBTC's Fighting Words program prior to premiering as part of an upcoming BWBTC season, and the playwright receives a $1,000 cash prize. See website.
GENRE: Plays **LENGTH:** Full-length **SPECIAL INTEREST:** Feminism/Women's Rights
FEE: No **AGENT ONLY:** No

BEVERLY HILLS CALIFORNIA MUSICAL THEATRE AWARD
PARENT ORGANIZATION: Beverly Hills Theatre Guild
WEBSITE: www.beverlyhillstheatreguild.org **PHONE:** (310) 273-3390
ADDRESS: Beverly Hills Theatre Guild, Box 148, Beverly Hills CA 90213
DESCRIPTION: See website for details. **GENRE:** Musicals

BIENNIAL PROMISING PLAYWRIGHT AWARD
WEBSITE: www.cplayers.com **EMAIL:** info@thecolonialplayers.org
PHONE: (410) 268-7373 **ADDRESS:** 108 E St, Annapolis MD 21401
DESCRIPTION: See website for details. **SUBMISSION MATERIALS:** Application, 2-pg synopsis, 10-pg sample, full script, SASE **GENRE:** Plays

CALIFORNIA YOUNG PLAYWRIGHTS CONTEST
PARENT ORGANIZATION: Playwrights Project
WEBSITE: www.playwrightsproject.org/programs/contest
EMAIL: write@playwrightsproject.com **PHONE:** (858) 384-2970
TWITTER: @PlaywrightsProj
ADDRESS: Playwrights Project, 2356 Moore St #204, San Diego CA 92110
DESCRIPTION: Est. 1984. Winners receive a production. This is an educational pro-

gram focused on the development of new plays - so if you're a winner, be prepared to revise your script with the support of a dramaturg, a director, and actors. Open to Californians under the age of 19 as of June 1, 2018.

SUBMISSION MATERIALS: See website. **DEADLINE:** 06/01/2018 **GENRE:** Plays

CANADIAN JEWISH PLAYWRITING COMPETITION

PARENT ORGANIZATION: The Miles Nadal Jewish Community Centre (MNjcc)
WEBSITE: mnjcc.org/browse-by-interest/arts-culture/theatre/theatre-development/346-the-canadian-jewish-playwriting-competition **EMAIL:** esthera@mnjcc.org **PHONE:** (416) 924-6211 **TWITTER:** @MilesNadalJCC
ADDRESS: Miles Nadal JCC, 750 Spadina Ave, Toronto ON M5R-3B2 Canada
DESCRIPTION: The Canadian Jewish Playwriting Competition runs bi-annually as a program of the Miles Nadal Jewish Community Centre in downtown Toronto. Playwrights need not be Jewish but the content needs to speak of a specifically Jewish experience. Playwrights must be Canadian or have a very strong Canadian connection.
SUBMISSION MATERIALS: See website. **DEADLINE TYPE:** Biennial **GENRE:** Plays
LENGTH: Full-length **SPECIAL INTEREST:** Jewish

CHARLES M. GETCHELL AWARD

WEBSITE: www.setc.org/scholarships-awards/getchell-new-play-contest
EMAIL: info@setc.org **PHONE:** (336) 272-3645 **FAX:** (336) 272-8810
ADDRESS: 1175 Revolution Mill Dr, Studio 14, Greensboro NC 27405
DESCRIPTION: One winner will receive a $1,000 cash award during the banquet gala and an all-expense paid trip to SETC, where both a critique and staged reading of the winning play will be held. The winning play will also be considered for publication in Southern Theatre magazine.
SUBMISSION MATERIALS: See website. **DEADLINE:** 07/01/2018 **GENRE:** Plays
LENGTH: Any Length **FEE:** Yes **AGENT ONLY:** No

CITY THEATRE NATIONAL AWARD FOR SHORT PLAYWRITING CONTEST

PARENT ORGANIZATION: City Theatre [FL]
WEBSITE: www.citytheatre.com **EMAIL:** susan@citytheatre.com
PHONE: (305) 755-9401 **ADDRESS:** 444 Brickell Ave, #229, Miami FL 33131
DESCRIPTION: See website for updates. Our mission is to identify, acknowledge and award excellence in short form dramatic writing. City Theatre will select up to twenty-five plays from among its annual Contest submissions for special recognition. Plays will be accepted yearly from August 30th-September 30th.
DEADLINE: 09/30/2018 **GENRE:** Plays **LENGTH:** 10-minute **FEE:** No **AGENT ONLY:** No

CLAUDER COMPETITION FOR NEW ENGLAND PLAYWRIGHTS

WEBSITE: www.portlandstage.org **EMAIL:** clauder@portlandstage.org
PHONE: (207) 774-1043 **FAX:** (207) 774-0576
ADDRESS: Portland Stage, Attn: Lit Manager, PO Box 1458, Portland ME 04104
DESCRIPTION: See website. **SUBMISSION MATERIALS:** Full script.

DEADLINE: 03/01/2018 **GENRE:** Plays **LENGTH:** Full-length **FEE:** No **AGENT ONLY:** No

CTAM PLAYWRITING CONTEST
PARENT ORGANIZATION: Community Theatre Association of Michigan
WEBSITE: communitytheatremichigan.org/index.php/playwriting-contest
PHONE: (231) 354-7291 **ADDRESS:** 5951 N Skeel Ave, #420, Oscoda MI 48750
DESCRIPTION: To encourage playwriting and promote Michigan playwrights and to encourage the production of new plays by community theatres, CTAM holds an annual Playwriting Contest. Author must be a Michigan resident. See website.
DEADLINE TYPE: Annual **GENRE:** Plays **LENGTH:** Full-length **FEE:** Yes **AGENT ONLY:** No

CUNNINGHAM COMMISSION FOR YOUTH THEATRE
WEBSITE: theatre.depaul.edu **EMAIL:** aables@depaul.edu
PHONE: (773) 325-7938 **FAX:** (773) 325-7920
ADDRESS: Depaul University, 2135 N Kenmore Ave, Chicago IL 60614
DESCRIPTION: See website.

DARREL AYERS TYA PLAYWRITING AWARD
WEBSITE: www.KCACTF.org **EMAIL:** ghenry@kennedy-center.org
PHONE: (202) 416-8857 **ADDRESS:** Kennedy Center, Washington DC 20566
DESCRIPTION: See website.
GENRE: Plays **LENGTH:** Any Length **SPECIAL INTEREST:** TYA **FEE:** Yes

DAVID CALICCHIO EMERGING AMERICAN PLAYWRIGHT PRIZE
PARENT ORGANIZATION: Marin Theatre Company
WEBSITE: www.marintheatre.org/productions/new-plays-program/new-play-awards
EMAIL: literarymanager@marintheatre.org **PHONE:** (415) 388-5200
FAX: (415) 388-1217 **ADDRESS:** 397 Miller Ave, Mill Valley CA 94941
DESCRIPTION: Est. 2007. Winning play receives 2 public staged readings at MTC as part of the theatre's annual New Play Reading Series. The playwright will receive a $2,500 award, as well as travel and accommodations for the rehearsal period.
GENRE: Plays **LENGTH:** Full-length **FEE:** No

DAVID MARK COHEN PLAYWRITING AWARD
WEBSITE: www.kcactf.org/kanin-playwriting/cohen.html
EMAIL: ghenry@kennedy-center.org **PHONE:** (202) 416-8857
FAX: (202) 416-8802 **ADDRESS:** Kennedy Center, Washington DC 20566
GENRE: Plays **FEE:** Yes **AGENT ONLY:** No

DIONYSIA NEW PLAY COMPETITION
PARENT ORGANIZATION: Khaos Company Theatre

WEBSITE: www.kctindy.com/2018-dionysia-compeition-submission-form.html
EMAIL: KCTIndy@outlook.com **ADDRESS:** Khaos Company Theatre, 1775 N Sherman Dr, Ste A, Indianapolis IN 46218
DESCRIPTION: See website.
SUBMISSION MATERIALS: Submission form online.
DEADLINE: 02/01/2018 **DEADLINE TYPE:** Annual **GENRE:** Plays
LENGTH: Full-length **FEE:** No

DOWN FOR #THECOUNT
PARENT ORGANIZATION: Bishop Arts Theatre Center
WEBSITE: bishopartstheatre.org/events/thecount-one-act-play-festival
EMAIL: teresa@bishopartstheatre.org **PHONE:** (214) 948-0716
ADDRESS: Bishop Arts Theatre Center, 215 S Tyler St, Dallas TX 75208
DESCRIPTION: Down For #TheCount seeks to level the playing field and give a platform to more female voices in American theatre. Guild members are given preferential consideration, otherwise Down For #TheCount entries are accepted by invitation only. See website.
DEADLINE: see website **DEADLINE TYPE:** Annual **GENRE:** Plays
LENGTH: 1-Act (under 1 hour) **SPECIAL INTEREST:** Feminism/Women's Rights **FEE:** No **AGENT ONLY:** No

DR. FLOYD GAFFNEY PLAYWRITING COMPETITION
PARENT ORGANIZATION: University of California (San Diego)
WEBSITE: theatre.ucsd.edu/playwritingcontest **EMAIL:** ahavis@ucsd.edu
PHONE: (858) 534-3791 **FAX:** (858) 534-8931
ADDRESS: 9500 Gilman Dr, MC0509, La Jolla CA 92093
DESCRIPTION: Est. 2006. The UC San Diego's Department of Theatre and Dance seeks from all enrolled undergraduate students submissions of previously unproduced, unpublished scripts highlighting the African-American experience in contemporary or historical terms. Adaptations from books and other forms are not allowed. A $1000 honorarium and a staged reading of the winning script plus travel and housing cost to and from UC San Diego to be present for the performance.
SUBMISSION MATERIALS: See website for info.
DEADLINE: 04/13/2018 **DEADLINE TYPE:** Annual **LENGTH:** Full-length
SPECIAL INTEREST: Black or African American **FEE:** No **AGENT ONLY:** No

ESSENTIAL THEATRE PLAYWRITING AWARD
PARENT ORGANIZATION: Essential Theatre
WEBSITE: www.essentialtheatre.com/playwriting-competition
EMAIL: pmhardy@aol.com **PHONE:** (404) 212-0815 **TWITTER:** @ATL_Essential
ADDRESS: 1414 Foxhall Ln, #10, Atlanta GA 30316
DESCRIPTION: The annual Essential Theatre Playwriting Award is for unproduced plays by current Georgia residents only. See website for details.

SUBMISSION MATERIALS: Full script (email or post.)
DEADLINE: 04/23/2018   **DEADLINE TYPE:** Annual   **GENRE:** Plays
LENGTH: Full-length   **FEE:** No   **AGENT ONLY:** No

EST/ALFRED P. SLOAN FOUNDATION SCIENCE & TECHNOLOGY PROJECT

PARENT ORGANIZATION: Ensemble Studio Theater (EST)
WEBSITE: www.ensemblestudiotheatre.org/est-sloan/submissions
EMAIL: literary@ensemblestudiotheatre.org   **PHONE:** (212) 247-4982
TWITTER: @ESTnyc   **ADDRESS:** 549 W 52nd St, New York NY 10019
DESCRIPTION: The EST/Sloan Project commissions, develops and presents new works delving into how we view and are affected by the scientific world. These plays examine the struggles and challenges scientists and engineers face from moral issues to the consequences of their discoveries. See website.
FEE: No   **AGENT ONLY:** No

FOUNDERS' AWARD FOR EMERGING PLAYWRIGHTS

PARENT ORGANIZATION: New York Stage and Film (NYSAF)
WEBSITE: www.newyorkstageandfilm.org/fellowships-residencies
EMAIL: info@newyorkstageandfilm.org   **PHONE:** 212-736-4240
ADDRESS: 214 W 29th St, Ste 1001, New York NY 10001
DESCRIPTION: The Founders' Award Recipient receives a one-month residency during the Powerhouse Theater Season, where they work with the rich community of artists, and New York Stage and Film's artistic staff. They receive a professional reading of their latest play at the end of the residency, and a monetary award.
GENRE: Plays   **LENGTH:** Full-length

FRANCESCA PRIMUS PRIZE

WEBSITE: americantheatrecritics.org/primus-prize
EMAIL: operations@americantheatrecritics.org   **PHONE:** (602) 956-2310
ADDRESS: American Theater Critics, 773 Nebraska Ave W, St Paul MN 55117
DESCRIPTION: The Francesca Primus Prize is an annual $10,000 award honoring outstanding contributions to the American theater by an emerging female playwright, one who has not yet achieved national prominence. The Primus Prize operates on an open submission basis—an applicant may submit herself or be nominated by another individual or organization. See website.
SUBMISSION MATERIALS: Submit portfolio of no more than 20 single-sided pages. Please include letter of recommendation, synopsis of body of work, and supporting materials sufficient to familiarize the committee with her achievement, possibly including reviews and/or a statement of the artist's philosophy. In addition (beyond those 20 pages), playwrights should also submit the produced script.
DEADLINE TYPE: Annual   **GENRE:** Plays   **FEE:** Yes   **AGENT ONLY:** No

FRED EBB AWARD

WEBSITE: fredebbfoundation.org/fred-ebb-award
EMAIL: fredebbfound@gmail.com
ADDRESS: Roundabout Theatre, 231 W 39th St, #1200, New York NY 10018

DESCRIPTION: Est. 2005. Each applicant must be a composer/lyricist or composer/lyricist team wishing to create work for the musical theatre, and must not yet have achieved significant commercial success. The winner will be selected in November, and will receive $60,000. The Foundation will also produce a one-night showcase of the winner's work.

SUBMISSION MATERIALS: CD of up to four songs from one or more musical theatre pieces with typewritten lyrics and a description of the dramatic context for each song; completed application form. See website for details and application.

DEADLINE TYPE: Annual **GENRE:** Musicals **LENGTH:** Full-length **AGENT ONLY:** No

FREMONT CENTRE THEATRE NEW PLAYWRIGHT CONTEST

WEBSITE: www.fremontcentretheatre.com
EMAIL: fct@fremontcentretheatre.com **PHONE:** (626) 441-5977
FAX: (626) 441-5976 **ADDRESS:** 1000 Fremont Ave, South Pasadena CA 91030
DEADLINE TYPE: Annual

GARY GARRISON NATIONAL TEN-MINUTE PLAY AWARD

PARENT ORGANIZATION: KC/ACTF
WEBSITE: www.kcactf.org **EMAIL:** ghenry@kennedy-center.org
PHONE: (202) 416-8864 **FAX:** (202) 416-8860
ADDRESS: Kennedy Center, Washington DC 20566
DESCRIPTION: See website.
SUBMISSION MATERIALS: Plays accepted only from college/university participating in KC/ACTF program. A regional selection process precedes the national award.
GENRE: Plays **LENGTH:** 10-minute **FEE:** Yes **AGENT ONLY:** No

GEORGE R. KERNODLE NEW PLAY AWARD

WEBSITE: fulbright.uark.edu/departments/theatre/callboard/kernodle-new-play-award.php **EMAIL:** rdgross@uark.edu **PHONE:** (479) 575-2953
FAX: (479) 575-7602 **ADDRESS:** 619 Kimpel Hall, Fayetteville AR 72701
DESCRIPTION: The University of Arkansas Department of Theatre administers the Kernodle New Play Award, a national playwriting competition named for George R. Kernodle, beloved U of A theatre professor and author of "Invitation to the Theatre". The award recognizes full-length plays that invite the audience's imagination and are inherently theatrical.
SUBMISSION MATERIALS: See website for submission details..
DEADLINE: 12/16/2017 **GENRE:** Plays **LENGTH:** Full-length **FEE:** No **AGENT ONLY:** No

GRAWEMEYER AWARD FOR MUSIC COMPOSITION

WEBSITE: www.grawemeyer.org/music **EMAIL:** charlie.leonard@louisville.edu
PHONE: (502) 852-1787 **ADDRESS:** Univ of Louisville School of Music, Louisville KY 40292
DESCRIPTION: Musical works including, but not limited to, choral, orchestral,

chamber, song-cycle, dance, opera, musical theater, extended solo. Accompanied by a prize of $100,000, which is presented in full during the awards ceremony. See website for details.

DEADLINE TYPE: Annual **GENRE:** Musicals **LENGTH:** Any Length
FEE: Yes **AGENT ONLY:** No

HAROLD & MIMI STEINBERG NATIONAL STUDENT PLAYWRITING AWARD

WEBSITE: www.kcactf.org **EMAIL:** ghenry@kennedy-center.org
PHONE: (202) 416-8864 **FAX:** (202) 416-8860
ADDRESS: Kennedy Center for the Performing Arts, Washington DC 20566
DESCRIPTION: For the outstanding student-written, full-length play premiering at a college or university participating in KCACTF program.
GENRE: Plays **LENGTH:** Full-length **FEE:** Yes **AGENT ONLY:** No

HAROLD MORTON LANDON TRANSLATION AWARD

WEBSITE: www.poets.org/academy-american-poets/american-poets-prizes
EMAIL: academy@poets.org **PHONE:** (212) 274-0343 **FAX:** (212) 274-9427
TWITTER: @POETSorg **ADDRESS:** 75 Maiden Ln, #901, New York NY 10038
DESCRIPTION: The translation prize is to honor a book of poems that has been translated into English. See full guidelines online.
DEADLINE: 02/15/2018

HENLEY ROSE PLAYWRIGHT COMPETITION FOR WOMEN

WEBSITE: yellowroseproductions.org/henleyrose **EMAIL:** henleyrosecompetition@gmail.com **PHONE:** (423) 773-5044 **TWITTER:** @yellowrosepro
ADDRESS: 810 Vista Oaks Ln, Knoxville Tennessee 37919
DESCRIPTION: The Henley Rose Playwright Competition for Women was founded by Yellow Rose Productions, with permission of Beth Henley, to encourage and recognize the new works of female playwrights. The Henley Rose Playwright Competition for Women aims to give voice to the stories of this generation and to bring into the spotlight important works that have been crafted. See website for details.
DEADLINE TYPE: Annual **GENRE:** Plays **LENGTH:** Any Length
SPECIAL INTEREST: Feminism/Women's Rights **FEE:** Waived for DG Members
AGENT ONLY: No

IHT/SRT INTERNATIONAL PLAYWRITING COMPETITION

WEBSITE: www.srt.com.sg **EMAIL:** office@srt.com.sg
PHONE: (656) 221-5585 **FAX:** (656) 221-1936
ADDRESS: DBS Arts Centre, 20 Merbau Rd, Singapore 239035 Singapore

INKSLINGER PLAYWRITING COMPETITION

WEBSITE: www.southeastern.edu/acad_research/programs/theatre/competition

EMAIL: Chad.Winters@southeastern.edu **PHONE:** (985) 549-2115
ADDRESS: Southeastern Louisiana University, Fine and Performing Arts Dept, Hammond LA 70402
DESCRIPTION: Southeastern Theatre is seeking original, unpublished, full-length plays geared for a university cast and audience. The winner will receive a full production in a 455-seat theatre, transportation to and from Hammond, Louisiana to attend the production, and up to two nights housing while attending the play. All submissions must be original and unpublished. Play should be intended for a college-aged cast and audience. **SUBMISSION MATERIALS:** See website for updates and details.
DEADLINE TYPE: Annual **GENRE:** Plays **LENGTH:** Full-length **FEE:** Yes **AGENT ONLY:** No

INSPIRATO PLAYWRITING CONTEST

PARENT ORGANIZATION: Theatre InspiraTO
WEBSITE: www.theatreinspirato.ca/submit-a-play
EMAIL: inspirato@ca.inter.net **PHONE:** (416) 483-2222
DESCRIPTION: Online submissions only. See website. The play must be a ten-minute play. The theme "all about her" must be an integral part of the play. The story can be a comedy, a drama, a parody, absurd or anything in between (in English only). We also accept musicals. The contest is open to anyone, in any part of the world, without geographic or age restrictions.
SUBMISSION MATERIALS: You may only submit one play. The cover page should have the title of the play, the playwright's name and the list of characters. The pages should be numbered. The format should be easy to read. We accept previously produced plays (but not plays that have produced at InspiraTO before). The playwright must own the rights to the play up to June 17, 2018 (i.e. the script cannot be owned by a publisher). We are particularly interested in scripts that aren't afraid to make bold choices: quality writing backed by imaginative staging.
DEADLINE: 11/20/2017 **DEADLINE TYPE:** Annual **GENRE:** Plays **LENGTH:** 10-minute **FEE:** No **AGENT ONLY:** No

INTERACT THEATRE NEW PLAY DEVELOPMENT AWARD

PARENT ORGANIZATION: InterAct Theatre Company [PA]
WEBSITE: www.interacttheatre.org/interact-new-play-development-award/
EMAIL: submissions@InterActTheatre.org **PHONE:** 215-568-8079
DESCRIPTION: In tandem with our 30th anniversary, InterAct Theatre Company in Center City Philadelphia is inaugurating a New Play Development Award this year. We are seeking promising plays that can benefit from additional development, and which have the potential to be premiered by InterAct in a future season. The play selected for this award will receive a multi-day developmental workshop at InterAct, along with a $1,000 cash award for the playwright.
DEADLINE TYPE: Annual **GENRE:** Plays **LENGTH:** Full-length **FEE:** No **AGENT ONLY:** No

INTERNATIONAL MUT COMPETITION FOR MUSICAL ENTERTAINMENT THEATRE

WEBSITE: www.gaertnerplatztheater.de **EMAIL:** mut@gaertnerplatztheater.de

ADDRESS: Gaertnerplatz 3, Munich, Bavaria 80469, Germany
DESCRIPTION: Creative composers, lyricists, and authors with an affinity for musical entertainment theatre are invited to develop dramatic concepts and apply. An international jury of artistic directors, dramaturgy experts, and publishers from the German and international music theatre scene, will select, without knowing who the writers are, a total of six concepts which will be presented to an audience at the final presentation at July 28, 2018 in the Gärtnerplatztheater. The winner gets €5,000, there's also an audience prize (€1,000) and a media prize (€1,000). See website.
DEADLINE TYPE: Annual **GENRE:** Musicals **LENGTH:** Full-length
FEE: No **AGENT ONLY:** No

JACKIE WHITE MEMORIAL CHILDREN'S PLAYWRITING CONTEST
WEBSITE: www.cectheatre.org/playwriting.html **EMAIL:** jwm@cectheatre.org
PHONE: (573) 874-5628 **ADDRESS:** 1400 Forum Blvd IC #214, Columbia MO 65203
DESCRIPTION: Est. 1988. In memory of Jackie Pettit White (1947-1991). This contest seeks to encourage playwrights to write quality plays for family audiences. Originally intended to find plays suitable for Theatre School production, the winning entries are produced for CEC's Summer Family Theatre Program, using actors of all ages. See website.
DEADLINE: 12/31/2017 **DEADLINE TYPE:** Annual **GENRE:** Plays **LENGTH:** Full-length **SPECIAL INTEREST:** TYA **FEE:** Yes **AGENT ONLY:** No

JANE CHAMBERS PLAYWRITING AWARD
PARENT ORGANIZATION: Association for Theatre in Higher Education (ATHE)
WEBSITE: www.athe.org/?page=Jane_Chambers **EMAIL:** jenscottmob@gmail.com
PHONE: (800) 918-9216 **ADDRESS:** East Carolina Univ, School of Theatre & Dance, Greenville NC 27858
DESCRIPTION: The Jane Chambers Playwriting Award recognizes plays and performance texts created by women that present a feminist perspective and contain significant opportunities for female performers. See website for details.
DEADLINE: 02/15/2018 **GENRE:** Plays
SPECIAL INTEREST: Feminism/Women's Rights **FEE:** No **AGENT ONLY:** No

JEAN KENNEDY SMITH PLAYWRITING AWARD
PARENT ORGANIZATION: KC/ACTF
WEBSITE: www.kcactf.org **EMAIL:** ghenry@kennedy-center.org
PHONE: (202) 416-8864 **FAX:** (202) 416-8860
ADDRESS: Kennedy Center, Education Div, Washington DC 20566
DESCRIPTION: Award for a student-written play addressing issues of disability (as defined by the ADA). Plays accepted only from college/university participating in KC/ACTF program.
GENRE: Plays **LENGTH:** Any Length **SPECIAL INTEREST:** Living with Disability **FEE:** Yes **AGENT ONLY:** No

JEWEL BOX THEATRE PLAYWRITING COMPETITION

WEBSITE: www.jewelboxtheatre.org/conteest **EMAIL:** jbtnewsletter@jewelboxtheatre.org **PHONE:** (405) 521-1786 **FAX:** (405) 525-6562
ADDRESS: 3700 N Walker Ave, Oklahoma City OK 73118
DESCRIPTION: Scripts will be accepted October 2, 2017 through January 19, 2018. The first 150 scripts will be accepted. The winner will be announced in April 2018, with a cash award of $750. In addition, the season selection committee will consider the play for full production in the 2019-2020 season. Plays should be of a strong ensemble nature with emphasis on character rather than spectacle. There is no censorship of subject matter for the competition.
DEADLINE: 01/19/2018 **GENRE:** Plays **FEE:** Yes **AGENT ONLY:** No

JOHN CAUBLE AWARD FOR OUTSTANDING SHORT PLAY

WEBSITE: www.kcactf.org **EMAIL:** ghenry@kennedy-center.org
PHONE: (202) 416-8864 **ADDRESS:** Kennedy Center, Washington DC 20566
GENRE: Plays **LENGTH:** 1-Act (under 1 hour) **FEE:** Yes **AGENT ONLY:** No

JOHN GASSNER MEMORIAL PLAYWRITING AWARD

PARENT ORGANIZATION: New England Theatre Conference (NETC)
WEBSITE: www.netconline.org/john-gassner-award.php
EMAIL: mail@NETConline.org **PHONE:** (617) 851-8535 **FAX:** (203) 288-5938
ADDRESS: NETC, 167 Cherry St #331, Milford CT 06460
DESCRIPTION: Fosters new playwrights and scripts through this important competition established by Molly Gassner, wife of theatre historian John Gassner. The winning script will be given a staged reading at the New England Theatre Conference Annual Convention in October.
SUBMISSION MATERIALS: Plays submitted to the competition must not have been published as of April 15, 2017, and must not have been produced by a professional or Equity company. See website for details.
GENRE: Plays **LENGTH:** Full-length **FEE:** No **AGENT ONLY:** No

JULIE HARRIS PLAYWRIGHT AWARDS

PARENT ORGANIZATION: Beverly Hills Theatre Guild
WEBSITE: www.beverlyhillstheatreguild.com **PHONE:** (310) 273-3390
ADDRESS: PO Box 148, Beverly Hills CA 90213
DESCRIPTION: This is a national competition to discover and to encourage American dramatists and was established by Neil Simon in 1977 to foster the development of quality plays for the theater. The competition was renamed in 1985 to honor Julie Harris in appreciation of her continuing encouragement to playwrights.
DEADLINE: 04/01/2018 **GENRE:** Plays **LENGTH:** Full-length
FEE: Yes **AGENT ONLY:** No

KENTUCKY WOMEN WRITERS CONFERENCE PLAYWRITING PRIZE

WEBSITE: womenwriters.as.uky.edu/playwriting-prize
EMAIL: kentuckywomenwriters@gmail.com **PHONE:** (859) 257-2874

ADDRESS: 232 E Maxwell St, Lexington KY 40503

DESCRIPTION: Submissions allowed from women playwrights residing anywhere in the world. The winner receives a world premiere production for a paying audience, with royalties, plus a cash prize of $500. See website for details.

DEADLINE TYPE: Biennial **GENRE:** Plays **SPECIAL INTEREST:** Feminism/Women's Rights **FEE:** No

KUMU KAHUA THEATRE/UHM THEATRE DEPARTMENT PLAYWRITING CONTEST

PARENT ORGANIZATION: Kumu Kahua Theatre
WEBSITE: www.kumukahua.org/contests-writing **EMAIL:** kumukahuatheatre@gmail.com **PHONE:** (808) 536-4222 **FAX:** (808) 536-4226
ADDRESS: 46 Merchant St, Honolulu HI 96813
DESCRIPTION: The playwriting contest is offered in three separate categories. One prize will be offered in each category. All plays must be original and not involve adaptation form any copyrighted source. They should not have received previous production in their current form. See website for details.
SUBMISSION MATERIALS: See website for details. **DEADLINE:** 01/04/2018
DEADLINE TYPE: Annual **GENRE:** Plays **LENGTH:** Full-length

L. ARNOLD WEISSBERGER AWARD

PARENT ORGANIZATION: Williamstown Theatre Festival
WEBSITE: www.wtfestival.org **EMAIL:** wtfinfo@wtfestival.org
PHONE: (413) 458-3200 **FAX:** (413) 458-3147
ADDRESS: PO Box 428, Williamstown MA 1267
DESCRIPTION: See website. **GENRE:** Plays

LATINO/LATINA PLAYWRITING AWARD

PARENT ORGANIZATION: KC/ACTF
WEBSITE: www.kcactf.org **EMAIL:** ghenry@kennedy-center.org
PHONE: (202) 416-8857 **ADDRESS:** Kennedy Center, Washington DC 20566
DESCRIPTION: See website. **GENRE:** Plays **LENGTH:** Full-length
SPECIAL INTEREST: Hispanic or Latinx **FEE:** Yes **AGENT ONLY:** No

LEAH RYAN'S FEWW PLAYWRITING PRIZE

PARENT ORGANIZATION: Leah Ryan's Fund for Emerging Women Writers
WEBSITE: www.leahryansfeww.com/apply.html
EMAIL: leahryansfeww@gmail.com **TWITTER:** @LeahRyanFEWW
DESCRIPTION: Leah Ryan's Fund for Emerging Women Writers (FEWW) and its annual prize were established in 2010 to honor the memory of Leah Ryan, and to encourage and support the work of women writers. It is the purpose of the prize to perpetuate the integrity, compassion and creativity that Leah herself possessed and inspired in others. Winner receives a cash prize of $2,500, a workshop at the Vassar Powerhouse Theater, and a reading of her play in New York City.
SUBMISSION MATERIALS: Online application only. See website for details.
DEADLINE: 01/08/2018 **DEADLINE TYPE:** Annual **GENRE:** Plays
LENGTH: Any Length **FEE:** Yes **AGENT ONLY:** No

LORRAINE HANSBERRY PLAYWRITING AWARD

PARENT ORGANIZATION: KC/ACTF
WEBSITE: www.kcactf.org **EMAIL:** ghenry@kennedy-center.org
PHONE: (202) 416-8864 **FAX:** (202) 416-8860
ADDRESS: Kennedy Center, Washington DC 20566
DESCRIPTION: For the outstanding play written by a student of African or Diasporan heritage. Plays accepted only from college/university participating in KC/ACTF program.
SUBMISSION MATERIALS: See website.
GENRE: Plays **LENGTH:** Any Length **SPECIAL INTEREST:** Black or African American
FEE: Yes **AGENT ONLY:** No

LUCKY SHORTS

WEBSITE: luckypennynapa.com **EMAIL:** info@luckypennynapa.com
PHONE: (707) 738-2920
ADDRESS: Lucky Penny Productions, 1357 Foster Road, Napa CA 94558
DESCRIPTION: Stories must relate to the theme of change/growth in the broadest sense. Humor is always welcome. Writers must reside in Napa, Sonoma, or Solano Counties. **GENRE:** Plays **LENGTH:** 10-minute **FEE:** No **AGENT ONLY:** No

MARIO FRATTI & FRED NEWMAN POLITICAL PLAY CONTEST

PARENT ORGANIZATION: Castillo Theatre
WEBSITE: www.castillo.org/playwriting-contest **EMAIL:** mchapman@allstars.org
PHONE: (212) 356-8485 **ADDRESS:** 543 W 42nd St, New York NY 10036
DESCRIPTION: The Castillo Theatre sponsors the Mario Fratti-Fred Newman Political Play Contest and reading series bi-annually. The contest is intended to encourage the writing of progressive plays that engage the political/social/cultural questions affecting the world today and/or historical events and issues that impact on our communities. See website for details.
DEADLINE: 07/01/2018 **GENRE:** Plays **LENGTH:** Any Length
FEE: No **AGENT ONLY:** No

MARK TWAIN PRIZE FOR COMIC PLAYWRITING

PARENT ORGANIZATION: KC/ACTF
WEBSITE: www.kcactf.org **EMAIL:** ghenry@kennedy-center.org
PHONE: (202) 416-8864 **FAX:** (202) 416-8860
ADDRESS: Kennedy Center, Washington DC 20566
DESCRIPTION: For the outstanding student-written comedy or play with a significant comic element from college/university participating in KC/ACTF program.
GENRE: Plays **LENGTH:** Any Length **FEE:** Yes **AGENT ONLY:** No

MAXIM MAZUMDAR NEW PLAY COMPETITION

WEBSITE: www.alleyway.com **EMAIL:** email@alleyway.com
PHONE: (716) 852-2600 **FAX:** (716) 852-2266

ADDRESS: 1 Curtain Up Alley, Buffalo NY 14202

DESCRIPTION: Est. 1990. Named for Maxim Mazumdar (1953-87). Winning full-length receives premiere production in mainstage season. Winning one-act receives premiere in Buffalo Quickies fest.

SUBMISSION MATERIALS: Full script, SASE **DEADLINE TYPE:** Annual **GENRE:** Plays **LENGTH:** 1-Act (under 1 hour)

MCLAREN MEMORIAL COMEDY PLAYWRITING COMPETITION

WEBSITE: www.mctmidland.org **EMAIL:** tracy@mctmidland.org
ADDRESS: Midland Community Theatre, 2000 W Wadley Ave, Midland TX 79705
GENRE: Plays **LENGTH:** Full-length **FEE:** Yes **AGENT ONLY:** No

MCNERNEY PLAYWRITING CONTEST

WEBSITE: theatre.cofc.edu/productions/todd-mcnerney-playwriting-contest.php
EMAIL: oleksiakm@cofc.edu **PHONE:** (843) 953-6306 **TWITTER:** @CofC
ADDRESS: College of Charleston Theatre Dept, 66 George St, Charleston SC 29424

DESCRIPTION: Winner – $400.00 cash prize, staged reading at the 2018 Piccolo Spoleto Festival, travel allowance to attend the reading. Runner-Up – $100.00 cash prize, staged reading at 2018 Piccolo Spoleto Festival

DEADLINE: 02/15/2018 **GENRE:** Plays **LENGTH:** Full-length **FEE:** Yes
AGENT ONLY: No

METLIFE NUESTRAS VOCES NATIONAL PLAYWRITING COMPETITION

WEBSITE: www.repertorio.nyc **EMAIL:** nuestrasvoces@repertorio.nyc
PHONE: (212) 225-9999 **ADDRESS:** Repertorio Espanol, 138 E 27th St, New York NY 10016

DESCRIPTION: Playwrights may be Latino or of any other ethnic or racial background as long as the play's subject matter and characters resonate with Latino audiences and accurately depicts the Hispanic experience. Grand Prize: $3,000 and a full production; 2nd Place: $2,000; 3rd Place: $1,000. See website for details.

GENRE: Plays **LENGTH:** Full-length
SPECIAL INTEREST: Hispanic or Latinx **FEE:** No **AGENT ONLY:** No

MILDRED & ALBERT PANOWSKI PLAYWRITING COMPETITION

WEBSITE: www.nmu.edu/theatre/playwritingcompetition
EMAIL: mejones@nmu.edu **PHONE:** (906) 227-2553 **FAX:** (906) 227-2567
ADDRESS: Northern Michigan University, 1401 Presque Isle Ave, Marquette MI 49855

DESCRIPTION: The theme for the 2018 competition is "A mystery about a Great Lakes legend or event." Details regarding acceptable submissions can be found on our website. **DEADLINE:** 12/01/2017 **GENRE:** Plays

MILKEN PLAYWRITING PRIZE

WEBSITE: www.milkenschool.org/playprize **EMAIL:** playprize@milkenschool.org
PHONE: (310) 440-3500 **ADDRESS:** 15800 Zeldins Way, Los Angeles CA 90049
GENRE: Plays **LENGTH:** 1-Act (under 1 hour) **FEE:** No **AGENT ONLY:** No

MORTON R. SARETT NATIONAL PLAYWRITING COMPETITION

WEBSITE: www.unlv.edu/programs/nct **EMAIL:** nct@unlv.edu
PHONE: (702) 895-3663 **ADDRESS:** Univ of Nevada, Las Vegas, 4505 Maryland Pkwy, Box 455036, Las Vegas NV 89154

MOSS HART & KITTY CARLISLE HART NEW PLAY INITIATIVE

WEBSITE: www.hartnpi.org/hartnpi-submissions **EMAIL:** kevin@gtc.org
ADDRESS: Attn: HartNPI, 59 E 59th St, New York, NY 10022
DESCRIPTION: The initiative builds upon the success of the Grove Theater Center New Play Initiative. And with productions in both Los Angeles and New York City, the Hart Initiative has a national impact.
SUBMISSION MATERIALS: Submitted scripts must be in pdf format and include a character list (with potential doubling if necessary), a short synopsis, and a title page. Further criteria can be found online. **DEADLINE:** 1/19/2018 **GENRE:** Plays
LENGTH: Full-length **FEE:** No **AGENT ONLY:** No

MUSICAL THEATRE AWARD

PARENT ORGANIZATION: Beverly Hills Theatre Guild
WEBSITE: www.beverlyhillstheatreguild.org
ADDRESS: PO Box 148, Beverly Hills CA 90213
DESCRIPTION: See website.

NATIONAL AUDIO THEATRE FESTIVALS (NATF) SCRIPT COMPETITION

WEBSITE: www.natf.org **EMAIL:** sue@natf.org **PHONE:** (516) 483-8321
FAX: (516) 538-7583 **ADDRESS:** 115 Dikeman St, Hempstead NY 11550
DESCRIPTION: See website.

NATIONAL LATINO PLAYWRITING AWARD

PARENT ORGANIZATION: Arizona Theatre Company
WEBSITE: www.arizonatheatre.org/national-latino-playwriting-award
EMAIL: kmonberg@arizonatheatre.org **PHONE:** (520) 884-8210
FAX: (520) 628-9129
ADDRESS: Arizona Theatre Company, 343 S Scott Ave, Tucson AZ 85701
DESCRIPTION: Latino playwrights residing in the United States, its territories or Mexico are encouraged to submit scripts for the award. Each script will be read and evaluated by a culturally diverse panel of theatre artists; finalists will be judged by ATC artistic staff. See website for updated deadline information.
SUBMISSION MATERIALS: See website.
DEADLINE: 11/15/2017 **GENRE:** Plays **LENGTH:** Full-length

SPECIAL INTEREST: Hispanic or Latinx **FEE:** No **AGENT ONLY:** No

NATIONAL NEW PLAY NETWORK
WEBSITE: www.nnpn.org **PHONE:** (202) 312-5270 **FAX:** (202) 289-2446
TWITTER: @NewPlayNetwork **ADDRESS:** 641 D St, NW, Washington DC 20004
DESCRIPTION: Please see website for contest dates.
GENRE: Plays **LENGTH:** Full-length **FEE:** Yes **AGENT ONLY:** No

NATIONAL ONE-ACT PLAYWRITING COMPETITION
WEBSITE: www.thelittletheatre.com **EMAIL:** asklta@thelittletheatre.com
PHONE: (703) 683-5778
ADDRESS: The Little Theatre of Alexandria, 600 Wolfe St., Alexandria VA 22314
GENRE: Plays **LENGTH:** 1-Act (under 1 hour) **FEE:** Yes **AGENT ONLY:** No

NATIONAL SCIENCE PLAYWRITING AWARD
PARENT ORGANIZATION: KC/ACTF
WEBSITE: www.kcactf.org **EMAIL:** ghenry@kennedy-center.org
PHONE: (202) 416-8864 **FAX:** (202) 416-4892 **ADDRESS:** Kennedy Center, Washington DC 20566
DESCRIPTION: Award for the outstanding student-written play on themes of science, technology and the impact of both on our lives from college/university participating in KCACTF program.
GENRE: Plays **LENGTH:** Any Length **FEE:** Yes **AGENT ONLY:** No

NATIONAL TEN MINUTE PLAY CONTEST
PARENT ORGANIZATION: Theatre Oxford
WEBSITE: www.theatreoxford.com/10-min-plays
EMAIL: theatreoxford@gmail.com **ADDRESS:** PO Box 1394, Oxford MS 38655
DESCRIPTION: Est. 1998. Production: casts 2-4, minimal set, props. Work must be unoptioned, unproduced, unpublished. See website for complete details.
SUBMISSION MATERIALS: Full script. **DEADLINE:** 03/01/2018 **DEADLINE TYPE:** Annual
GENRE: Plays **LENGTH:** 10-minute **FEE:** Yes **AGENT ONLY:** No

NATIONAL TRANSLATION AWARD
WEBSITE: www.literarytranslators.org/awards/national-translation-award
PHONE: (972) 883-2093 **FAX:** (972) 883-6303 **ADDRESS:** Univ of Texas at Dallas, Box 830688, Mail Sta JO 51, Richardson TX 75083
DESCRIPTION: Est. 1978. ALTA only accepts submissions from publishers for this award. Book must be translated from any language into English. Publishers are invited to submit translated works of poetry or prose published in the previous calendar year. Hybrid works and drama are welcome, and may be submitted to either category as determined appropriate by the publisher.
SUBMISSION MATERIALS: See website for details. **FEE:** Yes

NEW VOICES ONE-ACT PLAY COMPETITION
WEBSITE: www.youthplays.com/submit_play.php **EMAIL:** info@youthplays.com

PHONE: (424) 703-5315
ADDRESS: 7119 W Sunset Blvd #390, Los Angeles CA 90046
DESCRIPTION: The winner gets publication, a cash prize, and copies of Final Draft and Great Dialogue software! See website for details and submission form.
DEADLINE: 05/01/2018 **DEADLINE TYPE:** Annual **GENRE:** Plays
LENGTH: 1-Act (under 1 hour) **FEE:** No **AGENT ONLY:** No

NEW WORKS FESTIVAL [MA]
PARENT ORGANIZATION: Firehouse Center for the Arts
WEBSITE: www.firehouse.org/new-works-festival **EMAIL:** info@firehouse.org
PHONE: (978) 499-9931 **ADDRESS:** Firehouse Center for the Arts, Market Sq, Newburyport MA 01950
DESCRIPTION: The Firehouse is committed to the development of new work. This festival fosters the growth of New England playwrights while showcasing the talent of local and regional actors and directors. New England playwrights submit their 10-minute, one-act, and full-length plays to an independent panel who select the festival's shows in anonymous readings. Directors and their casts then work with selected playwrights to produce two weekends of theater.
DEADLINE TYPE: Annual **GENRE:** Plays **LENGTH:** Any Length

NEWWORKS@THEWORKS PLAYWRITING COMPETITION
PARENT ORGANIZATION: Playhouse on the Square
WEBSITE: playhouseonthesquare.org/shows/new-worksthe-works-competition.html
EMAIL: jordan@playhouseonthesquare.org **PHONE:** (901) 725-0776
ADDRESS: 66 S Cooper St, Memphis TN 38104
DESCRIPTION: The NewWorks@TheWorks Competition provides an outlet for new playwrights to showcase their work and have a chance to see their play produced on a professional level. Prize: a trip to Memphis to take part in the rehearsals and the development of the new work, a cash prize of $750, and a world premiere production in the upcoming season. See website for updates and submission guidelines.
DEADLINE TYPE: Annual **GENRE:** Plays **LENGTH:** Full-length
FEE: Yes **AGENT ONLY:** No

NORTH CAROLINA NEW PLAY PROJECT
WEBSITE: www.greensboro-nc.gov/index.aspx?page=1474
EMAIL: todd.fisher@greensboro-nc.gov **PHONE:** (336) 373-2974
ADDRESS: 200 N Davie St Ste 101, Greensboro NC 27401
DESCRIPTION: The Greensboro Playwrights' Forum is proud to sponsor the NC New Play Project, an annual workshop production. Playwrights from across North Carolina may submit their full-length scripts or related one-acts for consideration. See website for updates. **LENGTH:** Any length **FEE:** No **AGENT ONLY:** No

ONE ACT PLAY CONTEST
WEBSITE: tennesseewilliams.net/contests **EMAIL:** contests@tennesseewilliams.net
PHONE: (504) 581-1144 **ADDRESS:** Tennessee Williams/New Orleans Literary Festival, 938 Lafayette St, Ste 514, New Orleans LA 70113

DESCRIPTION: See website for details. **DEADLINE TYPE:** Annual **GENRE:** Plays **LENGTH:** 1-Act (under 1 hour) **FEE:** Yes **AGENT ONLY:** No

ONE-ACT PLAYWRITING COMPETITION

PARENT ORGANIZATION: The Little Theatre of Alexandria
WEBSITE: thelittletheatre.com/opportunities/#oneact
EMAIL: asklta@thelittletheatre.com **PHONE:** (703) 683-5778
ADDRESS: The Little Theatre of Alexandria, 600 Wolfe St, Alexandria VA 22314
DESCRIPTION: All submissions must be original, unpublished and unproduced (not staged for a paying audience as of date of entry) one-act plays. Time permitting, the Little Theatre of Alexandria will present a staged-reading or small-scale production of the top three shows. It is our intention to produce the winner of our contest in the NVTA One-Act Play Festival, which is held in late June or early July each year. In addition, cash awards of $350 for 1st Place, $250 for 2nd Place and $150 for 3rd Place are presented.
SUBMISSION MATERIALS: See website. **DEADLINE TYPE:** Annual **GENRE:** Plays **LENGTH:** 1-Act (under 1 hour) **FEE:** Yes **AGENT ONLY:** No

OPERA FOR ALL VOICES

PARENT ORGANIZATION: Santa Fe Opera
WEBSITE: www.santafeopera.org/discover/opera-for-all-voices
EMAIL: operaforall@santafeopera.org **PHONE:** (505) 946-2417
TWITTER: @santafeopera **ADDRESS:** 301 Opera Dr, Santa Fe NM 87506
DESCRIPTION: Opera for All Voices addresses the need for works with outstanding artistic quality that also appeal to a broader audience. The project also addresses the real need to attract new audiences to opera by commissioning substantial works that speak to all voices, created with modern attention spans in mind, and aims at breaking down pre-conceived notions about the limitations of our art form.
SUBMISSION MATERIALS: Synopsis, bio, audio/video files, score sample, libretto sample. **LENGTH:** Full-length **FEE:** No **AGENT ONLY:** No

ORIGINAL SHORTS PLAYWRITING CONTEST

PARENT ORGANIZATION: Theatre du Mississippi
WEBSITE: theatredumiss.org/get-involved/original-shorts/
EMAIL: originalshorts@theatredumiss.org
ADDRESS: Theatre du Mississippi, PO Box 184, Winona MN 55987
DESCRIPTION: Judges will select 4 winning scripts. Winners receive a $50 prize and a staged reading. Winning scripts will be assigned a director and will be performed with script in hand and with minimal production values. Audience feedback will be taken, and made available to playwrights after the performances. The plays will be performed sometime in Spring (usually April).
DEADLINE TYPE: Annual **LENGTH:** 1-Act (under 1 hour) **FEE:** No **AGENT ONLY:** No

PAUL STEPHEN LIM PLAYWRITING AWARD

PARENT ORGANIZATION: KC/ACTF
WEBSITE: www.kcactf.org **EMAIL:** ghenry@kennedy-center.org
PHONE: (202) 416-8864 **FAX:** (202) 416-8860

ADDRESS: Kennedy Center Washington DC 20566
GENRE: Plays **LENGTH:** Any Length **SPECIAL INTEREST:** Asian **FEE:** Yes
AGENT ONLY: No

PAULA VOGEL AWARD FOR PLAYWRITING
PARENT ORGANIZATION: KC/ACTF
WEBSITE: kcactf.org/kanin-playwriting/vogel.html
EMAIL: ghenry@kennedy-center.org **PHONE:** (202) 416-8864
FAX: (202) 416-8860 **ADDRESS:** Kennedy Center, Washington DC 20566
GENRE: Plays **LENGTH:** Any Length **SPECIAL INTEREST:** LGBT+
FEE: Yes **AGENT ONLY:** No

PEN CENTER USA LITERARY AWARDS
PARENT ORGANIZATION: PEN America
WEBSITE: penusa.org/awards **EMAIL:** stacy_valis@penusa.org
PHONE: (323) 424-4939 **ADDRESS:** PO Box 6037, Beverly Hills CA 90212
DESCRIPTION: See website for details.
SUBMISSION MATERIALS: Application, $35 check or credit card payment, full script (4 copies); submissions not returned. **FEE:** Yes **AGENT ONLY:** No

PEN/HEIM TRANSLATION FUND GRANT
PARENT ORGANIZATION: PEN America
WEBSITE: pen.org/literary-award/penheim-translation-fund-grants-2000-4000
EMAIL: awards@pen.org **PHONE:** (212) 334-1660 **FAX:** (212) 334-2181
ADDRESS: 588 Broadway, #303, New York NY 10012
DESCRIPTION: To support the translation of book-length works of prose, poetry, and drama. **SUBMISSION MATERIALS:** See website for details.
DEADLINE TYPE: Annual **LENGTH:** Full-length

PEN/LAURA PELS INTERNATIONAL FOUNDATION AWARDS FOR DRAMA
PARENT ORGANIZATION: PEN America
WEBSITE: pen.org/literary-award/penlaura-pels-international-foundation-for-theater-awards-for-master-american-dramatist-playwright-in-mid-career-and-emerging-playwright-7500-and-2500
EMAIL: arielle@pen.org **PHONE:** (212) 334-1660
ADDRESS: 588 Broadway, Ste 303, New York NY 10012
DESCRIPTION: Est. 1998. For Master American Dramatist: Candidates are proposed by the judges; nominations are not accepted. For American Playwright in Mid-career and Emerging American Playwright: Any playwright, writer, or member of the theater community may submit a nomination. However, a playwright may not nominate his or herself.
SUBMISSION MATERIALS: See website for details. **DEADLINE TYPE:** Annual
GENRE: Plays **FEE:** No **AGENT ONLY:** No

PLAY COMPETITION FOR YOUTH THEATRE

PARENT ORGANIZATION: Beverly Hills Theatre Guild
WEBSITE: www.beverlyhillstheatreguild.org   **PHONE:** (310) 273-3390
ADDRESS: PO Box 148, Beverly Hills CA 90213
DESCRIPTION: The competition aims to discover new theatrical works and to encourage established or emerging writers to create quality works for youth theatre. The Play Competition for Youth Theatre represents grades 6-8 and grades 9-12 and offers two prizes: First prize: $1,200, Second prize: $600.
SUBMISSION MATERIALS: query, application, full script
DEADLINE: 02/28/2018   **GENRE:** Plays   **LENGTH:** Full-length   **FEE:** No
AGENT ONLY: No

PLAYWRIGHTS FIRST
WEBSITE: www.playwrights-first.com   **PHONE:** (212) 410-9234
DESCRIPTION: Founded in 1993 by Carolyn French, a highly successful literary agent, Playwrights First is an organization which recognizes, rewards and advances playwrights of unusual promise. Submissions from 08/15/2018 to 09/15/2018. End date subject to change. Please check our website. Electronic submissions only. www.playwrights-first.com/how-to-submit.html
DEADLINE: 09/15/2018   **GENRE:** Plays   **LENGTH:** Full-length   **FEE:** No
AGENT ONLY: No

QUEST FOR PEACE PLAYWRITING AWARD
PARENT ORGANIZATION: KC/ACTF
WEBSITE: www.kcactf.org   **EMAIL:** ghenry@kennedy-center.org
PHONE: (202) 416-8864   **FAX:** (202) 416-4892
ADDRESS: Kennedy Center, Washington DC 20566
DESCRIPTION: See website for details.
GENRE: Plays   **LENGTH:** Any Length   **FEE:** Yes   **AGENT ONLY:** No

REVA SHINER COMEDY AWARD
PARENT ORGANIZATION: Bloomington Playwrights Project
WEBSITE: newplays.org/submit-a-play/reva-shiner-comedy
EMAIL: literarymanager@newplays.org   **PHONE:** (812) 334-1188
ADDRESS: 107 W 9th St, Bloomington IN 47404
DESCRIPTION: The Reva Shiner Comedy Award presents an unpublished full-length COMEDY with a cash prize of $1,000, a full production as part of the Bloomington Playwrights Project's Mainstage season, along with travel reimbursement. The submission fee is waved for Dramatists Guild members.
DEADLINE TYPE: Annual   **GENRE:** Plays   **LENGTH:** Full-length
FEE: Waived for DG Members   **AGENT ONLY:** No

RICHARD E. SHERWOOD AWARD
PARENT ORGANIZATION: Center Theatre Group
WEBSITE: www.centertheatregroup.org/programs/artists/sherwood-award
EMAIL: Sherwood@CTGLA.org   **TWITTER:** @CTGLA
ADDRESS: Music Center Annex, 601 W Temple St, Los Angeles CA 90012

DESCRIPTION: Since 1996, nineteen artists have received the $10,000 Sherwood Award, which was established in memory of Richard E. Sherwood as an endowed fund to support innovative, adventurous theatre artists working in Los Angeles. See website for updates and info. **DEADLINE TYPE:** Annual **GENRE:** All **LENGTH:** Full-length **FEE:** No **AGENT ONLY:** No

RICHARD RODGERS AWARDS FOR MUSICAL THEATER

WEBSITE: www.artsandletters.org **EMAIL:** academy@artsandletters.org
PHONE: (212) 368-5900 **ADDRESS:** American Academy of Arts and Letters, 633 W 155th St, New York NY 10032
DESCRIPTION: Created and endowed by Richard Rodgers in 1978 for the development of the musical theater. These awards subsidize full productions, studio productions, and staged readings by nonprofit theaters in New York City of works by composers and writers who are not already established in this field. The winners are selected by a jury of the American Academy of Arts and Letters. The Richard Rodgers Awards are the only awards for which the Academy accepts applications.
DEADLINE TYPE: Annual **GENRE:** Musicals **LENGTH:** Full-length **FEE:** No **AGENT ONLY:** No

ROBERT J. PICKERING AWARD FOR PLAYWRITING EXCELLENCE

WEBSITE: www.branchcct.org/pickering **PHONE:** (517) 279-7963
ADDRESS: Branch County Community Theatre, 14 S Hanchett St, Coldwater MI 49036
DESCRIPTION: Est. 1984. This award was established to provide a vehicle for playwrights to see their works produced. Prize: $200 for first place, $50 for second place, and $25 for third place.
SUBMISSION MATERIALS: full script, SASE **DEADLINE:** 12/31/2018 **GENRE:** Plays or Musicals **LENGTH:** Full-length **FEE:** No **AGENT ONLY:** No

ROSA PARKS PLAYWRITING AWARD

PARENT ORGANIZATION: KC/ACTF
WEBSITE: www.kcactf.org **EMAIL:** ghenry@kennedy-center.org
PHONE: (202) 416-8864 **FAX:** (202) 416-8860
ADDRESS: Kennedy Center, Washington DC 20566
DESCRIPTION: Awarded for the outstanding student or faculty written play on the theme of civil rights and social justice from college/university participating in KC/ACTF program.
GENRE: Plays **LENGTH:** Any Length **FEE:** Yes **AGENT ONLY:** No

SCHOLASTIC ART & WRITING AWARDS

WEBSITE: www.artandwriting.org **EMAIL:** info@artandwriting.org
PHONE: (212) 343-7729 **ADDRESS:** 557 Broadway, New York NY 10012
DESCRIPTION: See website for details.
GENRE: Plays **LENGTH:** Any Length **FEE:** No **AGENT ONLY:** No

SCRIPT TEASE OF SHORT PLAYS COMPETITION

PARENT ORGANIZATION: Scripteasers
WEBSITE: www.scripteasers.org/annual-competition
EMAIL: thescripteasers@msn.com **PHONE:** (619) 295-4040
ADDRESS: 3404 Hawk St, San Diego CA 92103
DESCRIPTION: Only open to writers in San Diego County. Cash prize, plus a reading at a regular Scripteasers meeting.
DEADLINE: 07/01/2018 **DEADLINE TYPE:** Annual **GENRE:** Plays **FEE:** No
AGENT ONLY: No

SHAKESPEARE'S NEW CONTEMPORARIES PROJECT

PARENT ORGANIZATION: American Shakespeare Center
WEBSITE: sncproject.com
EMAIL: sncproject@americanshakespearecenter.com
ADDRESS: 20 S New St, 4th Fl, Staunton, VA 24401
DESCRIPTION: The SNC Project strives to inspire playwrights to compose original works that serve as partner plays to Shakespeare's classics. The ASC selects companion plays, which are performed in repertory with their Shakespeare counterparts, through a blind submission process. Winning playwrights receive a cash prize of $25,000 as well as funds to support their travel and housing for the rehearsal process at the ASC's Blackfriars Playhouse in Staunton, Virginia. See website for details.
DEADLINE: 02/15/2018 **DEADLINE TYPE:** Rolling **GENRE:** Plays **FEE:** No
AGENT ONLY: No

SHUBERT FENDRICH MEMORIAL PLAYWRITING CONTEST

WEBSITE: www.pioneerdrama.com **EMAIL:** pioneer@pioneerdrama.com
PHONE: (303) 779-4035 **FAX:** (303) 779-4315
ADDRESS: PO Box 4267, Englewood CO 80155
DESCRIPTION: See website for updated information.

SKY COOPER NEW AMERICAN PLAY PRIZE

PARENT ORGANIZATION: Marin Theatre Company
WEBSITE: www.marintheatre.org/productions/new-plays-program/new-play-awards **EMAIL:** literarymanager@marintheatre.org **PHONE:** (415) 388-5200
TWITTER: @MarinTheatreCo **ADDRESS:** 397 Miller Ave, Mill Valley CA 94941
DESCRIPTION: Awarded annually to either an established or emerging playwright for an outstanding new work. The winner receives a $10,000 award and a developmental workshop as part of the theater's annual New Play Reading Series. The winning play will also be considered under option for a full production at MTC as part of the theater's annual main stage season. See website for details. **DEADLINE TYPE:** Annual
GENRE: Plays **LENGTH:** Full-length **FEE:** No **AGENT ONLY:** No

SOUTHERN PLAYWRIGHTS COMPETITION

WEBSITE: www.jsu.edu/english/southpla.html **EMAIL:** jmaloney@jsu.edu

PHONE: (256) 782-5412 **FAX:** (256) 782-5441
ADDRESS: Dept of English, 700 Pelham Road N, Jacksonville AL 36265
DESCRIPTION: Est. 1991. An annual award of $1,000 will be presented to the first-prize winner, as well as a consideration for production by the Jacksonville State University Department of Drama. Southern Playwrights Competition reserves the right to use the name of the play and the author's name in all publicity and promotions.
SUBMISSION MATERIALS: See website for updated information.
DEADLINE: 01/15/2018 **DEADLINE TYPE:** Annual **GENRE:** Plays
LENGTH: Full-length **AGENT ONLY:** No

STANLEY DRAMA AWARD
WEBSITE: www.wagner.edu/theatre/stanley-drama **EMAIL:** todd.price@wagner.edu
PHONE: (718) 420-4338 **ADDRESS:** Wagner College, 1 Campus Rd, Staten Island NY 10301
DESCRIPTION: Est. 1957. Work must be unoptioned, unproduced, unpublished. Prize: $2000. **DEADLINE TYPE:** Annual **GENRE:** Plays or Musicals
LENGTH: Full-length **FEE:** Yes **AGENT ONLY:** No

SUMMERFIELD G. ROBERTS AWARD
WEBSITE: www.srttexas.org/community.html **EMAIL:** aa-srt@son-rep-texas.net
PHONE: (979) 245-6644 **ADDRESS:** 1717 8th St, Bay City TX 77414
DESCRIPTION: A cash award of $2,500 is presented by the Sons of the Republic of Texas to the author of a work of creative writing on the Republic of Texas.
SUBMISSION MATERIALS: 5 copies of full script, SASE **DEADLINE:** 01/15/2018
FEE: No **AGENT ONLY:** No

SUSAN GLASPELL CONTEST [CENTENARY STAGE]
PARENT ORGANIZATION: Centenary Stage Company
WEBSITE: www.centenarystageco.org/call-for-plays-wps.php
EMAIL: info@centenarystageco.org **ADDRESS:** Attn: Catherine Rust, Program Director, 400 Jefferson St, Hackettstown NJ 07840
DESCRIPTION: Deadline for Open Submissions: November 2, 2017, Deadline for New Dramatists, Agent Submissions, and PW Center: January 15, 2018. One play from the WPS Festival will be selected by a panel of judges as the winner, to be featured in a subsequent CSC main-stage season as a full production, with an additional award of $1500 to the playwright.
SUBMISSION MATERIALS: Letter of recommendation **DEADLINE TYPE:** Annual
GENRE: Plays **LENGTH:** Full-length **FEE:** No **AGENT ONLY:** No

SUSAN SMITH BLACKBURN PRIZE
WEBSITE: www.blackburnprize.org/submission/usa
EMAIL: susansmithblackburn@gmail.com **PHONE:** (713) 308-2842
ADDRESS: 3239 Avalon Pl, Houston TX 77019
DESCRIPTION: Est. 1978. Plays accepted only from specified source theaters in US, UK, and Ireland. Writers should bring their work to the attention of the theatre companies listed on website.

SUBMISSION MATERIALS: See website for updated information.
DEADLINE TYPE: Annual   **LENGTH:** Any Length
SPECIAL INTEREST: Feminism/Women's Rights   **FEE:** No   **AGENT ONLY:** No

TENNESSEE WILLIAMS/NEW ORLEANS LITERARY FESTIVAL ONE-ACT PLAY CONTEST

WEBSITE: tennesseewilliams.net/contests/   **EMAIL:** info@tennesseewilliams.net
PHONE: (504) 581-1144   **FAX:** (504) 529-2430   **TWITTER:** @TWFestNOLA
ADDRESS: 938 Lafayette St, Ste 514, New Orleans LA 70113
DESCRIPTION: Plays must be unstaged, unrecognized, unproduced.
SUBMISSION MATERIALS: Submit via website or hard copy.
GENRE: Plays   **LENGTH:** 1-Act (under 1 hour)   **FEE:** Yes   **AGENT ONLY:** No

THEATER FOR YOUTH PLAYWRITING AWARD

PARENT ORGANIZATION: KC/ACTF
WEBSITE: www.kcactf.org   **EMAIL:** skshaffer@kennedy-center.org
PHONE: (202) 416-8857   **FAX:** (202) 416-8802
ADDRESS: Kennedy Center, Washington DC 20566
DESCRIPTION: Play must be entered by a college or university participating in the KCACTF program. A registration fee of $200 (associate level) or $250 (participating) must be paid to qualify.   **GENRE:** Plays   **LENGTH:** Any Length
SPECIAL INTEREST: TYA   **FEE:** Yes   **AGENT ONLY:** No

THEATRE CONSPIRACY

WEBSITE: artinlee.org/event/newplaycontest20
EMAIL: theatreconspiracyfl@gmail.com   **PHONE:** (239) 936-3239
ADDRESS: 10091 McGregor Blvd, Fort Myers FL 33919
DESCRIPTION: Work submitted to the contest must be a full length play with eight characters or less and have simple to moderate technical demands. Prize: $700.00 and full production.
GENRE: Plays   **LENGTH:** Full-length   **FEE:** Waived for DG Members   **AGENT ONLY:** No

THEATRE OF THE FIRST AMENDMENT PLAY FESTIVAL

PARENT ORGANIZATION: Nittany Theatre at the Barn
WEBSITE: nittanytheatre.org/theatre-of-the-first-amendment
EMAIL: nittanytheatre@gmail.com
DESCRIPTION: From eligible submissions, one play shall be selected for production on the main-stage of Nittany Theatre at the Barn (a 99 seat regional summer stock theatre) during Constitution Week. See website for updates and details.
GENRE: Plays   **LENGTH:** Full-length   **FEE:** No   **AGENT ONLY:** No

TNT POPS! NEW PLAY PROJECT

PARENT ORGANIZATION: Texas Nonprofit Theatres
WEBSITE: www.texastheatres.org/wf/programs/pops/pops18.html

EMAIL: tnt@texastheatres.org **PHONE:** (817) 731-2238
ADDRESS: 1300 Gendy St, Rm 263, Fort Worth TX 76107
DESCRIPTION: See website for updates.
GENRE: Plays **LENGTH:** Full-length **FEE:** Yes **AGENT ONLY:** No

TOWSON UNIVERSITY PRIZE FOR LITERATURE
WEBSITE: www.towson.edu/cla/departments/english/documents/towson_prize_for_literature_rev.pdf **EMAIL:** engl@towson.edu
PHONE: (410) 704-2871 **FAX:** (410) 704-3999
ADDRESS: 8000 York Rd, Towson MD 21252
DESCRIPTION: Est. 1979 the prize is awarded annually for a single book or book-length manuscript of fiction, poetry, drama, or imaginative nonfiction by a Maryland writer. The prize is granted on the basis of literary and aesthetic excellence as determined by a panel of distinguished judges appointed by the university.
SUBMISSION MATERIALS: See website for complete information before submitting.
DEADLINE: 06/15/2018 **DEADLINE TYPE:** Annual **GENRE:** Plays
LENGTH: Full-length **FEE:** No **AGENT ONLY:** No

UNIVERSITY OF CENTRAL MISSOURI COMPETITION
WEBSITE: www.ucmo.edu/theatre/about/write.cfm **EMAIL:** wilson@ucmo.edu
PHONE: (660) 543-4020 **FAX:** (660) 543-8006
ADDRESS: Theatre & Dance Dept, Warrensburg MO 64093
DESCRIPTION: Est. 2001. Has produced children's plays for over 25 years. Now focused on world-premiere originals, through national competition. See website for updates.
SUBMISSION MATERIALS: Submissions must be an original and unpublished work not produced professionally. Running time of production approximately 45-60 minutes. Please email one copy of the script in PDF or Word format to John Wilson.
DEADLINE TYPE: Annual **LENGTH:** 1-Act (under 1 hour)
SPECIAL INTEREST: TYA **FEE:** Yes **AGENT ONLY:** No

URBAN STAGES EMERGING PLAYWRIGHT AWARD
PARENT ORGANIZATION: Urban Stages
WEBSITE: urbanstages.org/submissions **EMAIL:** urbanstage@aol.com
PHONE: (212) 421-1380 **TWITTER:** @UrbanStages
ADDRESS: 555 8th Ave, Ste 1800, New York NY 10018
DESCRIPTION: Our $500 Emerging Playwright Award (coupled with press coverage) is given to playwrights who show excellence and dedication throughout this process from development to the stage. Submissions accepted year-round.
GENRE: Plays **LENGTH:** Full-length **FEE:** No **AGENT ONLY:** No

USA SONGWRITING COMPETITION
WEBSITE: www.songwriting.net/enter-usa-songwriting-competition
EMAIL: info@songwriting.net **PHONE:** (954) 537-3127 **TWITTER:** @usasong
ADDRESS: 2881 E Oakland Park Blvd, #414, Ft. Lauderdale FL 33306

DESCRIPTION: Since 1995, the USA Songwriting Competition®, the world's leading international songwriting event, has been honoring songwriters, composers, bands, and recording artists everywhere. This is open to all, regardless of nationality or country origin.
DEADLINE TYPE: Annual **FEE:** Yes **AGENT ONLY:** No

VERMONT PLAYWRIGHTS AWARD
WEBSITE: www.valleyplayers.com/vt-playwrights-award
EMAIL: valleyplayers@madriver.com **PHONE:** (802) 793-8362
ADDRESS: Valley Players, PO Box 441, Waitsfield VT 5673
DESCRIPTION: Est. 1982. The intent of the award is to promote the theater arts and to encourage and support the creation of original plays by residents of Vermont, New Hampshire and Maine. Cash prize: $1,000.
SUBMISSION MATERIALS: See website for updated information.
GENRE: Plays **LENGTH:** Full-length **FEE:** No **AGENT ONLY:** No

VERSE DRAMA PRIZE
WEBSITE: www.poetryfoundation.org/foundation/awards
EMAIL: info@poetryfoundation.org **PHONE:** 312-787-7070
TWITTER: @PoetryFound **ADDRESS:** 61 W Superior St, Chicago IL 60654
DESCRIPTION: Honors a living poet who has written a previously unpublished, outstanding original verse drama in English. The award is a cash purse of $10,000 and a staged reading of his or her winning manuscript in Chicago. Awards given annually or from time to time, as appropriate to maintain the prestige and quality of the prizes. No applications or unsolicited nominations are accepted. See website.
GENRE: Verse

W. KEITH HEDRICK PLAYWRITING CONTEST
WEBSITE: hrc-showcasetheatre.com/play_contest.html
EMAIL: jangrice2002@yahoo.com **PHONE:** (518) 851-7244
ADDRESS: Hudson River Classics, PO Box 940, Hudson NY 12534
DESCRIPTION: Est. 1993. HRC Showcase Theatre invites submissions of full-length plays to its annual contest from new, aspiring, or established playwrights. 70 and 90 pages in length. No one-person shows, musicals, or children's plays.
DEADLINE: 02/01/2018 **DEADLINE TYPE:** Annual **GENRE:** Plays

WHITING AWARDS
WEBSITE: www.whiting.org **EMAIL:** info@whiting.org **PHONE:** (718) 701-5962
ADDRESS: 16 Court St, Ste 2308, Brooklyn NY 11241
DESCRIPTION: Winners are chosen by a selection committee, a small group of recognized writers, literary scholars, and editors appointed every year by the Foundation. The Foundation does not accept applications or unsolicited nominations.
FEE: No **AGENT ONLY:** No

WICHITA STATE UNIVERSITY NEW PLAY COMPETITION
WEBSITE: www.wichita.edu **EMAIL:** bret.jones@wichita.edu

PHONE: (316) 978-3360   **FAX:** (316) 978-3202
ADDRESS: 1845 Fairmount, Campus Box 153, Wichita KS 67260   **GENRE:** Plays

WOODWARD/NEWMAN DRAMA AWARD
WEBSITE: newplays.org/submit-a-play/woodward-newman-drama
EMAIL: literarymanager@newplays.org   **PHONE:** (812) 334-1188
ADDRESS: 107 W 9th St, Bloomington IN 47404
DESCRIPTION: Offered by Bloomington Playwrights Project, it presents the best unpublished full-length drama of the year with a full production as part of the BPP's Mainstage season, along with travel reimbursement.
DEADLINE: 03/01/2018   **DEADLINE TYPE:** Annual   **GENRE:** Plays
LENGTH: Full-length   **FEE:** Waived for DG Members   **AGENT ONLY:** No

YALE DRAMA SERIES/DAVID C. HORN PRIZE
WEBSITE: yalebooks.com/series/yale-drama-series   **EMAIL:** yaledramaseries@yale.edu   **PHONE:** (203) 432-0975   **FAX:** (203) 436-0948
ADDRESS: PO Box 209040, New Haven CT 6520
SUBMISSION MATERIALS: Submit full script (unbound), cover pg (w/title, contact info, pg count), cast/scene list, Submissions not returned.
GENRE: Plays   **LENGTH:** Full-length   **FEE:** No   **AGENT ONLY:** No

YOUNG PLAYWRIGHT CONTEST
WEBSITE: www.capitalrep.org   **EMAIL:** mhall@capitalrep.org
PHONE: (518) 462-4531   **ADDRESS:** 111 N Pearl St, Albany NY 12207
SUBMISSION MATERIALS: Contest winners will see their short plays professionally produced on theREP's stage and will receive a series of workshops led by a professional playwright. Playwrights must be at least 13 years old and no older than 19 years at the time of submission, and must reside within a 90-mile radius of Albany, NY.
GENRE: Plays   **LENGTH:** 10-minute   **FEE:** No

YOUNG PLAYWRIGHTS IN PROCESS
PARENT ORGANIZATION: Indiana Repertory Theatre
WEBSITE: www.irtlive.com/learn-and-engage/young-playwrights-in-process
DESCRIPTION: Est. 2005. YPiP is an annual playwriting competition for Indiana students in grades 6-12 that encourages students across Indiana to create plays for live theatre that reflect and challenge their world.
DEADLINE TYPE: Annual   **GENRE:** Plays   **LENGTH:** 1-Act (under 1 hour)
FEE: No   **AGENT ONLY:** No

GRANTS & FELLOWSHIPS

2050 ARTISTIC FELLOWSHIP
PARENT ORGANIZATION: New York Theatre Workshop
WEBSITE: www.nytw.org/artist-workshop/2050-fellowships
PHONE: (212) 780-9037 **TWITTER:** @NYTW79
ADDRESS: New York Theatre Workshop, 83 E 4th St, New York NY 10003
DESCRIPTION: The 2050 Fellowship is named in celebration of the U.S. Census Bureau's projection that by the year 2050, there will be no single racial or ethnic majority in the United States. The 2050 Fellows are early career artists who, with their unique voices, give us perspective on the world in which we live; and who challenge us all to contend with this changing world.
SUBMISSION MATERIALS: The application period for the 2018/19 Fellowship has passed. Please check website in September 2018 to apply for the 2019/20 season.

ABOG FELLOWSHIP FOR SOCIALLY ENGAGED ART
WEBSITE: www.abladeofgrass.org/fellowship-program
PHONE: (646) 945-0860 **ADDRESS:** 81 Prospect St, Brooklyn NY 11201
DESCRIPTION: Artists or artist collectives working independently of a 501c3 nonprofit are eligible. If you are working under a registered 501c3, you are not eligible to apply. We look at the process and relationships of socially engaged art projects. See website for complete details and updated deadline information.
DEADLINE TYPE: Annual **GENRE:** All Genres **PREFERRED LENGTH:** Any Length
FEE: No **AGENT ONLY:** No

ABRONS ARTS CENTER AIRSPACE GRANT PROGRAM
PARENT ORGANIZATION: Abrons AIRspace Program
WEBSITE: www.abronsartscenter.org/artist-residencies/apply-to-airspace
DESCRIPTION: Abrons Arts Center's AIRspace Grant Program offers time-based residencies to five early-career* performing artists working in movement-based, theater, and performance practices. The program provides 150 hours of rehearsal time in any of our four studios, the option to present works-in-progress throughout the duration of the residency period, and other professional development opportunities. See website for details and updates.
DEADLINE TYPE: Annual **GENRE:** All Genres **PREFERRED LENGTH:** Any Length
FEE: No **AGENT ONLY:** No

ALABAMA STATE COUNCIL ON THE ARTS
WEBSITE: www.arts.alabama.gov/grants/grant_individual.aspx
PHONE: (334) 242-4076 **FAX:** (334) 240-3269 **TWITTER:** @ALStateArts
ADDRESS: 201 Monroe St, Montgomery AL 36130
DESCRIPTION: The Mission of the Alabama State Council on the Arts is to enhance the quality of life and economic vitality for all Alabamians by providing support for the state's diverse and rich artistic resources. The Council awards Artist Fellowships of $5,000 for artists working in crafts, dance, design, media/photography, music,

literature, theatre and the visual arts.

SUBMISSION MATERIALS: Grant applications will be evaluated according to the extent to which relevant criteria are addressed in the project. A brief description of how applicable criteria will be addressed in the proposed activities must be entered under the Project Narrative Tab within the eGRANT application.
DEADLINE: 03/01/2018 **DEADLINE TYPE:** Annual

ALASKA STATE COUNCIL ON THE ARTS
WEBSITE: www.education.alaska.gov/aksca/grants.html
PHONE: (888) 278-7424 **FAX:** (907) 269-6601
ADDRESS: 161 Klevin St, Ste 102, Anchorage AK 99508
DESCRIPTION: Est. 1966. ASCA represents, supports and advances the creative endeavors of individuals, organizations and agencies throughout Alaska. The Alaska State Council on the Arts offers grants to assist the development of the arts, distributing state and federal funds through programs to support both individual artists and arts organizations.
SUBMISSION MATERIALS: Deadlines and materials vary. See website for details and updates.

ALAVI FOUNDATION
WEBSITE: www.alavifoundation.us/grantprograms **PHONE:** (212) 944-8333
FAX: (646) 619-4272 **TWITTER:** @AlaviFdn
ADDRESS: 650 5th Ave, Ste 2406, New York NY 10019
DESCRIPTION: The Alavi Foundation has provided more than $50 million in funding for charitable activities in the United States since our founding in 1973. Throughout our history, we have been committed to funding cultural programs, universities, schools, free clinics and college scholarships.
SUBMISSION MATERIALS: Check website for updated information.

ALLEN LEE HUGHES FELLOWSHIP PROGRAM
PARENT ORGANIZATION: Arena Stage
WEBSITE: www.arenastage.org/education/education-programs/internships-fellowships **PHONE:** (202) 554-9066 **FAX:** (202) 488-4056
ADDRESS: 1101 6th St, Washington DC 20024
DESCRIPTION: The goal of Arena Stage's fellowship and internship program is to cultivate the next generation of theater professionals by providing the highest standard of training through immersion in the art and business of producing theater. Successful candidates for both programs are highly motivated individuals who have arts-related experience and training, as well as a passion for the exploration of the human condition through the dramatic forms.
SUBMISSION MATERIALS: Check website for updates. **DEADLINE TYPE:** Annual

AMERICAN ACADEMY IN ROME FELLOWSHIPS
WEBSITE: www.aarome.org/apply/affiliated-fellowships
PHONE: (212) 751-7200 **FAX:** (212) 751-7220
ADDRESS: 7 E 60th St, New York NY 10022
DESCRIPTION: See website for specific fellowship and award information.

GRANTS & FELLOWSHIPS

AMERICAN ANTIQUARIAN SOCIETY FELLOWSHIPS
WEBSITE: www.americanantiquarian.org/fellowships **PHONE:** (508) 471-2149
FAX: (508) 754-9069 **ADDRESS:** 185 Salisbury St, Worcester MA 1609
DESCRIPTION: The American Antiquarian Society offers three broad categories of visiting research fellowships, with tenures ranging from one to twelve months. All of the fellowships are designed to enable academic and independent scholars and advanced graduate students to spend an uninterrupted block of time doing research in the AAS library. Discussing this work with staff and other readers is a hallmark of an AAS fellowship. **SUBMISSION MATERIALS:** Check website for updated information.

AMERICAN SAMOA COUNCIL ON CULTURE, ARTS AND HUMANITIES
WEBSITE: www.americansamoa.gov/arts-council **PHONE:** (684) 633-4116
FAX: (684) 633-2269 **ADDRESS:** PO Box 1540, Office of the Governor, Pago Pago AS 96799
DESCRIPTION: The American Samoa Council on Arts, Culture and the Humanities (the Arts Council) is primarily funded by grants from the National Endowment for the Arts. Its dual mission is the maintenance of Samoan arts and culture and the presentation of art forms from the broader world beyond the archipelago. The Arts Council supports through subgrants and funded activities the practice and preservation of both Samoan material culture and performance traditions.
SUBMISSION MATERIALS: Check website for updated information.

AMERICAN-SCANDINAVIAN FOUNDATION
WEBSITE: www.amscan.org/fellowships-grants/grants-and-awards-for-americans
PHONE: (212) 779-3587 **FAX:** (212) 249-3444 **TWITTER:** @ScanHouse
ADDRESS: 58 Park Ave, New York NY 10016
DESCRIPTION: Information on grants and awards for educational and cultural exchange opportunities is available for individual applicants. See website for details and deadlines for Fellowships/Grants to study in Scandinavia, and also on their Translation Competition.
SUBMISSION MATERIALS: Check website for updated information.
DEADLINE TYPE: Annual

THE ARCH AND BRUCE BROWN FOUNDATION
WEBSITE: www.aabbfoundation.org
ADDRESS: c/o James Waller, 500 W Univ Pkwy, #16J, Baltimore MD 21210
DESCRIPTION: The Arch and Bruce Brown Foundation offers grants to production companies to offset expenses in producing LGBT-themed theatrical and other performing-arts works based on history. The foundation is not a production company; we provide support for performing-arts productions but do not produce work ourselves.
PLEASE NOTE: As of 2018, the foundation will no longer hold an annual playwriting competition, in order to concentrate its efforts and resources on production grants.
SUBMISSION MATERIALS: Online applications only. See website for details.
GENRE: All Genres **PREFERRED LENGTH:** Full-length **SPECIAL INTEREST:** LGBT+
FEE: No **AGENT ONLY:** No

ARIZONA COMMISSION ON THE ARTS

WEBSITE: azarts.gov/grants **PHONE:** (602) 771-6501 **FAX:** (602) 256-0282
TWITTER: @AZartscomm **ADDRESS:** 417 W Roosevelt St, Phoenix AZ 85003
DESCRIPTION: Awarding grants to arts organizations and schools is at the center of the Arizona Commission on the Arts' service. In this effort grant applicants are our partners, providing direct arts experiences throughout Arizona. The Arts Commission provides a variety of funding opportunities that enable schools, organizations and community groups to carry out projects and to maintain ongoing, high quality public arts programming.
SUBMISSION MATERIALS: Check website for updated information.
DEADLINE TYPE: Annual

ARLINGTON COUNTY CULTURAL AFFAIRS DIVISION

WEBSITE: www.arlingtonarts.org/resources/grants.aspx **PHONE:** (703) 228-1850
FAX: (703) 228-1851 **ADDRESS:** 3700 S Four Mile Run Dr, Arlington VA 22206
DESCRIPTION: Arlington Cultural Affairs is charged with fostering a creative environment that encourages collaboration, innovation, and community participation. We do this by providing material support to artists, and arts organizations, in the form of grants, facilities, and theater technology; through a commitment to integrating award-winning Public Art into our built environment; and with high quality performing, literary, visual, and new media programs across the County.
SUBMISSION MATERIALS: Check website for updated information.

ART PROJECT GRANT

PARENT ORGANIZATION: Iowa Arts Council
WEBSITE: iowaculture.gov/arts/grants **PHONE:** 515-281-3293
TWITTER: @iowaartscouncil **ADDRESS:** 600 E Locust, Des Moines IA 50319
DESCRIPTION: Apply for funding to support the creation and presentation of new artwork, development of an arts experience or formation of an arts education program. Project grants provide you support to positively impact the vitality of the arts in Iowa by creating arts opportunities that are accessible to all Iowans.
SUBMISSION MATERIALS: See website for current grants, deadlines, and submission guidelines. **GENRE:** All Genres **PREFERRED LENGTH:** Any Length

ARTIST TRUST

WEBSITE: www.artisttrust.org/index.php/for-artists/money
PHONE: (206) 467-8734 **FAX:** (206) 467-9633 **TWITTER:** @artisttrust
ADDRESS: 1835 12th Ave, Seattle WA 98122
DESCRIPTION: Artistic excellence is the highest priority in our funding programs. Artist Trust grants range from project funds and major merit awards to residencies across the United States. Recipients are selected by peer panels consisting of artists and arts professionals from around and outside the Northwest.
SUBMISSION MATERIALS: See website for details. Fellowships have a rotating list of eligible disciplines. **DEADLINE:** 06/25/2018 **DEADLINE TYPE:** Annual

GRANTS & FELLOWSHIPS

ASIAN CULTURAL COUNCIL
WEBSITE: www.asianculturalcouncil.org/our-programs/general-eligibility-guidelines
PHONE: (212) 843-0403   **FAX:** (212) 843-0343   **TWITTER:** @ACCNY
ADDRESS: 6 W 48th St, 12th Fl, New York NY 10036
DESCRIPTION: ACC accepts applications each fall (generally in September and October) for grants and fellowships to be awarded the following year. Applicants must submit their proposals online, using ACC's grant application platform. They may register for an account at any time, but will only be able to create/edit a submission during the open application period each fall.
SUBMISSION MATERIALS: Eligible disciplines and categories are subject to change from year to year. See website for updates.
DEADLINE TYPE: Annual   **SPECIAL INTEREST:** Asian

AURAND HARRIS CHILDREN'S THEATRE GRANTS AND FELLOWSHIP
PARENT ORGANIZATION: Children's Theater Foundation (CTFA)
WEBSITE: www.childrenstheatrefoundation.org/page9/page10
PHONE: (317) 272-9322   **ADDRESS:** 1114 Red Oak Dr, Avon IN 46123
DESCRIPTION: These grants benefit the field of theatre for children & youth; the utilization of drama or theatre in education for children grades K-12; or opportunities for theatre artists working in these fields.
SUBMISSION MATERIALS: See website for submission guidelines and application.
DEADLINE: 03/05/2018   **DEADLINE TYPE:** Annual
SPECIAL INTEREST: Theatre for Young Audiences

BERLIN ARTISTS-IN-RESIDENCE
WEBSITE: www.daad.de/der-daad/ueber-den-daad/foerderprogramme/de/29150-berliner-kuenstlerprogramm/   **PHONE:** (212) 758-3223
FAX: (212) 755-5780   **ADDRESS:** 871 United Nations Plz, New York NY 10017
DESCRIPTION: The Artists-in-Berlin Program, Berliner Künstlerprogramm, is one of the most renowned international programs offering grants to artists in the fields of visual arts, literature, music and film.
SUBMISSION MATERIALS: Contact New York office for details.

BEYOND THE PURE FELLOWSHIPS FOR WRITERS
PARENT ORGANIZATION: Intermedia Arts
WEBSITE: www.intermediaarts.org/beyond-the-pure-fellowships
ADDRESS: 2822 Lyndale Ave S, Minneapolis MN 55408
DESCRIPTION: Intermedia Arts' Beyond the Pure Fellowships for Writers awards grants of up to $5,000 to four to six emerging Minnesota writers. This program defines an emerging writer as a writer whose work demonstrates a sustained level of accomplishment and commitment, but who has not yet received widespread recognition from peers and/or industry as an established professional writer.
SUBMISSION MATERIALS: See website for updated information.

BRODY ARTS FUND

WEBSITE: www.calfund.org/nonprofits/grant-opportunities/arts/ccf-fellowship-visual-artists **PHONE:** (213) 413-4130
ADDRESS: 445 S Figueroa St, #3400, Los Angeles CA 90071
DESCRIPTION: The California Community Foundation (CCF) awards one-year fellowships to outstanding Los Angeles-based artists working in the visual arts through the CCF Fellowship for Visual Artists. The Fellowships for Visual Artists is a unique opportunity for artists because it is an investment in an artist's career rather than in a particular project.
SUBMISSION MATERIALS: Check website for updated information.
DEADLINE: 02/01/2018 **DEADLINE TYPE:** Annual

BROOKLYN ARTS COUNCIL (BAC)

WEBSITE: www.brooklynartscouncil.org/documents/2448
PHONE: (718) 625-0080 **FAX:** (718) 625-3294
ADDRESS: 20 Jay St, Ste 616, Brooklyn NY 11201
DESCRIPTION: BAC Grants annually distributes over $420,000 to help fund hundreds of projects from artists and cultural organizations across the borough.
SUBMISSION MATERIALS: Check website for updated information.

CALIFORNIA ARTS COUNCIL

WEBSITE: www.cac.ca.gov/programs **PHONE:** (916) 322-6555
FAX: (916) 322-6575 **TWITTER:** @CalArtsCouncil
ADDRESS: 1300 I St, #930, Sacramento CA 95814
DESCRIPTION: The California Arts Council invests in California nonprofit organizations via competitive grant programs, administered through a multistep public process. The California Arts Council is transitioning to a new grants management system. Guidelines and applications for most 2017-18 programs will be made available in mid-November 2017.
SUBMISSION MATERIALS: Check website for updated information.

CEC ARTSLINK

WEBSITE: www.cecartslink.org **PHONE:** (212) 643-1985 **FAX:** (212) 643-1996
TWITTER: @cecartslink **ADDRESS:** 435 Hudson St, 8th Fl, New York NY 10014
DESCRIPTION: Est. 1992. CEC ArtsLink invites artists, arts managers, and arts organizations from 37 countries to apply for ArtsLink Independent Projects awards to collaborate with US artists and arts organizations.
DEADLINE: 12/15/2017

CHAIM SCHWARTZ FOUNDATION

WEBSITE: www.chaimschwartz.org/how.htm
ADDRESS: 69 Olmsted Rd, Apt 109, Stanford CA 94305
DESCRIPTION: Created upon the death Sandra Schwartz Tangri to carry on the work of preserving and studying Yiddishkeit — that is, Yiddish language, culture, theater and art. It is a charitable, 501(c)(3) nonprofit; which is to say, it grants small amounts of money to recognized non-profit organizations for the purpose of preserving and en-

riching Yiddishkeit. The Foundation has no paid staff and a minimal operating budget, and its only activity is to disburse monies through its small grants program. It cannot fund scholarships or make other grants to individuals.

SUBMISSION MATERIALS: Visit website for updated information.
DEADLINE: 04/01/2018   **DEADLINE TYPE:** Annual   **SPECIAL INTEREST:** Jewish

CHARLES LAFITTE FOUNDATION
WEBSITE: www.charleslafitte.org//grants/overview
ADDRESS: 714 Hi Crest Dr, Auburn WA 98001
DESCRIPTION: Giving is personal for the Charles Lafitte Foundation, as we reflect the values and imperatives of our founders, Jeffrey and Suzanne Citron. Every member of the foundation is involved in all of our work, including researching organizations, reviewing grant requests, determining programs, and evaluating outcomes. Every grant is carefully considered. We believe that with each grant CLF awards, we are taking one step closer to a better world.
SUBMISSION MATERIALS: Visit website for updated information.

CHERRY LANE THEATRE MENTOR PROJECT
WEBSITE: www.cherrylanetheatre.org/programs/mentor_project/
EMAIL: company@cherrylanetheatre.org   **PHONE:** (212) 989-2020
ADDRESS: 38 Commerce St, New York NY 10014
DESCRIPTION: Cherry Lane's marquee program is our Obie Award-winning Mentor Project. Every year we pair three early-career playwrights in season-long, 1-on-1 mentoring relationships with experienced dramatists. Mentors guide their fellows through an intensive developmental process consisting of readings and rehearsals, while serving as a trusted source of career advice and professional support. The program culminates in fully-staged productions that remain critic-free to avoid commercial concerns that would inhibit the creative process. Each fellow receives a $5,000 stipend.

CHILDREN'S THEATER FOUNDATION (CTFA)
WEBSITE: www.childrenstheatrefoundation.org   **PHONE:** 9285271765
ADDRESS: CTFA c/o Moses Goldberg, 4211A Trillium Ln, Greensboro NC 27410
DESCRIPTION: Est. 1958. The Children's Theatre Foundation of America challenges and supports theatre artists to achieve excellence in service to young people. CTFA pursues its goals by funding proposals designed to advance the artistic and professional interests of theatre for youth in the USA.
SPECIAL INTEREST: Theatre for Young Audiences   **FEE:** No

CITY OF LOS ANGELES (COLA) PERFORMING ARTS FELLOWSHIPS
WEBSITE: www.culturela.org/grants-and-calls   **PHONE:** (213) 202-5566
FAX: (213) 202-5515   **TWITTER:** @Culture_LA
ADDRESS: 201 N Figueroa St, #1400, Los Angeles CA 90012
DESCRIPTION: Grants are available in a variety of disciplines and categories including dance, music, media, and the visual arts, as well as literature, educational programs, residencies, and professional fellowships. Grantees are selected through a competi-

tive peer review process and contracted for services across LA's neighborhoods.

DEADLINE TYPE: Rolling

CONNECTICUT OFFICE OF THE ARTS

WEBSITE: www.cultureandtourism.org/cct/cwp/view.asp?a=3933&q=462726&cctNav=|#programs **PHONE:** (860) 500-2300 **FAX:** (860) 256-2811 **ADDRESS:** 1 Constitution Plz, 2nd Fl, Hartford CT 6103 **DESCRIPTION:** The Connecticut Office of the Arts' Project Grants program encourages and supports arts-based projects of artistic excellence that are aligned with our READI (Relevance, Equity, Access, Diversity, Inclusion) framework. **SUBMISSION MATERIALS:** Deadlines and grant types vary. Visit website for updated information. **DEADLINE TYPE:** Annual

DC COMMISSION ON THE ARTS AND HUMANITIES

WEBSITE: www.dcarts.dc.gov/page/current-grant-opportunities **PHONE:** (202) 724-5613 **FAX:** (202) 727-4135 **ADDRESS:** 200 I St, SE, Washington DC 20003 **DESCRIPTION:** The DC Commission on the Arts and Humanities (CAH) provides grants, programs and educational activities that encourage diverse arts and humanities expressions and learning opportunities, so that all District of Columbia residents and visitors can experience the rich culture of our city. **SUBMISSION MATERIALS:** Visit website for updated information. **AGENT ONLY:** No

DELAWARE DIVISION OF THE ARTS

WEBSITE: www.arts.delaware.gov/grants-for-artists **PHONE:** (302) 577-8278 **TWITTER:** @ArtsDelaware **ADDRESS:** 820 N French St, Wilmington DE 19801 **DESCRIPTION:** The Division offers two grant options for artists including individual artist fellowships and opportunity grants. Applicants must be Delaware residents, 18 years of age or older, not enrolled in a degree-granting program. Fellowships: annual August 1 deadline. **SUBMISSION MATERIALS:** Visit website for updated information.

DENNIS & VICTORIA ROSS FOUNDATION (DVRF) PLAYWRIGHTS PROGRAM

WEBSITE: www.dvrf.org/about-the-program **PHONE:** 646-362-4316 **TWITTER:** @dvrfound **ADDRESS:** 251 Devoe St, PH, Brooklyn NY 11211 **DESCRIPTION:** This is an annual development opportunity based in New York City. DVRF will sponsor a 1-2 week intensive process where the writer is connected with a director and actors, and given space to concentrate on revisions. The program typically culminates in an industry presentation. We also offer workshops for finalists in the Program. Please see our website for deadlines and more information.

DRIEHAUS FOUNDATION

WEBSITE: www.driehausfoundation.org/guidelines **PHONE:** (312) 641-5772 **TWITTER:** @driehausfdn **ADDRESS:** 737 N Michigan Ave, Ste 2000, Chicago IL 60611 **DESCRIPTION:** Through strategic philanthropic partnerships, we seek to improve Chicago's built environment, to support cultural stewardship in the arts, to strengthen democracy through investigative journalism, and to advance economic opportunity for the working poor. Two deadlines for general operating support grants through the MacArthur Funds for Arts and Culture: • January 15, 2018 – All arts and culture organizations, regardless of discipline, with annual operating budgets under $150,000. • May 1, 2018 – All arts and culture organizations with annual operating budgets between $150,000 and $500,000

SUBMISSION MATERIALS: Visit website for updated information.

FLORIDA DIVISION OF CULTURAL AFFAIRS
WEBSITE: www.dos.myflorida.com/cultural/grants/grant-programs/general-program-support/ **PHONE:** (850) 245-6356 **FAX:** (850) 245-6497
ADDRESS: 500 S Bronough St, 3rd Fl, Tallahassee FL 32399
DESCRIPTION: General Program Support (GPS) funding is designed to support the general program activities of an organization that is realizing its stated mission and furthering the state's cultural objectives by conducting, creating, producing, presenting, staging, or sponsoring cultural exhibits, performances, educational programs, or events or providing professional services as a State Service Organization or Local Arts Agency. **SUBMISSION MATERIALS:** Visit website for updated information.

FULBRIGHT PROGRAM FOR US SCHOLARS
WEBSITE: us.fulbrightonline.org/about/types-of-awards **PHONE:** (212) 984-5525
ADDRESS: 809 United Nations Plz, 1400 K St., Suite 700, New York NY 10017
DESCRIPTION: See website for specific program information.
DEADLINE TYPE: Annual

FUND FOR NEW WORK
PARENT ORGANIZATION: Harlem Stage at The Gatehouse
WEBSITE: www.harlemstage.org/programs **PHONE:** (212) 281-9240
FAX: (212) 281-9318 **ADDRESS:** 150 Convent Ave, New York NY 10030
DESCRIPTION: Harlem Stage is a performing arts center that celebrates and perpetuates the unique and diverse artistic legacy of Harlem and the indelible impression it has made on American culture. We provide opportunity, commissioning and support for artists of color, make performances accessible to all audiences, and introduce children to the rich diversity, excitement and inspiration of the performing arts.
SUBMISSION MATERIALS: Email for specific information.

GEORGE BENNETT FELLOWSHIP
WEBSITE: www.exeter.edu/about-us/career-opportunities/fellowships/writer-residence-george-bennett-fellowship **PHONE:** (603) 777-3645
ADDRESS: 20 Main St, Exeter NH 03833
DESCRIPTION: The purpose of the George Bennett Fellowship is to provide time and freedom from material considerations to a person seriously contemplating or pursuing a career as a writer. The stipend for the one-year Fellow is $15,570, plus housing and meals. This position also offers medical and dental insurance, long-term disability coverage and access to an employee assistance program.
SUBMISSION MATERIALS: Resume, online application, statement of interest, writing sample **DEADLINE:** 11/30/2017 **DEADLINE TYPE:** Annual **FEE:** Yes:

GUAM COUNCIL ON THE ARTS & HUMANITIES AGENCY

WEBSITE: www.guamcaha.org/grants-programs **PHONE:** (671) 300-1204-8
ADDRESS: PO Box 2950, Hagatna 96932 Guam
DESCRIPTION: The Guam Council on the Arts and Humanities Agency awards grants in the disciplines of Arts-in-Education, Folk Arts, Media Arts, Performing Arts, Visual Arts, Special Projects and Underserved. All grants are made on a yearly basis and new applications must be submitted each year. Individuals or Non-Profit Organizations may apply for a grant.
SUBMISSION MATERIALS: See website for specific grant information.
\DEADLINE TYPE: Annual

HELEN MCCLOY/MWA SCHOLARSHIP FOR MYSTERY WRITING

WEBSITE: www.mysterywriters.org/about-mwa/helen-mccloy-scholarship/
ADDRESS: 1140 Broadway, Ste 1507, New York NY 10001
DESCRIPTION: The Helen McCloy/MWA Scholarship for Mystery Writing seeks to nurture talent in mystery writing—in fiction, nonfiction, playwriting, and screenwriting. The scholarship is open to U.S. citizens or permanent residents only and shall be used to offset tuition and fees for writing workshops, writing seminars, or university/college-level writing programs taking place in the U.S. in summer, fall, or winter of 2018 or early spring 2019. Applicants must select a specific writing class/workshop/seminar to which scholarship funds would be applied.
SUBMISSION MATERIALS: Writing sample, completed application, artist statement
DEADLINE: 02/28/2018 **GENRE:** Plays

HODDER FELLOWSHIP

WEBSITE: arts.princeton.edu/fellowships/hodder-fellowship
PHONE: (609) 258-6926 **FAX:** (609) 258-2230
ADDRESS: 185 Nassau St, Princeton NJ 8542
DESCRIPTION: The Hodder Fellowship will be given to artists and writers of exceptional promise to pursue independent projects at Princeton University during the academic year. Given the strength of the applicant pool, most successful Fellows have published a first book or have similar achievements in their own fields.
SUBMISSION MATERIALS: Deadline for 2018 has passed. See website for details and updates. **GENRE:** All genres **FEE:** No **AGENT ONLY:** No

IDAHO COMMISSION ON THE ARTS

WEBSITE: arts.idaho.gov/grants **PHONE:** (208) 334-2119 **FAX:** (208) 334-2488
ADDRESS: PO Box 83720, Boise ID 83720
DESCRIPTION: For annual grants, an applicant may submit one application per category per fiscal year. For quarterly Quickfunds grants, an applicant may submit one application per deadline and receive one Quickfunds grant each fiscal year. See website for specific grant information. **DEADLINE:** 01/31/2018

ILLINOIS ARTS COUNCIL
WEBSITE: www.arts.illinois.gov/grants-programs **PHONE:** (312) 814-6750
FAX: (312) 814-1471 **ADDRESS:** 100 W Randolph St, #10-500, Chicago IL 60601
DESCRIPTION: See website for specific grant and fellowship information.

INDIANA ARTS COMMISSION (IAC)
WEBSITE: www.in.gov/arts/3024.htm **PHONE:** (317) 232-1268 **FAX:** (317) 232-5595 **ADDRESS:** 100 N Senate Ave, Rm N505, Indianapolis IN 46204
DESCRIPTION: Grant categories alternate every fiscal year. See website for further information. **DEADLINE:** 02/01/2018

JAPAN FOUNDATION NEW YORK
WEBSITE: www.jfny.org/grant/grant.html **PHONE:** (212) 489-0299
FAX: (212) 489-0409 **ADDRESS:** 1700 Broadway, 15th Fl, New York NY 10019
DESCRIPTION: To encourage international cultural exchange, the Japan Foundation has various types of support programs. By making available the tools, opportunities, and venues that facilitate exchange activities, we invite individuals and organizations actively engaged in such a mission to participate in our programs. See website for specific grant information.

JEROME FELLOWSHIPS
PARENT ORGANIZATION: Playwrights' Center [MN]
WEBSITE: pwcenter.org/programs/jerome-fellowships
PHONE: (612) 332-7481 **FAX:** (612) 332-6037
ADDRESS: Playwrights' Center, 2301 Franklin Ave E, Minneapolis MN 55406
DESCRIPTION: The Playwrights' Center Jerome Fellowships are awarded annually, providing emerging American playwrights with funds and services to aid them in the development of their craft. Fellow will receive an $18,000 stipend in addition to $2,000 in development support. Fellows spend a year-long residency in Minnesota, working in an individualized and hands-on way with the Playwrights' Center artistic staff.
SUBMISSION MATERIALS: Online only. Full script, resume, artistic statement, letters of recommendation. **DEADLINE:** 01/11/2018

JEROME FOUNDATION GRANTS
PARENT ORGANIZATION: Playwrights' Center [MN]
WEBSITE: www.jeromefdn.org/apply **PHONE:** (651) 224-9431
FAX: (651) 224-3439 **ADDRESS:** 400 Sibley St, #125, Saint Paul MN 55101
DESCRIPTION: The Jerome Foundation promotes a dynamic culture through support for artists, collectives and/or ensembles across all disciplines in the early stages of their vocational artistic lives to create new work and for nonprofit arts organizations that offer programs, services and activities for such artists, collectives and/or ensembles. See website for specific grant information.

JONATHAN LARSON GRANTS
WEBSITE: americantheatrewing.org/program/jonathan-larson-grants
ADDRESS: American Theatre Wing, 230 W 41st St, Ste 1101, New York NY 10036
DESCRIPTION: The Jonathan Larson Grant is an unconditional annual investment in individual talent. The grant is awarded to four musical theatre composers, lyricists, and librettists, or writing teams, early in their career, to support artistic endeavors and safeguard long-term music writing careers.
SUBMISSION MATERIALS: The application for the 2018 grants is now closed. Check website for updated information. **GENRE:** Musicals

KENTUCKY ARTS COUNCIL
WEBSITE: artscouncil.ky.gov **PHONE:** (888) 833-2787 x479
ADDRESS: 500 Mero St, 21st Fl, Frankfort KY 40601
DESCRIPTION: See website for specific grant and fellowship information.

KLEBAN PRIZE IN MUSICAL THEATRE
WEBSITE: newdramatists.org/kleban-prize-musical-theatre
PHONE: (212) 757-6960 **ADDRESS:** 424 W. 44th St., New York NY 10036
DESCRIPTION: Created by Edward Kleban by an instruction in his Will, this prize is given annually to both a librettist and a lyricist. The Kleban Board of Directors sets the amount of the prize annually but in recent years the prize has been in the amount of $100,000 in each category payable in two annual installments.
SUBMISSION MATERIALS: Work sample, online application
DEADLINE: 05/15/2018 **GENRE:** Musicals

LAURA JANE MUSSER FUND RURAL ARTS PROGRAM
WEBSITE: www.musserfund.org/index.asp?page_seq=23
PHONE: (612) 825-2024
DESCRIPTION: The Musser Fund hopes to assist nonprofit arts organizations in rural communities to develop, implement or sustain exceptional artistic opportunities for adults and children in the areas of literary, visual, music, and performing arts. Visit website for application information. **DEADLINE:** 03/16/2018

LOS ANGELES CULTURAL AFFAIRS DEPT.
WEBSITE: culturela.org/grants-and-calls **PHONE:** (213) 202-5566
FAX: (213) 202-5515 **ADDRESS:** 201 N Figueroa St, #1400, Los Angeles CA 90012
SUBMISSION MATERIALS: See website for specific grant information.

LOUISIANA DIVISION OF THE ARTS
WEBSITE: www.crt.state.la.us/cultural-development/arts/arts-opportunities/index **PHONE:** (225) 342-8180
DESCRIPTION: See website for specific information regarding artist opportunities.

MACARTHUR FOUNDATION FELLOWSHIP
WEBSITE: www.macfound.org/info-grantseekers **PHONE:** (312) 726-8000
FAX: (312) 920-6258 **ADDRESS:** 161 N Clark St, Ste 700, Chicago IL 60601
DESCRIPTION: The MacArthur Fellowship is a five-year grant to individuals who show

exceptional creativity in their work and the prospect for still more in the future.

We limit our consideration only to those who have been nominated by someone from our constantly changing pool of invited external nominators. Applications or unsolicited nominations are not accepted

MAINE ARTS COMMISSION
WEBSITE: mainearts.maine.gov/Pages/Funding/Grants-Home
PHONE: (207) 287-2724 **FAX:** (207) 287-2725 **TWITTER:** @MaineArts
ADDRESS: 25 State House Station, Augusta ME 04333
DESCRIPTION: The Maine Arts Commission offers funding programs for organizations, individuals, educators, and municipalities. See website for specific grant information.

MANY VOICES FELLOWSHIPS
PARENT ORGANIZATION: Playwrights' Center [MN]
WEBSITE: pwcenter.org/programs/many-voices-fellowships
PHONE: (612) 332-7481 **FAX:** (612) 332-6037
ADDRESS: Playwrights' Center, 2301 Franklin Ave E, Minneapolis MN 55406
DESCRIPTION: Many Voices Fellowships are awarded annually to two artists of color with previous playwriting experience and/or training. Fellowships provide an $18,000 stipend and $2,000 in play development funds. Fellows spend a year-long residency in Minnesota, working in an individualized and hands-on way with the Playwrights' Center artistic staff—some of the most experienced and connected theater professionals in the country.
SUBMISSION MATERIALS: Online application. **DEADLINE:** 12/14/2017

MARYLAND STATE ARTS COUNCIL
WEBSITE: www.msac.org/programs/individual-artist-award
PHONE: (410) 767-6536 **FAX:** (410) 333-1062
ADDRESS: 175 W Ostend St, Ste E, Baltimore MD 21230
DESCRIPTION: Each year, MSAC recognizes the outstanding artistic achievements of artists from across Maryland with awards of $1,000, $3,000 and $6,000. These awards honor artists, showcasing their importance to the cultural fabric of our state, supporting their creative potential and strengthening their impact on the local level. See website for specific grant information.

MASSACHUSETTS CULTURAL COUNCIL
WEBSITE: www.massculturalcouncil.org/programs/programs.asp
PHONE: (617) 858-2700 **TWITTER:** @masscultural
ADDRESS: 10 St James Ave, 3rd Fl, Boston MA 02116
DESCRIPTION: See website for fellowship and grant information.
DEADLINE TYPE: Annual

MCKNIGHT FELLOWSHIP IN PLAYWRITING
PARENT ORGANIZATION: Playwrights' Center [MN]
WEBSITE: pwcenter.org/programs/mcknight-fellowships-in-playwriting
PHONE: (612) 332-7481

ADDRESS: Playwrights' Center, 2301 Franklin Ave E, Minneapolis MN 55406
DESCRIPTION: The McKnight Fellowships in Playwriting recognize playwrights whose work demonstrates exceptional artistic merit and excellence in the field, and whose primary residence is in the state of Minnesota. See website for details.
SUBMISSION MATERIALS: Online application. **DEADLINE:** 01/18/2018

MICHIGAN COUNCIL FOR THE ARTS & CULTURAL AFFAIRS
WEBSITE: www.michiganbusiness.org/community/council-arts-cultural-affairs/#mcaca-grants **PHONE:** (888) 522-0103
ADDRESS: 300 N Washington Sq, Lansing MI 48913
DESCRIPTION: The Michigan Council for Arts and Cultural Affairs (MCACA) coordinates grants to arts and culture organizations, cities and municipalities, and other nonprofit organizations to encourage, develop and facilitate an enriched environment of artistic, creative and cultural activity in Michigan. See website for specific grant information.

MID ATLANTIC ARTS FOUNDATION
WEBSITE: www.midatlanticarts.org/grants-programs/grants-for-artists
PHONE: 4105396656 **TWITTER:** @MidAtlanticArts **ADDRESS:** Mid Atlantic Arts Foundation, 201 N Charles St, Ste 401, Baltimore MD 21201
DESCRIPTION: Est. 1979. Mid Atlantic Arts Foundation's grant programs for artists allow artists to explore and create, provide touring engagements regionally and internationally, help to build audiences, and provide support and services to assist in career development. See website for specific grant information.

MINNESOTA STATE ARTS BOARD
WEBSITE: www.arts.state.mn.us/grants/artists.htm **PHONE:** (651) 215-1617
FAX: (651) 215-1602 **ADDRESS:** 400 Sibley St, #200, St. Paul MN 55101
DESCRIPTION: The Minnesota State Arts Board provides financial support to artists and organizations throughout the state to ensure that all Minnesotans have the opportunity to participate in the arts. See website for specific grant information.

MISSISSIPPI ARTS COMMISSION
WEBSITE: arts.ms.gov/grants **PHONE:** (601) 359-6546 **FAX:** (601) 359-6008
TWITTER: @MSarts **ADDRESS:** 501 N West St, #701-B, Jackson MS 39201
DESCRIPTION: MAC funds activities that promote public understanding and support of the arts and artistic excellence. See website for specific grant information.

MISSOURI ARTS COUNCIL
WEBSITE: www.missouriartscouncil.org/grants **PHONE:** (314) 340-6845
TWITTER: @MoArtsCouncil **ADDRESS:** 815 Olive St, Ste 16, St. Louis MO 63101
DESCRIPTION: The Missouri Arts Council provides funding for quality arts programming to eligible applicants. See website for specific grant information.

GRANTS & FELLOWSHIPS

NEA LITERATURE FELLOWSHIPS: CREATIVE WRITING

WEBSITE: www.arts.gov/grants-individuals/creative-writing-fellowships
EMAIL: LitFellowships@arts.gov   **PHONE:** (202) 682-5034   **TWITTER:** @NEAarts
ADDRESS: 109 E Jones St, Raleigh NC 27601

DESCRIPTION: Offers $25,000 grants in poetry to published creative writers that enable recipients to set aside time for writing, research, travel, and general career advancement. Applications are reviewed through an anonymous process in which the only criteria for review are artistic excellence and merit. This program operates on a two-year cycle with fellowships in prose and poetry available in alternating years.

SUBMISSION MATERIALS: See website for details. Online application only.
DEADLINE: 03/07/2018   **DEADLINE TYPE:** Biennial

NEA LITERATURE FELLOWSHIPS: TRANSLATION PROJECTS

WEBSITE: www.arts.gov/grants-individuals/translation-projects
EMAIL: LitFellowships@arts.gov   **PHONE:** (202) 682-5034   **TWITTER:** @NEAarts
ADDRESS: 109 E Jones St, Raleigh NC 27601

DESCRIPTION: The NEA supports published translators' projects for the translation of specific works of prose, poetry, or drama from other languages into English. Grants are for $12,500 or $25,000. Award amounts are determined by the NEA. Responses will be sent no sooner than August 2018. The National Endowment for the Arts' support of a project may begin any time between November 1, 2018, and November 1, 2019, and extend for up to two years.   **SUBMISSION MATERIALS:** See website for details. Online application only.   **DEADLINE:** 01/11/2018

NATIONAL MUSEUM OF THE AMERICAN INDIAN ARTIST LEADERSHIP PROGRAM

WEBSITE: nmai.si.edu/connect/artist-leadership-program
PHONE: (301) 238-1545   **FAX:** (301) 238-3200
ADDRESS: 4220 Silver Hill Rd, Suitland MD 20746

DESCRIPTION: Est. 1996. The National Museum of the American Indian's (NMAI) Artist Leadership Program (ALP) for Individual Artists enables indigenous artists to research, document, and network in Washington, D.C., then return home empowered with new artistic insights, skills, and techniques to share with their communities and the general public the value of Native knowledge through art.

SUBMISSION MATERIALS: Applications for Individual Artists and for Museums and Cultural Arts Organizations are not being accepted at this time. Please email alp@si.edu if you would like to be notified when a new call for proposals is open.

SPECIAL INTEREST: American Indian or Alaskan Native

NEBRASKA ARTS COUNCIL

WEBSITE: www.artscouncil.nebraska.gov/grants   **PHONE:** (402) 595-2122
FAX: (402) 595-2334   **ADDRESS:** 1004 Farnam St, LL, Omaha NB 68102

DESCRIPTION: The Nebraska Arts Council makes its biggest impact through the distribution of grants for arts projects and programming throughout the state. See website for specific grant information.

NEVADA ARTS COUNCIL
WEBSITE: nvculture.org/nevadaartscouncil/grants/5365-2/
PHONE: (775) 687-6680
ADDRESS: 716 N Carson St, Ste A, Carson City NV 89701
DESCRIPTION: Annual, quarterly and rolling grants available for artists, arts administrators, board members and educators. See website for specific grant information.

NEW MEXICO ARTS
WEBSITE: www.nmarts.org/grants **PHONE:** (505) 827-6490
FAX: (505) 827-6043 **ADDRESS:** PO Box 1450, Santa Fe NM 87504
DESCRIPTION: New Mexico Arts funds nonprofits and governmental organizations for arts activities. We support programs that foster arts education, arts economic development; performing and visual arts, and contemporary and traditional folk arts in New Mexico. See website for specific grant information.

NEW YORK STATE COUNCIL ON THE ARTS
WEBSITE: www.nysca.org/public/grants/index.htm **PHONE:** (212) 459-8800
ADDRESS: 300 Park Ave S, 10th Fl, New York NY 10010
DESCRIPTION: The New York State Council on the Arts awards grants to nonprofit organizations incorporated and doing business in New York State, Indian tribes in New York State, and units of government in municipalities in New York State. Individuals and unincorporated groups may not apply but an eligible nonprofit organization, known as a fiscal sponsor, may apply on behalf of an individual or unincorporated groupSee website for specific grant information.

NORTH CAROLINA ARTS COUNCIL
WEBSITE: www.ncarts.org/invest-arts/grants-artists **PHONE:** (919) 807-6512
FAX: (919) 807-6532 **TWITTER:** @NCArtsCouncil
ADDRESS: 109 E Jones St, Raleigh NC 27601
DESCRIPTION: The program operates on a two-year cycle. Songwriters, composers, and writers deadline: November 1, 2018. Artists residing in NC for at least one year prior to the deadline and who are at least 18 years old are eligible. They must be a U.S. citizen or holder of permanent resident alien status and must remain a NC resident and be physically present in the state during the grant period. Artists who received the fellowship grant in the past five years or are enrolled in an academic or degree-granting program at the time of application or during the grant period are not eligible.
SUBMISSION MATERIALS: See website for details and submission form.
DEADLINE: 11/01/2018

NORTH DAKOTA COUNCIL ON THE ARTS
WEBSITE: www.nd.gov/arts/grants **PHONE:** (701) 328-7590
ADDRESS: 1600 E Century Ave, Ste 6, Bismarck ND 58503
DESCRIPTION: Est. 1984. See website for specific grant and fellowship information.

NYFA FISCAL SPONSORSHIP
PARENT ORGANIZATION: New York Foundation for the Arts
WEBSITE: www.nyfa.org/Content/Show/Fiscal%20Sponsorship
PHONE: (212) 366-6900 **FAX:** (212) 366-1778 **TWITTER:** @nyfacurrent
ADDRESS: 20 Jay St, 7th Fl, Brooklyn NY 11201
DESCRIPTION: Fiscal sponsorship allows individual artists and emerging arts organizations in all disciplines the ability to raise funds using NYFA's tax-exempt status as a 501(c)(3)-classified organization. Under NYFA's fiscal sponsorship, artists and organizations can optimize the reach of their fundraising efforts. See website for application information.

NYSCA/NYFA ARTIST FELLOWSHIPS
PARENT ORGANIZATION: New York Foundation for the Arts
WEBSITE: www.nyfa.org/Content/Show/Artists'%20Fellowships
PHONE: (212) 366-6900 **FAX:** (212) 366-1778 **TWITTER:** @nyfacurrent
ADDRESS: 20 Jay St, 7th Fl, Brooklyn NY 11201
DESCRIPTION: NYSCA/NYFA Artist Fellowships, awarded in fifteen different disciplines over a three-year period, are $7,000 cash awards made to individual originating artists living and working in the state of New York for unrestricted use. These fellowships are not project grants but are intended to fund an artist's vision or voice, regardless of the level of his or her artistic development. See website for specific fellowship information.

OBAMA FOUNDATION FELLOWSHIP
WEBSITE: www.obama.org/fellowship **TWITTER:** @ObamaFoundation
DESCRIPTION: The Obama Foundation Fellowship program seeks to support outstanding civic innovators from around the world in order to amplify the impact of their work and to inspire a wave of civic innovation. See website for deadline information.
DEADLINE TYPE: Annual **FEE:** No **AGENT ONLY:** No

OHIO ARTS COUNCIL
WEBSITE: www.oac.ohio.gov/grants **PHONE:** (614) 466-2613 **FAX:** (614) 466-4494
ADDRESS: Rhodes State Office Twr, 30 E Broad St, 33rd Fl, Columbus OH 43215
DESCRIPTION: The Ohio Arts Council's current grant programs are grouped into four categories: operating support, project support, arts learning, and individual artists. See website for specific grant information.
DEADLINE: 09/01/2018 **DEADLINE TYPE:** Annual

OKLAHOMA ARTS COUNCIL
WEBSITE: www.arts.ok.gov/Grants.html **PHONE:** (405) 521-2931
FAX: (405) 521-6418 **TWITTER:** @OKArtsCouncil
ADDRESS: PO Box 52001-2001, Oklahoma City OK 73152
DESCRIPTION: The Oklahoma Arts Council provides grants to eligible organizations for arts programs that take place in communities and schools. See website for specific grant information.

OREGON ARTS COMMISSION

WEBSITE: www.oregonartscommission.org/grants?type=13
PHONE: (503) 986-0082 **FAX:** (503) 986-0260
ADDRESS: 775 Summer St NE, Ste 200, Salem OR 97301
DESCRIPTION: Along with our work in arts advocacy and policy development, the Arts Commission funds arts programs and individual artistic innovation throughout Oregon. See website for specific grant information.

PENNSYLVANIA COUNCIL ON THE ARTS

WEBSITE: www.arts.pa.gov/WHAT%20WE%20DO/FUNDING/apply-for-a-grant/Pages/default.aspx **PHONE:** (717) 525-5542 **FAX:** (717) 783-2538
ADDRESS: 216 Finance Bldg, Harrisburg PA 17120
DESCRIPTION: The PCA provides grants to individuals and organizations through its Arts Organizations and Arts Programs (AOAP) funding stream, and distributes grants at a localized level via its PA Partners in the Arts' (PPA) Project Stream and Program Stream. See website for specific grant information. **DEADLINE TYPE:** Annual

PEW GRANTS AND FELLOWSHIPS IN THE ARTS

WEBSITE: www.pcah.us/apply **PHONE:** (267) 350-4920
TWITTER: @PewCenterArts **ADDRESS:** Pew Center for Arts & Heritage, 1608 Walnut St, 18th Fl, Philadelphia PA 19103
DESCRIPTION: As a multidisciplinary grantmaker dedicated to fostering a vibrant community, the Center awards Project grants in Performance and Exhibitions & Public Interpretation, twelve annual Fellowships which provide unrestricted grants to individual artists working in all disciplines, and Advancement grants to support high-performing institutions undertaking bold, innovative organizational initiatives. See website for specific grant information.

THE BALL GRANT (THE PLAYWRITING COLLECTIVE)

WEBSITE: www.theplaywritingcollective.com/the-ball-grant
TWITTER: @PlaywritingCOLL **ADDRESS:** Bronx NY 10457
DESCRIPTION: The Ball Grant is financial resource dedicated to those lower class and marginalized writers and artists. The Playwriting Collective has been organized to create artistic and theatrical productions, readings, and showings centered within supporting voices from lower-economic backgrounds and other marginalized communities.
SUBMISSION MATERIALS: See website for updated information.
GENRE: Plays **PREFERRED LENGTH:** Full-length **FEE:** No **AGENT ONLY:** No

PRINCESS GRACE FOUNDATION USA PLAYWRITING FELLOWSHIP

WEBSITE: newdramatists.org/princess-grace **PHONE:** (212) 317-1470
ADDRESS: 150 E 58th St, 25th Fl, New York NY 10155
DESCRIPTION: The Princess Grace Awards is a national program dedicated to identifying and assisting emerging theater, dance, and film artists who are at the outset of their careers or at early stages of professional development. One fellowship is offered annually to an individual playwright, including residency at New Dramatists

and opportunity for winning play to be licensed and published by Samuel French, Inc.

SUBMISSION MATERIALS: All nominees (except playwrights, who may apply individually through www.newdramatists.org), must be nominated by a school department chair/dean or company artistic director. Self-nominations are not allowed. The nominating organization must be a registered 501 (c)(3) non-profit organization for at least three years.

DEADLINE: 03/15/2018   **DEADLINE TYPE:** Annual

PRINCETON ARTS FELLOWSHIP

WEBSITE: arts.princeton.edu/fellowships/princeton-arts-fellowship
PHONE: (609) 258-1500   **ADDRESS:** 185 Nassau St, Princeton NJ 08544
DESCRIPTION: Deadline for 2018 has passed. Please check website for updates. Princeton Arts Fellows spend two consecutive academic years (September 1-July 1) at Princeton University. The normal work assignment will be to teach one course each semester subject to approval by the Dean of the Faculty, but fellows may be asked to take on an artistic assignment in lieu of a class, such as directing a play or creating a dance with students. $81,000 annual stipend.

SUBMISSION MATERIALS: Resume, personal statement, references. Work samples are requested to be submitted online.   **DEADLINE TYPE:** Annual

PUBLIC THEATER EMERGING WRITERS GROUP

WEBSITE: www.publictheater.org/Programs--Events/Emerging-Writers-Group/
PHONE: (212) 539-8530   **ADDRESS:** 425 Lafayette St, New York NY 10003
DESCRIPTION: The Emerging Writers Group is a component of The Public Writers Initiative, a long-term program that provides key support and resources for writers at every stage of their careers. It creates a fertile community and fosters a web of supportive artistic relationships across generations.

QUEENS COUNCIL ON THE ARTS

WEBSITE: www.queenscouncilarts.org   **PHONE:** (347) 505-3016
TWITTER: @QNSArts   **ADDRESS:** 37-11 35th Ave, Astoria NY 11101
DESCRIPTION: Founded to foster and develop the arts in Queens County and to support individual Queens-based artists and arts organizations in presenting their cultural diversity for the benefit of the community. See website for grants and commission information.

SPECIAL INTEREST: American Indian or Alaskan Native; Asian; Black or African American; Deaf or Hearing-impaired; Feminism/Women's Rights; Gender Identity; Hispanic or Latinx; Jewish; LGBT+; Living with Disability; Muslim; Native Hawaiian or Other Pacific Islander

RADCLIFFE INSTITUTE FELLOWSHIPS

WEBSITE: www.radcliffe.edu/fellowships   **PHONE:** (617) 496-1324
TWITTER: @RadInstitute   **ADDRESS:** 8 Garden St, Byerly Hall, Cambridge MA 02138
DESCRIPTION: Fellows receive office or studio space and access to libraries and other resources of Harvard University during the fellowship year. Visual artists and film, video, sound, and new media artists may apply to come for either one or two semesters. In the event that they come for one semester, the stipend is $38,750.00. Fellows are expected to be free of their regular commitments so they may devote themselves full time to the work outlined in their proposal.

SUBMISSION MATERIALS: The deadline for 2018 application has passed. Please check website for updated information.

DEADLINE TYPE: Annual   **SPECIAL INTEREST:** Feminism/Women's Rights

RHODE ISLAND STATE COUNCIL ON THE ARTS
WEBSITE: www.arts.ri.gov/grants/overview   **PHONE:** (401) 222-3880
TWITTER: @risca1967   **ADDRESS:** 1 Capitol Hill, 3rd Fl, Providence RI 02908
DESCRIPTION: Offers a variety of grants for individuals and organizations in Rhode Island. See website for details.

ROBERT CHESLEY/VICTOR BUMBALO PLAYWRITING GRANT
PARENT ORGANIZATION: Helene Wurlitzer Foundation of New Mexico
WEBSITE: www.chesleyfoundation.org   **EMAIL:** vgb828@gmail.com
ADDRESS: PO Box 1891, Taos, NM 87571
DESCRIPTION: The award seeks to encourage LGBTQ themed work that makes a substantial contribution to the theatrical repertoire and community. This grant is made in partnership with the Helene Wurlitzer Foundation to provide residencies at the artists' colony in Taos, NM. The Wurlitzer and the Chesley/Bumbalo Foundations select the awardees. The Chesley/Bumbalo Foundation will underwrite the residency expenses and, in addition, will provide a stipend to the awardee. See website for details.
DEADLINE: 1/14/2018

SCHOMBURG CENTER SCHOLARS-IN-RESIDENCE
PARENT ORGANIZATION: New York Public Library
WEBSITE: schomburgcenter.org/scholarsinresidence   **PHONE:** (917) 275-6975
ADDRESS: Schomburg Center for Research in Black Culture, 515 Malcolm X Blvd, New York NY 10037
DESCRIPTION: The Schomburg Center for Research in Black Culture, a unit of The New York Public Library, invites applications for its Scholars-in-Residence Program for the 2018-2019 academic year. The program offers long-term and short-term research fellowships to scholars and writers pursuing projects in African diasporic studies in fields including history, politics, literature, and culture.
SUBMISSION MATERIALS: See website for application information.

SEVENTH GENERATION FUND FOR INDIGENOUS PEOPLES
WEBSITE: 7genfund.org/apply-grant   **ADDRESS:** PO Box 4569, Arcata CA 95518
DESCRIPTION: Seventh Generation Fund is an Indigenous identity-based organization dedicated to the self-determination of Native Peoples and the sovereignty of our distinct Nations that mobilizes financial, technical, and informational resources directly to Native communities to empower action. See website for specific grant information.

SOKOLOFF ARTS FELLOWSHIP
WEBSITE: www.sokoloffarts.org/fellowship   **PHONE:** (212) 634-7690

DESCRIPTION: In collaboration with TOWN STAGES' beautiful new arts and events complex in Manhattan, Sokoloff Arts is excited to offer artists a consolidated home for the life cycle of your project, a platform for the next phase of development, and an ultimate pipeline to success. Part residency, part incubator, and part home base, a Fellowship with Sokoloff Arts offers ultimate creative freedom to grow within our walls.
GENRE: All Genres **PREFERRED LENGTH:** Any Length

SOUTH CAROLINA ARTS COMMISSION
WEBSITE: www.southcarolinaarts.com/grants/artists/index.shtml
PHONE: (803) 734-8677 **FAX:** (803) 734-8526 **TWITTER:** @scartscomm
ADDRESS: 1800 Gervais St, Columbia SC 29201
DESCRIPTION: Fellowships for South Carolina residents in playwriting and music composition among other categories. See website for the fellowship rotation cycle and deadlines.

SOUTH DAKOTA ARTS COUNCIL
WEBSITE: www.artscouncil.sd.gov/grants/grantartist.aspx
PHONE: (800) 952-3625 **ADDRESS:** 711 E Wells Ave, Pierre SD 57501
DESCRIPTION: See website for list of available grants and information.
DEADLINE TYPE: Annual

SURDNA FOUNDATION
WEBSITE: www.surdna.org/grants/grants-overview.html **PHONE:** (212) 557-0010
TWITTER: @Surdna_Fndn **ADDRESS:** 330 Madison Ave, 30th Fl, New York NY 10017
DESCRIPTION: The Surdna Foundation makes grants to nonprofit organizations in the priority areas of Sustainable Environments, Strong Local Economies, and Thriving Cultures. They do not make grants to individuals. See website for specific grant information.

TCG GRANTS
PARENT ORGANIZATION: Theatre Communications Group
WEBSITE: www.tcg.org/Grants/GrantsAtAGlance.aspx **PHONE:** (212) 609-5900
FAX: (212) 609-5901 **TWITTER:** @TCG
ADDRESS: 520 8th Ave, 24th Fl, New York NY 10018
DESCRIPTION: See website for various grants and information.

TENNESSEE ARTS COMMISSION
WEBSITE: www.tn.gov/artscommission/topic/grants **PHONE:** (615) 741-1701
FAX: (615) 741-8559 **TWITTER:** @TN_Arts
ADDRESS: 401 Charlotte Ave, Nashville TN 37243
DESCRIPTION: The Tennessee Arts Commission offers a variety of distinct funding opportunities in the arts to serve diverse constituencies. See website for specific grant information.

TEXAS COMMISSION ON THE ARTS
WEBSITE: www.arts.state.tx.us **PHONE:** (512) 463-5535 **FAX:** (512) 475-2699

ADDRESS: PO Box 13406, Austin TX 78711

DESCRIPTION: Visit website to search current grants and other resources for artists residing in Texas.

TUTTEROW FELLOWS PROGRAM

PARENT ORGANIZATION: Chicago Dramatists
WEBSITE: www.chicagodramatists.org/Tutterow-Fellows
PHONE: (312) 633-0630   **TWITTER:** @ChiDrama
ADDRESS: 1105 W Chicago Ave, Chicago IL 60642
DESCRIPTION: Designed to support the emergent playwright, this two-year fellowship emphasizes training, practice and mentorship. Ideal candidates display significant potential for developing their craft, their voice and their network of collaborators during their fellowship at Chicago Dramatists. Two-thirds of each cohort are reserved for historically un-represented voices: writers of color, LGBTQIA, differently-abled, and/or neuro-divergent.
SUBMISSION MATERIALS: Resume, statement of intent, letter of recommendation, two writing samples   **DEADLINE:** 12/15/2017   **GENRE:** Plays
PREFERRED LENGTH: Full-length   **FEE:** No   **AGENT ONLY:** No

UTAH ARTS COUNCIL

WEBSITE: heritage.utah.gov/utah-division-of-arts-museums/grants
PHONE: (801) 236-7555   **FAX:** (801) 236-7556
ADDRESS: 617 E South Temple, Salt Lake City UT 84102
DESCRIPTION: A variety of grants primarily geared toward organizations. See website for information.   **DEADLINE TYPE:** Annual

VAN LIER NEW VOICES FELLOWSHIP

PARENT ORGANIZATION: The Lark
WEBSITE: www.larktheatre.org/get-involved/submit-play/van-lier-new-voices-fellowship-2018-application-guidelines   **PHONE:** (212) 246-2676
TWITTER: @LarkTheatre   **ADDRESS:** 311 W 43rd St, Ste 406, New York NY 10036
DESCRIPTION: The Van Lier New Voices Fellowship supports playwrights of color under 30 who demonstrate financial need. During a year-long residency, Fellows will work on multiple artistic projects through an individually-tailored program of Lark play development programs, and form relationships with other theatermakers at various career stages from all parts of the world. The Fellowship includes a cash award of $15,000, plus up to $3,000 in health insurance premium reimbursement, along with access to a wide range of Lark resources, including artistic program participation, office and rehearsal space, and staff support.
SUBMISSION MATERIALS: See website for updates & info.   **DEADLINE TYPE:** Annual
GENRE: Plays   **PREFERRED LENGTH:** Full-length   **FEE:** No   **AGENT ONLY:** No

VANDERBILT UNIVERSITY WRITER-IN-RESIDENCE

WEBSITE: apply.interfolio.com/45058   **ADDRESS:** Vanderbilt University, 2301 Vanderbilt Pl, Nashville TN 37235
DESCRIPTION: Vanderbilt University seeks applications for a Writer-in-Residence spe-

GRANTS & FELLOWSHIPS

cializing in screenwriting and playwriting for a joint appointment in Cinema and Media Arts (CMA) and Theatre. Undergraduate teaching load will be two courses each semester and will include an introductory course, "Writing for the Stage and Screen," upper level courses in screenwriting and playwriting, and working with students on independent and co-curricular projects. The successful candidate will have an MFA or Ph.D. in hand by August 1, 2018, professional experience writing in both modes, and evidence of teaching effectiveness. This is a non-tenure-track, non-renewable appointment for up to a three-year term.

SUBMISSION MATERIALS: Online only. Letter of interest, resume, letters of recommendation, writing sample **DEADLINE:** 12/01/2017

VERMONT ARTS COUNCIL
WEBSITE: www.vermontartscouncil.org/grants-and-services/artists
PHONE: (802) 828-3291 **TWITTER:** @VTArtsCouncil
ADDRESS: 136 State St, Montpelier VT 5633
DESCRIPTION: Est. 1994. Grants for artists and organizations. Application submission is online only. Must be a Vermont resident. See website for specific grant information.

VIRGIN ISLANDS COUNCIL ON THE ARTS
WEBSITE: www.vicouncilonarts.org/grant-programs-services/grant-guidelines/
PHONE: (340) 774-5984 **FAX:** (340) 774-6206
ADDRESS: 5070 Norre Gade, Ste 1, St Thomas VI 00802
DESCRIPTION: Deadlines: January 31st – Mini Grants, August 31st – Annual Grants. Must be in residence and active in the V.I. for a minimum of two years at time of application. See website for specific grant information.
DEADLINE: 01/31/2018

VIRGINIA COMMISSION FOR THE ARTS
WEBSITE: www.arts.virginia.gov/grants.html **PHONE:** (804) 225-3132
FAX: (804) 225-4327 **TWITTER:** @VirginiaArts
ADDRESS: 223 Governor St, 2nd Fl, Richmond VA 23219
DESCRIPTION: The Virginia Commission for the Arts builds and strengthens the cultural infrastructure through supporting Virginia's individual artists, arts entrepreneurs, businesses and institutions. See website for specific grant information.
SUBMISSION MATERIALS: Online applications only.

WASHINGTON STATE ARTS COMMISSION
WEBSITE: www.arts.wa.gov/grants **PHONE:** (360) 753-3860
FAX: (360) 586-5351 **TWITTER:** @ArtsWA
ADDRESS: PO Box 42675, Olympia WA 98504-2675
DESCRIPTION: See website for specific grant information.
SUBMISSION MATERIALS: Online applications only. **DEADLINE TYPE:** Annual

WEST VIRGINIA COMMISSION ON THE ARTS
WEBSITE: www.wvculture.org/arts/grants.html **PHONE:** (304) 558-0220
FAX: (304) 558-2779 **ADDRESS:** 1900 Kanawha Blvd, E Charleston WV 25305

DESCRIPTION: See website for specific grant information.

WILLIAM PENN FOUNDATION
WEBSITE: www.williampennfoundation.org/how-we-fund-creative-communities
PHONE: (215) 988-1830 **TWITTER:** @WilliamPennFdn
ADDRESS: 2 Logan Sq, 11th Fl, 100 N 18th St, Philadelphia PA 19103
DESCRIPTION: To foster a vibrant and creative Philadelphia, we support a variety of its arts and cultural organizations, educational experiences that increase student access to the arts, and development of high-quality public spaces as platforms for community and cultural expression.
SUBMISSION MATERIALS: The Foundation has a two-stage online application process which includes an initial inquiry and an invited full proposal. As a first step, we strongly suggest reviewing the program guidelines before making an inquiry. This will allow you to confirm that your proposed work aligns with the Foundation's strategic priorities and eligibility requirements. See website for details.

WISCONSIN ARTS BOARD
WEBSITE: artsboard.wisconsin.gov/pages/Community/GrantPrograms.aspx
PHONE: (608) 264-8191 **FAX:** (608) 267-9629
ADDRESS: 101 E Wilson St, 1st Fl, Madison WI 53702
DESCRIPTION: Individuals: Currently offering the Folk Arts Apprenticeship Program, designed to strengthen and preserve Wisconsin's heritage by supporting direct passage of knowledge and skills embedded in traditional arts. Skilled and experienced traditional or folk artists teach committed and talented apprentices of their choosing. The instructing artist should be locally or regionally respected in a traditional or folk art form important to a cultural community in Wisconsin. Both the instructing artist and apprentice should be committed to preserving and advancing the art form.
SUBMISSION MATERIALS: See website for details.
DEADLINE: 03/23/2018 **DEADLINE TYPE:** Annual **FEE:** No

WYOMING ARTS COUNCIL
WEBSITE: wyoarts.state.wy.us/grants/fy18-grants
PHONE: (307) 777-7742 **FAX:** (307) 777-5499
ADDRESS: 2301 Central Ave, 2nd Fl, Cheyenne WY 82001
DESCRIPTION: Grants and Fellowships for Wyoming residents in a variety of categories. See website for current information and deadlines.

THEATRES

2ND STORY
WEBSITE: www.2ndstory.com   **EMAIL**: info@2ndstory.com
PHONE: (773) 279-8580   **ADDRESS**: 3001 W Lawrence Ave, Chicago IL 60625
DESCRIPTION: 2nd Story is dedicated to creating and crafting story-sharing experiences that foster meaningful connections between individuals and communities. We believe that well-crafted, well-told stories can be a catalyst for change for artist and audience alike.

4TH STREET THEATER
WEBSITE: 4thstreetncca.org/6x10.php   **EMAIL**: ncca4thstreet@comcast.net
PHONE: (219) 926-7875   **ADDRESS**: PO Box 2281, Chesterton IN 46304
DESCRIPTION: Est. 1990. Producing award-winning theatre in Northwest Indiana.
FEE: No   **AGENT ONLY**: No

5TH AVENUE THEATRE
WEBSITE: www.5thavenue.org   **EMAIL**: info@5thavenue.org
PHONE: (206) 625-1418   **FAX**: (206) 292-9610
ADDRESS: 1308 5th Ave, Seattle WA 98101
DESCRIPTION: Our mission is to nurture, advance and preserve all aspects of America's great indigenous art-form: The Musical. We achieve this by creating extraordinary theatrical experiences that enrich, entertain, and inspire current and future audiences everywhere.   **PREFERRED GENRE**: Musicals

11TH HOUR THEATRE COMPANY
WEBSITE: www.11thhourtheatrecompany.org
EMAIL: info@11thhourtheatrecompany.org
PHONE: (917) 653-2490   **ADDRESS**: 2891 Senak Rd, Runnemede NJ 19001
DESCRIPTION: 11th Hour's mission is to have an enduring impact on our community by producing musical works of theatre. We use the expertise of industry leaders and up-and-coming artists to create an intimate and lasting experience with our audience.

12 PEERS THEATER
WEBSITE: www.12peerstheater.org   **EMAIL**: mhenderson@12peerstheater.org
PHONE: (412) 496-2194   **ADDRESS**: 100 5th Ave, Ste 308, Pittsburgh PA 15222
DESCRIPTION: Est. 2011. 12 Peers Theater's mission is to provide challenging and engaging theater through contemporary works exploring myth and cultural identity.
PREFERRED GENRE: All genres   **PREFERRED LENGTH**: Any Length   **FEE**: No
AGENT ONLY: No

13TH STREET REPERTORY COMPANY
WEBSITE: www.13thstreetrep.org   **EMAIL**: thirteenst@aol.com
PHONE: (212) 675-6677   **ADDRESS**: 50 W 13th St, New York NY 10011

DESCRIPTION: The 13th Street Repertory Company provides a place for actors, directors, playwrights and technicians to develop their craft in a caring, nurturing, professional environment. Five to seven shows run weekly, including children's shows on weekends.

16TH STREET THEATER
WEBSITE: 16thstreettheater.org **EMAIL:** scripts@16thstreettheater.org
PHONE: (708) 795-6704 **ADDRESS:** 6420 16th St, Berwyn IL 60402
SUBMISSION MATERIALS: We accept scripts through NNPN's New Play Exchange. Preference for Illinois resident writers able to commit to being "playwright-in-residence."
PREFERRED GENRE: Plays **PREFERRED LENGTH:** Full-length **FEE:** No

THE 20% THEATRE COMPANY TWIN CITIES
WEBSITE: www.tctwentypercent.org/submissions.html
EMAIL: info@tctwentypercent.org **PHONE:** (612) 227-1188
ADDRESS: 5152 Aldrich Ave N, Minneapolis MN 55430
DESCRIPTION: The 20% Theatre Company Twin Cities is committed to supporting and vigorously promoting the work of female and transgender theatre artists, and celebrating the unique contribution of these artists to social justice and human rights.
SUBMISSION MATERIALS: PLAYWRIGHTS: 20% Theatre Company Twin Cities is currently taking a break from accepting script submissions. We apologize for this inconvenience, and appreciate your patience.
FEE: No **AGENT ONLY:** No **SPECIAL INTEREST:** Feminism/Women's Rights

24TH STREET THEATRE
WEBSITE: www.24thstreet.org **EMAIL:** theatre@24thstreet.org
PHONE: (213) 745-6516 **ADDRESS:** 1117 W 24th St, Los Angeles CA 90007-1725
DESCRIPTION: We believe that the young people we reach today will grow up to be active participants in their communities who are notable for their generosity, independent thinking, and passion for the arts. We envision a change in the culture of Los Angeles: people animated by a greater sense of inter-connectedness, empathy and humanity. **PREFERRED LENGTH:** Any Length **FEE:** No **AGENT ONLY:** No
SPECIAL INTEREST: Theatre for Young Audiences

52ND STREET PROJECT
WEBSITE: www.52project.org **EMAIL:** hirsch@52project.org
PHONE: (212) 333-5252 **FAX:** (212) 333-5598
ADDRESS: 789 10th Ave, New York NY 10019
DESCRIPTION: The mission of The 52nd Street Project, a community-based arts organization, is to bring together kids from Hell's Kitchen in Manhattan, starting at age ten and lasting through their teens, with theater professionals to create original theater offered free to the general public.
FEE: No **AGENT ONLY:** No

1812 PRODUCTIONS
WEBSITE: www.1812productions.org **EMAIL:** info@1812productions.org
PHONE: (215) 592-9560 **FAX:** (215) 592-9580

ADDRESS: 421 N 7th St, #218, Philadelphia PA 19123

DESCRIPTION: 1812 Productions is dedicated to creating theatrical works of comedy and comedic works of theater that explore and celebrate our sense of community, our history, and our humanity.

A NOISE WITHIN (ANW)

WEBSITE: www.anoisewithin.org **EMAIL:** info@anoisewithin.org
PHONE: (626) 356-3100 **FAX:** (626) 356-3120
ADDRESS: 3352 E Foothill Blvd, Pasadena CA 91107
DESCRIPTION: A Noise Within produces classic theatre as an essential means to enrich our community by embracing universal human experiences, expanding personal awareness, and challenging individual perspectives. Our company of resident and guest artists performing in rotating repertory immerses student and general audiences in timeless, epic stories in an intimate setting.
PREFERRED GENRE: Plays **PREFERRED LENGTH:** Full-length
FEE: No **AGENT ONLY:** No

A. D. PLAYERS

WEBSITE: www.adplayers.org **EMAIL:** boxoffice@adplayers.org
PHONE: (713) 526-2721 **FAX:** (713) 439-0905
ADDRESS: 2710 W Alabama St, Houston TX 77098
DESCRIPTION: AD Players, originally known as After Dinner Players, was founded in 1967.
PREFERRED GENRE: Plays or Musicals **PREFERRED LENGTH:** Full-length **FEE:** No
AGENT ONLY: No

ABINGDON THEATRE COMPANY

WEBSITE: www.abingdontheatre.org **EMAIL:** tspeciale@abingdontheatre.org
PHONE: (212) 868-2055 **FAX:** (212) 868-2056
ADDRESS: 101 E 15th St, 2nd Fl, New York NY 10003
DESCRIPTION: Est. 1993. Abingdon Theatre Company is dedicated to developing and producing new American work by emerging and established artists. Production: cast limit 8. Response Time: 3 - 6 months. Work must be unproduced/unoptioned in NYC. Does not accept unsolicited scripts.
PREFERRED GENRE: Plays **PREFERRED LENGTH:** Full-length **FEE:** No
AGENT ONLY: Yes

ABOUT FACE THEATRE

WEBSITE: www.aboutfacetheatre.com **EMAIL:** literary@aboutfacetheatre.com
PHONE: (773) 784-8565 **FAX:** (773) 784-8557 **TWITTER:** @aboutfacechi
ADDRESS: 5252 N Broadway St, 2nd Fl, Chicago IL 60640
DESCRIPTION: About Face Theatre creates exceptional, innovative, and adventurous theatre and educational programming that advances the national dialogue on sexual and gender identity, and challenges and entertains audiences in Chicago and beyond.
PREFERRED GENRE: All genres **PREFERRED LENGTH:** Any Length **FEE:** No
AGENT ONLY: No **SPECIAL INTEREST:** Deaf or Hearing-impaired; LGBT+

ACT II PLAYHOUSE
WEBSITE: www.act2.org **EMAIL:** tony@act2.org **PHONE:** (215) 654-0200
ADDRESS: 56 E Butler PK, Ambler PA 19002
DESCRIPTION: Act II Playhouse is committed to creating and programming theatre in a venue whose intimacy draws audiences and actors into dynamic interaction. Act II produces new, classic, and contemporary plays and musicals that reflect the highest artistic standards. Our focus is on a variety of live performances that are accessible and entertaining. **PREFERRED GENRE:** Plays or Musicals **FEE:** No **AGENT ONLY:** No

ACT THEATRE (A CONTEMPORARY THEATRE)
WEBSITE: www.acttheatre.org **EMAIL:** artistic@acttheatre.org
PHONE: (206) 292-7660
ADDRESS: Kreielsheimer Pl, 700 Union St, Seattle WA 98101
DESCRIPTION: ACT is the only local theatre dedicated to producing contemporary work with promising playwrights and local performing artists since 1965.
PREFERRED LENGTH: Full-length **FEE:** No **AGENT ONLY:** No

ACTING COMPANY
WEBSITE: www.theactingcompany.org **EMAIL:** mail@theactingcompany.org
PHONE: (212) 258-3111 **FAX:** (212) 258-3299 **ADDRESS:** PO Box 898, New York NY 10108
DESCRIPTION: The Acting Company endures as the major touring classical theater in the United States. **FEE:** No **AGENT ONLY:** Yes

ACTORS' CENTER [VA]
WEBSITE: www.actorscenter.org **EMAIL:** staff@actorscenter.org
PHONE: (703) 413-3270 **FAX:** (703) 413-3271
ADDRESS: 601 S Clark St, Arlington VA 22202
DESCRIPTION: The Actors' Center empowers actors in the Washington, D.C., area to achieve their highest potential. We fulfill this mission by providing our members exclusive access to casting, training, and networking opportunities.

THE ACTORS COMPANY THEATRE (TACT)
WEBSITE: www.tactnyc.org **EMAIL:** newTACTics@tactnyc.org
PHONE: (212) 645-8228 **FAX:** (212) 462-2678
ADDRESS: 900 Broadway, #905, New York NY 10003
DESCRIPTION: Est. 1992, TACT is a company of theatre artists that reveals, reclaims, and reimagines great plays of literary merit, creating an intimate theatre experience for its audience by focusing on the text and the actor's ability to bring it to life.

ACTOR'S EXPRESS
WEBSITE: www.actors-express.com **EMAIL:** freddie@actorsexpress.com
PHONE: (404) 875-1606 **FAX:** (404) 875-2791
ADDRESS: 887 W Marietta St NW, #J-107, Atlanta GA 30318
DESCRIPTION: Our primary goals are four-fold: to nurture the next generation of playwrights through workshops, readings, and full productions of new plays; to

develop and nurture Atlanta's artistic community through rigorous theatre training; to catalyze the dialogue essential to the vitality of our neighborhood and our city; and to enhance Atlanta's reputation nationally as a thriving center for live performance.

At this time, Actor's Express is unable to accept unsolicited manuscripts directly from playwrights. Due to our small staff size, the acceptance of unsolicited work is simply not possible. While Actor's Express is committed to the production and development of new plays, our policy is designed to ensure that we are able to find new work in a way that is targeted and efficient.

PREFERRED GENRE: Plays **PREFERRED LENGTH:** Any Length
FEE: No **AGENT ONLY:** Yes

ACTORS' PLAYHOUSE AT THE MIRACLE THEATRE

WEBSITE: www.actorsplayhouse.org **EMAIL:** emaulding@actorsplayhouse.org
PHONE: (305) 444-9293 Ext 615 **FAX:** (305) 444-4181
ADDRESS: 280 Miracle Mile, Coral Gables FL 33134
DESCRIPTION: The mission of Actors' Playhouse is to enrich South Florida's cultural vitality with the highest caliber classic and contemporary live theatre productions; to provide comprehensive educational and outreach programs to multi-cultural audiences; to provide a supportive and creative work environment for Florida-based theatre professionals; to encourage the creation and production of new works for adults and children; and to maintain the identity of its home venue, the historic Miracle Theatre.
AGENT ONLY: No

ACTORS THEATRE OF LOUISVILLE

WEBSITE: www.actorstheatre.org **EMAIL:** boxoffice@actorstheatre.org
PHONE: (502) 584-1265 **ADDRESS:** 316 W Main St, Louisville KY 40202
DESCRIPTION: Est. 1964. Acclaimed for its artistic programming and business acumen, Actors Theatre presents over 500 performances of about 20 productions during its year-round season composed of a diverse array of contemporary and classical fare.

The theatre's other community outreach offerings include free apprentice showcase productions; public seminars and workshops; pre-and post-performance discussions; facility tours; discounted season tickets plans for students, senior citizens, people with disabilities and educators; audio described performances for low vision patrons and performances interpreted in American Sign Language.

SUBMISSION MATERIALS: Synopses and 10-page work samples will NOT be accepted or considered via e-mail or any electronic submission. We encourage literary agents and invited playwrights to submit full scripts by email (PDF and Word formats).
PREFERRED GENRE: Plays **AGENT ONLY:** Yes.

ACTORS THEATRE WORKSHOP [NY]

WEBSITE: www.actorstheatreworkshop.com
EMAIL: info@actorstheatreworkshop.com **PHONE:** (212) 947-1386
FAX: (212) 947-0642 **ADDRESS:** 145 W 28th St, 3rd Fl, New York NY 10001
DESCRIPTION: The Actors Theatre Workshop is an award-winning non-profit theatre, community center and educational institution that teaches innovative educational techniques and theatre principles to adults and children from all walks of life; produces classical and contemporary plays and documentary films that maintain the highest artistic standards; and develops new dramatic works that examine the social issues of the day.

ADIRONDACK THEATRE FESTIVAL
WEBSITE: www.atfestival.org **EMAIL:** atf@ATFestival.org
PHONE: (518) 798-7479 **FAX:** (518) 793-1334
ADDRESS: PO Box 3203, Glens Falls NY 12801
DESCRIPTION: Adirondack Theatre Festival (ATF) is a professional not-for-profit summer theatre located in Glens Falls, NY. ATF strives to challenge, entertain, and nourish its audience through the development and production of new and contemporary musicals and plays. This relationship engages the community as audience members and participants in workshops, discussions, and educational programming.

ADVENTURE STAGE CHICAGO
WEBSITE: www.adventurestage.org **EMAIL:** tom@adventurestage.org
PHONE: (773) 342-4141 **FAX:** (773) 278-2621
ADDRESS: 1012 N Noble St, Chicago IL 60642
DESCRIPTION: Adventure Stage Chicago, the participatory arts program of Northwestern Settlement, creates and tells heroic stories about and for young people. We do this to engage our community and inspire all of us to be heroes in our own lives.
PREFERRED LENGTH: Any Length **FEE:** No **AGENT ONLY:** Yes
SPECIAL INTEREST: Theatre for Young Audiences

AFROSOLO THEATRE COMPANY
WEBSITE: afrosolo.org **EMAIL:** info@afrosolo.org **PHONE:** (415) 771-2376
FAX: (415) 771-2312 **ADDRESS:** 762 Fulton St, #307, San Francisco CA 94102
DESCRIPTION: AfroSolo's mission is to nurture, promote, and present African American and African Diasporan art and culture through solo performances and the visual and literary arts. Through art, we bring people of all ethnicities together to explore and share the human spirit that binds us all.

AIRMID THEATRE COMPANY
WEBSITE: www.airmidtheatre.org **EMAIL:** info@airmidtheatre.org
PHONE: (631) 704-2888 **ADDRESS:** PO Box 2039, New York NY 10163
DESCRIPTION: Airmid aims to: Produce performances of significant dramatic works written by women throughout history; Engage in the ongoing research and recovery of classic plays by women; Expand the dramatic canon of works by women for study and production; Mentor emerging female theatre practitioners; Commission translations of non-English classic works of theatre by women.
FEE: No **AGENT ONLY:** Yes **SPECIAL INTEREST:** Feminism/Women's Rights

ALLEY THEATRE
WEBSITE: www.alleytheatre.org **EMAIL:** info@alleytheatre.org
PHONE: (713) 220-5700 **FAX:** (713) 315-5470
ADDRESS: 615 Texas Ave, 18th Fl, Houston TX 77002
DESCRIPTION: Est. 1947. Accepts script submissions from all Texas-based playwrights. Accepts scripts from out-of-state writers via agents only. Only produces full-length plays. Response time: 6-12 months.

PREFERRED GENRE: Plays **PREFERRED LENGTH:** Full-length **FEE:** No
AGENT ONLY: No

ALLIANCE REPERTORY COMPANY
WEBSITE: www.alliancerep.org **EMAIL:** alliancerepco@gmail.com
PHONE: (818) 566-7935 **ADDRESS:** 3204 W Magnolia Blvd, Burbank CA 91605
DESCRIPTION: The Alliance Repertory Theatre Company was founded in 1999 by Jerry Marino and Jeff Streger. We are a non-profit 501c3 company dedicated to producing distinctive, challenging and thought-provoking theater, and to providing local actors, directors and writers the opportunity to display and expand their talents.

ALLIANCE THEATRE
WEBSITE: www.alliancetheatre.org **EMAIL:** literary@woodruffcenter.org
PHONE: (404) 733-4650 **FAX:** (404) 733-4625
ADDRESS: 1280 Peachtree St NE, Atlanta GA 30309
DESCRIPTION: The Alliance Theatre will lead the national field by modeling radical inclusion and catalytic experiences on our stages, in our classrooms, and throughout Atlanta. We believe that acknowledging and embracing differences in identity is essential to a dynamic cultural conversation. This is why we are committed to equity, diversity, and inclusion in all areas of our organization and programming.
PREFERRED GENRE: All genres **PREFERRED LENGTH:** Full-length
FEE: No **AGENT ONLY:** No

ALTARENA PLAYHOUSE / ALAMEDA LITTLE THEATER
WEBSITE: www.altarena.org **EMAIL:** boxoffice@altarena.org
PHONE: (510) 764-9718 **ADDRESS:** 1409 High St, Alameda CA 94501
DESCRIPTION: Est. 1938. From re-envisioning the classics to promoting new works, our critically-acclaimed productions and our educational outreach programs foster greater appreciation and understanding of the theater arts in Alameda and throughout the Bay Area.

AMERICAN CONSERVATORY THEATER (ACT)
WEBSITE: www.act-sf.org **EMAIL:** publications@act-sf.org
PHONE: (415) 439-2445 **FAX:** (415) 433-2711
ADDRESS: 30 Grant Ave, 6th Fl, San Francisco CA 94108
DESCRIPTION: ACT's literary office accepts script submissions of plays, musicals, and ensemble-generated materials through professional agents and members of A.C.T.'s artistic staff. **PREFERRED GENRE:** Plays or Musicals

AMERICAN DRAMA GROUP (EUROPE)
WEBSITE: www.adg-europe.com **EMAIL:** info@adg-europe.com
PHONE: +49 (089) 34 38 03
ADDRESS: Grantly Marshall, Barerstrasse 19a, Munich 80333 Germany
DESCRIPTION: The goal of the American Drama Group Europe is to perform high quality theatre in as many countries in the world as possible.

AMERICAN OPERA PROJECTS (AOP)
WEBSITE: www.operaprojects.org **EMAIL:** info@operaprojects.org
PHONE: (718) 398-4024 **FAX:** (718) 398-3489
ADDRESS: 13 S Oxford St, Brooklyn NY 11217
DESCRIPTION: AOP's mission is to identify, develop and present innovative works of opera and music theater by established and emerging American artists, and to engage our audiences in unique and transformative theatrical experiences.
PREFERRED GENRE: Opera

AMERICAN REPERTORY THEATRE
WEBSITE: amrep.org **EMAIL:** information@amrep.org **PHONE:** (617) 495-2668
TWITTER: @americanrep **ADDRESS:** 64 Brattle St, Cambridge MA 2138
DESCRIPTION: The American Repertory Theater (A.R.T.) at Harvard University is a leading force in the American theater, producing groundbreaking work in Cambridge and beyond. The A.R.T. seeks to expand the boundaries of theater by programming events that immerse audiences in transformative theatrical experiences.

AMERICAN STAGE THEATRE COMPANY [FL]
WEBSITE: www.americanstage.org **EMAIL:** boxoffice@americanstage.org
PHONE: (727) 823-1600 **TWITTER:** @AmericanStage
ADDRESS: 163 3rd St N, St Petersburg FL 33701
DESCRIPTION: Since 1977 American Stage has been dedicated to telling meaningful, compelling stories with integrity and professionalism. As the Tampa Bay area's longest-running, most critically-acclaimed professional theatre company, we seek to bring the power of quality live theatre to each generation in our community.

AMERICAN THEATER COMPANY
WEBSITE: www.atcweb.org **EMAIL:** info@atcweb.org **PHONE:** (773) 929-5009
FAX: (773) 929-5171 **ADDRESS:** 1909 W Byron St, Chicago IL 60613
DESCRIPTION: American Theater Company challenges and inspires its community by exploring stories that ask the question, "What does it mean to be an American?" We provide a truly intimate home for the community to experience meaningful stories. We foster a nurturing environment for artists to take risks and create essential work.

AMERICAN THYMELE THEATRE
WEBSITE: americanthymeletheatre.yolasite.com
EMAIL: AmericanThymeleTheatre@gmail.com **PHONE:** (212) 781-3631
FAX: (212) 928-5074 **ADDRESS:** 229 E 85th St, #1280, New York NY 10028
DESCRIPTION: American Thymele Theatre (ATT) was founded in 1993. Its mission, to promote and disseminate Hellenic culture in America by producing plays with Greek themes.

AMPHIBIAN PRODUCTIONS
WEBSITE: www.amphibianproductions.org **EMAIL:** info@amphibianproductions.org
PHONE: (817) 923-3012 **FAX:** (817) 923-3470
ADDRESS: 1300 Gendy St, Fort Worth TX 76107

DESCRIPTION: The mission of Amphibian Stage Productions is to produce innovative and engaging live theatre that inspires new ideas, opens new doors, and increases our understanding of the vast world around us. **PREFERRED GENRE:** Plays

ANNENBERG CENTER FOR THE PERFORMING ARTS
WEBSITE: www.annenbergcenter.org **EMAIL:** rgoering@ac.upenn.edu
PHONE: (215) 898-6701 **ADDRESS:** 3680 Walnut St, Philadelphia PA 19104
DESCRIPTION: The Annenberg Center is dedicated to the advancement of a diverse and thriving cultural community through the pursuit of excellence, innovation and intellectual engagement in the performing arts. Affirming its core belief in the power of the arts to transform lives, the Annenberg Center embraces creative expression from the past and the present, of local and global origin, to expand the worlds of all who participate. As a destination and a resource, the Annenberg Center connects and engages artists, audiences, the University of Pennsylvania and the regional community through shared experiences in its high quality venues.

AQUILA THEATRE COMPANY
WEBSITE: www.aquilatheatre.com **EMAIL:** aquila@aquilatheatre.com
PHONE: (914) 401-9494
ADDRESS: 100 Washington Sq, #503, New York NY 10003
DESCRIPTION: Aquila Theatre's mission is to bring the greatest works to the greatest number. We believe passionately that everyone should be given the opportunity to engage with classical drama of the highest quality at an affordable price right in their own community, experience arts from other places and exchange ideas. We re-examine what constitutes a classical work and, in so doing, seek to expand the canon. We endeavor to create bold reinterpretations of classical plays for contemporary audiences that free the spirit of the original work and recreate the excitement of the live performance. Aquila presents its work each year in New York City, tours nationwide, provides extensive educational programming and is well known for its innovative humanities and arts based public programs. **PREFERRED GENRE:** Plays

ARDEN THEATRE COMPANY
WEBSITE: www.ardentheatre.org **EMAIL:** scripts@ardentheatre.org
PHONE: (215) 922-8900 **FAX:** (215) 922-7011
ADDRESS: 40 N 2nd St, Philadelphia PA 19106
DESCRIPTION: Arden Theatre Company is dedicated to bringing to life great stories by great storytellers – on the stage, in the classroom and in the community.
PREFERRED GENRE: Plays **PREFERRED LENGTH:** Full-length
FEE: No **AGENT ONLY:** Yes

ARENA STAGE
WEBSITE: www.arenastage.org **EMAIL:** institute@arenastage.org
PHONE: (202) 554-9066 **TWITTER:** @arenastage
ADDRESS: 1101 6th St SW, Washington DC 20024
DESCRIPTION: Arena Stage is alive as a center for American Theater in our nation's capital with productions, diverse and innovative works from around the country and the nurturing of new plays. Our focus is on American artists. We produce and present

all that is passionate, exuberant, profound, deep and dangerous in the American spirit. We explore issues from the past, present and future that reflect America's diversity and challenges.

SUBMISSION MATERIALS: Arena Stage does not accept unsolicited script submissions. Instead, projects come to our attention through agents, our national scouting process, and our pipeline of new work through our commissioning and development initiatives. **PREFERRED GENRE:** All genres **PREFERRED LENGTH:** Full-length
FEE: No **AGENT ONLY:** Yes

ARIZONA THEATRE COMPANY
WEBSITE: www.arizonatheatre.org **EMAIL:** kmonberg@arizonatheatre.org
PHONE: (520) 884-8210 **FAX:** (520) 628-9129
ADDRESS: 343 S Scott Ave, Tucson AZ 85701
DESCRIPTION: Est. 1967. Arizona Theatre Company is currently able to accept script submissions only when accompanied by a letter of recommendation from a literary agent; other unsolicited scripts that we receive will be recycled.
FEE: No **AGENT ONLY:** Yes

ARIZONA WOMEN'S THEATRE COMPANY
WEBSITE: www.azwtc.org **EMAIL:** jbstrimple@gmail.com
PHONE: (602) 738-4597
ADDRESS: 6501 E Greebway Pkwy, Ste 103, PMB 338, Scottsdale AZ 85254
DESCRIPTION: The Arizona Women's Theatre Company produces contemporary, provocative, thought provoking plays written by women. We provide an innovative forum for women's voices.
PREFERRED GENRE: Plays **FEE:** No **AGENT ONLY:** No
SPECIAL INTEREST: Feminism/Women's Rights

ARKANSAS ARTS CENTER CHILDREN'S THEATRE
WEBSITE: www.arkarts.com/childrens_theatre **EMAIL:** banderson@arkarts.com
PHONE: (501) 372-4000 **ADDRESS:** PO Box 2137, Little Rock AR 72203
DESCRIPTION: The Arkansas Arts Center is an active partner in the educational, economic and cultural life of a diverse community; inviting discovery, creativity and learning through engagement with the visual and performing arts.

ARKANSAS REPERTORY THEATRE
WEBSITE: www.therep.org **EMAIL:** info@therep.org **PHONE:** (501) 378-0445
TWITTER: @TheRep **ADDRESS:** PO Box 110, Little Rock AR 72201
DESCRIPTION: Arkansas Repertory Theatre exists to create a diverse body of theatrical work of the highest artistic standards. With a focus on dramatic storytelling that illuminates the human journey, The Rep entertains, engages and enriches local and regional audiences of all ages and backgrounds.
PREFERRED GENRE: Plays **PREFERRED LENGTH:** Full-length **FEE:** No
AGENT ONLY: Yes

ARS NOVA THEATER

WEBSITE: www.arsnovanyc.com **EMAIL:** artistic@arsnovanyc.com
PHONE: (212) 489-9800 **FAX:** (212) 489-1908 **TWITTER:** @arsnova
ADDRESS: 511 W 54th St, New York NY 10019
DESCRIPTION: Ars Nova is committed to developing and producing theater, comedy and music artists in the early stages of their professional careers. Our unique development programs are designed to support outside-the-box thinking and encourage innovative, genre-bending work. By providing a safe environment where risk-taking and collaboration are paramount, Ars Nova gives voice to a new generation of artists and audiences, pushing the boundaries of live entertainment by nurturing creative ideas into smart, surprising new work.
PREFERRED GENRE: Plays or Musicals **PREFERRED LENGTH:** Any Length
FEE: No **AGENT ONLY:** No **SPECIAL INTEREST:** All

ART STATION
WEBSITE: www.artstation.org **EMAIL:** davidt@artstation.org
PHONE: (770) 469-1105 **ADDRESS:** PO Box 1998, Stone Mountain GA 30086
DESCRIPTION: ART Station is a not-for-profit, professional, multi-cultural, multi-disciplinary (theatre, music, dance, visual and literary arts) arts center, theatre company and arts organization dedicated to the production, presentation, and celebration of the visual arts, literary arts, performing arts, arts education, and community arts outreach. ART Station is dedicated to providing professional quality arts events at reasonable prices and to providing jobs and showcase opportunities to quality artists in the region.
PREFERRED GENRE: Plays or Musicals **PREFERRED LENGTH:** Full-length
FEE: No **AGENT ONLY:** No

ARTICULATE THEATRE COMPANY
WEBSITE: www.articulatetheatre.com **EMAIL:** articulateATC@gmail.com
ADDRESS: 379 Lefferts Ave, #6A, Brooklyn NY 11225
DESCRIPTION: We strive to create theatre about timeless issues: theatre that is articulate, and also articulates those issues.

ARTSPOWER NATIONAL TOURING THEATRE
WEBSITE: www.artspower.org **EMAIL:** gblackman@artspower.org
PHONE: (973) 239-0100 **FAX:** (973) 239-0165
ADDRESS: 9 Sand Park Rd, Cedar Grove NJ 7009
DESCRIPTION: Our mission is to bring inspiring theatre to America's children that feeds their intellect while enhancing the cultural life of their communities, giving children and parents hope, and providing them with powerful examples of how to be kindhearted and fair minded members of society.
PREFERRED GENRE: Plays or Musicals **FEE:** No **AGENT ONLY:** No
SPECIAL INTEREST: Theatre for Young Audiences

ASIAN STORY THEATER
WEBSITE: www.asianstorytheater.com **EMAIL:** asianst@cox.net
PHONE: (619) 527-2816 **FAX:** (619) 527-0877

ADDRESS: 1250 Weaver St, San Diego CA 92114
DESCRIPTION: Asian Story Theater seeks to broaden multicultural awareness and understanding by dramatizing Asian and Pacific Island (API) stories, arts, and themes for family audiences.
SPECIAL INTEREST: Asian; Native Hawaiian or Other Pacific Islander

ATHENA PROJECT
WEBSITE: www.athenaprojectfestival.org
EMAIL: literarymanager@athenaprojectfestival.org
ADDRESS: 2344 E Iliff Ave, Denver CO 80210
DESCRIPTION: Athena Project's mission is to celebrate and nurture women's artistic expression, working actively for equality of opportunity, recognition and pay based on artistic merit alone.

ATLANTIC STAGE
WEBSITE: www.atlanticstage.com **EMAIL:** info@atlanticstage.com
PHONE: (877) 287-8587 **ADDRESS:** PO Box 7402, Myrtle Beach SC 299572
DESCRIPTION: Atlantic Stage is a professional resident artists committed to artistic excellence, community enrichment, and educational outreach. The purpose of Atlantic Stage is to enhance the cultural landscape of the Myrtle Beach area by providing quality theatrical productions of classical, contemporary and new works that are entertaining and enlightening. **PREFERRED GENRE:** Plays **FEE:** No

ATLANTIC THEATER COMPANY
WEBSITE: www.atlantictheater.org **EMAIL:** literary@atlantictheater.org
PHONE: (212) 691-5919 **FAX:** (212) 645-8755
ADDRESS: 76 9th Ave, #537, New York NY 10011
DESCRIPTION: Atlantic Theater Company produces great plays simply and truthfully utilizing an artistic ensemble. We believe that the story of a play and the intent of the playwright are at the core of the creative process.
PREFERRED GENRE: Plays or Musicals **PREFERRED LENGTH:** Full-length
FEE: No **AGENT ONLY:** Yes

AURORA THEATRE COMPANY
WEBSITE: www.auroratheatre.org **EMAIL:** literary@auroratheatre.org
PHONE: (510) 843-4042 **FAX:** (510) 843-4826
ADDRESS: 2081 Addison St, Berkeley CA 94704
DESCRIPTION: Aurora Theatre Company invigorates audiences and artists through the shared experience of professional, intimate theatre. Our work, while entertaining, is more than entertainment as we challenge ourselves and community to do better, think deeper, laugh louder and cast wider nets of empathy toward the world. Through our productions of both classic and new works, we support the Bay Area community by hiring local artists and artisans and likewise support all forms of diversity both onstage and off.
PREFERRED GENRE: Plays **PREFERRED LENGTH:** Full-length **FEE:** No

THEATRES

AURORA THEATRE, INC. [GA]
WEBSITE: www.auroratheatre.com **EMAIL**: info@auroratheatre.com
PHONE: (678) 226-6222 **FAX**: (678) 226-6240
ADDRESS: 128 E Pike St, Lawrenceville GA 30045
DESCRIPTION: Aurora Theatre is committed to producing quality, professional theatre for the Southeast, North Georgia, and our most ardent supporters, the residents of Gwinnett County. We will serve these communities by offering entertainment that nurtures a love of theatre and develops a new generation of theatergoers.

AUSTIN PLAYHOUSE
WEBSITE: www.austinplayhouse.com **EMAIL**: austinplayhouse@aol.com
PHONE: (512) 476-0084 **FAX**: (512) 476-3063
ADDRESS: PO Box 50533, Austin TX 78763
DESCRIPTION: Austin Playhouse is dedicated to providing opportunities for Austin artists and audiences to celebrate the human experience. Austin Playhouse will nourish your mind, delight your spirit, and enrich your life through professional productions of classic, contemporary and musical plays. **PREFERRED GENRE**: Plays or Musicals

B CURRENT
WEBSITE: www.bcurrent.ca **EMAIL**: office@bcurrent.ca **PHONE**: (416) 533-1500
FAX: (416) 533-1560 **ADDRESS**: Artscape Wychwood Barns, 601 Christie St. Studio 251, Toronto ON M5G-4C7 Canada
DESCRIPTION: b current is the hotbed for culturally-rooted theatre development in Toronto. Originally founded as a place for black artists to create, nurture, and present their new works, our company has grown to support artists from all diasporas.

BABES WITH BLADES
WEBSITE: www.babeswithblades.org **EMAIL**: newplays@BabesWithBlades.org
PHONE: (773) 904-0391 **ADDRESS**: 7016 N Greenview, #2, Chicago IL 60626
DESCRIPTION: Babes With Blades Theatre Company uses stage combat to place women and their stories center stage. Through performance, script development, training, and outreach, our ensemble creates theatre that explores the wide range of the human experience, and cultivates broader perspectives in the arts community and in society as a whole.
PREFERRED GENRE: Plays **PREFERRED LENGTH**: Any Length
FEE: No **AGENT ONLY**: No

BARKING LEGS THEATER
WEBSITE: www.barkinglegs.org **EMAIL**: info@barkinglegs.org
PHONE: (423) 624-5347 **FAX**: (423) 622-2511
ADDRESS: 1307 Dodds Ave, Chattanooga TN 37404
DESCRIPTION: Barking Legs Theater is a superb, intimate concert hall and performance venue that has established a reputation as a great place for musicians and listeners alike. **AGENT ONLY**: Yes

BARTER THEATRE

WEBSITE: www.bartertheatre.com **EMAIL:** dramaturge@bartertheatre.com
PHONE: (276) 628-2281 **ADDRESS:** PO Box 867, Abingdon VA 24212
DESCRIPTION: Laugh, scream, gasp and lose yourself in a world of adventure, comedy, romance and suspense. Escape to Barter Theatre and experience world-class entertainment. Let your imagination run wild and discover thrills like you never have before, watching stories unfold at the nation's longest running professional theatre.
FEE: No

BAX (BROOKLYN ARTS EXCHANGE)
WEBSITE: www.bax.org **EMAIL:** info@bax.org **PHONE:** (718) 832-0018
FAX: (718) 832-9189 **ADDRESS:** 421 5th Ave, Brooklyn NY 11215
DESCRIPTION: Our mission is to provide a nurturing, year-round, performance, rehearsal and educational venue in Brooklyn that encourages artistic risk-taking and stimulates dialogue among diverse constituencies.

BAY STREET THEATRE
WEBSITE: www.baystreet.org **EMAIL:** boxoffice@baystreet.org
PHONE: (631) 725-0818 **ADDRESS:** PO Box 810, Sag Harbor NY 11963
DESCRIPTION: Bay Street Theater & the Sag Harbor Center For The Arts is a year-round, not-for-profit professional theater and community cultural center which endeavors to innovate, educate, and entertain a diverse community through the practice of the performing arts. We serve as a social and cultural gathering place, an educational resource, and a home for a community of artists.
FEE: No **AGENT ONLY:** Yes

BEIJING PLAYHOUSE
WEBSITE: www.beijingplayhouse.com **EMAIL:** broadway@beijingplayhouse.com
DESCRIPTION: Beijing Playhouse is looking to identify writers who have previously produced comedy stage plays who would be interested in having their works adapted for the Chinese market. Seeking modern comedies and farces with 6-12 cast size with a strong production track record. For Beijing Playhouse's 2019/2020 season we may be looking for modern comedies that are specifically about China and targeted to the Chinese market. We are also looking for playwrights who are interested in having their produced comedies localized for a Chinese audience. The particulars around rights/royalties would be worked out with the playwright.
SUBMISSION DEADLINE: 08/30/2017 **PREFERRED GENRE:** Plays
PREFERRED LENGTH: Full-length **FEE:** No **AGENT ONLY:** No

BERKSHIRE THEATRE GROUP
WEBSITE: www.berkshiretheatregroup.org **EMAIL:** info@berkshiretheatre.org
PHONE: (413) 448-8084 **FAX:** (413) 448-8772
ADDRESS: 111 South St, Pittsfield MA 1201
DESCRIPTION: Berkshire Theatre Group's mission is to support wide ranging artistic exploration and acclaimed performances in theatre, dance, music and entertainment. Berkshire Theatre Group's celebrated four stages reflect the history of the American theatre; they represent a priceless cultural resource for the community. Our vision is to be a center for creative work that enriches, educates, invigorates and transforms

artists and audiences.
PREFERRED GENRE: Plays or Musicals **PREFERRED LENGTH:** Any Length
FEE: No **AGENT ONLY:** No

BLACK DAHLIA THEATRE LOS ANGELES
WEBSITE: www.thedahlia.com **EMAIL:** DahliaLiterary@gmail.com
PHONE: (323) 525-0085 **ADDRESS:** 5453 W Pico Blvd, Los Angeles CA 90019
DESCRIPTION: The Black Dahlia Theatre is dedicated to the development and production of new plays by both established and emerging writers.
PREFERRED GENRE: Plays **PREFERRED LENGTH:** Any Length
FEE: No **AGENT ONLY:** Yes

BLACK ENSEMBLE THEATER
WEBSITE: www.blackensembletheater.org **EMAIL:** info@blackensemble.org
PHONE: (773) 769-4451 **FAX:** (773) 769-4533 **TWITTER:** @blackensemble
ADDRESS: 4520 N Beacon, Chicago IL 60640
DESCRIPTION: The mission of the Black Ensemble Theater is to eradicate racism and its damaging effects upon our society through the utilization of theater arts.

BLACK REP
WEBSITE: www.theblackrep.org **EMAIL:** info@theblackrep.org
PHONE: (314) 534-3810 **TWITTER:** @stlBlackRep
ADDRESS: 6662 Olive Blvd, St. Louis MO 63130
DESCRIPTION: Founded in 1976 by Producing Director Ron Himes, The Black Rep is the largest, professional African-American theatre company in the nation and the largest African-American performing arts organization in Missouri.
PREFERRED GENRE: Plays **PREFERRED LENGTH:** Full-length **FEE:** No
AGENT ONLY: No **SPECIAL INTEREST:** Black or African American

BLOOMINGTON PLAYWRIGHTS PROJECT
WEBSITE: www.newplays.org **EMAIL:** literarymanager@newplays.org
PHONE: (812) 334-1188 **ADDRESS:** 107 W 9th St, Bloomington IN 47404
DESCRIPTION: The Bloomington Playwrights Project (BPP) strives to be a leading artistic force in the production and encouragement of new plays. The BPP provides opportunities for development, education, and production for promising and established writers and theater artists in a professional environment.
PREFERRED GENRE: Plays **PREFERRED LENGTH:** Full-length
FEE: No **AGENT ONLY:** No

BLOOMSBURG THEATRE ENSEMBLE (BTE)
WEBSITE: www.bte.org **EMAIL:** bte@bte.org **PHONE:** (570) 784-5530
FAX: (570) 784-4912 **ADDRESS:** 226 Center St, Bloomsburg PA 17815
DESCRIPTION: Bloomsburg Theatre Ensemble is a resident ensemble of theatre artists who make our work in rural Central Pennsylvania. We support our eclectic and evolving individual aesthetics. We are dedicated to: collective artistic empowerment, dynamic collaborations, and a symbiotic engagement with a wide range of audiences,

using entertainment and education to challenge, inspire, and excite.

BOND STREET THEATRE
WEBSITE: www.bondst.org **EMAIL:** info@bondst.org **PHONE:** (212) 254-4614
ADDRESS: 2 Bond St, New York NY 10012
DESCRIPTION: Founded in 1976, Bond Street Theatre initiates creative programming that inspires and educates youth, addresses human rights issues, provides tools for healing communities affected by conflict, and promotes the value of the arts in shaping a peaceful future. The company responds to humanitarian crises through the uplifting powers of the arts. The company has initiated innovative theatre and theatre-based programs in over 40 countries worldwide, and reached populations in refugee camps, schools, shelters, prisons, rural villages and urban centers.
PREFERRED LENGTH: Any Length **FEE:** No **AGENT ONLY:** No **SPECIAL INTEREST:** All

BOOMERANG THEATRE COMPANY
WEBSITE: www.boomerangtheatre.org **EMAIL:** literary@boomerangtheatre.org
ADDRESS: PO Box 237166, Ansonia Station, New York NY 10023
DESCRIPTION: Established in 1999, the Boomerang Theatre Company is dedicated to producing new, classic and neglected plays that add to the vibrancy of the national theatre canon. We annually present original and re-imagined plays as both outdoor performances and indoors rotating repertory seasons.
PREFERRED GENRE: Plays **PREFERRED LENGTH:** Full-length
FEE: No **AGENT ONLY:** No

BORDERLANDS THEATER
WEBSITE: www.borderlandstheater.org **EMAIL:** info@borderlandstheater.org
PHONE: (520) 882-8607 **FAX:** (520) 884-4264
ADDRESS: PO Box 2791, Tucson AZ 85702
DESCRIPTION: Championing the development and production of new plays while producing plays by established playwrights whose work resonates with the diversity of our audiences; partnering with regional civic organizations to foster diversity (geographic, cultural and ethnic) in play development and productions; and producing diverse and quality programs for youth.

BOULDER ENSEMBLE THEATRE COMPANY
WEBSITE: betc.org **EMAIL:** info@betc.org **PHONE:** (303) 351-2382
TWITTER: @BETCTheatre **ADDRESS:** 2590 Walnut St #1, Boulder CO 80302
DESCRIPTION: Boulder Ensemble Theatre Company presents profound theatrical stories that inspire our audiences and enrich our community.

BOX WINE THEATRE
WEBSITE: www.boxwinetheatre.com **EMAIL:** info@boxwinetheatre.com
DESCRIPTION: Box Wine Theatre believes that human nature is beautiful in its' flaws and we celebrate those flaws by producing stylistically or thematically unique shows which represent the comedy and tragedy that exists in all of us. Our goal is to bring a meaningful experience to our audience without a Broadway-sized budget while

sparking new ideas and encouraging the questioning of mainstream social norms and opinions.

BRAVA! FOR WOMEN IN THE ARTS
WEBSITE: www.brava.org **EMAIL:** spowers@brava.org **PHONE:** (415) 641-7657
ADDRESS: 2781 24th St, San Francisco CA 94110
FEE: No **AGENT ONLY:** No **SPECIAL INTEREST:** Feminism/Women's Rights

BRICOLAGE PRODUCTION COMPANY
WEBSITE: www.bricolagepgh.org **EMAIL:** submissions@wordplayshow.com
PHONE: (412) 471-0999 **TWITTER:** @BricolagePGH
ADDRESS: 937 Liberty Ave, Pittsburgh PA 15222
DESCRIPTION: Bricolage's mission is to immerse artists and audiences in adventurous theatrical experiences that foster connections and alter perceptions. We are a company that creates original works. We are not a presenting house and do not seek out plays to produce. Since 2012 we have veered away from presenting traditional theater scripts and are no longer accepting submissions of plays that follow the established rules of traditional theater.
PREFERRED LENGTH: 1-Act (under 1 hour) **FEE:** No **AGENT ONLY:** No

THE BRIDGE INITIATIVE: WOMEN IN THEATRE
WEBSITE: www.bridgeinit.com **EMAIL:** info@bridgeinit.com
DESCRIPTION: The Bridge Initiative: Women in Theatre incubates and celebrates professional female theatre artists, promoting gender parity across all theatrical disciplines.

BRISTOL RIVERSIDE THEATRE [PA]
WEBSITE: www.brtstage.org **EMAIL:** Keith@brtstage.org
PHONE: (215) 785-6664 **FAX:** (215) 785-2762
ADDRESS: PO Box 1250, Bristol PA 19007
DESCRIPTION: BRT is dedicated to being a premiere regional theatre for Bucks County and surrounding communities. Our mission is to engage audiences and artists alike with exceptional performances, inspired writing and superior productions that motivate us to think harder, to feel more deeply, to laugh more joyfully, and to reflect on ourselves and the world in which we live.

BROOKFIELD THEATRE FOR THE ARTS
WEBSITE: www.brookfieldtheatre.org **EMAIL:** BrookfieldTheatreCT@gmail.com
PHONE: (203) 775-0023 **ADDRESS:** 184 Whisconier Rd, Brookfield CT 6804
DESCRIPTION: The Brookfield Theatre for the Arts is an all volunteer, non-profit organization dedicated to providing quality community theater and educational opportunities to the Brookfield area. **FEE:** No **AGENT ONLY:** No

BRYANT-LAKE BOWL THEATER
WEBSITE: www.bryantlakebowl.com **EMAIL:** askus@bryantlakebowl.com

PHONE: (612) 825-8949 **FAX:** (612) 825-7109
ADDRESS: 810 W Lake St, Minneapolis MN 55408
DESCRIPTION: A vintage bowling alley, restaurant, and cabaret theater committed to supporting local and organic agriculture.

BURNING COAL THEATRE COMPANY
WEBSITE: www.burningcoal.org   **EMAIL:** coalnewworks@gmail.com
PHONE: (919) 834-4001 **ADDRESS:** 224 Polk St, Raleigh NC 27604
DESCRIPTION: We emphasize works that are felt and experienced viscerally, unlike more traditional, linear plays where audiences are most often asked to observe without participating. Using the best local, national and international artists available, we produce explosive re-examinations of overlooked classics, modern and contemporary plays that address issues and themes poignant in our community. With this in mind, we strive to achieve high-energy performances with minimalist production values. Race and gender non-specific casting is an integral component of our perspective, as well as an international viewpoint.
PREFERRED LENGTH: Any Length **FEE:** No **AGENT ONLY:** No

BUSHFIRE THEATRE OF PERFORMING ARTS
WEBSITE: www.bushfiretheatre.org   **EMAIL:** thebushfire@verizon.net
PHONE: (215) 747-9230 **FAX:** (215) 747-9236
ADDRESS: 224 S 52nd St, Philadelphia PA 19139
DESCRIPTION: We are dedicated to providing a performing arts experience featuring the works of African American playwrights and a resident ensemble of actors.

CALIFORNIA SHAKESPEARE THEATER
WEBSITE: www.calshakes.org   **EMAIL:** info@calshakes.org
PHONE: (510) 548-3422 **FAX:** (510) 843-9921
ADDRESS: 701 Heinz Ave, Berkeley CA 94710
DESCRIPTION: California Shakespeare Theater (Cal Shakes) redefines the classical theater for the 21st Century, making works of extraordinary artistry that engage with our contemporary moment so we might learn about ourselves and each other in the fullness of our world.

CAMELOT THEATRE
WEBSITE: www.camelottheatre.org   **EMAIL:** info@camelottheatre.org
PHONE: (541) 535-5250 **ADDRESS:** PO Box 780, Talent OR 97540
DESCRIPTION: Our mission is to be of service to the Rogue Valley, Oregon, by producing high-quality affordable plays, musicals and musical events while providing a supportive environment for professional and amateur theatre artists and technicians and inspiring and training adults, teens and children in the theatre arts.
PREFERRED GENRE: Plays or Musicals

CAMINO REAL PLAYHOUSE
WEBSITE: www.caminorealplayhouse.org   **EMAIL:** box_office@sbcglobal.net
PHONE: (949) 248-0808 **FAX:** (949) 248-0808

ADDRESS: 31776 El Camino Real, San Juan Capistrano CA 92675

DESCRIPTION: Our mission is to continue to delight and challenge our audiences with the intellectually challenging new works, re-imagined classics, and special events; to produce a broad range of theatrical presentations that nurture local artistic expression in our community of San Juan Capistrano.

CAPITAL REPERTORY THEATRE

WEBSITE: www.capitalrep.org **EMAIL:** mhall@capitalrep.org
PHONE: (518) 462-4531 **ADDRESS:** 111 N Pearl St, Albany NY 12207
DESCRIPTION: Est. 1981. Our mission is to create meaningful theatre with an authentic connection to the community we serve. **FEE:** No **AGENT ONLY:** No

CAPITAL STAGE

WEBSITE: capstage.org **EMAIL:** boxoffice@capstage.org **PHONE:** (916) 476-3116
ADDRESS: 2215 J St, Sacramento CA 95816
DESCRIPTION: Our mission is to entertain, engage and challenge our audience with bold, thought provoking theatre. **FEE:** No

CASA MAÑANA INC.

WEBSITE: www.casamanana.org **EMAIL:** wally.jones@casamanana.org
PHONE: (817) 321-5012 **FAX:** (817) 332-5711
ADDRESS: 930 W 1st St, #200, Ft Worth TX 76102
DESCRIPTION: Casa Mañana strives to create, nurture, and advance live professional theatre unparalleled in artistic excellence for the enrichment and education of our diverse community and its future generations of artists and patrons.

CASTILLO THEATRE

WEBSITE: www.castillo.org **EMAIL:** castillo@allstars.org
PHONE: (212) 356-8485 **ADDRESS:** 543 W 42nd St, New York NY 10036
DESCRIPTION: The Castillo Theatre was established in 1984 by a collective of political activist/artists. Privately funded from the beginning, Castillo's work features improvisation, the works of the late Fred Newman and of German avant-gardist and Brecht protégé, Heiner Müller (among others), and youth productions. It serves as a multi-racial home for Black theatre, and since 2007, has enjoyed a producing partnership with Woodie King, Jr.'s New Federal Theatre. Also sponsors the Mario Fratti-Fred Newman Political Play Contest.
FEE: No

CATALYST THEATER COMPANY [DC]

WEBSITE: www.catalysttheater.org **EMAIL:** david@dpotter.net
PHONE: (202) 494-3776
DESCRIPTION: Catalyst Theatre Company aims to glorify God by reaching Christians and non-Christians, inspiring and challenging both to grow and change, bringing hope to the lost and hurting. We do this by presenting the love of Christ through quality theatre. The Catalyst family strengthens its members by training, fellowship, prayer, and encouragement.

CELEBRATION THEATRE
WEBSITE: www.celebrationtheatre.com **EMAIL:** info@celebrationtheatre.com
PHONE: (323) 957-1884
ADDRESS: 1049 Havenhurst Dr #101-1, West Hollywood CA 90046
DESCRIPTION: We entertain, inspire, and empower with innovative productions that celebrate the LGBTQ community.
PREFERRED GENRE: Plays or Musicals   **PREFERRED LENGTH:** Any Length   **FEE:** No
AGENT ONLY: No   **SPECIAL INTEREST:** LGBT+

CELTIC ARTS CENTER (AN CLAIDHEAMH SOLUIS)
WEBSITE: www.celticartscenter.com   **EMAIL:** celt@celticartscenter.com
PHONE: (818) 760-8322
ADDRESS: 4843 Laurel Canyon Blvd, Studio City CA 91607
DESCRIPTION: Its mission is to preserve and foster the performing and visual arts, languages, music, folklore and traditions of the seven original Celtic nations—Brittany, Cornwall, Galicia, Ireland, the Isle of Man, Scotland and Wales—as well as that of their diaspora who continue to create and perform throughout the world.

CENTER STAGE [MD]
WEBSITE: www.centerstage.org   **EMAIL:** gwitt@centerstage.org   **PHONE:** (410) 986-4042   **ADDRESS:** 700 N Calvert St, Baltimore MD 21202
DESCRIPTION: Baltimore Center Stage is a professional, nonprofit institution committed to entertaining, engaging, and enriching audiences through bold, innovative, and thought-provoking classical and contemporary theater.
FEE: No   **AGENT ONLY:** No

CENTER THEATRE GROUP
WEBSITE: www.centertheatregroup.org   **EMAIL:** scripts@ctgla.org
PHONE: (213) 972-8033   **FAX:** (213) 972-0746
ADDRESS: 601 W Temple St, Los Angeles CA 90012
DESCRIPTION: Our mission is to serve the diverse audiences of Los Angeles by producing and presenting theatre of the highest caliber, by nurturing new artists, by attracting new audiences, and by developing youth outreach and arts education programs.

CENTRAL SQUARE THEATER
WEBSITE: www.centralsquaretheater.org   **EMAIL:** info@centralsquaretheater.org
PHONE: (617) 576-9278   **ADDRESS:** 450 Massachusetts Ave, Cambridge MA 2139
DESCRIPTION: Central Square Theater, is a state-of-the-art theatrical arts facility where audiences find, under one roof, the distinctive repertoires of two award-winning, professional companies, The Nora Theatre Company and Underground Railway Theater as well as collaborative projects drawing on their creative synergy.
FEE: Yes   **AGENT ONLY:** No

CENTRE STAGE [SC]
WEBSITE: centrestage.org   **EMAIL:** information@centrestage.org

PHONE: (864) 266-6733 **TWITTER:** @centrestagesc
ADDRESS: 501 River St, Greenville SC 29601
DESCRIPTION: Est. 1983. Centre Stage is a year-round, 285-seat professional theater offering a wide range of entertainment, plays and shows including musicals, comedy, drama, concerts and special events. **FEE:** Yes

CHARLESTON STAGE
WEBSITE: www.charlestonstage.com **EMAIL:** jwiles@charlestonstage.com
PHONE: (843) 577-5967 **ADDRESS:** PO Box 356, Charleston SC 29402
DESCRIPTION: Est. 1977. The mission of Charleston Stage is to produce live theatre of the highest caliber focusing on plays which excite and incite the imagination, and include indigenous and original works that celebrate the rich heritage and history of the South Carolina Lowcountry. Charleston Stage celebrates the spirit of discovery by providing a collaborative learning environment in which theatre professionals share their talents with the young people, teachers and schools in the community, and inspire participants to celebrate their own creativity. Not accepting new work at this time.
FEE: No **AGENT ONLY:** No

CHERRY LANE THEATRE
WEBSITE: www.cherrylanetheatre.org/programs **EMAIL:** info@cherrylanetheatre.org
PHONE: (212) 989-2020 **ADDRESS:** 38 Commerce St, New York NY 10014
DESCRIPTION: Our mission is to cultivate an urban artist colony, honor our groundbreaking history, and engage audiences as partners in creating theater that illuminates contemporary issues, and at its best, transforms the spirit. See website for details.

CHILDREN'S THEATRE COMPANY [MN]
WEBSITE: www.childrenstheatre.org **EMAIL:** eadams@childrenstheatre.org
PHONE: (612) 874-0500 **ADDRESS:** 2400 3rd Ave S, Minneapolis MN 55404
DESCRIPTION: Our mission is to create extraordinary theatre experiences that educate, challenge and inspire young people and their communities
PREFERRED GENRE: Plays or Musicals **PREFERRED LENGTH:** Full-length
SPECIAL INTEREST: Theatre for Young Audiences

CHILDREN'S THEATRE OF CINCINNATI [OH]
WEBSITE: www.thechildrenstheatre.com **EMAIL:** info@thechildrenstheatre.com
PHONE: (513) 569-8080 **FAX:** (513) 569-8084
ADDRESS: 4015 Red Bank Rd, Cincinnati OH 45227
DESCRIPTION: Our mission is to educate, entertain and engage audiences of all ages through professional theatrical productions and arts education programming.
PREFERRED GENRE: Theatre for Young Audiences **FEE:** No **AGENT ONLY:** No

CHILDSPLAY, INC
WEBSITE: www.childsplayaz.org **EMAIL:** jmillinger@childsplayaz.org
PHONE: (480) 921-5700 **ADDRESS:** 900 S Mitchell Dr, Tempe AZ 85281
DESCRIPTION: Our mission is to create theatre so strikingly original in form, content or both that it instills in young people an enduring awe, love and respect for the medium, thus preserving imagination and wonder, those hallmarks of childhood that

are the keys to the future."
PREFERRED GENRE: Plays or Musicals   **FEE**: No   **AGENT ONLY**: No
SPECIAL INTEREST: Theatre for Young Audiences

CHINESE THEATRE WORKS
WEBSITE: www.chinesetheatreworks.org   **EMAIL**: chinese.theatre.works@gmail.com
PHONE: (718) 392-3493
ADDRESS: 34-23 Steinway St, #241, Long Island City NY 11101
DESCRIPTION: Chinese Theatre Works is a non-profit organization based in New York City. Our mission is to preserve and promote the traditional Chinese performing arts (including opera, shadow theatre, puppetry, dance and music); to create new works that bridge Eastern and Western aesthetics and forms; and to foster understanding and appreciation of Chinese culture in audiences, students, artists and educators around the globe.

CIDER MILL PLAYHOUSE
WEBSITE: www.cidermillplayhouse.com   **EMAIL**: cmplayhousemarketing@gmail.com
PHONE: (607) 748-7363   **ADDRESS**: 2 S Nanticoke Ave, Endicott NY 13760
DESCRIPTION: Our mission is to produce and present a wide range of quality live theater offerings and advance the development of theater arts by utilizing local and national talent and cultivating and educating tomorrow's audiences.
FEE: No   **AGENT ONLY**: Yes

CINCINNATI BLACK THEATRE COMPANY
WEBSITE: www.cincyblacktheatre.com   **EMAIL**: cbtctickets@gmail.com
PHONE: (513) 241-6060   **FAX**: (513) 241-6671
ADDRESS: 5919 Hamilton Ave, Cincinnati OH 45224
DESCRIPTION: The mission of the Cincinnati Black Theatre Company is to keep alive the spirit of Black Theatre by offering top-notch theatrical productions, performance and employment opportunities, children's theatre, educational programs and community outreach in all aspects of theatre arts. CBTC is committed to increasing literacy, promoting diversity and multiculturalism, and pursuing community outreach and collaborations.

CINCINNATI PLAYHOUSE IN THE PARK
WEBSITE: www.cincyplay.com   **PHONE**: (513) 345-2242
ADDRESS: Attn: Literary Department, 962 Mt Adams Cir, Cincinnati OH 45202
DESCRIPTION: Cincinnati Playhouse in the Park accepts submissions for full-length plays, musicals and adaptations in any genre. The materials requested for both new and previously-produced works are the same. Playwrights should submit their work through established literary agents. Agents may submit complete manuscripts. If you do not have agent representation, send a letter of inquiry, playwright bio or resume, character breakdown, brief synopsis and 10 consecutive pages of sample dialogue. Please include your play's production history, if any. Musicals should be accompanied by a CD of selections from the score. Do not send sheet music or DVDs.

We will review your submission and let you know if we are interested in reading the entire script. Please include a stamped, self-addressed envelope if you wish to have

your materials returned. Unsolicited scripts will not be read. We do not accept electronically submitted materials.
PREFERRED GENRE: Plays or Musicals   **PREFERRED LENGTH:** Full-length
FEE: No   **AGENT ONLY:** Yes

CINCINNATI SHAKESPEARE FESTIVAL
WEBSITE: www.cincyshakes.com   **EMAIL:** boxoffice@cincyshakes.com
PHONE: (513) 381-2289   **FAX:** (513) 381-2298
ADDRESS: 719 Race St, Cincinnati OH 45202
DESCRIPTION: Cincinnati Shakespeare Company is a resident ensemble theatre company bringing Shakespeare and the Classics to life for audiences of all ages.

CINNABAR THEATER
WEBSITE: www.cinnabartheater.org   **EMAIL:** elly@cinnabartheater.org
PHONE: (707) 763-8920   **ADDRESS:** 3333 Petaluma Blvd N, Petaluma CA 94952
DESCRIPTION: Cinnabar's mission is to present a wide range of theatrical, musical, and operatic works that are relevant to contemporary life and challenging to audiences and artists alike. Cinnabar creates an environment that fosters the experimentation and exploration needed to produce high-quality performances, which can be enjoyed for their technique and artistry as well as their connection to life and living. Cinnabar is committed to training young people in the performing arts so they can make lasting and meaningful connections between the arts and their daily lives.
FEE: No   **AGENT ONLY:** No

CIRCLE THEATRE [TX]
WEBSITE: www.circletheatre.com   **EMAIL:** rosepearson@circletheatre.com
PHONE: (817) 877-3040   **ADDRESS:** 230 W 4th St, Ft Worth TX 76102
DESCRIPTION: Since 1981, Circle has brought the best work from today's playwrights to Fort Worth audiences.

CITY GARAGE
WEBSITE: www.citygarage.org   **EMAIL:** citygarage@citygarage.org
PHONE: (310) 319-9939
ADDRESS: 2525 Michigan Ave, Bldg T1, Santa Monica CA 90404
DESCRIPTION: City Garage has been producing innovative, award-winning theater in Santa Monica since 1987. The company creates and presents original works that explore contemporary ideas and issues in a distinctive, strongly physical, highly visual, multi-disciplinary style.   **FEE:** No   **AGENT ONLY:** No

CITY LIGHTS THEATER COMPANY (CLTC)
WEBSITE: www.cltc.org   **EMAIL:** citylights@cltc.org   **PHONE:** (408) 295-4200
FAX: (408) 295-8318   **ADDRESS:** 529 S 2nd St, San Jose CA 95112
DESCRIPTION: City Lights Theater Company creates provocative live productions that engage, inspire, and challenge audiences and artists alike through innovative

concepts, intimate staging, and uncompromising storytelling.

CITY LIT THEATER COMPANY
WEBSITE: www.citylit.org **EMAIL:** info@citylit.org **PHONE:** (773) 293-3682
FAX: (773) 293-3682 **ADDRESS:** 1020 W Bryn Mawr Ave, Chicago IL 60660
DESCRIPTION: Est. 1979. Devoted to stage adaptations of literary material.

CITY THEATRE [FL]
WEBSITE: www.citytheatre.com **EMAIL:** susan@citytheatre.com
PHONE: (305) 755-9401 **TWITTER:** @CityTheatreFL
ADDRESS: 444 Brickell Ave, #229, Miami FL 33131
DESCRIPTION: City Theatre's four-part mission is to: Develop and produce predominantly new work, specifically in the short play genre; Leverage our theatrical expertise to engage and educate the community; Provide leadership in the continued development of a world-class theatre community in South Florida; Provide thought leadership to the theatrical industry.
PREFERRED GENRE: Plays **PREFERRED LENGTH:** 10-minute **FEE:** No **AGENT ONLY:** No

CITY THEATRE COMPANY [PA]
WEBSITE: www.citytheatrecompany.org
EMAIL: submissions@citytheatrecompany.org **PHONE:** (412) 431-4400
ADDRESS: 1300 Bingham St, Pittsburgh PA 15203
DESCRIPTION: City Theatre's mission is to provide an artistic home for the development and production of contemporary plays of substance and ideas that engage and challenge a diverse audience.
PREFERRED GENRE: Plays **PREFERRED LENGTH:** Full-length
FEE: No **AGENT ONLY:** No

CLAGUE PLAYHOUSE
WEBSITE: www.clagueplayhouse.org **EMAIL:** info@clagueplayhouse.org
PHONE: (440) 331-0403 **ADDRESS:** 1371 Clague Rd, Westlake OH 44145
DESCRIPTION: The mission of Clague Playhouse is to present quality entertainment, to provide an educational environment for all ages through the art of theater, and to serve community needs in providing cultural arts awareness.

CLARENCE BROWN THEATRE (CBT)
WEBSITE: www.clarencebrowntheatre.org **EMAIL:** cbt@utk.edu
PHONE: (865) 974-6011 **FAX:** (865) 974-4867
ADDRESS: 206 McClung Twr, Knoxville TN 37996
DESCRIPTION: The Clarence Brown has a rich history and a mission equally focused on enriching the culture of Knoxville and training the next generation of great artists.

CLASSIC STAGE COMPANY (CSC)
WEBSITE: www.classicstage.org **EMAIL:** info@classicstage.org
PHONE: (212) 677-4210 **FAX:** (212) 477-7704
ADDRESS: 136 E 13th St, New York NY 10003

DESCRIPTION: Classic Stage Company (CSC) is committed to reimagining classic stories for contemporary audiences. It is a home for New York's finest established and emerging artists to grapple with great works of the world's repertory that speak directly to the issues of today.

CLASSICAL THEATRE OF HARLEM
WEBSITE: www.cthnyc.org **PHONE:** (212) 564-9983 **FAX:** (212) 564-9109
ADDRESS: 520 8th Ave, #313, New York NY 10018
DESCRIPTION: Since its founding in 1999, CTH has presented a repertory of works ranging from traditional classical playwrights (Anton Chekhov, Euripides, and William Shakespeare), to established 20th century playwrights (August Wilson, Langston Hughes, and Jean Genet), to new plays by emerging playwrights.

SYNETIC THEATRE
WEBSITE: synetictheater.org **EMAIL:** synetic@synetictheater.org
PHONE: (703) 824-6200 **FAX:** (703) 824-4827
ADDRESS: 4041 S 28th St, Arlington VA 22206
DESCRIPTION: Synetic redefines theater by blending innovative techniques and movement, investing in artists' growth, and creating unforgettable visceral experiences for every audience.

CLEVELAND OPERA THEATER
WEBSITE: www.clevelandoperatheater.org **EMAIL:** cwilson@clevelandoperatheater.org **PHONE:** (440) 285-1874
ADDRESS: 5000 Euclid Ave, #1001, Cleveland OH 44103
DESCRIPTION: Our vision is that people from all backgrounds, if given the opportunity, will be moved by the unique beauty and transformative qualities of opera. We believe that Opera is a vital and relevant art form possessing the unique power to communicate across boundaries of socio-economic status, cultures, and languages through the power of the human voice.
PREFERRED GENRE: Opera **PREFERRED LENGTH:** Full-length
FEE: No **AGENT ONLY:** No

CLEVELAND PLAY HOUSE
WEBSITE: www.clevelandplayhouse.com
EMAIL: submissions@clevelandplayhouse.com **PHONE:** (216) 400-7000
ADDRESS: 1901 E 13th St, Ste 200, Cleveland OH 44114
DESCRIPTION: Our mission is to inspire, stimulate and entertain diverse audiences across Northeast Ohio by producing plays and theatre education programs of the highest professional standards.
PREFERRED GENRE: Plays **PREFERRED LENGTH:** Full-length
FEE: No **AGENT ONLY:** Yes

CLEVELAND PUBLIC THEATRE
WEBSITE: www.cptonline.org **EMAIL:** artistic@cptonline.org
PHONE: (216) 631-2727 **ADDRESS:** 6415 Detroit Ave, Cleveland OH 44102

DESCRIPTION: Cleveland Public Theatre's mission is to raise consciousness and nurture compassion through groundbreaking performances and life-changing education programs.
PREFERRED GENRE: Plays **FEE:** No **AGENT ONLY:** No

CLUBBED THUMB
WEBSITE: www.clubbedthumb.org **EMAIL:** info@clubbedthumb.org
PHONE: (212) 260-0153
ADDRESS: 440 Lafayette St, 4th Fl, New York NY 10003
DESCRIPTION: Clubbed Thumb commissions, develops and produces funny, strange and provocative new plays by living American writers. Clubbed Thumb is a groundbreaker, with a precise curatorial vision and a remarkable track record for launching artists' careers; and an incubator, nurturing plays, collaborations, and above all artists, through thoughtfully deployed resources, opportunities, mentorship and hospitality.
PREFERRED GENRE: Plays **PREFERRED LENGTH:** 1-Act (under 1 hour)
FEE: No **AGENT ONLY:** No

THE COLLECTIVE NY
WEBSITE: www.thecollective-ny.org/collective-submission-guidelines
EMAIL: collective10@thecollective-ny.org **PHONE:** (212) 714-3993
TWITTER: @Collectivenyorg **ADDRESS:** 50 E 129th St, #2B, New York NY 10036
DESCRIPTION: Est 2007. The Collective unites professional artists who share a responsibility to create contemporary American theatre that is emotionally truthful, socially relevant, and defiantly accessible.
SUBMISSION MATERIALS: Scripts should engage truthful and behavior-driven storytelling. We are seeking new works that have not been produced or published, nor planned for production or publication, prior to submission. Production of a play counts as having been presented in multiple performances without scripts in hand. (Readings, workshops and workshop productions are excluded and plays that have received such are eligible for submission). Production of a screenplay counts as any work previously filmed and screened publicly via online or broadcast media, festivals and all other public screenings. See website for link to Submission Form.
PREFERRED GENRE: Plays **PREFERRED LENGTH:** 10-minute
FEE: No **AGENT ONLY:** No

COLONY THEATRE COMPANY
WEBSITE: www.colonytheatre.org **EMAIL:** barbarabeckley@colonytheatre.org
PHONE: (818) 558-7000 **ADDRESS:** 555 N 3rd St, Burbank CA 91502
DESCRIPTION: The Colony Theatre Company does not accept queries or scripts from individual playwrights. We require that all submissions be through agents or professional recommendations. We are seeking well-crafted, full-length plays and musicals of theatrical imagination and emotional resonance which treat universal human themes. Tell us a story, make us care, take us somewhere we've never been. We are not interested in partisan screeds, political correctness, or fashionable cynicism.
PREFERRED GENRE: Plays or Musicals **PREFERRED LENGTH:** Full-length
FEE: No **AGENT ONLY:** Yes

COLUMBUS CHILDREN'S THEATRE (CCT)
WEBSITE: www.colschildrenstheatre.org **EMAIL:** BGShows@aol.com
PHONE: (614) 224-6673 **FAX:** (614) 224-8844
ADDRESS: 177 E Naghten St, Columbus OH 43215
DESCRIPTION: Our mission is to inspire, enrich and empower the imaginations of children and their families through live theatre and theatre education.

COMMONWEAL THEATRE COMPANY
WEBSITE: www.commonwealtheatre.org **EMAIL:** info@commonwealtheatre.org
PHONE: (507) 467-2905 **FAX:** (507) 467-2468
ADDRESS: PO Box 15, Lanesboro MN 55949
DESCRIPTION: Our mission is to enrich the common good through actor based story telling which is both transcendent and relevant.

CONEJO PLAYERS THEATRE
WEBSITE: www.conejoplayers.org **EMAIL:** info@conejoplayers.org
PHONE: (805) 495-3715 **FAX:** (805) 435-8100
ADDRESS: 351 S Moorpark Rd, Thousand Oaks CA 91361
DESCRIPTION: Our mission: To share in providing the community with a year-round schedule of affordable live theatre produced to serve the cultural, educational, and entertainment needs of the community; To welcome and provide an avocational opportunity for all volunteers interested in the theatre arts to participate in the many activities of community theatre.

CONGO SQUARE THEATRE COMPANY
WEBSITE: www.congosquaretheatre.org **EMAIL:** tward@congosquaretheatre.org
PHONE: (773) 296-0968 **TWITTER:** @congosquareCHI
ADDRESS: 4434 S Lake Park Ave, Chicago IL 60653
DESCRIPTION: Est. 1999. Congo Square Theatre Company is a professional ensemble based organization who champions the African American experience by producing definitive and transformative theatre, spawned from the African Diaspora, to enlighten, educate, and inspire everyone. Congo Square Theatre Company seeks to establish itself as an institution of multicultural theatre globally.
FEE: No **AGENT ONLY:** Yes

CONTEMPORARY AMERICAN THEATRE COMPANY
WEBSITE: www.catco.org **EMAIL:** jbishara@catco.org **PHONE:** (614) 645-7558
ADDRESS: 55 East State St, Columbus OH 43215
DESCRIPTION: Producing commercially viable new work and regional and world premieres. Cultivating relationships with institutions of higher learning. Collaborating with other arts organizations. Exploring interesting spaces. Creating captivating programming and educational opportunities for all ages.
PREFERRED GENRE: Plays or Musicals **PREFERRED LENGTH:** Any Length **FEE:** No
AGENT ONLY: No **SPECIAL INTEREST:** Theatre for Young Audiences

CORNERSTONE THEATER COMPANY

WEBSITE: www.cornerstonetheater.org   **EMAIL:** info@cornerstonetheater.org
PHONE: (213) 613-1700   **ADDRESS:** 708 Traction Ave, Los Angeles CA 90013
DESCRIPTION: Cornerstone Theater Company makes new plays with and about communities. By combining the artistry of people with many levels of theatrical experience, we act upon the conviction that artistic expression is civic engagement and that access to a creative forum is essential to the wellness and health of every individual and community.
PREFERRED GENRE: Plays   **PREFERRED LENGTH:** Any Length
FEE: No   **AGENT ONLY:** Yes

COTERIE THEATRE
WEBSITE: www.coterietheatre.org   **EMAIL:** jchurch@coterietheatre.org
PHONE: (816) 474-6785 ext. 232   **FAX:** (816) 474-7112
ADDRESS: 2450 Grand Blvd, #144, Kansas City MO 64108
DESCRIPTION: The Coterie is a non-profit organization, established in 1979, with the mission of providing professional classic and contemporary theatre which challenges audience and artist and provides educational, dramatic outreach programs in the community. We seek to open lines of communication between races, sexes, and generations by redefining children's theatre to include families and diverse audiences.
PREFERRED GENRE: Plays   **PREFERRED LENGTH:** 1-Act (under 1 hour)   **FEE:** No
SPECIAL INTEREST: Theatre for Young Audiences

COURT THEATRE
WEBSITE: www.courttheatre.org   **EMAIL:** info@courttheatre.org
PHONE: (773) 702-7005   **FAX:** (773) 834-1897
ADDRESS: 5535 S Ellis Ave, Chicago IL 60637
DESCRIPTION: Court Theatre is the professional theatre of the University of Chicago, dedicated to innovation, inquiry, intellectual engagement, and community service.

CREEDE REPERTORY THEATRE
WEBSITE: www.creederep.org   **EMAIL:** info@creederep.com
PHONE: (719) 658-2540   **FAX:** (719) 658-2343
ADDRESS: PO Box 269, Creede CO 81130
DESCRIPTION: As a cultural home for artists, residents, and visitors of the West, Creede Repertory Theatre will create a diverse repertory season of plays, new works, and dynamic education programs.
PREFERRED GENRE: Plays   **PREFERRED LENGTH:** Full-length
FEE: No   **AGENT ONLY:** No

CROSSROADS THEATRE COMPANY
WEBSITE: www.crossroadstheatrecompany.org   **EMAIL:** membership@crossroadstheatrecompany.org   **PHONE:** (732) 545-8100
ADDRESS: PO Box 238, 7 Livingston Ave, New Brunswick NJ 8901
DESCRIPTION: The Crossroads Theatre Company is dedicated to creating and producing professional theatre of the highest standards of artistic excellence that celebrates the culture, history, spirit and voices of the entire African diaspora; presents honest

and positive portrayals of people of color from around the world; provides a nurturing working environment for writers and artistic collaborators through supporting the commissioning, development, presentation and documentation of new scripts; uses art to provoke and challenge a multicultural audience to a higher sense of communion; and educates audiences by creating bridges of understanding between people of all cultural backgrounds in this society and the world.

PREFERRED GENRE: Plays or Musicals **FEE:** No **AGENT ONLY:** No
SPECIAL INTEREST: Black or African American

CUMBERLAND COUNTY PLAYHOUSE
WEBSITE: www.ccplayhouse.com **EMAIL:** info@ccplayhouse.com
PHONE: (931) 484-4324 **FAX:** (931) 484-6299
ADDRESS: PO Box 484, Crossville TN 38557
DESCRIPTION: Theater that touches hearts, opens minds, and changes lives.

CURIOUS THEATRE COMPANY
WEBSITE: www.curioustheatre.org **EMAIL:** jennifer@curioustheatre.org
PHONE: (303) 623-2349 **FAX:** (303) 592-7953
ADDRESS: 1080 Acoma St, Denver CO 80204
DESCRIPTION: The mission of Curious Theatre Company is to engage the community in important contemporary issues through provocative modern theatre.
PREFERRED GENRE: Plays

CYRANO'S THEATRE COMPANY (CTC)
WEBSITE: www.cyranos.org **EMAIL:** cyrano@ak.net **PHONE:** (907) 274-2599
FAX: (907) 277-4698 **ADDRESS:** 413 D St, Anchorage AK 99501
DESCRIPTION: Cyrano's Theatre Company (Cyrano's) is the resident company at Cyrano's Off Center Playhouse in Anchorage, Alaska. It was formed in 1995 by a loose-knit group of volunteers committed to producing professional quality dramatic works while utilizing Alaska talent. We produce a wide variety of plays from new and original plays to Shakespeare, operating year round with a different play nearly every month. Nurturing regional talent is one of our most important goals. Cyrano's has employed actors and technicians from Juneau to Fairbanks and worked with UAA's Theatre Department graduates. In this respect, Cyrano's is a bridge or transition point from the academic to professional theater.

DAD'S GARAGE THEATRE COMPANY
WEBSITE: www.dadsgarage.com **EMAIL:** kevin@dadsgarage.com
PHONE: (404) 523-3141 **FAX:** (404) 688-6644
ADDRESS: 569 Ezzard St, Atlanta GA 30312
DESCRIPTION: Est. 1995. Dad's Garage transforms people, communities, and perspectives through laughter. **PREFERRED GENRE:** Plays
PREFERRED LENGTH: Any Length **FEE:** No **AGENT ONLY:** No

DALLAS CHILDREN'S THEATER
WEBSITE: www.dct.org **EMAIL:** artie.olaisen@dct.org **PHONE:** (214) 978-0110

ADDRESS: 5938 Skillman St, Dallas TX 75231

DESCRIPTION: Dallas Children's Theater is an outstanding venue for collaboration with local artists, designers, playwrights, and educators. Our directors and administrators are proud to contribute to the growing body of theater for youth with the commission and development of new plays. Familiar stories, literary works, histories, and biographies are also a part of our programming. Each season is thoughtfully chosen to produce plays that are engaging, enriching, and educational. Our productions promote social values, moral integrity, and reflect the cultural diversity of our community through casting and themes.

PREFERRED GENRE: Plays or Musicals **PREFERRED LENGTH:** Full-length **FEE:** No
AGENT ONLY: No **SPECIAL INTEREST:** Theatre for Young Audiences

DALLAS THEATER CENTER

WEBSITE: www.dallastheatercenter.org **EMAIL:** Lee.Trull@dallastheatercenter.org
PHONE: (214) 526-8210 **ADDRESS:** 2400 Flora St, Dallas TX 75201

DESCRIPTION: Dallas Theater Center accepts script submissions only from agents, writers and theater artists with whom we have an existing relationship. We are unable to accept any unsolicited scripts as the volume of material we consider each year and limited staff size prohibits this. Please note that DTC does not provide comments or suggestions about work that we dont intend to develop or produce. If you have any questions or need additional information, please contact us via e-mail.

SUBMISSION MATERIALS: If you are an artist currently living in the Dallas/Fort Worth area, please email a one page synopsis of your play to our Literary Department.

PREFERRED GENRE: Plays **PREFERRED LENGTH:** Full-length
FEE: No **AGENT ONLY:** Yes

DANISARTE

WEBSITE: www.danisarte.org **EMAIL:** Danisarte@aol.com **PHONE:** (212) 561-0191
ADDRESS: 1 Union Square S, Ste 17M, New York NY 10003

DESCRIPTION: Danisarte is New York based not-for-profit bilingual theatrical production company whose mission is to develop original productions with the goal of increasing understanding among people of many cultures & nations; develop & showcase their talents.

PREFERRED GENRE: Plays **PREFERRED LENGTH:** Any Length **FEE:** No
AGENT ONLY: No **SPECIAL INTEREST:** Hispanic or Latinx

DEAF WEST THEATRE

WEBSITE: www.deafwest.org **EMAIL:** info@deafwest.org **PHONE:** (818) 762-2998
ADDRESS: 5114 Lankershim Blvd., North Hollywood CA 91601

DESCRIPTION: DWT's unique approach to theatre enhances the theatrical experience for all while helping to bridge the gap between the deaf and hearing worlds.

FEE: No **AGENT ONLY:** No

DELAWARE THEATRE COMPANY

WEBSITE: www.delawaretheatre.org **EMAIL:** johannaschloss@delawaretheatre.org
PHONE: (302) 594-1104 **ADDRESS:** 200 Water St, Wilmington DE 19801

DESCRIPTION: The mission of Delaware Theatre Company is to create theatre of the highest professional quality in Delaware and thereby enrich the vitality of the area through artistic programming, education and community service.
PREFERRED GENRE: Plays   **PREFERRED LENGTH:** Full-length
FEE: No   **AGENT ONLY:** Yes

DENVER CENTER FOR THE PERFORMING ARTS (DCPA)
WEBSITE: www.denvercenter.org   **EMAIL:** info@dcpa.org
TWITTER: @DenverCenter   **ADDRESS:** 1101 13th St, Denver CO 80204
DESCRIPTION: Our shows are as diverse as the community we perform for, featuring everything from world premiere plays, well-loved classics, fun interactive theatre experiences and favorites from every genre. Our team believes and works toward a constantly-evolving theatre company that truly leads the national theatre conversation. Our passion for original works from fresh voices has led to the growth of the Colorado New Play Summit, an annual play festival featuring readings and performances of brand new shows. And in recognition of our body of work (including 138 world premieres), we received the 1998 Tony Award for Outstanding Regional Theatre.   **AGENT ONLY:** Yes

DESERT STAR PLAYHOUSE
WEBSITE: www.desertstar.biz   **EMAIL:** boxoffice@desertstar.biz
PHONE: (801) 266-2600   **ADDRESS:** 4861 S State St, Murray UT 84107
DESCRIPTION: Est. 1989. Desert Star produces original musical comedies.
PREFERRED GENRE: Musicals   **SPECIAL INTEREST:** Theatre for Young Audiences

DETROIT REPERTORY THEATRE
WEBSITE: www.detroitreptheatre.com   **EMAIL:** DetRepTh@aol.com
PHONE: (313) 868-1347   **ADDRESS:** 13103 Woodrow Wilson St, Detroit MI 48238
DESCRIPTION: The Repertory is recognized for its pioneer efforts in all phases of theatre and its strong community involvement. Born and bred in the heart of Detroit, the Repertory, since its inception, has remained in the theatre vanguard by staunchly advocating interracial casting, creating novel audience development techniques, stressing theatrical relevancy, inventing an array of cultural and educational community services and playing an active role in neighborhood revitalization.
SUBMISSION MATERIALS: Full script, cast list, SASE   **PREFERRED GENRE:** Plays
PREFERRED LENGTH: Full-length   **FEE:** No   **AGENT ONLY:** No

DEZART PERFORMS
WEBSITE: www.dezartperforms.org   **PHONE:** (760) 322-0179
ADDRESS: 611 S Palm Canyon, Ste 7538, Palm Springs CA 92264
DESCRIPTION: One of the Coachella Valley's preeminent theatre companies, we recognize that the performing arts enrich the life and culture of a community, promote greater understanding and provoke insightful discussion. See website for details.

DIRECTORS COMPANY
WEBSITE: www.directorscompany.org   **EMAIL:** directorscompany@gmail.com
PHONE: (212) 246-5877   **ADDRESS:** 311 W 43rd St, #409, New York NY 10036

DESCRIPTION: The Directors Company is an award-winning not-for-profit theatre company with an extraordinary record in its mission to develop and produce groundbreaking new plays and musicals initiated and generated by outstanding directorial talent, for the American theatre public.
PREFERRED GENRE: Plays or Musicals **FEE:** No **AGENT ONLY:** No

DISCOVERY THEATER
WEBSITE: www.discoverytheater.org **EMAIL:** info@discoverytheater.org
PHONE: (202) 633-8700 **FAX:** (202) 343-1073
ADDRESS: PO Box 23293, Washington DC 20026
DESCRIPTION: Discovery Theater has been presenting DC-area children with live educational performances for more than 30 years. As a program of the Smithsonian Associates, Discovery Theater serves as a child's gateway to the exhibitions, collections, and cultures contained in the museums on the National Mall and beyond.
SPECIAL INTEREST: Theatre for Young Audiences

DISTRICT OF COLUMBIA ARTS CENTER (DCAC)
WEBSITE: www.dcartscenter.org **EMAIL:** info@dcartscenter.org
PHONE: (202) 462-7833 **ADDRESS:** 2438 18th St, NW, Washington DC 20009
DESCRIPTION: The District of Columbia Arts Center (DCAC) serves the Washington, DC area by presenting high-caliber, challenging works, encouraging professionalism among artists, and by providing a forum for education and cultural exchange. DCAC was founded in 1989 as an alternative arts center for local artists in response to eroding support for local artists

DIXON PLACE
WEBSITE: www.dixonplace.org **EMAIL:** submissions@dixonplace.org
PHONE: (212) 219-0736 **ADDRESS:** 161A Christie St, New York NY 10002
DESCRIPTION: Est. 1986. Dixon Place is a Bessie and Obie Award-winning non-profit institution committed to supporting the creative process by presenting original works of theater, dance, music, puppetry, circus arts, literature & visual art at all stages of development. Presenting over 1000 creators a year, this local haven inspires & encourages diverse artists of all stripes & callings to take risks, generate new ideas & consummate new practices. Dixon Place is a local haven for creativity as well as an international model for the open exploration of the process of creation. If you have work that would be appropriate for Dixon Place, please read our open submissions policy.
DEADLINE TYPE: Rolling **PREFERRED GENRE:** Plays or Musicals
PREFERRED LENGTH: Any Length **FEE:** No **AGENT ONLY:** No

DOBAMA THEATRE
WEBSITE: www.dobama.org **EMAIL:** dobama@dobama.org
PHONE: (216) 932-6838 **FAX:** (216) 932-3259
ADDRESS: 2340 Lee Rd, Cleveland Heights OH 44118
DESCRIPTION: Dobama Theatre's mission is to premiere the best contemporary plays by established and emerging playwrights in professional productions of the highest quality. **PREFERRED GENRE:** Plays **PREFERRED LENGTH:** Full-length

DOUBLE EDGE THEATRE
WEBSITE: www.doubleedgetheatre.org **EMAIL:** office@doubleedgetheatre.org
PHONE: (413) 628-0277 **FAX:** (203) 886-3293
ADDRESS: 948 Conway Rd, Ashfield MA 1330
DESCRIPTION: Double Edge's mission: creating a 'living culture' by developing the highest quality of original theatre performance, based on the long-term imaginative work of the actor and his/her interaction with the communities in which the work takes place.

DRAMATIC WOMEN
WEBSITE: dramaticwomen.org **EMAIL:** ellena@silcom.com
PHONE: (805) 965-5826 **ADDRESS:** 111 Skylie Cir, Santa Barbara CA 93109
DESCRIPTION: Dramatic Women was founded in 1993 to explore and promote the participation of women in all areas of theatre and to produce original scripts by locally-based writers.
FEE: No **AGENT ONLY:** No **SPECIAL INTEREST:** Feminism/Women's Rights

DRAPER HISTORIC THEATRE
WEBSITE: www.drapertheatre.org **EMAIL:** info@drapertheatre.org
PHONE: (801) 572-4611 **ADDRESS:** PO Box 1191, Draper UT 84020
DESCRIPTION: Draper Historic Theatre, a non-profit organization, enriches families, individuals and the community by providing positive artistic experiences in theatre - including affordable, wholesome entertainment and pleasant, edifying performance and educational opportunities.
PREFERRED GENRE: Plays or Musicals
SPECIAL INTEREST: Theatre for Young Audiences

DRILLING COMPANY
WEBSITE: www.drillingcompany.org **EMAIL:** DrillingCompany@aol.com
PHONE: (212) 873-9050 **ADDRESS:** 236 W 78th St, New York NY 10024
DESCRIPTION: The Drilling Company discovers, develops, and produces new works by emerging American playwrights that represent a diverse community of ideas and cultures and explore different perspectives on the universal themes that define us as individuals and communities.
SUBMISSION MATERIALS: Full script, playwright bio **PREFERRED GENRE:** Plays
PREFERRED LENGTH: Any Length **FEE:** No **AGENT ONLY:** No

DUO MULTICULTURAL ARTS CENTER
WEBSITE: www.duotheater.org **EMAIL:** duotheater@gmail.com
PHONE: (212) 598-4320 **ADDRESS:** 62 E 4th St, New York NY 10003
DESCRIPTION: DMAC is a multicultural arts center for independent artists in the heart of the East Village. **FEE:** No **AGENT ONLY:** No **SPECIAL INTEREST:** All

EAST WEST PLAYERS
WEBSITE: www.eastwestplayers.org **EMAIL:** literary@eastwestplayers.org
PHONE: (213) 625-7000 **ADDRESS:** 120 Judge John Aiso St, Los Angeles CA

90012

DESCRIPTION: Founded in 1965, East West Players is the nation's longest-running professional theater of color and the largest producing organization of Asian American artistic work. Please note that our mission focuses on the Asian Pacific experience, and the majority of the new works we workshop and produce revolve around Asian and Asian American characters and/or themes. We are interested in both plays and musicals. Works need not be "issue-oriented," in that race/immigrant issues can be an unspoken component in the work.
SUBMISSION MATERIALS: Full script, cover sheet, resume, synopsis
PREFERRED GENRE: Plays or Musicals   **PREFERRED LENGTH:** Full-length   **FEE:** No
AGENT ONLY: No   **SPECIAL INTEREST:** Asian; Native Hawaiian or Other Pacific Islander

ECHO THEATRE [TX]
WEBSITE: www.echotheatre.org   **EMAIL:** mail@echotheatre.org
PHONE: (214) 904-0500   **ADDRESS:** PO Box 820698, Dallas TX 75382
DESCRIPTION: Because the words of women playwrights are not heard on world stages as often as their male colleagues, Echo Theater produces plays written by women that everyone can enjoy. The plays we present are as different as the women who write them, so you'll enjoy a variety of entertainment. Founded in April of 1998, Echo Theatre is based in Dallas, Texas and has built a national reputation for excellence.
PREFERRED GENRE: Plays   **FEE:** No   **AGENT ONLY:** No
SPECIAL INTEREST: Feminism/Women's Rights

ECHO THEATRE COMPANY [OK]
WEBSITE: www.echotheatreco.org   **EMAIL:** echotheatreco@gmail.com
PHONE: (870) 918-4371   **ADDRESS:** 1908 W Cameron St, Tulsa OK 74127
DESCRIPTION: Echo Theatre Company is interested in pieces that encompass the messiness that is being human. It is never our intention to provide easy answers but rather, through the creation of new works or the reenvisioning of existing works, to motivate our audiences to ask more questions.

EGYPTIAN THEATRE COMPANY
WEBSITE: www.egyptiantheatrecompany.org   **EMAIL:** boxoffice@parkcityshows.com
PHONE: (435) 645-0671   **FAX:** (435) 649-0446
ADDRESS: 328 Main St, PO Box 3119, Park City UT 84060
DESCRIPTION: The Egyptian Theatre is a community asset dedicated to enriching lives through the performing arts.

EL CENTRO SU TEATRO
WEBSITE: www.suteatro.org   **EMAIL:** john@suteatro.org
PHONE: (303) 296-0219   **FAX:** (303) 296-4614
ADDRESS: 4725 High St, Denver CO 80216
DESCRIPTION: Su Teatro's mission is to promote, produce, develop and preserve the cultural arts, heritage, and traditions of the Chicano/Latino community; to advance mutual respect for other cultures; and to establish avenues where all cultures may come together.   **SPECIAL INTEREST:** Hispanic or Latinx

EL PORTAL THEATRE
WEBSITE: www.elportaltheatre.com **EMAIL:** theelportal@aol.com
PHONE: (818) 508-0281 **FAX:** (818) 508-9698
ADDRESS: 11206 Weddington St, North Hollywood CA 91601
DESCRIPTION: El Portal Theatre is a historic landmark in the San Fernando Valley located in the heart of North Hollywood.

ELITE THEATRE COMPANY
WEBSITE: elitetheatre.org **EMAIL:** info@elitetheatre.org
PHONE: (805) 483-5118 **ADDRESS:** 2731 S Victoria Ave, Oxnard CA 93035
DESCRIPTION: The Elite Theatre Company's 2017 One-Act Play Writing Competition offers North American playwrights the opportunity to submit for judging no more than one (1) one-act play with a running time of no more than 30 minutes each. There will be up to 5 winners; each winner may have their one-act play(s) produced on stage by Elite Theatre Company, for a run of up to 12 performances.
PREFERRED GENRE: Plays **PREFERRED LENGTH:** 1-Act (under 1 hour) **FEE:** No

EMERGING ARTISTS THEATRE
WEBSITE: www.emergingartiststheatre.org **EMAIL:** eattheatre@gmail.com
PHONE: (212) 247-2429 **TWITTER:** @EATisTweeting
ADDRESS: 15 W 28th St, 3rd Fl, New York NY 10001
DESCRIPTION: Mission: to be an incubator for new voices from the page to the stage.
PREFERRED GENRE: Plays **FEE:** No **AGENT ONLY:** No

ENCOMPASS NEW OPERA THEATRE
WEBSITE: www.encompassopera.org **EMAIL:** encompassopera@yahoo.com
PHONE: (718) 398-4675 **FAX:** (718) 398-4684
ADDRESS: 138 S Oxford St, #1-A, Brooklyn NY 11217
DESCRIPTION: Encompass New Opera Theatre is dedicated to the creation, development and production of adventurous new music theatre and contemporary opera, as well as the revival of important musical works by American and international composers.
PREFERRED GENRE: Opera

ENRICHMENT WORKS
WEBSITE: www.enrichmentworks.org **EMAIL:** info@enrichmentworks.org
PHONE: (818) 780-1400
ADDRESS: 5605 Woodman Ave, #207, Valley Glen CA 91401
DESCRIPTION: Enrichment Works is looking for plays that address topics important to youth or topics studied in school. Plays should have 1-3 actors and run no more than 45 minutes. Please feel free to contact us with your finished script or to brainstorm an idea.
PREFERRED GENRE: Plays **PREFERRED LENGTH:** 1-Act (under 1 hour) **FEE:** No
AGENT ONLY: No **SPECIAL INTEREST:** Theatre for Young Audiences

ENSEMBLE STUDIO THEATER (EST)
WEBSITE: www.ensemblestudiotheatre.org/ **EMAIL:** boxoffice@estnyc.org

PHONE: (212) 247-4982 **TWITTER:** @ESTnyc
ADDRESS: 549 W 52nd St, New York NY 10019
DESCRIPTION: Through our unique collaborative process, Ensemble Studio Theatre develops and produces original, provocative, and authentic new plays that engage and challenge our audience and audiences across the country. Home to the EST/Alfred P. Sloan Foundation Science & Technology Project and the biannual One Act Marathon of Plays.

ENSEMBLE THEATRE COMPANY OF SANTA BARBARA [CA]

WEBSITE: www.ensembletheatre.com **EMAIL:** boxoffice@etcsb.org
PHONE: (805) 965-5400 **FAX:** (805) 568-3806
ADDRESS: PO Box 2307, Santa Barbara CA 93120
DESCRIPTION: Ensemble Theatre Company (ETC) is Santa Barbara's sole professional theater, now in its 38th season. Operating out of the state-of-the-art 300-seat New Vic, ETC presents five main stage productions per season. Education outreach programs include a Young Actors Conservatory, a Young Playwrights Program, student matinees and in-school workshops. ETC rents its venue to other local arts groups and non-profits.

ENSEMBLE THEATRE OF CINCINNATI [OH]

WEBSITE: ensemblecincinnati.org/ **EMAIL:** scripts@ensemblecincinnati.org
PHONE: (513) 421-3555 **ADDRESS:** 1127 Vine St, Cincinnati OH 45202
DESCRIPTION: Ensemble Theatre Cincinnati is a professional theatre dedicated to producing world and regional premieres of works that often explore compelling social issues. We fulfill our mission through our stage productions and educational outreach programs that enlighten, enliven, enrich and inspire our audiences.
PREFERRED GENRE: Plays **PREFERRED LENGTH:** Full-length

ETA CREATIVE ARTS FOUNDATION INC.

WEBSITE: www.etacreativearts.org **EMAIL:** info@etacreativearts.org
PHONE: (773) 752-3955 **FAX:** (773) 752-8727
ADDRESS: 7558 S Chicago Ave, Chicago IL 60619
DESCRIPTION: Do you want to see your play professionally produced at a nationally recognized theatre? ETA is always seeking new works to develop and produce.
SUBMISSION MATERIALS: Submissions accepted via email or post.

THE EUGENE O'NEILL THEATER CENTER

WEBSITE: www.theoneill.org **EMAIL:** litoffice@theoneill.org
PHONE: (860) 443-5378 **ADDRESS:** 305 Great Neck Rd, Waterford CT 6385
DESCRIPTION: O'Neill programs include the National Playwrights Conference, National Music Theater Conference, National Critics Institute, National Puppetry Conference, the Cabaret & Performance Conference, and National Theater Institute, which conducts semester-long intensive theater training, and a six-week summer program, Theatermakers. **PREFERRED GENRE:** Plays or Musicals
PREFERRED LENGTH: Full-length **FEE:** Yes **AGENT ONLY:** No

FIREHOUSE CENTER FOR THE ARTS
WEBSITE: www.firehouse.org **EMAIL:** info@firehouse.org
PHONE: (978) 462-7336 **ADDRESS:** Market Sq, Newburyport, MA 01950
DESCRIPTION: Our 191 seat theater is active throughout the year with Firehouse Produced events, partner presentations, and arts education programs. Everything we do is made better by the artists, audience, philanthropists, businesses, and volunteers that help us on a daily basis. Home of the New Works Festival.

FIRST STAGE CHILDREN'S THEATER
WEBSITE: www.firststage.org **EMAIL:** jfrank@firststage.org
PHONE: (414) 267-2929 **ADDRESS:** 325 W Walnut St, Milwaukee WI 53212
DESCRIPTION: Since 1987, First Stage has grown to become one of the nation's most acclaimed children's theaters and the second largest theater company in Milwaukee. First Stage touches hearts and transforms lives through professional theater productions that engage, enlighten and entertain. Committed to new play development, First Stage has presented nearly 50 world premieres in its history.
PREFERRED GENRE: Plays or Musicals **PREFERRED LENGTH:** Any Length **FEE:** No
AGENT ONLY: No **SPECIAL INTEREST:** Theatre for Young Audiences

FLAT ROCK PLAYHOUSE
WEBSITE: www.flatrockplayhouse.com **EMAIL:** Info@Flatrockplayhouse.Org
PHONE: (828) 693-0403 **FAX:** (828) 693-6795
ADDRESS: PO Box 310, Flat Rock NC 28731
DESCRIPTION: Flat Rock Playhouse, the State Theatre of North Carolina, enriches lives through the art of theatre by nurturing talent, inspiring creativity, and encouraging growth. **PREFERRED GENRE:** Plays or Musicals **PREFERRED LENGTH:** Full-length
FEE: No **AGENT ONLY:** No

THE FLEA THEATER
WEBSITE: theflea.org/for-artists/submissions **EMAIL:** draytonh@theflea.org
PHONE: (212) 226-0051 **TWITTER:** @TheFleaTheater
ADDRESS: 20 Thomas St, New York NY 10013
DESCRIPTION: The Flea was founded in 1996 by a group of downtown artists looking to raise a joyful hell in a small space. That same spirit of adventure and excitement, which defines Off-Off-Broadway, also defines The Flea. Part playground, part laboratory and part training ground, The Flea offers apprentice-style Resident Artist Programs for emerging actors, directors, writers, and small companies that are unique to the field.
SUBMISSION MATERIALS: We encourage you to send a play description, cast list and continuous 15-page excerpt rather than an entire script, so that we can evaluate whether your play might be at home on our stages. Before you contact us, please familiarize yourself with our programming, aesthetic, and company of actors. See website for details.

FLORIDA REPERTORY THEATRE
WEBSITE: www.floridarep.org **EMAIL:** jparrish@floridarep.org
PHONE: (239) 332-4665 **ADDRESS:** PO Box 2483, Fort Myers FL 33902

DESCRIPTION: Florida Rep is committed to providing a first-class regional theatre for Southwest Florida; to helping improve the quality of life in our community through all the arts; and to making the arts, especially theatre, accessible to all.
PREFERRED GENRE: Plays   **PREFERRED LENGTH:** Full-length
FEE: No   **AGENT ONLY:** Yes

FLORIDA STUDIO THEATRE
WEBSITE: floridastudiotheatre.org   **EMAIL:** crandazzo@floridastudiotheatre.org
PHONE: (941) 366-9017   **FAX:** (941) 955-4137   **TWITTER:** @FSTSarasota
ADDRESS: 1241 N Palm Ave, Sarasota FL 34236
DESCRIPTION: Writers must submit a script through their literary agent or with a letter of recommendation from a professional theatre. Florida-based writers without representation may submit a ten page dialogue sample, MP3 or CD if a musical, along with a query and brief synopsis) including casting requirements).
PREFERRED GENRE: Plays or Musicals   **PREFERRED LENGTH:** Full-length
FEE: No   **AGENT ONLY:** Yes

FOLGER SHAKESPEARE LIBRARY
WEBSITE: www.folger.edu   **EMAIL:** info@folger.edu   **PHONE:** (202) 544-4600
ADDRESS: 201 E Capitol St SE, Washington DC 20003
DESCRIPTION: Folger Shakespeare Library hosts a wide variety of events, performances, and activities, from theater to literary readings to family activities and more.
FEE: No   **AGENT ONLY:** No

FOOD FOR THOUGHT PRODUCTIONS
WEBSITE: www.foodforthoughtproductions.com   **EMAIL:** info@foodforthought-productions.com   **PHONE:** (212) 362-2560   **FAX:** (646) 366-9341
ADDRESS: 155 W 46th St, 6th Fl, New York NY 10036
DESCRIPTION: Food for Thought Productions, which started out as the brainchild of award winning writer Susan Charlotte, was launched in the Fall of 2000. This acclaimed theatre company presents a series of one-act plays by award-winning writers performed by an alternating repertory of Broadway stars and directors.
PREFERRED LENGTH: 1-Act (under 1 hour)

FORT WAYNE CIVIC THEATRE
WEBSITE: www.fwcivic.org   **EMAIL:** pcolglazier@fwcivic.org
PHONE: (260) 422-8641   **TWITTER:** @FWCivicTheatre
ADDRESS: 303 E Main St, Ft Wayne IN 46802
DESCRIPTION: Fort Wayne Civic Theatre entertains, educates, inspires, and enriches the community through exceptional live theatre experiences.

FOUNTAIN THEATRE
WEBSITE: www.fountaintheatre.com   **EMAIL:** info@fountaintheatre.com
PHONE: (323) 663-2235   **ADDRESS:** 5060 Fountain Ave, Los Angeles CA 90029
DESCRIPTION: The Fountain Theatre is a non-profit producing organization established in 1990 by co-Artistic Directors Deborah Lawlor and Stephen Sachs dedicated to providing a nurturing, creative home for multi-ethnic theatre and dance artists. Here

we develop provocative new works or explore a unique vision of established plays that reflect the immediate concerns and cultural diversity of contemporary Los Angeles and the nation. **PREFERRED LENGTH:** Full-length **FEE:** No **AGENT ONLY:** No

FREE STREET PROGRAMS
WEBSITE: www.freestreet.org **EMAIL:** info@freestreet.org
PHONE: (773) 772-7248 **FAX:** (773) 772-7248
ADDRESS: 1419 W Blackhawk St, Chicago IL 60622
DESCRIPTION: Founded in 1969 by Patrick Henry, Free Street Theater is dedicated to creating performance by, for, and with a wide-range of participants. As one of the the first racially-integrated theater companies in Chicago, Free Street has a long history of creating work that addresses pressing social issues from diverse points of view.

FREEDOM REPERTORY THEATRE
WEBSITE: www.freedomtheatre.org **EMAIL:** info@freedomtheatre.org
PHONE: (215) 765-2793 **FAX:** (215) 765-4191
ADDRESS: 1346 N Broad St, Philadelphia PA 19121
DESCRIPTION: Rooted in the African American tradition, New Freedom Theatre is an institution dedicated to achieving artistic excellence in professional theatre and performing arts training for the enrichment of the community.

FULTON THEATRE
WEBSITE: thefulton.org **EMAIL:** info@thefulton.org **PHONE:** (717) 397-7425
FAX: (717) 397-3780 **ADDRESS:** PO Box 1865, 12 N Prince St, Lancaster PA 17608
DESCRIPTION: The Fulton Theatre strives to make each production unique and unlike others you may have seen. Productions that are new to the community, relevant to the community, or different from what they have seen before. We have overheard many guests say, during previous productions, "I have seen this before, but this is better than I remember." Art evolves and it is our goal to bring you top-notch quality productions that are timely and relevant to your lives or the way you like to be entertained.
FEE: No **AGENT ONLY:** No

FUSION
WEBSITE: www.fusionabq.org **EMAIL:** dennis@fusionabq.org
PHONE: (505) 766-9412 **ADDRESS:** 700-708 1st St NW, Albuquerque NM 87102
DESCRIPTION: Regrettably, Fusion is unable to accept any unsolicited manuscript submissions.
PREFERRED GENRE: Plays **FEE:** No **AGENT ONLY:** Yes

GEFFEN PLAYHOUSE
WEBSITE: www.geffenplayhouse.com **EMAIL:** Literary@geffenplayhouse.org
PHONE: (310) 208-5454 **ADDRESS:** 10886 LeConte Ave, Los Angeles CA 90024
DESCRIPTION: Geffen Playhouse has been a hub of the Los Angeles theater scene since opening its doors in 1995. Noted for its intimacy and celebrated for its world-renowned mix of classic and contemporary plays, provocative new works and second productions, the non-profit organization continues to present a body of work

that has garnered national recognition.
PREFERRED GENRE: Plays **PREFERRED LENGTH:** Full-length
FEE: No **AGENT ONLY:** Yes

GEORGE STREET PLAYHOUSE
WEBSITE: www.georgestplayhouse.org
EMAIL: development@georgestplayhouse.org **PHONE:** (732) 846-2895
ADDRESS: 9 Livingston Ave, New Brunswick NJ 8901
DESCRIPTION: The mission of George Street Playhouse is to enrich people's lives by producing world-class theatre. **FEE:** No **AGENT ONLY:** Yes

GEVA THEATRE CENTER
WEBSITE: www.gevatheatre.org/play-submission/#3
EMAIL: jryon@gevatheatre.org **PHONE:** (585) 232-1366
ADDRESS: 75 Woodbury Blvd, Rochester NY 14607
DESCRIPTION: Geva Theatre Center accepts submissions of full-length plays, translations and adaptations. We are looking for bold, theatrical voices and are passionate about supporting the craft of both emerging and established writers in service of our commitment to developing new work for the American theatre. Playwrights with professional representation may have their agents send full manuscripts at any time. Please note that lawyers and law firms do not qualify as professional representation. To best accommodate our schedule of new play activities, we have an Inquiry Window, during which playwrights who are not working with an agent may send a submission inquiry. The dates of the next submission window are January 1, 2018 – April 30, 2018.
SUBMISSION DEADLINE: 04/30/2018 **DEADLINE TYPE:** Annual
PREFERRED GENRE: Plays **PREFERRED LENGTH:** Full-length **FEE:** No **AGENT ONLY:** No

GOLDEN THREAD PRODUCTIONS
WEBSITE: www.goldenthread.org **EMAIL:** information@goldenthread.org
PHONE: (415) 626-4061 **TWITTER:** @GoldenThread
ADDRESS: 1695 18th St, #C101, San Francisco CA 94107
DESCRIPTION: Est. 1996. The first American theatre company focused on the Middle East. We produce passionate and provocative plays from and about the Middle East that celebrate the multiplicity of its perspectives and identities. We are a developmental catalyst and vibrant artistic home to artists at various stages of their career. We bring the Middle East to the American stage, creating treasured cultural experiences for audiences of all ages and backgrounds.
PREFERRED GENRE: Plays or Musicals

GOODMAN THEATRE
WEBSITE: www.goodmantheatre.org
EMAIL: PlaySubmissions@GoodmanTheatre.org **PHONE:** (312) 443-3811
ADDRESS: 170 N Dearborn St, Chicago IL 60601
DESCRIPTION: By dedicating itself to three guiding principles—quality, diversity and

community—Goodman Theatre seeks to be the premier cultural organization in Chicago, providing productions and programs that make an essential contribution to the quality of life in our city.
PREFERRED GENRE: Plays **PREFERRED LENGTH:** Full-length **FEE:** No **AGENT ONLY:** Yes

GOODSPEED MUSICALS
WEBSITE: www.goodspeed.org **EMAIL:** dhilton@goodspeed.org
PHONE: (860) 873-8664 **ADDRESS:** 6 Main St, PO Box A, E Haddam CT 06423
DESCRIPTION: The Goodspeed campus will continue to serve as a thriving artist colony where the creative process informs the work on our stages and expanding educational programs. We aspire to serve as a safe haven where a singular commitment to discovery and innovation will enrich the field with the next generation of musical theatre artists.
PREFERRED GENRE: Musicals **PREFERRED LENGTH:** Full-length
FEE: No **AGENT ONLY:** Yes

GREAT LAKES THEATER FESTIVAL
WEBSITE: www.greatlakestheater.org **EMAIL:** mail@greatlakestheater.org
PHONE: (216) 241-5490 **FAX:** (216) 241-6315
ADDRESS: 1501 Euclid Ave, #300, Cleveland OH 44115
DESCRIPTION: The mission of Great Lakes Theater, through its main stage productions and its education programs, is to bring the pleasure, power and relevance of classic theater to the widest possible audience.
PREFERRED GENRE: Plays **PREFERRED LENGTH:** Full-length
FEE: No **AGENT ONLY:** No

GREENBRIER VALLEY THEATRE
WEBSITE: www.gvtheatre.org **EMAIL:** newvoicesplayfestival@gvtheatre.org
PHONE: (304) 645-3838 **ADDRESS:** 113 E Washington St, Lewisburg WV 24901
DESCRIPTION: Greenbrier Valley Theatre, the State Professional Theatre of West Virginia, is committed to its mission to create live, professional quality theatre in West Virginia and through theatre, to enlighten, enrich, and enliven the life of our region.
PREFERRED GENRE: Plays or Musicals **PREFERRED LENGTH:** Full-length
FEE: No **AGENT ONLY:** No

GREENWAY ARTS ALLIANCE (GAA)
WEBSITE: www.greenwayarts.org **EMAIL:** whitney@greenwayarts.org
PHONE: (323) 655-7679 **FAX:** (323) 655-7906
ADDRESS: 544 N Fairfax Ave, Los Angeles CA 90036
DESCRIPTION: Greenway Arts Alliance unites communities through art, education and social enterprise. Through our professional theatre productions, educational programs and the Melrose Trading Post, Greenway builds a vibrant artistic community.

GRETNA THEATRE
WEBSITE: www.gretnatheatre.org **PHONE:** (717) 964-3322
ADDRESS: PO Box 578, Mt Gretna PA 17064

DESCRIPTION: Gretna Theatre is a non-profit professional theatre with a primary focus on a summer season, dedicated to producing and presenting work that reaches out to our diverse community as it entertains, enriches, and educates its audience.

PREFERRED GENRE: Plays or Musicals   **PREFERRED LENGTH:** Full-length   **FEE:** No

GROWING STAGE – THE CHILDREN'S THEATRE OF NEW JERSEY

WEBSITE: www.growingstage.com   **EMAIL:** newplays@growingstage.com
PHONE: (973) 347-4946   **ADDRESS:** PO Box 36, Netcong NJ 7857

DESCRIPTION: Each year, four new, unpublished works for young audiences are chosen by a panel of artists and playwrights and presented by professional artists in two staged readings. The playwrights talk about their work, and artists and audience have the opportunity to join the discussion. At the conclusion of the festival, one of the new plays is chosen to be mounted as a Main Stage production.

FEE: No   **AGENT ONLY:** No   **SPECIAL INTEREST:** Theatre for Young Audiences

GUTHRIE THEATER

WEBSITE: www.guthrietheater.org   **EMAIL:** JoH@GuthrieTheater.org
PHONE: (612) 225-6000   **ADDRESS:** 818 S 2nd St, Minneapolis MN 55415

DESCRIPTION: The Guthrie Theater, founded in 1963, is an American center for theater performance, production, education and professional training. By presenting both classical literature and new work from diverse cultures, the Guthrie illuminates the common humanity connecting Minnesota to the peoples of the world.

PREFERRED GENRE: Plays   **PREFERRED LENGTH:** Full-length
FEE: No   **AGENT ONLY:** Yes

HARLEM STAGE AT THE GATEHOUSE

WEBSITE: www.harlemstage.org   **EMAIL:** marketing@harlemstage.org
PHONE: (212) 281-9240   **FAX:** (212) 281-9318
ADDRESS: 150 Convent Ave, New York NY 10031

DESCRIPTION: Harlem Stage is a performing arts center that celebrates and perpetuates the unique and diverse artistic legacy of Harlem and the indelible impression it has made on American culture. We provide opportunity, commissioning and support for artists of color, make performances accessible to all audiences, and introduce children to the rich diversity, excitement and inspiration of the performing arts.

SPECIAL INTEREST: Black or African American

HARTFORD STAGE

WEBSITE: www.hartfordstage.org   **EMAIL:** ewilliamson@hartfordstage.org
PHONE: (860) 525-5601   **ADDRESS:** 50 Church St, Hartford CT 6103

DESCRIPTION: Hartford Stage accepts plays ONLY from literary agents, except in the case of Connecticut playwrights, who may send a 10pp script selection. Beyond that, we are unable to accept scripts not submitted by an agent and such submissions will either be recycled or (if an SASE is enclosed) returned unread.

PREFERRED GENRE: Plays   **PREFERRED LENGTH:** Full-length
FEE: No   **AGENT ONLY:** Yes

HARWICH JUNIOR THEATRE
[CAPE COD THEATRE COMPANY]
WEBSITE: www.hjtcapecod.org **EMAIL**: info@capecodtheatrecompany.org
PHONE: (508) 432-2002
ADDRESS: 105 Division St, PO Box 168, West Harwich MA 2671
DESCRIPTION: The Cape Cod Theatre Company - Home of the Harwich Jr. Theatre educates, empowers, and inspires students of all ages and from all backgrounds to explore and expand their creative talents and aspirations, to experience and appreciate live theatre, and to develop and nurture a lifelong love of the performing arts.
PREFERRED GENRE: Plays or Musicals **FEE:** No **AGENT ONLY:** No
SPECIAL INTEREST: Theatre for Young Audiences

HEDGEROW THEATRE
WEBSITE: www.hedgerowtheatre.org **EMAIL:** company@hedgerowtheatre.org
PHONE: (610) 565-4211 **ADDRESS:** 64 Rose Valley Rd, Media PA 19063
DESCRIPTION: Hedgerow Theatre seeks to connect and enrich the lives of company, patrons, and community in the shared experience of ensemble theatre, through performance and theatre education of the highest quality.
FEE: No **AGENT ONLY:** No

THE HEIGHTS PLAYERS
WEBSITE: www.heightsplayers.org **EMAIL:** info@heightsplayers.org
PHONE: (718) 237-2752 **ADDRESS:** 26 Willow Pl, Brooklyn NY 11201
DESCRIPTION: Brooklyn's oldest, self-sustaining community theatre.

HERE ARTS CENTER
WEBSITE: www.here.org **EMAIL:** info@here.org **PHONE:** (212) 647-0202
FAX: (212) 647-0257 **ADDRESS:** 145 6th Ave, New York NY 10013
DESCRIPTION: HERE builds a community that nurtures career artists as they create innovative hybrid live performance in theatre, dance, music, puppetry, media and visual art. Our artist residencies support the singular vision of the lead artist through commissions, long-term development, and production support. HERE's programs and performances promote relationships among local, national, and international artists. Our space is a destination for audiences who are passionate about ground-breaking contemporary work and the creative process behind it.
PREFERRED GENRE: Plays or Musicals **SPECIAL INTEREST:** All

HIPPODROME THEATRE
WEBSITE: thehipp.org **EMAIL:** hipp@thehipp.org **PHONE:** (352) 373-5968
FAX: (352) 371-9130 **ADDRESS:** 25 SE 2nd Pl, Gainesville FL 32601
DESCRIPTION: The mission of the Hippodrome is to explore the truth of the human experience and the human spirit through the examination and presentation of dramatic work.

HISTORY THEATRE
WEBSITE: www.historytheatre.com **EMAIL:** newplays@historytheatre.com
ADDRESS: 30 E 10th St, St Paul MN 55101

DESCRIPTION: History Theatre entertains, educates, and engages through creating, developing, and producing new and existing works that explore Minnesota's past and the diverse American experience. Its work provides a unique lens which links our past to the present, explores our common heritage, and illuminates our understanding of what it means to be American.
SUBMISSION MATERIALS: Electronic submissions preferred. 10-page sample, synopsis, cast size, production requirements, cover letter. If the submission is a musical, a CD or digital file can accompany the script.
PREFERRED GENRE: Plays or Musicals   **PREFERRED LENGTH:** Full-length
FEE: No   **AGENT ONLY:** No

HOLE IN THE WALL THEATER
WEBSITE: www.hitw.org   **EMAIL:** info@hitw.org   **PHONE:** (860) 229-3049
ADDRESS: 116 Main St, New Britain CT 06052
DESCRIPTION: Established in 1972, incorporated in 1974.
PREFERRED GENRE: Plays   **PREFERRED LENGTH:** Full-length

HONOLULU THEATRE FOR YOUTH
WEBSITE: www.htyweb.org   **EMAIL:** artistic@htyweb.org
PHONE: (808) 839-9885   **ADDRESS:** 1149 Bethel St, Ste 700, Honolulu HI 96813
DESCRIPTION: HTY is committed to the support and development of new works, especially works focused on our unique geographic and cultural identity. There is a long history of supporting local writers and bringing in national and international collaborators interested in developing works that speak to our audience. If you are interested in submitting your work or being a part of this process we encourage you to get in touch.
DEADLINE TYPE: Rolling   **PREFERRED GENRE:** Plays or Musicals
PREFERRED LENGTH: 1-Act (under 1 hour)   **FEE:** No   **AGENT ONLY:** No
SPECIAL INTEREST: Theatre for Young Audiences

HORIZON THEATRE COMPANY [GA]
WEBSITE: www.horizontheatre.com   **EMAIL:** horizonco@mindspring.com
PHONE: (404) 523-1477   **FAX:** (404) 584-8815
ADDRESS: PO Box 5376, Atlanta GA 31107
DESCRIPTION: Horizon Theatre Company's mission is to connect people, inspire hope, and promote positive change through the stories of our times. We work towards achieving our mission by creating a welcoming home for a diverse community of audiences and artists to connect with each other, their communities, and the world. We create new diverse plays with developing artists, while also developing new audiences to experience those plays.

HOUSE THEATRE OF CHICAGO
WEBSITE: www.thehousetheatre.com   **EMAIL:** shawn@thehousetheatre.com
PHONE: (773) 769-3832
ADDRESS: 4611 N Ravenswood Ave #201, Chicago IL 60640
DESCRIPTION: The House is Chicago's premier home for intimate, original works of epic story and stagecraft. Founded and led by Artistic Director Nathan Allen and

driven by an interdisciplinary ensemble of Chicago's next generation of great storytellers, The House aims to become a laboratory and platform for the evolution of the American theatre as an inclusive and popular artform.

HUBBARD HALL CENTER FOR THE ARTS AND EDUCATION

WEBSITE: www.hubbardhall.org **EMAIL:** hhcarnival2017@gmail.com
PHONE: (518) 677-2495 **ADDRESS:** 25 E Main St, Cambridge NY 12816

DESCRIPTION: We are an arts incubator, a training ground for artists of all ages and backgrounds, a magnet for artistic activity, a safe haven for risk-taking, an economic driver for our region, and the beating heart of our community. We gather people from all walks of life to create, learn, and grow together, while developing, producing, and presenting world-class art and artists. We are dedicated to cultivating, sustaining, and promoting the cultural life of our rural community. We are also committed to restoring and preserving Hubbard Hall and all of the buildings on our campus as community cultural assets. **FEE:** No **AGENT ONLY:** No

THE HUMAN RACE THEATRE COMPANY

WEBSITE: www.humanracetheatre.org **EMAIL:** contact@humanracetheatre.org
PHONE: (937) 461-3823 **FAX:** (937) 461-7223 **TWITTER:** @HRTC_Dayton
ADDRESS: 126 N Main St, #300, Dayton OH 45402

DESCRIPTION: Est. 1986. We are Dayton's professional regional theatre company, exploring the human experience and promoting enlightenment, inclusion and understanding through quality entertainment. We operate a residency and workshop series designed to develop new plays and musicals. The Residency is a ten-day to two-week program that brings the playwright or writing team together for an un-interrupted work session with a handful of theatre artists. Our Workshop is a two-week program—working with professional performers/directors—and culminating in a performance in a staged reading format. We also produce premiere productions for both the Loft Theatre (a 212-seat thrust stage) and the Victoria Theatre (a 1,100-seat proscenium) on occassion, however, we tend to produce shows that 1) have already been produced, 2) we have a familiarity with the writers or 3) that we have developed at The Human Race.

SUBMISSION MATERIALS: We do not accept unsolicited submissions. You may send an introductory letter with a short description of your show. If we are interested, you will then be contacted. If you are contacted by us, please be prepared to send a full script (both plays and musicals), a CD recording of the music (preferably studio recording with a minimum of 6 songs from the show) and any pertinent information about the show, its history, previous readings or productions, and biographies of the writers.

HUNTINGTON THEATRE COMPANY

WEBSITE: www.huntingtontheatre.org **EMAIL:** chaugland@huntingtontheatre.org
PHONE: (617) 273-1503 **FAX:** (617) 353-8300
ADDRESS: 264 Huntington Ave, Boston MA 2115

DESCRIPTION: The Huntington Theatre Company engages, inspires, entertains and challenges audiences with theatrical productions that range from the classics to new works; we train and support the next generation of theatre artists; we provide arts education programs that promote life-long learning to a diverse community; and we

celebrate the essential power of the theatre to illuminate our common humanity.
PREFERRED GENRE: Plays or Musicals   **PREFERRED LENGTH:** Full-length
FEE: No   **AGENT ONLY:** No

IATI THEATRE
(INSTITUTO ARTE TEATRAL INTERNACIONAL)
WEBSITE: www.iatitheater.org   **EMAIL:** info@iatitheater.org
PHONE: (212) 505-6757   **ADDRESS:** 64 E 4th St, 2nd Fl, New York NY 10003
DESCRIPTION: Bilingual Latinx Theatre Company that provokes introspection through cutting-edge performing arts. We support multicultural, diverse and underserved communities while harnessing and empowering unique voices.
SUBMISSION MATERIALS: Online only, 90 mins. max. Accepts submissions during the month of June.   **SUBMISSION DEADLINE:** 06/30/2018   **DEADLINE TYPE:** Annual
PREFERRED GENRE: Plays   **PREFERRED LENGTH:** Full-length   **FEE:** No
AGENT ONLY: No   **SPECIAL INTEREST:** Hispanic or Latinx

ILLUSION THEATER
WEBSITE: www.illusiontheater.org   **EMAIL:** info@illusiontheater.org
PHONE: (612) 339-4944   **ADDRESS:** 528 Hennepin Ave, Minneapolis MN 55403
DESCRIPTION: Illusion Theater's mission is to generate theater that illuminates the illusions, myths and realities of our times and to catalyze personal and social change.
PREFERRED GENRE: Plays   **FEE:** No   **AGENT ONLY:** Yes

IMAGINATION STAGE
WEBSITE: www.imaginationstage.org   **EMAIL:** info@imaginationstage.org
PHONE: (301) 961-6060   **ADDRESS:** 4908 Auburn Ave, Bethesda MD 20814
DESCRIPTION: Imagination Stage empowers ALL young people to discover their voice and identity through performing arts education and professional theatre.
PREFERRED GENRE: Plays or Musicals   **FEE:** No   **AGENT ONLY:** No

IMPACT THEATRE [CA]
WEBSITE: www.impacttheatre.com   **EMAIL:** melissa@impacttheatre.com
ADDRESS: PO Box 12666, Berkeley CA 94712
DESCRIPTION: Since 1996 Impact Theatre has spoken to a new generation of theatre-goers and longtime enthusiasts alike who want to see something fresh and fearless on stage.   **PREFERRED GENRE:** Plays

IMPACT THEATRE REP [NY]
WEBSITE: impactreptheatre.org   **EMAIL:** impactdietrice@gmail.com
PHONE: 2129264516   **ADDRESS:** 253 W 138th St, Ste 100, New York NY 10030
DESCRIPTION: We are youth activists who view the creative arts and leadership training as a way to develop ourselves and change the world in a positive way. We believe that we must be the message that we bring through hardwork, focus, discipline, unity and the principles of S.O.S. safe space, outstanding effort and service to our family friends and community.

IN SERIES
WEBSITE: www.inseries.org **EMAIL:** inseries@inseries.org
PHONE: (202) 315-1323 **FAX:** (202) 315-1303
ADDRESS: Flashpoint, 916 G St, NW, Washington DC 20001
DESCRIPTION: Our mission is to work with and for D.C. area artists to create innovative theatrical programming around a classical music core of opera, cabaret, and song. In Series productions embrace fresh approaches to the classics and blend the performing arts in unconventional ways. The In Series is committed to excellence, affordability, and access to our shared, multifaceted musical heritage, as exemplified by our annual Latino culture programs.
PREFERRED GENRE: Opera **SPECIAL INTEREST:** Hispanic or Latinx

INDIANA REPERTORY THEATRE
WEBSITE: www.irtlive.com **EMAIL:** rroberts@irtlive.com
PHONE: (317) 635-5277 **ADDRESS:** 140 W Washington St, Indianapolis IN 46204
DESCRIPTION: If you would like to submit your script for consideration by the IRT, please send a digital copy to Richard | Roberts, Dramaturg.
PREFERRED GENRE: Plays **PREFERRED LENGTH:** Full-length
FEE: No **AGENT ONLY:** No

INSIDE OUT THEATRE COMPANY
WEBSITE: www.insideouttheatre.org **EMAIL:** info@insideouttheatre.org
PHONE: (954) 385-3060 **ADDRESS:** PO Box 267355, Ft Lauderdale FL 33326
DESCRIPTION: Inside Out Theatre is dedicated to producing works that address social and community concerns and help stimulate positive change. We believe the theatre is a significant instrument to access important truths and insights about one's self and the society in which one lives and is a powerful tool for transformation.
PREFERRED GENRE: Plays or Musicals

INTAR (INTERNATIONAL ARTS RELATIONS) THEATRE
WEBSITE: www.intartheatre.org **EMAIL:** intar@intartheatre.org
PHONE: (212) 695-6134 **ADDRESS:** 500 W 52nd St, 4th Fl, New York NY 10019
DESCRIPTION: We do not accept unsolicited scripts. However approximately 10 pages of a Full-length script can be sent to INTAR Attn. Lou Moreno.
PREFERRED GENRE: Plays or Musicals **PREFERRED LENGTH:** Any Length **FEE:** No
AGENT ONLY: No **SPECIAL INTEREST:** Hispanic or Latinx

INTERACT CENTER [MN]
WEBSITE: www.interactcenter.com **EMAIL:** jeanne@interactcenter.com
PHONE: (612) 339-5145 **ADDRESS:** 212 3rd Ave N, #140, Minneapolis MN 55401
DESCRIPTION: Interact Center creates art that challenges perceptions of disability.

INTERACT STORY THEATRE [MD]
WEBSITE: www.interactstory.com **EMAIL:** info@interactstory.com
PHONE: (301) 879-9305 **ADDRESS:** 32 Pennydog Ct, Wheaton MD 20902
DESCRIPTION: InterAct Story Theatre is a multidisciplinary arts-in-education organiza-

tion and touring theatre for young audiences.

FEE: No **AGENT ONLY:** No **SPECIAL INTEREST:** Theatre for Young Audiences

INTERACT THEATRE COMPANY [CA]
WEBSITE: www.interactla.org **EMAIL:** info@interactla.org
PHONE: (818) 765-8732 **ADDRESS:** PO Box 349, North Hollywood CA 91603
DESCRIPTION: Est. 1992. Interact's Play Development Lab, moderated by Anita Khanzadian, meets on the last Monday of each month at SCLA at 7:00 p.m.
PREFERRED GENRE: Plays

INTERACT THEATRE COMPANY [PA]
WEBSITE: www.interacttheatre.org **EMAIL:** boxoffice@interacttheatre.org
PHONE: (215) 568-8079 **ADDRESS:** 302 S Hicks St, Center City PA 19102
DESCRIPTION: InterAct's mission is to produce new plays that explore the challenging political and social questions of our times. We strongly recommend that you read our mission statement and list of previously produced plays before submitting.
SUBMISSION MATERIALS: Online only. Query letter, biography, 10 page sample.
PREFERRED GENRE: Plays **PREFERRED LENGTH:** Full-length **FEE:** No **AGENT ONLY:** No

INTERBOROUGH REPERTORY THEATER INC. (IRT)
WEBSITE: www.irttheater.org **EMAIL:** krushton@irttheater.org
PHONE: (212) 206-6875 **TWITTER:** @irttheater
ADDRESS: 154 Christopher St, #3-B, New York NY 10014
DESCRIPTION: Est. 1986. IRT is a grassroots laboratory for independent theater and performance in New York City, providing space and support to a new generation of artists. Tucked away in the old Archive Building in Greenwich Village, IRT's mission is to build a community of emerging and established artists by creating a home for the development and presentation of new work. IRT Theater is focused in two primary areas. First, IRT fosters independent artists by providing space, support, and most important, time to create their work through its Archive Residency and 3B Development Series, in which there are several residencies reserved for Deaf artists. Second, IRT mentors the next generation of theater artists through its educational program.

INTERMEDIA ARTS
WEBSITE: www.intermediaarts.org **EMAIL:** info@IntermediaArts.org
ADDRESS: 2822 Lyndale Ave S, Minneapolis MN 55408
DESCRIPTION: Intermedia Arts is a catalyst that builds understanding among people through art.

INTERNATIONAL CITY THEATRE
WEBSITE: www.ictlongbeach.org **EMAIL:** ict@ictlongbeach.org
PHONE: (562) 495-4595 **FAX:** (562) 436-7895
ADDRESS: 1 World Trade Center, #300, Long Beach CA 90831
DESCRIPTION: International City Theatre's mission is to entertain, educate, inspire and provoke thoughtful dialogue through live theatre.

PREFERRED GENRE: Plays

INTIMAN THEATRE
WEBSITE: www.intiman.org   **EMAIL:** info@intiman.org   **PHONE:** (206) 315-5838
TWITTER: @IntimanTheatre   **ADDRESS:** PO Box 19537, Seattle WA 98109
DESCRIPTION: Intiman Theatre produces theatre that is relevant to our time and as diverse as the community in which we live.
PREFERRED GENRE: Plays

IRISH ARTS CENTER
WEBSITE: www.irishartscenter.org   **EMAIL:** submissions@irishartscenter.org
PHONE: (212) 757-3318   **ADDRESS:** 553 W 51st St, New York NY 10019
DESCRIPTION: Founded in 1972, Irish Arts Center is a New York-based arts and cultural center dedicated to projecting a dynamic image of Ireland and Irish America for the 21st century, building community with artists and audiences of all backgrounds, forging and strengthening cross-cultural partnerships, and preserving the evolving stories and traditions of Irish culture for generations to come.
PREFERRED GENRE: Plays or Musicals   **PREFERRED LENGTH:** Any Length
FEE: No   **AGENT ONLY:** No

IRISH CLASSICAL THEATRE COMPANY (ICTC)
WEBSITE: www.irishclassicaltheatre.com   **EMAIL:** boxoffice@irishclassical.com
PHONE: (716) 853-1380   **FAX:** (716) 853-0592
ADDRESS: 625 Main St, Buffalo NY 14203
DESCRIPTION: The Irish Classical Theatre Company is a performing arts theatre located in Buffalo, NY. It presents outstanding productions at The Andrews Theatre, Western New York's only true theatre-in-the-round.
PREFERRED GENRE: Plays   **PREFERRED LENGTH:** Full-length

IRISH REPERTORY THEATRE
WEBSITE: www.irishrep.org   **EMAIL:** kara@irishrep.org   **PHONE:** (212) 727-2737
ADDRESS: 132 W 22nd St, New York NY 10011
DESCRIPTION: Irish Repertory Theatre is unable to accept full unsolicited scripts for our Reading Series or our regular production season unless it is an agent submission.
SUBMISSION MATERIALS: For consideration, please submit, by regular mail only and in care of literary manager Kara Manning, a query letter, 20 page sample, synopsis, audio (if musical), brief biography and SASE if you'd like your material to be returned. No email submissions unless solicited as such.
DEADLINE TYPE: Rolling   **PREFERRED GENRE:** Plays or Musicals
PREFERRED LENGTH: Full-length   **FEE:** No   **AGENT ONLY:** Yes

IRONDALE ENSEMBLE PROJECT
WEBSITE: www.irondale.org   **EMAIL:** irondalert@aol.com
PHONE: (718) 488-9233   **FAX:** (718) 788-0607
ADDRESS: 85 S Oxford S., Brooklyn NY 11217
DESCRIPTION: Irondale is a theatre company — essentially, a performance think tank — that brings together artists who collaborate over long periods of time, who speak a

common performance language and who believe that theatre can educate as well as entertain.

JEFFERSON PERFORMING ARTS SOCIETY

WEBSITE: www.jpas.org **EMAIL:** info@jpas.org **PHONE:** (504) 885-2000
FAX: (504) 885-3437 **ADDRESS:** 1118 Clearview Pkwy, Metairie LA 70001
DESCRIPTION: JPAS is a nonprofit professional arts organization whose mission is to promote arts performance, training, and outreach by providing a diverse range of quality programs that entertain, educate, and enrich the cultural and economic vitality of Jefferson Parish, Greater New Orleans and the Gulf South.

ISLAND CITY STAGE

WEBSITE: islandcitystage.org **EMAIL:** md@islandcitystage.org
PHONE: (954) 519-2533 **TWITTER:** @IslandCityStage
ADDRESS: 2038 N Dixie Hwy, #102B, Wilton Manors FL 33305
DESCRIPTION: Mission: To create professional theatrical productions and quality programs that engage the community in the LGBTQ experience.
Founded in 2012, Island City Stage has gained the reputation of being a multi-award winning professional theater that provides stellar performances for those in the Greater Fort Lauderdale/Wilton Manors/Oakland Park communities. We specialize in developing new work in addition to featuring the works of playwrights who expose audiences to different voices and experiences. These works are brought to life on stage through the talents of professional artists, both union and non-union, whose credits include Broadway, off-Broadway, national tours, major regional theatres, film and television. **FEE:** No **AGENT ONLY:** No **SPECIAL INTEREST:** LGBT+

JEWISH ENSEMBLE THEATRE

WEBSITE: www.jettheatre.org **EMAIL:** c.bremer@jettheatre.org
PHONE: (248) 788-2900
ADDRESS: 6600 W Maple Rd, West Bloomfield MI 48322
DESCRIPTION: JET serves as a force for Jewish continuity, a platform for new voices, and a bridge of understanding to the general community. One of only two professional equity theatres in Oakland County, JET produces on its main stage both award-winning plays and plays making their world premiere or their pre-Broadway debut.

JEWISH PLAYS PROJECT

WEBSITE: www.jewishplaysproject.org/submit **EMAIL:** jcp@jewishplaysproject.org
ADDRESS: 1436 S 13th St, Philadelphia PA 19147
DESCRIPTION: The Jewish Plays Project puts bold, progressive Jewish conversations on world stages. The JPP's innovative and competitive development vehicle invests emerging artists in their Jewish identity; engages Jewish communities in the vetting, selecting and championing of new voices; and secures mainstream production opportunities for the best new plays.

PREFERRED GENRE: Plays **PREFERRED LENGTH:** Full-length **FEE:** No
AGENT ONLY: No **SPECIAL INTEREST:** Jewish

JEWISH THEATER OF NEW YORK

WEBSITE: www.jewishtheater.org **EMAIL:** thejtny@aol.com
PHONE: (212) 494-0050
ADDRESS: PO Box 845, Times Sq Station, New York NY 10108
DESCRIPTION: Our mission is to develop and produce plays and musicals that present a new, thought-provoking perspective on Jewish culture, identity and history; to examine Jewish life through various periods of history; to expose tendencies towards anti-Semitism, as well as their causes and effects; to explore the question of whether Judaism is a race, a religion, or merely a system of thought; to address contemporary social issues affecting Jewish communities in the United States, Europe, Middle East and elsewhere; and to promote dialogue in both Jewish and non-Jewish communities alike about issues affecting Jewish life & culture.
PREFERRED GENRE: Plays or Musicals **PREFERRED LENGTH:** Full-length **FEE:** No
AGENT ONLY: No **SPECIAL INTEREST:** Jewish

JEWISH WOMEN'S THEATRE

WEBSITE: www.jewishwomenstheatre.org
EMAIL: ronda@jewishwomenstheatre.org **PHONE:** (310) 315-1400
ADDRESS: 521 Latimer Rd, Santa Monica CA 90402
DESCRIPTION: Jewish Women's Theatre produce themed Salons, which include short plays, poems, monologues, memoirs and songs. Please check the website for themes this season and submit accordingly. Deadlines vary throughout the year. E-mail submissions. We like short stories, poems, songs, 10 minute one acts, personal essays.
SUBMISSION DEADLINE: 12/15/2017 **DEADLINE TYPE:** Rolling
PREFERRED LENGTH: 10-minute **FEE:** No **AGENT ONLY:** No **SPECIAL INTEREST:** Jewish

JOBSITE THEATRE

WEBSITE: www.jobsitetheater.org/script-submissions **TWITTER:** @jobsitetheater
ADDRESS: 1010 N Macinnes Pl, Tampa FL 33602
DESCRIPTION: Jobsite Theater is an incorporated professional, nonprofit theater company that has been serving the Tampa Bay area since 1998. Most of our productions occur in the Shimberg Playhouse at the David A. Straz, Jr. Center for the Performing Arts, Tampa, where we are the official theater company in residence. Jobsite Theater is dedicated to the creation of socially and politically relevant theater and the pursuit of performing it to the broadest possible audience. Jobsite has established and will continue to evolve a collective of like-minded artists, creating a supportive environment where artists of all disciplines may experiment, hone, and apply their skills in a professional laboratory environment. **PREFERRED LENGTH:** Any Length **FEE:** No

JOHN DREW THEATER AT GUILD HALL OF EAST HAMPTON

WEBSITE: www.guildhall.org **EMAIL:** info@guildhall.org **PHONE:** (631) 324-0806
ADDRESS: 158 Main St, East Hampton NY 11937
DESCRIPTION: Guild Hall is an arts, entertainment, and education center for the community. Its primary focus is to inform, inspire, and enrich our diverse audiences by presenting programs of the highest quality in the visual and performing arts, to collaborate with artists of eastern Long Island, to foster the artistic spirit and to provide a

meeting place for all.

PREFERRED GENRE: All genres **PREFERRED LENGTH:** Any Length

JUBILEE THEATRE
WEBSITE: www.jubileetheatre.org **EMAIL:** tickets@jubileetheatre.org
PHONE: (817) 338-4204 **FAX:** (817) 338-4206
ADDRESS: 506 Main St, Ft Worth TX 76102
DESCRIPTION: Our Mission is to create and produce theatrical works that give voice to the African-American experience. **SPECIAL INTEREST:** Black or African American

KAIROS ITALY THEATER
WEBSITE: www.kitheater.com **EMAIL:** info@kitheater.com
PHONE: (212) 254-4025 **ADDRESS:** 60 E 8th St, #12B, New York NY 10003
DESCRIPTION: KIT's mission is to create a cultural exchange program between Italy, the US and the international community, to unveil the artistic and creative sides of these two countries to the world. In the States, Kairos Italy Theater is dedicated to spreading the Italian Culture and to creating an Italian Cultural Network in order to support and further increase the knowledge of Italy in the States.
PREFERRED GENRE: Plays **PREFERRED LENGTH:** Any Length
FEE: No **AGENT ONLY:** No

KANSAS CITY REPERTORY THEATRE
WEBSITE: www.kcrep.org **EMAIL:** publicity@kcrep.org **PHONE:** (816) 235-2727
ADDRESS: 4949 Cherry St, Kansas City MO 64110
DESCRIPTION: Unfortunately, due to the volume of scripts we receive, we are unable to accept unsolicited submissions.
PREFERRED GENRE: Plays **PREFERRED LENGTH:** Full-length
FEE: No **AGENT ONLY:** Yes

KAVINOKY THEATRE
WEBSITE: www.kavinokytheatre.com **EMAIL:** kavinokytheatre@dyc.edu
PHONE: (716) 829-7668 **FAX:** (716) 829-7790
ADDRESS: 320 Porter Ave, Buffalo NY 14221
DESCRIPTION: Est. 1980. The Kavinoky Theatre has produced over 200 shows in the last 37 years and has earned a reputation for consistently high-quality productions, a solid subscriber base, and has received more awards than any other theatre in Buffalo.

KEEGAN THEATRE
WEBSITE: www.keegantheatre.com **EMAIL:** keegantheatre@keegantheatre.com
PHONE: (703) 892-0202 **TWITTER:** @keegantheatre
ADDRESS: PO Box 17407, Arlington VA 22216
DESCRIPTION: Powerful productions of classic and modern plays and musicals, offered to the community at affordable, neighborhood prices. Our work is fueled by the highest caliber acting and design, scripts that put real people out there on the stark edges of life, and a directing approach that honors clear, authentic storytelling.

KEEN COMPANY

WEBSITE: www.keencompany.org **EMAIL:** info@keencompany.org
PHONE: (212) 216-0963 **FAX:** (212) 216-9629
ADDRESS: 520 8th Ave, #328, New York NY 10018
DESCRIPTION: Keen Company does not accept unsolicited submissions. We consider submissions of new work from writers with whom we have relationships, from agents, and by professional recommendation.

KHAOS COMPANY THEATRE

WEBSITE: www.kctindy.com **EMAIL:** KCTIndy@outlook.com
ADDRESS: 1775 N Sherman Dr, Ste A, Indianapolis IN 46218
DESCRIPTION: Khaos Company Theatre is the Urban Theatre for Professional Emerging Artists providing paid opportunities and filling the void between community and unionized experience in a unique simplistic environment.

KIDS' ENTERTAINMENT

WEBSITE: www.kidsentertainment.net **EMAIL:** info@kidsentertainment.net
PHONE: (416) 971-4836 **FAX:** (416) 971-4841
ADDRESS: 500 St Clair Ave, Ste 808, Toronto ON M6C1A8 Canada
DESCRIPTION: Kids' Entertainment exists to foster and promote only the best in theatre for young audiences. With a roster full of international theatre companies and performance artists, Kids' Entertainment specializes in theatre shows that educate and inspire youth and family audiences.
FEE: No **AGENT ONLY:** No **SPECIAL INTEREST:** Theatre for Young Audiences

KITCHEN DOG THEATER

WEBSITE: www.kitchendogtheater.org **EMAIL:** tina@kitchendogtheater.org
PHONE: (214) 953-2258 **ADDRESS:** Trinity River Arts Center, 2600 N Stemmons Freeway, Ste 180, Dallas TX 75207
DESCRIPTION: It is the mission of Kitchen Dog Theater to provide a place where questions of justice, morality, and human freedom can be explored. We choose plays that challenge our moral and social consciences, invite our audiences to be provoked, challenged, and amazed. We believe that the theater is a site of individual discovery as well as a force against conventional views of the self and experience. It is not a provider of answers, but an invitation to question. Since theater of this kind is not bound by any tradition, Kitchen Dog Theater is committed to exploring these questions whether they are found in the classics, contemporary works, or new plays.
PREFERRED GENRE: Plays **PREFERRED LENGTH:** Full-length

KUMU KAHUA THEATRE

WEBSITE: www.kumukahua.org **EMAIL:** kumukahuatheatre@hawaiiantel.net
PHONE: (808) 536-4222 **FAX:** (808) 536-4226
DDRESS: 46 Merchant St, Honolulu HI 96813
DESCRIPTION: Our mission is to provide theatrical opportunities for the expression of local community lifestyles, whether contemporary or historical; to stage locally written plays set in Hawai'i or dealing with some aspect of the Hawaiian experience of residents; to provide training and theatrical experiences for local playwrights,

directors, performers and other theatrical artists; and to develop an increasingly large audience sensitive to plays and theatre pieces dealing specifically and truthfully with local subject matter.

PREFERRED GENRE: Plays **SPECIAL INTEREST:** Native Hawaiian or Other Pacific Islander

L.A. THEATRE WORKS (LATW)

WEBSITE: www.latw.org **EMAIL:** latw@latw.org **PHONE:** (310) 827-0808
ADDRESS: 681 Venice Blvd, Venice CA 90291
DESCRIPTION: Est. 1974. Live performances and studio recordings for broadcast over public radio. Agent, no unsolicited. L.A. Theatre Works' mission is to record and preserve great performances of important stage plays, maximizing the use of new technologies to make world-class theatre accessible to the widest possible audience, and to expand the use of theatre as a teaching tool. Also core to our mission is selecting and maximizing material that sheds light on important issues and stirs debate.
PREFERRED GENRE: Radio plays **PREFERRED LENGTH:** Any Length
FEE: No **AGENT ONLY:** Yes

LA JOLLA PLAYHOUSE

WEBSITE: www.lajollaplayhouse.org **EMAIL:** information@ljp.org
PHONE: (858) 550-1070 **TWITTER:** @ljplayhouse
ADDRESS: PO Box 12039, La Jolla CA 92039
DESCRIPTION: Est. 1947. We accept full-length scripts submitted by literary agents and 10-page samples from Southern California resident playwrights only. Submissions accepted year-round. La Jolla Playhouse advances theatre as an art form and as a vital social, moral and political platform by providing unfettered creative opportunities for the leading artists of today and tomorrow. With our youthful spirit and eclectic, artist-driven approach we will continue to cultivate a local and national following with an insatiable appetite for audacious and diverse work.

LA MAMA EXPERIMENTAL THEATER CLUB

WEBSITE: www.lamama.org **EMAIL:** web@lamama.org **PHONE:** (212) 254-6468
ADDRESS: 74-A E 4th St, New York NY 10003
DESCRIPTION: Est. 1961. La MaMa is recognized as the seedbed of new work by artists of all nations and cultures. To date, La MaMa has presented more than 150,000 artists from over 70 nations. Professional recommendation. We support the people who make art, and it is to them that we give $2 million of in-kind support including free theatre and rehearsal space, and audio/visual package, tech support, marketing support, and ticketing services. We enable artists to explore their ideas and translate them into a theatrical language that can communicate to any person in any part of the world.
PREFERRED GENRE: Plays **PREFERRED LENGTH:** Any Length **FEE:** No

LABYRINTH THEATER COMPANY

WEBSITE: labtheater.org **PHONE:** (212) 513-1080 **TWITTER:** @LabTheaterNYC
ADDRESS: 155 Bank St, New York NY 10014
DESCRIPTION: Est. 1992. Labyrinth produces new works for the stage, giving voice to new perspectives that are powerful, groundbreaking, and that have changed the face

of America's theatrical landscape. Not currently accepting new play submissions. Check website for updates.

PREFERRED GENRE: Plays **PREFERRED LENGTH:** Any Length
FEE: No **AGENT ONLY:** No

LAKESHORE PLAYERS THEATRE
WEBSITE: www.lakeshoreplayers.org **EMAIL:** office@lakeshoreplayers.org
PHONE: (651) 426-3275
ADDRESS: 4820 Stewart Ave, White Bear Lake MN 55110
DESCRIPTION: Lakeshore Players' mission is to provide community enrichment and education through the performing arts. A community based nonprofit theater under professional management, Lakeshore is committed to strengthening our community by helping people of all ages and experiences to participate in the performing arts. Lakeshore Players Theatre is accepting submissions for 10-minute plays for festival in June.
PREFERRED GENRE: Plays **FEE:** No **AGENT ONLY:** No

LAMB'S PLAYERS THEATRE (LPT)
WEBSITE: www.lambsplayers.org **EMAIL:** robert@lambsplayers.org
PHONE: (619) 437-6050 **FAX:** (619) 437-6053
ADDRESS: PO Box 182229, Coronado CA 92178
DESCRIPTION: NO UNSOLICITED SUBMISSIONS. Est. 1971. Response Time: 6 wks query, 6 mos script. OUR MISSION: To Tell Good Stories Well. We look for narratives that: probe and question the values and choices of contemporary culture; celebrate the joys, strengths and diverse traditions of family and community; explore the spiritual dimension of life; champion the moral imagination.

LAMICRO THEATER
WEBSITE: www.lamicrotheater.org **EMAIL:** info@lamicrotheater.org
PHONE: (212) 929-0332
ADDRESS: PO Box 20019, London Terrace, New York NY 10011
DESCRIPTION: Est. 2003. Bilingual productions of contemporary and emerging playwrights; explore new ideas and generate dialogue concerning the realities faced by our diverse communities. LaMicro Theater's mission is to present high-quality Spanish, Latin American, and U.S. Latino theater in English and bilingual productions. We want to expose our audiences to contemporary and emerging playwrights whose work will lead us to explore new ideas and generate dialogue concerning the realities facedby our diverse communities. LaMicro is committed to presenting under-produced playwrights and also to experiment with new media technology and work in collaboration with contemporary artists. LaMicro wants to produce plays that attract non-traditional audiences, including spectators who might never before have been to the theater.
FEE: No **AGENT ONLY:** No **SPECIAL INTEREST:** Hispanic or Latinx

LE PETIT THEATRE DU VIEUX CARRE
WEBSITE: www.lepetittheatre.com **EMAIL:** boxoffice@lepetittheatre.com
PHONE: (504) 522-2081 **ADDRESS:** 616 St Peter St, New Orleans LA 70116
DESCRIPTION: Est. 1916. Le Petit Théâtre du Vieux Carré, a nonprofit organization, is

passionately dedicated to presenting the highest quality theatrical performances to entertain and educate the diverse population of the region and enhance the economic vitality of the greater New Orleans area. By offering a full season of contemporary and classic dramas, comedies, musicals, and children's productions, as well as master classes and special events, the theatre embraces the work of the city's professional artists both onstage and backstage, all the while nurturing and mentoring up-and-coming talent with its array of outreach programs.

LEAPING THESPIANS

WEBSITE: www.leapingthespians.com **EMAIL:** info@leapingthespians.com

DESCRIPTION: Leaping Thespians is an award-winning woman's theatre company bringing stories of queer lives to anyone who wants to watch. The company debuted in the 1990's in Nelson BC, was revived in Vancouver in 2001, and has been creating shows ever since. Leaping Thespians has written five original shows and has produced variety shows and acts with other groups in Vancouver. We are always interested in reading scripts of at least one hour's length, where all parts can be played by women. Send synopsis, production history, script sample.

REFERRED LENGTH: Full-length **FEE:** No

AGENT ONLY: No **SPECIAL INTEREST:** Feminism/Women's Rights

LEXINGTON CHILDREN'S THEATRE

WEBSITE: www.lctonstage.org **EMAIL:** info@lctonstage.org

PHONE: (859) 254-4546 **ADDRESS:** 418 W Short St, Lexington KY 40507

DESCRIPTION: Est. 1938. Lexington Children's Theatre is a fully professional, non-profit organization dedicated to the intellectual and cultural enrichment of young people and families. LCT creates imaginative and compelling theatre experiences for young people and families.

FEE: No **AGENT ONLY:** No **SPECIAL INTEREST:** Theatre for Young Audiences

LINCOLN CENTER THEATER

WEBSITE: www.lct.org/about/script-submissions **EMAIL:** scriptquestions@lct.org

PHONE: (212) 362-7600 **TWITTER:** @LCTheater

ADDRESS: 150 W 65th St, New York NY 10023

DESCRIPTION: America's largest not-for-profit theater, producing a year-round program of plays and musicals at the Beaumont, the Newhouse, the Tow and at various other theaters around New York City.

PREFERRED GENRE: Plays or Musicals **PREFERRED LENGTH:** Full-length

FEE: No **AGENT ONLY:** Yes

LITERALLY ALIVE

WEBSITE: www.literallyalive.com **EMAIL:** brenda@literallyalive.com

PHONE: (212) 475-1237

ADDRESS: The Players Theatre, 115 MacDougal St, New York NY 10012

DESCRIPTION: NYC based theatre company that produces original musicals based on classic children's literature. We are committed to engaging children in the arts, which develops their imagination and instills the mental flexibility necessary to utilize creative, problem solving in their adult life. High-quality theatrical productions which

offer engaging costumes and sets, as well as performances by talented professional actors, reach across the footlights and welcome the child in.
PREFERRED GENRE: Musicals **PREFERRED LENGTH:** Any Length **FEE:** No
AGENT ONLY: No **SPECIAL INTEREST:** Theatre for Young Audiences

LITTLE FISH THEATRE (LFT)
WEBSITE: www.littlefishtheatre.org **EMAIL:** holly@littlefishtheatre.org
PHONE: (310) 512-6030 **FAX:** (310) 507-0269
ADDRESS: 777 Centre St, San Pedro CA 90731
DESCRIPTION: Est. 2002. Little Fish Theatre is an Artists' ensemble whose mission is to present quality productions year-round, drawing material from the wealth of new, contemporary and classic plays that lend themselves to an intimate performance space. We aim to explore provocative, stimulating theatrical entertainment, while providing a nurturing environment for theatre artists and an inviting nexus for local and visiting audiences to our 65-seat venue in the San Pedro / LA Waterfront Arts District. Not currently accepting Full-length plays. Go to website for short play festival guidelines.
PREFERRED GENRE: Plays **PREFERRED LENGTH:** 10-minute **FEE:** No
AGENT ONLY: No

THE LITTLE THEATRE OF ALEXANDRIA
WEBSITE: www.thelittletheatre.com **EMAIL:** asklta@thelittletheatre.com
PHONE: (703) 683-5778 **ADDRESS:** 600 Wolfe St, Alexandria VA 22314
DESCRIPTION: Founded in 1934, The Little Theatre of Alexandria began as a small play-reading group. Full productions ensued, and in 1939 the group bought a rickety former blacksmith's shop located in Ramsey Alley, between Lee and Fairfax Streets, for rehearsal space and construction of sets and costumes. Since 1934, the theatre has mounted over 350 productions. Home of the One-Act Playwriting Competition.
PREFERRED LENGTH: Any Length **FEE:** No **AGENT ONLY:** No

LONG BEACH PLAYHOUSE
WEBSITE: www.lbplayhouse.org **EMAIL:** boxoffice@lbplayhouse.org
PHONE: (562) 949-1014 **FAX:** (562) 494-1014
ADDRESS: 5021 E Anaheim St, Long Beach CA 90804
DESCRIPTION: Established in 1929. Mission: To celebrate the human experience while encouraging the participation of artist and audience alike. Established over 20 years ago, the New Works Literary Committee and Annual New Works Festival is a part of Long Beach Playhouse's commitment to the arts. Check website for festival deadlines.

LONG WHARF THEATRE
WEBSITE: www.longwharf.org **EMAIL:** literary@longwharf.org
PHONE: (203) 787-4284 **FAX:** (203) 776-2287
ADDRESS: 222 Sargent Dr, New Haven CT 06511
DESCRIPTION: Our mission is to create theatre of the highest quality that inspires discourse and reflection about each of us and the world in which we live. Submission procedure: agent submission or professional recommendation only, no unsolicited scripts or samples. Best submission time: year-round. Response time: 6-9 months.

LOOKINGGLASS THEATRE [IL]
WEBSITE: www.lookingglasstheatre.org **EMAIL:** info@lookingglasstheatre.org
PHONE: (773) 477-9257
ADDRESS: 875 N Michigan Ave, Ste 1430, Chicago IL 60611
DESCRIPTION: Lookingglass is an ensemble-based company that primarily produces new work, both original plays and adaptations, created by our ensemble. Therefore, Lookingglass Theatre Company does not accept unsolicited scripts or script samples for consideration.
PREFERRED GENRE: Plays **PREFERRED LENGTH:** Full-length **AGENT ONLY:** Yes

LORRAINE HANSBERRY THEATER
WEBSITE: www.lhtsf.org **EMAIL:** lhtsf@lhtsf.org
PHONE: (415) 345-3980 **FAX:** (415) 345-3983
ADDRESS: 762 Fulton St, Ste 204, San Francisco CA 94102
DESCRIPTION: Established 1981. The core mission of the Lorraine Hansberry Theatre is to create Theater work by, for, and about African American people and other people of color. We accept submissions of new scripts from established and emerging playwrights. Will accept hard copies or email submissions. Sorry, we cannot return scripts. Please do not send your only copy.

LOST NATION THEATER
WEBSITE: www.lostnationtheater.org **EMAIL:** info@lostnationtheater.org
PHONE: (802) 229-0492
ADDRESS: City Hall, 39 Main St, Montpelier VT 05602
DESCRIPTION: Est. 1977. By calling our company Lost Nation Theater, we feel we're locating ourselves on an imaginative frontier— breaking boundaries, taking dramatic action, and courageously making things happen. But at the same time, we're grounding ourselves in a well-known place and discovering who we are as we're shaped by that evolving landscape. Essentially, Lost Nation Theater derives inspiration from a three-dimensional vision that: 1) celebrates the exciting and boundless possibilities of our human potential; 2) nurtures our individual emotional intelligence and our collective civilization; and 3) forges the inclusive, transformative connections that make us better people and communities. Playwrights Submissions accepted during November! Please use the playwrights & show proposals submission form on the website to upload a 10-page sample.
SUBMISSION DEADLINE: 11/30/2017 **FEE:** No **AGENT ONLY:** No

LUCKY PENNY PRODUCTIONS
WEBSITE: www.luckypennynapa.com **EMAIL:** info@luckypennynapa.com
PHONE: (707) 738-2920 **ADDRESS:** 1357 Foster Rd, Napa CA 94558
DESCRIPTION: Established 2009. As Napa Valley's Premier Theatre Company, Lucky Penny Productions creates, develops and presents professional quality theatre, and fosters educational opportunities for youth and adults in our community. Lucky Penny Productions offers regular opportunities for writers to submit works for special events. Go to website under Submission Opportunities to learn more.

LUNA STAGE

WEBSITE: www.lunastage.org **EMAIL**: submissions@lunastage.org
PHONE: (973) 395-5551 **ADDRESS**: 555 Valley Rd, West Orange NJ 07052
DESCRIPTION: Established 1992. The mission of Luna Stage is to develop and produce thought-provoking theatre that gives voice to emerging American playwrights and new life to contemporary and classic plays that speak to our times. As producer, educator and innovator, Luna Stage is committed to collaborating with artists of multiple disciplines and partnering with our community to illuminate the diverse perspectives of our society. Please note, we will be taking a hiatus from accepting open script submissions for the remainder of 2017. We expect to begin accepting open submissions again as of January 2018, but please check back on the website for updates prior to submitting.
PREFERRED LENGTH: Full-length **FEE**: No **AGENT ONLY**: No

LYRIC STAGE COMPANY OF BOSTON
WEBSITE: www.lyricstage.com **EMAIL**: info@lyricstage.com
PHONE: (617) 585-5680 **FAX**: (617) 585-5689
ADDRESS: 140 Clarendon St, Boston MA 02116
DESCRIPTION: Est. 1974. Our mission is to produce intimate, challenging and entertaining theatre; reflect the tastes and backgrounds of 21st century Boston; and provide a home for Boston-based theatre artists to establish and expand their careers. Opportunities incl. Growing Voices new work development program. Check website for current submission information.

MA'AT PRODUCTION ASSN. OF AFRIKAN CENTERED THEATRE (MPAACT)
WEBSITE: www.mpaact.org **EMAIL**: information@mpaact.org
ADDRESS: PO Box 10039, Chicago IL 60610
DESCRIPTION: MPAACT exists to develop, nurture, and sustain Afrikan Centered Theatre (ACT), an artistic expression grounded in the many cultures and traditions of the Afrikan continent and its Diaspora. With a vision focused on creating new work and collaborative art, MPAACT produces and educates with the goal of increasing understanding and appreciation of (ACT) and its interrelated disciplines.

MAGIC THEATRE
WEBSITE: www.magictheatre.org **EMAIL**: plays@magictheatre.org
PHONE: (415) 441-8822 **FAX**: (415) 771-5505
ADDRESS: Ft Mason Ctr, 2 Marina Blvd, Bldg D, San Francisco CA 94123
DESCRIPTION: Magic Theatre is dedicated to the cultivation of bold new plays, playwrights, and audiences – and to producing explosive, entertaining, and ideologically robust plays that ask substantive questions about, and reflect the rich diversity of, the world in which we live. Magic believes that demonstrating faith in a writer's vision by providing a safe yet rigorous artistic home, where a full body of work can be imagined, supported, and produced, allows writers to thrive. We encourage local writers to submit work to us. Local is defined as residing within the nine San Francisco Bay Area counties (Alameda, Contra Costa, Marin, Napa, San Mateo, Santa Clara, Solano and Sonoma). Writers from outside the Bay Area may only submit work through agents. We no longer accept query packages or musicals. We only accept full-length plays.
SUBMISSION MATERIALS: Please submit full-length scripts as PDF documents. Due

to the number of script submissions we have been receiving, response times may be longer than usual. **PLEASE NOTE:** We will be unable to return your script. Please keep this in mind when preparing your materials.

PREFERRED GENRE: Plays **PREFERRED LENGTH:** Full-length **FEE:** No **AGENT ONLY:** No

MAINSTREET MUSICALS, INC.

WEBSITE: www.mainstreetmusicals.org **EMAIL:** info@mainstreetmusicals.org

ADDRESS: c/o Tim Jerome, 1 Jervis Rd, Yonkers NY 10705

DESCRIPTION: MAINSTREET MUSICALS Inc. - a national non-profit, tax-exempt organization - is a consortium of theater professionals and their non-profit, commercial, and educational partners. Utilizing professional script evaluation, industry competitions, and local concert-reading presentations, MainStreet promotes development opportunities for original musical theater works throughout regional America. Please note: all submissions are made through our website.

PREFERRED GENRE: Musicals **PREFERRED LENGTH:** Full-length

FEE: Yes **AGENT ONLY:** No

MANHATTAN THEATRE CLUB (MTC)

WEBSITE: www.manhattantheatreclub.com **EMAIL:** questions@mtc-nyc.org

PHONE: (212) 399-3000 **FAX:** (212) 399-4329

ADDRESS: 311 W 43rd St, New York NY 10036

DESCRIPTION: Founded in 1970, MTC is committed to the creation of new plays and musicals through an intensive Artistic Development Program that offers commissions, script evaluation, dramaturgical support, readings and workshops. Using the work on its stages, MTC's Education Program promotes active participation in the arts through in-class instruction, student and family matinees, teacher training, internships and internet-based distance learning. In constantly seeking new ways to innovate, MTC keeps theatre alive and relevant.

PREFERRED GENRE: Plays or Musicals **AGENT ONLY:** Yes

THE MASQUERS PLAYHOUSE

WEBSITE: www.masquers.org **EMAIL:** info@masquers.org

PHONE: (510) 232-3888 **ADDRESS:** PO Box 71037, Richmond CA 94807

DESCRIPTION: Est. 1955.

MARIN THEATRE COMPANY

WEBSITE: www.marintheatre.org **EMAIL:** literarymanager@marintheatre.org

PHONE: (415) 388-5200 **FAX:** (415) 388-1217

ADDRESS: 397 Miller Ave, Mill Valley CA 94941

DESCRIPTION: Marin Theatre Company produces world-class theater for the Marin County and Bay Area communities. We strive to set a national standard for intimate theater experiences of the highest quality, featuring provocative plays by passionate playwrights. We pursue a dialogue with our community that addresses our national and local concerns and interests and assists us in finding a new understanding of our lives. We create future artists and arts patrons through innovative programs for youth.

PREFERRED GENRE: Plays **PREFERRED LENGTH:** Full-length

FEE: No **AGENT ONLY:** No

MA-YI THEATER COMPANY

WEBSITE: www.ma-yitheatre.org **EMAIL:** info@ma-yitheatre.org
PHONE: (212) 971-4862 **FAX:** (212) 971-4876
ADDRESS: 520 8th Ave, #309, New York NY 10018
DESCRIPTION: Founded in 1989, Ma-Yi Theater Company is a Drama Desk and Obie Award-winning not-for-profit 501(c)(3) organization whose primary mission is to develop and produce new and innovative plays by Asian American writers. Since its founding, Ma-Yi has distinguished itself as one of the country's leading incubators of new work shaping the national discourse about what it means to be Asian American today.
PREFERRED GENRE: Plays **PREFERRED LENGTH:** Full-length **FEE:** No **AGENT ONLY:** No
SPECIAL INTEREST: Asian;Native Hawaiian or Other Pacific Islander

MCC THEATER

WEBSITE: www.mcctheater.org **EMAIL:** mcc@mcctheater.org
PHONE: (212) 727-7722 **ADDRESS:** 231 W 29th St, #303, New York NY 10001
DESCRIPTION: Due to the high volume of scripts and the careful attention the members of the Literary Department give to each script received, MCC Theater does not accept unsolicited manuscripts.
SUBMISSION MATERIALS: Interested writers are welcome to submit synopses and dialogue samples no longer than ten pages and are assured a timely reply. Writers looking to submit musicals may include an electronic link to selections from the score as well. Email submissions@mcctheater.org
PREFERRED GENRE: Plays or Musicals **PREFERRED LENGTH:** Full-length
FEE: No **AGENT ONLY:** Yes

MCCARTER THEATER CENTER

WEBSITE: www.mccarter.org **EMAIL:** literary@mccarter.org
PHONE: (609) 258-6500 **ADDRESS:** 91 University Pl, Princeton NJ 08540
DESCRIPTION: McCarter Theatre is committed to nurturing new plays and artists through commissions, readings, workshops, retreats and productions. We identify new artists by carefully following the work around us through contact with other theaters, festivals, graduate programs and playwright development organizations, and through conversations with our colleagues around the country. Agents and artists with a relationship with McCarter who have a project they believe will be of particular interest to McCarter are invited to contact the artistic staff. If the project fits our needs and we believe it may be a possible fit for development or production in the next few seasons, we will respond with a request to read the script.
PREFERRED GENRE: Plays **PREFERRED LENGTH:** Full-length **FEE:** No **AGENT ONLY:** Yes

MEADOW BROOK THEATRE

WEBSITE: www.mbtheatre.com **EMAIL:** communications.mbt@gmail.com
PHONE: (248) 370-3322 **FAX:** (248) 370-3108
ADDRESS: 207 Wilson Hall, Oakland Univ, Rochester MI 48309
DESCRIPTION: Our Mission is to provide a season of innovative, Broadway quality theatre productions that make audiences smile, laugh and cry, enriching the cultural experience of the community in southeast Michigan.

MEDICINE SHOW THEATRE

WEBSITE: www.medicineshowtheatre.org

EMAIL: medicineshow@medicineshowtheatre.org **PHONE:** (212) 262-4216

ADDRESS: 549 W 52nd St, 3rd Fl, New York NY 10019

DESCRIPTION: We are interested in comedy in its largest sense – innovative, experimental, abstract, brilliant. Especially interested in receiving plays by women and/or with parts for women. We are not interested in scripts that would make good TV sitcoms, TV dramas, or movies. We do not do realistic or naturalistic plays. We want challenges that help us grow as live theatre artists. Submissions accepted year-round.

PREFERRED GENRE: Plays **PREFERRED LENGTH:** Full-length **FEE:** No

MERRIMACK REPERTORY THEATRE

WEBSITE: www.mrt.org **EMAIL:** emily.ruddock@mrt.org

PHONE: (978) 654-4678 **ADDRESS:** 132 Warren St, Lowell MA 1852

DESCRIPTION: MRT is not currently accepting or reading unsolicited scripts.

PREFERRED GENRE: Plays **PREFERRED LENGTH:** Full-length

FEE: No **AGENT ONLY:** Yes

METRO THEATER COMPANY

WEBSITE: www.metrotheatercompany.org **EMAIL:** julia@metroplays.org

PHONE: (314) 932-7414 **ADDRESS:** 3311 Washington Ave, St. Louis MO 63103

DESCRIPTION: We do not accept unsolicited scripts. Commissioned playwrights are individuals who have established a relationship with us over time.

SUBMISSION MATERIALS: Letter of introduction, resume, sample of dialogue (3-5 pages max), scenario for proposed play, SASE, letters of recommendation from directors who have worked with you. Response time: 2-3 mos.

PREFERRED GENRE: Plays **PREFERRED LENGTH:** Full-length **FEE:** No **AGENT ONLY:** Yes

METROPOLITAN PLAYHOUSE

WEBSITE: www.metropolitanplayhouse.org

EMAIL: connect@metropolitanplayhouse.org **PHONE:** (212) 995-8410

ADDRESS: 220 E 4th St, New York NY 10009

DESCRIPTION: Metropolitan Playhouse explores America's theatrical heritage to illuminate contemporary American culture. The Playhouse produces early American plays, new plays drawn from American culture and history, and plays from around the world that resonate with the American canon.

MIAMI LIGHT PROJECT

WEBSITE: www.miamilightproject.com **EMAIL:** info@miamilightproject.com

PHONE: (305) 576-4350 **FAX:** (305) 576-6480

ADDRESS: 3000 Biscayne Blvd, #100, Miami FL 33137

DESCRIPTION: Founded in 1989, Miami Light Project is a not-for-profit cultural organization which presents live performances by innovative dance, music and theater artists from around the world; supports the development of new work by South Florida-based artists; and offers educational programs for students of every age.

MIAMI THEATER CENTER, INC.
WEBSITE: www.mtcmiami.org **EMAIL:** idalmis@mtcmiami.org
PHONE: (305) 751-9550 **TWITTER:** @MTCMiami
ADDRESS: 9806 NE 2nd Ave, Miami Shores FL 33138
DESCRIPTION: Mission: To create transformative live arts experiences and educational opportunities for people of all ages, abilities, and cultural and socioeconomic backgrounds, and to provide affordable rehearsal, performance, and screening facilities for artists and arts organizations. **FEE:** No **AGENT ONLY:** No

MILL MOUNTAIN THEATRE
WEBSITE: www.millmountain.org **EMAIL:** mmtmail@millmountain.org
PHONE: (540) 342-5730 **FAX:** (540) 342-5745
ADDRESS: 1 Market Sq, 2nd Fl, Roanoke VA 24011
DESCRIPTION: Mill Mountain Theatre strives to inspire, entertain, enrich, educate and challenge audiences of Southwest Virginia through high-quality, professional theatrical productions and experiences. We are dedicated to nurturing the next generation of theatre artists and audiences through conservatory and outreach classes and programming; and are committed to ensuring the long term economic and artistic sustainability of the performing arts in the Roanoke Valley and Southwest Virginia.

MILWAUKEE REPERTORY THEATER
WEBSITE: www.milwaukeerep.com **EMAIL:** dsladky@milwaukeerep.com
PHONE: (414) 224-1761 **FAX:** (414) 224-9097
ADDRESS: 108 E Wells St, Milwaukee WI 53202
DESCRIPTION: Producing entertaining, thought-provoking, accessible, adventurous, and compelling world premiere plays, musicals, and theater events—of recognized excellence, and that express strong local relevance and carry wider national appeal—provides the strongest possible mechanism with which to reflect our core values and to advance our mission in service of our community.
PREFERRED GENRE: Plays or Musicals **PREFERRED LENGTH:** Full-length
AGENT ONLY: Yes

MIRACLE THEATRE GROUP
WEBSITE: www.milagro.org **EMAIL:** jefe@milagro.org **PHONE:** (503) 236-7253
FAX: (503) 236-4174 **ADDRESS:** 2322 SE Yamhill, Portland OR 97214
DESCRIPTION: Teatro Milagro, Milagro's touring & arts education program, presents its original bilingual plays and educational residencies to diverse and underserved communities across the nation.
PREFERRED GENRE: Plays **PREFERRED LENGTH:** Full-length **FEE:** No **AGENT ONLY:** No
SPECIAL INTEREST: Hispanic or Latinx

MIXED BLOOD THEATRE COMPANY
WEBSITE: www.mixedblood.com **EMAIL:** literary@mixedblood.com
PHONE: (612) 338-6131 **ADDRESS:** 1501 S 4th St, Minneapolis MN 55454
DESCRIPTION: Using theater to illustrate and animate, Mixed Blood changes attitudes, behavior, and policy by paying positive attention to difference.

PREFERRED LENGTH: Full-length **FEE:** No **AGENT ONLY:** No

MONTANA REPERTORY THEATER
WEBSITE: www.montanarep.org **PHONE:** (406) 243-6809
FAX: (406) 243-5726 **ADDRESS:** School of Theatre & Dance, Univ of Montana, Missoula MT 59812
DESCRIPTION: Montana Repertory Theatre was established as a professional touring company in 1967, providing professional theatre to our own and neighboring Western states at an affordable cost. Our mission is to tell the great stories of our world to enlighten, develop, and celebrate the human spirit in an ever-expanding community.

MOSAIC YOUTH THEATRE
WEBSITE: www.mosaicdetroit.org **EMAIL:** rick@mosaicdetroit.org
PHONE: (313) 554-6910 **FAX:** (313) 544-6920
ADDRESS: 610 Antoinette St, Detroit MI 48202
DESCRIPTION: Mosaic Youth Theatre of Detroit's critically acclaimed student-driven performances and national and international tours have brought worldwide attention to Detroit as a center for arts and culture while shining a spotlight on the area's talented young people and creating new and diverse audiences for the performing arts.

MOVING ARTS
WEBSITE: www.movingarts.org **EMAIL:** info@movingarts.org
PHONE: (323) 472-5646 **ADDRESS:** 1822 Hyperion Ave, Los Angeles CA 90027
DESCRIPTION: Moving Arts is committed to creating, producing and promoting adventurous theatrical new work by diverse Los Angeles artists for diverse audiences.
PREFERRED GENRE: Plays **PREFERRED LENGTH:** Any Length **FEE:** No **AGENT ONLY:** Yes

MPAACT
WEBSITE: www.mpaact.org **EMAIL:** submissions@mpaact.org
ADDRESS: PO Box 10039, Chicago IL 60610
DESCRIPTION: MPAACT exists to develop, nurture, and sustain Afrikan Centered Theatre (ACT), an artistic expression grounded in the many cultures and traditions of the Afrikan continent and its Diaspora. With a vision focused on creating new work and collaborative art, MPAACT produces and educates with the goal of increasing understanding and appreciation of (ACT) and its interrelated disciplines.
PREFERRED GENRE: Plays **PREFERRED LENGTH:** Any Length **FEE:** No
SPECIAL INTEREST: Black or African American

MU PERFORMING ARTS
WEBSITE: www.muperformingarts.org **EMAIL:** info@muperformingarts.org
PHONE: (651) 789-1012 **FAX:** (651) 789-1015
ADDRESS: 355 Wabash St N, #140, St Paul MN 55102
DESCRIPTION: Mu produces great performances born of arts, equity, and justice from the heart of the Asian American experience.
SPECIAL INTEREST: Asian; Native Hawaiian or Other Pacific Islander

MUSIC THEATRE OF CONNECTICUT

WEBSITE: www.musictheatreofct.com   **EMAIL:** admin@musictheatreofct.com
ADDRESS: PO Box 344, Westport CT 6880
DESCRIPTION: Music Theatre of Connecticut produces an annual series of Equity productions featuring New York professionals (MTC MainStage), numerous annual student productions, and a conservatory-style School of Performing Arts with curriculum-based training for students ages four through high school, including the nationally-recognized College-Bound in the Performing Arts program for performance career-focused high school students.
PREFERRED GENRE: Musicals

NACL THEATRE
(NORTH AMERICAN CULTURAL LABORATORY)
WEBSITE: www.nacl.org   **EMAIL:** nacl@nacl.org   **PHONE:** (845) 557-0694
FAX: (845) 557-0393   **ADDRESS:** 110 Highland Lake Rd, Highland NY 12743
DESCRIPTION: Mission: To cultivate a culture of creativity through the development and presentation of innovative ensemble theatre, education, and sustainable community service.   **PREFERRED GENRE:** Plays

NAPLES PLAYERS ETC
WEBSITE: www.naplesplayers.org   **EMAIL:** balexander@naplesplayers.org
PHONE: (239) 434-7340   **ADDRESS:** 701 5th Ave S, Naples FL 34102-6662
DESCRIPTION: The Naples Players continually seeks to enrich, educate, and entertain our community through a superior theatre experience. TNP is inspiring passion for the performing arts through life-long opportunities to participate in vibrant theatrical experiences.   **FEE:** No   **AGENT ONLY:** No

NASHVILLE REPERTORY THEATRE
WEBSITE: www.nashvillerep.org   **EMAIL:** nate@nashvillerep.org
PHONE: (615) 244-4878   **ADDRESS:** 161 Rains Ave, Nashville TN 37203
DESCRIPTION: Nashville Repertory Theatre strives to be a vital professional regional theatre that is an indispensable part of our community's creative life, widely embraced and deeply valued as an essential source for illuminating artistic experiences and exciting entertainment, and recognized as a model of sustainability that is home for a thriving community of professional artists and whose name is synonymous with excellence in every aspect.
PREFERRED GENRE: Plays or Musicals   **PREFERRED LENGTH:** Full-length
FEE: No   **AGENT ONLY:** No

THE NATIONAL THEATRE [DC]
WEBSITE: thenationaldc.org   **PHONE:** (202) 628-6161   **FAX:** (202) 628-3208
TWITTER: @NatTheatreDC
ADDRESS: 1321 Pennsylvania Ave NW, Washington DC 20004
DESCRIPTION: Est. 1835. Our mission is to be the Stage for the Nation.

NATIONAL THEATRE OF THE DEAF
WEBSITE: www.ntd.org   **EMAIL:** bbeekman@ntd.org   **PHONE:** (860) 574-9063
FAX: (860) 574-9107   **ADDRESS:** 325 Pequot Ave, New London CT 6320

DESCRIPTION: Our mission is to present theatrical work of the highest quality, performing in the unique style we created through blending American Sign Language and spoken word.

FEE: No   **AGENT ONLY:** No   **SPECIAL INTEREST:** Deaf or Hearing-impaired

NATIONAL YIDDISH THEATER FOLKSBIENE
WEBSITE: www.nytf.org   **EMAIL:** info@nytf.org   **PHONE:** (212) 213-2120
FAX: (212) 213-2186   **ADDRESS:** 36 Battery Pl, New York NY 10280
DESCRIPTION: National Yiddish Theatre Folksbiene's mission is to celebrate the Yiddish experience through the performing arts by transmitting the rich cultural legacy in exciting new ways that bridge social and cultural divides.
PREFERRED GENRE: Plays or Musicals   **PREFERRED LENGTH:** Any Length   **FEE:** No
AGENT ONLY: No   **SPECIAL INTEREST:** Jewish

NAUTILUS MUSIC THEATRE
WEBSITE: www.nautilusmusictheater.org   **EMAIL:** staff@nautilusmusictheater.org
PHONE: (651) 298-9913   **TWITTER:** @NautilusMT
ADDRESS: 308 Prince St, #190, St Paul MN 55101
DESCRIPTION: Est. 1986 as a program of the Minnesota Opera and spun off independently in 1992. It provides opportunities for the artistic growth of music-theater artists who create, develop, and produce new operas and other forms of music-theater that are emotionally expansive, dramatically engaging, and spiritually stimulating. We form partnerships between creators, performers, and audiences in order to contribute to the quality and diversity of new American music-theater, and we envision an extended family of artists and audiences that uses music-theater as a tool to support the individual and collective growth of the human spirit.

NEAR WEST THEATRE
WEBSITE: www.nearwesttheatre.org   **EMAIL:** info@nearwesttheatre.org
PHONE: (216) 961-9750   **ADDRESS:** 6702 Detroit Ave, Cleveland OH 44102
DESCRIPTION: Near West Theatre builds loving relationships and engages diverse people in strengthening their sense of identity, passion, and purpose, individually and in community, through transformational theatre arts experiences.
FEE: No   **AGENT ONLY:** No

NEW CONSERVATORY THEATRE CENTER
WEBSITE: www.nctcsf.org   **EMAIL:** ed@nctcsf.org   **PHONE:** (415) 861-4914
FAX: (415) 861-6988   **TWITTER:** @NCTCSF
ADDRESS: 25 Van Ness Ave, LL, San Francisco CA 94102
SUBMISSION MATERIALS: Script submissions by invitation after letter of inquiry, including synopsis, character breakdown, and production history.
PREFERRED GENRE: Plays or Musicals   **PREFERRED LENGTH:** Any Length   **FEE:** No
AGENT ONLY: Yes   **SPECIAL INTEREST:** LGBT+; Theatre for Young Audiences

NEW EDGECLIFF THEATRE
WEBSITE: www.newedgecliff.com   **EMAIL:** Gprocaccino@aol.com
PHONE: (888) 588-0137   **ADDRESS:** 1612 Otte Ave, Cincinnati OH 45223

DESCRIPTION: Our mission is to create a powerful artistic experience utilizing local professionals and stressing the fundamental communion between actor and audience.

NEW FEDERAL THEATRE
WEBSITE: www.newfederaltheatre.com **EMAIL:** newfederal@aol.com
PHONE: (212) 353-1176 **ADDRESS:** c/o All Stars' Project, Inc., 543 W 42nd St, New York NY 10036
DESCRIPTION: Specializing in minority drama, NFT has brought the joy of the living stage to many minorities who live in the surrounding Lower East Side community and the greater Metropolitan area.
PREFERRED GENRE: Plays **PREFERRED LENGTH:** Full-length
FEE: No **AGENT ONLY:** No

NEW GEORGES
WEBSITE: www.newgeorges.org/artists **EMAIL:** sonya@newgeorges.org
PHONE: (646) 336-8077 **TWITTER:** @newgeorges
ADDRESS: 109 W 27th St, #9-A, New York NY 10001
SUBMISSION MATERIALS: Please keep in mind: we don't read submitted plays to consider them for production. We happily read submissions to find voices we want to know better and artists who may make productive members of the artistic community from which our work springs. We work flexibly, project-to-project, so we don't do season planning in the traditional sense. Submit with that expectation, and we can go from there. Please see website for full details before submitting.
PREFERRED GENRE: Plays **PREFERRED LENGTH:** Full-length **FEE:** No
AGENT ONLY: No **SPECIAL INTEREST:** Feminism/Women's Rights

THE NEW GROUP
WEBSITE: www.thenewgroup.org **EMAIL:** info@thenewgroup.org
PHONE: (212) 244-3380 **FAX:** (212) 244-3438 **TWITTER:** TheNewGroupNYC
ADDRESS: 410 W 42nd St, New York NY 10036
DESCRIPTION: An award-winning, artist-driven company with a commitment to developing and producing powerful, contemporary theater. While constantly evolving, we strive to maintain an ensemble approach to all our work and an articulated style of emotional immediacy in our acting and productions. In this way, we seek a theater that is adventurous, stimulating and most importantly "now," a true forum for the present culture.
SUBMISSION MATERIALS: We request that playwrights submit, via mail, a letter of inquiry and a 10 page sample of the play, along with a resume and synopsis (SASE required for response) to ATTN: SUBMISSIONS. The play must not have been previously produced in New York City, and should be a challenging, character-based script with a contemporary setting and sensibility. Due to the volume of submissions, please be patient in awaiting a response. Please DO NOT email work to us.
PREFERRED GENRE: Plays **PREFERRED LENGTH:** Full-length **FEE:** No **AGENT ONLY:** No

NEW JERSEY REPERTORY COMPANY
WEBSITE: www.njrep.org **EMAIL:** njrep@njrep.org **PHONE:** (732) 229-3166

ADDRESS: 179 Broadway, Long Branch NJ 7740

DESCRIPTION: NJ Rep accepts unsolicited scripts year-round. Please limit your submission to one script per year, unless additional material is requested. We currently cannot consider plays that require more than 4 actors. NJ Rep prefers plays that are previously unproduced and unpublished.

SUBMISSION MATERIALS: Synopsis, character breakdown, production history. Musicals should include MP3's of songs. Please allow at least 12 months for notification. Electronic submissions only. You will be contacted only if your script is being considered. Please include an email address and telephone number for notification.

PREFERRED GENRE: Plays or Musicals **PREFERRED LENGTH:** Full-length **FEE:** No **AGENT ONLY:** No

NEW JERSEY SHAKESPEARE FESTIVAL

WEBSITE: www.njshakespeare.org **EMAIL:** boxoffice@shakespearenj.org
ADDRESS: 36 Madison Ave, Madison NJ 7940
DESCRIPTION: The Shakespeare Theatre of New Jersey is the state's largest professional theatre company dedicated to the presentation of Shakespeare's canon and other classic dramatic entertainments for the cultural enrichment of the community.

NEW ORLEANS OPERA ASSN.

WEBSITE: www.neworleansopera.org **EMAIL:** robertlyall@neworleansopera.org
PHONE: (504) 529-2278 **FAX:** (504) 529-7668
ADDRESS: 1010 Common St, #1820, New Orleans LA 70115
DESCRIPTION: Our mission is to enrich the lives of all people by producing opera of the highest artistic quality and providing education opportunities through traditional and innovative approaches. **PREFERRED GENRE:** Opera

NEW PERSPECTIVES THEATRE COMPANY

WEBSITE: www.newperspectivestheatre.org
EMAIL: contact@newperspectivestheatre.org **PHONE:** (212) 630-9945
FAX: (212) 594-2553 **ADDRESS:** 456 W 37th St, New York NY 10018
DESCRIPTION: New Perspectives was founded in 1991 as a multi-racial ensemble dedicated to using theatre as an agent for positive social change. Artistically, we are interested in returning theatre to its ancient role of gathering the community to examine social, political and spiritual issues that affect us as individuals and as a whole. Our emphasis on multi-racial casting and the development of new works by women and writers of color is an attempt to bring to that examination a range of voices that reflect the true diversity of contemporary America. Our aim is not to exclude, but to cast a wider net.

NEW REPERTORY THEATRE

WEBSITE: www.newrep.org **EMAIL:** bridgetoleary@newrep.org
PHONE: (617) 923-7060 **ADDRESS:** 200 Dexter Ave, Watertown MA 2472
DESCRIPTION: Through the passion and electricity of live theater performed to the highest standards of excellence, New Rep seeks to spark community conversations on crucial contemporary issues.
PREFERRED GENRE: Plays **PREFERRED LENGTH:** Full-length **FEE:** No **AGENT ONLY:** No

NEW STAGE THEATRE
WEBSITE: www.newstagetheatre.com **EMAIL:** mail@newstagetheatre.com
PHONE: (601) 948-3533 **FAX:** (601) 948-3538 **TWITTER:** @NewStageTheatre
ADDRESS: 1100 Carlisle St, Jackson MS 39202
DESCRIPTION: New Stage produces five plays each year in its subscription series, in addition to a Holiday show, an annual SchoolFest matinee, and a kids-only summer camp show that features local area talent. Main stage productions range from master works to contemporary classics to new plays. Additionally, the theatre presents a second season called Unframed at New Stage Theatre Series featuring cutting-edge plays directed and performed by local artists. **PREFERRED GENRE:** Plays

NEW YORK DEAF THEATRE
WEBSITE: www.newyorkdeaftheatre.org **EMAIL:** info@newyorkdeaftheatre.org
TWITTER: @NYDeafTheatre
ADDRESS: 138 S Oxford St, Ste 4F, Brooklyn NY 11217
DESCRIPTION: The New York Deaf Theatre, LTD (NYDT) was established in 1979 by a group of Deaf actors and theatre artists who wanted to create opportunities for the production of a dramatic art form that was not found elsewhere in New York City: plays in American Sign Language (ASL). A nonprofit, professional theatre, NYDT is the longest running company of its kind in the greater New York City area and the third oldest Deaf Theatre company in America.
SPECIAL INTEREST: Deaf or Hearing-impaired

NEW YORK STAGE AND FILM (NYSAF)
WEBSITE: www.newyorkstageandfilm.org **EMAIL:** info@newyorkstageandfilm.org
PHONE: (212) 736-4240 **TWITTER:** @NYStageandFilm
ADDRESS: 214 W 29th St, Ste 1001, New York New York 10001
DESCRIPTION: New York Stage and Film is a non-profit company dedicated to both emerging and established artists in the development and production of theater and film. Since 1985, we've been a vital incubator for artists and their work, a catalyst for stories that start with us and continue across the country and around the world. Due to our small staff size, we do not accept unsolicited script submissions.
SUBMISSION MATERIALS: Email only. 10-page sample, synopsis, CV/Resume, project history. If there is interest in requesting the complete submission, someone will be in touch. As a general rule, we do not consider plays that have already received productions. **PREFERRED GENRE:** Plays or Musicals **PREFERRED LENGTH:** Full-length
FEE: No **AGENT ONLY:** No

NEW YORK THEATRE WORKSHOP
WEBSITE: www.nytw.org **EMAIL:** literary@NYTW.org **PHONE:** (212) 780-9037
ADDRESS: 83 E 4th St, New York NY 10003
DESCRIPTION: New York Theatre Workshop provokes, produces and cultivates the work of artists whose visions inspire and challenge all of us.
PREFERRED GENRE: Plays **PREFERRED LENGTH:** Full-length **FEE:** No **AGENT ONLY:** No

NIGHTWOOD THEATRE
WEBSITE: www.nightwoodtheatre.net **EMAIL:** submissions@nightwoodtheatre.net

PHONE: (416) 944-1740
ADDRESS: 15 Case Goods Ln, Studio 306, Toronto ON M5A 3C4 Canada
DESCRIPTION: We do not accept unsolicited script submissions.
FEE: No **AGENT ONLY:** Yes **SPECIAL INTEREST:** Feminism/Women's Rights

NITTANY THEATRE AT THE BARN
WEBSITE: nittanytheatre.org **EMAIL:** nittanytheatre@gmail.com
ADDRESS: Boal Estate Dr, Boalsburg PA 16827 USA
DESCRIPTION: Est. 1953. Nittany Theatre at the Barn is the oldest arena barn theatre in Pennsylvania and one of the oldest in the nation. Preserving this treasured legacy drives our dedication to provide the finest in theatrical entertainment for residents and visitors of Happy Valley. To better serve our audience, we've renovated and enlarged the stage area, replaced and reupholstered our seats, and installed state-of-the-art LED lighting and Broadway quality sound systems, all while retaining the charm and intimacy of our ¾ thrust stage of 99 sweet seats. Theatre of the First Amendment Play Festival, founded in 2017, is a national playwright competition (with a $3,500 cash prize) in search of a theatrical tribute of freedom of speech in the United States. **PREFERRED GENRE:** Plays **FEE:** No **AGENT ONLY:** No

NORTH CAROLINA BLACK REPERTORY COMPANY
WEBSITE: www.ncblackrep.org **EMAIL:** submissions@ncblackrep.org
PHONE: (336) 723-2266 **ADDRESS:** 610 Coliseum Dr, Winston-Salem NC 27106
DESCRIPTION: Est. 1979. NCBRC is committed to exposing diverse audiences to Black classics, the development and production of new works, improving artistic quality, and sustaining Black theatre internationally. NCBRC was founded as a vehicle from which theatre professionals can earn a living through their craft. NCBRC also produces the National Black Theatre Festival.

SUBMISSION MATERIALS: Submissions are open for the North Carolina Black Repertory Company's 2018-2019 main stage season. To submit, email submissions@ncblackrep.org with the subject line: [Title of Your Play] 2018-2019 Script Submission. In the body of the email, include the following: Play title, playwright name, playwright bio, contact info, character breakdown, set description, production history, short synopsis. Attach the first 10 pages of the script in PDF format.

PREFERRED GENRE: Plays **PREFERRED LENGTH:** Full-length
SPECIAL INTEREST: Black or African American

NORTH CAROLINA THEATRE FOR YOUNG PEOPLE
WEBSITE: nctyp.weebly.com **EMAIL:** r_briley@uncg.edu **PHONE:** (336) 334-5575 **ADDRESS:** 406 Tate St, PO Box 26170, Greensboro NC 27402-6170
DESCRIPTION: The mission of North Carolina Theatre for Young People is to produce plays to engage young audiences, K-9, in the art of the live theatre. We strive to present highly mobile and flexible productions that can be presented effectively in a variety of performance settings. Our plays are chosen from the best available to include a variety of styles and content in order to aquaint our audiences with the richness of theatre for young audiences literature. We seek to encourage and foster the development of new scripts, develop residencies in creative drama and theatre for schools, and explore the theory that theatre-going by young people will contribute to the development of adult audiences of tomorrow.

PREFERRED GENRE: Plays   **PREFERRED LENGTH**: 1-Act (under 1 hour)   **FEE**: No
AGENT ONLY: No   **SPECIAL INTEREST**: Theatre for Young Audiences

NORTH COAST REPERTORY THEATRE (NCRT)
WEBSITE: www.northcoastrep.org   **EMAIL**: chris@northcoastrep.org   P
HONE: (858) 481-2155   **FAX**: (858) 481-0530
ADDRESS: 987 Lomas Santa Fe Dr, Ste D, Solana Beach CA 92075
DESCRIPTION: North Coast Rep Theatre accepts new play submissions all year. Plays must have no more than 8 characters. When submitting your work, please consider our theatre's size, past productions, and minimal casting needs. We also have a New Works Reading Series. Please indicate in your submission if you'd be interested in having your work considered as part of this series.
SUBMISSION MATERIALS: Submit by mail. Synopsis (500 words max), character list, 10 pg sample, short summary of how your play may work at our theatre and within our typical seasons
DEADLINE TYPE: Rolling   **PREFERRED GENRE**: Plays   **PREFERRED LENGTH**: Full-length

NORTHERN SKY THEATRE
WEBSITE: www.northernskytheater.com   **EMAIL**: dave@northernskytheater.com
PHONE: (920) 854-6117   **FAX**: (920) 854-9106
ADDRESS: PO Box 273, Fish Creek WI 54212
DESCRIPTION: The mission of Northern Sky Theater is to create, develop and present professional musical and dramatic productions that will further the knowledge and appreciation of the culture and heritage of the United States.
PREFERRED GENRE: Plays or Musicals   **PREFERRED LENGTH**: Full-length
FEE: No   **AGENT ONLY**: No

NORTHERN STAGE
WEBSITE: www.northernstage.org   **EMAIL**: adeva@northernstage.org
PHONE: (802) 296-7000
ADDRESS: PO Box 4287, White River Junction VT 5001
DESCRIPTION: Our mission is to change lives, one story at a time.
PREFERRED GENRE: Plays   **PREFERRED LENGTH**: Full-length   **FEE**: No   **AGENT ONLY**: No

NORTHLIGHT THEATRE
WEBSITE: www.northlight.org   **EMAIL**: submissions@northlight.org
PHONE: (847) 679-9501   **ADDRESS**: 9501 N Skokie Blvd, Skokie IL 60077
DESCRIPTION: Northlight Theatre aspires to promote change of perspective and encourage compassion by exploring the depth of our humanity across a bold spectrum of theatrical experiences. We seek to entertain, enlighten, and electrify our audiences through contemporary dramas, intimate musicals and refreshed classics.
PREFERRED GENRE: Plays or Musicals   **PREFERRED LENGTH**: Full-length
FEE: No   **AGENT ONLY**: Yes

OBSIDIAN THEATRE COMPANY
WEBSITE: www.obsidiantheatre.com   **EMAIL**: pd@obsidiantheatre.com

PHONE: (416) 463-8444
ADDRESS: 1089 Dundas St E, Toronto ON M4M-1R9 Canada
DESCRIPTION: Obsidian Theatre has been developing new Black voices through our Playwrights Unit, our Development Series, and our Resident Playwrights for over 15 years. Our Playwrights Unit runs from September to June each year. Submissions for the Playwrights Unit are accepted starting in April annually.
PREFERRED GENRE: Plays **PREFERRED LENGTH:** Full-length **FEE:** No **AGENT ONLY:** No
SPECIAL INTEREST: Black or African American

OHENRY PRODUCTIONS
WEBSITE: www.ohenryproductions.com/submit
EMAIL: scripts@ohenryproductions.com **PHONE:** (917) 727-4706
ADDRESS: 295 Madison Ave, 22nd Fl, New York NY 10017
DESCRIPTION: OHenry Productions has an open submission policy. Due to the volume of submissions, we can not guarantee we will be able to personally respond to every submission, though we try our best.
SUBMISSION MATERIALS: Script, demo tape **PREFERRED GENRE:** Plays or Musicals **PREFERRED LENGTH:** Full-length **FEE:** No **AGENT ONLY:** No

OLDCASTLE THEATRE COMPANY
WEBSITE: www.oldcastletheatreco.org **EMAIL:** oldcastletheatre@gmail.com
PHONE: (802) 447-1267 **FAX:** (802) 442-3704
ADDRESS: PO Box 1555, Bennington VT 5201
DESCRIPTION: Formed by five New York actors in 1972, the troupe began touring in Vermont because one of its founding members, Eric Peterson, was originally from Bennington. Plays developed at Oldcastle have been produced in more than 25 states and in such foreign countries as South Africa, Canada, Spain and Argentina. OTC presents at least one new play each season and has premiered plays by such well-known writers as Elliot Hays, Reginald Rose and Bob Shanks.
PREFERRED GENRE: Plays **PREFERRED LENGTH:** Full-length

OLNEY THEATRE CENTER
WEBSITE: www.olneytheatre.org **PHONE:** (301) 924-4485 **FAX:** (301) 924-2654
ADDRESS: 2001 Olney-Sandy Spring Rd, Olney MD 20832
DESCRIPTION: A professional, award-winning regional theater established in 1937, Olney Theatre Center operates under an Actors' Equity Association Council of Stock Theaters (COST) contract, one of only two theaters in the country to operate under such a contract. Olney Theatre produces and presents extraordinary theater and performance on its four-theater campus for an ever-more diverse set of audiences in our community, and educates the next generation of theatermakers to follow in our footsteps. **PREFERRED GENRE:** Plays or Musicals **AGENT ONLY:** Yes

OMAHA THEATER COMPANY AT THE ROSE
WEBSITE: www.rosetheater.org **EMAIL:** michaelm@rosetheater.org
PHONE: (402) 502-4624 **ADDRESS:** 2001 Farnam St, Omaha NE 68102
DESCRIPTION: The Rose is a professional, non-Equity, producing theater offering a full season of productions for young and family audiences. The Rose also offers a full

range of education programs including a teen theater program and summer production camps for youth. We accept unsolicited script submissions related to any of our programming needs, including: Main Stage Productions, Teens 'N' Theater Productions.
SUBMISSION MATERIALS: Contact information, identification of which Rose Theater program the script fits, summary, 10 page sample, cast size
PREFERRED GENRE: Plays or Musicals **PREFERRED LENGTH:** 1-Act (under 1 hour)
FEE: No **AGENT ONLY:** No **SPECIAL INTEREST:** Theatre for Young Audiences

ORLANDO SHAKESPEARE THEATER
WEBSITE: orlandoshakes.org **EMAIL:** cynthiaw@orlandoshakes.org
PHONE: (407) 447-1700 **ADDRESS:** 812 E Rollins St, Orlando FL 32803
DESCRIPTION: Mission: To enrich our community with engaging professional theater, inspiring educational experiences, and thought-provoking new plays.

OUT OF BOX THEATRE
WEBSITE: www.outofboxtheatre.com **EMAIL:** info@outofboxtheatre.com
PHONE: (678) 653-4605 **TWITTER:** @outofboxtheatre
ADDRESS: 123 Cheatham Rd, Acworth GA 30101
DESCRIPTION: Est. 2012. Known for producing offbeat, exciting, daring, & thrilling works that aren't always widely performed. We aim to provide a home for shows and artists that want to step outside the norm and stretch their creative horizons. We are continuing to develop our programs, including our offering of resources for playwrights with Out of Box Original Works.

PACIFIC CONSERVATORY THEATRE
WEBSITE: www.pcpa.org **EMAIL:** literary@pcpa.org **PHONE:** (805) 928-7731
ADDRESS: 800 S. College Dr, Santa Maria CA 93454
DESCRIPTION: Est. 1964. PCPA is a professional conservatory theatre, committed to reflecting and transforming our diverse community with the art of live theatre. We believe that the theater has a vital role and responsibility in the community to enrich cultural literacy and improve the quality of life. We commit to serving our current audience, cultivating our future audience and training the next generation of theatre professionals. We aspire to adhere to the best theatrical traditions and to set new standards of excellent artistry, ethics, and professional practice for the future of the theatre.
PREFERRED GENRE: Plays or Musicals **PREFERRED LENGTH:** Full-length
FEE: No **AGENT ONLY:** No

PALM BEACH DRAMAWORKS
WEBSITE: www.palmbeachdramaworks.org
EMAIL: blinser@palmbeachdramaworks.org **PHONE:** (561) 514-4042
ADDRESS: 201 Clematis St, West Palm Beach FL 33401
DESCRIPTION: Palm Beach Dramaworks is a professional not-for-profit theatre company that engages and entertains audiences with provocative and timeless productions that personally impact each individual.
PREFERRED GENRE: Plays **PREFERRED LENGTH:** Full-length **AGENT ONLY:** Yes

PAN ASIAN REPERTORY THEATRE

WEBSITE: www.panasianrep.org   **EMAIL:** info@panasianrep.org
PHONE: (212) 868-4030   **FAX:** (212) 868-4033   **TWITTER:** @PanAsianRep
ADDRESS: 520 8th Ave, #314, New York NY 10018
DESCRIPTION: Our mission is to celebrate the artistic expressiveness of Asian and American theatre artists under the highest standards of professional theatre and professional productions; to encourage the production of new plays, especially those with contemporary Asian American themes; to draw upon the unique heritage of Asian Americans by utilizing the style, music and movement of Asian performing arts traditions in order to explore new theatrical forms; to nurture emerging Asian American talent through professionally led workshops and on-the-job training; and to introduce Asian American Theatre to the general theatre-going public as well as the differently-abled; to deepen the appreciation and understanding of Asian American cultural heritage.
PREFERRED GENRE: Plays   **PREFERRED LENGTH:** Full-length   **SPECIAL INTEREST:** Asian

PANGEA WORLD THEATER

WEBSITE: www.pangeaworldtheater.org   **EMAIL:** pangea@pangeaworldtheater.org
PHONE: (612) 822-0486   **FAX:** (612) 821-1070
ADDRESS: 711 W Lake St, #101, Minneapolis MN 55408
DESCRIPTION: Since our inception in 1995, Pangea World Theater has worked with artists from many communities locally, nationally and internationally to create new aesthetic realities for an increasingly diverse audience.

PASSAGE THEATRE

WEBSITE: www.passagetheatre.org   **EMAIL:** passagelit@gmail.com
PHONE: (609) 392-0766   **FAX:** (609) 392-0318
ADDRESS: PO Box 967, Trenton NJ 8605
DESCRIPTION: At its best, theater transforms – inspires understanding of the rich diversity of the human experience, gives voice to the silent, and dignity to the dispirited. Through the creation and production of theater, we chart a passage to grace – in ourselves, in others, and throughout our community.
PREFERRED GENRE: Plays or Musicals   **PREFERRED LENGTH:** Any Length
FEE: No   **AGENT ONLY:** No

PEAR THEATRE

WEBSITE: www.thepear.org   **EMAIL:** info@thepear.org   **PHONE:** (650) 254-1148
ADDRESS: 1110 La Avenida St, Mountain View CA 94043
DESCRIPTION: Est. 2002. We are experienced actors, directors, writers, and teachers. Our goals are to produce new plays by local writers and innovative stagings of classic works; to encourage playwrights to grow through workshops, staged readings, and productions of their plays; and to offer performance classes to all ages. Writers: we have an active playwright's guild and play development program that cultivates new works.

PENGUIN REP THEATRE

WEBSITE: www.penguinrep.org   **EMAIL:** info@penguinrep.org

PHONE: (845) 786-2873   **ADDRESS:** PO Box 91, Stony Point NY 10980

DESCRIPTION: Since its founding in 1977, Penguin Rep has entertained more than 400,000 people with outstanding productions of 150 plays. And not just any plays either, but new works by established and emerging writers.

PREFERRED GENRE: Plays   **PREFERRED LENGTH:** Full-length   **FEE:** No   **AGENT ONLY:** Yes

PENNSYLVANIA YOUTH THEATRE

WEBSITE: www.123pyt.org   **EMAIL:** office@123pyt.org   **PHONE:** (610) 332-1400
ADDRESS: 25 W 3rd St, Bethlehem PA 18015

DESCRIPTION: Pennsylvania Youth Theatre (PYT) is a professional, non-profit performing arts organization whose mission is to educate, entertain, and enrich the lives of young people and their families through the art of theatre. Through a comprehensive performing arts curriculum, literature-based performances, and vigorous outreach programs, PYT challenges children to develop their talents, to think creatively, and to acquire an appreciation and understanding of the arts.

FEE: No   **AGENT ONLY:** No   **SPECIAL INTEREST:** Theatre for Young Audiences

PENUMBRA THEATRE COMPANY

WEBSITE: www.penumbratheatre.org   **EMAIL:** sarah.bellamy@penumbratheatre.org
PHONE: (651) 288-6795   **ADDRESS:** 270 N Kent St, St Paul MN 55102

DESCRIPTION: Penumbra Theatre creates professional productions that are artistically excellent, thought provoking, and relevant and illuminates the human condition through the prism of the African American experience.

PREFERRED GENRE: Plays   **PREFERRED LENGTH:** Any Length   **FEE:** No   **AGENT ONLY:** No
SPECIAL INTEREST: Black or African American

PEOPLE'S LIGHT AND THEATRE COMPANy

WEBSITE: www.peopleslight.org   **EMAIL:** pisasale@peopleslight.org
PHONE: (610) 647-1900   **ADDRESS:** 39 Conestoga Rd, Malvern PA 19355

DESCRIPTION: People's Light, a professional theatre in Chester County, Pennsylvania, makes plays drawn from many sources to entertain, inspire, and engage our community. We extend our mission of making and experiencing theatre through arts education programs that excite curiosity about, and deepen understanding of, the world around us. These plays and programs bring people together and provide opportunities for reflection, discovery, and celebration.

PREFERRED GENRE: Plays   **PREFERRED LENGTH:** Full-length   **FEE:** No   **AGENT ONLY:** Yes

PERSEVERANCE THEATRE (PT)

WEBSITE: www.perseverancetheatre.org   **EMAIL:** info@perseverancetheatre.org
PHONE: (907) 364-2421   **FAX:** (907) 364-2603
ADDRESS: 914 3rd St, Douglas AK 99824

DESCRIPTION: Perseverance Theatre has awarded participation into The Playwright's Circle to five playwrights. The award includes commission, including development support, for a two-year period of time to write and develop a new Alaskan play. The goal of the Playwright's Circle is to develop diverse, new Alaskan plays in a group that will include Alaska Native writers who are writing for Native Actors, and representing voices that were previously unheard.

PREFERRED GENRE: Plays **PREFERRED LENGTH:** Full-length
SPECIAL INTEREST: American Indian or Alaskan Native

PETALUMA RADIO PLAYERS
WEBSITE: www.petalumaradioplayers.com **EMAIL:** info@petalumaradioplayers.com
ADDRESS: 10 4th St, Petaluma CA 94952
DESCRIPTION: We're looking for 10, 15, 20 and 30-minute radio plays or stage plays that can easily be adapted to radio. We'll consider all genres including comedies, dramas, thrillers, historical fiction, adventure, noir and more. Our Troupe will read your play within two weeks at one of our Thursday evening script review sessions, then notify you whether or not we decide to put your play into our development cycle. We do pay stipends and we do request broadcast rights for air on KPCA-fm (103.3 fm / Petaluma, CA) as well as via KPCA's podcast: KPCA.fm, You retain all other rights to your play.
SUBMISSION MATERIALS: Email script as either a pdf or Word file. In your Subject line, please write: 'SUBMISSION'. Please include contact information.
PREFERRED GENRE: Radio plays **PREFERRED LENGTH:** Any Length **FEE:** No

PHILADELPHIA THEATRE COMPANY
WEBSITE: www.philadelphiatheatrecompany.org
EMAIL: literary@philadelphiatheatrecompany.org **PHONE:** (215) 985-1400
FAX: (215) 985-5800 **ADDRESS:** 215 S Broad St, 10th Fl, Philadelphia PA 19102
DESCRIPTION: Philadelphia Theatre Company (PTC) produces, develops, and presents entertaining and imaginative contemporary theater focused on the American experience that ignites the intellect and touches the soul.
PREFERRED GENRE: Plays or Musicals **PREFERRED LENGTH:** Full-length
FEE: No **AGENT ONLY:** No

PHOENIX ARTS ASSOCIATION THEATRE [CA]
WEBSITE: www.phoenixtheatresf.org **EMAIL:** phoenixtheatresf@gmail.com
PHONE: (415) 336-1020 **ADDRESS:** 414 Mason St, San Francisco CA 94102
DESCRIPTION: We are dedicated to producing theatre that strives for artistic excellence; is affordable and accessible; provides a nurturing environment for new voices to be heard where the plays, artists and audiences reflect the vitality and diversity of our community. We present as many San Francisco and World premiere works as possible by contemporary playwrights and occasional classics. We encourage and nurture new work by Bay Area Theatre artists & writers. Above all, we are committed to creating theatre that ennobles the strength and beauty of the human spirit. **PREFERRED GENRE:** Plays **FEE:** No **AGENT ONLY:** No

PHOENIX STAGE COMPANY
WEBSITE: www.phoenixstagecompany.org **EMAIL:** info@phoenixstagecompany.org
PHONE: (860) 417-2505 **TWITTER:** @PhoenixStageCo
ADDRESS: 133 Main St, Oakville CT 06779

DESCRIPTION: Phoenix Stage Company is a community theater with a strong focus on supporting new works and new playwrights. They produce the annual PSC One-Act Festival, established in 2012. See website for details.
PREFERRED GENRE: Plays **PREFERRED LENGTH:** 1-Act (under 1 hour)
FEE: No **AGENT ONLY:** No

PHOENIX THEATRE [AZ]
WEBSITE: www.phoenixtheatre.com **EMAIL:** info@phoenixtheatre.com
PHONE: (602) 258-1974 **ADDRESS:** 100 E McDowell Rd, Phoenix AZ 85004
DESCRIPTION: Phoenix Theatre creates exceptional theatrical experiences by using the arts to articulate messages that inspire hope and understanding.

PHOENIX THEATRE [IN]
WEBSITE: www.phoenixtheatre.org **EMAIL:** litman@phoenixtheatre.org
PHONE: (317) 635-7529 **TWITTER:** @Phoenix_Theatre
ADDRESS: 749 N Park Ave, Indianapolis IN 46202
DESCRIPTION: The leadership of the Indianapolis-based Phoenix Theatre believes that our city deserves to be emotionally and intellectually engaged in works that contribute to or comment on the national dialogue, that a diversity of voices and viewpoints is vital to the well-being of this city and all who enter the Phoenix Theatre, and that our welcoming, intimate space provides a safe place where risks can be taken and transformative conversations created. We are committed to producing only contemporary theatre, so that through our productions we are inviting a dialogue on current affairs to Indianapolis and are helping to create a more enlightened, aware local community.
SUBMISSION DEADLINE: 05/31/2018 **DEADLINE TYPE:** Annual
PREFERRED LENGTH: Any Length **FEE:** No **AGENT ONLY:** Yes

PILLSBURY HOUSE THEATRE
WEBSITE: www.pillsburyhouseandtheatre.org
EMAIL: raymondn@pillsburyhousetheatre.org **PHONE:** (612) 825-0459
ADDRESS: 3501 Chicago Ave S, Minneapolis MN 55407
DESCRIPTION: Pillsbury House Theatre's mission is to create challenging theatre to inspire choice, change and connection. Through the mainstage season and other community engagement programs, Pillsbury House Theatre (PHT) illuminates the differences that make each person unique and the similarities that bring people together, within an artistic environment that promotes understanding and leads to positive action.
PREFERRED GENRE: Plays **PREFERRED LENGTH:** Full-length **FEE:** No **AGENT ONLY:** Yes

PIONEER THEATRE COMPANY
WEBSITE: www.pioneertheatre.org **EMAIL:** karen.azenberg@PTC.utah.edu
PHONE: (801) 581-6356 **TWITTER:** @pioneertheatre
ADDRESS: Univ of Utah, 300 S 1400 E, SPMT Rm 325, Salt Lake City UT 84112
DESCRIPTION: Est. 1962. Pioneer Theatre Company offers a wide range of exceptional theatre exploring the breadth of the human experience—challenging the intellect, stirring emotions, igniting imaginations and encouraging conversation.

PREFERRED GENRE: Plays or Musicals   **PREFERRED LENGTH:** Full-length
FEE: No   **AGENT ONLY:** No

PIVEN THEATRE
WEBSITE: www.piventheatre.org   **EMAIL:** scott@piventheatre.org
PHONE: (847) 866-8049   **TWITTER:** @piventheatre
ADDRESS: 927 Noyes St, #110, Evanston IL 60201
DESCRIPTION: Our mission is to preserve a process of creative exploration that celebrates each individual's unique voice through an ensemble-based, community-oriented approach to theatre training and performance.
PREFERRED GENRE: Plays

PLAN-B THEATRE COMPANY
WEBSITE: www.planbtheatre.org   **EMAIL:** jerry@planbtheatre.org
PHONE: (801) 297-4200   **TWITTER:** @planbtheatreco
ADDRESS: 138 W 300 S, Salt Lake City UT 84101
DESCRIPTION: Est. 1991. Plan-B develops and produces unique and socially conscious theatre created by Utah playwrights. We share stories with a local point-of-view as well as global stories from a local perspective. See website for more info and opportunities.
PREFERRED GENRE: Plays   **PREFERRED LENGTH:** Any Length   **FEE:** No   **AGENT ONLY:** No
SUBMISSION MATERIALS: Submit script via email in PDF format.

PLAY WITH YOUR FOOD
WEBSITE: www.jibproductions.org   **EMAIL:** info@jibproductions.org
PHONE: (203) 247-4083
ADDRESS: JIB Productions, Inc, PO Box 2161, Westport CT 6880
DESCRIPTION: Play With Your Food is a professional one-act and short play reading series generally held at lunch-time. We accept ongoing submissions of well-written short plays, between 7 and 30 minutes long.
SUBMISSION MATERIALS: Submit by email or post.
PREFERRED GENRE: Plays   **FEE:** No   **AGENT ONLY:** No

PLAYHOUSE ON THE SQUARE
WEBSITE: www.playhouseonthesquare.org
EMAIL: jordan@playhouseonthesquare.org   **PHONE:** (901) 725-0776
ADDRESS: 66 S Cooper St, Memphis TN 38104
DESCRIPTION: Playhouse on the Square is Memphis' only professional resident theatre. Playhouse on the Square remains committed to its mission to produce a challenging and diverse repertoire of theatrical work, to provide a nurturing artistic home where artists can practice their craft and share their talent, and to make all productions available through access, outreach, & education. Home of NewWorks@ TheWorks Plawriting Competition.

PLAYMAKERS OF BATON ROUGE

WEBSITE: playmakersbr.org **EMAIL:** michael@playmakersbr.org
PHONE: (225) 578-6996 **ADDRESS:** PO Box 4286, Baton Rouge LA 70821
DESCRIPTION: To submit a script for consideration, please first send your resume to michael@playmakersbr.org.
PREFERRED GENRE: Plays **PREFERRED LENGTH:** Any Length **FEE:** No **AGENT ONLY:** No

PLAYMAKERS REPERTORY COMPANY
WEBSITE: www.playmakersrep.org **EMAIL:** prcboxoffice@unc.edu
PHONE: (919) 962-4846
ADDRESS: 150 Country Club Rd, Chapel Hill NC 27516
DESCRIPTION: PlayMakers Repertory Company is the LORT-D professional theatre in residence at the University of North Carolina at Chapel Hill.
PREFERRED GENRE: Plays **PREFERRED LENGTH:** Full-length

PLAYWRIGHTS HORIZONS
WEBSITE: www.playwrightshorizons.org **EMAIL:** lit@phnyc.org
PHONE: (212) 564-1235 **ADDRESS:** 416 W 42nd St, New York NY 10036
DESCRIPTION: Playwrights Horizons accepts unsolicited manuscripts of full-length, original plays by living American writers. As a writers' theater who believes there are as many distinctive styles and voices as there are playwrights, we remain open to as wide a range of plays — and approaches to playwriting — as possible. We are looking for idiosyncratic, accomplished, original theatrical voices.
SUBMISSION MATERIALS: Full script, bio, resume, other print supporting materials (e.g. reviews). Response time: 6-8 mos. Play submissions should be sent to Sarah Lunnie, Literary Director. Musical submissions (script and CD) should be sent to the attention of Kent Nicholson, Director of Musical Theater.
PREFERRED GENRE: Plays or Musicals **PREFERRED LENGTH:** Full-length
FEE: No **AGENT ONLY:** No

PLAYWRIGHTS LOCAL
WEBSITE: www.playwrightslocal.org/submissions
EMAIL: dtodd@playwrightslocal.org **TWITTER:** @PlaywrightsLcl
ADDRESS: 2624 Idlewood Rd, Cleveland Heights OH 44118
DESCRIPTION: Playwrights Local seeks original, unproduced plays for our 2017-2018 season and events. Submissions are open to all playwrights age 18 or older who are permanent residents of any county in Northeast Ohio.
SUBMISSION MATERIALS: Submissions closed for 2017/2018 season. Check website for updates. **PREFERRED GENRE:** Plays **PREFERRED LENGTH:** Any Length **FEE:** No

PORCHLIGHT MUSIC THEATRE
WEBSITE: www.porchlightmusictheatre.org
EMAIL: michael@porchlightmusictheatre.org **PHONE:** (773) 777-9884
ADDRESS: 4200 W Diversey Ave, Chicago IL 60639
DESCRIPTION: Porchlight Music Theatre accepts Full-length scripts year-round from literary agents and theatre professionals with whom we have an existing professional relationship.

SUBMISSION MATERIALS: We invite unrepresented writers to submit a brief bio, short synopsis, and ten pages of sample dialogue and music on CD or sent electronically.
PREFERRED GENRE: Musicals **PREFERRED LENGTH:** Full-length
FEE: No **AGENT ONLY:** Yes

PORTLAND CENTER STAGE AT THE ARMORY [OR]
WEBSITE: www.pcs.org **EMAIL:** boxoffice@pcs.org **PHONE:** (502) 445-3700
TWITTER: @PCS_Armory **ADDRESS:** 128 NW 11th Ave, Portland OR 97209
DESCRIPTION: The Armory is currently able to accept script submissions only from theatrical literary agents and from artists with whom we have an existing professional relationship. **AGENT ONLY:** Yes

PORTLAND STAGE COMPANY [ME]
WEBSITE: www.portlandstage.org **EMAIL:** literary@portlandstage.org
PHONE: (207) 774-1043 **ADDRESS:** PO Box 1458, Portland ME 04104
DESCRIPTION: The two primary ways playwrights can submit new plays for consideration at Portland Stage are through the Little Festival of the Unexpected (Portland Stage's annual new play development festival, open to all playwrights) and Clauder Competition (for New England-based Playwrights only).
PREFERRED GENRE: Plays **PREFERRED LENGTH:** Full-length **FEE:** No **AGENT ONLY:** No

POWERHOUSE THEATRE
WEBSITE: powerhouse.vassar.edu **EMAIL:** powerhouse@vassar.edu
PHONE: (845) 437-5907 **FAX:** (845) 437-7209
ADDRESS: Box 225, 124 Raymond Ave, Poughkeepsie NY 12604-0225
DESCRIPTION: For six weeks every summer the Powerhouse Season brings fully-produced plays, musical workshops, and readings of works-in-progress to the college campus. In all, more than 200 professional artists come to Powerhouse each season and bring to life 20-25 new works.
PREFERRED GENRE: Plays **PREFERRED LENGTH:** Full-length

PREGONES/PRTT
WEBSITE: pregonesprtt.org **EMAIL:** info@pregones.org **PHONE:** (718) 585-1202
TWITTER: @pregonesprtt **ADDRESS:** 571-575 Walton Ave, Bronx NY 10451
DESCRIPTION: Following years of enterprising activity on stage and in the community, Pregones Theater and Puerto Rican Traveling Theater recently merged into a single Latino arts organization with performance venues in The Bronx and Manhattan. The transformation builds upon congruence of mission, values, and programs, and sustained engagement of a growing network of diverse artists and audiences throughout and beyond NYC. Moving forward, Pregones/PRTT champions a cultural legacy of broad impact through (1) creation and performance of original musical theater and plays rooted in Puerto Rican/Latino cultures, and (2) presentation of other artists who share our twin commitment to the arts and civic enrichment.
PREFERRED GENRE: Plays or Musicals **PREFERRED LENGTH:** Full-length **FEE:** No
AGENT ONLY: No **SPECIAL INTEREST:** Hispanic or Latinx

PREMIERE STAGES AT KEAN UNIVERSITY

WEBSITE: www.premierestagesatkean.com **EMAIL:** premiere@kean.edu
PHONE: (908) 737-4092 **TWITTER:** @PremiereStages
ADDRESS: 1000 Morris Ave, J235, Union NJ 07083
DESCRIPTION: Premiere Stages is the professional Equity theatre in residence at Kean University. Dedicated to producing new work, Premiere runs an annual Play Festival that develops a minimum of four new plays each year, one of which is fully produced. In addition to this flagship program, the theatre runs multiple commissioning projects (including Liberty Live, a partnership with the Liberty Hall Museum that celebrates the rich and diverse history of New Jersey) and presents the New Jersey premieres of celebrated contemporary plays each summer. Playwrights who are interested in submitting plays should visit: www.premierestagesatkean.com/play-development
FEE: No **AGENT ONLY:** No

PRESENT COMPANY
WEBSITE: presentcompany.org **EMAIL:** info@fringenyc.org
ADDRESS: 518 E 6th St, #BW, New York NY 10009
DESCRIPTION: We created and produce The New York International Fringe Festival (FringeNYC), which has become the largest multi-arts festival in North America. Forged on the off-off-Broadway tradition of self-sufficiency and creativity, the festival is an annual celebration of downtown theater and an opportunity to introduce the vibrancy, diversity, and innovation of indie theatre to a larger audience.
PREFERRED GENRE: Plays **PREFERRED LENGTH:** Any Length **FEE:** Yes **AGENT ONLY:** No

PRIMARY STAGES
WEBSITE: www.primarystages.org **EMAIL:** info@primarystages.org
PHONE: (212) 840-9705 **ADDRESS:** 307 W 38th St, #1510, New York NY 10018
DESCRIPTION: Primary Stages does not accept unsolicited submissions. Only agents may submit scripts. Unrepresented artists may send information on readings or productions to our mailing address. Please note that our staff receives a large number of submissions and invitations and makes an effort to cover as many as possible.
PREFERRED GENRE: Plays **PREFERRED LENGTH:** Full-length **FEE:** No **AGENT ONLY:** Yes

PRIME STAGE THEATRE
WEBSITE: www.primestage.com **EMAIL:** wbrinda@primestage.com
PHONE: (724) 773-0700 **ADDRESS:** PO Box 99446, Pittsburgh PA 15233
DESCRIPTION: The mission of Prime Stage is to entertain, inspire and enrich through professional theatre by bringing literature to life.
PREFERRED GENRE: Plays **PREFERRED LENGTH:** Full-length **FEE:** No **AGENT ONLY:** No

PROP THTR
WEBSITE: www.propthtr.org **EMAIL:** info@propthtr.org **PHONE:** (773) 539-7838
ADDRESS: 3502-4 N Elston Ave, Chicago IL 60618
DESCRIPTION: Prop Thtr functions as an incubator for new talent, exposing audiences and artists to fresh outlooks on life through the development of new plays and playwrights. We concentrate on stories that expand our perception of who we are as human beings. The Prop Thtr augments its new works and new workers program with fresh examinations of great and provocative literature and fostering long-term

relationships with playwrights and with other like-minded theater companies.
PREFERRED GENRE: Plays

PUBLIC THEATER
WEBSITE: www.publictheater.org/en/About/Artist-Submissions
EMAIL: submissions@publictheater.org   **PHONE:** (212) 539-8530
ADDRESS: 425 Lafayette St, New York NY 10003
DESCRIPTION: The Literary Office does not accept unsolicited scripts. If you would like us to review your work, please send us a Synopsis Submission.
SUBMISSION MATERIALS: Email or post. 10-page dialogue sample, synopsis, brief (100-200 word) statement about how your piece fits with the Public's Mission. For musicals, you may include up to 3 sample songs.
PREFERRED GENRE: Plays or Musicals   **PREFERRED LENGTH:** Full-length
FEE: No   **AGENT ONLY:** Yes

PULSE ENSEMBLE THEATRE
WEBSITE: www.pulseensembletheatre.org
EMAIL: playwrightslab@pulseensembletheatre.org   **PHONE:** (212) 695-1596
ADDRESS: 248 W 35th St, 15th Fl, New York NY 10001
DESCRIPTION: Established in 1989, PULSE ENSEMBLE THEATRE is one of the oldest ensemble theatre companies in New York City. In its new home and under its new structure, Pulse is committed to two major productions a year: one summer Shakespeare site-specific outreach project, and one new script from its Playwrights' Lab.
PREFERRED GENRE: Plays   **PREFERRED LENGTH:** Full-length   **FEE:** No   **AGENT ONLY:** No

PURPLE ROSE THEATRE COMPANY
WEBSITE: www.purplerosetheatre.org   **EMAIL:** mountain@purplerosetheatre.org
PHONE: (734) 433-7782   **ADDRESS:** 137 Park St, Chelsea MI 48118
DESCRIPTION: The Purple Rose Theatre Company (PRTC) is the home of world-class, original American theatre. The PRTC is a professional theatre company with roots in the Midwest that takes a handcrafted, artisanal approach to producing new and classic American plays that are nothing less than one-of-a-kind experiences. The PRTC is a 501(c)(3) nonprofit professional theatre operating under a Small Professional Theatre agreement with the Actors' Equity Association.
PREFERRED GENRE: Plays   **PREFERRED LENGTH:** Full-length   **FEE:** No   **AGENT ONLY:** No

QUEENS THEATRE
WEBSITE: www.queenstheatre.org   **EMAIL:** roburbinati@gmail.com
PHONE: (718) 760-0686   **ADDRESS:** 14 United Nations Ave S, Flushing NY 11352
DESCRIPTION: Queens Theatre is the premier performing arts venue in Queens. Queens Theatre's mission is to provide quality and diverse performing arts activities that are economically and geographically accessible to the 2.2 million residents of Queens, the most ethnically diverse county in the nation, and the surrounding metropolitan region. To foster greater cultural awareness and appreciation, the Theatre presents and produces programs that reflect this diversity and features international, national and local artists.   **FEE:** No   **AGENT ONLY:** No

QUEENSBURY THEATRE
WEBSITE: www.queensburytheatre.org **EMAIL:** lwesteen@queensburytheatre.org
PHONE: (713) 467-4497 **ADDRESS:** 12777 Queensbury Ln, Houston TX 77024
DESCRIPTION: The Tribble School explores the heart of great music, theatre and dance. We exist to provide a positive and nurturing environment, where students of all ages and backgrounds can develop skills; tell meaningful stories; and connect – with self, the truth of the moment, their fellow artists, and community.

THE RADIO THEATRE PROJECT
WEBSITE: www.radiotheatreproject.org
ADDRESS: 620 1st Ave S, St. Petersburg FL 33701
DESCRIPTION: Please see website for audio dramaturgy and format.
PREFERRED GENRE: Radio plays **PREFERRED LENGTH:** 1-Act (under 1 hour)
FEE: No **AGENT ONLY:** No

RAINBOW'S COMEDY PLAYHOUSE
WEBSITE: www.rainbowcomedy.com **EMAIL:** info@rainbowcomedy.com
PHONE: (717) 687-4301
ADDRESS: 3065 Lincoln Hwy E, PO Box 56, Paradise PA 17562
DESCRIPTION: Est. 1984. Professional non-Equity dinner theater.
PREFERRED GENRE: Comedy **PREFERRED LENGTH:** Full-length
FEE: No **AGENT ONLY:** No

RATTLESTICK PLAYWRIGHTS THEATRE
WEBSITE: www.rattlestick.org **EMAIL:** info@rattlestick.org
PHONE: (212) 627-2556 **ADDRESS:** 244 Waverly Pl, New York NY 10014
DESCRIPTION: Est. 1994. The mission of Rattlestick Playwrights Theater is to present diverse, challenging and provocative plays that might not otherwise be produced and to foster the future voices of the American theater. Unique in its dedication, Rattlestick guarantees a second production to any playwright we take on, regardless of the reception of the first. At this time, we are unfortunately unable to responsibly respond to unsolicited submissions.
PREFERRED GENRE: Plays **PREFERRED LENGTH:** Full-length
FEE: No **AGENT ONLY:** Yes

RED BARN THEATRE
WEBSITE: www.redbarntheatre.com **EMAIL:** mmcdon3444@aol.com
PHONE: (305) 296-9911 **FAX:** (305) 293-3035
ADDRESS: 319 Duval St (Rear), Key West FL 33040
DESCRIPTION: Est. 1981. The Mission of Red Barn Theatre is to provide professional opportunities in a creative, nurturing environment for actors, directors, playwrights, designers, musicians and choreographers.

RED BULL THEATER
WEBSITE: www.redbulltheater.com **EMAIL:** craig@redbulltheater.com
PHONE: (212) 343-7394 **ADDRESS:** 191 7th Ave, #2S, New York NY 10011

DESCRIPTION: Est. 2003. Red Bull Theater is dedicated to the exploration and creation of heightened language plays. With the Jacobean plays of Shakespeare and his contemporaries as our cornerstone, Red Bull Theater engages today's theatergoers through intimate and imaginative performances of great classic stories from all eras and cultures.

SUBMISSION MATERIALS: See website for updates. If you have a play that you feel is right for Red Bull Theater, please have your agent send a letter of inquiry to artistic director Jesse Berger. Include your bio, a synopsis of your play with character breakdown, and the play's production or development history. We will contact you only if we are interested in pursuing your submission further. The only exception to this is our annual open-submission Short New Play Festival. Please do not mail unsolicited submissions. We are unable to return manuscripts or respond to unsolicited inquiries.

PREFERRED GENRE: Plays **PREFERRED LENGTH:** Any Length **FEE:** No **AGENT ONLY:** Yes

RED ORCHID THEATRE

WEBSITE: www.aredorchidtheatre.org **EMAIL:** literary@aredorchidtheatre.org
PHONE: (312) 943-8722 **ADDRESS:** 1531 N Wells St, Chicago IL 60610

DESCRIPTION: Est. 1993. A Red Orchid Theatre is an ensemble of artists dedicated to the proliferation of live theatre in the modern world. We believe that theatre is the greatest sustenance for the human spirit and approach our work with a palpable sense of social compassion, aesthetic rigor, and honesty. By presenting new plays from all over the world and by reviving insightful works from the past that bear new relevance today, we aim to seek out and build new audiences for the modern stage.

SUBMISSION MATERIALS: We are not currently accepting unsolicited material. We will accept submissions through agents or referrals. If we are interested in your play, we will contact you, so please do include all of your contact information with your script. No phone calls please. **AGENT ONLY:** Yes

RELATIVE THEATRICS

WEBSITE: www.relativetheatrics.com **EMAIL:** relativetheatrics@gmail.com
ADDRESS: 710 E Garfield, #278, Laramie WY 82070

DESCRIPTION: Relative Theatrics strives to present thought-provoking theatre that examines the joining qualities of the human race. We produce an annual festival, classes, and a development workshop. Please check back for information about future dates and submission guidelines.

REP STAGE

WEBSITE: www.repstage.org **EMAIL:** lwilde@howardcc.edu
PHONE: (410) 772-4942 **FAX:** (410) 772-4040 **ADDRESS:** Howard Community College, 10901 Little Patuxent Pkwy, Columbia MD 21044

DESCRIPTION: Rep Stage produces exceptional theatre by creating a collaborative artistic space in which regional theatre professionals tell evocative, engaging stories. At this time, Rep Stage is NOT accepting any unsolicited scripts.

PREFERRED GENRE: Musicals **AGENT ONLY:** Yes

REPERTORIO ESPANOL

WEBSITE: www.repertorio.org **EMAIL:** r.federico@repertorio.org
PHONE: (212) 225-9999 **ADDRESS:** 138 E 27th St, New York NY 10016

DESCRIPTION: st. 1968. Repertorio Espanol was founded to introduce the best of Latin American, Spanish and Hispanic-American theatre in distinctive, quality productions, and to bring theatre to a broad audience in New York City and across the country. Dedicated to the next generation of Latino artists, Repertorio has been cultivating playwrights by establishing the annual MetLife Nuestras Voces National Playwriting Competition (submit plays via the website).
PREFERRED LENGTH: Full-length **FEE:** No **AGENT ONLY:** No
SPECIAL INTEREST: Hispanic or Latinx

REPERTORY THEATRE OF ST. LOUIS
WEBSITE: www.repstl.org **EMAIL:** sgordon@repstl.org **PHONE:** (314) 968-7340
ADDRESS: 130 Edgar Rd, St Louis MO 63119
DESCRIPTION: Est. 1966. The Repertory Theatre of St. Louis is dedicated to excellence in producing an eclectic range of live theatre. The Repertory Theatre of St. Louis does not accept unsolicited manuscripts. We do welcome a cover letter, resume, synopsis and 10-page sample from anyone who wishes for their work to be considered. The cover letter should specify whether the play has been previously produced. Submissions made under these guidelines may be sent to Seth Gordon, Associate Artistic Director, by mail or by email.

RIANT THEATRE
WEBSITE: www.therianttheatre.com **EMAIL:** TheRiantTheatre@gmail.com
PHONE: (646) 623-3488 **ADDRESS:** PO Box 1902, New York NY 10013
DESCRIPTION: Providing a nurturing environment to develop new plays and outstanding artists. We accomplish this through our various programs and activities that we offer such as semi-annual Strawberry One-Act Fest, Core Project workshop. Deadline for submissions for the April Strawberry Festival is November 15, 2017. Late submissions is anything received after November 15, 2017. To obtain an application email us at RiantTheatre@gmail.com. To submit full-length plays, musicals, variety acts, cabaret acts, improv shows, sketch comedy shows and readings email us and request an application for the Strawberry Theatre Festival. **PREFERRED GENRE:** All genres

RIVENDELL THEATRE ENSEMBLE
WEBSITE: www.rivendelltheatre.org **EMAIL:** literary@rivendelltheatre.org
PHONE: (773) 334-7728 **ADDRESS:** 5775 N Ridge Ave, #1, Chicago IL 60660
DESCRIPTION: Established 1994. Rivendell Theatre Ensemble is dedicated to advancing the lives of women through theatre. Seeking out innovative plays that explore the unique female experience. Full scripts are accepted by agent submission only. Rivendell accepts full scripts via agent submission only. Playwrights may submit a script synopsis of no more than one page along with a character breakdown, production history, and current resume. We will be in touch if these materials are of interest to us. Please email your script submission materials to our literary department. Our response time is typically two weeks for queries, three months for complete scripts.
PREFERRED GENRE: Plays **FEE:** No **AGENT ONLY:** Yes
SPECIAL INTEREST: Feminism/Women's Rights

RIVERSIDE THEATRE [FL]
WEBSITE: www.riversidetheatre.com **EMAIL:** info@riversidetheatre.com

PHONE: (772) 231-5860 **FAX:** (772) 234-5298
ADDRESS: 3250 Riverside Park Dr, Vero Beach FL 32963
DESCRIPTION: Est. 1985. Riverside Theatre, Inc. is committed to providing a total theatre arts experience that entertains, challenges, and educates both adults and children. Not accepting unsolicited scripts at this time.
PREFERRED GENRE: Plays or Musicals **PREFERRED LENGTH:** Full-length **FEE:** No **AGENT ONLY:** Yes **SPECIAL INTEREST:** Theatre for Young Audiences

RIVERSIDE THEATRE [IA]
WEBSITE: www.riversidetheatre.org **EMAIL:** Sean.lewis@riversidetheatre.org
PHONE: (319) 887-1360 **ADDRESS:** 213 N Gilbert St, Iowa City IA 52245
DESCRIPTION: Est. 1981. Riverside Theatre is a professional theatre that connects artists and audiences through intimate, engaging, and provocative productions from the classics to new works, and provides an artistic home for regional theatre professionals. Scripts may be submitted by agents and professional representatives as well as all NNPN member theatres. Additionally, some unsolicited work may be considered on the strength of a professional recommendation or existing professional relationship. Please email any queries directly to Artistic Director.
PREFERRED GENRE: Plays **PREFERRED LENGTH:** Any Length **FEE:** No **AGENT ONLY:** Yes

RIVERTOWN THEATERS FOR THE PERFORMING ARTS
WEBSITE: www.rivertowntheaters.com **EMAIL:** info@rivertowntheaters.com
PHONE: (504) 461-9475 **ADDRESS:** 325 Minor St, Kenner LA 70062
DESCRIPTION: Theatre 13 was founded in 2009 by New Orleans theatre artists Gary Rucker and Kelly Fouchi as a side project to the already successful FourFront Theatre, which they co-founded in 2008. The mission of Theatre 13 is to bring new and exciting productions to the New Orleans area while providing local theatre artists an opportunity to perform and create. Theatre 13 produces a wide range of professional theatrical performances, from musicals to children's theatre to more controversial and thought-provoking works. In 2012, the City of Kenner awarded Theatre 13 the management contract for what is now known as The Rivertown Theaters for the Performing Arts.

ROAD LESS TRAVELED PRODUCTIONS
WEBSITE: roadlesstraveledproductions.org **EMAIL:** jelston@roadlesstraveledproductions.org **ADDRESS:** PO Box 542, Buffalo NY 14205
DESCRIPTION: RLTP is dedicated to the development and production of new theatrical works by Western New York and Southern Ontario playwrights through a variety of programming. Road Less Traveled Productions challenges audiences through provocative storytelling and passionate artistry. Our mission is to develop the canon of contemporary voices through production of new and notable works by regional and national playwrights, creating unforgettable live theatre experiences that bring value to our lives. Check website for submission guidelines and deadlines for National Residency program and Regional Residency programs.

ROAN PRODUCTIONS
WEBSITE: www.roanproductions.com **EMAIL:** info@roanproductions.com

PHONE: (646) 415-8206 **ADDRESS:** 30-43 41st St, Ste 1, Astoria NY 11103
DESCRIPTION: RoaN Productions produces works that challenge, inspire, and entertain audiences through its reverence for language, spirit of adventure, and through the staging of unique and unparalleled new works and classics. RNP's artistic policy includes: a feminine perspective, a strong collaborative environment, and non-traditional casting. RoaN Reading Series is seeking screenplays with strong female roles. Please email for more information or to submit your work.
PREFERRED LENGTH: Full-length **FEE:** No **AGENT ONLY:** No
SPECIAL INTEREST: Feminism/Women's Rights

RORSCHACH THEATRE
WEBSITE: www.rorschachtheatre.com
EMAIL: literarydepartment@rorschachtheatre.com **PHONE:** (202) 715-6707
ADDRESS: 1421 Columbia Rd NW, #303, Washington DC 20009
DESCRIPTION: Through uncommon uses of environment and intimate passionate performances, Rorschach Theatre seeks to lure its audiences beyond the limits of ordinary theatrical experience so that they may discover new elements of their own humanity. New work is important to Rorschach Theatre.
SUBMISSION MATERIALS: Synopsis and 10-page dialogue sample or, an agent submission of a full script. Please include a resume and cover letter that summarizes the play's developmental history. We cannot guarantee response. We are especially interested in plays that are epic in scope but intimate in their exploration of human psychology. Plays that include elements of mythology and the supernatural while remaining contemporary in their themes and settings. Plays that might be described as magic realism. Plays that might be described by some literary managers as "impossible." Please no domestic comedies or kitchen sink dramas. For all inquiries, please email with the following in the subject line: SUBMISSION / name of playwright / name of play / date / DRAFT

ROSS VALLEY PLAYERS
WEBSITE: www.rossvalleyplayers.com **EMAIL:** raw@rossvalleyplayers.com
PHONE: (415) 456-9555 **ADDRESS:** PO Box 886, Ross CA 94957
DESCRIPTION: Ross Valley Players produce diverse, professionally-oriented, high quality live theatre that evokes, entertains, and enlivens the human spirit. We invite the participation of an evolving and expanding community. Opportunities incl. RAW (Ross Alternative Works) staged readings. Bay Area residents only. Check website for guidelines and deadlines.

ROUND HOUSE THEATRE
WEBSITE: www.roundhousetheatre.org **EMAIL:** roundhouse@roundhousetheatre.org
PHONE: (240) 644-1099 **ADDRESS:** 1 Veterans Pl, Silver Spring MD 20910
DESCRIPTION: Est. 1978. Round House Theatre is a home for outstanding ensemble acting and lifelong learning. We seek to captivate audiences with stories that inspire compassion, evoke emotions, and demand conversation.
PREFERRED LENGTH: Any Length **FEE:** No **AGENT ONLY:** No

ROUNDABOUT THEATRE COMPANY

WEBSITE: www.roundabouttheatre.org   **EMAIL:** info@roundabouttheatre.org
PHONE: (212) 719-9393   **FAX:** (212) 869-8817
ADDRESS: 231 W 39th St, #1200, New York NY 10018
DESCRIPTION: Est. 1965, Roundabout Theatre Company has grown from a small 150-seat theatre in a converted supermarket basement to become the nation's most influential nonprofit theatre company, as well as one of New York City's leading cultural institutions. With five stages on and off-Broadway, Roundabout now reaches over a million theatregoers, students, educators and artists across the country and around the world every year.   **AGENT ONLY:** Yes

ROUST THEATRE COMPANY
WEBSITE: www.rousttc.com   **EMAIL:** roust.info@gmail.com
PHONE: (212) 340-9058
ADDRESS: 425 W 110th St, #11E, New York NY 10024
DESCRIPTION: Roust is dedicated to radical and epoch making theatre. Strong focus on social change and narratives that have been traditionally underrepresented in mass media. We accept new, previously unproduced plays from both literary agents and directly from playwrights as unsolicited manuscripts, with some limitations. 'Unproduced' means not previously seen on a stage in a professional capacity, it does not include being previously produced as a staged reading. And we like to receive plays that fit our mission!
SUBMISSION MATERIALS: Please attach your script to the submission form on our website. Be sure to include a synopsis.
PREFERRED GENRE: Plays   **PREFERRED LENGTH:** Full-length   **FEE:** No   **AGENT ONLY:** No

ROUTE 66 THEATRE COMPANY
WEBSITE: www.route66theatre.org   **EMAIL:** submissions@route66theatre.org
PHONE: (773) 450-8177   **ADDRESS:** 1333 N Milwaukee Ave, Chicago IL 60622
DESCRIPTION: Route 66 Theatre Company introduces, develops, produces, and exports new work for the stage that embrace the American spirit of exploration and risk. Sponsors new play developmental workshop, Test Drive. The annual workshop awards one playwright with a developmental workshop that is focused on the playwright and what they need to move their script toward being production-ready. Playwrights must either reside in the Chicago area, or be willing to cover their own expenses to travel to Chicago for the workshop dates. Check website for submission information.
PREFERRED GENRE: Plays   **PREFERRED LENGTH:** Full-length   **FEE:** No   **AGENT ONLY:** No

ROYAL COURT THEATRE
WEBSITE: www.royalcourttheatre.com   **EMAIL:** literary@royalcourttheatre.com
PHONE: +44 (0) 207-565-5000   **ADDRESS:** Literary Office, Royal Court, Sloane Sq, London SW1W 8AS United Kingdom
DESCRIPTION: Only accepts hard copies of scripts.
PREFERRED GENRE: Plays   **PREFERRED LENGTH:** Full-length   **FEE:** No   **AGENT ONLY:** No

SACRAMENTO THEATRE COMPANY
WEBSITE: www.sactheatre.org   **EMAIL:** launm@sactheatre.org
PHONE: (916) 446-7501   **FAX:** (916) 446-4066
ADDRESS: 1419 H St, Sacramento CA 95814

DESCRIPTION: Sacramento Theatre Company (STC) strives to be the leader in integrating professional theatre with theatre arts education. STC produces engaging professional theatre, provides exceptional theatre training, and uses theatre as a tool for educational engagement.

SALT LAKE ACTING COMPANY
WEBSITE: www.saltlakeactingcompany.org
EMAIL: shannon@saltlakeactingcompany.org **PHONE:** (801) 363-7522
ADDRESS: 168 W 500 N, Salt Lake City UT 84103
DESCRIPTION: Since its inception in 1994, SLAC's New Play Sounding Series (NPSS) has nurtured emerging and established playwrights alike in the development of their new work. The NPSS creates a constructive, low risk arena for artists to navigate the challenges that come with writing and developing new plays.
PREFERRED GENRE: Plays **PREFERRED LENGTH:** Full-length **FEE:** No **AGENT ONLY:** Yes

SAN DIEGO REPERTORY THEATRE
WEBSITE: www.sdrep.org **PHONE:** (619) 231-3586 **TWITTER:** @SanDiegoREP
ADDRESS: 79 Horton Plz, San Diego CA 92101-6144
DESCRIPTION: Est. 1976. San Diego REP is happy to accept scripts from agents and theater professionals with whom we have an existing relationship. In general, we no longer accept unsolicited scripts from unrepresented writers. However, we continue to offer an open submission policy for plays and musicals from Latino(a) writers across the country because we are committed to supporting today's Latino(a) voices. In addition, local writers residing in the Southern California area may submit a query letter about their new work that includes a current email contact and:
- A brief biography of your writing history, noting awards and production history,
- A paragraph about why your play is a good match for the San Diego REP,
- A one-page synopsis of the play including number of cast, genre & run-time,
- For musicals, please also include a CD with sample songs from the score.

PREFERRED GENRE: Plays or Musicals **PREFERRED LENGTH:** Full-length
FEE: No **AGENT ONLY:** Yes

SANTA CRUZ ACTORS' THEATRE
WEBSITE: www.sccat.org **EMAIL:** sccactorstheatre@gmail.com
PHONE: (831) 335-4409 **ADDRESS:** PO Box 7084, Santa Cruz CA 95061
DESCRIPTION: Since 1995, playwrights from around the country have sent in their raw scripts to Santa Cruz Actors' Theatre, in the hopes that their piece might be one of the eight selected to become a full-fledged production. Submissions are accepted year-round, but must meet the summer deadline of July 1. Over the following six months, eight plays are anonymously selected by a panel of judges consisting of local writers, directors, and theater enthusiasts, assigned to directors at random, and rehearsed for three months, before premiering in front of a sold-out audience. The only criteria for entering: Each play must be 10 minutes or less.
SUBMISSION DEADLINE: 07/01/2018 **PREFERRED GENRE:** Plays
PREFERRED LENGTH: 10-minute **FEE:** No **AGENT ONLY:** No

SANTA FE OPERA
WEBSITE: www.santafeopera.org **EMAIL:** boxoffice@santafeopera.org

PHONE: (505) 946-2417   **FAX:** (505) 986-5999   **TWITTER:** @santafeopera
ADDRESS: 301 Opera Dr, Santa Fe NM 87506-2823
DESCRIPTION: The Santa Fe Opera's mission is to advance the operatic art form by presenting ensemble performances of the highest quality in a unique setting with a varied repertoire of new, rarely performed, and standard works; to ensure the excellence of opera's future through apprentice programs for singers, technicians and arts administrators; and to foster and enrich an understanding and appreciation of opera among a diverse public.
PREFERRED GENRE: Opera   **FEE:** No   **AGENT ONLY:** No

SEACOAST REPERTORY THEATRE
WEBSITE: www.seacoastrep.org   **EMAIL:** info@seacoastrep.org
PHONE: (603) 433-4793   **ADDRESS:** 125 Bow St, Portsmouth NH 3801
DESCRIPTION: The Seacoast Repertory Theatre is committed to the cultural richness of the Seacoast region through the shared experience of live theater and its youth, teen, and senior educational programs. We contribute by producing creative, thoughtful, and high quality year-round programming as well as collaborating with like-minded arts and cultural organizations.
PREFERRED GENRE: Plays or Musicals   **PREFERRED LENGTH:** Full-length
FEE: No   **AGENT ONLY:** No

SEATTLE CHILDREN'S THEATRE
WEBSITE: www.sct.org   **EMAIL:** courtneys@sct.org   **PHONE:** (206) 441-3322
ADDRESS: 201 Thomas St, Seattle WA 98109
DESCRIPTION: Seattle Children's Theatre accepts work either directly from literary agents or with a recommendation of an artistic director, literary manager, or dramaturg affiliated with a professional theatre.
PREFERRED GENRE: Plays   **PREFERRED LENGTH:** Full-length   **FEE:** No   **AGENT ONLY:** Yes
SPECIAL INTEREST: Theatre for Young Audiences

SEATTLE JEWISH THEATER COMPANY
WEBSITE: www.seattlejewishtheater.com   **EMAIL:** seattlejewishtheatercompany@gmail.com   **PHONE:** (212) 581-8655
ADDRESS: 5225 50th Ave NE, #203, Seattle WA 98105
DESCRIPTION: The Seattle Jewish Theater Company was launched in spring 2011 to bring classic and contemporary Jewish theater to the Seattle area.
PREFERRED GENRE: Plays   **PREFERRED LENGTH:** Any Length   **FEE:** No
AGENT ONLY: No   **SPECIAL INTEREST:** Jewish

SEATTLE REPERTORY THEATRE
WEBSITE: www.seattlerep.org   **EMAIL:** submissions@seattlerep.org
PHONE: (206) 443-2210
ADDRESS: 155 Mercer St, PO Box 900923, Seattle WA 98109
DESCRIPTION: The Seattle Repertory Theatre is committed to discovering and nurturing playwrights and their work. Our New Play Program offers the perfect balance

of passion for the creative process with the resources needed to help bring the next great American play to life.

PREFERRED GENRE: Plays **PREFERRED LENGTH:** Full-length **FEE:** No **AGENT ONLY:** Yes

SECOND STAGE THEATRE
WEBSITE: www.2st.com **EMAIL:** rmcglone@2st.com **PHONE:** (212) 787-8302
ADDRESS: 305 W 43rd St, New York NY 10036
DESCRIPTION: Second Stage Theater produces an adventurous range of premieres, musicals, bold new interpretations of contemporary plays, and unique theatrical experiences from America's most dynamic writers of the 21st century. Through the discovery of emerging talent, the commissioning of new work, and the creation of a training base for directors, Second Stage reflects the diverse city and the world we live in today and reaches an ever-growing audience through its Broadway runs, national tours and regional productions.
PREFERRED GENRE: Plays or Musicals **PREFERRED LENGTH:** Full-length
FEE: No **AGENT ONLY:** Yes

SHADOW BOX THEATRE [NY]
WEBSITE: www.shadowboxtheatre.org **EMAIL:** sbt@shadowboxtheatre.org
PHONE: (212) 724-0677 **FAX:** (212) 724-0767
ADDRESS: 325 West End Ave, #12-B, New York NY 10023
DESCRIPTION: The Shadow Box Theatre's mission is to touch the minds and hearts of children through shadow and three dimensional puppet based theatre arts.

SHADOWLIGHT PRODUCTIONS
WEBSITE: www.shadowlight.org **EMAIL:** lreed@shadowlight.org
PHONE: (415) 648-4461 **ADDRESS:** 22 Chattanooga St, San Francisco CA 94114
DESCRIPTION: The mission of ShadowLight Productions is to expose the general public to the art of Shadow Theater. The means of providing such exposure includes but is not limited to live theater, film, and other media. We strive to help preserve indigenous shadow theater traditions, and to explore and expand the possibilities of the shadow theatre medium by creating innovative interdisciplinary, multicultural works.
PREFERRED GENRE: Plays **PREFERRED LENGTH:** Full-length **FEE:** No **AGENT ONLY:** Yes

SHOTGUN PLAYERS
WEBSITE: www.shotgunplayers.org **EMAIL:** info@shotgunplayers.org
PHONE: (510) 841-6500 **TWITTER:** @ShotgunPlayers
ADDRESS: 1901 Ashby Ave, Berkeley CA 94703
DESCRIPTION: Est. 1992. Shotgun Players is a company of artists determined to create bold, relevant, affordable theatre that inspires and challenges audience and artist alike to re-examine our lives, our community, and the ever-changing world around us. Our commitment to new play development has made Shotgun Players a vital part of the arts community in the Bay Area and beyond. We commission at least one new play each season, and we celebrated our 20th anniversary with an entire season of new works. **PREFERRED GENRE:** Plays

SHOTGUN PRODUCTIONS INC.

WEBSITE: www.shotgunproductions.org **EMAIL**: literary@shotgun-productions.org
PHONE: (212) 689-2322 **ADDRESS**: 165 E 35 St, #7-J, New York NY 10016
DESCRIPTION: Shotgun Productions is a not-for-profit theatrical production company committed to developing and producing original, contemporary works for the stage by emerging and established artists.
PREFERRED GENRE: Plays **PREFERRED LENGTH**: Full-length
FEE: No **AGENT ONLY**: Yes

THE SIDE PROJECT
WEBSITE: www.thesideproject.net **EMAIL**: scripts@thesideproject.net
PHONE: (773) 973-2150 **FAX**: (312) 335-4277
ADDRESS: 1439 W Jarvis Ave, Chicago IL 60626
DESCRIPTION: The side project connects Chicago's most innovative and engaging writers, directors, designers, and performers in an ongoing exploration of the power of hyper-intimate theatre. Our projects develop out of relationships with artists, an appreciation of their work and processes, and an understanding of where they want to go. Our focus is not simply on world-premiere plays, but on world-premiere collaborations: creating never-before-seen teams of artists, each of whom has a body of work which speaks to the others in unique and exciting ways.
SUBMISSION MATERIALS: Send full scripts with synopsis via email or via USPS Attn: LITERARY. **FEE**: No **AGENT ONLY**: No

SIGNATURE THEATRE [VA]
WEBSITE: www.sigtheatre.org **EMAIL**: gardnerm@sigtheatre.org
PHONE: (703) 820-9771 **FAX**: (703) 820-7790
ADDRESS: 4200 Campbell Ave, Arlington VA 22206
DESCRIPTION: Signature Theatre is a Tony Award®-winning, non-profit professional theater company with a mission to produce contemporary musicals and plays, reinvent classic musicals, develop new work, and reach its community through engaging educational and outreach opportunities.
PREFERRED GENRE: Plays or Musicals **PREFERRED LENGTH**: Full-length

SIGNATURE THEATRE COMPANY [NY]
WEBSITE: www.signaturetheatre.org **EMAIL**: jembrey@signaturetheatre.org
PHONE: (212) 967-1913 **ADDRESS**: 480 W 42nd St, New York NY 10036
DESCRIPTION: Est. 1990. Premieres and revivals produced in a season of work by current and past playwrights in residence. Signature Theatre Company does not accept unsolicited scripts or inquiries. **FEE**: No **AGENT ONLY**: Yes

SIGNSTAGE
WEBSITE: www.chsc.org/Main/SignStage.aspx **EMAIL**: wmorgan@chsc.org
PHONE: (216) 325-7119 **ADDRESS**: 11635 Euclid Ave, Cleveland OH 44106
DESCRIPTION: Mission: To produce educational programs and performances about Deaf Culture that promotes awareness and demonstrates the value of cultural diversity between the Deaf and Hearing communities.
FEE: No **AGENT ONLY**: No **SPECIAL INTEREST**: Deaf or Hearing-impaired

SIMPATICO THEATRE PROJECT
WEBSITE: simpaticotheatre.org **EMAIL:** simpatico@simpaticotheatre.org
PHONE: (215) 423-0254 **ADDRESS:** PO Box 2277, Philadelphia PA 19103
DESCRIPTION: Simpatico Theatre explores stories that celebrate, challenge, and expand our definitions of community and compassion. We stage thought-provoking work that's grounded in social justice, civil rights, and community service. Our grassroots dedication to bridging communities fuels our work, reveals avenues of advocacy for our audiences, and leads to transformative collaborations in our city.
PREFERRED GENRE: Plays **PREFERRED LENGTH:** Full-length

SINGAPORE REPERTORY THEATRE
WEBSITE: www.srt.com.sg **EMAIL:** office@srt.com.sg **PHONE:** (65)67338166
FAX: (65)67338167 **ADDRESS:** KC Arts Ctr, 20 Merbau Rd, Singapore 239035
DESCRIPTION: Mission: To stage theatre of the highest calibre, developing and collaborating with the best talent in the world, and to be known as the most professional and progressive theatre company in Asia.
PREFERRED GENRE: Plays or Musicals **PREFERRED LENGTH:** Full-length

SITI COMPANY
WEBSITE: www.siti.org **EMAIL:** inbox@siti.org **PHONE:** (212) 868-0860
FAX: (212) 868-0837 **ADDRESS:** 520 8th Ave, #310, New York NY 10018
DESCRIPTION: SITI Company is committed to providing a gymnasium-for-the-soul where the interaction of art, artists, audiences and ideas inspire the possibility for change, optimism and hope.

SKYLIGHT MUSIC THEATRE
WEBSITE: www.skylightmusictheatre.org
EMAIL: kendallj@skylightmusictheatre.org **PHONE:** (414) 291-7811
FAX: (414) 291-7815 **ADDRESS:** 158 N Broadway, Milwaukee WI 53202
DESCRIPTION: Emphasizing the development of emerging American artists, directors and designers, Skylight Music Theatre attracts important new talent from around the country. With extended rehearsal and production periods, Skylight artists are able to hone their skills, expand their repertoire and gain invaluable experience.
PREFERRED GENRE: Musicals

SOHO REPERTORY THEATRE INC.
WEBSITE: www.sohorep.org **EMAIL:** sohorep@sohorep.org
PHONE: (212) 941-8632 **ADDRESS:** 401 Broadway, Ste 300, New York NY 10013
DESCRIPTION: Soho Rep. is a leading hub for innovative contemporary theater in New York City. We are dedicated to artistic excellence by supporting distinctive, diverse, and pioneering theater. We empower artists to make their boldest work and invite audiences to share in that intimate and transformative live experience. Soho Rep. creates a dynamic context for both artists and audiences that promotes and sustains conversation in the field and the cultural fabric of the city.
PREFERRED GENRE: Plays **PREFERRED LENGTH:** Full-length **FEE:** No **AGENT ONLY:** Yes

SOUTH CAMDEN THEATRE COMPANY

WEBSITE: www.southcamdentheatre.org   **EMAIL:** info@southcamdentheatre.org
PHONE: (856) 409-0365
ADDRESS: Waterfront South Theatre, 400 Jasper St, Camden NJ 8104
DESCRIPTION: As Camden's first professional theater we enhance the community by creating quality artistic productions while anchoring The Waterfront South Arts District. We strive to promote South Camden's rebirth as a destination by providing a positive experience for its residents and those from the surrounding region. Our goal is to entertain, engage, and educate.
PREFERRED LENGTH: Full-length   **FEE:** No   **AGENT ONLY:** No

SOUTH COAST REPERTORY THEATRE

WEBSITE: www.scr.org   **EMAIL:** theatre@scr.org   **PHONE:** (714) 708-5500
TWITTER: @SouthCoastRep
ADDRESS: Literary Department, PO Box 2197, Costa Mesa CA 92628
DESCRIPTION: Playwrights with professional representation may have their agents send full manuscripts at any time. Please note that—for this purpose—lawyers and law firms do not qualify as "professional representation." SCR accepts submissions for full-length plays, musicals, translations and adaptations and works for young audiences (approximately fourth-grade level). Unproduced plays are considered for possible inclusion in the NewSCRipts reading series, the Pacific Playwrights Festival and for production on SCR stages. Submissions are accepted year-round; there is no submission deadline for any opportunity.
SUBMISSION MATERIALS: Playwrights without representation may send a query letter, brief synopsis, complete list of characters and 10-page excerpt by mail. Unsolicited full-length scripts will not be reviewed. We do not accept materials submitted electronically.
DEADLINE TYPE: Rolling   **PREFERRED GENRE:** Plays or Musicals
PREFERRED LENGTH: Full-length   **FEE:** No   **AGENT ONLY:** Yes

SOUTHERN APPALACHIAN REPERTORY THEATRE

WEBSITE: www.sartplays.org   **EMAIL:** bgregg@mhu.edu   **PHONE:** (828) 689-1384
ADDRESS: PO Box 1720, 44 University St, Mars Hill NC 28754
DESCRIPTION: Southern Appalachian Repertory Theatre is a professional theatre company in residence at the historic Owen Theatre on the campus of Mars Hill University. Since its founding in 1975 by visionary director and theatre educator Jim Thomas, SART has produced scores of plays, musicals, and original works, many portraying the rich culture and heritage of Southern Appalachia.
PREFERRED GENRE: Plays or Musicals   **PREFERRED LENGTH:** Full-length   **FEE:** No
AGENT ONLY: No

SOUTHERN REP

WEBSITE: www.southernrep.com   **EMAIL:** helen@southernrep.com
PHONE: (504) 523-9857
ADDRESS: 333 Canal St, PO Box 34, New Orleans LA 70130
DESCRIPTION: Southern Rep Theatre is committed to the development and production of new plays and playwrights. Our program 4D creates teams of dramatists, directors, and dramaturgs in New Orleans to create three new full-length plays every

season. The Ruby Prize is our $10,000 Biennial award to a woman playwright of color named in honor of Ruby Bridges, who showed incredible perseverance in the face of formidable obstacles. Finalists for the Ruby Prize present their work in the New Play Bacchanal, a multi-day series of several staged readings open to the public for low or no cost. **PREFERRED GENRE:** Plays **PREFERRED LENGTH:** Full-length

SPRINGER OPERA HOUSE
WEBSITE: www.springeroperahouse.org **PHONE:** (706) 324-5714
FAX: (706) 324-4461 **ADDRESS:** 103 10th St, Columbus GA 31901
DESCRIPTION: The Springer is one of America's most vibrant professional theatre companies with a popular Mainstage Series, an innovative second-space series called Studio II, a Theatre for Young Audience Series featuring some of this region's most talented student actors and a national touring program called Springer Theatricals.
PREFERRED GENRE: Opera

ST. BART'S PLAYERS
WEBSITE: www.stbartsplayers.org **EMAIL:** info@stbartsplayers.org
PHONE: (212) 378-0217 **ADDRESS:** 109 E 50th St, New York NY 10022
DESCRIPTION: St. Bart's Players, founded in 1927, is a non-profit, volunteer-driven organization dedicated to presenting high-caliber quality theater at affordable prices.

ST. LOUIS BLACK REPERTORY COMPANY
WEBSITE: www.theblackrep.org **EMAIL:** info@theblackrep.org
PHONE: (314) 534-3807 **FAX:** (314) 534-4035
ADDRESS: 1717 Olive St, 4th Fl, St Louis MO 63103
DESCRIPTION: The Black Rep produces quality professional dramas, comedies and musicals by primarily African-American and third world playwrights.
PREFERRED GENRE: Plays or Musicals **PREFERRED LENGTH:** Full-length
SPECIAL INTEREST: Black or African American

STAGE 773
WEBSITE: www.stage773.com **EMAIL:** info@stage773.com
PHONE: (773) 929-7367 **ADDRESS:** 1225 W Belmont Ave, Chicago IL 60657
DESCRIPTION: Stage 773 is a vibrant anchor of the Belmont Theatre District and home to Chicago's finest off-Loop talent. As a performance and tenant venue, our four stages provide entertainment for everyone: comedy, theatre, dance, musicals and more. We are a not-for-profit, connecting and catalyzing the theater community, while showcasing established artists and incubating up-and-coming talent.
PREFERRED GENRE: Plays or Musicals **PREFERRED LENGTH:** Full-length
FEE: No **AGENT ONLY:** No

THE STAGE COMPANY
WEBSITE: www.stagecompany.org **EMAIL:** stagecompanycarbondale@gmail.com
PHONE: (618) 549-2028 **FAX:** (618) 457-0596
ADDRESS: PO Box 463, Carbondale IL 62903
DESCRIPTION: The Stage Company was born in 1982 when a small but enthusiastic

group met to explore the possibility of founding a community theater in Southern Illinois. We encourage participation of people from all walks of life. Interested in joining? Please come see a show, talk to an usher about joining, or come to our monthly meeting-third Wednesday of every month at 7 pm at the Varsity Center, or contact a member (any officer, director, actor or technician) for information.
SUBMISSION MATERIALS: Application, full script, submissions returned with SASE.

STAGES REPERTORY THEATRE
WEBSITE: www.stagestheatre.com **EMAIL:** scripts@stagestheatre.com
PHONE: (713) 527-0220 **ADDRESS:** 3201 Allen Pkwy, #101, Houston TX 77019
DESCRIPTION: Through this robust scope of activities Stages encourages conversation about important ideas, provides insight into other cultures and viewpoints, and helps develop each new generation of artists, audiences and citizens.
PREFERRED GENRE: Plays **PREFERRED LENGTH:** Full-length **FEE:** No **AGENT ONLY:** No

STAGES THEATRE COMPANY
WEBSITE: www.stagestheatre.org **EMAIL:** jcoulombe@stagestheatre.org
PHONE: (952) 979-1123 **ADDRESS:** 1111 Main St, Hopkins MN 55343
DESCRIPTION: Stages Theatre Company is committed to the enrichment and education of children and youth in a professional theatre environment that stimulates artistic excellence and personal growth.
PREFERRED GENRE: Plays **PREFERRED LENGTH:** 1-Act (under 1 hour) **FEE:** No
AGENT ONLY: No **SPECIAL INTEREST:** Theatre for Young Audiences

STAGE WEST
WEBSITE: www.stagewest.org **EMAIL:** boxoffice@stagewest.org
PHONE: (817) 784-9378 **FAX:** (817) 348-8392
ADDRESS: 821 W Vickery Blvd, Fort Worth TX 76107
DESCRIPTION: Stage West's goal is to broaden and intensify the theatrical experience for our patrons with consistently excellent acting, directing and plays. Through this, the company nurtures the artistic growth of area actors, directors, designers, playwrights and musicians.

STAGEWORKS, INC.
WEBSITE: www.stageworkstheatre.org **EMAIL:** khartley@stageworkstheatre.org
PHONE: (813) 215-8984 **TWITTER:** @StageworksTampa
ADDRESS: West Bldg, 1120 E Kennedy Blvd T33602, Tampa FL 33602
DESCRIPTION: Stagewrights is a script development group that meets twice a month at Stageworks (with a summer break). Meetings are usually held on the 2nd and 4th Tuesdays of the month. At the first monthly meeting, playwrights bring up to ten pages of a script. Members read the scripts aloud and provide constructive feedback. At the second meeting actors perform a script-in-hand reading of a new play or one act of a play, with a talkback. Meetings are designed for playwrights to get feedback on new drafts as works develop. **PREFERRED GENRE:** Plays **FEE:** No **AGENT ONLY:** No

STATE THEATRE COMPANY
WEBSITE: www.austintheatre.org **EMAIL:** info@austintheatre.org

PHONE: (512) 692-0509 **FAX**: (512) 472-7199
ADDRESS: PO Box 1566, Austin TX 78767
DESCRIPTION: Inspired by the power of the arts to change lives, the Austin Theatre Alliance strives to engage all Central Texans through extraordinary live performances and films, to ignite the intellect and imagination of our youth, and to ensure the preservation of the crown jewels of downtown Austin.

STEPPENWOLF THEATRE COMPANY
WEBSITE: www.steppenwolf.org **EMAIL**: customerservice@steppenwolf.org
PHONE: (312) 335-1888 **ADDRESS**: 1650 N Halsted St, Chicago IL 60614
DESCRIPTION: Steppenwolf Theatre Company accepts full-length scripts year-round from literary agents and theater professionals with whom we have an existing professional relationship.
SUBMISSION MATERIALS: In recognition of our commitment to fostering local voices, we invite unrepresented writers in the Chicagoland area to submit a query consisting of a brief bio, short synopsis and ten pages of sample dialogue during the months of July and August only. We encourage electronic submission if at all possible.
PREFERRED GENRE: Plays **PREFERRED LENGTH**: Full-length **FEE**: No **AGENT ONLY**: Yes

STEPPING STONE THEATRE FOR YOUTH DEVELOPMENT
WEBSITE: www.steppingstonetheatre.org
EMAIL: info@steppingstonetheatre.org **PHONE**: (651) 225-9265
FAX: (651) 225-1225 **ADDRESS**: 55 Victoria St N, St Paul MN 55104
DESCRIPTION: SteppingStone Theatre focuses on developing the whole child through educational theater programs and fully staged productions. Our supportive, non-competitive environment helps youth build self-esteem and confidence in a community that celebrates diversity.
FEE: No **AGENT ONLY**: No **SPECIAL INTEREST**: Theatre for Young Audiences

STONEHAM THEATRE
WEBSITE: www.stonehamtheatre.org **EMAIL**: weylin@stonehamtheatre.org
PHONE: (781) 279-7885 **FAX**: (781) 279-2374
ADDRESS: 395 Main St, Stoneham MA 2180
DESCRIPTION: Greater Boston Stage Company is committed to producing one world premiere play each season as part of the Don Fulton New Play Project. We accept submissions from March 1 to August 1 each year from playwrights and agents as part of the process for selecting these plays. In addition to potential selection for a full production as part of the Don Fulton New Play Project, we may also consider your play for a reading or workshop.
SUBMISSION DEADLINE: 08/01/2018 **DEADLINE TYPE**: Annual
PREFERRED GENRE: Plays **PREFERRED LENGTH**: Full-length **FEE**: No **AGENT ONLY**: No

STRANGE SUN THEATER COMPANY
WEBSITE: www.strangesuntheater.com
ADDRESS: 65 W 90th St, #4, New York NY 10024
DESCRIPTION: Theater is magic in its most basic form, with the power to reveal the

complex difficulties and unexpected joys of all our lives. We believe the dialogue among artist, audience and community, shared in the spirit of simplicity and truth, has the power to evoke this magic. We are compelled to call upon the magic of theater by bringing the finest theater artists together with dynamic audiences to focus this strange sun upon our shared humanity, releasing us from the ordinary, igniting within us, the power of possibility.

PREFERRED LENGTH: Full-length **FEE**: No **AGENT ONLY**: No

STRAZ CENTER
[TAMPA BAY PERFORMING ARTS CENTER]
WEBSITE: www.strazcenter.org **PHONE**: (813) 222-1000 **FAX**: (813) 222-1057
ADDRESS: 1010 N W C MacInnes Pl, Tampa FL 33602
DESCRIPTION: Built on an abandoned gravel lot in a city that was lacking cultural offerings, the Straz Center began as the dream of a community. Today the Straz Center is the largest performing arts center in the Southeast and the only one with an on-site performing arts conservatory. The Straz Center was incorporated in 1980 and opened in 1987.

STUDIO@620
WEBSITE: www.thestudioat620.org **EMAIL**: info@studio620.org
PHONE: (727) 895-6620 **TWITTER**: @studio620
ADDRESS: 620 1st Ave S, St. Petersburg FL 33701
DESCRIPTION: Mission: To provide a place where people can experience artistic and educational programs in innovative ways. To bring people from diverse cultural backgrounds and experiences together as artists, audiences and volunteers. To work collaboratively with artistic, educational, and cultural organizations in and beyond our community. To develop artistic and educational programs that integrate a variety of art forms in order to encourage new cultural experiences both for the audience and the artists. **FEE**: No **AGENT ONLY**: No **SPECIAL INTEREST**: All

STUDIO X AT THE STUDIO THEATRE
WEBSITE: www.studiotheatre.org **EMAIL**: literary@studiotheatre.org
PHONE: (202) 232-7267 **FAX**: (202) 588-5262 **TWITTER**: @Studio_Theatre
ADDRESS: 1501 14th St NW, Washington DC 20005
DESCRIPTION: Studio X is a new producing arm at Studio Theatre designed to support work that breaks new ground in its style or content. Complementing the subscribed work of the Main Series, Studio X will be a home for three or four innovative productions outside of the Main Series each season, including out-of-the-box immersive productions, groundbreaking work by international artists and ensembles, and bold world premiere projects.

DEADLINE TYPE: Rolling **PREFERRED LENGTH**: Full-length
FEE: No **AGENT ONLY**: Yes

SUNDANCE INSTITUTE THEATRE
WEBSITE: www.sundance.org/programs/theatre-program
EMAIL: institute@sundance.org **PHONE**: (310) 360-1981
ADDRESS: 321 W 44th St, Ste 805, New York NY 10036

DESCRIPTION: The Sundance Institute Theatre Program provides a unique catalytic process of artistic engagement for independent theatre-makers in the U.S. and globally through a range of artist-driven developmental opportunities that connect, support and sustain artists across their careers.
FEE: No   **AGENT ONLY**: No

SUN VALLEY CENTER FOR THE ARTS
WEBSITE: www.sunvalleycenter.org   **EMAIL**: information@sunvalleycenter.org
PHONE: (208) 788-6520   **FAX**: (208) 788-1053
ADDRESS: PO Box 329, Hailey ID 83333
DESCRIPTION: The Sun Valley Center for the Arts is a non-profit educational arts organization founded in 1971, whose mission is to enrich our community through transformative arts and educational experiences.

SYNCHRONICITY THEATRE
WEBSITE: www.synchrotheatre.com   **EMAIL**: info@synchrotheatre.com
PHONE: (404) 974-3291
ADDRESS: 1389 Peachtree St, Ste 350, Atlanta GA 30309
DESCRIPTION: Synchronicity Theatre produces smart, gutsy and bold theatre to spark community connections and uplift the voices of women and girls. The theatre was founded in 1997 as a company by and for women artists dedicated to bringing challenging, meaningful theatre to Atlanta audiences.
PREFERRED GENRE: Plays   **PREFERRED LENGTH**: Full-length
FEE: No   **AGENT ONLY**: Yes

SYRACUSE STAGE
WEBSITE: www.syracusestage.org   **EMAIL**: kebass@syr.edu
PHONE: (315) 443-4008   **ADDRESS**: 820 E Genesee St, Syracuse NY 13210
DESCRIPTION: The Syracuse Stage Literary Office is not accepting unsolicited scripts at this time. Unsolicited scripts cannot be read or returned.
PREFERRED GENRE: Plays   **PREFERRED LENGTH**: Full-length   **FEE**: No   **AGENT ONLY**: Yes

TADA! YOUTH THEATER
WEBSITE: www.tadatheater.com   **EMAIL**: mhaws@tadatheater.com
PHONE: (212) 252-1619   **ADDRESS**: 15 W 28th St, 3r Fl, New York NY 10001
DESCRIPTION: Since 1984, TADA!'s mission is to provide young people from different backgrounds with musical theater programs that inspire them to be creative, learn, and think differently.
PREFERRED GENRE: Musicals   **PREFERRED LENGTH**: Full-length   **FEE**: No
AGENT ONLY: No   **SPECIAL INTEREST**: Theatre for Young Audiences

TARGET MARGIN THEATER
WEBSITE: www.targetmargin.org   **EMAIL**: info@targetmargin.org
PHONE: (718) 398-3095   **FAX**: (718) 398-3613   **TWITTER**: @targetmargin
ADDRESS: 138 S Oxford St, #5-A, Brooklyn NY 11217
DESCRIPTION: Target Margin Theater was founded in 1991 by David Herskovits on the

principle that works of art return us to real truths more powerfully by their divergence from a strict illustration of reality. Through classic and contemporary texts, we seek continuously to expand our conception of what can take place in a theater.

TEATRO CIRCULO

WEBSITE: teatrocirculowordpress.wordpress.com
EMAIL: joliveras@teatrocirculo.org **PHONE**: (212) 505-1808
ADDRESS: 65 E 4th St, 3rd Fl, New York NY 10003
DESCRIPTION: Founded by a group of Latin artists with a strong academic background committed to preserving and promoting our cultural heritage through the presentation of creative, inclusive and educational theater works. It is our purpose to expose the public to the best works of Spanish and Latin American playwrights, both contemporary and classical, and to foster an appreciation of the richness of Latin American and Iberian cultures in the context of the pluralism that characterizes NYC.
FEE: No **AGENT ONLY**: No **SPECIAL INTEREST**: Hispanic or Latinx

TEATRO DALLAS

WEBSITE: www.teatrodallas.org **EMAIL**: info@teatrodallas.org
PHONE: (214) 689-6492 **TWITTER**: @teatrodallas1
ADDRESS: 1331 Record Crossing Rd, Dallas TX 75235
DESCRIPTION: Est. 1985. We recognize the theater's power to foster understanding of both cultural differences and similarities, and it is our hope to promote a sense of community while celebrating our diverse traditions.
PREFERRED GENRE: Plays **PREFERRED LENGTH**: Any Length **FEE**: Yes
AGENT ONLY: No **SPECIAL INTEREST**: Hispanic or Latinx

TEATRO DE AL LUNA

WEBSITE: www.teatrodelaluna.org **EMAIL**: info@teatrodelaluna.org
PHONE: (202) 882-6227 **TWITTER**: @teatrodelaluna
DESCRIPTION: Est. 1991 to provide the Washington capital area – both to its Spanish-speaking community and to its English-speaking community as well – with a source of high quality theater as seen from a Latin American perspective.

TEATRO DEL PUEBLO

WEBSITE: www.teatrodelpueblo.org **EMAIL**: al@teatrodelpueblo.org
PHONE: (651) 224-8806 **ADDRESS**: 209 Page St W, St Paul MN 55107
DESCRIPTION: Teatro del Pueblo promotes Latino culture through the creation and presentation of performing arts. Teatro develops and supports Latino artists, provides educational opportunities for all to experience Latino culture, and promotes cross-cultural dialogue.
PREFERRED GENRE: Plays or Musicals **PREFERRED LENGTH**: 1-Act (under 1 hour)
FEE: No **AGENT ONLY**: No **SPECIAL INTEREST**: Hispanic or Latinx

TEATRO LATEA

WEBSITE: www.teatrolatea.org **EMAIL**: info@teatrolatea.org
PHONE: (212) 529-1948 **ADDRESS**: 107 Suffolk St, New York NY 10002
DESCRIPTION: Est. 1982. Teatro LATEA (Latin American Theater Experiment As-

sociates) is a theater production company, which for over 30 years has run its own performance/rehearsal space in The Clemente located in the Lower East Side of Manhattan. Since its inception LATEA has opened its doors to a multitude of performers, artists and theater companies to forge theatrical experiences in this 76 seat experimental space. The mission of LATEA involves promoting multicultural theater and developing underrepresented audiences while presenting a variety of theatrical works with a Latino emphasis.

FEE: No **AGENT ONLY:** No **SPECIAL INTEREST:** Hispanic or Latinx

TEATRO SEA

WEBSITE: www.teatrosea.org **EMAIL:** sea@teatrosea.org **PHONE:** (212) 529-1545
TWITTER: @TeatroSEA **ADDRESS:** 107 Suffolk St, Ste 202, New York NY 10002
DESCRIPTION: Est. 1985. SEA is the premiere Bilingual Arts-in-Education Organization and Latino Children's Theatre in the United States. SEA has created and produced a combination of educational theatre productions and art workshops/programs specifically designed to examine, challenge and create possible solutions for current educational, social and community issues.

FEE: No **AGENT ONLY:** No

TEATRO VISION

WEBSITE: www.teatrovision.org **EMAIL:** elisamarina@teatrovision.org
PHONE: (408) 928-5582 **FAX:** (408) 928-5589 **TWITTER:** @Teatro_Vision
ADDRESS: 1700 Alum Rock Ave, San Jose CA 95116
DESCRIPTION: Teatro Visión creates theater rooted in Chicanx and Latinx experiences to inspire the people of Santa Clara Valley and beyond to feel, think, and act to create a better world.

TEATRO VISTA

WEBSITE: www.teatrovista.org/forartists **EMAIL:** plays@teatrovista.org
PHONE: (773) 599-9280 **TWITTER:** @TeatroVista
ADDRESS: 2936 N Southport, Ste 210, Chicago IL 60657
DESCRIPTION: We are committed to sharing and celebrating the riches of Latinx culture with Chicago audiences and are dedicated to sharing new work by new playwrights in cutting-edge productions.
SUBMISSION MATERIALS: Teatro Vista is always seeking new full-length plays. We are especially interested in work that speaks to our mission, values, and vision. Please email full scripts as PDFs and include your contact information. Feel free to send any other supporting materials such as your biography, resume, or reviews.
PREFERRED GENRE: Plays **PREFERRED LENGTH:** Full-length **FEE:** No **AGENT ONLY:** No
SPECIAL INTEREST: Hispanic or Latinx

TEATRO VIVO

WEBSITE: www.teatrovivo.org **EMAIL:** info@teatrovivo.org
PHONE: (512) 474-6379 **TWITTER:** @teatrovivotx
ADDRESS: 3103 Breeze Terr, Austin TX 78722
DESCRIPTION: Teatro Vivo is dedicated to producing quality bilingual theater accessible to all theater audiences and artists. Teatro Vivo reflects the heart and soul of the

Latino reality by opening a unique window for all to share in this experience.
PREFERRED GENRE: Plays **PREFERRED LENGTH:** Full-length **FEE:** No
SPECIAL INTEREST: Hispanic or Latinx

TECTONIC THEATER PROJECT
WEBSITE: www.tectonictheaterproject.org
EMAIL: admin@tectonictheaterproject.org **PHONE:** (212) 579-6111
TWITTER: @TectonicTheater
ADDRESS: 520 8th Ave, Ste 313, New York NY 10024
DESCRIPTION: Est. 1991. Dedicated to developing innovative works that explore theatrical language and form, fostering an artistic dialogue with audiences on the social, political, and human issues that affect us all. In service to this goal, Tectonic supports readings, workshops, and full theatrical productions, as well as training for students around the country in our play-making techniques.
PREFERRED GENRE: Plays **PREFERRED LENGTH:** Full-length **FEE:** No **AGENT ONLY:** No

TENNESSEE WOMEN'S THEATRE PROJECT
WEBSITE: www.twtp.org **EMAIL:** maryanna@twtp.org **PHONE:** (615) 681-7220
TWITTER: @twtp_dot_org **ADDRESS:** PO Box 158525, Nashville TN 37215
DESCRIPTION: Est. 1971. TNT's mission is to support and serve the theatre community of Texas, specifically: to promote high standards in theatre arts; to continue to provide professional training and development for individuals involved in theatre; to promote the development of educational theatre; to provide a forum for the exchange of information and ideas by persons engaged in theatre; to aid and encourage the formation of new theatre groups and support established theatre organizations; to provide information and advocacy for the needs of theatres in Texas within the limits of the law.
FEE: No **AGENT ONLY:** No **SPECIAL INTEREST:** Feminism/Women's Rights

TEXAS NONPROFIT THEATRES
WEBSITE: www.texastheatres.org **EMAIL:** info@texastheatres.org
PHONE: (817) 731-2238 **TWITTER:** @TexasTheatres
ADDRESS: 1300 Gendy St, Ft Worth TX 76107
DESCRIPTION: Mission: to present theatrical productions of the highest quality to Middle Tennessee audiences; to produce plays that express the human condition in the female voice; to provide acting, directing, design and management opportunities for women in professional theater; to bring live theater to new, underserved audiences.

THALIA SPANISH THEATRE
WEBSITE: www.thaliatheatre.org **EMAIL:** info@thaliatheatre.org
PHONE: (718) 729-3880 **TWITTER:** @TeatroThalia
ADDRESS: 41-17 Greenpoint Ave, Sunnyside NY 11104
DESCRIPTION: Est. 1977. First and only bilingual Hispanic theatre in Queens. Unique productions of plays, musicals, and dance of Spanish and Latin American culture. Submissions accepted year-round.
FEE: No **AGENT ONLY:** No **SPECIAL INTEREST:** Hispanic or Latinx

THEATER 2020

WEBSITE: www.theater2020.com **EMAIL**: theater2020@gmail.com
TWITTER: @Theater2020 **ADDRESS**: 57 Montague St, Ste 7-I, New York NY 11201
DESCRIPTION: Theater 2020, Inc., Visions for a New Millennium is dedicated to producing classic and contemporary plays and musicals for a 21st Century audience and to providing a nurturing atmosphere for both emerging artists and seasoned professionals. We are dedicated to reaching out to the community and to producing quality theater at affordable prices, utilizing established professionals and fostering young artists as they emerge into the theatrical mainstream, with a particular emphasis on providing more opportunities for women in theater.
SUBMISSION MATERIALS: Submissions accepted year-round by email only.
PREFERRED GENRE: Plays or Musicals **PREFERRED LENGTH**: Any Length
FEE: No **AGENT ONLY**: No

THEATER ALLIANCE

WEBSITE: www.theateralliance.com **EMAIL**: submissions@theateralliance.com
PHONE: (202) 399-7993 **TWITTER**: @ThtrAllianceDC
ADDRESS: 1365 H St, NE, Washington DC 20002
DESCRIPTION: A catalyst for innovation and diversity, Theater Alliance produces thought-provoking and socially pertinent work, successfully uniting audiences of all backgrounds through the power of creative presentation and participation. Theater Alliance has a small staff and cannot accept unsolicited script submissions. We encourage you to learn more about the Theater Alliance mission and production history to determine if your work would be a good fit. If you feel it would, please submit by emailing submissions@theateralliance.com with a cover page and a 5 page sample of your script.
DEADLINE TYPE: Rolling **PREFERRED GENRE**: Plays **FEE**: No

THEATER BREAKING THROUGH BARRIERS

WEBSITE: www.tbtb.org **EMAIL**: tbtbinfo@gmail.com **PHONE**: (212) 243-4337
TWITTER: @TBTBTheater
ADDRESS: 400 W 43rd St, #43R, New York NY 10036
DESCRIPTION: Est. 1979. TBTB is the only off-Broadway theater, and one of the few professional theaters in the country, dedicated to advancing actors and writers with disabilities and changing the image of people with disabilities from dependence to independence.
PREFERRED GENRE: All genres **PREFERRED LENGTH**: Any Length **FEE**: No
AGENT ONLY: No **SPECIAL INTEREST**: Living with Disability

THE THEATER CENTER

WEBSITE: www.thetheatercenter.com **EMAIL**: press@thetheatercenter.com
PHONE: (212) 921-7862 **FAX**: (212) 921-7928
ADDRESS: 210 W 50th St, New York NY 10019
DESCRIPTION: The Theater Center is a multi-theater entertainment complex located on the corner of 50th Street and Broadway in New York City. The complex opened on May 22, 2006. It is a 20,000-square-foot (1,900 m2) state of the art entertainment center consisting of two theaters with a total seating capacity of 398, rehearsal

studios, contemporary lobbies, WiFi, two bars with cabaret-style seating and two merchandise stands.

PREFERRED GENRE: All genres **PREFERRED LENGTH**: Any Length

THEATRE EXILE
WEBSITE: theatreexile.org **EMAIL**: info@theatreexile.org
PHONE: (215) 922-4462 **TWITTER**: @TheatreExile
ADDRESS: 525 S 4th St, #475, Philadelphia PA 19147
DESCRIPTION: Dedicated to enhancing the cultural experiences of Philadelphians through the staging of works that engage the imagination. We produce challenging plays that explore the complexities of the human condition and contain a sense of Philadelphia grit and passion. We strive to reach new theater audiences throughout the community by presenting both new works as well as established plays that are often reinterpreted in original ways. We believe in freedom of expression formulated through innovation, exploration and provocation. At the same time, we provide a safe and creative environment in which local artists can grow, experiment and find their own voice. Home to the Studio X-hibition New Play Development.

THEATRE INSPIRATO
WEBSITE: www.theatreinspirato.ca **EMAIL**: inspirato@ca.inter.net
PHONE: (416) 483-2222
ADDRESS: 124 Broadway Ave, Ste 112, Toronto ON M4P-IV8 Canada
DESCRIPTION: Theatre inspiraTO, the producers of the inspiraTO Festival, Canada's largest ten-minute play festival, is entering its 13th year. Each season, playwrights from around the globe are asked to submit a ten-minute play based on a theme. 24 ten-minute plays are selected. The inspiraTO Festival is held in Toronto in early June and provides over 100 theatre artists an opportunity to participate, network, learn and grow their craft.

SUBMISSION DEADLINE: 11/20/2017 **DEADLINE TYPE**: Annual **PREFERRED GENRE**: Plays or Musicals **PREFERRED LENGTH**: 10-minute **FEE**: No **AGENT ONLY**: No

THEATRE LAB
WEBSITE: www.fau.edu/theatrelab/about/get-involved/index.php
EMAIL: theatrelab@fau.edu **PHONE**: (561) 297-4784
ADDRESS: Florida Atlantic University, 777 Glades Rd, Boca Raton FL 33431
DESCRIPTION: The professional resident company of Florida Atlantic University. Established in 2015 on the Boca Raton campus, Theatre Lab's mission is to inspire, develop, and produce new work, audiences, and artists for the American Theatre. Dedicated to the play-making process through the development and production of new work. We create a laboratory for seasoned theater professionals to share their work with students, faculty, and the entire community. The goal is to gain an in-depth understanding of every aspect of new play development and making great theatre accessible. **AGENT ONLY**: No

THEATRE MEMPHIS
WEBSITE: theatrememphis.org **EMAIL**: rhartzog@theatrememphis.org
PHONE: (901) 682-8323 **TWITTER**: @TheatreMemphis

ADDRESS: 630 Perkins Extd, Memphis TN 38117

DESCRIPTION: Est. 1920. Theatre Memphis is a community theatre whose mission is "to provide outstanding theatrical experiences to enrich the live of our audiences, participants and community."

THEATRE DU MISSISSIPPI

WEBSITE: www.theatredumiss.org   **EMAIL**: admin@theatredumiss.org

PHONE: (507) 858-7543   **TWITTER**: @TheatreDuMiss

ADDRESS: PO Box 184, Winona MN 55987

DESCRIPTION: Founded in 1997, Theatre du Mississippi is committed to the development and production of high-quality programs in the performing arts, particularly those that address important contemporary or historical issues. Our aim is to integrate artistic excellence and originality with a sense of community in the Winona area and beyond. In addition to our regular season, we produce the annual Original Shorts Playwriting Contest.

PREFERRED LENGTH: Any Length   **FEE**: No   **AGENT ONLY**: No

THEATRE FOR A NEW AUDIENCE

WEBSITE: www.tfana.org   **EMAIL**: info@tfana.org   **PHONE**: (212) 229-2819

TWITTER: @TheatreforaNewA

ADDRESS: 154 Christopher St, #3D, New York NY 10014

DESCRIPTION: The mission of Theatre for a New Audience is to develop and vitalize the performance and study of Shakespeare and classic drama. In 2001, Theatre for a New Audience became the first American theater to be invited to bring a production of Shakespeare to the Royal Shakespeare Company, Stratford-upon-Avon. We do not accept unsolicited scripts.   **FEE**: No   **AGENT ONLY**: Yes

THEATER FOR THE NEW CITY

WEBSITE: www.theaterforthenewcity.net   **EMAIL**: literary@theaterforthenewcity.net

PHONE: (212) 254-1109   **FAX**: (212) 979-6570   **TWITTER**: @TNCinNYC

ADDRESS: 155 1st Ave, New York NY 10003

DESCRIPTION: Est. 1970. THEATER FOR THE NEW CITY is a unique Cultural Institution that has earned a nationwide reputation for its dedication to nurturing established and emerging playwrights who experiment with new forms and to presenting other experimental and developmental theaters with a very active program of Community Art Services and Festivals which continue to expand theater accessibility.

SUBMISSION MATERIALS: Please send a ten-page sample of the script, brief synopsis, bio and desired outcome to us via email at tncdreamup@gmail.com

PREFERRED GENRE: Plays or Musicals   **PREFERRED LENGTH**: Any Length

FEE: No   **AGENT ONLY**: No

THEATRE OF NOTE

WEBSITE: www.theatreofnote.com   **EMAIL**: psc@theatreofnote.com

PHONE: (323) 856-8611

ADDRESS: 1517 N Cahuenga Blvd, Hollywood CA 90028

DESCRIPTION: Est. 1981. Ensemble-based organization is dedicated to providing a creative environment in which to collaborate and develop maverick theater. NOTE produces an average of four mainstage shows a year, with a focus on premiere productions—shows that are brand new to the world, to the West Coast, to California, or to Los Angeles. NOTE also produces the annual Hollywood Performance Marathon, the NOTEworthy new play development workshops, and our educational outreach program, the Young Writers Project.

SUBMISSION MATERIALS: We accept submissions year-round. Please send scripts via email to the NOTEworthy Committee at mgrdir@theatreofnote.com.

THEATRE ODYSSEY [FL]
WEBSITE: www.theatreodyssey.org   **EMAIL:** theatreodyssey@gmail.com
PHONE: (941) 799-7224   **TWITTER:** @theatre_odyssey
ADDRESS: PO Box 1383, Sarasota FL 34234
DESCRIPTION: Est. 2006. The play selection process begins with qualified readers, who remain anonymous so as not to be influenced by a writer's identity. An independent scoring system using a uniform matrix guides the readers in choosing the most worthy plays for production. Three highly respected judges choose the best play each year at the annual festival. See website for submission guidelines.
PREFERRED LENGTH: 10-minute

THEATRE IN THE RAW
WEBSITE: www.theatreintheraw.ca   **EMAIL:** theatreintheraw@telus.net
PHONE: (604) 708-5448   **TWITTER:** @intherawtheatre
ADDRESS: 3521 Marshall St, Vancouver BC V5N 4S2 Canada
DESCRIPTION: Est. 1994. Our company is dedicated to artistic grassroots theatre in the Lower Mainland of Vancouver, as well as to presentations beyond B.C. borders. We are risk takers, creating and responding to the cultural needs of those in the Canadian and International community. Home of TITR's Biennial One-Act Contest, please inquire prior to submitting.
DEADLINE TYPE: Biennial   **PREFERRED GENRE:** Plays
PREFERRED LENGTH: 1-Act (under 1 hour)

THE THEATRE AT ST CLAUDE
WEBSITE: www.thetheatreatstclaude.com
EMAIL: booking@thetheatreatstclaude.com   **PHONE:** (504) 638-6326
TWITTER: @Theatre_StClaud
ADDRESS: 2240 St Claude Ave, New Orleans LA 70117
DESCRIPTION: Located in the heart of the historic Fabourg Marigny, The Theatre at St. Claude is in search of an audience that revels in the whisper of conspiracy, delights in a collective gasp, and enjoys a taste for the curious oddity. New Orleans premiere venue for the wild, weird, and wondrous, The Theatre at St. Claude invites you to become part of its year round programming of music and performance.

THEATRE IN THE SQUARE
WEBSITE: www.theatreinthesquare.net   **EMAIL:** info@theatreinthesquare.net
PHONE: (770) 426-4800   **FAX:** (770) 422-7436   **TWITTER:** @MTheatreSquare
ADDRESS: 11 Whitlock Ave, Marietta GA 30064

DESCRIPTION: Est. 1982. Marietta's New Theatre in the Square seeks to stimulate your senses with productions that bring you both comedy and drama in a tight-knit proscenium, black box venue. Marietta's New Theatre in the Square aims to create a legacy of cultural exploration in the North Georgia region. Marietta's New Theatre in the Square focuses on programs that create educate, and inspire the reflection of the community we live.

THEATRE OF YUGEN
WEBSITE: www.theatreofyugen.org **EMAIL**: info@theatreofyugen.org
PHONE: (415) 621-0507 **TWITTER**: @TheatreofYugen
ADDRESS: 2840 Mariposa St, San Francisco CA 94110
DESCRIPTION: Est. 1978. Traditional and new works of East-West fusion primarily based on Noh and Kyogen. Our plays tend to incorporate music and dance and as such we prefer short poetic scripts with minimal dialogue. Submissions accepted year-round.
PREFERRED LENGTH: 1-Act (under 1 hour) **FEE**: No **AGENT ONLY**: No

THEATRE RHINOCEROS
WEBSITE: www.therhino.org **EMAIL**: info@therhino.org
PHONE: (415) 552-4100 **TWITTER**: @FollowTheRhino
ADDRESS: 1 Sansome St, Ste 3500, San Francisco CA 94104
DESCRIPTION: Est. 1977. The mission of Theatre Rhinoceros is to develop and produce works of theatre that enlighten, enrich, and explore both the ordinary and extraordinary aspects of our queer community. Agent submissions only.
SUBMISSION MATERIALS: Theatre Rhinoceros does not accept unsolicited manuscripts. We are, however, interested in hearing about plays that deal specifically with marginalized communities within the larger LGBT world. If you feel this describes your play, please send us a synopsis and first ten pages of manuscript to info@therhino.org. We do accept agent submissions.
PREFERRED GENRE: Plays or Musicals **PREFERRED LENGTH**: Full-length **FEE**: No **AGENT ONLY**: Yes **SPECIAL INTEREST**: LGBT+

THEATRESQUARED
WEBSITE: theatre2.org **PHONE**: (479) 445-6333 **TWITTER**: @TheatreSquared
ADDRESS: 505 W Spring St, Fayetteville AR 72701
DESCRIPTION: Est. 2005. TheatreSquared's locally produced and nationally acclaimed productions reach 40,000 patrons each year. The company is Northwest Arkansas's only year-round professional theatre, offering a unique audience experience in an intimate space at Walton Arts Center's Nadine Baum Studios. In 2011, TheatreSquared was recognized by the American Theatre Wing, founder of the Tony Awards, as one of the nation's ten most promising emerging theatres. A professional company, TheatreSquared employs trained artists from across the country to create its 220 annual performances and is contracted with Actors' Equity. The theatre is also Arkansas's home for professional playwrights, developing scripts through the Arkansas New Play Festival in Fayetteville and Bentonville and producing new works and world premieres each year.

THEATRE THREE, INC. [TX]

WEBSITE: www.theatre3dallas.com **EMAIL:** theatre3literary@gmail.com
PHONE: (214) 871-3300 **FAX:** (214) 871-3139
ADDRESS: 2800 Routh St, Dallas TX 75201
DESCRIPTION: Est. 1961. Theatre Three illuminates the human experience with exemplary, intimate theatre by nurturing authors, artists and audiences. Theatre Three does not accept unsolicited scripts. Theatre Three is an associate member of the National New Play Network. Submitting your play to NPX, newplayexchange.org, is another opportunity to get your play read by us and other member theatres.
SUBMISSION MATERIALS: Please include the following with your submission:
• A one page description of the play/musical including: synopsis, production details including cast size and breakdown and design requirements, production and workshop history, and a statement detailing why this piece is a good fit for Theatre Three and its mission.
• The 10 pages of the script that you think best represent the story.
• Bio of the creatives-playwright, lyricist, composer, etc.
• Contact information
Please email materials to theatre3literary@gmail.com. We will follow up with a request for the full script if we are interested.
AGENT ONLY: Yes

THEATREWORKS SILICON VALLEY

WEBSITE: www.theatreworks.org **EMAIL:** gsardelli@theatreworks.org
PHONE: (650) 463-1950 **TWITTER:** @TheatreWorksSV
ADDRESS: PO Box 50458, Palo Alto CA 94303
DESCRIPTION: Est. 1970. TheatreWorks is one of America's outstanding professional theatres. Our work celebrates the human spirit through innovative productions, new works, and education programs inspired by and engaging our diverse Silicon Valley community. Home of the New Works Festival and Writer's Retreat. See website for details.
SUBMISSION MATERIALS: TheatreWorks accepts full-length scripts year-round from literary agents and theatre professionals with whom we have an existing professional relationship. **FEE:** No **AGENT ONLY:** Yes

THEATREWORKS USA

WEBSITE: www.theatreworksusa.org **EMAIL:** bpasternack@twusa.org
PHONE: (212) 647-1100 **TWITTER:** @theatreworksusa
ADDRESS: 151 W 26th St, New York NY 10001
DESCRIPTION: Est. 1961. We create, produce, and provide access to professional theatre for young and family audiences nationwide, including disadvantaged youth and under-served communities. Since our founding in 1961, we have presented more than 96.5 million children and their families with opportunities to enjoy our theatrical productions in 49 states and Canada.
SUBMISSION MATERIALS: Professional recommendations or agent submissions only. Query letter (note theme addressed), synopsis, 30-pg writing sample, full script, audio, submissions returned with SASE.
PREFERRED GENRE: All genres **PREFERRED LENGTH:** Full-length **FEE:** No
AGENT ONLY: Yes **SPECIAL INTEREST:** Theatre for Young Audiences

THEATRICAL OUTFIT

WEBSITE: www.theatricaloutfit.org   **PHONE**: (678) 528-1490
ADDRESS: Box 1555, Atlanta GA 30301
DESCRIPTION: Est. 1976. Produces world-class theatre that starts the conversations that matter.
SUBMISSION MATERIALS: Due to our staff size and resources, Theatrical Outfit does not accept unsolicited script submissions. Trust that we are hard at work considering and supporting writers by reading numerous plays each year. Currently, we are solidifying programming through our 2017-2018 season and are hard at work crafting a New Play Development Program to consider longer range projects.
FEE: No   **AGENT ONLY**: Yes

THE CHILDREN'S THEATRE COMPANY [MN]
WEBSITE: www.childrenstheatre.org   **EMAIL**: info@childrenstheatre.org
PHONE: (612) 874-0500   **TWITTER**: @ChildrensTheatr
ADDRESS: 2400 3rd Ave S, Minneapolis MN 55404
DESCRIPTION: Our mission is to create extraordinary theatre experiences that educate, challenge and inspire young people and their communities.
PREFERRED GENRE: Plays or Musicals   **PREFERRED LENGTH**: Any Length   **FEE**: No
AGENT ONLY: No   **SPECIAL INTEREST**: Theatre for Young Audiences

THUNDERCLAP PRODUCTIONS
WEBSITE: www.thunderclapproductions.com
EMAIL: info@thunderclapproductions.com   PHONE: (281) 954-4399
TWITTER: @ThunderclapProd   **ADDRESS**: 5248 Arboles Dr, Houston TX 77035
DESCRIPTION: Est. 2011. Thunderclap Productions is a Houston-based nonprofit production company dedicated to producing new, lesser-known, and under-performed plays, musicals, and screenplays. We have a commitment to making the arts accessible to all patrons and a special interest in producing works that highlight issues of social justice and inequity. We are not currently accepting submissions at this time, while we catch up on backlogged scripts to our rolling call. Please check website for posts about specific calls for scripts and forthcoming instructions about our new guidelines for submitting plays or musicals to our company.
PREFERRED GENRE: Plays or Musicals   **PREFERRED LENGTH**: Any Length
FEE: No   **AGENT ONLY**: No

TOMO SURU PLAYERS
WEBSITE: www.tomosuruplayers.com   **EMAIL**: tomosuru@gmail.com
PHONE: (604) 417-0714   **TWITTER**: @TomoSuru
ADDRESS: 303-828 Gilford St, Vancouver BC V6G 2N6 Canada
DESCRIPTION: Dedicated to providing opportunities for young people to experience theatre in the pursuit of enhancing their talent and career.
PREFERRED GENRE: Plays   **PREFERRED LENGTH**: Full-length   **FEE**: No

TOUCHSTONE THEATRE
WEBSITE: www.touchstone.org   **EMAIL**: jp@touchstone.org
PHONE: (610) 867-1689   **ADDRESS**: 321 E 4th St, Bethlehem PA 18015

DESCRIPTION: Est. 1981. Touchstone Theatre is a professional not-for-profit theatre dedicated to the creation of original work. At its center is a resident ensemble of theatre artists rooted in the local community of Bethlehem, the Greater Lehigh Valley of Pennsylvania and the international community of Ensemble Theatres. We only accept proposals for collaborative work with movement-based company ensemble.
FEE: No   **AGENT ONLY**: No:

TOWN HALL THEATRE COMPANY (THT)
WEBSITE: www.townhalltheatre.com   **EMAIL**: BoxOffice@TownHallTheatre.com
PHONE: (925) 283-6673   **FAX**: (925) 283-3481   **TWITTER**: @TownHallTheatre
ADDRESS: 3535 School St, Lafayette CA 94549
DESCRIPTION: Est. 1944. Formerly Dramateurs (1944-92). The mission of Town Hall Theatre is to serve the diverse audiences of Lamorinda and the Bay Area by presenting theatre of the highest professional standards that embodies a spirit of intelligent exploration of the human experience. We believe in nurturing new theatre artists through our arts education programs, and in bringing artists, audiences and community together in fellowship.

TRANSPORT GROUP
WEBSITE: www.transportgroup.org   **EMAIL**: krista@transportgroup.org
PHONE: (212) 564-0333   **TWITTER**: @TransportGrp
ADDRESS: 520 8th Ave, Ste 305, New York NY 10018
DESCRIPTION: Transport Group is a nonprofit, off-Broadway theatre company in New York City that stages new works and re-imagines revivals by American writers. Our visually progressive productions of emotionally classic stories explore the challenges of relationships and identity in modern America.
SUBMISSION MATERIALS: Transport Group accepts submissions of plays and musicals that engage the American experience in the 20th and 21st centuries. We welcome full submissions from represented playwrights. If you are without representation please email a bio, synopsis, and a 10-page dialogue sample, for musicals, song samples (mp3s preferred). Email submissions preferred and accepted year-round.
DEADLINE TYPE: Rolling   **PREFERRED GENRE**: Plays or Musicals
PREFERRED LENGTH: Full-length   **FEE**: No   **AGENT ONLY**: Yes

TRIANGLE PRODUCTIONS!
WEBSITE: www.tripro.org   **EMAIL**: don@trianglepro.org
PHONE: (503) 239-5919   **TWITTER**: @tripro
ADDRESS: 8420 SW Canyon Ln, #13, Portland OR 97225-3968
DESCRIPTION: Est. 1989. Triangle Productions! has enjoyed a unique niche in the arts landscape of Oregon by producing rich stories told through diverse perspectives, particularly the gay perspective. Using the company's mission, each show is chosen with the goal of promoting diversity and acceptance.

TRINITY REPERTORY COMPANY
WEBSITE: www.trinityrep.com   **EMAIL**: tdobrowsky@trinityrep.com
PHONE: (401) 351-4242   **TWITTER**: @trinityrep   **ADDRESS**: The Mabel T. Woolley Literary Dept, 201 Washington St, Providence RI 2903

DESCRIPTION: Trinity Rep's mission is to reinvent the public square with dramatic art that stimulates, educates and engages our diverse community in a continuing dialogue. In 2006, Artistic Director Curt Columbus instituted an annual creative workshop at Trinity Rep to nurture and develop new ideas and artists. During this time playwrights with projects at various stages of development work with Trinity Rep actors and directors to bring their plays closer to being ready for a full production.
PREFERRED GENRE: Plays **PREFERRED LENGTH**: Full-length **FEE**: No **AGENT ONLY**: Yes

TRIUMVIRATE ARTISTS, INC.
WEBSITE: www.triumvirateartists.com **EMAIL**: johnessay@gmail.com
TWITTER: @triumvirateart **ADDRESS**: 364 W 46th St, New York NY 10036
DESCRIPTION: We produce new plays that will, wherever possible, utilize the talents of gifted theatre professionals over the age of 55: actors, directors, playwrights, stage managers, scenic and costume designers, tech staff et al. We also plan to reach out to our aging population by bringing programs and performances to those no longer able to attend theatre.
PREFERRED GENRE: Plays **PREFERRED LENGTH**: Any Length **FEE**: No

TRUSTUS THEATRE
WEBSITE: www.trustus.org **EMAIL**: chad@trustus.org **PHONE**: (803) 254-9732
TWITTER: @trustustheatre **ADDRESS**: 520 Lady St, Columbia SC 29201
DESCRIPTION: Est. 1985. Trustus Theatre and the Trustus Company endeavors to enrich the lives and deepen the experiences of our artists and patrons by producing works that examine humanity in the 21st Century. The theatre's goal is to select challenging scripts that will start and nurture dialogues that promote discussion within the community with productions that are brought to life through dynamic storytelling and inventive designs. See website for details and updates.
PREFERRED GENRE: Plays **FEE**: Yes **AGENT ONLY**: No

TWO RIVER THEATRE COMPANY (TRTC)
WEBSITE: www.trtc.org **EMAIL**: achapin@trtc.org **PHONE**: (732) 345-1400
FAX: (732) 345-1414 **TWITTER**: @TwoRiverTheater
ADDRESS: 21 Bridge Ave, Red Bank NJ 7701
DESCRIPTION: We create great American theater by developing and producing new works and world masterpieces that most richly direct our gaze to the life of the human spirit. We cultivate an audience that cherishes the intimate joy of theater, enriched when shared by a community of others.
SUBMISSION MATERIALS: We are able to accept script submissions from agents only. If you are unrepresented, feel free to send us information about upcoming productions and readings. This information can be sent by email or hard copy to Anika Chapin, Literary Manager. **PREFERRED LENGTH**: Full-length **FEE**: No **AGENT ONLY**: Yes

UNDERSCORE THEATRE
WEBSITE: underscoretheatre.org **EMAIL**: literary@underscoretheatre.org
TWITTER: @_theatre **ADDRESS**: PO Box 408748, Chicago IL 60640
DESCRIPTION: An ensemble of artists dedicated to creating new, original musical theatre in Chicago. We strive to create opportunities for new writers and composers to develop their work through constructive feedback from their peers in our UNDERSCORE EXPERIMENTS workshop series, and performance opportunities in a variety

of contexts, from informal staged readings, discussion groups, and writing sessions, to our bimonthly UNDERSCORE PRESENTS cabarets showcasing songs from up-and-coming composers, to our annual Chicago Musicals Festival where we premier complete new works, to our Mainstage productions. We are proud to maintain an open submission policy.

SUBMISSION MATERIALS: Email only. See website for submission details.

PREFERRED GENRE: Musicals **PREFERRED LENGTH:** Full-length **FEE:** No

UNICORN THEATRE

WEBSITE: www.unicorntheatre.org/?page=about-new-play-development
EMAIL: clevin@unicorntheatre.org
PHONE: (816) 531-7529 **FAX:** (816) 531-0421 **TWITTER:** @UnicornTheatre
ADDRESS: 3828 Main St, Kansas City MO 64111
DESCRIPTION: Est. 1974. Unicorn Theatre fosters the next generation of great American writers and artists, creating innovative and intimate theatrical experiences that transcend the ordinary. We inspire the community to think and feel deeply; to see the world in new and different ways. Unicorn strives to be one of the preeminent homes for new plays in the country.

SUBMISSION MATERIALS: Unicorn Theatre will utilize the New Play Exchange to read and evaluate new works. We receive hundreds of plays each season and we do our best to read and respond to every single one. So that we can best serve and respond to the works we receive, we will no longer accept unsolicited plays outside of the In-Progress New Play Reading Series.

PREFERRED GENRE: Plays **FEE:** No **AGENT ONLY:** No

UPSTREAM ARTISTS' COLLECTIVE

WEBSITE: www.upstreamartistscollective.org/submt
EMAIL: keith@upstreamartistscollective.org **TWITTER:** @upstreamartists
ADDRESS: 37 Grand Ave, Brooklyn NY 11205
DESCRIPTION: A group of interdisciplinary artists making theater with an environmental conscience seeking to reexamine what it means to be human on a global scale for the purposes of understanding our relationship to a changing climate. Upstream develops new work and reexamines existing work with an eco-arts aesthetic and makes this work accessible to audiences of all ages, colors, identities, incomes, and abilities.

SUBMISSION MATERIALS: Upstream will accept general script submissions at any time. All submissions must include a full script, character breakdown and description (including any doubling possibilities), and a brief synopsis. No snail mail scripts or scripts in Word documents will be considered. Incomplete submissions will not be considered. **PREFERRED LENGTH:** Full-length **FEE:** No **AGENT ONLY:** No

URBANITE THEATRE

WEBSITE: www.urbanitetheatre.com **EMAIL:** info@urbanitetheatre.com
PHONE: (941) 321-1397 **TWITTER:** @urbanitetheatre
ADDRESS: 1487 2nd St, Sarasota FL 34236
DESCRIPTION: Urbanite Theatre brings compelling, intimate live theater experiences to downtown Sarasota. Our commitment to fresh works, burgeoning playwrights, and

actor-driven productions provides the region with exciting, contemporary playgoing opportunities.

PREFERRED GENRE: Plays   **PREFERRED LENGTH**: Full-length   **FEE**: No   **AGENT ONLY**: No

URBAN STAGES
WEBSITE: urbanstages.org/submissions   **EMAIL**: urbanstage@aol.com
PHONE: (212) 421-1380   **TWITTER**: @UrbanStages
ADDRESS: 555 8th Ave, Rm 1800, New York NY 10018
DESCRIPTION: Mission: to champion new works by artists of diverse cultural backgrounds and to make these works available to all.
SUBMISSION MATERIALS: No email submissions. Plays MAY HAVE BEEN developed or produced elsewhere, BUT NEVER PRODUCED in New York City. With your submission, please include biography and/or history of the play, character breakdown, synopsis, and SASE. See website for details.
PREFERRED GENRE: Plays   **PREFERRED LENGTH**: Full-length   **FEE**: No   **AGENT ONLY**: No

UTAH SHAKESPEARE FESTIVAL
WEBSITE: www.bard.org   **EMAIL**: guestservices@bard.org
PHONE: (435) 586-7880   **FAX**: (435) 865-8003   **TWITTER**: @UtahShakespeare
ADDRESS: 351 W Center St, Cedar City UT 84720
DESCRIPTION: The Utah Shakespeare Festival presents life-affirming classic and contemporary plays in repertory, with Shakespeare as our cornerstone. These plays are enhanced by interactive festival experiences which entertain, enrich, and educate.

VANTAGE THEATRE
WEBSITE: www.vantagetheatre.com   **EMAIL**: vantagetheatre@gmail.com
PHONE: (858) 456-9664   **ADDRESS**: 1251 W Muirlands Dr, La Jolla CA 92037
DESCRIPTION: VANTAGE THEATRE presents thought-provoking professional theatrical productions. We concentrate on presenting original plays, as well as known contemporary or classic theatre produced from a different "vantage point" We seek to present the "AHA" moment-- not only to entertain, but also to illuminate, enlighten, and elevate. Site- specific producing and the creation of producing partners at each site assists us to fulfill our mission of bringing theatre in new ways to new venues, reaching new audiences.
PREFERRED GENRE: Plays   **PREFERRED LENGTH**: Any Length   **FEE**: No   **AGENT ONLY**: No

VENICE LITTLE THEATRE (VLT)
WEBSITE: www.venicestage.com   **EMAIL**: murraychase@venicestage.com
PHONE: (941) 488-1115   **FAX**: (941) 484-9437   **TWITTER**: @VeniceTheatre
ADDRESS: 140 W Tampa Ave, Venice FL 34285
DESCRIPTION: We exist to celebrate and nurture creative expression, to foster human communication and understanding, and to delight and challenge our audiences through theatre and the performing arts of the highest quality.

VENUS THEATRE
WEBSITE: www.venustheatre.org   **EMAIL**: submissionsofvenus@gmail.com

PHONE: (202) 236-4078 **TWITTER**: @venus_theatre
ADDRESS: 21 C St, Laurel MD 20707
DESCRIPTION: A women's theatre company that perform plays by talented women playwrights and employs talented female actors, directors, designers, and others.
SUBMISSION MATERIALS: Please submit an introductory paragraph, a synopsis, a bio and/or author's history of the play, character breakdown, brief description or synopsis of the play, and script to: submissionsofvenus@gmail.com. See website for details.
FEE: No **AGENT ONLY**: No **SPECIAL INTEREST**: Feminism/Women's Rights

VICTORY GARDENS THEATER
WEBSITE: www.victorygardens.org **EMAIL**: edaniels@victorygardens.org
PHONE: (773) 549-5788 **TWITTER**: @VictoryGardens
ADDRESS: 2433 N Lincoln Ave, Chicago IL 60614
DESCRIPTION: Victory Gardens develops and produces new plays from its Ensemble Playwrights through readings, workshops and productions, and provides necessary resources to further cultivate their individual voices and craft. Through their seven year residencies, the playwrights are involved in the artistic life of the theater. During that time, the playwrights also engage audiences throughout Chicago's diverse communities and participate in Victory Gardens educational and community programs. After the residency concludes, the playwrights will join the Alumni, whereby they will maintain an artistic relationship with Victory Gardens.
PREFERRED GENRE: Plays **PREFERRED LENGTH**: Full-length **FEE**: No **AGENT ONLY**: Yes

VICTORY THEATRE CENTER
WEBSITE: thevictorytheatrecenter.org **EMAIL**: victoryadmin@mindspring.com
PHONE: (818) 841-4404 **TWITTER**: @VictoryTheatre
ADDRESS: 3326 W Victory Blvd, Burbank CA 91505
DESCRIPTION: Est. 1979. Our mission is to be a creative hub for audiences and artists to engage with one another through ground-breaking theatrical productions, educational opportunities, and social events in an intimate setting that can't help resulting in intoxicating conversation. Submissions accepted year-round.
SUBMISSION MATERIALS: Because The VTC is one of only a few venues that produces original material, the volume of submitted scripts is high. It will take time for your material to be processed. Please be assured your work will be read. We prefer that playwrights email their plays as a PDF to victoryadmin@mindspring.com
PREFERRED GENRE: Plays **PREFERRED LENGTH**: Full-length **FEE**: No **AGENT ONLY**: No

VILLAGE THEATRE
WEBSITE: www.villagetheatre.org **EMAIL**: bivie@villagetheatre.org
PHONE: (425) 392-1942 **TWITTER**: @TheVillageVault
ADDRESS: 303 Front St N, Issaquah WA 98027
DESCRIPTION: Mission: To be a regionally recognized and nationally influential center of excellence in family theatre.
PREFERRED GENRE: Musicals **PREFERRED LENGTH**: Full-length
FEE: No **AGENT ONLY**: No

VINEYARD THEATRE
WEBSITE: www.vineyardtheatre.org **EMAIL**: mweiner@vineyardtheatre.org

PHONE: (212) 353-3366   **TWITTER**: @vineyardtheatre
ADDRESS: 108 E 15th St, New York NY 10003
DESCRIPTION: A nonprofit theatre company dedicated to new work, bold programming, and the support of artists. One of America's preeminent centers for the creation of new plays and musicals, Vineyard Theatre has consistently premiered provocative, groundbreaking works by both new and established writers.
PREFERRED GENRE: Plays or Musicals   **PREFERRED LENGTH**: Full-length
FEE: No   **AGENT ONLY**: Yes

VIRGINIA REPERTORY THEATRE
WEBSITE: va-rep.org   **EMAIL**: contact@virginiarep.org   **PHONE**: (804) 783-1688
TWITTER: @VirginiaRep   **ADDRESS**: 114 W Broad St, Richmond VA 23220
DESCRIPTION: Virginia Repertory Theatre creates professional productions of the great comedies, dramas, and musicals – past, present and future. We seek to be a regional theatre of national standing. We embrace the art form in its entirety, presenting plays of all genres and national origins, serving an audience of all ages and backgrounds. In keeping with the legacies of Barksdale and Theatre IV, the hallmark of our nonprofit company is community engagement. To that end, we seek national caliber excellence in the arts, education, children's health, and community leadership.
SUBMISSION MATERIALS: Unfortunately, due to the high volume of submissions on hand, Virginia Rep is not able to accept unsolicited scripts.
PREFERRED GENRE: Plays or Musicals   **PREFERRED LENGTH**: Any Length   **FEE**: No
AGENT ONLY: Yes   **SPECIAL INTEREST**: All; Theatre for Young Audiences

VIRGINIA STAGE COMPANY
WEBSITE: www.vastage.com   **EMAIL**: pmullins@vastage.org
PHONE: (757) 627-1234   **TWITTER**: @VAstage
ADDRESS: PO Box 3770, Norfolk VA 23514
DESCRIPTION: Est. 1978. Virginia Stage Company strives to celebrate our community's rich diversity and reaches out to the broadest possible constituency for all our work. Our ongoing agenda at VSC includes brainstorming new ways for people to experience theater as both our society and our artform evolve.
PREFERRED GENRE: All genres   **FEE**: No   **AGENT ONLY**: No

VITAL THEATRE COMPANY
WEBSITE: www.vitaltheatre.org   **EMAIL**: info@vitaltheatre.org
PHONE: (212) 579-0528   **TWITTER**: @VitalTheatre
ADDRESS: 2162 Broadway, Fl 4, New York NY 10024
DESCRIPTION: Est. 1999. VITAL THEATRE COMPANY is a community of artists who believe that a shared theatrical experience profoundly affects people's lives. We create stories that challenge our audience to ask questions, make discoveries and engage in dialogue.
PREFERRED GENRE: Theatre for Young Audiences   **PREFERRED LENGTH**: Full-length
FEE: No   **AGENT ONLY**: Yes

VS. THEATRE COMPANY
WEBSITE: www.vstheatre.org   **EMAIL**: jclark@vstheatre.org

PHONE: (323) 739-4411 **TWITTER:** @VS_Theatre
ADDRESS: 5453 West Pico Blvd, Los Angeles CA 90019
DESCRIPTION: Est. 2004. VS. Theatre Company, is a small, dedicated group of passionate artists devoted to producing original works and Los Angeles Premieres by the best contemporary playwrights in America. At this time, VS. is only accepting agent solicited scripts.
PREFERRED GENRE: Plays **PREFERRED LENGTH:** Full-length **FEE:** No **AGENT ONLY:** Yes

THE WALLIS ANNENBERG CENTER FOR THE PERFORMING ARTS
WEBSITE: thewallis.org **EMAIL:** info@thewallis.org **PHONE:** (310) 246-3800
TWITTER: @TheWallisBH
ADDRESS: 9390 N Santa Monica Blvd, Beverly Hills CA 90210
DESCRIPTION: Est. 2013. The mission of The Wallis is to create, present and celebrate unique performing arts events and educational programs that reflect the rich cultural diversity of our community.
SUBMISSION MATERIALS: We only accepts full-length scripts and project proposals year-round from literary agents and arts professionals with whom we have an ongoing professional relationship.
PREFERRED LENGTH: Full-length **FEE:** No **AGENT ONLY:** Yes
SPECIAL INTEREST: Theatre for Young Audiences

WALNUT STREET THEATRE
WEBSITE: www.walnutstreettheatre.org **PHONE:** (215) 574-3550
TWITTER: WalnutStTheatre **ADDRESS:** 825 Walnut St, Philadelphia PA 19103
DESCRIPTION: Est. 1809. America's oldest theatre, the Official State Theatre of Pennsylvania, and a National Historic Landmark. The mission of Walnut Street Theatre Company is to sustain the tradition of professional theatre and contribute to its future viability and vitality.
SUBMISSION MATERIALS: 1-2 pg synopsis, 5-10 pg excerpt, character breakdown, bio(s), demo CD for musicals, SASE. Please DO NOT send full script unsolicited. Response time: 6 mos. Submissions should be sent attn: Literary Manager.
PREFERRED GENRE: Plays or Musicals **PREFERRED LENGTH:** Full-length
FEE: No **AGENT ONLY:** No

WASATCH THEATRE COMPANY
WEBSITE: www.wasatchtheatre.org **EMAIL:** wasatchtheatre@hotmail.com
ADDRESS: 10776 Pine Grove Way S, Jordan UT 84095
DESCRIPTION: The mission of Wasatch Theatre Company is: to provoke thought and action by selecting and producing a variety of theatrical experiences and encounters; to specialize in a presentational style of production making use of minimal resources; to increase awareness of, respect for, and participation in theatre.

WASHINGTON STAGE GUILD
WEBSITE: www.stageguild.org **EMAIL:** info@stageguild.org
PHONE: (240) 582-0050 **FAX:** (240) 582-0051 **TWITTER:** @WashStageGuild
ADDRESS: 1901 14th St, NW, Washington DC 20011

DESCRIPTION: The Washington Stage Guild (incorporated as Theatre Downtown, Inc.) produces eloquent plays of idea and argument, passion and wit – plays from all periods of world drama enacted by a classical ensemble with a contemporary sensibility – smart plays for a smart town!

WATERTOWER THEATRE
WEBSITE: www.watertowertheatre.org
EMAIL: artistic@watertowertheatre.org   **PHONE**: (972) 450-6230
FAX: (972) 450-6244   **TWITTER**: @WTTheatre
ADDRESS: 15650 Addison Rd, Addison TX 75001
DESCRIPTION: WaterTower Theatre's mission is to create innovative, diverse theatre that builds community by fostering empathy and dialogue.
SUBMISSION MATERIALS: Resume, brief synopsis, 10-pg sample. Musical submissions: up to four audio samples (.mp3 or .wav preferred). Submissions should be emailed as PDFs with the subject line: PLAY SUBMISSION - Last Name, First Name - TITLE.
PREFERRED GENRE: Plays or Musicals   **PREFERRED LENGTH**: Full-length
AGENT ONLY: No

WEATHERVANE PLAYHOUSE
WEBSITE: www.weathervaneplayhouse.com
EMAIL: mycp@weathervaneplayhouse.com   **PHONE**: (330) 836-2626
TWITTER: WeathervanePlay   **ADDRESS**: 1301 Weathervane Ln, Akron OH 44313
DESCRIPTION: Weathervane Community Playhouse produces high-quality live theater with volunteer artists, designers, and technicians under professional direction, provides education and training in theater arts and appreciation, and engages and entertains its audience and constituents to enrich the quality of life in Northeast Ohio.

WEIRD SISTERS WOMEN'S THEATRE COLLECTIVE
WEBSITE: www.weirdsisterscollective.com
DESCRIPTION: Est. 2004. In addition to producing plays by, about, and for women, we also hold informal salons, readings, and workshops where we explore women's issues and celebrate women's work.
FEE: No   **AGENT ONLY**: No   **SPECIAL INTEREST**: Feminism/Women's Rights

WELLFLEET HARBOR ACTORS THEATER
WEBSITE: www.what.org   **EMAIL**: jeffry@what.org   **PHONE**: (508) 349-9428
TWITTER: WHATorg   **ADDRESS**: PO Box 797, 2357 Rte 6, Wellfleet MA 2667
DESCRIPTION: The Mission of Wellfleet Harbor Actors Theater is to present professional quality theater to its audiences; to provide an alternative theater experience not found elsewhere in the region; to advance and preserve the art of the theater for the education and appreciation of the public.
PREFERRED LENGTH: Full-length   **FEE**: No   **AGENT ONLY**: No

WEST END STUDIO THEATRE
WEBSITE: www.westperformingarts.com   **EMAIL**: admin@westperformingarts.com
PHONE: (831) 425-9378   **ADDRESS**: 335 Spreckels Dr, Ste F, Aptos CA 95003
DESCRIPTION: We provide educational experiences in literature, performing, ex-

pressive and creative arts through classes and productions. We give young artists and audiences the invaluable knowledge that their imaginations have had a positive and profound impact on their world. **FEE:** No **AGENT ONLY:** No

WESTCLIFFE CENTER FOR THE PERFORMING ARTS
WEBSITE: www.jonestheater.com **PHONE:** (719) 783-3004
ADDRESS: PO Box 790, Westcliffe CO 81252
DESCRIPTION: The Westcliffe Center for the Performing Arts was incorporated in 1992 and received its not-for-profit status the following year. Our goals are to provide a Center for the Performing Arts in the picturesque Wet Mountain Valley of Colorado. We encourage new playwrights and provide classes and theater training each summer through the co-operation of local universities.
PREFERRED GENRE: Plays or Musicals

WESTERN STAGE
WEBSITE: www.westernstage.com **EMAIL:** jselover@hartnell.edu
PHONE: (831) 755-6987 **FAX:** (831) 755-6954 **TWITTER:** westernstage
ADDRESS: 334 1/2 Capitol St, Salinas CA 93901
DESCRIPTION: Est. 1974. TWS is committed to enriching the culture of its community by bringing together professional artists, theatre students, and community members to produce a dynamic season of plays that enhances the lives of both the artist and audience; developing new works that speak to the history and culture of the Salinas Valley; and providing educational opportunities to allow students of all skill levels to explore and develop their unique talents. Special consideration given to works which are particularly relevant to Latino audiences.
PREFERRED GENRE: All genres **PREFERRED LENGTH:** Full-length
FEE: No **AGENT ONLY:** No

WESTON PLAYHOUSE
WEBSITE: www.westonplayhouse.org **EMAIL:** sstettler@westonplayhouse.org
PHONE: (802) 824-8167 **FAX:** (802) 717-1032 **TWITTER:** @westonplayhouse
ADDRESS: 703 Main St, Weston VT 05161
DESCRIPTION: Est. 1935. The company builds on and enhances the unique assets of its Vermont village campus to produce a diverse, entertaining, and challenging season of live professional theatre and high impact events; enrich the theatergoing experience with education and outreach programs for all ages; and make significant contributions to the American theatre through training programs, play development, and retreats. See website for info on our New Works Program, New Musical Award, Artists Retreat, Workshops, and Full Productions. **AGENT ONLY:** Yes

WESTPORT COUNTRY PLAYHOUSE
WEBSITE: www.westportplayhouse.org **EMAIL:** bhuisking@westportplayhouse.org
PHONE: (203) 227-5137 **FAX:** (203) 221-7482 **TWITTER:** @WCPlayhouse
ADDRESS: 25 Powers Ct, Westport CT 6880
DESCRIPTION: The Westport Country Playhouse is a nationally recognized, not-for-profit, professional theater under the artistic direction of Mark Lamos and management leadership of Michael Barker. The mission of Westport Country Playhouse is to enrich, enlighten, and engage our community through the power of professionally

produced theater worth talking about and the welcoming experience of our Playhouse campus. Westport Country Playhouse accepts scripts for plays and musicals only when submitted by an agent. The Playhouse does not accept unsolicited scripts nor does it accept film treatments or screenplays. Response time is six to nine months. Scripts will be returned only by pre-stamped, self-addressed mailing envelope included with the script submission.
PREFERRED GENRE: Plays or Musicals **PREFERRED LENGTH**: Full-length
FEE: No **AGENT ONLY**: Yes

WHITE HORSE THEATER COMPANY
WEBSITE: www.whitehorsetheater.com **EMAIL**: cymarion@whitehorsetheater.com
PHONE: (212) 592-3706 **ADDRESS**: 205 3rd Ave, #6-N, New York NY 10003
DESCRIPTION: Est. 2003. White Horse Theater Company is a nonprofit organization dedicated to producing and developing American plays. We seek to investigate and celebrate American culture by re-examining American classics and nurturing new American voices. We aim to champion great American playwrights by revitalizing their masterworks and shedding new light on their seldom-produced works. We strive to support emerging American playwrights by offering them developmental readings, labs and workshops. White Horse is committed to making high-quality theater and sharing our passion for American plays and playwrights with our fellow artists and audiences. **FEE**: No **AGENT ONLY**: No

WILDCLAW THEATRE
WEBSITE: www.wildclawtheatre.com **EMAIL**: literary@wildclawtheatre.com
TWITTER: @WildClawTheatre **ADDRESS**: 3900 N Monticello, Chicago IL 60613
DESCRIPTION: Home of Deathscribe International Festival of Horror Radio Plays Writers may submit up to two radio plays to Deathscribe in any given year. Five scripts will be selected from all submissions. These five pieces will be performed on stage in front of a live audience. The writer of the winning piece, chosen by a celebrity panel of judges, will receive the coveted Bloody Axe Award, as well as a $100 cash prize.
SUBMISSION MATERIALS: See website for submission information.
PREFERRED GENRE: Radio plays **PREFERRED LENGTH**: 10-minute
FEE: No **AGENT ONLY**: No

WILL GEER THEATRICUM BOTANICUM
WEBSITE: www.theatricum.com **EMAIL**: info@theatricum.com
PHONE: (310) 455-2322 **FAX**: (310) 455-3724 **TWITTER**: @theatricum
ADDRESS: PO Box 1222, Topanga CA 90290
DESCRIPTION: Est. 1973. Our mission is to elevate, educate and entertain audiences of all ages by presenting thought-provoking classics, socially relevant plays, and education programs in a beautiful, natural outdoor sanctuary for the arts. By passing on a sense of history to young people and adults alike, great works of art inform their present and inspire their future. A true renaissance theatre, we offer a diversity of programming from Shakespeare to poetry to folk music to the development of future playwrights – all to help understand the world we live in and to embrace our shared humanity. The submission window is September 1 – November 1 annually. We will close this window after the first 200 submissions are received. These works will be considered for development and also production. See website for details.

SUBMISSION DEADLINE: 11/01/2018 **DEADLINE TYPE:** Annual **PREFERRED GENRE:** Plays

WILLIAMS STREET REP
WEBSITE: wsrep.org **EMAIL:** boxoffice@rauecenter.org **PHONE:** 815.356.9212
TWITTER: @WSRep **ADDRESS:** 108 Minnie St, Crystal Lake IL 60014
DESCRIPTION: Non-profit theater company in Chicago's NW suburb. McHenry County's only professional theater company. Housed at the Raue Center for the Arts.
PREFERRED GENRE: Plays **PREFERRED LENGTH:** Full-length **FEE:** No **AGENT ONLY:** No

WILMA THEATER
WEBSITE: www.wilmatheater.org **EMAIL:** KMecleary@WilmaTheater.org
PHONE: (215) 893-9456 **TWITTER:** @TheWilmaTheater
ADDRESS: 265 S Broad St, Philadelphia PA 19107
DESCRIPTION: Est. 1979. The Wilma Theater creates living, adventurous art. We engage artists and audiences in imaginative reflection on the complexities of contemporary life. We present bold, original, well-crafted productions that represent a range of voices, viewpoints, and styles.
PREFERRED LENGTH: Full-length **FEE:** No **AGENT ONLY:** Yes

WP THEATER
WEBSITE: wptheater.org **EMAIL:** literary@womensproject.org
PHONE: (212) 765-1706 **TWITTER:** @WPTheater
ADDRESS: 55 West End Ave, New York NY 10023
DESCRIPTION: WP THEATER (Formerly known as Women's Project Theater) is the nation's oldest and largest theater company dedicated to developing, producing and promoting the work of female-identified and trans theater artists at every stage in their careers. WP Theater supports a rotating Lab of five playwrights. Our commitment to the current and alumnae writers from the Playwrights Lab, limits the number of productions available to writers outside the Lab. If you would like to invite a WP staff member to come see a reading, workshop or production, please email literary@womensproject.org. We receive many requests and are only able to attend a limited number of events.
SUBMISSION MATERIALS: Submission Procedure: WP Theater does not accept unsolicited scripts. Plays must be submitted through a bona fide industry agent.
FEE: No **AGENT ONLY:** Yes **SPECIAL INTEREST:** Feminism/Women's Rights

WOMEN'S THEATRE COMPANY
WEBSITE: www.womenstheater.org **EMAIL:** info@womenstheater.org
PHONE: (973) 335-3038 **TWITTER:** @Womenstheater
ADDRESS: 1130 Knoll Rd, Lake Hiawatha NJ 7034
DESCRIPTION: The Women's Theater Company has provided a distinct voice and imprint on the state's professional theatre community since its start in 1993. Unlike any of the other nearly 30 professional theatre companies in NJ, the Women's Theater is dedicated to development, promotion and inclusion of women in all aspects of theatre production. The voices of these women have begun to be heard thanks to the commitment of the Women's Theater to do just that.
PREFERRED GENRE: All genres **PREFERRED LENGTH:** Full-length **FEE:** No

AGENT ONLY: No **SPECIAL INTEREST:** Feminism/Women's Rights

WOOLLY MAMMOTH THEATRE COMPANY
WEBSITE: www.woollymammoth.net **EMAIL:** submissions@woollymammoth.net
PHONE: (202) 393-3939 **TWITTER:** @woollymammothtc
ADDRESS: 641 D St NW, Washington DC 20004
DESCRIPTION: Est. 1980 to create rousing, visceral, enlightening theatre experiences that galvanize diverse artists and audiences to engage with our world in unexpected and often challenging ways. not accept unsolicited scripts. However, in an effort to support the Washington, DC artistic community, we do accept unsolicited ten-page samples exclusively from writers living in the DC area.
PREFERRED GENRE: Plays **PREFERRED LENGTH:** Full-length **FEE:** No **AGENT ONLY:** Yes

WORKING THEATER
WEBSITE: www.theworkingtheater.org **EMAIL:** mark@theworkingtheater.org
ADDRESS: 520 8th Ave, Ste 303, New York NY 10018
DESCRIPTION: Great theater strives to tell stories that illuminate, challenge and alter our perceptions, that show us who we are and transform us in the process.
SUBMISSION MATERIALS: To submit your work to us, please either do so through an agent or send us a synopsis of the play and a ten-page sample of the text, along with a bio or resume. Then please be patient. We have a small staff and it sometimes takes us a while to get back to you. Thanks! We're happy to receive your material through the internet (to help save a tree or two), so please email workingtheaterscripts@gmail.com.

WORKSHOP THEATER COMPANY
WEBSITE: www.workshoptheater.org **EMAIL:** info@workshoptheater.org
PHONE: (212) 695-4173 **FAX:** (212) 695-3384
ADDRESS: 312 W 36th St, 4th Fl, New York NY 10018
DESCRIPTION: Est. 1994. The Workshop Theater is a vital resource for artists and audiences to explore new works. From staged readings to polished productions, over 170 professional playwrights, actors and directors are given the tools of our development process to bring their works to life. See website for details.

WRITERS THEATRE
WEBSITE: www.writerstheatre.org **EMAIL:** literary@writerstheatre.org
PHONE: (847) 242-6001 **TWITTER:** @WritersTheatre
ADDRESS: 321 Park Ave, Glencoe IL 60022
DESCRIPTION: Est. 1992. Writers Theatre is committed to commissioning, developing and producing new plays, musicals and adaptations. Since our founding in 1992, we have produced 26 world premieres: 7 plays, 14 adaptations, 3 musicals. In addition to these premieres, WT is also committed to providing playwrights the chance to continue refining their new work after it debuts, via developmental workshop opportunities and fully-staged second productions. See website for details.
PREFERRED GENRE: Plays or Musicals **PREFERRED LENGTH:** Full-length
FEE: No **AGENT ONLY:** Yes

WRITERS THEATRE OF NEW JERSEY
WEBSITE: www.wtnj.org **EMAIL**: literary@wtnj.org **PHONE**: (973) 514-1787
ADDRESS: PO Box 1295, Madison NJ 7940
DESCRIPTION: Est. 1986. Submissions must meet one of the criteria listed on our site. Submissions accepted year-round by e-mail only.
PREFERRED GENRE: Plays **PREFERRED LENGTH**: Any Length **FEE**: No **AGENT ONLY**: No

XOREGOS PERFORMING COMPANY
WEBSITE: xoregos.com **EMAIL**: xoregos@juno.com **PHONE**: (212) 239-8405
ADDRESS: 496 9th Ave, #4-A, New York NY 10018
DESCRIPTION: The Xoregos Performing Company explores the classical theater repertoire as well as new playwrights' works, premieres, old dances, poetry, and arcane musical choices in its programs.

YALE REPERTORY THEATRE
WEBSITE: www.yalerep.org **EMAIL**: literary.office@yale.edu
PHONE: (203) 436-9098 **TWITTER**: @yalerep
ADDRESS: PO Box 208244, New Haven CT 6520
DESCRIPTION: Est. 1966. Yale Repertory Theatre accepts submissions of full-length plays, musicals, translations, and adaptations. All submissions are considered for productions at Yale Rep and for development opportunities with the Binger Center for New Theatre. Playwrights must submit their work either through established agents or by first sending a letter of inquiry, accompanied by a brief synopsis, cast breakdown, a ten-page dialogue sample, and a résumé. The Literary Office will review these materials and contact playwrights regarding Yale Rep's interest in reading a full manuscript. See website for details.
DEADLINE TYPE: Rolling **PREFERRED GENRE**: Plays or Musicals
PREFERRED LENGTH: Full-length **FEE**: No **AGENT ONLY**: No

YORK SHAKESPEARE COMPANY
WEBSITE: www.yorkshakespeare.org **EMAIL**: casting@yorkshakespeare.org
TWITTER: @YorkShakespeare
DESCRIPTION: Producing high-quality classical and contemporary theater in rotating repertory for the last 15 years.
SUBMISSION MATERIALS: Unsolicited scripts should be emailed to casting@yorkshakespeare.org.
PREFERRED GENRE: Plays or Musicals **PREFERRED LENGTH**: Any Length
FEE: No **AGENT ONLY**: No

YORK THEATRE COMPANY
WEBSITE: www.yorktheatre.org **EMAIL**: submissions@yorktheatre.org
PHONE: (212) 935-5820 **FAX**: (212) 832-0037
ADDRESS: 619 Lexington Ave, New York NY 10022
DESCRIPTION: Est. 1985. Electronic submissions (email/Dropbox) are preferred, but not necessary. The York's mission concerns musicals and the occasional play with music. Non-musical plays will be declined unread.

PREFERRED GENRE: Musicals   **PREFERRED LENGTH:** Full-length
FEE: No   **AGENT ONLY:** No

YOUNG PLAYWRIGHTS THEATER (YPT)
WEBSITE: www.youngplaywrightstheater.org   **EMAIL:** tpowell@yptdc.org
PHONE: (202) 387-9173   **FAX:** (202) 387-9175
ADDRESS: 2437 15th St NW, Washington DC 20009
DESCRIPTION: Young Playwrights' Theater seeks to create social justice by providing all young people with the opportunity to realize the power and value of their own voices. A nationally recognized leader in arts education, YPT proves the benefit of the arts in the classroom by demonstrating the direct and positive impact of an active, arts-integrated process on student learning, and strives to close the academic achievement gap by increasing equitable access to arts education for all students.

YOUTH PERFORMANCE CO
WEBSITE: www.youthperformanceco.com   **EMAIL:** info@youthperformanceco.org
PHONE: (612) 623-9180   **FAX:** (612) 623-1020
ADDRESS: 3338 University Ave SE, Minneapolis MN 55414
DESCRIPTION: Youth Performance Company is a youth-inspired theatre that serves the community and fuels the creative spirit of youth by developing, empowering and advancing young artists.
FEE: No   **AGENT ONLY:** No   **SPECIAL INTEREST:** Theatre for Young Audiences

ZEITGEIST MULTI-DISCIPLINARY ARTS CENTER
WEBSITE: www.zeitgeistnola.org   **EMAIL:** rene@zeitgeistnola.org
PHONE: (504) 827-5858   **TWITTER:** @ZeitgeistNOLA
ADDRESS: 1220A N Robertson St, New Orleans LA 70116
DESCRIPTION: Zeitgeist Multi-Disciplinary Arts Center has been bringing alternative art to New Orleans since November 1986 – 31 years and still counting! We are an entirely volunteer, artist-run organization that does not receive grants or public funds. Presenting film, video, performance art, visual art and literary events seven nights a week, all year round, Zeitgeist is considered one of the premier alternative arts center in the South.

ZOETIC STAGE
WEBSITE: www.zoeticstage.org   **EMAIL:** literary@zoeticstage.com
PHONE: (305) 741-3180   **TWITTER:** @ZoeticStageMIA
ADDRESS: 7545 SW 54 Court, Miami FL 33143
DESCRIPTION: Zoetic Stage accepts new, previously unproduced full-length plays from literary agents. We are unable to accept unsolicited manuscripts by playwrights who are not represented (lawyers and law firms do not qualify as representation). Florida residents may submit a manuscript without representation.
PREFERRED GENRE: Plays   **PREFERRED LENGTH:** Full-length   **FEE:** No   **AGENT ONLY:** Yes

COLLEGES & UNIVERSITIES

ACADEMY OF ART UNIVERSITY
WEBSITE: www.academyart.edu **EMAIL:** info@academyart.edu
PHONE: (800) 544-2787 **FAX:** (415) 618-6287
ADDRESS: 79 New Montgomery St, San Francisco CA 94105

ARIZONA STATE UNIVERSITY
WEBSITE: filmdancetheatre.asu.edu/degree-programs/theatre-dramatic-writing-mfa-mfa **EMAIL:** Guillermo.Reyes@asu.edu
PHONE: (480) 965-0519 **FAX:** (480) 965-5351
ADDRESS: School of Theatre and Film, Box 872002, Tempe AZ 85287
DESCRIPTION: The concentration in dramatic writing under the MFA in theatre will include course work in playwriting, screenwriting, historical studies in theatre, dramatic theory, directing new work, literary management, electives and related topics such as writing for solo performance, storytelling, devising and collaborative writing.

ART/MOSCOW ART INSTITUTE
WEBSITE: amrep.org **EMAIL:** information@amrep.org **PHONE:** (617) 496-2000
FAX: (617) 495-1705 **ADDRESS:** 64 Brattle St, Cambridge MA 02138
DESCRIPTION: MLA degree. The dramaturgy program provides practical and academic training for literary directors, dramaturgs, playwrights, and theater critics. Includes a 3-month residency in Moscow where students are taught by Russian dramaturgs and critics and assist in the development of Institute productions. See website for details.

BOSTON PLAYWRIGHTS' THEATRE AT BOSTON UNIVERSITY
WEBSITE: www.bu.edu/bpt/playwriting-program.html **EMAIL:** ksnodgra@bu.edu
PHONE: (617) 353-5443 **FAX:** (617) 353-6196 **TWITTER:** @PlaywrightsBPT
ADDRESS: 949 Commonwealth Ave, Boston MA 02215
DESCRIPTION: After more than 30 years of building our nationally recognized Playwriting Program—founded by Nobel Laureate Derek Walcott in 1981—we now offer a three-year MFA in Playwriting that combines the best of our traditions with a new and exciting collaboration with the award-winning School of Theatre at Boston University. Our playwriting students' voices are encouraged, nurtured, and challenged, and we have a profound and positive impact on their artistry by incorporating them into a vibrant community of artists. We accept only four or five graduate students every two years—2016, 2018, and so on. This assures you of individual, hands-on attention from our faculty during all phases of the MFA degree program.

BROOKLYN COLLEGE - CUNY
WEBSITE: www.brooklyn.cuny.edu/web/academics/schools/socialsciences/graduate/english/mfa/playwriting.php
EMAIL: BHarris@brooklyn.cuny.edu **PHONE:** (718) 951-5197
ADDRESS: English Dept, 2900 Bedford Ave, Brooklyn NY 11210

COLLEGES & UNIVERSITIES

BROWN UNIVERSITY
WEBSITE: www.brown.edu/Departments/Theatre_Speech_Dance/grad/playwritingmfa.html **EMAIL:** erik_ehn@brown.edu **PHONE:** (401) 863-3283 **ADDRESS:** PO Box 1897, 83 Waterman St, Providence RI 02912

CALIFORNIA INSTITUTE OF THE ARTS
WEBSITE: www.theater.calarts.edu/programs/writing **EMAIL:** tpreston@calarts.edu **PHONE:** (661) 253-7853 **ADDRESS:** 24700 McBean Pkwy, Valencia CA 91355

CARNEGIE MELLON UNIVERSITY
WEBSITE: www.drama.cmu.edu **EMAIL:** rhandel@andrew.cmu.edu **ADDRESS:** Purnell Center for the Arts, 5000 Forbes Ave, Pittsburgh PA 15213

CATHOLIC UNIVERSITY OF AMERICA
WEBSITE: www.drama.cua.edu/graduate/mfa-playwriting.cfm **EMAIL:** kleinj@cua.edu **PHONE:** (202) 319-5360 **ADDRESS:** Dept of Drama, 620 Michigan Ave NE, Washington DC 20064

COLUMBIA COLLEGE [IL]
WEBSITE: www.colum.edu/theatre **EMAIL:** jgreen@colum.edu **PHONE:** (312) 369-7130 **ADDRESS:** 72 E 11th St, Chicago IL 60605

CORNISH COLLEGE OF THE ARTS
WEBSITE: www.cornish.edu/theater **EMAIL:** admission@cornish.edu **PHONE:** (206) 323-1400 **ADDRESS:** 1000 Lenora St, Seattle WA 98121

DREXEL UNIVERSITY, WESTPHAL COLLEGE
WEBSITE: drexel.edu/westphal/academics/undergraduate/SCRP/ **PHONE:** (215) 895-1920 **ADDRESS:** 3141 Chestnut St, Philadelphia PA 19104

FORDHAM UNIVERSITY/PRIMARY STAGES MFA IN PLAYWRITING
WEBSITE: www.fordham.edu/info/21309/playwriting_mfa **EMAIL:** carlaj.fordham@gmail.com **PHONE:** (212) 636-6306 **ADDRESS:** 113 W 60th St, Rm 423, New York NY 10023

GODDARD COLLEGE
WEBSITE: www.goddard.edu/mfa-creative-writing **EMAIL:** deborah.brevoort@goddard.edu **PHONE:** (802) 322-1619 **FAX:** (802) 454-1029 **ADDRESS:** 123 Pitkin Rd, Plainfield VT 05667

HOLLINS UNIVERSITY PLAYWRIGHT'S LAB
WEBSITE: www.hollins.edu/grad/playwriting/index.html **EMAIL:** tristau@hollins.edu **PHONE:** (540) 362-6386 **ADDRESS:** 7916 Williamson Rd, Roanoke VA 24020

HUNTER COLLEGE - CUNY
WEBSITE: www.hunter.cuny.edu/theatre/graduate-program/m.f.a.-in-playwriting
EMAIL: bml882@hunter.cuny.edu **PHONE:** (212) 772-4000
ADDRESS: 695 Park Ave, New York NY 10065
DESCRIPTION: Brighde Mullins is the Director of the Rita & Burton Goldberg MFA in Playwriting.

INDIANA UNIVERSITY
WEBSITE: www.indiana.edu/~thtr/academics/MFA_playwriting.shtml
EMAIL: pgil@iu.edu **PHONE:** (812) 855-4535
ADDRESS: 257 N Jordan Ave, Rm A300U, Bloomington IN 47405

JUILLIARD
WEBSITE: www.juilliard.edu/drama/playwriting **EMAIL:** admissions@juilliard.edu
PHONE: (212) 799-5000 Ext 223
ADDRESS: Playwrights Program, 60 Lincoln Center Plaza, New York NY 10023

LESLEY UNIVERSITY
WEBSITE: www.lesley.edu/academics/graduate/creative-writing-writing-for-stage-screen **EMAIL:** luadmissions@lesley.edu
ADDRESS: 29 Everett St, Cambridge MA 02138
DESCRIPTION: One of the few low-residency MFA programs whose graduate students work on their scripts with local professional actors and directors. During your first year in the Stage & Screen track, you will write a full-length script in both disciplines. For your second year, you can choose to concentrate in either stage or screen, or you can choose to write another full-length play and another screenplay. Either way, you will leave the program with four full-length scripts and three ten-minute plays. You may write additional scripts (like short screenplays, TV scripts and one-acts) for your Interdisciplinary Studies. In lieu of a traditional workshop for your fourth semester, you will receive a Play Lab reading where one of your completed full-length plays is presented as a reading to our Stage & Screen students, faculty and the public. In the process, you will work with professional Boston area actors and a director as well as have a consult with that director. Your play presented is also qualified for the Kennedy Center American College Theater Festival.

LONG ISLAND UNIVERSITY/POST CAMPUS
WEBSITE: www.liu.edu/post/theatre **EMAIL:** jfraser@liu.edu
PHONE: (516) 299-4280 **FAX:** (516) 299-3824
ADDRESS: 720 Northern Blvd, Brookville NY 11548

NEW HAMPSHIRE INSTITUTE OF ART
WEBSITE: www.nhia.edu **EMAIL:** GradAdmissions@nhia.edu
PHONE: (603) 623-0313 **TWITTER:** @NHIArt
ADDRESS: 148 Concord St, Manchester NH 03104-4858
DESCRIPTION: The MFA in Writing for Stage and Screen program focuses on develop-

ing each student's own creative process and the works that evolve from that process. It's structured to attract exceptionally talented writers from throughout the US and beyond who are seeking to immerse themselves in an intensive, challenging artistic experience. The Writing for Stage and Screen program guides students through (1) the creation of new work for both stage and screen, (2) the initial testing of that work with SAG and AEA actors and other industry professionals, and (3) the preparation to enter the professional playing field with the skills, know-how, and networking necessary to launch a meaningful writing career. Application deadlines are May 1 and December 1.

NEW SCHOOL FOR DRAMA
WEBSITE: www.newschool.edu/drama/playwriting
EMAIL: performingarts@newschool.edu **PHONE:** (212) 229-5859
ADDRESS: 66 W 12th St, New York NY 10011

NEW YORK UNIVERSITY, GOLDBERG DEPARTMENT OF DRAMATIC WRITING
WEBSITE: www.ddw.tisch.nyu.edu/page/graduate.html
EMAIL: tisch.ddw@nyu.edu **PHONE:** (212) 998-1940 **FAX:** (212) 998-1940
ADDRESS: 721 Broadway, 7th Fl, New York NY 10003

NEW YORK UNIVERSITY, GRADUATE MUSICAL THEATRE WRITING
WEBSITE: www.tisch.nyu.edu/grad-musical-theatre-writing
EMAIL: musical.theatre@nyu.edu **PHONE:** (212) 998-1830
ADDRESS: 715 Broadway, 2nd Fl, New York NY 10003

NORTHERN KENTUCKY UNIVERSITY
WEBSITE: rtscience.nku.edu/departments/theatre/prospective.html
EMAIL: jonesk@nku.edu **PHONE:** (859) 572-6160
ADDRESS: Nunn Drive, Highland Heights KY 41099

NORTHWESTERN UNIVERSITY
WEBSITE: www.communication.northwestern.edu/programs/mfa_writing_screen_stage/welcome **EMAIL:** write@northwestern.edu
PHONE: (847) 467-1157 **TWITTER:** @NUMFAWrite
ADDRESS: School of Communication, 70 Arts Circ Dr, Evanston IL 60208
DESCRIPTION: Our two-year MFA in Writing for the Screen and Stage is founded upon these five principles, principles that have also guided Northwestern's highly successful undergraduate Creative Writing for the Media Program.

OHIO UNIVERSITY
WEBSITE: www.ohioplaywriting.org **EMAIL:** ohioplaywriting@gmail.com
PHONE: (740) 593-4818 **ADDRESS:** Kantner Hall 307, Athens OH 45701

PACE UNIVERSITY

WEBSITE: pace.edu/academics/graduate-students/degrees/actors-studio-drama-school%E2%80%94acting-directing-and-playwriting-mfa
EMAIL: actorsstudiomfa@pace.edu   **PHONE:** (800) 874-7223
ADDRESS: 1 Pace Plz, New York NY 10038

POINT PARK UNIVERSITY
WEBSITE: www.pointpark.edu/Academics/Schools/COPA/COPADeptsMajors/LowResMFA   **EMAIL:** mpelfrey@PointPark.edu   **PHONE:** 412-392-3451
ADDRESS: 201 Wood St, Pittsburgh PA 15222
DESCRIPTION: Point Park University's Conservatory of Performing Arts offers Downtown Pittsburgh's first low-residency MFA in writing for the screen and stage.

QUEENS COLLEGE - CUNY
WEBSITE: www.english.qc.cuny.edu/graduate-programs/mfa-in-creative-writing
EMAIL: mfadirector@qc.cuny.edu   **PHONE:** (718) 997-4671
ADDRESS: 6530 Kissena Blvd, Flushing NY 11367

RUTGERS UNIVERSITY (NEW BRUNSWICK)
WEBSITE: www.masongross.rutgers.edu/theater/programs-of-study/playwriting-mfa
EMAIL: ktolin@mgsa.rutgers.edu   **PHONE:** (849) 932-9891
ADDRESS: Mason Gross School of the Arts, 2 Chapel Dr, New Brunswick NJ 8901

SAN FRANCISCO STATE UNIVERSITY
WEBSITE: www.online.sfsu.edu/~rconboy   **EMAIL:** rconboy@sfsu.edu
PHONE: (415) 338-1891   **ADDRESS:** 1600 Holloway Ave, San Francisco CA 94132

SMITH COLLEGE
WEBSITE: www.smith.edu/admission-aid/how-apply/graduate-students/mfa-playwriting   **EMAIL:** lberkman@smith.edu
PHONE: (413) 585-3206   **FAX:** (413) 585-3229
ADDRESS: Theatre Dept, Mendenhall Ctr, Northampton MA 01063
DESCRIPTION: MFA in Playwriting provides specialized training to candidates who have given evidence of professional promise in playwriting. The Department of Theatre places great emphasis on collaborative work among designers, performers, directors and writers, thus offering a unique opportunity for playwrights to have their work nurtured and supported by others who work with it at various levels.

SOUTHERN ILLINOIS UNIVERSITY (CARBONDALE)
WEBSITE: cola.siu.edu/theater/graduate/graduate-degree/master-of-fine-arts/playwriting.php   **EMAIL:** jjuntunen@siu.edu   **PHONE:** (618) 453-5741
ADDRESS: Dept of Theater, Comm Bldg, Mail Code 6608, Carbondale IL 62901

SUNY PURCHASE
WEBSITE: www.purchase.edu/academics/playwriting-and-screenwriting/
EMAIL: christina.anderson@purchase.edu   **PHONE:** (914) 251-6833
ADDRESS: 735 Anderson Hill Rd, Purchase NY 10577

COLLEGES & UNIVERSITIES

TEXAS STATE UNIVERSITY (SAN MARCOS)
WEBSITE: www.theatreanddance.txstate.edu/Graduate-Degrees/MFA-Dramatic-Writing.html **PHONE:** (512) 245-2147
ADDRESS: 601 Univ Dr, San Marcos TX 78666

UNIVERSITY OF CALIFORNIA (LOS ANGELES)
WEBSITE: www.tft.ucla.edu/programs/theater-department/graduate-degrees/playwriting-mfa **EMAIL:** theatergrad@tft.ucla.edu
ADDRESS: 10920 Wilshire Blvd 5th Fl, Los Angeles CA 90024

UNIVERSITY OF CALIFORNIA (SAN DIEGO)
WEBSITE: www.theatre.ucsd.edu/academics/gradAdmissions/PlaywritingApply.html
EMAIL: ahavis@ucsd.edu **PHONE:** (858) 534-1046 **FAX:** (858) 534-1080

UNIVERSITY OF HOUSTON
WEBSITE: www.uh.edu/kgmca/theatre-and-dance/theatre/undergraduate/playwriting
PHONE: (713) 743-3003 **FAX:** (713) 743-2648
ADDRESS: 3351 Cullen Blvd, Rm 133, Houston TX 77204
DESCRIPTION: The Bachelor of Fine Arts (BFA) in Playwriting/Dramaturgy gives students extensive practical experience in both playwriting and dramaturgy.

UNIVERSITY OF IOWA
WEBSITE: www.theatre.uiowa.edu/academic-programs/mfa-programs/playwrights-workshop **EMAIL:** art-borreca@uiowa.edu **PHONE:** (319) 353-2700
ADDRESS: 107 Theatre Bldg, Iowa City IA 52242

UNIVERSITY OF MASSACHUSETTS (AMHERST)
WEBSITE: www.umass.edu/theater/playlab.php **EMAIL:** gina@theater.umass.edu
PHONE: (413) 545-3490 **ADDRESS:** Fine Arts Ctr 112, Amherst MA 01003

UNIVERSITY OF NEBRASKA AT OMAHA
WEBSITE: www.unomaha.edu/college-of-communication-fine-arts-and-media/writers-workshop/mfa-program/index.php
EMAIL: cfam@unomaha.edu **PHONE:** (402) 554.3857 **TWITTER:** @UNOmaha
ADDRESS: Weber Fine Arts Bldg 314, 6505 University Dr S, Omaha NE 68182
DESCRIPTION: The University of Nebraska at Omaha's low-residency MFA in Writing program is composed of four 16-week at-home semesters and five 10-day conference-style residencies. Over the course of the program, you will earn 60 credit hours toward a Masters of Fine Arts degree in one of four genres: Adult or Young Adult Fiction, Poetry, Playwriting, or Creative Nonfiction.

UNIVERSITY OF NEW MEXICO
WEBSITE: inearts.unm.edu/academics/departments/theatre-dance/dramatic-writing/ **EMAIL:** fineartsdean@unm.edu **PHONE:** (505) 277-2112
ADDRESS: Center for the Arts, MSC04 2570, Albuquerque NM 87131

NOTES

UNIVERSITY OF NEW ORLEANS
WEBSITE: www.uno.edu/creative-writing-mfa **EMAIL:** cww@uno.edu
PHONE: (504) 280-6276 **ADDRESS:** Dept of English, 201 Liberal Arts Bldg, 2000 Lakeshore Dr, New Orleans LA 70148
DESCRIPTION: The UNO Creative Writing Workshop (CWW) is our resident graduate program in fiction writing, nonfiction writing, poetry writing, playwriting and screenwriting.

UNIVERSITY OF SOUTHERN CALIFORNIA
WEBSITE: dramaticarts.usc.edu/programs/graduate/dramatic-writing
EMAIL: sdagrad@usc.edu **PHONE:** (213) 740-1292
ADDRESS: 1029 Childs Way, Los Angeles CA 90089

UNIVERSITY OF TEXAS (AUSTIN)
WEBSITE: theatredance.utexas.edu/graduate-programs/mfa-playwriting
EMAIL: andrea.grapko@austin.utexas.edu **PHONE:** (512) 471-5793
ADDRESS: 300 E 23rd St, Austin TX 78712

WEBSTER UNIVERSITY
WEBSITE: www.webster.edu **PHONE:** (800) 981-9801 **TWITTER:** @websteru
ADDRESS: 470 E Lockwood Ave, St Louis MO 63119 USA
DESCRIPTION: Webster University's Bachelor of Music in Music Direction for Musical Theatre is a pre-professional degree, designed for students who wish to pursue a career as a professional music director for musical theatre. Extensive applied instruction and classes on technique, coaching, and musical theatre performance styles, as well as ensemble experience, constitute the core of the curriculum.

YALE UNIVERSITY SCHOOL OF DRAMA
WEBSITE: drama.yale.edu/program/playwriting **EMAIL:** ysd.admissions@yale.edu
PHONE: (203) 432-0254 **ADDRESS:** PO Box 208325, New Haven CT 6520

ALWAYS VERIFY THE INFORMATION LISTED IN THIS DIRECTORY. These listings have been updated and checked as of November 1, 2017. This Directory is only updated once a year. The information inside can and will change throughout the year. Where applicable, we have listed websites, addresses, and emails. Be diligent. Take the time to verify the deadlines, submission materials, etc. Internet access and research will be required for most submissions.

DEVELOPMENTAL WORKSHOPS

29TH STREET PLAYWRIGHTS COLLECTIVE

WEBSITE: www.29thStreetPlaywrightsCollective.org
EMAIL: 29thStPlaywrightscollective@gmail.com **PHONE:** (646) 260-8102
TWITTER: @EmmaGSherman
ADDRESS: 270 Seaman Ave, Apt F6, New York NY 10034
DESCRIPTION: See our website for our goals, how we do what we do, and guidelines for submitting. Anyone chosen to attend will be able to test out the group to see if it would suit their purposes.
SUBMISSION MATERIALS: Please send an email expressing your interest, what you seek in a group, and your current goals for your work. Also send a short work sample, an artistic statement and bio. **FEE:** No

AMERICAN LYRIC THEATER COMPOSER LIBRETTIST DEVELOPMENT PROGRAM (CLDP)

PARENT ORGANIZATION: American Lyric Theater
WEBSITE: www.altnyc.org/composer-librettist-development-program
PHONE: (646) 216-8298 **TWITTER:** @ALTNYC
ADDRESS: 410 W 42nd St, New York NY 10036
DESCRIPTION: Until ALT started the Composer Librettist Development Program (CLDP), there was not a single full-time training program for opera composers and librettists at any opera company in the United States. To date, the program has provided intensive, personalized mentorship to 38 gifted emerging artists. Beyond works developed at ALT, distinguished alumni of the CLDP are now creating works for companies around the country, including Houston Grand Opera, Opera Philadelphia, Chicago Lyric Opera, Los Angeles Opera, Beth Morrison Projects, and the Metropolitan Opera. **GENRE:** Opera **FEE:** No

ARS NOVA PLAY GROUP

PARENT ORGANIZATION: Ars Nova Theater
WEBSITE: www.arsnovanyc.com/playgroup **TWITTER:** @arsnova
ADDRESS: 511 W 54th St, New York NY 10019
DESCRIPTION: Play Group is a two year residency in which members become a part of the Ars Nova Resident Artist community. In addition to biweekly meetings where members share new work and receive feedback from their Play Group peers, residents enjoy two Play Group writing retreats; and the opportunity to further develop and showcase one of their plays in a weeklong workshop that can culminate in a public reading. Applications for Play Group 2018 are now closed.
SUBMISSION MATERIALS: See website for updates and info.
GENRE: Plays **PREFERRED LENGTH:** Full-length **FEE:** No **AGENT ONLY:** No

ASCAP FOUNDATION/DREAMWORKS MUSICAL THEATRE WORKSHOP IN LA

PARENT ORGANIZATION: American Society of Composers, Authors & Publishers

WEBSITE: www.ascap.com/help/career-development/workshops#workshopla
EMAIL: mkerker@ascap.com   **PHONE:** (323) 883-1000
FAX: (323) 883-1049   **TWITTER:** @ASCAP
ADDRESS: 7920 W Sunset Blvd, 3rd Fl, Los Angeles CA 90046
DESCRIPTION: Stephen Schwartz serves annually as artistic director for the ASCAP/DreamWorks Musical Theatre Workshop in Los Angeles. Workshop participants will have the opportunity to present selections from their original works in progress for professional critique. Each session will feature prominent guests from all aspects of musical theatre, including producers, directors, critics, performers and composers. ASCAP does not provide lodging, or cover costs of transportation if your musical is selected. You must bring your own actors and accompanist. A piano will be provided.
SUBMISSION MATERIALS: See website for updates and information.
GENRE: Musicals   **FEE:** No   **AGENT ONLY:** No

ASCAP MUSICAL THEATRE WORKSHOP IN NY

PARENT ORGANIZATION: American Society of Composers, Authors & Publishers
WEBSITE: www.ascap.com/help/career-development/workshops#workshopny
EMAIL: mkerker@ascap.com   **PHONE:** (212) 621-6234   **FAX:** (212) 621-6558
TWITTER: @ASCAP   **ADDRESS:** 1 Lincoln Plaza, 7th Fl, New York NY 10023
DESCRIPTION: Stephen Schwartz serves annually as artistic director for the ASCAP Musical Theatre Workshop in New York. Workshop participants will have the opportunity to present selections from their original works in progress for professional critique. Each session will feature prominent guests from all aspects of musical theatre, including producers, directors, critics, performers and composers. ASCAP does not provide lodging, or cover costs of transportation if your musical is selected. You must bring your own actors and accompanist. A piano will be provided.
SUBMISSION MATERIALS: See website for updates and details.
GENRE: Musicals   **FEE:** No   **AGENT ONLY:** No

BMI LEHMAN ENGEL MUSICAL THEATRE WORKSHOP

PARENT ORGANIZATION: BMI (Broadcast Music Inc)
WEBSITE: www.bmi.com/theatre_workshop/application_requirements
EMAIL: theatreworkshop@bmi.com   **PHONE:** (212) 830-2508
FAX: (212) 262-2508   **TWITTER:** @bmi   **ADDRESS:** Patrick Cook, Director, Musical Theatre, 7 World Trade Ctr, 250 Greenwich St, New York NY 10007
DESCRIPTION: The Workshop runs September through May in New York City. Prospective members must make their own living arrangements in the city or be able to commute weekly. See website for details and application.
SUBMISSION MATERIALS: • Composer: Three contrasting compositions - uptempo, comedy song, ballad. Please include copy of score which includes lyrics.
• Lyricist: Three contrasting lyrics in PDF format - uptempo, comedy song, ballad.
• Composer/Lyricist: Three contrasting songs - uptempo, comedy song, ballad. Please include copy of score which includes lyrics.
• Librettist: A script sample of at least ten consecutive pages. Material written for the stage is preferred, but screenplays or teleplays are acceptable. Material need not include songs. Please include a sample of comedy writing.

DEVELOPMENTAL WORKSHOPS

DEADLINE TYPE: Annual **GENRE:** Musicals **PREFERRED LENGTH:** Any Length **FEE:** No **AGENT ONLY:** No

BRAVE NEW WORKS
PARENT ORGANIZATION: Playwriting Center, The
WEBSITE: theater.emory.edu/home/Playwriting%20Center/Brave%20New%20Works/index.html **EMAIL:** lpaulse@emory.edu
DESCRIPTION: The Playwriting Center of Theater Emory produces Brave New Works. This festival provides theater professionals and students with the space and resources to conduct creative experimentation, to create new works for the stage, and to test the dramatic product on an audience. For three weeks, the Brave New Works festival of new and evolving plays gives playwrights a laboratory to work with a director and actors, revise and rewrite their scripts, and share the results with members of the Emory and Atlanta community.
SUBMISSION MATERIALS: The next Brave New Works festival will be presented in February 2018. Planning and script selection is currently underway, but unfortunately we can not accept unsolicited manuscripts.
DEADLINE TYPE: Biennial **FEE:** No **AGENT ONLY:** Yes

CAPE COD THEATRE PROJECT
WEBSITE: www.capecodtheatreproject.org/apply
EMAIL: info@capecodtheatreproject.org **PHONE:** (508) 457-4242
TWITTER: @CapeCodTheatre **ADDRESS:** PO Box 410, Falmouth MA 2541
DESCRIPTION: Each week in July, professional actors, directors and playwrights flock to Falmouth to develop new plays at the Cape Cod Theatre Project. Each weekend in July - on Thursday, Friday and Saturday at 8 pm - audiences get to experience a newly developed play for the first time.
SUBMISSION MATERIALS: To apply, please email a PDF of the script to capecodlit@gmail.com. Please label the document using your first and last name as well as the play's title. For example: janesmithplaytitle.pdf. Include in your email a short bio & a brief artistic statement on how you propose to use your development time at CCTP. The bio and statement of intentions should be one page combined, sent as a PDF or Microsoft Word Doc and labeled with your first and last name. For example: janesmithbio.doc. See website for updates and details.
DEADLINE TYPE: Annual **GENRE:** Plays **PREFERRED LENGTH:** Full-length

CHARLES MARYAN'S PLAYWRIGHTS'-DIRECTORS' WORKSHOP
WEBSITE: www.charlesmaryan.com **EMAIL:** chuck@charlesmaryan.com
PHONE: (212) 864-0542 **TWITTER:** @cmaryan
ADDRESS: 777 West End Ave, #6C, New York NY 10025
DESCRIPTION: On contacting us by email, a playwright can make an appointment for a complimentary phone consultation with Charles Maryan. In general, a playwright will send their script and receive an evaluation of the play with notes and suggestions, as well as a discussion by phone, Skype or if in New York City, by in-person appointment. Response time: 2 weeks. Fee: $250. See website for other services and fees.
GENRE: All Genres **PREFERRED LENGTH:** Any Length **FEE:** No **AGENT ONLY:** No

CORE WRITER PROGRAM

PARENT ORGANIZATION: Playwrights' Center [MN]
WEBSITE: www.pwcenter.org/programs   **EMAIL:** juliab@pwcenter.org
PHONE: (612) 332-7481
ADDRESS: Playwrights' Center, 2301 Franklin Ave E, Minneapolis MN 55406
DESCRIPTION: The Playwrights' Center invites committed professional playwrights to apply for the Core Writer program. Created in recognition of the particular needs of emerging and established writers, the program offers significant resources intended to further a playwright's career and is available to writers nationally.
SUBMISSION MATERIALS: Full-length play script, Playwriting resume, Artistic statement, Core Writer goals (PDF or Word doc).

CPT NEW PLAY DEVELOPMENT

PARENT ORGANIZATION: Cleveland Public Theatre
WEBSITE: www.cptonline.org/performances/new-work-development/the-dark-room
EMAIL: avaldez@cptonline.org   **PHONE:** (216) 631-2727   **TWITTER:** @CPTCLE
ADDRESS: Cleveland Public Theatre, 6415 Detroit Ave, Cleveland OH 44102
DESCRIPTION: CPT is a national leader in providing platforms for new work and emerging artists. Programs include ENTRY POINT: JAN 18 – 21, TEST FLIGHT: MAR 29 – APR 28, and CATAPULT: Year round, ongoing. See website for details.

DALLAS PLAYWRIGHTS' WORKSHOP

WEBSITE: www.dallastheatercenter.org/subpage.php?sid=146&parent_id=6
EMAIL: literary@dallastheatercenter.org   **PHONE:** (214) 526-8210
TWITTER: @DallasTheater
DESCRIPTION: Dallas Playwrights' Workshop is intended for emerging and mid-career playwrights who reside in DFW and have previously written at least one play and are able to demonstrate a unique, compelling voice.
SUBMISSION MATERIALS: Dallas Theater Center accepts script submissions only from agents, writers and theater artists with whom we have an existing relationship. We are unable to accept any unsolicited scripts as the volume of material we consider each year and limited staff size prohibits this.
GENRE: All genres   **PREFERRED LENGTH:** Any Length   **AGENT ONLY:** No

DAVID HENRY HWANG WRITERS INSTITUTE

WEBSITE: www.eastwestplayers.org/professional-enrichment/writers-institute
EMAIL: literary@eastwestplayers.org   **PHONE:** (213) 625-7000
TWITTER: @EWPlayers
ADDRESS: 120 N Judge John Aiso St, Los Angeles CA 90012
DESCRIPTION: Named after Tony Award-winning playwright David Henry Hwang (FOB, The Dance and the Railroad, M. Butterfly), the David Henry Hwang Writers Institute is the most active Asian Pacific American playwright development program in the country. Offering a series of writing classes designed to foster new work for the stage, the Institute is a nationally recognized force in the creation of plays that embrace the voice of multi-ethnic America and especially the Asian Pacific American experience.

SUBMISSION MATERIALS: Please note that our mission focuses on the Asian Pacific experience, and the majority of the new works we workshop and produce revolve around Asian and Asian American characters and/or themes. We are interested in both plays and musicals. Works need not be "issue-oriented," in that race/immigrant issues can be an unspoken component in the work. We are particularly interested in new comedies, musicals, and works that unearth the history of Asians in America.
SPECIAL INTEREST: Asian **FEE:** Yes **AGENT ONLY:** No

FIELDWORK
WEBSITE: www.thefield.org/content/fieldwork **EMAIL:** wilfredo@thefield.org
PHONE: (212) 691-6969 **TWITTER:** @TheFieldNYC
ADDRESS: 75 Maiden Ln, Ste 906, New York NY 10038
DESCRIPTION: Participants meet weekly to share developing works and exchange peer-to-peer feedback. Incisive and stimulating critiques are guided by an experienced facilitator. Fieldwork is open to a wide array of art creators: solo theater artists, spoken word performers, choreographers, composers, writers, directors and more.
SUBMISSION MATERIALS: Join online mailing list to receive information.
FEE: Yes **AGENT ONLY:** No

FIREHOUSE STUDIO
PARENT ORGANIZATION: Firehouse Theatre
WEBSITE: www.firehousetheatre.org/firehouse-studio
EMAIL: tennessee@firehousetheatre.org **TWITTER:** @firehouserva
ADDRESS: Firehouse Theatre, 1609 W Broad St, Richmond VA 23220
DESCRIPTION: Firehouse Studio is a program of Firehouse Theatre that provides space and resources for the development of experimental and collaborative performance projects. Work in the Studio is about process and innovation. The goal is not to make cultural products necessarily, but to give space for creative human interaction, to challenge perception, and awaken ideas.
SUBMISSION MATERIALS: See website for details and application.
DEADLINE TYPE: Rolling **GENRE:** Plays **FEE:** No **AGENT ONLY:** No

FRIGID NEW YORK
WEBSITE: www.horsetrade.info **EMAIL:** submissions@horsetrade.info
PHONE: (212) 777-6088 **ADDRESS:** 85 E 4th St, New York NY 10003
DESCRIPTION: FRIGID New York's continuing mission is to seek out new art, new artists, and new audiences. We provide a home for independent theater artists, we nurture their development, and we help to establish their careers by promoting their work to local, national, and international audiences.
SUBMISSION MATERIALS: We are seeking new full-length scripts that have never had a full production in New York City. Please send a cover letter, resume and a .pdf or .doc file of your script to submissions@horsetrade.info. Please note we accept all new scripts on a rolling basis, we can not guarentee a timely response.
DEADLINE TYPE: Rolling **GENRE:** Plays **PREFERRED LENGTH:** Full Length
FEE: No **AGENT ONLY:** No

HIGH DESERT PLAY DEVELOPMENT WORKSHOP

PARENT ORGANIZATION: New Mexico State University
WEBSITE: www.nmsutheatre.com/highdesert.php **EMAIL:** matcreyn@nmsu.edu
PHONE: (575) 646-4517 **ADDRESS:** NMSU Theatre Arts, American Southwest Theatre Company, PO Box 30001, MSC 3072, Las Cruces NM 88003-8001
DESCRIPTION: Est. 2005. A bi-annual program that solicits new plays from 15-20 nationally-renowned emerging playwrights. Two scripts are selected to participate in a week-long developmental reading program, and one of the two scripts is selected for a fully-mounted production the next season. The playwright is in-residence for one or two weeks of the rehearsal or performance process. We do not claim ownership or a future in the play; we offer feedback to the playwright only as requested; and we allow the playwright to classify the play as either a workshop production or as a world premiere as they see fit.
SUBMISSION MATERIALS: We do not accept unsolicited scripts, if you are a playwright and are interested in being considered for our program, please contact us.
FEE: No **AGENT ONLY:** Yes

INGRAM NEW WORKS PROJECT

PARENT ORGANIZATION: Nashville Repertory Theatre
WEBSITE: nashvillerep.org/ingram-new-works **EMAIL:** nate@nashvillerep.org
PHONE: (615) 244-4878 **TWITTER:** @nashrep
ADDRESS: Nashville Repertory Theatre, 161 Rains Ave, Nashville TN 37203
DESCRIPTION: Created in 2009 with the support of co-founder Martha R. Ingram to provide an opportunity for theatre artists to develop new theatre works while in residency at Nashville Rep. The program has evolved to include a New Works Lab for emerging playwrights. Lab Playwrights develop new works for the stage alongside the Ingram New Works Fellow in a yearlong residency culminating in the annual Ingram New Works Festival.
SUBMISSION MATERIALS: See website for more information.

LA MAMA EXPERIMENTS

PARENT ORGANIZATION: La MaMa Experimental Theater Club
WEBSITE: lamama.org/programs/play-reading/
EMAIL: LaMaMaExperiments@gmail.com **PHONE:** (212) 254-6468
ADDRESS: 74-A E 4th St, New York NY 10003
DESCRIPTION: Check website for updated information.

THE LARK

WEBSITE: www.larktheatre.org **EMAIL:** andreah@larktheatre.org
PHONE: (212) 246-2676 **ADDRESS:** 311 W 43rd St, Ste 406, New York NY 10036
DESCRIPTION: Est. 1994. The Lark Play Development Center is a laboratory for new voices and new ideas. We provide playwrights and their collaborators with resources to develop their work in a supportive yet rigorous environment and encouraging artists to define their own goals and creative processes in pursuit of a unique vision.

LAST FRONTIER THEATRE CONFERENCE PLAY LAB

PARENT ORGANIZATION: Last Frontier Theatre Conference
WEBSITE: www.theatreconference.org/play-lab **EMAIL:** dlmoore@alaska.edu
PHONE: (907) 834-1614 **ADDRESS**: PO Box 97, Valdez AK 99686
DESCRIPTION: Selected plays receive public readings, with both public and private feedback sessions led by theatre professionals. Authors must register for the Conference and be in attendance for their reading. Authors are asked to submit using the online form on the Play Lab link on the website.
SUBMISSION MATERIALS: See website for updates and info.
DEADLINE TYPE: Annual **GENRE:** Plays **PREFERRED LENGTH:** Any Length **FEE:** No

MARSHA HANNA NEW PLAY WORKSHOPS

PARENT ORGANIZATION: The Human Race Theatre Company
WEBSITE: www.humanracetheatre.org/works/new-works
EMAIL: kevin@humanracetheatre.org **ADDRESS:** The Human Race Theatre Company, 126 N Main St, Ste 300, Dayton OH 45402
DESCRIPTION: Named after The Human Race Theatre Company's late Artistic Director, Marsha Hanna, who passed away in 2011, the New Play Workshops program provides playwrights a residency opportunity in order to further develop a new play in a workshop setting, guided by a seasoned director and supported by professional actors. The process culminates in the staged reading of the play.
SUBMISSION MATERIALS: We do not accept unsolicited submissions. You may send an introductory letter with a short description of your show. If we are interested, you will then be contacted.
GENRE: Plays **PREFERRED LENGTH:** Full-length **FEE:** No **AGENT ONLY:** Yes

MUSICAL CAFE

WEBSITE: www.musicalcafe.org **EMAIL:** musicals@playcafe.org
ADDRESS: PO Box 12162, Berkeley CA 94712
DESCRIPTION: Musical Cafe is a musical theatre development and education program for Northern California-based writers and composers. Our prime offering, the Musical Cafe Showcase Series, alternates between San Francisco and the East Bay. Each Showcase is a public presentation of new, original, locally-sourced musical theatre works-in-progress.
SUBMISSION MATERIALS: Synopsis, work samples, contact information
DEADLINE: 11/30/2017 **GENRE:** Musicals **PREFERRED LENGTH:** Any Length **FEE:** No
AGENT ONLY: No

MUSICAL STAGES: NC STATE UNIVERSITY NEW MUSICALS PROGRAM

WEBSITE: https://theatre.arts.ncsu.edu/get-involved/musical-stages/
EMAIL: kadougan@ncsu.edu **PHONE:** (919) 515-8490
ADDRESS: Campus Box 7306, Raleigh NC 27695
DESCRIPTION: Selected projects will be given a 30-hour rehearsal followed by two performances of a staged or concert reading in Raleigh, NC as part of NC State University Theatre's season.

SUBMISSION MATERIALS: 2017/2018 deadline has passed. Check website for updated information. **GENRE:** Musicals **PREFERRED LENGTH:** Full-length **FEE:** No **AGENT ONLY:** No

MUSICAL THEATRE WORKSHOPS

PARENT ORGANIZATION: The Human Race Theatre Company
WEBSITE: www.humanracetheatre.org/works/new-works
EMAIL: kevin@humanracetheatre.org **ADDRESS:** The Human Race Theatre Company, 126 N Main St, Ste 300, Dayton OH 45402
DESCRIPTION: The Human Race's Musical Theatre Workshops program focuses on the development of original musicals, providing an avenue for that very important "second production" and to encouraging appreciation of rarely produced musicals. Through a process of residencies, workshops and staged readings, the program not only contributes to the art form, but helps build an audience for new musicals. For years, the highlight of the MTW program has been the Festival of New Musicals.
SUBMISSION MATERIALS: We do not accept unsolicited submissions. You may send an introductory letter with a short description of your show. If we are interested, you will then be contacted. **AGENT ONLY:** Yes

NAUTILUS COMPOSER-LIBRETTIST STUDIO

PARENT ORGANIZATION: Nautilus Music Theatre
WEBSITE: www.nautilusmusictheater.org **EMAIL:** staff@nautilusmusictheater.org
PHONE: (651) 298-9913 **TWITTER:** @NautilusMT
ADDRESS: 308 Prince St, #190, St Paul MN 55101
DESCRIPTION: Website under construction. The Nautilus Composer-Librettist Studio is provides an opportunity for five writers and five composers to work with five professional performers, exploring the possibilities and basic elements of music-theater. The studio focuses on the process of collaboration through a series of brief exploratory assignments for the writers and composers. The exercises are then sight-read by the performers in brief working sessions. The participants rotate partners, and the process is repeated four more times. Within the two-week period, all composers work with all writers and all performers. Toward the end of the studio, an informal reading of all the compositions is held.
DEADLINE TYPE: Annual **GENRE:** Musicals **FEE:** No **AGENT ONLY:** No

NEW CITY, NEW BLOOD READING SERIES

PARENT ORGANIZATION: Theater for the New City
WEBSITE: theaterforthenewcity.net/submissions.htm
EMAIL: tncdreamup@gmail.com **ADDRESS:** 155 1st Ave, New York NY 10003
DESCRIPTION: The newest division of the Resident Theater Program, NEW CITY, NEW BLOOD, is a reading series for worthy plays in earlier stages of development.
SUBMISSION MATERIALS: If you would like your work to be considered, please send a ten-page sample of the script, brief synopsis, bio and subject line: "New City, New Blood submission" to us via email tncdreamup@gmail.com
DEADLINE TYPE: Rolling **GENRE:** Plays **PREFERRED LENGTH:** Full-length **FEE:** No **AGENT ONLY:** No

THE NEW HARMONY PROJECT

WEBSITE: www.newharmonyproject.org
EMAIL: submissions@newharmonyproject.org **PHONE**: (317) 464-1103
ADDRESS: PO Box 441062, Indianapolis IN 46244
DESCRIPTION: Our 2018 script submission window is now closed. Please follow us on social media or sign up for our newsletter to stay up to date on the process.
GENRE: Plays **PREFERRED LENGTH**: Full-length **FEE**: No **AGENT ONLY**: No

NEW MUSICALS INC.

WEBSITE: nmi.org **EMAIL**: admin@nmi.org **PHONE**: (818) 506-8500
FAX: (818) 506-8500 **ADDRESS**: 5628 Vineland Ave, North Hollywood CA 91601
DESCRIPTION: New Musicals Inc. hosts many programs which support new musicals in development. We develop several dozen musicals each year for producers and writers all around the country through table readings, workshops, concerts, and occasional productions. **GENRE**: Musicals

NEW VISIONS/NEW VOICES

PARENT ORGANIZATION: The Kennedy Center
WEBSITE: education.kennedy-center.org/education/nvnv.html
EMAIL: kctya@kennedy-center.org **PHONE**: (202) 416-8830
FAX: (202) 416-8297 **ADDRESS**: Education Division, The Kennedy Center, PO Box 101510, Arlington VA 22210
DESCRIPTION: New Visions/New Voices is a week-long biennial workshop/festival for playwrights and theaters to stimulate and support the creation of new plays and musicals for young audiences and families. The next New Visions/New Voices will be April 27-29, 2018. **DEADLINE TYPE**: Biennial **GENRE**: Plays or Musicals
SPECIAL INTEREST: Theatre for Young Audiences **FEE**: No **AGENT ONLY**: No

NEW VOICES PROJECT

PARENT ORGANIZATION: New Musicals Inc.
WEBSITE: nmi.org/develop/new-voices-project
EMAIL: admin@nmi.org **PHONE**: (818) 506-8500
ADDRESS: New Musicals Inc., 5628 Vineland Ave, North Hollywood CA 91601
DESCRIPTION: New Voices Project nurtures new musical theatre writers under the age of 26 by offering them private and public workshops of their writing.
SUBMISSION MATERIALS: Bio, artist statement, work samples. Submissions open Jan. 1, 2018. See website for details. **DEADLINE**: 02/15/2018 **DEADLINE TYPE**: Annual
GENRE: Musicals **FEE**: No **AGENT ONLY**: No

NEW WORKS INITIATIVE

WEBSITE: www.montclair.edu/arts/theatre-and-dance/new-works-initiative/
EMAIL: stovera@mail.montclair.edu **PHONE**: (973) 655-4817
ADDRESS: Montclair State University, MSU LI-126G, Montclair NJ 07043
DESCRIPTION: NWI is an Artist-in-Residence program and developmental platform in the Department of Theatre and Dance in Montclair State University's College of the Arts. NWI's mission is to bring together established and emerging playwrights,

composers, choreographers, theatre-makers, and professional directors with MSU theatre students to explore adventurous theatrical works.
SUBMISSION MATERIALS: Check website for submission instructions.
DEADLINE: 12/01/2017   **FEE:** No   **AGENT ONLY:** No

NOTEWORTHY
PARENT ORGANIZATION: Theatre of NOTE
WEBSITE: www.theatreofnote.com/noteworthy
EMAIL: mgrdir@theatreofnote.com   **PHONE:** (323) 856-8611
TWITTER: @TheatreOfNOTE
ADDRESS: 1517 N Cahuenga Blvd, Los Angeles CA 90028
DESCRIPTION: Theatre of NOTE's staged reading series, established to foster relationships with playwrights as they develop new works (with the hopes of producing these pieces on our stage).
SUBMISSION MATERIALS: We accept submissions year-round. Please send scripts via email to the NOTEworthy Committee at mgrdir@theatreofnote.com.
DEADLINE TYPE: Rolling   **GENRE:** Plays   **PREFERRED LENGTH:** Full-length
FEE: No   **AGENT ONLY:** No

OBSIDIAN'S PLAYWRIGHTS UNIT
WEBSITE: www.obsidiantheatre.com/artist-centre/for-playwrights-2/
EMAIL: pd@obsidiantheatre.com   **PHONE:** (416) 463-8444
ADDRESS: 1089 Dundas St E, Toronto ON M4M-1R9 Canada
DESCRIPTION: The Playwrights Unit is an intensive yearlong process that runs annually from Sept-June. The Unit has an emphasis on professional development and the business of being a professional artist in Canada. Submissions for the Playwrights Unit are accepted starting in April annually.

ORIGINATE + GENERATE (O+G)
PARENT ORGANIZATION: Aurora Theatre Company
WEBSITE: www.auroratheatre.org/o+g   **EMAIL:** education@auroratheatre.org
PHONE: (510) 843-4042   **FAX:** (510) 843-4826   **TWITTER:** @AuroraTheatreCo
ADDRESS: Aurora Theater, 2081 Addison St, Berkeley CA 94704
DESCRIPTION: Aurora Theatre Company's program for the development of new works builds upon the successes of Aurora's Global Age Project. With O+G, Aurora serves as an incubator of new works, offering extensive personalized support to local playwrights and theatre creators as they craft their pieces specifically for Aurora's stages.

PATAPHYSICS PLAYWRITING WORKSHOPS
PARENT ORGANIZATION: The Flea Theater
WEBSITE: theflea.org/for-artists/pataphysics-playwriting-workshops/
EMAIL: pataphysics@theflea.org   **PHONE:** (212) 226-0051
ADDRESS: 20 Thomas St, New York NY 10013
DESCRIPTION: The Pataphysics Playwriting Workshops at The Flea Theater are intimate, four-session intensives for new work and new ways of working. Check website for updated information.

DEVELOPMENTAL WORKSHOPS

TEST DRIVE DEVELOPMENT WORKSHOP
PARENT ORGANIZATION: Route 66 Theatre Company
WEBSITE: route66theatre.org/new-play-workshop
EMAIL: submissions@route66theatre.org **PHONE**: (773) 450-8177
ADDRESS: Route 66 Theatre Co, 6255 N Sheridan, #28, Chicago IL 60660
DESCRIPTION: Our annual workshop awards one playwright with a developmental workshop that is focused on the playwright and what they need to move their script toward being production-ready. A director, workshop curator, two dramaturg mentors, and a panel of special guest directors, artistic directors, and literary managers will provide support, criticism, ideas, and suggestions.
SUBMISSION MATERIALS: Check website for updated information.

THEATER AT SOLEL
WEBSITE: templesolel.com/about/programs-special-events
EMAIL: lmkjewishplays@gmail.com **PHONE**: (954) 815-4024
TWITTER: TempleSolelHwd **ADDRESS**: 4011 Buchanan St, Hollywood FL 33021
DESCRIPTION: Theater at Solel presents readings of short plays on Jewish topics, and invites the audience to discuss and debate their meanings. Contact for more information.
GENRE: Plays **PREFERRED LENGTH**: Any Length **SPECIAL INTEREST**: Jewish **FEE**: No

TRU VOICES PLAY AND MUSICAL READING SERIES
WEBSITE: www.truonline.org/tru-voices **EMAIL**: truplaysubmissions@gmail.com
PHONE: (212) 864-3753 **FAX**: (212) 864-6301
ADDRESS: 309 W 104th St, 1D, New York NY 10025
DESCRIPTION: Created to nurture producers as well as writers, TRU VOICES seeks producer-driven projects, and also matches writers with producers. Each reading is followed by a "Dollars and Sense" panel discussion with prominent New York producers, general managers and artistic directors focusing on potential venues, marketing and budgeting of the work.
SUBMISSION MATERIALS: Submissions for 2018 have closed. Check website for updated information. **GENRE**: Plays or Musicals **PREFERRED LENGTH**: Full-length
FEE: Yes **AGENT ONLY**: No

VOICES OF OUR NATIONS ARTS
WEBSITE: vonacommunity.org/community/index.php/apply.html
EMAIL: info@vonacommunity.org **PHONE**: (732) 842-3932
DESCRIPTION: VONA/Voices is open to all adult writers-of-color at any level of experience. There are no degree, publication or documentation requirements to apply. See website for workshop descriptions and updated deadline information.
SPECIAL INTEREST: All

WRITE NOW
WEBSITE: writenow.co/competition **EMAIL**: jmillinger@childsplayaz.org
PHONE: (480) 921-5700 **ADDRESS**: 900 S Mitchell Dr, Tempe AZ 85281
DESCRIPTION: Write Now provides a forum through which each playwright receives constructive criticism and the support of a development team consisting of a

professional director and dramaturg. Finalists will spend approximately one week in workshop with their development team. At the end of the week, each play will be read as a part of the Write Now convening.

SUBMISSION MATERIALS: Write Now will begin accepting submissions for the 2019 competition in Spring 2018. Check website for submission guidelines.

DEADLINE TYPE: Biennial **GENRE**: Plays **PREFERRED LENGTH**: Full-length
SPECIAL INTEREST: Theatre for Young Audiences **FEE**: No **AGENT ONLY**: No

YOUNG WRITERS PROJECT
PARENT ORGANIZATION: Theatre of NOTE
WEBSITE: www.theatreofnote.com/young-writers-project
EMAIL: mgrdir@theatreofnote.com **PHONE**: (323) 856-8611
TWITTER: @TheatreOfNOTE
ADDRESS: 1517 N Cahuenga Blvd, Los Angeles CA 90028
DESCRIPTION: The Young Writers Project is NOTE's 10-year-old outreach program featuring original work from young LA playwrights, produced for Theatre of NOTE by Jonathan Klein. Each year, five writers from five high schools are chosen to participate in a workshop-based writing experiment that culminates in the staged production of five short plays, one play representing each school. Check website for details.
GENRE: Plays **FEE**: No **AGENT ONLY**: No

YOUNG WRITERS SHOWCASE
PARENT ORGANIZATION: Geva Theatre Center
WEBSITE: www.gevatheatre.org/artists/play-submission/#3
EMAIL: youngwriters@gevatheatre.org **PHONE**: (585) 232-1366
ADDRESS: 75 Woodbury Blvd, Rochester NY 14607
DESCRIPTION: Geva Theatre Center invites aspiring playwrights from the Greater Rochester area, ages 13-18, to submit short plays for consideration for the Young Writers Showcase. We recommend submitting plays of no more than 10 pages and with no more than eight characters.
SUBMISSION MATERIALS: Contact info, SASE, full script **DEADLINE**: 03/01/2018
GENRE: Plays **PREFERRED LENGTH**: 10-minute **FEE**: No **AGENT ONLY**: No

OTHER EDUCATIONAL OPPORTUNITIES

AROUND THE BLOCK PLAYWRITING COURSE
WEBSITE: www.aroundtheblock.org/around_block_playwriting_course
EMAIL: info@aroundtheblock.org   **PHONE:** (212) 673-9187
ADDRESS: 5 E 22nd St, #9-K, New York NY 10010
DESCRIPTION: Course offered: Principles of Playwriting – what they are and how to apply them, taught by Carlos Jerome. The course will meet each week, Saturdays, 10:30 am – 1 pm, starting March 4, for 15 weeks.

DRAMATISTS GUILD INSTITUTE
PARENT ORGANIZATION: Dramatists Guild of America Inc.
WEBSITE: www.dginstitute.org   **EMAIL:** dginstitute@dramatistsguild.com
PHONE: (212) 398-9366   **TWITTER:** @dg_institute
ADDRESS: 1501 Broadway, Ste 701, New York NY 10036
DESCRIPTION: We will regard the Institute as a true place of education, expecting that our faculty and students will combine their energies with the resources of the Dramatists Guild to elevate the creative landscape of the American theatre through the development of new plays and musicals. See website for full details.

EDUCATION AND COMMUNITY ENGAGEMENT PROGRAM
PARENT ORGANIZATION: Chicago Dramatists
WEBSITE: www.chicagodramatists.org   **EMAIL:** clantz@chicagodramatists.org
ADDRESS: 1105 W Chicago Ave, Chicago IL 60642
DESCRIPTION: See website for updated information.

EINHORN SCHOOL OF PERFORMING ARTS (ESPA)
PARENT ORGANIZATION: Primary Stages
WEBSITE: www.primarystages.org/ESPA   **EMAIL:** espa@primarystages.org
PHONE: (212) 840-9705   **TWITTER:** @primaryESPA
ADDRESS: 307 W 38th St, Ste 1510, New York NY 10018
DESCRIPTION: The Primary Stages Einhorn School of Performing Arts (ESPA)'s multidisciplinary classes have trained playwrights, actors, and directors in all stages of their development and from all corners of the globe. Our focus is on nurturing, advocating, and honoring emerging artists by providing them countless developmental opportunities, space to write and rehearse, and a family of collaborators. ESPA is open to all artists, in all stages of their careers.

THE LITTLE THEATRE OF ALEXANDRIA PLAYWRITING CLASS
WEBSITE: www.thelittletheatre.com   **EMAIL:** asklta@thelittletheatre.com
PHONE: (703) 683-5578   **ADDRESS:** 600 Wolfe St, Alexandria VA 22314

PRACTICE-BASED, LOW-RESIDENCY
MFA
WRITING FOR STAGE AND SCREEN

[He]ld in Peterborough and Sharon NH, with an outstanding faculty of nationally [re]cognized playwrights and screenwriters focusing on the writing process from [pre]-draft story development through the finished draft and beyond.

NHIA — NEW HAMPSHIRE INSTITUTE OF ART

Sharon Campus
457 NH Route 123, Sharon NH
603.836.2588 | gradadmissions@nhia.edu
www.nhia.edu/graduate-studies

PLUS programs in Visual Arts | Photography | Writing

WRITING FOR THE SCREEN AND STAGE
LOW-RESIDENCY M.F.A. | POINT PARK UNIVERSITY

CORE FACULTY

Matt Pelfrey *(MTV's SKINS/ In the Heat of the Night)*

Elise D'Haene *(Red Shoe Diaries, Little Mermaid II)*

Molly Rice *(The Saints Tour, Don't Stop)*

RECENT VISITORS

Gab Cody *(Fat Beckett)*

Tim Griffin *(Entourage)*

Jason Grote *(Mad Men/Hannibal)*

Gordy Hoffman *(Love Liza)*

Chris Moore *(Good Will Hunting/American Pie)*

Tammy Ryan *(Lost Boy Found in Whole Foods/Soldier's Heart)*

Ellen Sandler *(Everybody Loves Raymond)*

Scholarships Available

Find out more:
PointPark.edu/MFAScreenAndStage

POINT PARK UNIVERSITY — Pittsburgh, Pa.

NORTHWEST CHILDREN'S THEATER & SCHOOL
WEBSITE: www.nwcts.org **EMAIL:** info@nwcts.org **PHONE:** (503) 222-2190
ADDRESS: 1819 NW Everett St, Portland OR 97209

SENIOR PLAYWRITING
PARENT ORGANIZATION: Delaware Theatre Company
WEBSITE: www.delawaretheatre.org/senior-playwriting
EMAIL: asteele@delawaretheatre.org **TWITTER:** @DelawareTheatre
DESCRIPTION: Through a partnership between DTC and Ingleside Retirement Apartments, the Playwriting for Seniors Program was born. Now reaching a number of facilities, the program allows participants to meet and share stories of their past while also learning the fundamentals of playwriting. Ingleside residents meet once a week for ten weeks to write, edit and perform original monologues drawn from their own life histories.

SOUTH COAST REPERTORY PLAYWRITING CLASSES
WEBSITE: www.scr.org/classes/adult-acting-and-playwriting-classes
EMAIL: holly@scr.org **PHONE:** (714) 708-5510 **FAX:** (714) 545-0395
ADDRESS: PO Box 2197, Costa Mesa CA 92628
DESCRIPTION: Classes are offered four times a year with a cost of $315 for 8 weeks. If you register 10 days before the session begins, you will receive a $20 discount for early registration. Most classes are offered every session but can not be guaranteed.

THE THEATRE LAB SCHOOL OF DRAMATIC ARTS
WEBSITE: www.theatrelab.org **EMAIL:** contact@theatrelab.org
PHONE: (202) 824-0449 **FAX:** (202) 824-0458
ADDRESS: 733 8th St NW, Washington DC 20001

EMERGENCY FUNDS

ACTORS FUND [LA]
WEBSITE: www.actorsfund.org **EMAIL**: intakela@actorsfund.org
PHONE: (888) 825-0911 **TWITTER:** @TheActorsFund
ADDRESS: 5757 Wilshire Blvd, Ste 400, Los Angeles CA 90036
DESCRIPTION: We provide free and confidential assistance nationally to everyone who works in performing arts and entertainment—including actors, dancers, musicians, stagehands, playwrights and many more. Whether you work on stage or on camera, behind the scenes or below the line, you can contact The Actors Fund for support.

ACTORS FUND [NY]
WEBSITE: www.actorsfund.org **EMAIL**: intakeny@actorsfund.org
PHONE: (212) 221-7300 ext.119 **TWITTER:** @TheActorsFund
ADDRESS: 729 7th Ave, 10th Fl, New York NY 10019
DESCRIPTION: We provide free and confidential assistance nationally to everyone who works in performing arts and entertainment—including actors, dancers, musicians, stagehands, playwrights and many more. Whether you work on stage or on camera, behind the scenes or below the line, you can contact The Actors Fund for support.

ALLIANCE OF ARTISTS COMMUNITIES EMERGENCY FUNDS FOR INDIVIDUAL ARTISTS
WEBSITE: www.artistcommunities.org **EMAIL:** info@artistcommunities.org
DESCRIPTION: The fund disburses mini-grants of up to $1,000 to artists who have already been accepted and scheduled for a residency, but who would not otherwise be able to participate due to a sudden change in circumstances. The Alliance also serves artists affected by natural disasters by mobilizing its network of residency programs to offer residencies to eligible artists. This process is activated as-needed, and will be announced by the Alliance online, through CERF+, and throughout its network.

AMERICAN SOCIETY OF JOURNALISTS & AUTHORS WRITERS EMERGENCY ASSISTANCE FUND
WEBSITE: www.asja.org/for-writers/weaf **EMAIL:** weaf@asja.org
PHONE: (212) 997-0947 **FAX:** (212) 937-2315 **TWITTER**: ASJAhq
ADDRESS: 1501 Broadway, Ste 302, New York NY 10036
DESCRIPTION: Helping established freelance writers across the country who, because of advanced age, illness, disability, a natural disaster, or an extraordinary professional crisis, are unable to work. Membership in ASJA not required. No grants to beginning freelancers seeking funding for writing projects; no grants to fund works-in-progress of any kind. Maximum grant: $3,500. The following types of writing do not count toward qualifications for ASJA Associate membership:

• Fiction or poetry
• Work from markets that direct writers to use their advertisers as sources
• Most self-published or subsidy-published books and materials (see caveat above)
• PR, advertising, or other writings paid for, in whole or in part, by the subject(s) of the piece(s).

ARTISTS' FELLOWSHIP, INC
WEBSITE: www.artistsfellowship.com/home.html **EMAIL:** info@artistsfellowship.org
PHONE: (212) 255-7740 ext.216 **ADDRESS:** 47 5th Ave, New York NY 10003
DESCRIPTION: The Artists' Fellowship, Inc. is a private, charitable foundation that assists professional fine artists (painters, graphic artists, sculptors) and their families in times of emergency, disability, or bereavement.

AUTHORS LEAGUE FUND
WEBSITE: www.authorsleaguefund.org **EMAIL:** staff@authorsleaguefund.org
PHONE: (212) 268-1208 **FAX:** (212) 564-5363
ADDRESS: 155 Water St, #206, Brooklyn NY 11201
DESCRIPTION: Since 1917, the Authors League Fund has been helping professional writers and dramatists who find themselves in financial need because of medical or health-related problems, temporary loss of income, or other misfortune. Emergency assistance for book authors, journalists, and dramatists facing unexpected financial hardship. Help with necessary expenses, such as rent, medical bills, groceries, utilities, etc.

BROOKLYN ARTS FUND
PARENT ORGANIZATION: Brooklyn Arts Council (BAC)
WEBSITE: brooklynartscouncil.submittable.com/submit
EMAIL: bac@brooklynartscouncil.org **PHONE:** (718) 625-0080
ADDRESS: 20 Jay St, Ste 616, Brooklyn NY 11201
DESCRIPTION: The Brooklyn Arts Fund aims to cultivate Brooklyn's artists, arts organizations, and audiences through its support of performances, exhibitions, pop-up galleries, workshops, reading series, festivals, public art and more, all across the borough. This program is appropriate for arts and culture makers developing projects that contribute to the rich creative experiences that engage audiences all across the borough. Competitive applicants will clearly identify the audience they strive to reach, and articulate how the project's outcome(s) will impact the cultural life of the borough. This program is appropriate for arts and culture makers developing projects that contribute to the rich creative experiences that engage audiences all across the borough. Competitive applicants will clearly identify the audience they strive to reach, and articulate how the project's outcome(s) will impact the cultural life of the borough. Brooklyn-based 501c3 organizations and individual artists with Brooklyn residency may apply directly to this program.

CARNEGIE FUND FOR AUTHORS
WEBSITE: www.carnegiefundforauthors.org **PHONE:** (516) 877-2141
ADDRESS: Lenox Hill Station, PO Box 409, New York NY 10021
DESCRIPTION: Grants for published authors in need of emergency financial assistance as a result of illness/injury to self, spouse, or dependent child, or who has had other misfortune that has placed the applicant in pressing and substantial pecuniary need. We accept applications from any American author who has written at least one book of reasonable length that has been published commercially and received reader acceptance.

EMERGENCY FUNDS

CERF+
WEBSITE: cerfplus.org **EMAIL:** info@cerfplus.org **PHONE:** 802-229-2306
ADDRESS: 535 Stone Cutters Way, Ste 202, Montpelier VT 05602
DESCRIPTION: CERF+ is a national non-profit arts organization serving artists who work in craft disciplines for over 30 years by providing a safety net to support strong and sustainable careers. CERF+'s core services are education programs, advocacy, network building and emergency relief. Our emergency financial relief program, the Craft Emergency Relief Fund, provides grants up to $6,000 and interest-free loans up to $9,000 to artists working in craft disciplines who are facing a career threatening emergency or disaster

CREATIVE RESISTANCE FUND
WEBSITE: freedimensional.org/resources/money
EMAIL: inquiry@freedimensional.org
ADDRESS: C/O freeDimensional, PO Box 2, New York NY 10276
DESCRIPTION: An online database of emergency fund listings.

DRAMATISTS GUILD FOUNDATION
WEBSITE: www.dgf.org **EMAIL:** Rachel@DGFund.org **PHONE:** (212) 391-8384
TWITTER: @DGFound **ADDRESS:** 356 W 40th St, 2nd Fl, New York NY 10018
DESCRIPTION: If you are a writer in need, we can help. DGF Emergency Grants provide financial assistance to individual playwrights, composers, lyricists, and bookwriters nationwide in dire need of funds due to severe hardship or unexpected illness. Visit dgf.org/grants. DGF also institutes several programs designed to meet you where you are as a writer and help bridge you to your full potential. For more information on any of these programs, visit dgf.org or email info@dgf.org.

FOUNDATION FOR CONTEMPORARY ARTS
WEBSITE: www.foundationforcontemporaryarts.org/grants/emergency-grants
EMAIL: grants@contemporary-arts.org **PHONE:** (212) 807-7077
ADDRESS: 820 Greenwich St, New York NY 10014
DESCRIPTION: In keeping with FCA's mission to encourage, sponsor, and promote work of a contemporary, experimental nature, applicants must demonstrate that their artistic practice falls within this context. Emergency Grants provides prompt funding for innovative visual and performing artists who have unanticipated, sudden opportunities to present their work to the public when there is insufficient time to seek other sources of funding and/or incur unexpected or unbudgeted expenses for projects close to completion with committed exhibition or performance dates. Grants range in amount from $200 to $2,500.

THE HAVEN FOUNDATION
WEBSITE: www.thehavenfdn.org **ADDRESS:** PO Box 128, Brewer ME 04412
DESCRIPTION: Founded by Stephen King, the mission of The Haven Foundation is to strengthen and sustain the careers of freelance professional writers, artists and others connected with the entertainment industry across the United States ("qualified persons"). The Foundation accomplishes its mission through direct financial assistance to qualified persons, including financial support. See website for details.

EMERGENCY FUNDS

HUMAN RIGHTS WATCH / HELLMAN-HAMMETT GRANTS

WEBSITE: www.hrw.org/human-rights-watch/hellman-hammett-grants
EMAIL: hhgrants@hrw.org **PHONE:** (212) 290-4700
ADDRESS: 350 5th Ave, 34th Fl, New York NY 10118-3299
DESCRIPTION: Human Rights Watch administers the Hellman/Hammett grant program for writers all around the world who have been victims of political persecution and are in financial need. The grants are named for the late American playwright Lillian Hellman and her longtime companion, the novelist Dashiell Hammett. The program also gives small emergency grants to writers who have an urgent need to leave their country or who need immediate medical treatment after serving prison terms or enduring torture. See website for details.

MARY MASON MEMORIAL LEMONADE FUND

WEBSITE: www.theatrebayarea.org/?page=LemonadeFund
EMAIL: dale@theatrebayarea.org **PHONE:** (415) 430-1140
FAX: (415) 430-1145 **TWITTER:** @theatrebayarea
ADDRESS: 1119 Market St, 2nd Fl, San Francisco CA 94103
DESCRIPTION: A confidential resource for theatre practitioners with terminal or life-threatening illnesses who are in need of supplemental financial assistance to improve the quality of their lives as they deal with medical conditions. Since 2000, Theatre Bay Area has distributed over $100,000 to theatre workers in need through the Lemonade Fund. Much of it is made possible by generous donations by fellow artists. See website for information and application.

MAX'S KANSAS CITY PROJECT

WEBSITE: maxskansascity.org **EMAIL:** maxskc@aol.com
PHONE: (845) 679-2593 **FAX:** (845) 679-2593 **TWITTER:** maxskcproject
ADDRESS: PO Box 53, Woodstock NY 12498
DESCRIPTION: We are dedicated to providing emergency funding and resources to financially distressed individuals in the creative and performing arts for housing, medical and legal aid. One time grants are awarded ranging from $500-$1000. Special consideration is given, but not limited to, Max's Kansas City's extended family, (those who worked at Max's or were Max's patrons).

PEN AMERICA WRITERS' EMERGENCY FUND

PARENT ORGANIZATION: Pen America
WEBSITE: pen.org/writers-emergency-fund **EMAIL:** feprogram@pen.org
PHONE: (212) 334-1660 **FAX:** (212) 334-2181 **TWITTER:** @PENamerican
ADDRESS: 588 Broadway #303, New York NY 10012
DESCRIPTION: Est. 1921. An emergency fund for professional—published or produced—writers in acute, emergency financial crisis. Depending on the situation, the Fund gives grants of up to $2,000. The maximum amount is given only under especially dire circumstances and when monies are available. It is the Fund's preference not to give repeated grants within a three-year period. See website for details and application.

SFWA EMERGENCY MEDICAL FUND

WEBSITE: www.sfwa.org/about/benevolent-funds/emergency-medical-fund
EMAIL: emf@sfwa.org **TWITTER:** @sfwa **ADDRESS:** Science Fiction & Fantasy Writers of America, PO Box 3238, Enfield CT 06083
DESCRIPTION: SFWA is an organization for published authors and industry professionals in the fields of science fiction, fantasy, and related genres. The Emergency Medical Fund (EMF) is established to help genre writers pay medical expenses not otherwise covered by insurance. The fund is meant to cover only short-term (i.e. Emergency situations that interfere with the ability to write.) Requests must specify the recipient, a description of the circumstances, and the amount of support needed. Additional information may be requested by the EMF Committee. See website for details.

SPRINGBOARD FOR THE ARTS

WEBSITE: springboardforthearts.org **PHONE:** (651) 292-4381
TWITTER: @SpringboardArts
ADDRESS: 308 Prince St, Ste 270, St Paul MN 55101
DESCRIPTION: Springboard for the Arts is an economic and community development organization for artists and by artists. Our work is about building stronger communities, neighborhoods, and economies, and we believe that artists are an important leverage point in that work. Springboard for the Arts' mission is to cultivate vibrant communities by connecting artists with the skills, information, and services they need to make a living and a life.

TURN2US

WEBSITE: www.turn2us.org.uk **PHONE:** +44 (0)808-802-2000
TWITTER: @turn2us_org
ADDRESS: 200 Shepherds Bush Rd, Hammersmith W6 7NL United Kingdom
DESCRIPTION: Turn2us is a national charity set up in 1897 to fight poverty in the UK. We help people in financial need gain access to welfare benefits, charitable grants and other financial help – online, by phone and face to face.

WOODCOCK FUND

PARENT ORGANIZATION: Writers' Trust of Canada
WEBSITE: www.writerstrust.com/Programs/WoodcockFund **EMAIL:** jdavies@writerstrust.com **PHONE:** (416) 504-8222 **TWITTER:** @writerstrust
ADDRESS: 600-460 Richmond St W, Toronto ON M5V 1Y1 Canada
DESCRIPTION: The Woodcock Fund provides emergency funding to professional Canadian writers in mid-project who are facing an unforeseen financial need that threatens the completion of their book, and who lack the resources to meet that situation. Each grant is given as one-time assistance for a specific emergency. (The program does not consider requests for chronic situations or project funding; nor can it consider situations resulting from general indebtedness or lack of employment.) See website for details.

MEMBERSHIP & SERVICE ORGANIZATIONS

ACTORS FEDERAL CREDIT UNION (AFCU)
WEBSITE: www.actorsfcu.com **EMAIL:** mservices@actorsfcu.com
PHONE: (212) 869-8926 **FAX:** (212) 278-8655 **TWITTER:** @ActorsFCU
ADDRESS: 165 W 46th St, 14th Fl, New York NY 10036
DESCRIPTION: AFCU is a cooperatively run, not-for-profit financial organization chartered in 1962. Any paid-up member of Equity, SAG-AFTRA, AGMA, or member in good standing of any of our 151 member organizations – including the Dramatists Guild – is eligible to apply.

ALLIANCE FOR JEWISH THEATRE
WEBSITE: alljewishtheatre.org **EMAIL:** info@alljewishtheatre.org
PHONE: (312) 608-9781 **TWITTER:** @AJTtweets
ADDRESS: 1810 W Farwell, #1A, Chicago IL 60626
DESCRIPTION: A 501(c)(3) nonprofit organization made up of theatre-artists, theatres, and other people connected to theatre to promote the creation, presentation, and preservation of both traditional and non-traditional theatrical endeavors by, for, and about the Jewish experience.

ALLIANCE OF ARTISTS COMMUNITIES
WEBSITE: www.artistcommunities.org **EMAIL:** info@artistcommunities.org
PHONE: (401) 351-4320 **FAX** (401) 351-4507 **TWITTER:** @artistresidency
ADDRESS: 144 Westminster St, Ste 301, Providence RI 02903
DESCRIPTION: The Alliance gives a collective voice on behalf of its members, small and large, that leverages support for the field as a whole; promotes successful practices in the field; and advocates for creative environments that support the work of today's artists. Website includes a directory of residencies.

ALLIANCE OF LOS ANGELES PLAYWRIGHTS
WEBSITE: www.laplaywrights.org **EMAIL:** DanB@LAPlaywrights.org
PHONE: (323) 696-ALAP (2527) **TWITTER:** @LAPlaywrights
ADDRESS: 7190 Sunset Blvd, #1050, Los Angeles CA 90046
DESCRIPTION: A service and support organization dedicated to protecting the rights and addressing the professional needs of the Los Angeles playwriting community. Founded in 1993, ALAP has a large and diverse membership of area playwrights ranging from students and beginning writers to established professionals. ALAP is all-volunteer, and is a nonprofit 501(c)(3) organization.

ALLIANCE OF RESIDENT THEATERS (ART/NY)
WEBSITE: www.art-newyork.org **EMAIL:** tgramps@art-newyork.org
PHONE: (212) 244-6667 **FAX:** (212) 714-1918 **TWITTER:** @artny72
ADDRESS: 520 8th Ave, #319, New York NY 10018

MEMBERSHIP & SERVICE ORGANIZATIONS

DESCRIPTION: Est. 1972, the Alliance of Resident Theatres/New York is an arts service organization dedicated to supporting New York City's vibrant community of nonprofit theatres.

ALTERNATE ROOTS INC.
WEBSITE: www.alternateroots.org **EMAIL**: carlton@alternateroots.org
PHONE: (404) 577-1079 **FAX**: (404) 577-7991 **TWITTER**: @Alternate_ROOTS
ADDRESS: 115 Martin Luther King Jr Dr, Atlanta GA 30303
DESCRIPTION: As a member-driven national resource for artists and cultural organizers, we seek to champion social and economic justice and the work of people in our field. The ROOTS Region covers the Southern area of the United States: Alabama, Arkansas, Florida, Georgia, Kentucky, Louisiana, Maryland, Mississippi, North Carolina, South Carolina, Tennessee, Texas, Virginia, West Virginia, and Washington, D.C.

AMERICAN ALLIANCE FOR THEATRE & EDUCATION
WEBSITE: www.aate.com **EMAIL**: john.newman@uvu.edu
PHONE: (202) 909-1194 **TWITTER**: @AATENow
ADDRESS: 718 7th St NW, Washington DC 20001
DESCRIPTION: Works to ensure that every young person experiences quality theatre arts in their lives provided by proficient, talented artists and educators. AATE is a registered 501(c)3 non-profit organization. Through its membership of theatre artists, inservice and pre-service teachers, professors, directors, scholars and playwrights, AATE serves more than a million students in 48 U.S. states and 19 countries worldwide.

AMERICAN ASSOCIATION OF COMMUNITY THEATRE
WEBSITE: www.aact.org **EMAIL**: newplayfest@aact.org
PHONE: (866) 687-2228 **ADDRESS**: 1300 Gendy St, Ft Worth TX 76107
DESCRIPTION: AACT Helps Theatres Thrive. Est. 1986, AACT is a nonprofit corporation that serves both individuals and organizations by providing expertise, assistance and support so that community theatres can provide the best possible theatrical experience for participants and audience alike.

AMERICAN INDIAN COMMUNITY HOUSE
WEBSITE: www.aich.org **EMAIL**: jcyrus@aich.org **PHONE**: (212) 598-0100
FAX: (212) 598-4909 **TWITTER**: @AICHNYC
ADDRESS: 11 Broadway, 2nd Fl, New York NY 10004
DESCRIPTION: Est. 1969, AICH is a 501(c)(3) nonprofit organization serving the health, social service, and cultural needs of Native Americans residing in New York City. AICH also sponsors programs in cultural enrichment through a performing arts program and the first permanent Native American gallery in New York City.

AMERICAN TRANSLATORS ASSN. (ATA)
WEBSITE: www.atanet.org **EMAIL**: ata@atanet.org **PHONE**: (703) 683-6100
FAX: (703) 683-6122 **TWITTER**: @atanet

MEMBERSHIP & SERVICE ORGANIZATIONS

ADDRESS: 225 Reinekers Ln, #590, Alexandria VA 22314

DESCRIPTION: Est. 1959. ATA was established to advance the translation and interpreting professions and foster the professional development of individual translators and interpreters.

AMERICANS FOR THE ARTS
WEBSITE: www.artsusa.org **EMAIL**: info@afta.org **PHONE**: (202) 371-2830
FAX: (202) 371-0424 **TWITTER**: @Americans4Arts
ADDRESS: 1000 Vermont Ave NW, 6th Fl, Washington DC 20005

DESCRIPTION: Our mission is to serve, advance, and lead the network of organizations and individuals who cultivate, promote, sustain, and support the arts in America. Connecting your best ideas and leaders from the arts, communities, and business, together we can work to ensure that every American has access to the transformative power of the arts.

ARTSPACE PROJECTS, INC.
WEBSITE: www.artspace.org/our-places **EMAIL**: info@artspace.org
PHONE: (612) 333-9012 **TWITTER**: @artspaceusa
ADDRESS: 250 3rd Ave N, Ste 400, Minneapolis MN 55401

DESCRIPTION: Est. 1979. Artspace's mission is to create, foster, and preserve affordable space for artists and arts organizations. It is a national leader in the field of developing affordable space that meets the needs of artists through the adaptive reuse of historic buildings and new construction. See website for available leasing information.

ASCAP (AMERICAN SOCIETY OF COMPOSERS, AUTHORS & PUBLISHERS)
WEBSITE: www.ascap.com **EMAIL**: mkerker@ascap.com
PHONE: (212) 621-6234 **TWITTER**: @ASCAP
ADDRESS: 1 Lincoln Plz, New York NY 10023

DESCRIPTION: Est. 1914. Membership organization for composers, lyricists, and publishers of musical works. Programs include winter and spring Musical Theater Workshops directed by Stephen Schwartz and Songwriters Showcases in NY and LA. Author must be published, recorded, or performed.

ASSOCIATION FOR THEATRE IN HIGHER EDUCATION (ATHE)
WEBSITE: www.athe.org/?page=Awards **EMAIL**: erice@athe.org
PHONE: (800) 918-9216 **FAX**: (800) 809-6374 **TWITTER**: @TheatreHigherEd
ADDRESS: 1000 Westgate Dr, Ste 252, St Paul MN 55114

DESCRIPTION: Est. 1986. Organization promoting excellence in theater education through publications, conferences, advocacy, projects, and collaborative efforts with other organizations.

ASSOCIATION OF AUTHORS' REPRESENTATIVES, INC.
WEBSITE: aaronline.org **EMAIL**: administrator@aaronline.org
ADDRESS: 302A W 12th St, #122, New York NY 10014

DESCRIPTION: We are a professional organization of over 400 agents who work with both book authors and playwrights. Our members must meet the highest standards and subscribe to our Canon of Ethics. If you are looking for an agent, browse our roster to see which agents might be right for your project. aaronline.org/Find

ASSOCIATION OF WRITERS & WRITING PROGRAMS (AWP)
WEBSITE: www.awpwriter.org **EMAIL**: awp@gmu.edu **PHONE**: (703) 993-4301
FAX: (703) 993-4302 **TWITTER**: @awpwriter
ADDRESS: George Mason Univ, Mail Stop 1E3, Fairfax VA 22030
DESCRIPTION: Est. 1967. Provides support, advocacy, resources, and community to nearly 50,000 writers, 550 college and university creative writing programs, and 150 writers' conferences and centers. Our mission is to foster literary achievement, advance the art of writing as essential to a good education, and serve the makers, teachers, students, and readers of contemporary writing.

AUSTIN SCRIPT WORKS (ASW)
WEBSITE: www.scriptworks.org **EMAIL**: info@scriptworks.org
PHONE: (512) 454-9727 **ADDRESS**: PO Box 9787, Austin TX 78766
DESCRIPTION: Est. 1997. Austin Script Works supports playwrights by providing opportunities at all stages of the writing process from inception to production, through a variety of programming.

BEVERLY HILLS THEATRE GUILD
WEBSITE: www.beverlyhillstheatreguild.com **PHONE**: (310) 273-3390
ADDRESS: PO Box 148, Beverly Hills CA 90213
DESCRIPTION: Est. 1977. The Beverly Hills Theatre Guild was established to develop and maintain greater community interest in the theatre. BHTG is a non-profit organization made up of a diverse group of members who work together to encourage new works in the theatre and musical theatre and to enrich theatrical experiences in the community. We welcome new members who are interested in participating in The Guild through either active or financial support.

BILLY ROSE THEATRE DIVISION
WEBSITE: www.nypl.org/locations/divisions/billy-rose-theatre-division
EMAIL: theatrediv@nypl.org **PHONE**: (212) 870-1637 **FAX**: (212) 870-1868
TWITTER: @nypl **ADDRESS**: 40 Lincoln Center Plz, 3rd Fl, New York NY 10023
DESCRIPTION: Research facility with historical and current docs of performing arts and popular entertainment, incl. books, personal papers, scripts and promptbooks from theater, film, TV and radio. Tape archive incl. Broadway, Off-Broadway and regional productions.

BLACK THEATRE NETWORK
WEBSITE: www.blacktheatrenetwork.org
EMAIL: President@Blacktheatrenetwork.org **PHONE**: (850) 656-9061
ADDRESS: 8306 Bluebird Way, Lorton VA 22079
DESCRIPTION: Comprised of artists, educators, scholars, students and theatre lovers

who are dedicated to the exploration and preservation of the theatrical visions of the African Diaspora. BTN's main function is to expose the beauty and complexity of the inherited theatre work of our African American ancestors, and to take this work to a higher level through the 21st century and beyond. We seem to unite those who share this rich inheritance to assure that we all work TOGETHER.

BLACK WOMEN'S PLAYWRIGHTS' GROUP

WEBSITE: www.blackwomenplaywrights.org **EMAIL**: info@bwpg.org
PHONE: (202) 832-7329 **TWITTER**: @BLKWMPLYWRIGHTS
ADDRESS: 2229 Newton St, NE, Washington DC 20018
DESCRIPTION: BWPG serves African American playwrights writing for the professional theater. It is an institution that reflects and serves our community, gives voice and an artistic haven to women who are writing their first play and to those who have won many honors and awards. Founded in 1989 and incorporated in 1993, the mission of BWPG is to support and promote the work of our members as well as provide leadership and advocacy on critical issues within the theater world.

BMI (BROADCAST MUSIC INC)

WEBSITE: www.bmi.com **EMAIL**: theater@bmi.com **TWITTER**: @bmi
ADDRESS: 7 World Trade Ctr, 250 Greenwich St, New York NY 10007
DESCRIPTION: Est. 1939. Performing rights society that collects royalties on behalf of songwriters, composers, and music publishers.

BROOKLYN WRITERS SPACE

WEBSITE: www.brooklynwriters.com **EMAIL**: info@brooklynwriters.com
PHONE: 718-788-2697 **ADDRESS**: 185 1st St, 2nd Fl, Brooklyn NY 11215
DESCRIPTION: The Brooklyn Writers Space provides a dedicated place for writers of all genres that is quiet and fosters their literary success. Currently offering two locations. Accepting applications here: brooklynwriters.com/wp/application-form

CENTRE DES AUTEURS DRAMATIQUES (CEAD)

WEBSITE: www.cead.qc.ca **EMAIL**: cead@cead.qc.ca **PHONE**: (514) 288-3384
FAX: (514) 288-7043 **TWITTER**: @LeCEAD
ADDRESS: 261 rue du St-Sacrement, #200, Montreal QC H2Y 3V2 Canada
DESCRIPTION: Est. 1965. CEAD has nearly 250 members and is at the service of authors. It is a center of support, promotion and distribution of francophone dramaturgy in Quebec and Canada. Center for Dramatic Development, it occupies a unique place in the theatrical landscape as much by the number of authors authors as by the objectives of research and excellence that it pursues. Website in French.

CENTRE FOR INDIGENOUS THEATRE

WEBSITE: www.indigenoustheatre.com
EMAIL: rosestella@indigenoustheatre.com **PHONE**: (416) 506-9436
FAX: (416) 506-9430 **ADDRESS**: Ste 209, 180 Shaw St, Toronto ON M6J 2W5 Canada
DESCRIPTION: Est. 1994. A 3 year full-time program. The Centre embraces the spirit, energy and inspiration derived from the culture, values and traditions of Indigenous

people. From these roots, we seek to elaborate a contemporary Indigenous performance culture through training and professional development opportunities for emerging and established Native theatre artists.

CHICAGO DRAMATISTS

WEBSITE: www.chicagodramatists.org **EMAIL**: clantz@chicagodramatists.org
PHONE: (312) 633-0630 **TWITTER**: @ChiDrama
ADDRESS: 1105 W Chicago Ave, Chicago IL 60642
DESCRIPTION: Est. 1979. Chicago Dramatists nurtures playwrights, develops new plays, and enriches the national theatre repertory. We develop plays through originality, connectivity, harmony, vibrancy, and collaboration.

COMMUNITY THEATRE ASSOCIATION OF MICHIGAN

WEBSITE: communitytheatremichigan.org **PHONE**: (231) 354-7291
ADDRESS: 5951 N Skeel Ave, #420, Oscoda MI 48750
DESCRIPTION: Designed to help community theatre groups thrive while developing the skills and talents of individual members as well.

CULTURECAPITAL.COM

WEBSITE: www.cultural-alliance.org **PHONE**: (202) 638-2406
FAX: (202) 638-3388 **TWITTER**: @MetroDCArts
ADDRESS: 1436 U St NW, #103, Washington DC 20009
DESCRIPTION: Est. 2008 by the Cultural Alliance of Greater Washington, CultureCapital.com connects people to the heart of the thriving arts and culture community throughout Metro DC including the District of Columbia; Montgomery, Prince George's, Arlington and Fairfax Counties; and the City of Alexandria. CultureCapital.com is now a program of HumanitiesDC, a nonprofit organization whose goal is to enrich the quality of life, foster intellectual stimulation, and promote cross-cultural understanding and appreciation of local history in all neighborhoods of DC through humanities programs and grants.

DANISH DRAMATISTS

WEBSITE: www.dramatiker.dk **EMAIL**: admin@dramatiker.dk
PHONE: +45 33454035 **FAX**: +45 33454039
ADDRESS: Autorhuset, Nørre Voldgade 12, 2nd th, Copenhagen 1358 Denmark
DESCRIPTION: Est. 1906. Danish Dramatists' purpose is to take care of the dramatic and professional interests of the drama and to work for the most favorable terms for dramatists and scriptwriters. The federation carries out the joint agreements of the members, and provides consultancy in contractual matters as well as legal assistance in professional cases. Danish Dramatists are members of the NDU - Nordisk Dramatikerunion - whose main purpose is to support the rights of Nordic dramatists and to preserve their general economic interests globally.

DANSK FORFATTERFORENING - DANISH AUTHORS' SOCIETY

WEBSITE: www.danskforfatterforening.dk **EMAIL**: df@danskforfatterforening.dk
PHONE: +45 22630048 **ADDRESS**: Strandgade 6, København K 1401 Denmark

DESCRIPTION: Danish Authors' Society was founded in 1894 and today comprises approximately 1,300 authors, translators, and illustrators.

DRAMATISTS GUILD OF AMERICA INC.
WEBSITE: www.dramatistsguild.com **EMAIL**: info@dramatistsguild.com
PHONE: (212) 398-9366 **FAX**: (212) 944-0420 **TWITTER**: @dramatistsguild
ADDRESS: 1501 Broadway, Ste 701, New York NY 10036
DESCRIPTION: Est. 1919. Works for the professional rights of writers of stage works and the conditions under which those works are created and produced. Also fights to secure fair royalties and protect subsidiary rights, artistic control, and copyright ownership. See website for details.

DRAMATISTS GUILD FOUNDATION
WEBSITE: www.dgf.org **EMAIL**: Rachel@DGFund.org **PHONE**: (212) 391-8384
TWITTER: @DGFound **ADDRESS**: 356 W 40th St, 2nd Fl, New York NY 10018
DESCRIPTION: If you are a writer in need, we can help. DGF Emergency Grants provide financial assistance to individual playwrights, composers, lyricists, and bookwriters nationwide in dire need of funds due to severe hardship or unexpected illness. Visit dgf.org/grants. DGF also institutes several programs designed to meet you where you are as a writer and help bridge you to your full potential. For more information on any of these programs, visit dgf.org or email info@dgf.org.

DRAMATISTS LEGAL DEFENSE FUND
WEBSITE: www.dldf.org **EMAIL**: info@dldf.org **PHONE**: (212) 398-9366
ADDRESS: 1501 Broadway, Ste 701, New York NY 10036
DESCRIPTION: The DLDF believes that the advancement of our society relies on the unfettered expression of our words. The Dramatists Guild has created the Dramatists Legal Defense Fund to advocate and to educate, and to provide you with a new resource in defense of the First Amendment and on behalf of a robust public domain.

EDUCATIONAL THEATRE ASSOCIATION
WEBSITE: www.schooltheatre.org/home **EMAIL**: dlafleche@schooltheatre.org
PHONE: (513) 421-3900 **FAX**: (513) 421-7077 **TWITTER**: @schooltheatre
ADDRESS: 2343 Auburn Ave, Cincinnati OH 45219
DESCRIPTION: Mission: shaping lives through theatre education by honoring student achievement in theatre and enriching their theatre education experience; supporting teachers by providing professional development, networking opportunities, resources, and recognition; and influencing public opinion that theatre education is essential and builds life skills.

THE FIELD
WEBSITE: thefield.org **EMAIL**: claire@thefield.org **PHONE**: (212) 691-6969
FAX: (212) 255-2053 **TWITTER**: @TheFieldNYC
ADDRESS: 75 Maiden Ln, Ste 906, New York NY 10038
DESCRIPTION: Est. 1986. Founded by artists for artists. The Field is a 501(c)(3) nonprofit organization that provides fiscal sponsorship, professional development services, and creative resources to thousands of performing artists in New York City and beyond.

MEMBERSHIP & SERVICE ORGANIZATIONS

FRACTURED ATLAS
WEBSITE: www.fracturedatlas.org **EMAIL**: support@fracturedatlas.org
PHONE: (888) 692-7878 **TWITTER**: @FracturedAtlas
ADDRESS: 248 W 35th St, 10th Fl, New York NY 10001
DESCRIPTION: Est. 2002. Fractured Atlas empowers artists, arts organizations, and other cultural sector stakeholders by eliminating practical barriers to artistic expression, so as to foster a more agile and resilient cultural ecosystem.

GREENSBORO PLAYWRIGHTS' FORUM
WEBSITE: www.greensboro-nc.gov/index.aspx?page=1475
EMAIL: todd.fisher@greensboro-nc.gov **PHONE**: (336) 373-2974
ADDRESS: 200 N Davie St, #2, Greensboro NC 27401
DESCRIPTION: Est. 1993 as part of the ongoing and growing programs of the City Arts Drama Center. Its mission is to aid playwrights of the Piedmont Triad and North Carolina in getting published or produced through contacts, marketing, and improving their skill as dramatic writers.

INTERNATIONAL CENTER FOR WOMEN PLAYWRIGHTS
WEBSITE: www.womenplaywrights.org
EMAIL: administrator@womenplaywrights.org **TWITTER**: @ICWP
DESCRIPTION: ICWP is virtual organisation; a peer support group for playwrights. We are not a producing house and do not have a physical venue. Please do not send us scripts. Playwrights are invited to become members and receive news of opportunities, join our online discussions, participate in script feedback groups and other membership activities.

INTERNATIONAL INTELLECTUAL PROPERTY ALLIANCE [IIPA]
WEBSITE: www.iipawebsite.com **EMAIL**: info@iipaWEBSITE.com
PHONE: 202-355-7900 **ADDRESS**: 1818 N St NW, 8th Fl, Washington DC 20036
DESCRIPTION: Est. 1984, IIPA is a private sector coalition of trade associations representing U.S. copyright-based industries in bilateral and multilateral efforts working to improve international protection and enforcement of copyrighted materials and open up foreign markets closed by piracy and other market access barriers.

INTERNATIONAL THEATRE INSTITUTE - U.S. CENTER
WEBSITE: www.tcg.org/International/ITI/USCenterofITI.aspx **EMAIL**: iti@tcg.org
PHONE: (212) 609-5900 **ADDRESS**: 520 8th Ave, 24th Fl, New York NY 10018
DESCRIPTION: Mission: to promote the international exchange of knowledge and practice in theatre arts in order to consolidate peace and friendship between peoples, to deepen mutual understanding and increase creative co-operation between all people in the theatre arts.

NOTES

MEMBERSHIP & SERVICE ORGANIZATIONS

INTERNATIONAL WOMEN'S WRITING GUILD (IWWG)
WEBSITE: www.iwwg.org **EMAIL:** iwwgquestions@iwwg.org
PHONE: (212) 737-7536 **FAX:** (212) 737-9469 **TWITTER:** @IWWG
ADDRESS: PO Box 810, Gracie Sta, New York NY 10028
DESCRIPTION: We're a global community of women with diverse backgrounds who share core common values.

L.A. STAGE ALLIANCE
WEBSITE: www.lastagealliance.com **EMAIL:** info@lastagealliance.com
PHONE: (213) 614-0556 **TWITTER:** LAStageAlliance
ADDRESS: 4200 W Chevy Chase Dr, Los Angeles CA 90039
DESCRIPTION: Since 1975, LA STAGE has worked to support artists and engage audiences of Greater LA through a series of programs, events, and advocacy efforts. All of our initiatives aim to serve and strengthen the sector — both at an individual and community level. Specifically, we provide resources that facilitate audience engagement, collaborative marketing, community building, and professional development.

LEAGUE OF CHICAGO THEATRES
WEBSITE: www.chicagoplays.com **EMAIL:** ben@chicagoplays.com
PHONE: (312) 554-9800 **TWITTER:** @ChicagoPlays
ADDRESS: 17 N Wabash Ave, Ste 520, Chicago IL 60602
DESCRIPTION: Est. 1979. Serves a membership of more than 200 theaters, a rich and varied theater community ranging from storefront, non-union theaters with budgets under $10,000 to major cultural centers with multi-million dollar shows. No other theater service organization in the country has such a diverse theater membership.

LEAGUE OF PROFESSIONAL THEATRE WOMEN
WEBSITE: www.TheatreWomen.org **EMAIL:** Membership@TheatreWomen.org
PHONE: 888-297-3117 **TWITTER:** @LPTWomen
ADDRESS: 520 8th Avenue, 24th Fl, New York NY 10018
DESCRIPTION: The League of Professional Theatre Women is a membership non-profit organization that champions women in theatre. Learn more: www.theatrewomen.org

THE LILLY AWARDS FOUNDATION
WEBSITE: www.thelillyawards.org **EMAIL:** info@thelillyawards.org
PHONE: (212) 398-0843 **TWITTER:** @TheLillyAwards
ADDRESS: C/O Dramatists Guild of America, 1501 Broadway, Ste 701, New York NY 10036
DESCRIPTION: The Lilly Awards Foundation is a 501(c)(3) nonprofit organization whose mission is to celebrate the work of women in the theater and promote gender parity at all levels of theatrical production.

LITERARY MANAGERS & DRAMATURGS OF THE AMERICAS (LMDA)
WEBSITE: www.lmda.org **EMAIL:** lmdanyc@gmail.com

PHONE: (800) 680-2148 **TWITTER**: @LMDAmericas
ADDRESS: PO Box 604074, Bayside NY 11360
DESCRIPTION: Est. 1985. Volunteer membership organization with conferences, quarterly journal, newsletter, advocacy caucuses, dramaturgy prize, and more.

MISSISSIPPI THEATRE ASSOCIATION
WEBSITE: www.mta-online.org **EMAIL**: execdir@mta-online.org
PHONE: (601) 201-9564 **TWITTER**: @mstheatre
ADDRESS: PO Box 625, Ocean Springs MS 39566
DESCRIPTION: Mission: to foster appreciation of and participation in children's, college, community, high school, professional, and university theatre in Mississippi.

MONTANA ARTS COUNCIL
WEBSITE: art.mt.gov **EMAIL**: mac@mt.gov **PHONE**: 406-444-6430
FAX: (406) 444-6548 **TWITTER**: montanaarts
ADDRESS: PO Box 202201, Helena MT 59620
DESCRIPTION: The Montana Arts Council is the agency of state government established to develop the creative potential of all Montanans, advance education, spur economic vibrancy and revitalize communities through involvement in the arts.

MYSTERY WRITERS OF AMERICA
WEBSITE: mysterywriters.org **EMAIL**: mwa@mysterywriters.org
PHONE: (212) 888-8171 **TWITTER**: @EdgarAwards
ADDRESS: 1140 Broadway, Ste 1507, New York NY 10001
DESCRIPTION: MWA is the premier organization for mystery writers, professionals allied to the crime writing field, aspiring crime writers, and those who are devoted to the genre. MWA is dedicated to promoting higher regard for crime writing and recognition and respect for those who write within the genre. We provide scholarships for writers, sponsor MWA Literacy programs, sponsor symposia and conferences, present the Edgar® Awards, and conduct other activities to further a better appreciation and higher regard for crime writing.

THE NATIONAL ARTS CLUB
WEBSITE: www.nationalartsclub.org **EMAIL**: info@thenationalartsclub.org
TWITTER: @NatnlArtsClub
DESCRIPTION: Est. 1898. Our mission is to stimulate, foster & promote public interest in the arts & educate the American people in the fine arts.

NATIONAL AUDIO THEATRE FESTIVALS (NATF)
WEBSITE: www.natf.org **EMAIL**: hearnowfestival@gmail.com
PHONE: (516) 483-8321 **FAX**: (516) 538-7583 **TWITTER**: @NatAudioTheatre
ADDRESS: 115 Dikeman St, Hempstead NY 11550
DESCRIPTION: Est. 1979. The mission of the NATF is to serve the advancement of audio theatre and evolving media arts through education and presentation. NATF currently incorporates the learning skills once offered at it's annual week-long workshops into the HEAR Now Festivals Workshop 101 program.

NATIONAL COALITION AGAINST CENSORSHIP
WEBSITE: ncac.org **EMAIL**: ncac@ncac.org **PHONE**: (212) 807-6222
FAX: (212) 807-6245 **TWITTER**: @ncacensorship
ADDRESS: 19 Fulton St, Ste 407, New York NY 10038
DESCRIPTION: NCAC's mission is to promote freedom of thought, inquiry and expression and oppose censorship in all its forms. The Coalition formed in response to the 1973 Supreme Court decision in Miller v. California, which narrowed First Amendment protections for sexual expression and opened the door to obscenity prosecutions. 56 national not-for-profit organizations make up the National Coalition Against Censorship including the Dramatists Guild and the Dramatists Legal Defense Fund. These diverse organizations, representing the artistic, educational, religious, and labor communities, join together in the interest of protecting First Amendment rights.

NATIONAL LEAGUE OF AMERICAN PEN WOMEN, INC.
WEBSITE: www.nlapw.org **EMAIL**: contact@nlapw.org **PHONE**: (202) 785-1997
ADDRESS: 1300 17th St NW, Washington DC 20036
DESCRIPTION: Est. 1897. NLAPW's mission is to encourage, recognize, and promote the production of creative work of professional standard in Art, Letters, and Music, and through outreach activities provide educational, creative, and professional support to members and non-members in these disciplines. The core values of the NLAPW are respect, knowledge, creation and preservation of the arts.

NATIONAL WRITERS ASSOCIATION FOUNDATION (NWAF)
WEBSITE: www.nationalwriters.com **EMAIL**: authorsandy@hotmail.com
PHONE: (303) 841-0246 **FAX**: (303) 841-2607 **TWITTER**: @NatlWritersAsn
ADDRESS: PO Box 4187, Parker CO 80134
DESCRIPTION: NWAF exists to enhance the future of writers by fostering continuing education through awarding scholarships and providing no or low cost workshops and seminars. A non-profit organization, we provide education and an ethical resource for writers at all levels of experience.

NEW DRAMATISTS
WEBSITE: www.newdramatists.org **EMAIL**: emilymorse@newdramatists.org
PHONE: (212) 757-6960 **TWITTER**: @NewDramatists
ADDRESS: 424 W 44th St, New York NY 10036
DESCRIPTION: To provide playwrights with time, space and resources in the company of gifted peers to create work, realize their artistic potential, and make lasting contributions to the theatre. Visit website to read further mission cornerstones.

NEW ENGLAND THEATRE CONFERENCE (NETC)
WEBSITE: www.netconline.org **EMAIL**: mail@netconline.org
PHONE: (617) 851-8535 **ADDRESS**: 167 Cherry St, #331, Milford CT 06460
DESCRIPTION: The New England Theatre Conference promotes excellence in theatre for our region, and supports quality theatre and performance in all of its diversity. We believe that theatre is essential to the quality of life for everyone. NETC is composed

of individuals and organizations in the six-State region of New England, who are active or interested in the performing arts.

NEW JERSEY THEATRE ALLIANCE
WEBSITE: njtheatrealliance.org **EMAIL**: info@njtheatrealliance.org
PHONE: 973-731-6582 **FAX**: (973) 731-5520 **TWITTER**: @NJTheatre
ADDRESS: 7 King Pl, Morristown New Jersey 07960
DESCRIPTION: NJTA unites, promotes, strengthens, and cultivates New Jersey's professional theatres. We advance the theatre community by developing innovative, collaborative, and engaging programs and services for member theatres and their diverse audiences.

NEW MUSIC USA
WEBSITE: www.newmusicusa.org **EMAIL**: info@newmusicusa.org
PHONE: (212) 645-6949 **TWITTER**: @NewMusicUSA
ADDRESS: 90 Broad St, Ste 1902, New York NY 10004
DESCRIPTION: Est. 1939. We see ourselves first and foremost as advocates. Our mission is to support and promote new music created in the United States. We do that in many ways, fostering connections, deepening knowledge, encouraging appreciation, and providing financial support. In recognition of the possibility and power inherent in the virtual world, we've worked to build a strong internet platform to serve our constituency. And that constituency is broad and diverse, from composers and performers to presenters and producers, casual listeners to die-hard fans. We're truly committed to serving the WHOLE new music community.

NEW PLAYWRIGHTS FOUNDATION
WEBSITE: www.newplaywrights.org **EMAIL**: dialogue@newplaywrights.org
PHONE: (310) 393-3682 **ADDRESS**: PO Box 54, Santa Monica CA 90406
DESCRIPTION: Est. 1969. A non-profit 501(c)3 corporation. The writers workshop meets every other Thursday, usually in Santa Monica, to read work aloud and offer feedback. NPF has produced members' works for stage, film, and video. Writers, actors, directors, producers, composers, and others are encouraged to attend workshop meetings free of charge. Writers may submit after participating in three meetings and making a $25 (annual) tax-deductible donation to NPF.

NEW YORK FOUNDATION FOR THE ARTS
WEBSITE: www.nyfa.org **EMAIL**: help@nyfa.org **PHONE**: (212) 366-6900
FAX: (212) 366-1778 **TWITTER**: @nyfacurrent
ADDRESS: 20 Jay St, 7th Fl, Brooklyn NY 11201
DESCRIPTION: Each year, NYFA provides over $650,000 in cash grants to individuals pursuing artistic excellence in all forms, as well as a variety of artist-in-residence opportunities. See website for details.

NEW YORK MUSIC FESTIVAL (NYMF)
WEBSITE: www.nymf.org **EMAIL**: info@nymf.org **PHONE**: (212) 664-0979
FAX: (212) 664-0978 **TWITTER**: @NYMF
ADDRESS: 242 W 38th St, #1102, New York NY 10018

DESCRIPTION: Est. 2004. The New York Musical Festival nurtures the creation, production, and public presentation of stylistically, thematically, and culturally diverse new musicals to ensure the future vitality of musical theater.

NORTH CAROLINA WRITERS' NETWORK
WEBSITE: www.ncwriters.org   **EMAIL**: mail@ncwriters.org
PHONE: (336) 293-8844   **TWITTER**: @WritingestState
ADDRESS: PO Box 21591, Winston-Salem NC 27120
DESCRIPTION: North Carolina Writers' Network connects, promotes, and serves the writers of this state. We provide education in the craft and business of writing, opportunities for recognition and critique of literary work, resources for writers at all stages of development, support for and advocacy of the literary heritage of North Carolina, and a community for those who write. We believe that writing is necessary both for self-expression and a healthy community, that well-written words can connect people across time and distance, and that the deeply satisfying experiences of writing and reading should be available to everyone.

NORTHWEST PLAYWRIGHTS ALLIANCE (NPA)
WEBSITE: www.northwestplaywrights.org   **EMAIL**: info@northwestplaywrights.org
ADDRESS: PO Box 1088, McCleary WA 98557
DESCRIPTION: Est. 2004, the NPA connects playwrights, actors, directors, and audiences to support the development and production of new performance works in the Pacific Northwest.

NYC PLAYWRIGHTS
PARENT ORGANIZATION: Mergatroyd Productions
WEBSITE: www.nycplaywrights.org   **EMAIL**: info@nycplaywrights.org
TWITTER: @nycplaywrights
DESCRIPTION: NYCPlaywrights provides playwright submission opportunities; discounts; free shows and other theatre items for New York City and the world.

OPERA AMERICA
WEBSITE: www.operaamerica.org   **EMAIL**: Info@operaamerica.org
PHONE: (212) 796-8620   **FAX**: (212) 796-8631
ADDRESS: 330 7th Ave, 16th Fl, New York NY 10001
DESCRIPTION: The association provides members with an array of publications and online resources, regional workshops, an annual conference and network-specific services such as conference calls, listservs and direct contact with staff with expertise in opera production, administration and education. OPERA America provides members with tools to maximize the effectiveness of financial and human resources, expand the scope of repertoire and programs, and extend their reach to new and diverse audiences. Founded in 1970, OPERA America has an international membership that includes nearly 150 Professional Company Members, 300 Associate and Business Members, 2,000 Individual Members and over 16,000 subscribers to its electronic news service.

MEMBERSHIP & SERVICE ORGANIZATIONS

SHUBERT ARCHIVES
WEBSITE: www.shubertarchive.org **EMAIL**: information@shubertarchive.org
PHONE: (212) 944-3895 **FAX**: (212) 944-4139
ADDRESS: 149 W 45th St, New York NY 10036
DESCRIPTION: Est. 1976. Repository for over 6m docs related to the Shubert brothers and Shubert Org, incl. costume/set designs, scripts, music, publicity, photos, letters, business records, and architectural plans.

SONGWRITERS GUILD OF AMERICA FOUNDATION (SGAF)
WEBSITE: www.songwritersguild.com **EMAIL**: ny@songwritersguild.com
PHONE: (212) 768-7902 **FAX**: (212) 768-7902
ADDRESS: 1560 Broadway, #1306, New York NY 10036

SOUTHEASTERN THEATRE CONFERENCE (SETC)
WEBSITE: www.setc.org **EMAIL**: tiza@setc.org **PHONE**: (336) 272-3645
FAX: (336) 272-8810 **TWITTER**: @SETCTweet
ADDRESS: 1175 Revolution Mill Dr, Studio 14, Greensboro NC 27405
DESCRIPTION: SETC is the strongest and broadest network of theatre practitioners in the United States. We provide extensive resources and year-round opportunities for our constituents. Our services, publications, and products contribute significantly to the careers of emerging artists, seasoned professionals and academicians. SETC energizes the practical, intellectual and creative profile of theatre in America.

STAGE (SOCIETY FOR THEATRICAL ARTISTS' GUIDANCE AND ENHANCEMENT)
WEBSITE: www.stage-online.org **EMAIL**: stage-online@sbcglobal.net
PHONE: (214) 630-7722 **FAX**: (214) 630-4468
ADDRESS: 1106 Lupo Dr, Dallas TX 75207
DESCRIPTION: Est. 1981. Nonprofit promoting theater, broadcast, and film by serving as info clearinghouse and training center for north central Texas. The cost of an Adult membership for your first year is $75.00 membership fee plus a one time application fee of $15.00 = $90.

STAGESOURCE
WEBSITE: www.stagesource.org **EMAIL**: info@stagesource.org
PHONE: (617) 720-6066 **FAX**: (617) 720-4275 **TWITTER**: @StageSourceBos
ADDRESS: 15 Channel Center St, Ste 103, Boston MA 02108
DESCRIPTION: Est. 1985. StageSource provides leadership and services to advance the art of theater in the Greater Boston region. Our mission is to unite theater artists, theater companies, and related organizations in vision and goals that inspire and empower our community to realize its greatest artistic potential.

TASMANIAN WRITERS' CENTRE
WEBSITE: www.tasmanianwriters.org
EMAIL: admin@tasmanianwriters.org **PHONE**: +61 (03) 6224 0029

MEMBERSHIP & SERVICE ORGANIZATIONS

PROFESSIONAL ASSOCIATION OF CANADIAN THEATRES (PACT)
WEBSITE: www.pact.ca **EMAIL**: info@pact.ca **PHONE**: (416) 595-6455
FAX: (416) 595-6450 **TWITTER**: @PACTtweets
ADDRESS: 215 Spadina Ave, #210, Toronto ON M5T 2C7 Canada
DESCRIPTION: PACT is a member-driven organization of professional Canadian theatres which serves as the collective voice of its members. For the betterment of Canadian theatre, PACT provides leadership, national representation and a variety of programs and practical assistance to member companies, enabling members to do their own creative work.

THE PURPLE CIRCUIT
WEBSITE: www.buddybuddy.com/pc.html **EMAIL**: purplecir@aol.com
PHONE: (818) 953-5096 **ADDRESS**: 921 N Naomi St, Burbank CA 91505
DESCRIPTION: The Purple Circuit exists to promote LGBTQ theater and performance throughout the world. The Circuit maintains directory of LGBT friendly venues, free listing of playwrights, submission opportunities, and online newsletter.

RITHÖFUNDASAMBAND ÍSLANDS (WRITERS' UNION OF ICELAND)
WEBSITE: www.rsi.is/english **EMAIL**: rsi@rsi.is **PHONE**: + 354 568 3190
ADDRESS: Gunnarshús, Dyngjuvegi 8, Reykjavik 104 Iceland
DESCRIPTION: The Writers' Union of Iceland (RSÍ) is a professional organisation for authors founded in 1974. Until then, Icelandic writers had a union since 1928 when writers got their own chapter within the Artists Union of Iceland. From 1945, Icelandic writers formed two unions which worked closely together from 1957 until they eventually merged. The Writers' Union of Iceland currently has some 470 members, including poets, novelists, dramatists, scriptwriters, writers of children's books, authors of academic works, and translators.

SALAMANCA ARTS CENTRE
WEBSITE: www.salarts.org.au **EMAIL**: info@salarts.org.au
PHONE: +61 (03) 6234 8414 **TWITTER**: @salarts
ADDRESS: 77 Salamanca Pl, Hobart Tasmania 7000 Australia
DESCRIPTION: Salamanca Arts Centre is the custodian of seven heritage buildings that are home to studio artists in residence, numerous arts organisations working across the visual and performing arts, festivals & events, literature, writing & film, and to designers, makers, retailers of, and commercial galleries for contemporary art and craft.

SASKATCHEWAN WRITERS GUILD
WEBSITE: www.skwriter.com **EMAIL**: info@skwriter.com
PHONE: (306) 757-6310 **ADDRESS**: PO Box 3986, Regina SK S4P 3R9 Canada
DESCRIPTION: Est. 1969. The Saskatchewan Writers' Guild acts as an advocate to improve the status of Saskatchewan writers, encourages the development of writers of all ages and levels through educational opportunities and strives to improve public access to Saskatchewan writers and their work. Membership is open to writers and those interested in Saskatchewan writing.

PLAYWRIGHTS GUILD OF CANADA
WEBSITE: www.playwrightsguild.ca **EMAIL**: membership@playwrightsguild.ca
PHONE: (416) 703-0201 **TWITTER**: @PGuildCanada
ADDRESS: 401 Richmond St W, Ste 350, Toronto ON M5V 3A8 Canada
DESCRIPTION: Playwrights Guild of Canada is a registered national arts service association mandated to advance the creative rights and interests of professional Canadian playwrights, promote Canadian plays nationally and internationally, and foster an active, evolving community of writers for the stage.

PLAYWRIGHTS CENTER SAN FRANCISCO (PCSF),
WEBSITE: www.playwrightscentersf.org
EMAIL: submission@playwrightscentersf.org **PHONE**: (415) 626-0453
ADDRESS: 118 Costanza Dr, Martinez CA 94553
DESCRIPTION: The mission of the The Playwrights' Center of San Francisco (PCSF) is to encourage and develop local playwrights and promote script writing, audience development, and related arts.

PLAYWRIGHTS PROJECT
WEBSITE: www.playwrightsproject.org **EMAIL**: write@playwrightsproject.org
PHONE: (858) 384-2970 **FAX**: (858) 384-2974 **TWITTER**: @PlaywrightsProj
ADDRESS: 3675 Ruffin Rd, Ste 330, San Diego CA 92123
DESCRIPTION: Mission: to advance literacy, creativity, and communication by empowering individuals to voice their stories through playwriting programs and theatre productions. We accomplish these goals by providing playwriting workshops in schools and underserved communities, producing community readings, conducting the annual California Young Playwrights Contest for writers under the age of 19, and professionally producing winning scripts in its annual festival of Plays by Young Writers.

PLAYWRIGHTS' CENTER [MN]
WEBSITE: www.pwcenter.org **EMAIL**: info@pwcenter.org
PHONE: (612) 332-7481 **FAX**: (612) 332-6037 **TWITTER**: @pwcenter
ADDRESS: 2301 Franklin Ave E, Minneapolis MN 55406
DESCRIPTION: Founded in 1971 by five writers seeking artistic and professional support, the Playwrights' Center today serves more playwrights in more ways than any other organization in the country. One of the nation's most generous and well-respected theater organizations, the Playwrights' Center focuses on both supporting playwrights and promoting new plays to production at theaters across the country.

PLAYWRIGHTS' FORUM [MD]
WEBSITE: theplaywrightsforum.org **EMAIL**: pforum7@yahoo.com
PHONE: (301) 816-0569 **ADDRESS**: PO Box 5322, Rockville MD 20848
DESCRIPTION: Est. 1982. One of America's premier playwriting workshops. We offer an exciting program of activities for playwrights at every level of development, enhanced by the participation of leading universities and professional theatres in the Mid-Atlantic region.

MEMBERSHIP & SERVICE ORGANIZATIONS

ORANGE COUNTY PLAYWRIGHTS ALLIANCE
WEBSITE: ocplaywrights.org **EMAIL:** ocpabox@gmail.com
PHONE: (714) 902-5716
ADDRESS: 21112 Indigo Cir, Huntington Beach CA 92646
DESCRIPTION: Committed to free expression and risk-taking, Orange County Playwrights Alliance (OCPA) celebrates, promotes and supports the diversity of playwrights with Orange County in common and provides innovative and educative theatrical experiences for the community at large.

PACIFIC NORTHWEST WRITERS ASSOCIATION
WEBSITE: www.pnwa.org **EMAIL:** pnwa@pnwa.org **PHONE:** (425) 673-2665
ADDRESS: 317 NW Gilman Blvd, Ste 2, Issaquah WA 98027
DESCRIPTION: Since 1955, writers in the NW have been dedicated to helping writers connect to other writers, publishers, agents, and editors across the country. Zola Helen Ross and Lucille McDonald came together to form the Pacific Northwest Writers Association and since the beginning many people have dedicated their time to ensure its continuation. Over the years we have expanded our efforts so that writers receive a trusted resource within this ever-changing publishing industry while staying true to our mission of helping writers carve out their place and provide them with a platform for their literary voice.

PEN AMERICA
WEBSITE: www.pen.org **EMAIL:** info@pen.org **PHONE:** (212) 334-1660
FAX: (212) 334-2181 **TWITTER:** @PENamerican
ADDRESS: 588 Broadway, Ste 303, New York NY 10012
DESCRIPTION: PEN America stands at the intersection of literature and human rights to protect open expression in the United States and worldwide. We oversee a variety of programming, festivals, awards, committees, and emergency funds.

THE PLAYERS CLUB
WEBSITE: www.theplayersnyc.org **EMAIL:** info@theplayersnyc.org
ADDRESS: 16 Gramercy Park S, New York NY 10003
DESCRIPTION: Est 1888. The Players is a private social club that draws its membership from the international theatre community, the related fields of film, television, music, and publishing, as well as respected patrons of the arts.

PLAYMARKET
WEBSITE: www.playmarket.org.nz **EMAIL:** info@playmarket.org.nz
PHONE: +64 9 365 2648 **FAX:** (644) 382-8461
ADDRESS: PO Box 9767, Wellington 6141 New Zealand
DESCRIPTION: Empowering and representing New Zealand playwrights. Our purpose is developing New Zealand's best playwrights and their plays through:
a) Promoting our playwrights' work nationally and internationally; b) Upholding playwrights' standards and rights; c) Providing access to New Zealand scripts; d) Identification and development of playwrights of excellence.

FAX: +61 (03) 6224 0029   **TWITTER**: @TasWriters
ADDRESS: 77 Salamanca Pl, #E101, Hobart Tasmania 7000 Australia
DESCRIPTION: The Centre gives you a wealth of benefits ranging from discounted tickets to exclusive services. Established writers may seek teaching opportunities in our statewide workshop program, career support through our high-profile readings, festival partnerships and feature events, access to visiting writers for networking, and free marketing for their book launches. For emerging writers, we offer guidance, outstanding literary events, services such as manuscript assessment and connection to a wide literary community.

TEXAS NONPROFIT THEATRES
WEBSITE: www.texastheatres.org   **EMAIL**: info@texastheatres.org
PHONE: (817) 731-2238   **TWITTER**: @TexasTheatres
ADDRESS: 1300 Gendy St, Ft Worth TX 76107
DESCRIPTION: Est. 1971. TNT's mission is to support and serve the theatre community of Texas, and specifically to promote high standards in theatre arts; to continue to provide professional training and development for individuals involved in theatre; to promote the development of educational theatre; to provide a forum for the exchange of information and ideas by persons engaged in theatre; to aid and encourage the formation of new theatre groups and support established theatre organizations; to provide information and advocacy for the needs of theatres in Texas within the limits of the law.

THEATER RESOURCES UNLIMITED
WEBSITE: www.truonline.org   **EMAIL**: trustaff1@gmail.com
PHONE: (212) 714-7628   **FAX**: (212) 864-6301   **TWITTER**: @TRUonline
ADDRESS: 309 W 104th St, 1D, New York NY 10025
DESCRIPTION: Est. 1992. TRU was formed to promote a spirit of cooperation and support within the general theatre community by providing information and a variety of entertainment-related services and resources that strengthen the capacity of producing organizations, individuals producers, self-producing artists and other theater professionals.

THEATRE BAY AREA
WEBSITE: www.theatrebayarea.org   **EMAIL**: tba@theatrebayarea.org
PHONE: (415) 430-1140   **TWITTER**: @theatrebayarea
ADDRESS: 1119 Market St, 2nd Fl, San Francisco CA 94103
DESCRIPTION: Est. 1976. At Theatre Bay Area, we believe that the arts are essential to a healthy and democratic society. We work to nourish our creative community and expand access to the arts for all. We are the largest arts service organization of our kind, supporting the radical creativity of our members with unparalleled access to educational, financial and professional resources. Now engaging millions of arts participants each year, our members' work is situated at the dynamic intersections of technology, arts, entertainment and culture. The result—our region is one of the most vibrant and unique cultural destinations in the world.

THEATRE DEVELOPMENT FUND (TDF)
WEBSITE: www.tdf.org   **EMAIL**: dleshay@tdf.org   **PHONE**: (212) 912-9770 ext. 320

TWITTER: @TDFNYC **ADDRESS:** 520 8th Ave, #801, New York NY 10018
DESCRIPTION: a not-for-profit organization, was created with the conviction that the live theatrical arts afford a unique expression of the human condition that must be sustained and nurtured. TDF's twofold mission is to identify and provide support, including financial assistance, to theatrical works of artistic merit and to encourage and enable diverse audiences to attend live theatre and dance in all their venues.

THEATRE FOR YOUNG AUDIENCES/USA
WEBSITE: www.tyausa.org **EMAIL:** info@tyausa.org
PHONE: (917) 438-7010 **TWITTER:** @TYA_USA
ADDRESS: c/o NYC Children's Theater, 340 E 46th St, New York NY 10017
DESCRIPTION: TYA/USA serves and represents the national field of theatre for young audiences.

THEATRE PROJECT
WEBSITE: www.theatreproject.org **EMAIL:** chris@theatreproject.org
PHONE: (410) 539-3091 **FAX:** (410) 539-2137
ADDRESS: 45 W Preston St, Baltimore MD 21201
DESCRIPTION: Est. 1971. Theatre Project—through the presentation of a diverse array of original and experimental theatre, music, and dance—connects the artists and audiences of Baltimore with a global community of performers. We seek to nurture those artists who are actively experimenting with new forms of expression and support both performers of international reputation and emerging local companies creating new work.

THEATRE WEST
WEBSITE: www.theatrewest.org **EMAIL:** theatrewest@theatrewest.org
PHONE: (323) 851-4839 **TWITTER:** @TheatreWest
ADDRESS: 3333 Cahuenga Blvd W, Hollywood CA 90068
DESCRIPTION: Est. 1962. The oldest continually running theatre company in Los Angeles. It is a democratic artistic cooperative of actors, writers, directors, administrators, executive and artistic Board members and technical professionals dedicated to the artistic growth of its members. Our threefold mission statement is to conduct workshops to further our member's artistic growth, present performances grown from those workshops and to do outreach to the greater community. Dues paying company members enjoy access to workshops in acting, playwrighting, musical theatre and Shakespeare.

UNITED STATES COPYRIGHT OFFICE
WEBSITE: www.copyright.gov **PHONE:** (202) 707-3000
ADDRESS: 101 Independence Ave SE, Washington DC 20003
DESCRIPTION: Though registration isn't required for protection, copyright law provides several advantages. See website for details and registration.

VOLUNTEER LAWYERS FOR THE ARTS
WEBSITE: vlany.org/ **EMAIL:** vlany@vlany.org **PHONE:** 212-319-2787
TWITTER: @VLANY **ADDRESS:** 1 E 53rd St, 6th Fl, New York NY 10022

MEMBERSHIP & SERVICE ORGANIZATIONS

DESCRIPTION: Est. 1969. Provider of pro bono legal and mediation services, educational programs, publications, and advocacy to the arts community in NYC. Fees: based on client's finances.

WASHINGTON AREA ARCHIVE OF THE PERFORMING ARTS (WAPAVA)
WEBSITE: www.wapava.org **PHONE**: (703) 248-0026 **FAX**: (703) 248-0028
ADDRESS: PO Box 7582, Arlington VA 22207
DESCRIPTION: Est. 1993. WAPAVA is a nonprofit organization, incorporated in Washington, DC, and is one of only three major continuous Actors' Equity-approved video performance archives in America. WAPAVA is a resource for theater professionals and scholars; students and educational programs; specialized researchers in local/national theater history; and the public. See website for location and details.

WOMEN IN THE ARTS & MEDIA COALITION
WEBSITE: www.womenartsmediacoalition.org
EMAIL: stageopps@womenartsmediacoalition.org
PHONE: (212) 592-4511 **TWITTER**: @WomenArtsMedia
ADDRESS: 244 5th Ave, Ste 2932, New York NY 10001
DESCRIPTION: The Women in the Arts & Media Coalition combines our member organizations' abilities and strengths, focusing on issues of concern to women in the arts and media. We are committed to being the link between our member organizations as we collaborate to empower women in our industry through advocacy, mentoring, networking, and events.

WOMEN PLAYWRIGHTS INTERNATIONAL
WEBSITE: www.wpichile2018.com/wpi
EMAIL: northamericareadingswpichile18@gmail.com
DESCRIPTION: WPI is an opportunity to meet, to build networks, to create genuine, lasting contacts between women playwrights and theatre professionals. Our aim is to have a supporting impact on cooperations and to build bridges between people from different parts of the world. WPI was founded in 1988 and held its first conference in Buffalo, NY. Two hundred women from over 30 countries were in attendance. Since then, women playwrights have gathered in Canada, Ireland, Greece, Australia, the Philippines, Indonesia, India, Sweden, and South Africa.

WOMEN PLAYWRIGHTS' INITIATIVE
WEBSITE: www.womenplaywrights.wordpress.com
EMAIL: womenplaywrights@gmail.com **PHONE**: (407) 380-1812
ADDRESS: PO Box 1546, Orlando FL 32802
DESCRIPTION: Fosters the development and production of plays written by women through educational outreach, workshops, readings and productions.

WOMEN'S THEATRE ALLIANCE
WEBSITE: www.wtachicago.org **EMAIL**: wtachicago@gmail.com
PHONE: (312) 408-9910 **ADDRESS**: 2936 N Southport Ave, Chicago IL 60657
DESCRIPTION: Est. 1992, WTA is a union of theatre artists (female and male) and

theatre organizations which support women, helping to promote leadership and provide opportunity within the theatre community. Alliance members are encouraged to share their advice, knowledge and expertise in the hopes of creating an environment of mutual support and unity in which women's theatre can flourish. WTA works to build a unified voice so that we can more effectively be advocates for women in theatre, publicize and promote our members and increase positive public awareness of our goals.

WOMENARTS

WEBSITE: www.womenarts.org **PHONE**: (510) 868-5096
TWITTER: @WomenArts **ADDRESS**: 1442A Walnut St, #67, Berkeley CA 94709
DESCRIPTION: Est. 1994. A worldwide community of artists and allies that works for empowerment, opportunity, and visibility for women artists. We provide a variety of free online networking, fundraising and advocacy services, and we organize Support Women Artists Now Day (SWAN Day), an annual international holiday celebrating women's creativity in all its forms. We believe in the power of women artists to create, connect, and change the world. WomenArts does not have a grants program, and we do not have enough staff to respond to fundraising questions.

WOW CAFE

WEBSITE: www.wowcafe.org **EMAIL**: wowcafetheater@gmail.com
PHONE: (917) 725-1482 **TWITTER**: @wowcafetheatre
ADDRESS: 59-61 E 4th St, #4, New York NY 10003
DESCRIPTION: WOW Café Theatre is a women's theater collective in NYC's East Village, which promotes the empowerment of women through the performing arts.

WRITERS GUILD OF AMERICA EAST

WEBSITE: www.wgaeast.org **EMAIL**: kobrien@wgaeast.org
PHONE: (212) 767-7800 **TWITTER**: @WGAEast
ADDRESS: 250 Hudson St, Ste 700, New York NY 10013
DESCRIPTION: A labor union of thousands of professionals who are the primary creators of what is seen or heard on television and film in the U.S., as well as the writers of a growing portion of original digital media content. On joining the Guild, writers from an extraordinarily vast range of backgrounds and abilities unite to promote, protect, and maintain important artistic and professional principles. The Guild's assistance is provided regardless of the writers' degree of success.

WRITERS GUILD OF AMERICA WEST

WEBSITE: www.wga.org **EMAIL**: membership@wga.org
PHONE: (323) 951-4000 **TWITTER**: @WGAWest
ADDRESS: 7000 W 3rd St, Los Angeles CA 90048
DESCRIPTION: A labor union composed of the thousands of writers who write the content for television shows, movies, news programs, documentaries, animation, and Internet and mobile phones (new media) that keep audiences constantly entertained and informed.

MEMBERSHIP & SERVICE ORGANIZATIONS

THE WRITERS ROOM
WEBSITE: www.writersroom.org **EMAIL**: writersroom@writersroom.org
PHONE: (212) 254-6995 **ADDRESS**: 740 Broadway, 12th Fl, New York NY 10003
DESCRIPTION: Est. 1978 by four writers who met in the New York Public Library on 42nd Street and Fifth Avenue, The Writers Room (WR) is New York City's first and most acclaimed professional writers' colony – as well as the nation's original writers' collective. Membership fee required. See website for details.

WRITERS' GUILD OF GREAT BRITAIN
WEBSITE: www.writersguild.org.uk **EMAIL**: admin@writersguild.org.uk
PHONE: +44 (0)207 330 777 **TWITTER**: @TheWritersGuild
ADDRESS: 1st Fl, 134 Tooley St, London SE1 2TU United Kingdom
DESCRIPTION: WGGB is a trade union representing professional writers in TV, film, theatre, radio, books, comedy, poetry, animation and videogames. Our members also include emerging and aspiring writers.

PRODUCTS & OTHER SERVICES

ALASKA QUARTERLY REVIEW (AQR)
WEBSITE: aqreview.org **EMAIL:** uaa_aqr@uaa.alaska.edu
PHONE: (907) 786-6916 **FAX:** (907) 786-6916
ADDRESS: University of Alaska Anchorage, 3211 Providence Dr, Anchorage AK 99508
PREFERRED GENRE: All genres **DESCRIPTION:** Est. 1982. Fiction, short plays, poetry and literary nonfiction in traditional and experimental styles.

AMERICAN THEATRE MAGAZINE
PARENT ORGANIZATION: Theatre Communications Group
WEBSITE: www.americantheatre.org **EMAIL:** info@tcg.org
PHONE: (212) 609-5900 ext. 370 **TWITTER:** @AmericanTheatre
ADDRESS: 520 8th Ave, 24th Fl, New York NY 10018
DESCRIPTION: American Theatre magazine is the nation's only general-circulation magazine devoted to theatre. Founded in 1984 by the pioneering arts service organization Theatre Communications Group, the magazine featured cowboy-hatted playwright Sam Shepard on its first cover in April of that year. Published 10 times a year, the magazine now has an estimated readership of 50,000, mostly within the theatre profession.

ASIAN THEATRE JOURNAL
WEBSITE: www.uhpress.hawaii.edu/journals **EMAIL:** uhpjourn@hawaii.edu
PHONE: (888) 847-7377 **FAX:** (800) 650-7811
ADDRESS: 2840 Kolowalu St, Honolulu HI 96822
DESCRIPTION: Dedicated to performing arts of Asia, traditional, modern, original, and translated plays.

CALLALOO
WEBSITE: www.callaloo.tamu.edu **EMAIL:** callaloo@tamu.edu
PHONE: (979) 458-3108
ADDRESS: 4212 TAMU, Texas A&M University, College Station TX 77843
DESCRIPTION: Est. 1976. Callaloo is the premier literary and cultural journal of the African Diaspora.
PREFERRED GENRE: All genres **PREFERRED LENGTH:** Any Length
SPECIAL INTEREST: Black or African American **FEE:** No **AGENT ONLY:** No

CANADIAN THEATRE REVIEW
WEBSITE: www.utpjournals.com **EMAIL:** journals@utpress.utoronto.ca
PHONE: (416) 667-7810 **FAX:** (416) 667-7881
ADDRESS: Univ of Toronto Press Inc, Journal, 5201 Dufferin St, Toronto ON M3H 5T8 Canada

CAPILANO REVIEW
WEBSITE: www.thecapilanoreview.ca **EMAIL:** contact@thecapilanoreview.ca

ADDRESS: 281 Industrial Ave, Vancouver BC V6A 2P2 Canada
DESCRIPTION: Est. 1972. Unpublished poetry, drama, visual arts. Online submissions only.
PREFERRED LENGTH: Any Length **FEE:** No **AGENT ONLY:** No

CLOCKHOUSE
WEBSITE: www.clockhouse.net/main/submit **EMAIL:** submissions@clockhouse.net
PHONE: (312) 607-1001 **ADDRESS:** 352 9th St, Brooklyn NY 11215
DESCRIPTION: Clockhouse is a national literary journal published in partnership with Goddard College by the Clockhouse Writers' Conference, the alumni association for graduates of Goddard's MFA in Creative Writing Program.
PREFERRED GENRE: All genres **FEE:** No **AGENT ONLY:** No

CONFRONTATION MAGAZINE
WEBSITE: www.confrontationmagazine.org **EMAIL:** confrontationmag@gmail.com
PHONE: (516) 299-2720 **ADDRESS:** LIU Post English Dept, 720 Northern Blvd, Brookville NY 11548
DESCRIPTION: Response time: 3-4 mos. Reading period for all submissions: August 16 – April 15. All mailed manuscripts received during the non-reading period will be returned unread. E-mail submissions are accepted only from writers living outside the U.S.
PREFERRED GENRE: Plays **PREFERRED LENGTH:** 10-Min / 10 Pages **FEE:** No
AGENT ONLY: No

DRAMATICS MAGAZINE
WEBSITE: www.schooltheatre.org/resources/dramatics
EMAIL: gbossler@schooltheatre.org **PHONE:** (513) 421-3900
FAX: (513) 421-7077 **ADDRESS:** 2343 Auburn Ave, Cincinnati OH 45219
DESCRIPTION: Est. 1929. National monthly magazine for high school theatre students & teachers, printing one-acts and full-lengths. Plays should contain roles that are within the acting range of high school students, and the subject matter should address concerns of interest to teenagers and young adults. Large casts are desirable. We buy one-time, non-exclusive publication rights to plays. The playwright retains all other rights. Response time: 5 mos.
PREFERRED GENRE: Plays **PREFERRED LENGTH:** Any Length **FEE:** No **AGENT ONLY:** No

THE DRAMATIST
PARENT ORGANIZATION: Dramatists Guild of America Inc.
WEBSITE: dramatistsguild.com/dramatist-magazine
EMAIL: publications@dramatistsguild.com **PHONE:** (212) 398-9366
TWITTER: @DramatistsGuild **ADDRESS:** Dramatists Guild of America, 1501 Broadway, Ste 701, New York NY 10036
DESCRIPTION: Est. 1964. The official journal of Dramatists Guild of America, Inc. *The Dramatist* is, first and foremost, a member service, written by members for members. It is the only national publication dedicated to the business and craft of writing for theatre. Publishes seven issues annually with an international circulation of 8,000.
SUBMISSION MATERIALS: All article pitches and/or submissions are subject to peer review by our Publications Committee. Email only.

IPSILON MUSIC SERVICES
WEBSITE: www.ipsilonmusic.com **EMAIL:** ipsilonmusic@gmail.com **PHONE:** (646) 265-5666 **ADDRESS:** 604 Riverside Dr, Ste 3-C, New York NY 10031

DESCRIPTION: Lead sheets, piano/vocals, orchestra scores, etc., transcribed, edited, meticulously prepared to order. State-of-the-art, publishing-quality printouts. Arranging and producing for demos, readings, and productions. New York's finest.

KENYON REVIEW
WEBSITE: www.kenyonreview.org **EMAIL:** kenyonreview@kenyon.edu **PHONE:** (740) 427-5208 **FAX:** (740) 427-5417 **ADDRESS:** Finn House, 102 W Wiggin St, Gambier OH 43022

MASTERWRITER
WEBSITE: www.masterwriter.com **PHONE:** (805) 892-2656 **ADDRESS:** 1323 E Valley Rd, Montecito CA 93108

DESCRIPTION: MasterWriter was originally designed by songwriters for songwriters and contained all the tools and reference that are essential for the modern songwriter. The program has since evolved into a collection of writing tools for every type of writer.

PAJ: A JOURNAL OF PERFORMANCE AND ART
WEBSITE: www.mitpressjournals.org/paj **EMAIL:** submissions.paj@gmail.com **PHONE:** (212) 243-3885 **ADDRESS:** PO Box 532, Village Station, New York NY 10014

DESCRIPTION: Est. 1976. PAJ is a triannual periodical offering expanded coverage of performance, video, dance, drama, film, music, photography, installations, and media. Since its inception, PAJ has published more than 1000 plays and performance texts, translated from 20 languages.

PREFERRED GENRE: Plays **FEE:** No **AGENT ONLY:** No

PROSCENIUM JOURNAL
WEBSITE: prosceniumjournal.com **EMAIL:** submissions@prosceniumjournal.com **PHONE:** (503) 593-3548 **ADDRESS:** 1515 SW Morrison St, Portland OR 97202

DESCRIPTION: Proscenium Journal is the first quarterly journal dedicated to publishing high-caliber theatrical works. Proscenium publications are free of charge and readily accessible online, allowing playwrights to share their work with newer and larger audiences. Proscenium is now accepting submissions for the sixth issue of Proscenium Journal and the third annual Proscenium Live Festival of New Work.

PREFERRED GENRE: Plays **PREFERRED LENGTH:** Any Length **FEE:** No **AGENT ONLY:** No

SDC JOURNAL
WEBSITE: www.sdcweb.org/sdc-journal **EMAIL:** SDCJournal@SDCweb.org **PHONE:** (212) 391-1070 **ADDRESS:** 321 W 44th St, Ste 804, New York NY 10036

DESCRIPTION: Published quarterly, SDC Journal is distributed to SDC Members nationwide and is available to industry constituents, theatre education programs, and the theatre-going public at large. SDC Journal's mission is to give voice to an empowered collective of Directors and Choreographers working in all jurisdictions and venues across the country, encourage advocacy, and highlight artistic achievement.

PRODUCTS & OTHER SERVICES

ST. PETERSBURG REVIEW
WEBSITE: stpetersburgreview.com **EMAIL:** submission@stpetersburgreview.com
ADDRESS: PO Box 2888, Concord NH 03302
DESCRIPTION: Est. 2007. Publishes quality work from established and emerging writers and artists with a special emphasis on translations and fostering an international literary community that, among other things, provides a forum for freedom of artistic expression especially for those writing and/or living in global conflict areas.

THEATER MAGAZINE
WEBSITE: theatermagazine.org **EMAIL:** theater.magazine@yale.edu
PHONE: (203) 432-1568 **FAX:** (203) 432-8336 **ADDRESS:** PO Box 208244, New Haven CT 06520
SUBMISSION MATERIALS: Est. 1968. Yale's journal of criticism, plays, and reportage.

WRITE BROTHERS INC.
WEBSITE: www.screenplay.com **EMAIL:** service@screenplay.com
PHONE: (818) 843-6557 **FAX** (818) 843-8364 **TWITTER:** @Write_Brothers
ADDRESS: 638 Lindero Canyon Rd, Ste 267, Oak Park CA 91377
DESCRIPTION: Since 1982, Write Brothers® Inc. (formerly called Screenplay Systems™) has been a world leader in film and television screenwriting and production software.

NOTES

Final Draft proudly supports the DGA

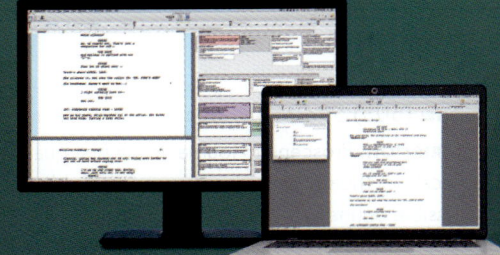

New Features: Story Map™ • Beat Board™ • Collaboration • Alternate Dialogue

Members Save 30%! Use Code: **DGwriter17** during checkout

BOOKSTORES

BOOKS & BOOKS – CORAL GABLES
WEBSITE: www.booksandbooks.com/venue/the-store-at-coral-gables
PHONE: (305) 442-4408   **TWITTER**: @BooksandBooks
ADDRESS: 265 Aragon Ave, Coral Gables FL 33134
DESCRIPTION: Est. 1982. Located in an exquisite 1927 building listed in the Coral Gables Register of Historic Places where we host over 60 author events a month, featuring presidents and Nobel prize winners, athletes and artists, celebrities and poets, and a variety of other community-based events.
Hours: Monday to Thursday: 9 AM - 11 PM, Friday - Saturday: 9 AM - midnight, Sunday: 9 AM - 11 PM

THE DRAMA BOOK SHOP
WEBSITE: www.dramabookshop.com   **EMAIL**: info@dramabookshop.com
PHONE: (212) 944-0595   **FAX**: (212) 730-8739   **TWITTER**: @dramabookshop
ADDRESS: 250 W 40th St, New York NY 10018
DESCRIPTION: Founded in 1917 by the Drama League, the Drama Book Shop became an independent store in 1923. It has moved several times, but since 2001 it has been located in a 5,000-square-foot space on West 40th Street in Manhattan. The basement houses a 60-seat black-box theater, and a staff of about 20, many of whom are actors or have theater-related interests, assists the thousands of students, theater professionals, and award-winning artists who pass through the shop's doors. In 2011 the Drama Book Shop received a Tony Honor for Excellence in the Theatre. Given since 1990, these awards are bestowed on individuals, organizations, and institutions that have demonstrated profound achievement in theater but are ineligible in any of the established Tony categories.

PRAIRIE LIGHTS
WEBSITE: www.prairielights.com   **EMAIL**: info@prairielights.com
PHONE: (319) 337-2681   **TWITTER**: @Prairie_Lights
ADDRESS: 15 South Dubuque St, Iowa City IA 52240
DESCRIPTION: Est. 1978. Perhaps the strength of reputation lies in the reading series of local, national and international writers. Store Hours Mon-Sat 10-9, Sunday 10-6. Cafe open at 9am.

SAMUEL FRENCH HOLLYWOOD BOOKSHOP
WEBSITE: www.samuelfrench.com/bookstore   **TWITTER**: @SamFrenchBkshp
ADDRESS: 7623 Sunset Blvd, Hollywood CA 90046
DESCRIPTION: The bookshop is located on the corner of Sunset and Stanley in Hollywood, five blocks east of Fairfax Ave. There is two hour parking on Stanley and we do have a parking lot behind the bookshop.
Hours: 10am - 6pm Monday through Saturday, 10am - 5pm Sunday.

TATTERED COVER BOOK STORE

WEBSITE: www.tatteredcover.com **EMAIL**: books@tatteredcover.com
PHONE: (303) 322-7727 **FAX**: (303) 399-2279 **TWITTER**: @TatteredCover
ADDRESS: 2526 E Colfax Ave, Denver CO 80206
DESCRIPTION: Est. 1971. Tattered Cover is a large indie bookstore and cafe with the cozy feel and comfort of smaller bookshops, furnished with comfortable sofas and overstuffed chairs and and a world-class newsstand. We sell new and used books, in addition to crisp pre-discounted bargain editions. We are a Denver institution, a community gathering place, and an experience you can't download. The Tattered Cover has a long history of hosting LIVE author events, averaging over 400 authors, illustrators, and public figures each year.

Hours: Mon - Sat, 9am to 9pm; Sun 10am to 6pm

Other locations in Historic LoDo, Aspen Grove, Union Station, and at Denver International Airport on Concourses A, B & C.

TRIDENT BOOKSELLERS & CAFE

WEBSITE: www.tridentbookscafe.com **PHONE**: (617) 267-8688
TWITTER: @TridentBooks **ADDRESS**: 338 Newbury St, Boston MA 02115
DESCRIPTION: Since 1984, Trident Booksellers & Cafe has been providing Back Bay residents, students, and tourists with sustenance for the mind and body. Trident is the perfect place to catch up with friends, study for your exam, grab brunch, or browse our wide selection of books and magazines. We offer free wifi, an award-winning magazine selection, a full service restaurant, books, cards, gifts, and, above all, a unique Boston experience.

Hours: 8am-midnight 7 days a week. The closest T stop is Hynes Convention Center on the Green Line.

PLAYWRIGHTS WELCOME

Developed for the Dramatists Guild of America Members, Playwrights Welcome is a national ticketing initiative created by Samuel French along with Dramatists Play Service, Dramatic Publishing, Music Theatre International, Playscripts, and Rodgers and Hammerstein. This program was made out of a desire to support the artistic health of our industry's writers, and by extension the vibrancy of the American theatre.

Below, you'll find the list of participating theatres as of October 2017. New theatres are being added on a regular basis, so be sure to check this website for updates: www.samuelfrench.com/playwrightswelcome

If you're interested in seeing a show at one of the below theatres, simply show up at their box office before to curtain and ask if they have any Playwrights Welcome tickets available. If they do, you will need to present your current Dramatists Guild membership card as well as your ID. Please remember that every box office is different, so some theatres may have different ticketing processes for Playwrights Welcome tickets. Not a Guild member? Join here: www.dramatistsguild.com/register

Alliance Theater – Atlanta, GA

American Stage – St Petersburg, FL

Amphibian Stage – Fort Worth, TX

Atlantic Theater – NYC, NY

Axis Theatre – New York, NY

Barrington Stage Company – Pittsfield, MA

Berkeley Rep – Berkeley, CA

Bishop Arts Theatre Center – Dallas, TX

Boston Playwrights' Theatre – Boston, MA

Boulder Ensemble Theatre Company – Boulder, CO

Center Stage – Baltimore, MD

Children's Theatre Company – Minneapolis, MN

Community College of Baltimore County – Baltimore, MD

Coterie Theatre – Kansas City, MO

Dallas Theater Center – Dallas, TX

Denver Theater Center – Denver, CO

PLAYWRIGHTS WELCOME

Dorset Theatre Festival – Dorset, VT

Dreamcatcher Repertory Theatre – Summit, NJ

Ford's Theatre – Washington, DC

Forward Theater Company – Madison, WI

Geffen Playhouse – Los Angeles, CA

Goodman Theater – Chicago, IL

Guthrie Theatre – Minneapolis, MN

Hartford Stage – Hartford, CT

Huntington Theatre Company – Boston, MA

The Idiopathic Ridiculopathy Consortium – Philly, PA

The Indie on Main – Keyser, WV

Intiman Theater – Seattle, WA

Iron Crow Theatre – Baltimore, MD

JET – West Bloomfield, MI

La Jolla – La Jolla, CA

La Mirada Theater – La Mirada, CA

Lab Theater Project – Tampa, FL

Magic Theatre – San Francisco, CA

Manatee Performing Arts Center – Bradenton, FL

McCarter Theatre – Princeton, NJ

Nashville Repertory Theatre – Nashville, TN

Old Globe – San Diego, CA

Palm Beach Dramaworks – West Palm Beach, FL

Paramount – Aurora, IL

Playwrights Local – Cleveland, OH

Portland Center Stage – Portland, OR

NOTES

PLAYWRIGHTS WELCOME

NOTES

Premiere Stages at Kean University – Union, NJ

Rattlestick Playwrights Theater – New York, NY

Renaissance Theaterworks – Milwaukee, WI

Ritz Community Theater – Snyder, TX

Road Less Traveled Productions – Buffalo, NY

Roundabout Theater – NYC, NY

San Francisco Playhouse – San Francisco, CA

Seattle Rep – Seattle, WA

Shakespeare Theatre Company – Washington, DC

Signature Theatre – Arlington, VA

StreetSigns – Pittsboro, NC

PASSAGE THEATRE – Trenton, NJ

The Pearl Theatre Company – New York, NY

Theatre Aspen – Aspen, CO

Theatre Britain – Plano, TX

Theatre Elision – Minneapolis, MN

Theatre Under the Stars – Houston, TX

Two River Theater Company – Red Bank, NJ

Urban Stages – New York, NY

Vineyard Theater – NYC, NY

Victory Gardens Theater – Chicago, IL

Village Theater – Issaquah, WA

The Welders – Washington, DC

The Wilbury Theatre Group – Providence, RI

Westport Playhouse – Westport, CT

Yale Rep Theatre – New Haven, CT

Develop Your Story   Write It!

Special Dramatists Guild Member Discounts with Promo Code

Dramatica® Pro for Windows: $99 * & Dramatica® Story Expert™ for Mac: $99 *

The ultimate creative writing partners for story development

"Dramatica is my indispensable tool both for bringing form to my new novels and in the repair and tune-up of stories that I am revising. It has added new, grander dimensions to my craft. These are power tools no storyteller should be without."

Tracy Hickman,
New York Times Best-selling Author

The Dramatica software is useful for developing all types of stories in all types of forms, whether they are scripts, novels, plays, graphic novels, mini-series, or any other creative narrative form. It's like having a successful author as your writing partner, sitting by your side.

Movie Magic® Screenwriter™ 6 / 6.5 - $99 *

The script writing choice of playwrights, novelists, Hollywood professionals, and graphic novelists

"I've used Movie Magic Screenwriter for many years. Nothing is as simple, powerful, intuitive and versatile."

Paul Haggis, *Writer, Director*
Crash, Million Dollar Baby

"Movie Magic Screenwriter is an incredibly valuable tool, it allows a writer to express the words without having obstacles. Writers cannot afford interruptions when inspired, it could kill the story. I love my Movie Magic Screenwriter."

Kim Sky, *Writer*
Just Another Romantic Wrestling Comedy

* Use the promo code DGDISCOUNT during checkout to receive the discounts!

Shop now online at **Screenplay.com** to take advantage of these Dramatist Guild member specials.

Copyright © 2017 Write Brothers Inc. Dramatica and Write Brothers are registered trademarks of Write Brothers Inc. ALL RIGHTS RESERVED.

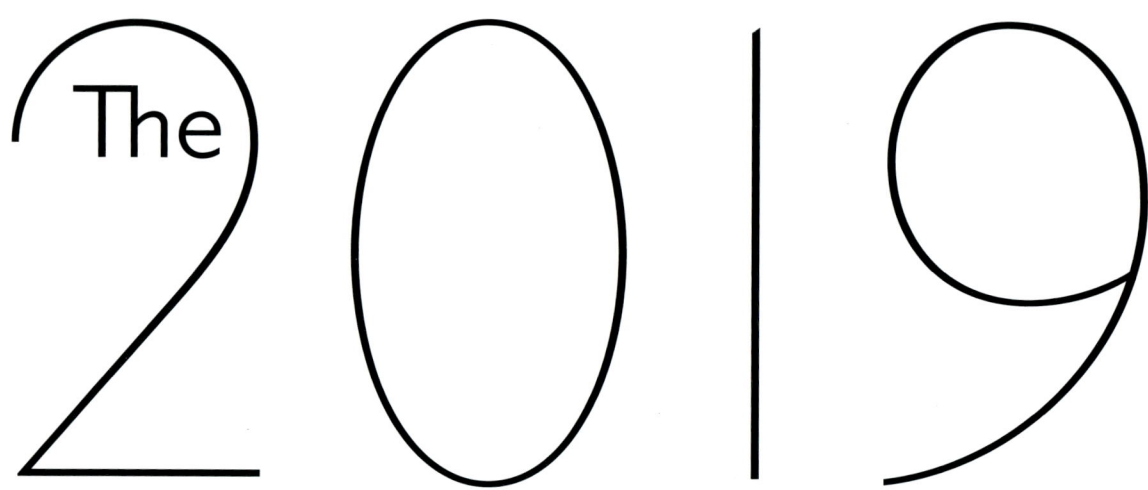

The 2019 Resource Directory

is scheduled to go on sale
NOVEMBER 15, 2018!

THE SUBMISSION LETTER AND PRODUCTION RESUME

Though there is no right or wrong way to write a letter of introduction to your work, realize an effective submission letter should be short, professional, and with just enough information so the reader knows you've submitted exactly what was called for in the solicitation. And while it's tempting to entice the reader to want to read the script with an overly expressive narrative in your submission latter, consider that this is the first exposure to your writing (of any kind) that will be read by someone in the producing organization. Be mindful, then, how you represent yourself on paper, and allow your play or musical to speak for itself.

A common question is often asked when writers construct a production resume: what do you do if you don't have a lot of readings or productions to list on your resume? Whatever you do, don't misrepresent yourself; don't say you've had a reading or a production that you haven't had. You'll eventually be found out and will look worse than someone who has a thin resume. If you don't have a lot of production experience with your writing, write a brief synopsis of each of the plays you've written, cite any classes or workshops you've taken as a playwright, and detail any other experience you have in the theatre (as stage manager, director, actor, dramaturg, etc.). People are more likely to be sympathetic to you being young in the theatre than they are to you being someone who misrepresents themselves.

A more accomplished playwright's resume should list productions or readings of plays (by theatre and date), awards, grants, writers colonies, workshops, festivals, and any special recognition received as a writer. Give the reader a sense of the whole of your writing career, including memberships in theatre groups, professional organizations, and related writing work. Include your address and phone number at the top or bottom of your resume, on the cover sheet of your play, and obviously on the return envelope. Again, there are any number of variations on how to construct a writer's resume, but a template to inspire your thinking can be found on the following page.

358 SUBMISSION LETTER AND PRODUCTION RESUME

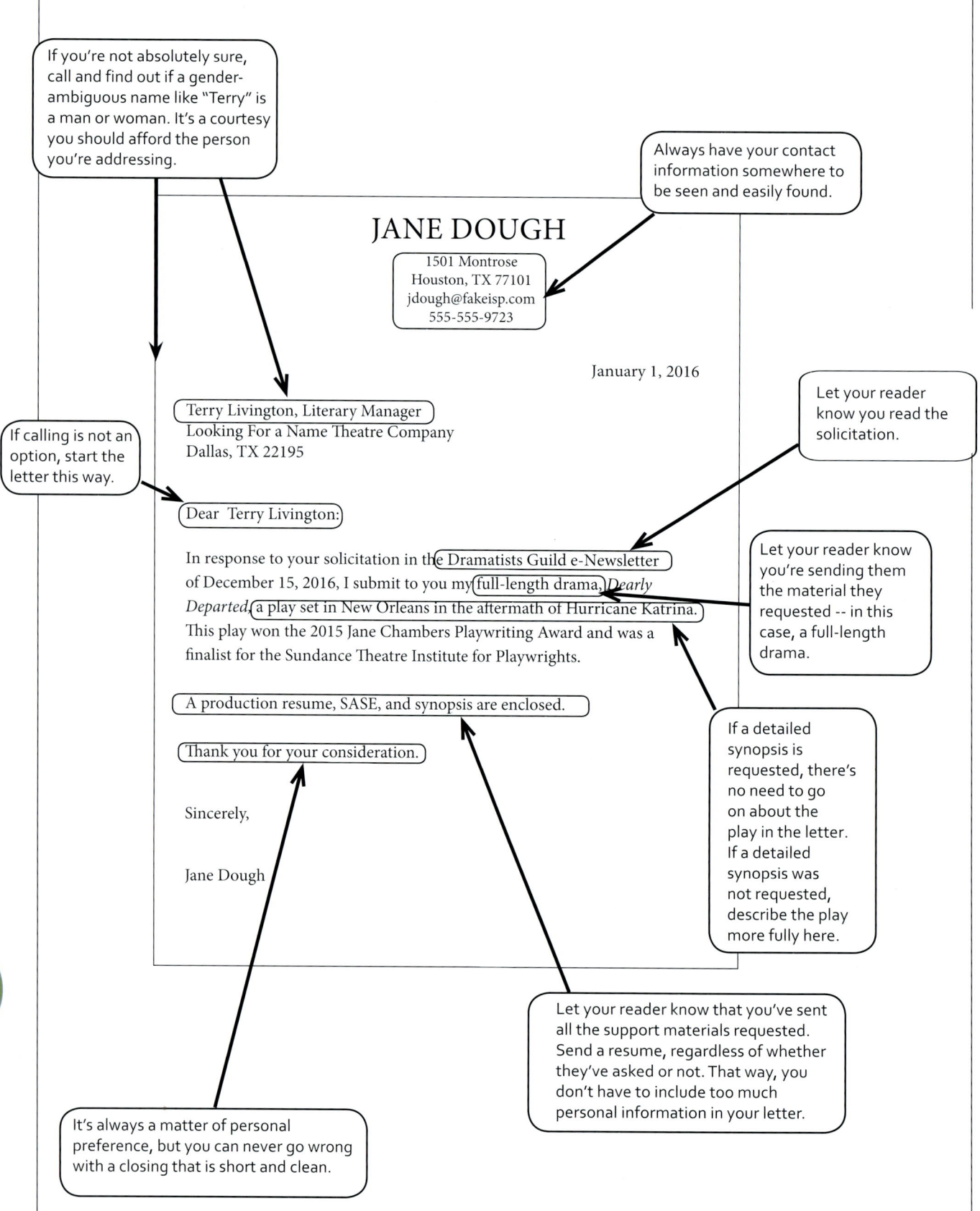

JANE DOUGH

1501 Montrose
Houston, TX 77101
jdough@fakeisp.com
555-555-9723

January 1, 2016

Terry Livington, Literary Manager
Looking For a Name Theatre Company
Dallas, TX 22195

Dear Terry Livington:

In response to your solicitation in the Dramatists Guild e-Newsletter of December 15, 2016, I submit to you my full-length drama, *Dearly Departed*, a play set in New Orleans in the aftermath of Hurricane Katrina. This play won the 2015 Jane Chambers Playwriting Award and was a finalist for the Sundance Theatre Institute for Playwrights.

A production resume, SASE, and synopsis are enclosed.

Thank you for your consideration.

Sincerely,

Jane Dough

Annotations:

- If you're not absolutely sure, call and find out if a gender-ambiguous name like "Terry" is a man or woman. It's a courtesy you should afford the person you're addressing.
- Always have your contact information somewhere to be seen and easily found.
- If calling is not an option, start the letter this way.
- Let your reader know you read the solicitation.
- Let your reader know you're sending them the material they requested -- in this case, a full-length drama.
- If a detailed synopsis is requested, there's no need to go on about the play in the letter. If a detailed synopsis was not requested, describe the play more fully here.
- Let your reader know that you've sent all the support materials requested. Send a resume, regardless of whether they've asked or not. That way, you don't have to include too much personal information in your letter.
- It's always a matter of personal preference, but you can never go wrong with a closing that is short and clean.

SUBMISSION LETTER AND PRODUCTION RESUME 359

> Cite the name of the play and genre.

> Note your most current address, phone number and email address. If they want to contact you, make it easy for them.

> Cite publications as if they were productions. Why not let whoever know that your work's been published?

> Cite the name of the theatre that produced the play and where it was produced.

> Because a lot of theatres are specific about the kind of second production they'll provide, note the nature of the production.

> Date your events from the most recent to the least recent.

> Professional memberships, education, writers groups you belong to and the like should be noted.

> List your degrees and any courses you may have taken related to play or music writing.

JANE DOUGH

jdough@fakeisp.com
555-555-9723
1501 Montrose
Houston, TX 77101

Production History

Dearly Departed (full-length drama)
Winner, Jane Chambers Playwriting Award (July, 2015)
Finalist, 2008 Sundance Theatre Institute for Playwrights (May, 2013)
Early scenes published in The Best Stage Scenes of 2008, Smith & Kraus, Inc. (April, 2013)

Forty-Love, Roger (full-length drama)
Winner, Arthur Ashe Award (July, 2012)
Finalist, 2008 Sundance Theatre Institute for Playwrights (May, 2012)

Silly Billy (ten-minute play)
Boston Theatre Marathon (May, 2010)

Daily Puppy Dot Com (full-length musical)
Summer Shorts Festival, Decatur, IL. (November, 2009)
Turnip Theatre Festival, New York City, Equity Showcase (September 2009)

Awards

Residency MacDowell Colony (January 2014)
Texas State Foundation for the Arts, Artists Grant (January, 2011)
The Young Playwrights Award, Texas Education Theatre Association (May, 2007)

Member Associations

Dramatists Guild of America, Associate Member
Minneapolis Playwrights Center
Writers Focusing Writers, Houston, TX
Austin Scriptworks, Austin, TX

Education

MFA in Playwriting, University of Houston (with Edward Albee) (May, 2006)
BFA in Acting, The University of Michigan (May, 2003)

SUGGESTED FORMATS FOR PLAYS AND MUSICALS

Included in this document are suggested formats for plays and musicals drawn from suggestions of distinguished dramatists, literary managers, teachers of dramatic writing, producers, professional theatres, and publishers. It is the Guild's belief that these formats present a standard that will work well for most professional opportunities. A few additional elements to consider:

1. Formatting works towards two purposes: easy reading and the ability to approximate the performance time of the written story. Admittedly, not all stories or styles of writing will work within a standard format. Therefore, use your better judgment in deciding the architecture of the page.

2. There is an industry standard (though some may say old-fashioned) of using the 12-point Courier font. With the proliferation of computers and word-processing programs, there are literally hundreds of fonts to choose from. Whatever your choice, we recommend that you maintain a font size of 12 points – thereby assuring some reliable approximation of performance time.

3. Though you wrote the story, someone has to read it before anyone sees it. Therefore, make your manuscript easy to read by employing a standard format with clearly delineated page numbers, scene citations and act citations. Headers and footers are optional.

4. If you're using a software program to format your work such as Final Draft or Movie Magic, be aware that you have the ability to create your own format in these programs that can be uniquely named, saved and applied to all of your manuscripts.

5. Usually between the title page and the first page of the story and/or dialogue, there is a page devoted to character break-down. What's important to note on this page is the age, gender and name of each character. Some dramatists write brief character descriptions beside each name.

6. While it is cost-effective for both photocopying and mailing, realize that some institutions prefer that you don't send double-sided documents. We recommend that you inquire about preference.

7. There is no right or wrong way to signify the end of a scene or act. Some writers do nothing but end the scene; others write "black out," "lights fade down," "End Act I" or some other signifier that the scene or act has concluded.

8. The binding margin should be 1.5 inches from the edge. All other margins (top, bottom, right) should be 1.0 inch from the edge.

Text is centered in the page and includes the title, genre, and author.

A Dog's Life
———————————
A full-length play

By Rachel Thompson

Include as much information as needed for someone to contact you.

Contact:
Rachel Thompson
3255 Temple Drive
Lake Charles, LA 32782
rthompson@yahoo.com

If you have an agent, you won't need to provide the personal information above.

Represented by:
David Stark
The Stark Agency
250 W. 47th, Ste. 310
New York, NY 10036

© All rights reserved. 2018

From Eugene O'Neill's The Emperor Jones *(suggested first page format)*

The scene citation is centered to the page. —— SCENE 8

Dawn. Same as Scene Two, the dividing line of forest and plain. The nearest tree trunks are dimly revealed but the forest behind them is still a mass of glooming shadow. The tom-tom seems on the very spot, so loud and continuously vibrating are its beats. LEM enters from the left, followed by a small squad of his soldiers, and by the Cockney trader, SMITHERS. LEM is a heavyset, ape-faced old savage of the extreme African type, dressed only in a loin cloth. A revolver and cartridge belt are about his waist. His soldiers are in different degrees of rag-concealed nakedness. All wear broad palm leaf hats. Each one carries a rifle. SMITHERS is the same as in Scene One. One of the soldiers, evidently a tracker, is peering about keenly on the ground. He grunts and points to the spot where JONES entered the forest. LEM and SMITHERS come to look.

In setting the beginnings of scenes, make you notations run from the center the page t the right margin, a italicize t text.

Character names, in these directions, are placed in all CAI to distinguish their action. Bu after these initial directions, the charac ter names return to regular formatting

SMITHERS
(after a glance, turns away
in disgust)
That's where 'e went in right enough. Much good it'll do yer. 'E's miles orf by this an' safe to the Coast damn 'S 'ide! I tole yer yer'd lose 'im, didn't I?—wastin' the 'ole bloomin' night beatin' yer bloody drum and castin' yer silly spells! Gawd blimey, wot a pack!

LEM
(gutturally)
We cotch him. You see.

(He makes a motion to his soldiers
who squat down on their haunches in
a semi-circle.)

From Tennessee Williams' Not About Nightingales
MODERN PLAY FORMAT

BOSS
You've probably come here to question me about that ex-convicts story in that damned yellow sheet down there in Wilkes county – That stuff about getting Pellagra in here – Jimmy, hand me that sample menu!

JIM
She's not a reporter.

BOSS
Aw. – What is your business, young lady?

EVA
I understand there's a vacancy here. Mr. McBurney, my landlady's brother-in-law, told her that you were needing a new stenographer and I'm sure that I can qualify for the position. I'm a college graduate, Mr. Whalen, I've had three years of business experience – references with me – but, oh – I've – I've had such abominable luck these last six months. – the last place I worked – the business recession set in they had to cut down on their sales-force – they gave me a wonderful letter – I've got in with me.

                                      She opens her purse and spills contents on floor.

BOSS
Anybody outside?

EVA
Yes. That woman.

BOSS
What woman?

EVA
The one from Wisconsin. She's still waiting –

BOSS
I told you I don't want to see her.
                  (talking into phone)
How's the track, Bert? Fast? Okay.

                                      Sailor Jack's mother, MRS. BRISTOL, has quietly entered. She carries a blanket.

MRS. BRISTOL
I beg your pardon, I – You see I'm Jack Bristol's mother, and I've been wanting to have a talk with you so long about – about my boy!

From Tennessee Williams' Not About Nightingales

TRADITIONAL PLAY FORMAT

Dialogue begins 1.5 inches from left side to account for binding. Dialogue is single-spaced.

Essential page numbering**

16.

Stage action is indented 3 inches from left; put in parenthesis. A blank line is inserted before and after.

```
                        BOSS
              (removes cover from basket)
Speak of biscuits and what turns up but a nice batch of
homemade cookies! Have one young lady - Jim boy!

              (Jim takes two.)

                        BOSS
Uh-huh, you've got an awful big paw, Jimmy!
              (laughs)
Show the new Arky-what's-it to Miss Daily news - or is it
the Morning Star? Have a chair! I'll be right with you -
              (vanishes for a moment)
Sweat, sweat, sweat's all I do these hot breezy days!

                        JIM
              (sotto voce)
He thinks you're a newspaper woman.

                        BOSS
Turn on that fan.
              (emerging)
Well, now, let's see -

                        EVA
To begin with I'm not -

                        BOSS
You've probably come here to question me about that ex-
convicts story in that damned yellow sheet down there in
Wilkes county - That stuff about getting Pellagra in here
 - Jimmy, hand me that sample menu!

                        JIM
She's not a reporter.

                        BOSS
Aw. - What is your business, young lady?

              (She opens her purse and spills
                contents on floor.)
```

Dialogue extends to 1.0 inch from right margin

Stage action reliant on the proceeding dialogue is indented to the left of the character name.

Character name in all caps; in the center of the page.

Standard font for this formatting is 12.0 point.

Stage action is indented 3.0 inches from left margin and enclosed in parenthesis.

***There are many ways to paginate your play, from the straight forward numerical sequence of 1, 2, 3 to an older format of I-2-16, (meaning Act 1, Scene 2, Page 16).*

From APPLAUSE, Book by Betty Comden, Adolph Green
Music by Charles Strouse, Lyrics by Lee Adams (suggested musical format)

Essential page numbering**

56.

Dialogue begins 1.5 inches from left side to account for binding. Dialogue is single-spaced.

Stage action is indented 3 inches from left; put in parenthesis. A blank line is inserted before and after.

Character name in all caps; in the center of the page.

Dialogue extends to 1.0 inch from right margin

Stage action reliant on the proceeding dialogue is indented to the left of the character name.

Stanzas are separated by a blank line and distinguish themselves by dramatic thought and/or changes from verse to chorus to bridges, etc.

Lyrics are in all CAPS, separated line to line by either musical phrasing and/or the rhyming scheme and clearly indented from the left margin.

For duets, or characters singing counterpoint, create two colums side by side, following the same format here.

                        KAREN
                      (to Margo)
Margo, you've been kicking us all around long enough. Someone ought to give *you* a good swift one for a change!

                    (She leaves.)

                         EVE
Miss Channing . . . if I ever dreamed that anything I did could possibly cause you any unhappiness, or come between you and your friends . . . please believe me.

                        MARGO
                (in a low, weary voice)
Oh, I do. And I'm full of admiration for you.
                (stands, approaches Eve)
If you can handle yourself on the stage with the same artistry you display off the stage . . . well, my dear, you are in the right place.

            (She speaks the following lines as the music
             of WELCOME TO THE THEATRE begins.)

Welcome to the theater, to the magic, to the fun!

                    (She sings.)

            WHERE PAINTED TREES AND FLOWERS GROW
            AND LAUGHTER RINGS FORTISSIMO,
            AND TREACHERY'S SWEETLY DONE!

            NOW YOU'VE ENTERED THE ASYLUM,
            THIS PROFESSION UNIQUE
            ACTORS ARE CHILDREN
            PLAYING HIDE-AND-EGO-SEEK . . .

            SO WELCOME, MISS EVE HARRINGTON,
            TO THIS BUSINESS WE CALL SHOW,
            YOU'RE ON YOUR WAY
            TO WEALTH AND FAME,
            UNSHEALTH YOUR CLAWS,
            ENJOY THE GAME!
            YOU'LL BE A BITCH
            BUT THEY'LL KNOW YOUR NAME
            FROM NEW YORK . . . TO KOKOMO

            WELCOME TO THEATRE,
            MY DEAR, YOU'LL LOVE IT SO!

**There are many ways to paginate your play, from the straight forward numerical sequence of 1, 2, 3 to an older format of 1-2-16, (meaning Act 1, Scene 2, Page 16).

FURTHER READING

Cited articles for further reading in this section are available free of charge to Dramatists Guild members via our website: www.dramatistsguild.com/ba-archive

Not a member of the Guild? Apply for membership here: www.dramatistsguild.com/how-do-i-join

BUSINESS AFFAIRS ON REPRESENTATION – FAQ

*Current Guild members: further reading suggestions may be found at www.dramatistsguild.com/ba-archive

WHAT DOES AN AGENT DO?

Agents use their contacts to get your plays read and produced. They negotiate contracts, explain these contracts to you, and monitor those contracts to guarantee timely payment. Agents can open doors to producers and venues, and can give you credibility with producers. They represent you in business situations so that you can devote more time and energy to the creative process. An agent or manager can give business advice, help direct your career, and be a valuable ally and support system as you grow professionally.

Further Reading: THE ROLE OF THE AGENT; REPRESENTATION; and DO YOU NEED A MANAGER?

ARE AGENTS LICENSED?

Literary agents are not employment agents and are therefore not licensed under most states' laws. Most (though not all) reputable agents are members of the Association of Authors' Representatives (www.aar-online.org) which has its own guidelines for appropriate standards.

Further Reading: PAY OR PLAY.

HOW DO I GET AN AGENT?

The Guild's Resource Directory—updated annually—contains a list of agents who specialize in theatre. Additionally, the Association of Authors' Representatives (www.aar-online.org) has an online database with agents' information and what kind of authors they represent.

If you are having a production, you should consider inviting agents to attend. If you're working with a director or designers or actors who like your work, you may try to get her or him to recommend you to their own representatives. You can also be referred to an agent by a theatre's literary manager, artistic director, or by a producer or other theatre professional.

You should understand however, that it is difficult for new or emerging writers to obtain representation. There are also opportunities to submit your work to theatres, festivals, and contests that do not require an agent or other representation.

Further Reading: THE ROLE OF THE AGENT; REPRESENTATION; and DO YOU NEED A MANAGER?

WILL THE GUILD HELP ME GET AN AGENT?

The Guild cannot help you to get an agent. We can, however, help guide you through the steps you need to take. We can also advise you about the history and reputation of various agents, managers, attorneys, theatres, and producers as reported to us by our membership.

Further Reading: PAY OR PLAY, THE ROLE OF THE AGENT; REPRESENTATION; and DO YOU NEED A MANAGER?

IS A PUBLISHER AN AGENT, TOO?

Yes. Play publishers are in the business of licensing the stock & amateur production rights of the plays they publish. They retain a commission and pay the author the rest of the licensing fee. They do not own the author's copyright nor do they have rights reserved for the author.

Further Reading: ELECTRONIC PUBLISHING; GUIDE TO PUBLISHING/LICENSING TERMS; PUBLISHING AND YOUR COPYRIGHT; and TO PRINT OR NOT TO PRINT.

BUSINESS AFFAIRS ON
COPYRIGHT – FAQ

*Current Guild members: further reading suggestions may be found at www.dramatistsguild.com/ba-archive

WHAT DOES "PUBLIC DOMAIN" MEAN? WHAT IS IN THE PUBLIC DOMAIN?

A work of authorship is in the "public domain" if it is no longer under copyright protection or if it failed to meet the requirements for copyright protection. Works in the public domain may be used freely without the permission of the former copyright owner.

Further Reading: Public Domain and the Copyright Duration Chart.

HOW DO I REGISTER MY COPYRIGHT?

The government's website (www.copyright.gov) provides comprehensive information and instructions for copyright registration. Your registration is effective as of the day that the Copyright Office receives your completed application, application fee, and deposit of the work, whether it be by email or mail. The Guild advises its members to become acquainted with submitting works to the Copyright Office electronically.

WHEN SHOULD I REGISTER MY COPYRIGHT?

Generally, there are three points in the life of a work at which copyright registration and revised registration makes the most sense:

When you have finished a work and are prepared to start submitting it to theatres, festivals, agents, directors, producers, or other theatre professionals;

When after substantial changes have been incorporated into your work;

When a work is published. (The publisher will usually register the published version of the work in your name.)

CAN I COPYRIGHT REVISIONS TO MY WORK?

When substantial changes (i.e., more than mere edits or minor alternations) have been incorporated into your work, the revised version of your work must be registered to protect any new elements added. This generally occurs after you have presented a full production.

WHAT DOES REGISTERING MY COPYRIGHT ACCOMPLISH?

Registering the copyright in your work with the U.S. Copyright Office is the one and only way you can avail yourself of the various rights and remedies provided by U.S. Copyright Law and defend your work against infringement.

Further Reading: A Writer's Guide to Copyright Infringement; New Developments in Copyright; and The Varied Copyrights of Theatre.

CAN'T I JUST MAIL A COPY OF MY SCRIPT TO MYSELF OR REGISTER IT WITH THE WRITERS GUILD OR THE DRAMATISTS GUILD?

Despite what you may have heard, the practice of establishing a "poor man's copyright" (where you mail the manuscript to yourself or register it with an organization like the Writer's Guild) is of little legal significance. That is why the Dramatists Guild does not provide such a service. The only way to protect your copyright is to register it with the Copyright Office at the Library of Congress, in Washington D.C.

Further Reading: A Writer's Guide to Copyright Infringement and New Developments in Copyright.

CAN I USE THE LIFE STORY OF A REAL PERSON IN MY PLAY?

When writing about real people, there are issues of copyright, libel, rights of privacy, and rights of publicity to consider.

There are several permissions that a writer may need (or choose) to obtain to safeguard against such legal matters. Interview release forms, for example, can be signed by the interviewee to ensure the author free use of materials gathered during an interview session. Furthermore, some writers acquire "life story" rights (sometimes even when not legally required), in order to remove any threat of a lawsuit that could encumber a play. Writers may additionally wish to obtain permission from an individual or estate to use a range of copyrightable material (i.e. letters and diaries) within a work or to otherwise have access to materials and private information.

Involving the subject in this way has the added benefit of brining an air of legitimacy to a work. However, if the real person is controversial or particularly litigious, requesting such permission may unnecessarily put you on the subject's radar.

Further Reading: The Real Person In Your Play - Part I, Part II, Part III and the Real Person Seminar.

IF I TRANSLATE SOMEONE'S PLAY OR A TRANSLATOR TRANSLATES MY PLAY, WHO OWNS THE COPYRIGHT?

Whether you are translating or being translated it is always best to try to own your copyright. It is not uncommon, however, for an author of an original work to commission a translation on a "work for hire" basis.

If you are translating a public domain work, copyright your work immediately because there may be competing translations.

Further Reading: The Art of Translation.

CAN I WRITE A PLAY BASED ON SOMEONE ELSE'S COPYRIGHTED WORK? CAN I WRITE A MUSICAL OR USE MUSIC OWNED BY ANOTHER SONGWRITER?

Writers can adapt or incorporate someone else's work into their own if one of the following conditions are met: (1) if the existing work is in the public domain, (2) if the use constitutes a "fair use," or (3) if the writer has a license to do so. Without qualifying for one of these three permissive scenarios, the use of another author's work may constitute copyright infringement.

Further Reading: Acquiring Underlying Rights; Parody is No Laughing Matter; Parody: A Case Study;

Reviewing the Revue; The Life of a Song; Underlying Rights; Writing a Play or Musical Based on an Existing Work; Your Playing Their Song; Public Domain; A Writer's Guide to Copyright Infringement; New Developments in Copyright and Don't Steal This Book – Adapt It!.

WHAT IS "WORK FOR HIRE"? SHOULD I DO WORK FOR HIRE, OR OTHERWISE SELL OR ASSIGN MY COPYRIGHT?

"Work for hire" can exist only under two conditions. First, it can exist in an employer-employee relationship where the work is part of the author's employment. Indicia that you are an employee includes use of the employer's work space and equipment, daily supervision by the employer, a regular salary from the employer, and health and pension benefits.

Second, a "work for hire" can be formed if (a) there is a written agreement that explicitly states the product will be a work for hire and (b) the product fits into one of nine cateogries. While these nine categories include authorship within the motion picture and television industries, authorship within theatre is NOT included.

Typically, a "work for hire" agreement to a dramatist includes the sentence, "If for any reason the Author's work should be considered not a work for hire, Author hereby assigns the copyright in perpetuity to the [producer/theatre/etc.]." In other words, this agreement is a copyright assignment. Copyright assignments are far from standard practice in the theatre industry.

Further Reading: Author's Bill of Rights and the U.S. Copyright Act.

DO DIRECTORS HAVE A COPYRIGHT IN THEIR VERSION OF MY STAGE DIRECTIONS? IS THERE A "DIRECTOR'S COPYRIGHT"?

No. Statues and courts have not recognized a copyright in stage direction and the Department of Justice has entered at least one civil law suit on behalf of the Copyright Office specifically to state that there is no such thing as a "director's copyright." The product of a director's work is conceptual, not tangible, and copyright does not protect ideas, only the specific expression of an idea fixed in a tangible medium.

Any changes a director may suggest in an author's stage directions are subject to the author's approval and, under any Guild contract, all approved changes become the author's sole property. Directors do not become co-authors of a play simply by offering dramaturgical advice to a playwright or offering ideas that the author is free to accept or reject. Such contributions are conceptual and considered part of directors' customary services in the course of their employment. Directors do not become co-authors unless they make a copyrightable contribution to a work and the author intends the director to be co-author.

Further Reading: Directors at the Gates II; No Copyright for Directors; The Director-Dramatist Relationship; Script and Artistic Approval Clauses; Working Together; The Seventh Annual Media and Society Lecture; and Why Is "Director's Copyright" A Bad Idea & Should Playwrights Pay Directors a Percentage of Their Income?

CONTRACT DISCLAIMER

Dramatists Guild contract forms are the copyrighted property of The Dramatists Guild of America, Inc., and are intended solely for use by DG members. Please note that the receipt by a DG member of any DG contract does not grant a right to the recipient to distribute or copy the contract for the benefit of non-members. Furthermore, the text of our contract forms should not be revised (except to fill in blanks and select specified options within a form) without prior consultation with a DG business affairs representative. Unauthorized copying, distribution, or revision of DG agreements constitutes an infringement of copyright, and so, as a consequence thereof, the DG reserves the right to pursue all its rights and remedies under the law against any such infringing party.

DG SAMPLE CONTRACT GUIDE

APPROVED PRODUCTION CONTRACT FOR MUSICALS*
Form contract for Broadway/First Class musical productions. Requires Guild certification. The Executive Director must approve all requests for APCs.

APPROVED PRODUCTION CONTRACT FOR PLAYS*
Form contract for Broadway/First Class straight plays. Requires Guild certification. The Executive Director must approve all requests for APCs.

SMALL THEATRE CONTRACT - NATIONAL PREMIERE
Form of 99 Seat Theatre Contract (NY, LA, and National) - Three form contracts for small theatres presenting premiere productions or AEA showcases.

FORM OF LICENSING AGREEMENT
A basic license; it grants the rights for a producer to produce a production without granting the subsidiary rights and future options that might go along with a premiere. This contract is short, straightforward and not intimidating, and it is especially useful when an author and producer are looking to enter into a very simple agreement, especially for amateur and school/university productions.

FORM OF COLLABORATION AGREEMENT (PLAYS OR MUSICALS)
Two form agreements for collaboration between authors. It is in the best interest of parties to enter into a collaboration agreement early in the creative process, to avoid potential difficulties that could arise at a later time.

FORM OF COMMISSION AGREEMENT
Agreement between a commissioning producer and author(s) to write and revise a script. The author(s) retain(s) the sole ownership of the play and maintain(s) control over additions, changes, and modifications. This agreement covers only the writing of a new piece and the producer's right to acquire the option to produce the work. It does not cover the production of the work's premiere, for which a separate contract must be entered into.

FORM OF OPTION UNDERLYING RIGHTS (PLAYS OR MUSICALS)
Two forms of an option agreement used for an author to obtain the basic right to adapt a work as a play/musical from an existing work in which a second author holds copyright. These forms only deal with the acquisition of the option to adapt a copyrighted work and hold a staged reading. It does not guarantee the right to stage an actual production beyond the initial presentation. Given the complex process of acquiring underlying rights, the Guild recommends that members consult with an attorney.

Contracts marked with an (*) require a $7 mailing fee <u>and</u> approval of the Executive Director or Associate Director before they can be released. Members can request a copy of a contract by emailing contracts@dramatistsguild.com. Contracts will be emailed as Adobe Acrobat PDF files within one business day. The contract will be password-protected.

INDEX

2nd Story 169
4th Street Theater 82, 169
4th Street Theatre - 6x10 Play Festival 82
5th Avenue Theatre 169
8 Tens @ 8 Festival 117
8x10 TheatreFest 82
10-Minute Play Festival 82
11th Hour Theatre Company 169
12 Peers Theater 169
13th Street Repertory Company 169
16th Street Theater 170
The 20% Theatre Company Twin Cities ... 170
21st Century Voices New Play Festival 82
24th Street Theatre 170
29th Street Playwrights Collective 299
52nd Street Project 170
1812 Productions 170
2050 Artistic Fellowship 145

A

Abingdon Theatre Company 171
About Face Theatre 171
About Love Festival 83
Above the Line Agency 39
Abrams Artists Agency 39
Abrons AIRspace Program 65, 145
Abrons Arts Center AIRspace Grant Program . 145
Academy of Art University 292
Act II Playhouse 172
Acting Company 172
Activate: Midwest New Play Festival 83
Actors' Center [VA] 172
The Actors Company Theatre (TACT) 105, 172
Actor's Express 172
Actors Federal Credit Union (AFCU) 324
Actors Fund [LA] 319
Actors Fund [NY] 319
Actors' Playhouse at the Miracle Theatre . 173
Actors Theatre of Louisville 95, 173
Actors Theatre Workshop [NY] 173
ACT Theatre (A Contemporary Theatre) . 172
Adirondack Theatre Festival 174
A. D. Players 171
Adventure Stage Chicago 174
African American and African Playwrights Creative Residency 65
AfroSolo Theatre Company 174
Agence Artistique Duchesne 40
Agency for the Performing Arts [LA] 40
Agency for the Performing Arts [NY] 40
Airmid Theatre Company 174
Alabama Shakespeare Festival - Southern Writers' Project 83
Alabama State Council on the Arts 145
ALAP New Works Lab 83
Alaska Native Plays Competition 117
Alaska Quarterly Review (AQR) 346
Alaska State Council on the Arts 146
Alavi Foundation 146
Alfred Music Publishing 55
Allen Lee Hughes Fellowship Program 146
Alley Theatre 174
Alliance for Jewish Theatre 324
Alliance of Artists Communities 324
Alliance of Artists Communities Emergency Funds for Individual Artists 319
Alliance of Los Angeles Playwrights 324
Alliance of Resident Theaters (ART/NY) 324
Alliance Repertory Company 175
Alliance Theatre 175
Alpern Group 40
Altarena Playhouse/Alameda Little Theater ... 175
Alternate ROOTS Inc. 325
Altos de Chavon 65
American Academy in Rome Fellowships . 146
American Alliance for Theatre & Education ... 325
American Antiquarian Society Fellowships 147
American Association of Community Theatre 82, 325
American Conservatory Theater (ACT) ... 175
American Drama Group (Europe) 175
American Indian Community House 325
American Lyric Theater Composer Librettist Development Program (CLDP) 299
American Opera Projects (AOP) 176
American Repertory Theatre 176
American Samoa Council on Culture, Arts and Humanities 147
American-Scandinavian Foundation 147
American Scandinavian Foundation Translation Prize 117
Americans for the Arts 326
American Society of Composers, Authors & Publishers 299, 300, 326
American Society of Journalists & Authors Writers Emergency Assistance Fund ... 319
American Stage [FL] 82
American Stage Theatre Company [FL] ... 176
American Theater Company 176
American Theatre Magazine 346
American Thymele Theatre 176
American Translators Association (ATA) ... 117, 325
American Translators Association (ATA) Honors and Awards 117
A.M. Heath & Company, Ltd. 39
Amphibian Productions 176
Amy's Horse 84
Anam Cara Writer's and Artist's Retreat 66
Law Office of Andrew B. Peretz P.A. 50
Anna Zornio Memorial Children's Theatre Playwriting Award 117
Annenberg Center for the Performing Arts 177
Ann Rittenberg Literary Agency 40
Annual Blank Theatre Company Young Playwrights Festival 118
Ann Wright Representatives 40

NOTES

A Noise Within (ANW) 171
AO International Talent Agency 39
Appalachian Festival of Plays & Playwrights 84
Applause Theatre & Cinema Books 55
Aquila Theatre Company 177
The Arch and Bruce Brown Foundation 147
Arden Theatre Company 177
Arena Stage 146, 177
Arizona Commission on the Arts 148
Arizona State University 292
Arizona Theatre Company 132, 178
Arizona Women's Theatre Company 178
Arkansas Arts Center Children's Theatre .. 178
Arkansas New Play Festival 84
Arkansas Repertory Theatre 178
Arkansas Theatre Collective 82
Arkansas Writers Conference 84
Arlington County Cultural Affairs Division 148
Around The Block Playwriting Course 316
Ars Nova Play Group 299
Ars Nova Theater 178
ArtAge Publications' Senior Theatre
    Resource Center 55
Arte Publico Press 55
Arthur W. Stone New Play Award 118
Articulate Theatre Company 179
Artist's Cottage, The 66
Artists' Fellowship, Inc 320
Artist Trust 148
ART/Moscow Art Institute 292
Art Project Grant 148
Artscape Gibraltar Point 66
Arts & Letters Prize in Drama 118
Arts Management Services, LLC 40
Artspace Projects, Inc. 326
ArtsPower National Touring Theatre 179
ART Station 179
ASCAP Foundation/DreamWorks Musical
    Theatre Workshop in LA 299
ASCAP Musical Theatre Workshop in NY 300
Ashland New Plays Festival 85
Asian American Writers Workshop 55
Asian Cultural Council 149
Asian Story Theater 179
Asian Theatre Journal 346
Aspland Management 40
Association for Theatre in Higher Education
    (ATHE) 127, 326
Association of Authors' Representatives, Inc.
    326
Association of Writers & Writing Programs
    (AWP) 327
ATHE Award for Excellence In Playwriting. 118
ATHE Awards 118
Athena Project 180
Atlantic Center for the Arts 66
Atlantic Stage 180
Atlantic Theater Company 180
August Wilson New Play Initiative 118
Aurand Harris Children's Theatre Grants and
    Fellowship 149
Aurand Harris Memorial Playwriting Award 119
Aurora Theatre Company 180, 308
Aurora Theatre, Inc. [GA] 180
Austin Latino New Play Festival 85
Austin Playhouse 181
Austin Script Works (ASW) 327
Authors League Fund 320

B

Babes With Blades 181
Babes With Blades - Joining Sword and Pen 119
Baker's Plays 55
The Playwriting Collective Ball Grant 162
The Ball Grant (The Playwriting Collective) ...
    162
Baltic Centre for Writers & Translators
    (BCWT) 67
Baltimore Playwrights Festival 85
The Barbara Hogenson Agency, Inc 40
Barking Legs Theater 181
Barter Theatre 84, 181
Law Offices of Bartley F. Day 50
BAU Institute 67
BAU Institute Arts Residency 67
BAX (Brooklyn Arts Exchange) 182
Bay Area Playwrights Festival 85
Bay Street Theatre 182
b current 181
Beacon Artists Agency 40
Beaufort Books 55
Beijing Playhouse 182
Berkshire Theatre Group 182
Berlin Artists-in-Residence 149
BETC Generations Residency 67
Beverly Hills California Musical Theatre
    Award 119
Beverly Hills Theatre Guild 119, 128, 132, 136,
    327
Beyond the Pure Fellowships for Writers .. 149
Biennial Promising Playwright Award 119
Big Dog Publishing 55
Bilingual Foundation of the Arts (BFA) 86
Bill & Peggy Hunt Playwright Festival 86
Billy Rose Theatre Division 327
Bishop Arts Theatre Center 122
Black Box New Play Festival 86
Black Dahlia Theatre Los Angeles 183
Black Ensemble Theater 87, 183
Black & Latino Playwrights Conference 86
Black Playwrights Festival 87
Black Rep 183
Black Theatre Network 327
Black Women's Playwrights' Group 328
Blank Theatre Company Young Playwrights
    Festival 87
Bloomington Playwrights Project 137, 144, 183
Bloomsburg Theatre Ensemble (BTE) 183
Blue Mountain Center 67, 68
BMI (Broadcast Music Inc) 300, 328
BMI Lehman Engel Musical Theatre

Workshop 300	Carnegie Mellon University 293
Bogliasco Foundation 68	Casa Mañana Inc. 187
Bohemia Group 41	Case Arts Law LLC 48
The Bohrman Agency 47	Castillo Theatre 130, 187
Bond Street Theatre 183	Catalyst Series 88
Books & Books – Coral Gables 350	Catalyst Theater Company [DC] 187
Boomerang Theatre Company 93, 184	Catholic University of America 293
Boosey and Hawkes 56	CEC ArtsLink 150
Borderlands Theater 184	Celebration Theatre 187
Boston Playwrights' Theatre at Boston University 292	Celtic Arts Center (An Claidheamh Soluis) ... 188
Boston Theater Marathon 87	Centenary Stage Company 140
Boulder Ensemble Theatre Company 184	Center Stage [MD] 116, 188
Boulder International Fringe Festival 87	Center Theatre Group 137, 188
Box Wine Theatre 109, 184	Central Square Theater 188
Brava! for Women in the Arts 185	Centre des auteurs dramatiques (CEAD) 328
Brave New Works 301	Centre for Indigenous Theatre 328
Breaking Ground Festival 87	Centre Stage [SC] 88, 188
Breckenridge Creative Arts: Tin Shop and Robert Whyte House Residency 68	Centre Stage [SC] New Play Festival 88
	Centrum Artistic Residencies Program 70
Bret Adams Agency 41	CERF+ 321
BRIClab Residency 68	Chaim Schwartz Foundation 150
Bricolage Production Company 116, 185	Charles Lafitte Foundation 151
The Bridge Initiative: Women in Theatre .. 185	Charles Maryan's Playwrights'-Directors' Workshop 301
Bristol Riverside Theatre [PA] 185	
Broadway Play Publishing, Inc. 56	Charles M. Getchell Award 120
Brody Arts Fund 150	Charleston Stage 189
Brookfield Theatre for the Arts 185	Charlotte Gusay Literary Agency 41
Brooklyn Arts Council (BAC) 150	Cherry Lane Theatre 151, 189
Brooklyn Arts Fund 320	Cherry Lane Theatre Mentor Project 151
Brooklyn College - CUNY 292	Chicago Dramatists 78, 165-66, 316
Brooklyn Publishers 56	Children's Theater Foundation (CTFA) 151
Brooklyn Writers Space 328	Children's Theatre Company [MN] 189
Brown Foundation Fellows Program at the Dora Maar House 69	Children's Theatre of Cincinnati [OH] 189
	Childsplay, Inc 189
Brown University 293	Chinese Theatre Works 189
Bryant-Lake Bowl Theater 185	Cider Mill Playhouse 190
Burning Coal Theatre Company 186	Cincinnati Black Theatre Company ... 101, 190
Bushfire Theatre of Performing Arts 186	Cincinnati Fringe Festival 88
Byrdcliffe Arts Colony Artist-in-Residence (AIR) 69	Cincinnati Fringe Next Festival 89
	Cincinnati Playhouse in the Park 190
C	Cincinnati Shakespeare Festival 191
California Arts Council 150	Cinnabar Theater 191
California Institute of the Arts 293	Circle Theatre [TX] 191
California Shakespeare Theater 186	City Garage 191
California Young Playwrights Contest 119	City Lights Theater Company (CLTC) 191
Callaloo 346	City Lit Theater Company 191
Camargo Core Program 69	City of Los Angeles (COLA) Performing Arts Fellowships 151
Cambridge University Press 56	
Camelot Theatre 186	City Theatre Company [PA] 192
Camino Real Playhouse 112, 186	City Theatre [FL] 120, 192
Canadian Jewish Playwriting Competition 120	City Theatre National Award for Short Playwriting Contest 120
Canadian Theatre Review 346	
Cane Law LLP 48	City Wrights Playwrights Conference 89
Cape Cod Theatre Project 301	Clague Playhouse 192
Capilano Review 346	Clarence Brown Theatre (CBT) 192
Capital Repertory Theatre 105, 187	Classical Theatre of Harlem 192
Capital Stage 88, 187	Classic Stage Company (CSC) 192
Capital Stage - Playwrights Revolution 88	Clauder Competition for New England Playwrights 121
Carnegie Fund for Authors 320	

Cleveland Opera Theater 193
Cleveland Play House 103, 193
Cleveland Public Theatre 193, 302
Clintons Solicitors 48
Clockhouse 347
Clubbed Thumb 193
Coe College 89
Coe College Playwriting Festival 89
The Collective NY 194
College of Literary Translators of Seneffe (CTLS) 70
Colony Theatre Company 194
Colorado New Play Summit 89
Columbia College [IL] 293
Columbus Children's Theatre (CCT) 194
Commonweal Theatre Company 195
Community Theatre Association of Michigan . 121, 329
Conejo Players Theatre 195
Confrontation Magazine 347
Congo Square Theatre Company 118, 195
Connecticut Office of the Arts 152
Contemporary American Theater Festival..90
Contemporary American Theatre Company... 195
Contemporary Drama Service 56
Core Writer Program 302
Cornerstone Theater Company 195
Cornish College of the Arts 293
Coterie Theatre 196
Court Theatre 196
Cowan, DeBaets, Abrahams & Sheppard .. 48
CPT New Play Development 302
Creative Ammo Inc. 91
Creative Resistance Fund 321
Creede Repertory Theatre 95, 196
Crossroads Theatre Company 196
CTAM Playwriting Contest 121
CultureCapital.com 329
Cumberland County Playhouse 197
Cunningham Commission for Youth Theatre .. 121
Curious Theatre Company 197
Currency Press 56
Curtis Brown Group Ltd. [UK] 41
Curtis Brown Ltd. [US] 41
Cutting Ball Theater 110
Cyrano's Theatre Company (CTC) 197

D

Dad's Garage Theatre Company 197
Dallas Children's Theater 197
Dallas Playwrights' Workshop 302
Dallas Theater Center 198
Daniel Aharoni & Partners LLP 49
Danisarte 198
Danish Authors' Society (Dansk Forfatterforening) 329
Danish Dramatists 329
Dartmouth Management 41
David Calicchio Emerging American Playwright Prize 121
David Henry Hwang Writers Institute 302
David H. Friedlander, Esq. 49
David Mark Cohen Playwriting Award 122
Day & Koch LLP 49
Dayton Playhouse Futurefest 90
DC Commission on the Arts and Humanities . 152
Deaf West Theatre 198
Deathscribe Festival 90
Delaware Division of the Arts 152
Delaware Theatre Company 90, 198, 318
Delaware Young Playwrights Festival (DYPF) . 90
Dennis & Victoria Ross Foundation (DVRF) Playwrights Program 152
Denver Center for the Performing Arts (DCPA) 89, 198
Desert Star Playhouse 199
Detroit Repertory Theatre 199
Dezart Performs 199
Dionysia New Play Competition 122
DiPerna Associates 49
Directors Company 199
Discovery New Musical Theatre Festival 91
Discovery Theater 199
District of Columbia Arts Center (DCAC) 200
Dixon Place 200
Djerassi Resident Artists Program 70
D. Krausz and Associates, Attorneys at Law ... 49
Dobama Theatre 200
Donaldson & Callif, LLP 49
Dorland Mountain Arts Colony 70
Double Edge Theatre 200
Down For #TheCount 122
Downtown Urban Arts Festival 91
The Drama Book Shop 350
Dramatic Publishing Company 57
Dramatics Magazine 347
Dramatic Women 201
The Dramatist 347
Dramatists Guild Foundation 321, 330
Dramatists Guild Institute 316
Dramatists Guild of America Inc. 316, 347
Dramatists Legal Defense Fund 330
Dramatists Play Service, Inc. 57
Draper Historic Theatre 201
Drexel University, Westphal College 293
Dr. Floyd Gaffney Playwriting Competition ... 122
Driehaus Foundation 152
Drilling Company 201
Drinker Biddle & Reath LLP 49
Dr TaxGuy, LLC 38
Duo Multicultural Arts Center 201

E

East End Fringe Festival 91
East West Players 201

Echo Theatre Company [OK]..........110, 202
Echo Theatre [TX] 202
EcoDrama Playwright Festival..................91
Edinburgh Festival Fringe 92
Edmonton International Fringe Festival.....92
Educational Theatre Association 330
Education and Community Engagement Program..316
Edward F. Albee Foundation, The..............71
Egyptian Theatre Company...................202
Einhorn School of Performing Arts (ESPA)316
El Centro Su Teatro 202
Eldridge Publishing Company, Inc. 57
Elephant Eye Theatrical, LLC 41
Elite Theatre Company 203
El Portal Theatre................................. 202
Emerging Artists Theatre 92, 203
Emerging Artist Theatre New Work Series .92
Empire Publishing Service....................... 57
Encompass New Opera Theatre 203
Enrichment Works................................ 203
Ensemble Studio Theater (EST)......100, 123, 203
Ensemble Theatre Company of Santa Barbara [CA] 204
Ensemble Theatre of Cincinnati [OH]....204
Eric Glass Ltd...41
Essential Theatre 123
Essential Theatre Playwriting Award 123
EST/Alfred P. Sloan Foundation Science & Technology Project 123
eta Creative Arts Foundation Inc. 204
EU 92
The Eugene O'Neill Theater Center102, 103, 204
European Translators' College.................71
Evening of New Plays 93

F
Fade To Black Play Festival.....................93
The Field 330
Fieldwork.. 303
Fifi Oscard Agency, Inc. 41
Finger Lakes Musical Theatre Festival 93
Firehouse Center for the Arts 134, 204
Firehouse Studio 303
Firehouse Theatre............................... 303
First Flight New Play Festival 93
First Stage Children's Theater................205
Flat Rock Playhouse 205
Florida Division of Cultural Affairs 153
Florida Repertory Theatre.................... 205
Florida Studio Theatre 206
Focus Publishing................................... 57
Folger Shakespeare Library 206
Food for Thought Productions 206
Fordham University/Primary Stages MFA in Playwriting 293
Fort Wayne Civic Theatre.................... 206
Foundation for Contemporary Arts 321
Founders' Award for Emerging Playwrights 123

Fountain Theatre 206
Fox Plays... 57
Fractured Atlas................................... 331
Francesca Primus Prize 123
Frankfurt, Kurnit, Klein and Selz.............50
Franklin, Weinrib, Rudell & Vassallo PC 50
Fred Ebb Award.................................. 124
Freedom Repertory Theatre 207
Free Street Programs 207
Fremont Centre Theatre New Playwright Contest.. 124
Fresh Fruit Festival................................94
FRIGID New York............................... 303
Fulbright Program for US Scholars 153
Fulton Theatre 207
Fund for New Work 153
Fusion 207

G
Gage Group, Inc. 42
Ganer, Grossbach and Ganer 38
Gary Garrison National Ten-Minute Play Award 124
Law Office of Gary N. DaSilva 50
Geffen Playhouse 207
Gelfand, Rennert, & Feldman.................50
Gell: A Finger Lakes Creative Retreat........71
George Bennett Fellowship 153
George R. Kernodle New Play Award....124
Georges Borchardt Agency 42
George Street Playhouse..................... 208
Georgia Theatre Conference 94
Gersh Agency [LA]................................ 42
Gersh Agency [NY] 42
Geva Theatre Center....................208, 314
Law Office of Ghenya B. Grant 51
Giordano, Cohen, Fastiggi, Luciano, & Co., P.A. 38
Gloria Stern Literary Agency....................42
Goddard College 293
Going to the River 94
Golden Thread Productions 110, 208
Goodman Theatre 208, 309
Goodspeed Musicals 209
Law Office of Gordon P. Firemark 51
Grawemeyer Award for Music Composition .. 125
Great Lakes Theater Festival 209
Great Plains Theatre Conference 94
Greenbrier Valley Theatre.................... 209
Green Integer 58
Greensboro Fringe Festival 95
Greensboro Playwrights' Forum 331
Greenspan Artists Management..............42
Greenway Arts Alliance (GAA) 209
Gretna Theatre 209
Ground Floor Summer Residency Lab 71
Grove Atlantic Press............................. 58
Growing Stage - The Children's Theatre of New Jersey.................................. 210
Grubman Shire & Meiselas, P.C. 42

G. Schirmer, Inc. / Associated Music
    Publishers, Inc. 58
GSK Talent (Grant, Savic, Kopaloff) 42
Guam Council on the Arts & Humanities
    Agency 154
Gurman Agency LLC 42
Guthrie Theater.................................. 210

H

Hal Leonard 55, 58, 62
Hambidge Center................................. 71
Harden Curtis Associates 42
Harlem Stage at The Gatehouse 153, 210
Harold Clurman Playwrights Division........ 72
Harold & Mimi Steinberg National Student
    Playwriting Award 125
Harold Morton Landon Translation Award 125
Harry Fox Agency, Inc. 43
Hartford Stage 210
Harwich Junior Theatre [Cape Cod Theatre
    Company].................................... 210
The Haven Foundation 321
HaveScripts.com 58
Hawthornden Retreat for Writers 72
Headlands Center for the Arts 72
Headwaters New Play Festival 95
Hedgebrook Women Writers in Residence 72
Hedgerow Theatre............................... 211
The Heights Players............................. 211
Heinemann 58
Helene Wurlitzer Foundation of New Mexico
    73
Helen McCloy/MWA Scholarship for Mystery
    Writing 154
Helen Merrill Ltd. 43
Henley Rose Playwright Competition for
    Women 125
HERE Arts Center 211
High Desert Play Development Workshop ....
    304
Hippodrome Theatre............................ 211
Hirsch Wallerstein Hayum Matlof + Fishman .
    50
History Theatre 211
Hodder Fellowship 154
Hole in the Wall Theater 212
Hollins University Playwright's Lab 293
Honolulu Theatre for Youth................... 212
Horizon Theatre Company [GA] 104, 212
House Theatre of Chicago.................... 212
Hubbard Hall Center for the Arts and
    Education 213
Hubbard Hall Winter Carnival of New Work...
    95
Humana Festival 95
The Human Race Theatre Company 305, 306
Human Rights Watch/Hellman-Hammett
    Grants... 322
Hunter College - CUNY 294
Huntington Theatre Company 213

I

IATI Theatre (Instituto Arte Teatral
    Internacional) 214
Idaho Commission on the Arts............... 154
IHT/SRT International Playwriting
    Competition 126
Illinois Arts Council............................. 155
Illusion Theater 214
Imagination Stage 214
Impact Theatre [CA] 214
Impact Theatre Rep [NY] 214
Indiana Arts Commission (IAC) 155
Indiana Repertory Theatre 144, 215
Indiana University 294
Ingram New Works Project................... 304
Inkslinger Playwriting Competition 126
Innes Smolansky, Attorney at Law........... 50
Innovative Artists [LA........................... 43
In Series 214
Inside Out Theatre Company 215
InspiraTO Playwriting Contest............... 126
INTAR (International Arts Relations) Theatre
    215
Interact Center [MN] 215
InterAct Story Theatre [MD] 215
Interact Theatre Company [CA]............. 216
InterAct Theatre Company [PA] 126, 216
InterAct Theatre New Play Development
    Award 126
Interborough Repertory Theater Inc. (IRT) 216
Intermedia Arts 149, 216
International Center for Women Playwrights..
    331
International City Theatre..................... 216
International College of Literary Translators
    (CITL) 73
International Creative Management (ICM)
    [CA]... 43
International Creative Management (ICM)
    [NY]... 43
International Creative Management (ICM)
    [UK]... 43
International Intellectual Property Alliance
    [IIPA] 331
International Playwrights Festival............ 96
International Theatre Institute - U.S. Center..
    331
International Women's Writing Guild
    (IWWG) 332
Intiman Theatre 216
Iowa Arts Council 148
Ipsilon Music Services......................... 348
Irish Arts Center 217
Irish Classical Theatre Company (ICTC).. 217
Irish Repertory Theatre 217
Irondale Ensemble Project................... 217
Irvington Town Hall Theater: Stage Door
    Playwrights Festival 96
Ithaca Fringe Festival 96
IWP Residency 73

J

Jackie White Memorial Children's Playwriting Contest 127
JAC Publishing & Promotions 58
Jana Luker Agency 43
Jane Chambers Playwriting Award 127
Japan Foundation New York 155
JAW: A Playwrights Festival 97
Jean Kennedy Smith Playwriting Award 127
Jefferson Performing Arts Society 218
Law Office of Jeffrey L. Graubart, P.C. 51
Jerome Fellowships 155
Jerome Foundation Grants 155
JET Fest 97
Jewel Box Theatre Playwriting Competition ... 127
Jewish Ensemble Theatre 218
Jewish Plays Project 218
Jewish Theater of New York 218
Jewish Women's Theatre 219
Law Office of J.J. Sherman, P.C. 51
Jobsite Theatre 219
John Cauble Award for Outstanding Short Play 128
John Drew Theater at Guild Hall of East Hampton 219
John Gassner Memorial Playwriting Award 128
John J. Tormey III, PLLC 50
Jonathan Clowes Ltd. 43
Jonathan Larson Grants 156
Jubilee Theatre 219
Judi Farkas Management 43
Judy Boals, Inc. 43
Judy Daish Associates LTD. 44
Juilliard 294
Julie Harris Playwright Awards 128

K

Kairos Italy Theater 220
Kansas City Repertory Theatre 220
Kavinoky Theatre 220
Keegan Theatre 220
Keen Company 220
The Kennedy Center 307
Kennedy Center American College Theater Festival 97, 124, 127, 129-30, 133, 135, 137-8, 141
Kentucky Arts Council 156
Kentucky Women Writers Conference 97, 128
Kentucky Women Writers Conference Playwriting Prize 128
Kenyon Playwrights' Conference 97
Kenyon Review 348
Khaos Company Theatre 122
Kids' Entertainment 221
Kids Rule the 8x10 Festival 98
Kimerling and Wisdom 38
Kimmel Harding Nelson (KHN) Center for the Arts 73
King's Shorts Festival of Ten Minute Plays . 98
Kings Theatre 98
Kitchen Dog Theater 98, 221
Kitchen Dog Theater New Works Festival .. 98
Klaustrid Artist-in-Residence Program 74
Kleban Prize in Musical Theatre 156
Knight Hall Agency 44
Kumu Kahua Theatre 129, 221
Kumu Kahua Theatre/UHM Theatre Department Playwriting Contest 129

L

LAByrinth Theater Company 222
La Centrale Galerie Powerhouse 74
Laguardia Performing Arts Center Rough Draft Festival 99
La Jolla Playhouse 222
Lakeshore Players 10-Minute Play Festival . 99
Lakeshore Players Theatre 99, 223
La MaMa Experimental Theater Club 222, 304
La MaMa Experiments 304
La MaMa Playwright Retreat 74
Lamb's Players Theatre (LPT) 223
LaMicro Theater 223
Lanesboro Residency Program Fellowships 74
The Lark 94, 109, 166, 304
L. Arnold Weissberger Award 129
L.A. Stage Alliance 332
Last Frontier Theatre Conference 99, 305
Last Frontier Theatre Conference Play Lab 305
L.A. Theatre Works (LATW) 222
Latino/Latina Playwriting Award 129
Laura Jane Musser Fund Rural Arts Program ... 156
Lazarus & Harris LLP 52
Lazy Bee Scripts 58
League of .... Chicago Theatres 332
League of Professional Theatre Women .. 332
Leah Ryan's FEWW Playwriting Prize 129
Leah Ryan's Fund for Emerging Women Writers 129
Leaping Thespians 224
Leavens, Strand, Glover & Adler, LLC 52
Legacies Agency 44
Leighton Artists Studios 74
Le Petit Theatre du Vieux Carre 223
Lesley University 294
Levine, Plotkin & Menin 52
Lexington Children's Theatre 224
Lichter, Grossman, Nichols, Adler & Feldman, Inc. 52
Lift-Off New Play Series 99
Lillenas Publishing Company 58
The Lilly Awards Foundation 332
Limelight Scripts 59
Lincoln Center Theater 224
Linn Sand Agency 44
Literally Alive 224
Literary Artists Representatives 44
Literary Managers & Dramaturgs of the

Americas (LMDA) 332
Little Festival of the Unexpected 100
Little Fish Theatre (LFT) 107, 225
The Little Theatre of Alexandria .. 133-4, 225, 316
Law Offices of Lloyd J. Jassin 51
Loeb & Loeb 52
Long Beach Playhouse 225
Long Island University/Post Campus 294
Long Wharf Theatre 225
Lookingglass Theatre [IL] 225
Lorraine Hansberry Playwriting Award...... 130
Lorraine Hansberry Theater................. 226
Los Angeles Cultural Affairs Dept. 156
Los Angeles Women's Theatre Festival 100
Lost Nation Theater 226
Louisiana Division of the Arts 156
Lucky Penny Productions 226
Lucky Shorts 130
Luna Stage 226
Lyric Stage Company of Boston 227

M

Ma'at Production Assn. of Afrikan Centered Theatre (MPAACT) 227
MacArthur Foundation Fellowship 156
MacDowell Colony 75
Mach 33 Festival................................100
MacNaughton Lord Representation 44
Magic Theatre 227
Maine Arts Commission....................... 157
MainStreet Musicals, Inc..................... 228
Manatt, Phelps & Philips LLP 44
Manhattan Theatre Club (MTC)........... 228
Many Voices Fellowships..................... 157
Marathon of One-Act Plays 100
Margot Miles & Matt Harvey Literary Talent Agency 44
Marin Theatre Company 121, 139, 228
Mario Fratti & Fred Newman Political Play Contest..130
Marks Paneth & Shron LLP 38
Mark Twain Prize for Comic Playwriting ... 130
Marsha Hanna New Play Workshops....... 305
The Marton Agency, Inc. 47
Maryland State Arts Council 157
Mary Mason Memorial Lemonade Fund . 322
The Masquers Playhouse 228
Massachusetts Cultural Council 157
MasterWriter 348
Maxim Mazumdar New Play Competition . 131
Max's Kansas City Project.................... 322
Ma-Yi Theater Company..................... 228
McCarter Theater Center.................... 229
MCC Theater 229
McIntosh & Otis, Inc. 44
McKnight Fellowship in Playwriting......... 157
McKnight National Playwriting Residency and Commission 75
McLaren Memorial Comedy Playwriting Competition 131

McLaughlin & Stern 44
McNerney Playwriting Contest.............. 131
Meadow Brook Theatre 229
Medicine Show Theatre 229
Meister Seelig & Fein LLP 52
Menaker & Herrmann LLP.................... 52
Merrimack Repertory Theatre.............. 230
Metlife Nuestras Voces National Playwriting Competition 131
Metropolitan Playhouse 230
Metro Theater Company..................... 230
Miami Light Project............................. 230
Miami Theater Center, Inc................... 230
Michael Blaha, Esq. 52
Michigan Council for the Arts & Cultural Affairs 158
Mid Atlantic Arts Foundation................ 158
Midtown International Theatre Festival.....101
Midwest Regional Black Theatre Festival ..101
Mildred & Albert Panowski Playwriting Competition 131
The Miles Nadal Jewish Community Centre (MNjcc)......................................120
Milken Playwriting Prize 132
Millay Colony for the Arts..................... 75
Mill Mountain Theatre......................... 231
Milwaukee Repertory Theater 110, 231
Mind's Ear Audio Productions 59
Mind the Gap BritBits Short Play Festival ..101
Mind The Gap Theatre........................101
Minnesota Fringe Festival 101
Minnesota Shorts Festival of Plays 102
Minnesota State Arts Board 158
Miracle Theatre Group 231
Mississippi Arts Commission 158
Mississippi Theatre Association............. 333
Missoula Colony 75
Missouri Arts Council 158
Mixed Blood Theatre Company 231
Montana Arts Council 333
Montana Repertory Theater................. 231
Monteiro Rose Agency Inc. 45
Moose Hide Books 59
Morton R. Sarett National Playwriting Competition 132
Mosaic Youth Theatre......................... 232
Moving Arts...................................... 232
MPAACT 232
Mu Performing Arts 232
Musical Cafe 305
Musical Stages: NC State University New Musicals Program 305
Musical Theatre Award 132
Musical Theatre International................. 59
Musical Theatre Workshops 306
Music Theatre of Connecticut.............. 232
Mysteries by Moushey Inc. 59
Mystery Writers of America 333

N

NACL Theatre (North American Cultural

Laboratory) 233
Naples Players ETC 233
Nashville Repertory Theatre 233, 304
National Alliance for Musical Theatre (NAMT) 102
The National Arts Club 333
National Association of Talent Representatives 45
National Audio Theatre Festivals (NATF) 132, 333
National Audio Theatre Festivals (NATF) Script Competition 132
National Black Theatre Festival 102
National Coalition Against Censorship ... 334
National Endowment for the Arts 65, 147, 159
National Latino Playwriting Award 132
National League of American Pen Women, Inc. 334
National Museum of the American Indian Artist Leadership Program 159
National Music Theater Conference – The Eugene O'Neill Theater Center 102
National New Play Network 67, 132
National One-Act Playwriting Competition ... 133
National Playwrights Conference – The Eugene O'Neill Theater Center 103
National Science Playwriting Award 133
National Ten Minute Play Contest 133
National Theatre of the Deaf 233
National Translation Award 133
National Winter Playwrights Retreat 76
National Writers Association Foundation (NWAF) 334
National Yiddish Theater Folksbiene 234
Native Voices Annual Short Play Festival .. 103
Nautilus Composer-Librettist Studio 306
Nautilus Music Theatre 306
The Navigators Theatre Company 99
NEA Literature Fellowships: Creative Writing. 159
NEA Literature Fellowships: Translation Projects 159
Near West Theatre 234
Nebraska Arts Council 159
Nevada Arts Council 160
New City, New Blood Reading Series 306
New Conservatory Theatre Center 234
New Dramatists 334
New Edgecliff Theatre 234
New England Theatre Conference (NETC) ... 119, 128, 334
New Federal Theatre 235
New Georges 235
New Ground Theatre Festival 103
The New Group 235
New Hampshire Institute of Art 294
The New Harmony Project 307
New Jersey Repertory Company 113, 235
New Jersey Shakespeare Festival 236
New Jersey Theatre Alliance 335
New Mexico Arts 160
New Mexico State University 304
NewMusicals.com 59
New Musicals Inc. 307
New Music USA 335
New Orleans Opera Assn. 236
New Orleans Writers' Residency 76
New Perspectives Theatre Company 236
New Playwrights Foundation 335
New Repertory Theatre 236
New School For Drama 295
New South Play Festival 104
New Stage Theatre 236
newTACTics (New Play Festival) 105
New Visions/New Voices 307
New Voice Play Festival 104
New Voices One-Act Play Competition .. 133
New Voices Project 307
New Works Festival 98-9, 104
New Works Festival at Long Beach Playhouse 105
New Works Festival [MA] 133
New Works Initiative 307
NewWorks@TheWorks Playwriting Competition 134
New York Deaf Theatre 237
New York Foundation for the Arts 77, 161, 335
New York International Fringe Festival (FringeNYC) 105
New York Mills Arts Retreat 76
New York Music Festival (NYMF) 335
New York Stage and Film (NYSAF) .. 123, 237
New York State Council on the Arts 160
New York Theater Festival 113, 115
New York Theatre Workshop 145, 237
New York University 295
New York University, Goldberg Department of Dramatic Writing 295
New York University, Graduate Musical Theatre Writing 295
Next Act! 105
Next Stage Press 59
Next Stage Theatre Festival (NSTF) 105
Niad Management 45
Nicolosi & Co., Inc. 45
Nightwood Theatre 237
Nittany Theatre at the Barn 141, 238
Law Offices of Noel L. Silverman 51
Norman Maine Publishing 60
North Carolina Arts Council 160
North Carolina Black Repertory Company 102, 238
North Carolina New Play Project 134
North Carolina Theatre for Young People 238
North Carolina Writers' Network 336
North Coast Repertory Theatre (NCRT) 238
North Dakota Council on the Arts 160
Northern Kentucky University 295
Northern Sky Theatre 239

NOTES

Northern Stage 239
Northlight Theatre 239
North Park Playwright Festival 106
Northwest Children's Theater & School .. 318
Northwestern University 295
Northwest Playwrights Alliance (NPA) ... 336
Norton Island Residency Program 76, 77
NOTEworthy 308
NYC Playwrights 336
NYFA Fiscal Sponsorship 161
NYFA in Residence 77
NYSCA/NYFA Artist Fellowships 161

O

Obama Foundation Fellowship 161
Obsidian's Playwrights Unit 308
Obsidian Theatre Company 239
OHenry Productions 240
Ohio Arts Council 161
Oklahoma Arts Council 161
Oldcastle Theatre Company 240
Old Opera House Theatre Co 104
Olney Theatre Center 240
Omaha Theater Company at The Rose ... 240
One Act Play Contest 134
One-Act Playwriting Competition 133-4
One Company's Writer's Residency Retreat at DoLittle Farm 77
Open Eye Theater 113
Opera..... 135, 176, 193, 203, 215, 236, 258, 263, 336
Opera America 336
Opera for All Voices 135
Opus 3 Artists 45
Orange County Playwrights Alliance 337
The Orchard Project 77
Oregon Arts Commission 162
Original Shorts Playwriting Contest 135
Original Works Publishing 60
Originate + Generate (O+G) 308
Orlando International Fringe Theatre Festival. 106
Orlando Shakespeare Theater 108, 241
Out of Box Theatre 241

P

Pace University 295
Pacific Conservatory Theatre 241
Pacific Northwest Writers Association 337
PAJ: A Journal of Performance and Art ... 348
Palm Beach Dramaworks 241
Pan Asian Repertory Theatre 241
Pangea World Theater 242
Pan Theater Ten Minute Play Fest 106
Paradigm [LA] 45
Paradigm [NY] 45
Park Plays Festival 106
Passage Theatre 242
Pataphysics Playwriting Workshops 308
Paula Vogel Award for Playwriting 136
Paul Stephen Lim Playwriting Award 135
Paul, Weiss, Rifkind, Wharton & Garrison .. 53

Pear Theatre 242
Peikoff Mahan Law Office 53
Pen America 322, 337
PEN America 136
PEN America Writers' Emergency Fund .. 322
PEN Center USA Literary Awards 136
Penguin Rep Theatre 242
PEN/Heim Translation Fund Grant 136
PEN/Laura Pels International Foundation Awards for Drama 136
Penn State NU Musical Theatre Festival .. 107
Pennsylvania Council on the Arts 162
Pennsylvania Youth Theatre 243
Penumbra Theatre Company 243
People's Light and Theatre Company 243
Peregrine Whittlesey Agency 45
Performer Stuff 60
Perseverance Theatre (PT) 243
Petaluma Radio Players 244
Peter D. Singh, Jr. 53
Law Offices of Peter M. Thall 51
Peters, Fraser & Dunlop Ltd. 45
Pew Grants and Fellowships in the Arts 162
Philadelphia Children's Festival 107
Philadelphia Theatre Company 244
Philadelphia young playwrights' Festival ... 107
Philip Spitzer Literary Agency 46
Phillly Fringe 107
Phoenix Arts Association Theatre [CA] ... 244
Phoenix Stage Company 244
Phoenix Theatre [AZ] 107, 245
Phoenix Theatre Festival of New American Theatre 107
Phoenix Theatre [IN] 245
Pick of the Vine Short Play Festival 107
Pillsbury House Theatre 245
Pioneer Drama Service 60
Pioneer Theatre Company 245
Pittsburgh New Works Festival (PNWF) ... 108
Piven Theatre 246
Plan-B Theatre Company 246
Planet Connections Theatre Festivity 108
Play Competition for Youth Theatre 136-7
The Players Club 337
Players Press, Inc. 60
Playfest 108
PlayGround 309
Playhouse on the Square 134, 246
Playmakers of Baton Rouge 246
PlayMakers Repertory Company 247
Playmarket 337
PlayPenn 108, 309
PlayPenn Conference 108
Playscripts, Inc. 60
Plays In Progress Series 108
Playstage Junior 61
Play With Your Food 246
Playwrights' Center [MN] ... 75, 155, 157, 302
Playwrights' Center of San Francisco 310
Playwrights Center San Francisco (PCSF), ...

338	ReOrient Festival of Short Plays 110
Playwrights First 137	Repertorio Espanol 252
Playwrights' Forum [MD] 338	Repertory Theatre of St. Louis 253
Playwrights Foundation 85, 309	Rep Lab Short Play Festival 110
Playwrights Gallery 309	Rep Stage 252
Playwrights Guild of Canada 338	Residency Flat in Gröndal's House 78
Playwrights Horizons 247	Resident Playwright Program 78
Playwrights Local 247	Reva Shiner Comedy Award 137
Playwrights Project 119-20, 137, 144, 338	Reverb Play Festival 110
Playwrights Unit 309	Rhinebeck Writers Retreat 78
Playwrights Voiced 109	Rhode Island State Council on the Arts ... 164
Playwrights' Week 109	Riant Theatre 253
The Playwriting Center 310	Richard E. Sherwood Award 137
Point Park University 296	Law Offices of Richard Garmise, PLLC 51
Pond Plays 61	Richard Rodgers Awards for Musical Theater . 138
Porchlight Music Theatre 247	
Portland Center Stage at the Armory [OR] 97, 248	RISK IS THIS...New Experimental Plays Festival 110
Portland Stage Company [ME] 100, 248	Rivendell Theatre Ensemble 253
Powerhouse Theatre 248	Riverside Theatre [FL] 253
Prairie Lights 350	Riverside Theatre [IA] 254
Pregones/PRTT 248	Rivertown Theaters for the Performing Arts 254
Premiere Stages at Kean University .. 109, 248	
Premiere Stages Play Festival 109	RLTP Playwright In Residence 78
Present Company 249	Road Less Traveled Productions 254
Primary Stages 249, 310, 316	RoaN Productions 254
Primary Stages Reading Series 310	Robert A. Freedman Dramatic Agency, Inc. ... 46
Prime Stage Theatre 249	
Princess Grace Foundation USA Playwriting Fellowship 162	Roberta L. Korus, Attorney at Law 53
	Law Offices of Robert G Pimm 52
Princeton Arts Fellowship 163	Robert J. Pickering Award for Playwriting Excellence 138
Prism International 61	
Professional Association of Canadian Theatres (PACT) 339	Robert M. Pesce, CPA 38
	Roberts Ritholz Levy Sanders Chidekel & Fields LLP 53
Prop Thtr 249	
Proscenium Journal 348	Robinson, Brog, Leinwand, Greene, Genovese & Gluck 53
Public Theater 163, 249	
Public Theater Emerging Writers Group ... 163	Rocky Mountain National Park Artist-in-Residence Program 78
Pulse Ensemble Theatre 250, 310	
Pulse Ensemble Theatre Playwrights' Lab. 310	Rodgers & Hammerstein Organization 62
The Purple Circuit 339	Rorschach Theatre 255
Purple Rose Theatre Company 250	Rosalie Calabrese Management 46
Q	Rosa Parks Playwriting Award 138
Queensbury Theatre 250	Ross Alternative Works (RAW) 311
Queens College - CUNY 296	Ross Valley Players 255, 311
Queens Council on the Arts 163	Roundabout Theatre Company 255
Queens Theatre 106, 250	Round House Theatre 255
Quest for Peace Playwriting Award 137	Roust Theatre Company 256
R	Route 66 Theatre Company 256, 313
Rabin Panero & Herrick 53	Royal Court Theatre 256
Radcliffe Institute Fellowships 163	RSO Advisors 39
The Radio Theatre Project 251	Rutgers University (New Brunswick) 296
Ragdale Foundation 77	**S**
Rainbow's Comedy Playhouse 251	Sacramento Theatre Company 256
Rattlestick Playwrights Theatre 251	Salamanca Arts Centre 339
Raucous Caucus 109	Salt Lake Acting Company 257
Red Barn Theatre 251	Salt Lake Acting Company Playwrights Lab 311
Red Bull Theater 251	Samuel French Hollywood Bookshop 350
Red Orchid Theatre 252	Samuel French, Inc. 62, 110, 163
Relative Theatrics 109, 252	Samuel French Off-Off Broadway Short-Play

Festival 110	Soho Rep Writer/Director Lab 311
San Diego Repertory Theatre 257	Soiree Fair, Inc. 46
San Francisco Fringe Festival................... 111	Sokoloff Arts Fellowship........................ 164
San Francisco State University 296	Songwriters Guild of America Foundation (SGAF) 340
Santa Cruz Actors' Theatre 257	
Santa Fe Opera 135, 257	SOUND BITES 10-Minute Musical Festival ... 112
Saper Law 54	
Saskatchewan Writers Guild 339	South Camden Theatre Company 261
Scholastic Art & Writing Awards............. 138	South Carolina Arts Commission............ 164
Schreck, Rose, and Dapello................... 54	South Coast Repertory Playwriting Classes.... 318
Scott Mauro Entertainmnet 46	
Scripteasers................................. 139, 311	South Coast Repertory Theatre 262
Script Tease of Short Plays Competition .. 139	South Dakota Arts Council 165
SDC Journal 348	Southern Appalachian Repertory Theatre 262
Seacoast Repertory Theatre 258	Southern Illinois University (Carbondale) 296
Seattle Children's Theatre 258	Southern Playwrights Competition 139
Seattle Jewish Theater Company 258	Southern Rep 262, 312
Seattle Repertory Theatre 258	Southern Rep's 4D 312
Second Stage Theatre 259	SPACE on Ryder Farm........................... 79
Sendroff & Baruch, LLP 54	Spielman, Koenigsberg and Parker (SKP) .. 38
Senior Playwriting 318	Springboard for the Arts 323
Seven Devils Playwrights Conference........ 111	Springer Opera House........................ 263
Seventh Generation Fund for Indigenous Peoples 164	Stage 773 263
	The Stage Company 263
Sewanee Writers' Conference 111	Stage Left Theatre Playwright Residencies 312
SFWA Emergency Medical Fund 323	STAGE (Society for Theatrical Artists' Guidance and Enhancement) 340
Shadow Box Theatre [NY] 259	
Shadowlight Productions..................... 259	StageSource 340
The Sharland Organisation..................... 46	Stages Repertory Theatre 264
Shawnee Press 62	Stages Theatre Company..................... 264
Shedler and Cohen 38	Stage West 264
Shenandoah International Playwrights 78	Stageworks, Inc.................................. 264
She NYC Arts and She LA Arts................. 111	Stanley Drama Award 139
Shotgun Players................................. 259	State Theatre Company 264
Shotgun Productions Inc. 259	St. Bart's Players 263
Shovel Town 10-Minute Play Festival, The . 112	Steele Spring Stage Rights..................... 63
ShowOff! Ten-Minute Playwriting Festival . 112	Steppenwolf Theatre Company 265
Shubert Archives 340	Stepping Stone Theatre for Youth Development 265
Shubert Fendrich Memorial Playwriting Contest.. 139	
	Sterling Lord Literistic 46
Shukat Arrow Hafer Weber & Herbsman, LLP 54	St. Louis Black Repertory Company........ 263
	Stoneham Theatre 265
The Side Project.................................260	St. Petersburg Review......................... 349
Siena Art Institute Summer Residency Program.. 78	Strange Sun Theater Company 265
	Stratford Shakespeare Festival [ON] 112
Signature Theatre Company [NY]..........260	Straz Center [Tampa Bay Performing Arts Center] 266
Signature Theatre [VA]........................260	
SignStage 260	Studio@620 266
Simpatico Theatre Project 260	Studio X at The Studio Theatre 266
Singapore Repertory Theatre................. 261	Studio X-hibition New Play Development 312
Sinister Wisdom 62	Summerfest Festival 113
SITI Company..................................... 261	Summerfield G. Roberts Award 140
S. Jean Ward 53	Summer Pride Festival........................... 112
Sky Cooper New American Play Prize...... 139	Summer Shortcuts 113
Skylight Music Theatre......................... 261	Summer Shorts 113
SMC Artists.. 46	Sundance Institute Theatre 266, 312
Smith and Kraus 62	Sundance Institute Theatre Program 312
Smith College 296	Sun Valley Center for the Arts............... 266
Soho Repertory Theatre Inc. 311	SUNY Purchase................................. 296
SoHo Repertory Theatre Inc. 261	Surdna Foundation 165

Susan Glaspell Contest [Centenary Stage].... 140
Susan Schulman Literary Agency 47
Susan Smith Blackburn Prize.................. 140
S. Verlag Fischer................................... 46
Synchronicity Theatre 267
Synetic Theatre 193
Syracuse Stage 267

T
TADA! Youth Theater 267
Target Margin Theater......................... 267
Tasmanian Writers' Centre 340
Tattered Cover Book Store 351
TCG Grants 165
Teatro Circulo.................................... 267
Teatro Dallas 268
Teatro de al Luna 268
Teatro del Pueblo 268
Teatro Latea 268
Teatro SEA.. 269
Teatro Vision...................................... 269
Teatro Vista 269
Teatro Vivo 85, 269
Tectonic Theater Project 269
Tennessee Arts Commission 165
Tennessee Williams/New Orleans Literary Festival One-Act Play Contest.......... 140
Tennessee Women's Theatre Project...... 270
Test Drive Development Workshop 313
Texas Commission on the Arts............... 165
Texas Nonprofit Theatres 141, 270, 341
Texas State University (San Marcos) 297
Thalia Spanish Theatre 270
The Agency [UK] 47
Theater 2020 270
Theater Alliance 271
Theater at Solel.................................. 313
Theater Breaking Through Barriers 271
Theater Emory 310
Theater for the New City.............. 273, 306
Theater for Youth Playwriting Award......... 141
Theater Magazine 349
Theater Resources Unlimited 341
The Theatre at St Claude..................... 274
Theatre Bay Area 341
Theatre Brut Short-Play Festival 113
Theatre Communications Group......165, 346
Theatre Conspiracy 141
Theatre Development Fund (TDF).......... 341
Theatre du Mississippi 135, 272
Theatre Exile 271, 312
Theatrefolk 63
Theatre for a New Audience................. 273
TheatreForum 64
Theatre for Young Audiences/USA 342
Theatre InspiraTO 126, 272
Theatre in the Raw 274
Theatre in the Square 274
Theatre Lab....................................... 272
The Theatre Lab School of Dramatic Arts. 318
Theatre Memphis 272
Theatre Now New York......................... 112
Theatre Odyssey [FL] 274
Theatre of NOTE 273, 308, 314
Theatre of the First Amendment Play Festival. 141
Theatre of Yugen 275
Theatre Oxford 133
Theatre Project 342
Theatre Rhinoceros............................. 275
TheatreSquared............................ 84, 275
Theatre Three, Inc. [TX] 275
Theatre Three [NY] 113
Theatre Three [NY] One-Act Play Festival . 113
Theatre West 342
TheatreWorks Silicon Valley 276
Theatreworks USA 276
Theatrical Outfit 276
Theatrical Rights Worldwide................... 64
The Flea Theater................................ 205
The Little Theatre of Alexandria Playwriting Class 316
The National Theatre [DC] 233
The Theater Center............................. 271
Thunderclap Productions 277
Tiny Storefront Concert Series 114
TNT POPS! New Play Project 141
Tomo Suru Players 277
Toronto Fringe Festival.................. 105, 114
Touchstone Theatre 277
Town Hall Theatre Company (THT) 278
Towson University Prize for Literature....... 142
Transport Group 278
Triangle Productions!........................... 278
Trident Booksellers & Cafe 351
Trinity Repertory Company 278
Triumvirate Artists, Inc. 279
Trustus Theatre.................................. 279
TRU Voices Play and Musical Reading Series . 313
Tsu Tsu Unlimited 47
TURN2US 323
Tutterow Fellows Program 165
Two River Theatre Company (TRTC) 279
Tyrone Guthrie Centre.......................... 79

U
Ucross Foundation Residency Program 79
UMass New Play Lab............................. 80
Underscore Theatre 279
Unicorn Theatre 280
United Agents [A P Watt]....................... 39
United States Copyright Office 342
United Talent Agency [LA]..................... 47
United Talent Agency [NY] 47
University of California (Los Angeles) 297
University of California (San Diego) 122, 297
University of Central Missouri Competition... 142
University of Hawai'i Press 64
University of Houston 297

University of Iowa 297
University of Massachusetts (Amherst)... 297
University of Missouri Press..................... 64
University of Nebraska at Omaha 297
University of New Mexico 297
University of New Orleans.................... 298
University of Southern California........... 298
University of Texas (Austin).................. 298
Upstream Artists' Collective 280
Urbanite Theatre 280
Urban Stages 142, 280
Urban Stages Emerging Playwright Award. 142
USA Songwriting Competition 142
U.S. - Japan Creative Artists' Program 79
Utah Arts Council 166
Utah Shakespeare Festival 116, 281

V

Vancouver Fringe Festival....................... 114
Vanderbilt University Writer-in-Residence 166
Van Lier New Voices Fellowship............. 166
Vantage Theatre 281
VCCA (Virginia Center for the Creative Arts). 80
Venice Little Theatre (VLT) 281
Venus Theatre 281
Vermont Arts Council 167
Vermont Playwrights Award.................. 143
Vermont Pride Theater.......................... 112
Verse Drama Prize................................ 143
Victory Gardens Theater....................... 282
Victory Theatre Center 282
Village Theatre..................................... 282
Villa Montalvo Artist Residency Program... 80
Vineyard Theatre 282
Virginia Commission for the Arts 167
Virginia Repertory Theatre 283
Virginia Stage Company 283
Virgin Islands Council on the Arts 167
Vital Theatre Company 283
Voices Of Our Nations Arts 313
Volunteer Lawyers for the Arts 342
VS. Theatre Company........................... 283

W

The Wallis Annenberg Center for the
    Performing Arts 284
Walnut Street Theatre........................... 284
Warner International Playwrights Festival..96, 115
Warner Theatre 96, 115
Wasatch Theatre Company 284
Washington Area Archive of the Performing
    Arts (WAPAVA) 343
Washington Square Arts and Film............. 54
Washington Stage Guild 284
Washington State Arts Commission 167
Watertower Theatre 284
Weathervane Playhouse 285
Webster University 298
Weird Sisters Women's Theatre Collective 285

Wellfleet Harbor Actors Theater 285
Westcliffe Center for the Performing Arts 285
West End Studio Theatre 285
Western Stage..................................... 286
Weston Playhouse................................ 286
Westport Country Playhouse 286
West Virginia Commission on the Arts 167
White Horse Theater Company............. 287
Whiting Awards 143
Wichita State University New Play
    Competition 144
WildClaw Theatre 90, 287
Will Geer Theatricum Botanicum 287
William Kerwin Agency 48
William Morris Endeavor [NY] 48
William Penn Foundation 167
Williams Street Rep............................... 287
Williamstown Theatre Festival.......... 115, 129
Wilma Theater 288
Winslett Studnicky McCormick & Bomser
    LLP 54
Winterfest Festival................................. 115
Wisconsin Arts Board............................ 168
W. Keith Hedrick Playwriting Contest...... 143
WomenArts 344
Women in the Arts & Media Coalition.... 343
Women Playwrights' Initiative 343
Women Playwrights International 343
Women's Theatre Alliance 343
Women's Theatre Company 288
Women's Work Lab 80
Woodcock Fund 323
Woodstock Byrdcliffe Guild 80
Woodward/Newman Drama Award 144
Woolly Mammoth Theatre Company 288
WordPlay... 116
Words Cubed 116
Working Theater 289
WorkShop Theater Company................ 289
WOW Cafe 344
WP Theater 288
Write Brothers Inc................................. 349
Write Now 313
Writers Guild of America East 344
Writers Guild of America West............... 344
Writers' Guild of Great Britain 345
Writers Omi at Ledig House.................... 81
Writers' Residence in Gunnarshús............. 81
The Writers Room................................ 345
Writers Theatre 289
Writers Theatre of New Jersey............... 289
Writers' Trust of Canada 323
Writers' Union of Iceland
    (Rithöfundasamband Íslands).......... 339
WW Norton and Company 64
Wylie Agency 48
Wyoming Arts Council 168

X

Xoregos Performing Company.............. 289

Y

Yaddo 81
Yale Drama Series/David C. Horn Prize ...144
Yale Repertory Theatre 290
Yale University School of Drama 298
York Shakespeare Company 290
York Theatre Company 290
Young Playwright Contest..................... 144
Young Playwrights Festival........... 87, 90, 116
Young Playwrights in Process 144
Young Playwrights Theater (YPT) 290
Young Writers Project 314
Young Writers Showcase...................... 314
Youth Performance Co........................ 291
YouthPlays 64

Z

Zeitgeist Multi-Disciplinary Arts Center ..291
Zoetic Stage....................................... 291